The Dream and Human Societies

Published under the Auspices of the
Near Eastern Center
University of California
Los Angeles

Based on the proceedings of the international Colloquium on "Le Rêve et les sociétés humaines," sponsored and organized by the Near Eastern Center, University of California, Los Angeles, and held at the Cercle Culturel de Royaumont, Abbaye de Royaumont, Asnières-sur-Oise, June 17 to June 23, 1962

The Dream and Human Societies

Edited by
G. E. VON GRUNEBAUM *and* ROGER CAILLOIS

University of California Press
BERKELEY AND LOS ANGELES
1966

UNIVERSITY OF CALIFORNIA PRESS
Berkeley and Los Angeles, California

CAMBRIDGE UNIVERSITY PRESS
London, England

© 1966 by The Regents of the
University of California
Library of Congress Catalog Card Number: 66-16285

Designed by Jane Brenner

PRINTED IN THE UNITED STATES OF AMERICA

Foreword

Many factors made the editing of the proceedings of the international Colloquium on "Le Rêve et les sociétés humaines," held in France in June, 1962, a complex and, at times, a tricky task: twenty-five authors representing more than a dozen disciplines from neurophysiology to comparative religion and ranging from ancient Greece to modern Brazil; as many conceptual frameworks and terminologies; contributions presented in the closely related yet sharply contrasting stylistic traditions of French and English scholarship; and withal the need to make the specialist's knowledge accessible to that general reader into whom the specialist himself is transformed when he leaves his chosen field.

Wherever names and terms from Eastern tongues must be inserted in Western texts, transliteration becomes the first butt of criticism. A slowly stiffening convention is making it easier to match the Arabic to the Latin alphabet, and we have followed the precedent set by earlier publications of the Near Eastern Center in which efforts were made toward harmony with prevailing custom in the English printing world. Philologically exact transliteration has been abandoned in the instance of words that, by inclusion in *Webster's Third New International Dictionary,* have attained the right of citizenship in the English language: Muhammad, shah, qadi, Shiʻite, and their likes thus appear as they do in Webster. Dealing as he does almost exclusively with Persian materials, Henry Corbin has transliterated the names and terms of his study in tune with Persian pronunciation rather than with the standard values of the Arabic script, a procedure left unchanged in all essentials. On occasion, yielding to the special requirements of a passage or to the request of an author, English custom in the handling of Greek names was abandoned for closer adherence to the original form.

The initiative taken by the Near Eastern Center, University of California, Los Angeles, could not have been sustained but for the encouragement and material assistance rendered by the U.S. Public Health

Service, the National Science Foundation, and by the Affaires Culturelles et Techniques of the French Ministry of Foreign Affairs in response to the recommendation of Mr. M. Lejeune, Membre de l'Institut de France, who was Associate Director of the Centre National de la Recherche Scientifique, Paris, at the time of the Colloquium.

A large number of collaborators have put us in their debt. Dr. Marcel Leibovici of the C.N.R.S., for two years with the Near Eastern Center and now with the San Fernando Valley State College, Northridge, California, made his wide knowledge of subject and researchers effectively available. Mr. Michel Zéraffa collaborated with Dr. Leibovici during the actual proceedings. The help rendered by Mr. Alain Crespelle, Director of the Centre Culturel de Royaumont, by far exceeded his official duties. Not only are we obligated to him for a number of valuable suggestions, but first and foremost for the atmosphere that welded some two dozen invitees into one effective group.

Then came the task of making a book out of a collection of conference papers, and with its completion a deep sense of obligation and gratitude to another set of collaborators. My thanks to Mrs. Teresa Joseph for the intensity and thoroughness of her work are restrained only by the fear that responsibility for remaining errors might be attributed to her rather than to me. The inadequacies of the first translation of the French papers were remedied by the collaboration with myself of Mrs. Helen A. Dillon of the Near Eastern Center, and of my daughter Tessa. Miss Gia Aivazian, Mrs. Evelyn N. Oder, and Mrs. Dorothea M. Gallup, all of the Near Eastern Center, have done most valuable bibliographical and editorial work. Special thanks are due my colleague Professor D. M. Farquhar for his help in transliterating a string of Chinese names, and Miss Elaine K. Miller, Department of Spanish, University of California, Los Angeles, for translating from Spanish to English the paper by María Zambrano. The Orion Press kindly permitted the use of a sizable section of the introductory essay of Roger Caillois in *The Dream Adventure* (New York, 1963).

It is a matter of profound regret that Dorothy Eggan did not live to see the publication of a book to which she contributed an outstanding chapter. A great scholar and a sensitive friend, those she studied miss her as much as those she enriched by her work. Her essay in this volume is like the capstone in the monument she has erected for herself in a life of unceasing devotion to scholarship, far-reaching and humane.

G. E. von Grunebaum

University of California
Los Angeles
November 3, 1965

Contributors

ROGER BASTIDE
    Professor of Social Anthropology, Sorbonne

ANGELO BRELICH
    Professor and Director, Institute for the History of Religion, University of Rome

FRÉDÉRIC BREMER
    Professor and Director, Laboratory of Physiopathology, University of Brussels

ROLAND CAHEN
    School of Medicine, Sorbonne

ROGER CAILLOIS
    Editor-in-chief, Diogène, *Paris*

HENRY CORBIN
    Professor of Islamic Studies, École des Hautes Études, Sorbonne; Director, Department of Iranian Studies, Institut Franco-iranien, Tehran; and Editor, Bibliothèque iranienne

WILLIAM C. DEMENT, M.D.
    Associate Professor of Psychiatry, Stanford University, Palo Alto, California

GEORGE DEVEREUX
    Professor of Research in Ethnopsychiatry, School of Medicine, Temple University, Philadelphia, Pa.

MARTIN EBON
    Administrative Secretary, Parapsychology Foundation, New York

Contributors

DOROTHY EGGAN
> Fellow, American Anthropological Association. Deceased July 18, 1965

MIRCEA ELIADE
> Sewell L. Avery Distinguished Service Professor of History of Religions, University of Chicago

TOUFY FAHD
> Professor of Islamology and Arab Literature and Director of Institute of Islamic Studies, University of Strasbourg

G. E. VON GRUNEBAUM
> Professor of History and Director of Near Eastern Center, University of California, Los Angeles

A. IRVING HALLOWELL
> Professor Emeritus of Anthropology, University of Pennsylvania

WESTON LA BARRE
> Professor of Anthropology, Duke University, Durham, North Carolina

JEAN LECERF
> Professor Emeritus, École Nationale des Langues Orientales Vivantes, Paris

SONJA MARJASCH, Ph.D.
> Practicing analyst; teacher at C. G. Jung Institute, Zurich

CARL ALFRED MEIER, M.D.
> Psychiatrist, practicing analyst of the Jungian School; Professor of Psychology, Swiss Federal Institute of Technology (ETH)

FRITZ MEIER
> Professor of Islamic Studies, University of Basel, Switzerland

ALFONSO MILLÁN
> Professor, Faculty of Medicine, National University of Mexico

A. LEO OPPENHEIM
> Professor of Assyriology, Oriental Institute, University of Chicago; Editor-in-chief, University of Chicago Assyrian Dictionary

ENZO PACI
> Professor of Theoretical Philosophy, University of Milan; Editor-in-chief, Aut Aut: Rivista di filosofia e di cultura

FAZLUR RAHMAN
> Director, Islamic Research Institute, Karachi, Pakistan

EMILIO SERVADIO, LL.D.
    Honorary Professor of Psychology, University of Rome; President, Italian Psychoanalytic Society

MARÍA ZAMBRANO
    Professor Emeritus of Philosophy, Madrid, Barcelona, Morelia

Contents

1 *Introduction: The Cultural Function of the Dream as Illustrated by Classical Islam*
                    G. E. VON GRUNEBAUM   3

2 *Logical and Philosophical Problems of the Dream*
                    ROGER CAILLOIS   23

3 *The Neurophysiological Problem of Sleep*
                    FRÉDÉRIC BREMER   53

4 *The Psychophysiology of Dreaming*
                    WILLIAM C. DEMENT   77

5 *The Dynamics of So-Called Paranormal Dreams*
                    EMILIO SERVADIO   109

6 *The Psychology of the Dream: Its Instructive and Therapeutic Uses*
                    ROLAND CAHEN   119

7 *On the Dream Psychology of C. G. Jung*
                    SONJA MARJASCH   145

8 *Parapsychological Dream Studies*
                    MARTIN EBON   163

9 Toward a Phenomenological Analysis
   of Sleep and the Dream
                              ENZO PACI   179

10 Dreams and Literary Creation
                              MARÍA ZAMBRANO   189

11 The Sociology of the Dream
                              ROGER BASTIDE   199

12 Pathogenic Dreams in Non-Western Societies
                              GEORGE DEVEREUX   213

13 The Dream, Charisma, and the Culture-Hero
                              WESTON LA BARRE   229

14 Hopi Dreams in Cultural Perspective
                              DOROTHY EGGAN   237

15 The Role of Dreams in Ojibwa Culture
                              A. IRVING HALLOWELL 267

16 The Place of Dreams in the Religious World
   Concept of the Greeks
                              ANGELO BRELICH   293

17 The Dream in Ancient Greece and Its Use in
   Temple Cures (Incubation)
                              CARL ALFRED MEIER 303

18 Dreams and Social Character in Mexico
                              ALFONSO MILLÁN   321

19 Initiation Dreams and Visions among the
   Siberian Shamans
                              MIRCEA ELIADE   331

20 Mantic Dreams in the Ancient Near East
                              A. LEO OPPENHEIM   341

21 *The Dream in Medieval Islamic Society*
TOUFY FAHD   351

22 *The Dream in Popular Culture: Arab and Islamic*
JEAN LECERF   365

23 *The Visionary Dream in Islamic Spirituality*
HENRY CORBIN   381

24 *Dream, Imagination, and ʿĀlam al-mithāl*
FAZLUR RAHMAN   409

25 *Some Aspects of Inspiration by Demons in Islam*
FRITZ MEIER   421

Index   431

The Dream and Human Societies

I

Introduction

The Cultural Function of the Dream as Illustrated by Classical Islam

G. E. VON GRUNEBAUM

Like nations, sciences have their moments of advance and retreat. Unlike nations, though, sciences readily establish condominium over contested territory, but they fail to perceive that such condominium also prevails where they believe themselves to be in exclusive possession. So the borders—not to say the area—of nature and culture oscillate and overlap as the development of natural and cultural sciences draws the two regions closer or pushes them farther apart, makes them seem to coincide or barely to touch.

This century has witnessed a signal increase in the scope of the cultural sciences. The realization of the social conditioning of physiological behavior has spread —consider only what anthropology has taught with regard to postures, elementary movements, habits of relaxation and sleep. May one go so far as to claim the admission of cultural factors whenever psychological influence on physiological fact is recognized? Conversely, the physiological infrastructure not only of language, but of literature and music, the plastic arts—in short, of all aesthetic creation—has come to be accepted, although it may still be disregarded in actual research. But whatever the scholarly practice may be, the *Kulturforscher* at least recognizes that (1) a wide variety of psychological phenomena need to be investigated for their cultural components (or motivation), and that (2) a correspondingly wide variety of cultural phenomena need to be studied for their physiological or "natural" facets. More stringently put, the *Kulturforscher* has learned that to understand the cultural variables of a phenomenon he has first to ascertain its "natural" invariables.

Among the phenomena to which this methodological principle applies, the dream ranks with the most conspicuous. Its physiological basis is uncontestable, its social and cultural range coterminous with human society—if we may disregard here the dreaming observable in animals. An indispensable part of the human existence, it is dependent on the endeavors of a considerable number of sciences, from neurophysiology to literary history and from medicine to comparative religion, if one is to describe it completely and a fortiori to explain it adequately. The simultaneous unity and functional diversity of the elemental human experience are brought home dramatically by this need for concerted attack from every one of the numerous points of departure implied in the divers contexts in which the dream makes its appearance.

The wealth of material to be considered by any and all of the sciences concerned with its elucidation, and, in fact, the very efficiency of their individual advancement, have tended to prevent the coordination of effort which the investigation of the dream needs. This Colloquium is intended to counteract the isolation of researches in two ways: (1) by emphasizing the urgency of interdisciplinary cooperation, and (2) by demonstrating concretely the usefulness, on every level and in every relevant branch of learning, of drawing on the results and sharing the problems of those who have chosen different approaches to the multifaceted phenomena of the dream. To the best of my knowledge, our Colloquium is the first systematic attempt to provide the oneirologists of every persuasion with at least an aperçu of the state of knowledge attained in neighboring fields which are yet remote in terms of current organization of research.

The aim could only be representative selection, not completeness, particularly with regard to function and significance of the dream in different cultural settings, both present and past. A certain emphasis on the Near East is accidental, yet heuristically defensible because of the intense concern that Muslim civilization has shown for the dream. Other emphases or omissions may be equally accidental; but suggestion and example may do more for the growth of our studies than a prematurely encyclopedic treatment, which could hardly produce anything at this stage but pretentious monotony.

For our purpose, we designate Descartes as the first fully self-conscious spokesman of the recent West, and we term all civilizations before his time, Eastern or Western, "medieval" or, more blandly, "pre-modern." I wish to indicate by these adjectives—which are too pale and at the same time too precise, too much and too little related to concrete historical situations—that those civilizations possess, in varying degrees, these characteristics: (*a*) Their theory of knowledge is predominantly realist. Concepts, principles of order and organization, in short, names and universals, any entity construed or abstracted for delineation and mastery of the particular, are attributed existence. (*b*) Ultimate reality is transcendental, and this worldly reality is its sign or symbol. Being, consequently, becomes susceptible of gradation, with the hierarchy of being frequently felt to coincide with the hierarchy of graded participation in moral perfection. (*c*) The craving for absolute and largely static truth—for change degrades, and becoming is inferior to being—excludes acquiescence in psychological or operational truth. The human experience reflects not merely the human condition but an objective reality independent of the structure of the human "soul." Introspection does not stop at self-cognition but aspires to the exteriorization or reification of psychological experiences and its causes. (*d*) Accordingly, the universe and, with it, the individual life are centered on God or on fate; man's purpose is outside himself and so are the source and the rationale of the incidents that make up his life. (*e*) As there are no firm criteria to distinguish fact from figment, figment from theory, and again theory from fact, man is reduced to speculation and deduction, exposed to wonderment and fear to an extent no longer imaginable to ourselves, hence subjected to alternations of extreme emotions which make him grasp at any cue by which to secure orientation in a universe that by its very construction defies orientation. (*f*) Hence, also, man's dedication to an ideal of cosmic and social stability with fixed lines of causation and symbolization. The universe—at least its directly relevant segment—tends to be limited or closed. At the same time, this quest for stability and security is defeated *ab initio* by the unwillingness to accept the epistemological consequences of the frailty of human cognition; revelations and dreams, signs of any kind, are expected to remedy from the outside what man is unable to achieve from within. (*g*) Accordingly, psychological phenomena tend to be interpreted as representing objective, nonpsychological "outside" reality; they constitute a means of obtaining objective, factual information about this outside reality and, up to a point, of controlling it. (*h*) There is, to put it differently, no mandatory or even no clearly perceived dividing line between the natural and the supernatural, any more than (*i*) between the possible and the impossible.[1]

This axiomatics, or mentality, creates of necessity (*a*) an intense concern for the dream that is (*b*) experienced and viewed as indicating, most of all, nonsubjective and nonpsychological (that is, suprapersonal and objective) facts and conditions (*c*) when it does not fulfill the function of a means of communication between the dreamer and the superhuman or supernatural powers. In other words, the dream is seen as possessed of cognitive force in regard to otherwise inaccessible sectors of objective reality, especially such as the future and the Hereafter, or, more generally, truths bearing on man's relation to the divine.

Thus the role of the dream, with its heuristic transpersonal symbolism, was firmly and legitimately embedded in the medieval civilization of Islam as well as in the outlook prevalent throughout our own Middle Ages. To account for certain contemporary attitudes toward the dream, it is useful to remember that the particulars of a cultural approach tend to linger even though their structural justification has long disappeared. Below and sometimes even on the surface of our own cultural life astrology persists, despite the fact that it is incompatible with our concepts of infinite universe and of causation, in short with the major assumptions of both our cosmology and our epistemology. The same goes for the reaction to the dream as it continues to animate sizable sections of the population throughout the West. Like an erratic bloc surviving from a past geological age the popular quest for material guidance from dreams, fed by curiosities and anxieties, continues on the medieval pattern. Logical contradiction, a divided intellectual universe, are less troublesome than the urge that the dream would seem to gratify so well. This reminder of the inconsistencies of conceptual frameworks, both on the individual and (even more so) on the collective plane, will help to account for the persistence of a certain type of dream interpretation, as well as of astrology, in the face of hesitations suggested by the implications of the accepted religious doctrine.

The ubiquity of the dream in Muslim civilization is touched upon in my communication only with regard to its "great tradition," its upper stratum, where its appropriateness to the scientific world view is significant. It cannot be emphasized enough that to the medieval Muslim, scholar or lay, the cognitive power of the dream does not present an epistemological problem. Not a single time does the latest authority on *oneirokritika,* the theologian ʿAbdalghanī an-Nābulusī (1641–1731), the

---

[1] In connection with (*h*) and (*i*), cf. L. Febvre, *Le Problème de l'incroyance au XVIe siècle: La religion de Rabelais* (2d ed.; Paris, 1947), pp. 473–481.

compiler of an encyclopedic guide to dream interpretation, arranged by the alphabet of the object seen in the dream, in the six hundred pages of his *Taʿṭīr al-anām fī taʿbīr al-manām,* question the objective validity of oneiric data. The cognitive significance of the dream is sufficiently established and explained by the observation that "the prophets were wont to consider dreams as revelation to them of the sacred laws: 'Prophecy has passed, and only the bearers of good tidings remain—good dreams which a man sees or which are shown him in sleep.'"[2]

Only the classification of the dreams and the methodology of dream interpretation are required. The reality of the objective significance of the dream is guaranteed by the Holy Book itself where Joseph is given knowledge of dreams and is addressed by God with the words:

> "Thus your Lord will prefer you and teach you the interpretation of events,"[3] meaning the science of dreams, the prime science since the beginning of the world, which the prophets and messengers did not cease to study and act upon. . . . To invalidate the significance of dreams, some unbelievers have stated that what a man sees in his sleep is dictated by the dominant of the four humors. If black bile dominates, he sees impurities [or: misfortunes], blackness, horrors, and terrors; if yellow bile dominates, he sees fire, lights, blood, and stuffs dyed yellow (*muʿaṣfarāt*); if phlegm dominates, whiteness, water, rivers and waves he sees; and if blood dominates, he sees wine, aromatic plants, lutes, and pipes [lit.: string and woodwind instruments]. But this constitutes only one type of dream, to which the whole range of dreams cannot be limited. For we know for certain that while the humors do dictate some dreams, some dreams are sent by the devil and some originate in the self. The latter, the truest of the three, are "confused [or: incoherent] dreams" (*aḍghāth*), so-called because they are mixed. They are like a bundle formed of plants, a *ḥuzma* that a person picks from the earth, containing plants both large and small, red and green, withered and fresh. . . .

It has been said that dreams are of three kinds: dreams of glad tidings from God; they are those good dreams cited in the tradition; dreams of warning from the devil; and dreams that originate in the

---

[2] Abdalghanī an-Nābulusī, *Taʿṭīr al-anām fī taʿbīr al-manām* (Cairo, 1316), I, 2. The *ḥadīth* was accepted by Buhkārī (cf. his *Ṣaḥīḥ,* 91:5). The translations from the *Taʿṭīr al-anām* throughout the chapter were prepared by D. P. Little in collaboration with me. The relationship of dream and prophecy is discussed in the remarkable study by Toufy Fahd, "Les Songes et leur interprétation selon l'Islam," in A.-M. Esnoul, P. Garelli, *et al.,* eds., *Les Songes et leur interprétation,* Sources orientales, Vol. II (Paris, 1959), pp. 125-157, at p. 137; Talmudic sayings of the same type ("The dream is the sixtieth part of prophecy," and the like) are referred to on p. 156 n. 37.
[3] Koran 12:6.

self. Dreams of warning from the devil are false and have no interpretation [or: significance]. . . . As examples of dreams that originate in the aspirations of the self, a person sees himself with one whom he loves; or, sees something of which he is afraid, or, being hungry, sees himself eating; being replete, sees himself vomit; sleeping in the sun, sees himself burning in fire; there being pain in his members, sees himself tortured.

False dreams are divided into seven types: (1) those that originate in the self, in desire, ambition, and confusion; (2) [sexual] dreams that necessitate ablution and have no interpretation; (3) warnings from the devil—threats and nightmares—which do no damage; (4) dreams that are shown by sorcerers, both *jinnī* and human, and are just as much a burden upon dreamers as those sent by the devil;[4] (5) falsity shown by Satan, not counted among dreams; (6) dreams shown by the humors when they are at variance and turbid; (7) "reversion," that is, when a dreamer sees himself in the present as if he were twenty years younger.

The truest dreams are those of good tidings. If in the dream there are tranquillity, repose, splendid garments, and wholesome, appetizing food, the dream is true and confusion is at a minimum. True dreams are divided into five types: (1) the trustworthy, manifest dream—a part of prophecy, in accordance with the words of the Exalted: "God has confirmed for his messenger the vision with truth. You shall enter the Holy Mosque, if God wills, secure."[5] . . . It has been said: "Blessed the one who sees a dream clearly, for clear dreams without mediation of the angel of the dreams are sent by none but the Creator." (2) Good dreams, which are glad tidings from God, just as adverse tidings are a means by which God alerts you. . . . (3) Dreams that the angel of dreams shows you, his name being Ṣiddīqūn, in accordance with what God has taught him from the original copy of the Book and has inspired him in providing a sure likeness for each and every thing. (4) The symbolic dream, which is from spirits. For example, a person sees in sleep one of the angels saying to him, "Your wife wants to give you poison to drink by the hand of your friend So and So," thereby hinting to him that the friend is committing adultery with his wife. But his dream indicates that the adultery is hidden, just like the poison. (5) The dream that is valid for the viewer and exerts an overpowering influence upon him, whereupon he makes evil into good and good into

---

[4] For (3) and (4) cf., as representative of our own attitude as late as the sixteenth century, the verses of Ronsard in which he identifies the demons bringing the dreams as messengers of the godhead:

> Postes divins, divins postes de Dieu
> Qui ses segrets nous apportez grand erre.

(Quoted by Febvre, *op. cit.*, pp. 205–206.)
[5] Koran 48:27.

evil. For example, he dreams that he is playing a *ṭunbūr* [a long-necked string instrument] in a mosque; thereafter he turns to God in repentance for abomination and the forbidden and becomes well known for his good deeds. Or he dreams that he is reading the Koran in the baths, or dancing; thereafter he gains notoriety for committing abomination or soliciting for whores, for the bath is a place of uncovering the genitals, a place that the angels do not enter, just as the devil does not enter a mosque. The dream of menstruation and ritual impurity is valid, for unbelievers and Magians do not believe in ritual ablution. Joseph interpreted the vision of the king, an unbeliever; the dreams of the young are valid, for Joseph was a boy of seven when he dreamed the dream that came true.[6]

The classification of dreams is followed by what may be called a minimum methodology of their interpretation. The psychophysical basis for the dreamer's awareness of his vision is this: "Man sees dreams with the spirit and understands them with the intelligence. . . . When a man sleeps, his spirit spreads like the light of a lamp or the sun. By this light and the brightness of God he sees that which the angel of dreams shows him. . . . When the senses are reawakened to their activities, the spirit is reminded of what the angel of dreams has shown and suggested to it."[7]

Nābulusī protects himself against any objection on the ground of incompleteness by observing that there are many paths to interpretation; the methods of the interpreter are expandable in accordance with his knowledge. There are, however, certain basic traits in the structure of the dream which bear on interpretation.

The elements of a dream consist of the genus, species and nature of things. Genus, for example, may be trees, beasts of prey, and birds, all these representing men. Species involves knowing the species of the tree, the beast and the bird. If the tree is a palm, the man represented by it is an Arab, for the origin of most palms is the land of the Arabs. If the bird is a peacock, the man is a non-Arab, or, if

---

[6] Nābulusī, *op. cit.*, I, 3-4. Poisoning as a symbol of a wife's adultery occurs in Artemidorus, *Oneirocritica* IV. 71. A simpler classification was offered by the qadi Sharīk b. ʿAbdallāh an-Nakhaʿī (d. 177/793-794). When the caliph al-Mahdī had seen him in a dream leading the community prayer in competition with himself and was persuaded that the vision indicated the judge's opposition to his rule, Sharīk pointed out that there were four classes of dreams: (1) divine inspiration; (2) converse of man with his own soul; (3) confused visions (or mere dreams, *aḥlām*); and (4) tricks played by Satan on the dreamer (*talaʿʿub ash-shaiṭān*). The caliph realizes that his dream was of the last class and bestows a robe of honor on the judge (Tauḥīdī [d. 1023], *al-Baṣāʾir waʾdh-dhakhāʾir*, ed. A. Amīn and A. Ṣaqr [Cairo, 1373/1953], pp. 218-219).
[7] Nābulusī, *op. cit.*, I, 5.

an ostrich, he is an Arab Bedouin. Nature involves observing the nature of the tree; by so doing one determines the nature of the man. If the tree is a walnut, one determines that the man's conduct and arguments are harsh in a dispute. If it is a palm, one determines that he is a man who serves the good. But if the subject is a bird, one knows that he is a man who travels. Then one observes the nature of the bird; if it is a peacock, he is a non-Arab king, handsome and rich. If it is an eagle, he is likewise a king, but if it is a crow, he is a sinful, treacherous man, and a liar.[8]

The connection that the interpreter establishes between the dream elements and "objective" reality is largely associative. It is preferable that the association be directed by applicable passages from the Koran and the *sunna;* but, in fact, the correct association may be found in "current sayings and common expressions." [9] The truthfulness of a personage seen in a dream depends on what may be expected from him in life: a child will be truthful in a dream because in life he does not yet know how to lie. If animals speak in dreams, they tell the truth, and so do the dead since they are "in the abode of truth." [10] As the environment influences the dreamer, so it influences the dreams. Because of regional differences in regard to "water, climate, and location" the interpretation of the several schools of interpreters differs. "Thus, dreaming in a torrid land of snow, ice, or cold indicates high prices and famine. But if such is dreamed in a cold land, it means fertility and plenty. For the people of India, mud and mire mean prosperity; for others, hardship and distress. Then, too, for Indians, breaking wind signifies good news and pleasure but for others is a disgusting mode of expression. To some countries, fish signify punishment; in others, from one to four fish mean marriage; to Jews—calamity." [11] Even in its Hippocratean disguise this awareness of the cultural conditioning of dream content and dream significance is remarkably clear. Nābulusī is conscious that people will approach the interpreter with invented dreams. It is not for the interpreter to establish their genuineness. "If the answer is auspicious, the merit is the interpreter's; if bad, it is at the cost of the willful questioner." [12]

How thoroughly the medieval Muslim was penetrated by the importance of his dreams is to be gauged from autobiographical documents such as the diary of the Ḥanbalite doctor Ibn al-Bannā' of Baghdad (1005-1079). In the preserved portion, which extends from August 3, 1068, to

---

[8] *Ibid.,* p. 7.
[9] *Ibid.,* p. 6.
[10] *Ibid.*
[11] *Ibid.,* p. 5.
[12] *Ibid.,* p. 6.

September 4, 1069, no less than twenty-three dreams are narrated, some of them at considerable length. Not all of these are his own; for Ibn al-Bannāʾ appears to have enjoyed a reputation as an interpreter and so was frequently approached by others for an explanation of theirs. These dreams bear on purely personal matters as well as political events and doctrinal questions.[13]

Similarly, the dream plays a prominent part in the autobiography of the Damascene historian Abū Shāma (1203-1268). Indeed, approximately one-fourth of it is taken up by dreams. The author justifies his indulging in these ultraprivate reports by the Koranic verse *wa-ammā bi-niʿmati rabbi-ka fa-ḥaddith* ("as for the benefactions of thy Lord, tell of them").[14] The gift of dreams was shared by the brother of the Shafiʿite scholar. The community recognized that the caliph ʿUmar (634-644) would frequently appear to Abū Shāma in his dreams and transmit through them his ideas concerning the war against the Franks and other matters regarding Islam. This happened in the year 624/1226-27.[15] Typologically, the justification proffered by Abū Shāma for relating his dreams belongs with the mystic ash-Shaʿrānī's (d. 1565) justifying self-glorification as fulfillment of the believer's duty to avow the acts of grace, *minan,* which God had deigned to confer on him.[16]

There is hardly any phase in the life of the community and the individual where dreams will not play a part. Less with a view to classifying the superabundant material than to increasing its manageableness, certain distinct categories of dreams or dream interference may be distinguished.

1. *The dreamer receives personal messages.*—Thus the Prophet may appear simultaneously to an individual and a prospective protector who extricates him from a difficult situation.[17] The poet Niẓāmī (d. 1209)

---

[13] Cf. G. Makdisi, "Autograph Diary of an Eleventh-Century Historian of Baghdad," *Bulletin of the School of Oriental and African Studies* (London), XVIII (1956), 9-31, 239-260; XIX (1957), 13-48, 281-303, 426-443.

[14] Koran 93:11; R. Bell, *The Qurʾān* (Edinburgh, 1937-1939) translates: "And as for the goodness of thy Lord, discourse of it."

[15] Abū Shāma, *Kitāb ar-rauḍatain,* ed. and trans. Barbier de Meynard (Paris, 1898-1906), II, 207-210, App. (trans., II, 211-216).

[16] Cf. G. E. von Grunebaum, *Der Islam im Mittelalter* (Zurich and Stuttgart, 1963), pp. 566 ff. n. 45.

[17] E.g., Hilāl aṣ-Ṣābī, *Wuzarāʾ,* ed. ʿA. A. Farrāj (Cairo, 1958), pp. $360^{ult.}$-362^5. The famous philosopher Abū Sulaimān al-Manṭiqī (d. 985 or 1000) and his friend, the qadi Ibn Sayyār, have similar dreams almost simultaneously—an indication of their deep-rooted friendship (M. Bergé, "Une Anthologie sur l'amitié d'Abū Ḥayyān at-Tawḥīdī," *Bulletin d'études orientales* [Damascus], XVI [1958-1960; published 1961], 15-60, at p. 40, quoting Tauḥīdī, "Risāla fī 'ṣ-ṣadāqa wa'ṣ-ṣadīq," in *Risālatāni* [Constantinople, 1301], p. 3^{8-13}).

exhorts the Indo-Muslim ʿIṣāmī (wrote 1349-1350) to undertake his historical work, later known as *Futūḥ as-salāṭīn*.[18] Before his last journey to Khurasan, Hārūn ar-Rashīd (786-809) sees a hand with red earth coming forth from under his bed while a voice is heard to say: "This is the earth, *turba,* of Hārūn." The court physician asks the caliph to resist the "confused vision"; but needless to say, it proves a true omen.[19] A dream conversation with Aristotle was one of the reasons that induced the caliph al-Maʾmūn to promote translations into Arabic of Greek philosophical texts.[20] A pious North African, convinced that he will die a martyr for the faith, sees in a dream God bless a part of his head—the exact spot where later he receives his mortal wound.[21] The great Andalusian heresiographer, jurist, and litterateur, Ibn Ḥazm (994-1064), records that he has seen some of his deceased friends in his dreams, but others, not. "At the time when one of those was still living we agreed that if possible we should visit [the survivor] in a dream. However, I did not see him after he had preceded me into the other world. And I do not know whether he forgot or was distracted [from appearing]." [22] The present prime minister of Malaya, Tunku Abdul Rahman, recently traveled to Ajmer because "a humble man in Malaya dreamt thrice in the course of a few weeks in 1959 that the pir or saint buried there desired the Tunku to pay a visit" to his tomb "if his difficulties were to be solved. . . . In the third and last dream, the pir is said to have brandished a sword." On hearing this the Tunku decided on making the pilgrimage at an early date.[23]

---

[18] P. Hardy, *Historians of Medieval India* (London, 1960), p. 95.
[19] Ibn Kathīr, *al-Bidāya wa'n-nihāya* (Cairo, 1351-1358), X, 213, *s.a.* 193/808-809. Translated from a different source, the dream is included in E. Schroeder, *Muhammad's People* (Portland, Me., 1955), pp. 339-341.
[20] Cf., e.g., Ibn an-Nadīm, *Fihrist* (Cairo, 1348/1929-1930), p. 339. Maʾmūn, however, was not the only prominent person to whom Aristotle appeared. The famous "illuminationist" thinker Suhrawardī (executed in 1191), too, has left a record of a dream interview with the protophilosopher (R. Walzer, *Greek into Arabic* [Oxford, 1962], p. 28). Not to overdraw the picture, reference should be made to the existence of a more cautious, even skeptical attitude. Thus, Samauʾal al-Maghribī (d. 1175), defending himself against the allegation that he had accepted Islam merely on account of a dream, insisted that "a sensible man will not be deceived about his affairs by dreams without proof or demonstration" (Samauʾal al-Maghribī, *Ifḥām al-Yahūd,* ed. and trans. M. Perlmann [New York, 1964], p. 87).
[21] H. R. Idris, "Contribution à l'histoire de l'Ifrikya . . . d'après le Riyāḍ En Nufūs d'Abū Bakr El Māliki," *Revue des études islamiques* (1935), 105-177; (1936), 45-104, at pp. 52-53, hereafter cited as *REI.*
[22] *Kitāb al-akhlāq wa's-siyar,* ed. and trans. N. Tomiche (Beirut, 1961), sec. 84.
[23] Cf. *Times of India* (Bombay), Oct. 9, 1962, p. 1, col. 3; article entitled "Tunku Plans To Visit Ajmer Darga." I am beholden to D. R. S. Desai, Assistant, Department of History, University of California, Los Angeles, for acquaintance with this news report.

2. *The dream constitutes a private prophecy.*—After long years in prison the fallen vizier of al-Mahdī (775–785), Yūnus b. ar-Rabīʿ, is visited in his sleep by an apparition reciting verse to him which suggests his early release. The implied announcement comes true after the dream has recurred three times.[24] The pious Rushaid, of "Slav" origin, dreamed that he had urinated in the mihrab of a mosque. The famous Buhlūl b. Rāshid of Qairawān (d. 799) explained this vision as presaging that a son would be born to him, who would become an outstanding religious scholar, a prediction, it is hardly necessary to add, that came true.[25] When on the accession of Qānṣūh al-Ghūrī (1501–1516), more than seven hundred years later, the famous polymath Jalāl ad-Dīn as-Suyūṭī (d. 1505) comes out of hiding he reports that the Prophet had announced to him in a dream the early end of al-ʿĀdil Ṭūmānbāy who had sentenced him to death.[26] Abū 'l-ʿAbbās Ibn al-Furāt, the brother of the famous vizier, appears to Abū ʿAbdallāh az-Zanjī telling him his brother's worries would end the next day. In the morning the caliph al-Muktafī (902–908) did, in fact, give him an appointment.[27] In 1169 Asad ad-Dīn Shīrkūh, the Zengid general in Egypt, has a dream which he interprets as foretelling that he would arrest and replace his rival, the Fatimid commander Shāwar. Encouraged by this dream he proceeds with his plot which leads to the capture and execution of his opponent.[28]

The private dream may lead to a personality change. A shrew changes her ways after dreaming that five men would whip her because her husband had complained of her to a saint; the saint, in turn, had informed God who thereupon sent the apparition.[29] A more celebrated instance is the dream that decided Nāṣir-i Khusraw in 1045 to end his dissipation and go on pilgrimage.[30] Even more famous, and more consequential for the Muslim community, is the dream that induced al-Ashʿarī (d. 935) to foresake the *kalām* of the Muʿtazila and establish "Ashʿarite" orthodoxy.[31] The Qarakhānid chieftain Satūq Bughrā Khān

---

[24] E. Köcher, "Yaʿqūb b. Dāʾūd, Wezir al-Mahdīs," *Mitteilungen des Instituts für Orientforschung*, III (1955), 378–420, at p. 408.
[25] Cf. Abū 'l-ʿArab Muḥammad b. Aḥmad b. Tamīm, *Kitāb ṭabaqāt ʿulamāʾ Ifrīqiya*, ed. and trans. M. Ben Cheneb (Algiers, 1914–1920), I, 110 (trans., II, 189).
[26] [Ibn Iyās], *Journal d'un bourgeois du Caire*, trans. G. Wiet (Paris, 1955–1960), I, 4.
[27] Ṣābī, *op. cit.*, p. 251¹⁻²; note that it is again Abū 'l-ʿAbbās who, in 924, announces to his brother, the vizier, his impending execution (D. Sourdel, *Le Vizirat ʿabbāside de 749 à 936* [Damascus, 1959–1960], II, 434).
[28] Abū Shāma, *op. cit.*, I, 144.
[29] Idris, *REI* (1936), 54.
[30] *Safar-Nāma*, trans. Ch. Schefer (Paris, 1881), pp. 3–4.
[31] The story has often been told with more or less embroidery added (R. J. McCarthy, *The Theology of al-Ashʿarī* [Beirut, 1953], pp. 150–151, 152–153, 154–155;

(d. 955), the first of his tribe to embrace Islam, took this step under the impact of a dream in which conversion was commanded him by heaven.³²

3. *Dreams elucidate theological doctrine.*—Abū Dulaf, in 226/841, sees his father in a desolate house; the father recites verses to him assuring him of the reality of the examination after death and expressing the wish that death actually were a coming to rest, *rāḥa kull shaiʾ*, which, however, it is not; for on dying we are roused and interrogated.³³ Similarly, al-Bājī tells Abū 'l-Faḍl al-Ghaḍāmisī (d. 349/960) in a dream that he has come through this examination. "On my death, my soul was given back to me. I perceived all you did to me: the washing [of my body], the shroud, prayer. When you had put me in the ground someone called me shouting to me to recite. My tongue recited the Sura Yāsīn [Sura 36]. The two [interrogating] angels arrived. The one said to the other: 'Examine him!' 'Do you not hear him recite the heart of the Koran?' replied the other; and they went off without further interrogation."³⁴ These dreams serve the double purpose of clarifying the moot question of the "examination in the grave" and of reassuring the survivors with regard to the fate in the Hereafter of particular persons. Zubaida, the wife of Hārūn ar-Rashīd, who died in 831, is seen in heaven by ʿAbdallāh b. al-Mubārak. She had been admitted to Paradise because of the work she had done on the pilgrim road to Mecca; her face, however, was pale because of the moaning of the Muʿtazilite Bishr al-Marīsī (d. 833) which she had heard rise from Hell and which had made her shiver.³⁵

Death reveals the truth about a person's religious condition. The mystic Abū Bakr al-Warrāq (d. 903) is weeping when he is seen in a dream by a dervish. He is asked: "Why do you cry?" Al-Warrāq replies: "How could I help crying? Of ten dead who today were carried to the cemetery where I rest, not a one died a believer."³⁶ The intensity of the communication that some Sufis maintain with the transcendental world by means of the dream can only be noted. It is in the nature of their approach to themselves and to reality that the distinction between personal message

---

see also p. 170; all versions are translated from Ibn ʿAsākir [d. 1176], *Tabyīn kadhib al-muftarī*, ed. Ḥusām ad-Dīn al-Qudsī [Damascus, 1347/1928–1929], pp. 38–39, 40–43, 147).

³² Cf. W. Barthold, *Histoire des Turcs d'Asie Centrale* (Paris, 1945), p. 64; the story does, however, present chronological difficulties.

³³ Ibn Kathīr, *op. cit.*, X, 294.

³⁴ Idris, *REI* (1935), 278.

³⁵ Ibn Kathīr, *op. cit.*, X, 271¹²⁻¹⁶, *s.a.* 216/831. The name of ʿAbdallāh b. al-Mubārak must be an erroneous choice by the transmitter, for this celebrated preacher and fighter for the faith died in 181/797–798.

³⁶ Cf. H. Ritter, *Das Meer der Seele* (Leiden, 1955), p. 72, after ʿAṭṭār, *Ilāhī-Nāma*, ed. H. Ritter (Leipzig, 1940), pp. 278–279.

and theological enlightenment, or confirmation of their type of religiosity as conveyed by a dream, is difficult to establish.[37] Dreams that clarify the position of the deceased in the Hereafter at the same time frequently instruct on the correct solution of controversial theological issues. There are a number of dreams in which the Prophet is shown siding with the then still living Aḥmad b. Ḥanbal against his Muʿtazilite adversary, the chief judge Aḥmad b. abī Duʾād, whose death (which occurred in 854) and punishment are announced.[38] After Ibn Ḥanbal's death (in 855) he is often seen by faithful dreamers deciding theological problems.[39] Saḥnūn, the great doctor (d. 854), to whom Mālikism is deeply indebted for its spread in North Africa, after his death announced by means of a dream that to read the Koran with a text before one's eyes was preferable to reciting it by heart, thus deciding a controversy of long standing.[40] It is of course well known that Christian hierarchs, too, used this manner of communication to set the hearts of the faithful at rest. A dream bore witness that Pope Benedict VIII (1012-1024) had been received into heaven as a result of Cluniac intercession.[41]

At times the stage setting of the dream is quite elaborate. Thus Rabīʿ al-Qaṭṭān (d. 339/950-951) had this dream experience in support of strict predestinarianism. Walking in the air as one does on the ground he became aware of a number of tents and a considerable crowd by them. He got the feeling that he was near God. A voice told him that he was asked to enter; he noticed the chamberlains and was introduced to God whom he saw seated on His royal couch. God told him: "Ask." Rabīʿ asked to be taught something useful. Thereupon he was projected into space, chest first, as if he were swimming in water. He saw people like ants, some had a light, others did not. God said to him: "On earth, those [with the light] desire Us; among them We have chosen a small number and have given them knowledge; one of them is al-Ḥajjāj b. abī Yaʿqūb ad-Daqqāq." [42] In this dream God is introduced quite naïvely, but the

---

[37] The easiest access to the peculiar "dreamworld" of Sufism is through Ritter, *Meer,* Index, *s.v.* "Traum," pp. 767–768.
[38] Ibn Kathīr, *op. cit.,* X, 321^{24}–322^4, *s.a.* 240/854–855.
[39] *Ibid.,* X, 342–343, *s.a.* 241/855–856.
[40] Idris, *REI* (1935), 287.
[41] Cf. G. Tellenbach, *Libertas: Kirche und Weltanschauung im Zeitalter des Investiturstreites* (Stuttgart, 1936), p. 96. For contrast, note the dream in which Pierre Barthélemy sees Bishop Adhémar de Puy in Hell three days after his death on Aug. 1, 1098; cf. P. Alphandéry and A. Dupront, *La Chrétienté et l'idée de croisade* (Paris, 1954-1959), I, 108–109. The cliché goes back to antiquity. In the (lost) dialogues of Antisthenes (*ca.* 440–370 B.C.), Socrates appears in their dreams to his disciples sitting by his grave and offers them instruction; cf. O. Gigon, *Grundprobleme der antiken Philosophie* (Bern and Munich, 1959), p. 80.
[42] Idris, *REI* (1935), 140–141.

dream vision of the Lord, attested as an actual experience by many who assert having seen Him in various shapes—as a beardless youth, a woman, a Turk with his cap put on at a coquettish angle—was to become a theological problem. The crucial point was, of course, the elimination of anthropomorphic conceptions. Al-Ghazzālī (d. 1111) teaches that God, being above shape and form, cannot in fact be seen in the ruʾyat Allāh; what appears to the dreamer is a likeness, a symbol, mithāl.[43] The experience of being instructed through a dream is not entirely confined to the Muslim pious. The Christian philosopher Ibn Zurʿa (d. 1008) sees in 368/978-979 his teacher Yaḥyà b. ʿAdī, then four years dead, in a dream during which he communicates to him certain teachings in astonishing detail.[44] Discouraging for the powerful but heartening for the simple pious is the dream in which Maḥmūd of Ghazna (998-1030) revealed his insight acquired in the next world, that his kingship had been but illusion and error. God alone rules and is worthy to rule. Having understood his impotence and confusion Maḥmūd is ashamed of having been sultan. It would have been better for him to spend his life as a beggar; now he has to account for every grain he expended.[45] The cosmic importance that the saint, in contradistinction to the king, possesses comes through in the dream in which Abū Mūsà sees the heavenly throne placed on his head. When he goes to relate the vision to his master Bāyazīd Bisṭāmī (d. 874), he finds that the sheikh has died that very night. During the funeral Abū Mūsà, prevented by the crowd from carrying the coffin at one of its ends, puts his head under it while the procession is moving toward the cemetery. The dream had slipped his mind. Suddenly his master appears to him and says: This is the meaning of last night's dream. That heavenly throne is the body of Bāyazīd.[46]

It deserves notice that the pattern of theological argumentation through dreams has persisted into our own time. In Iraq, during a recent polemical exchange on problems of modernism, the Prophet appeared in a dream to one of the controversialists to confound the heretic in person.[47] Similarly, it was by way of a dream that in 1953 the saint whose tomb protected a market in eastern Algeria announced his consent that this

---

[43] Cf. Ritter, Meer, pp. 447-449, for examples of pertinent dreams and for an analysis of al-Ghazzālī's Risāla fī taḥqīq ruʾyat Allāh fī 'l-manām.

[44] Cf. S. Pines, "La longue recension de la théologie d'Aristote dans ses rapports avec la doctrine ismaélienne," REI (1954), 7-20, at p. 9 n. 2; and Scripta Hierosolymitana, IX (1961), 155-156.

[45] Ritter, Meer, p. 112, after ʿAṭṭār (d. 1220; less reliable reports identify the year of his death as 1229 or 1234), Manṭiq aṭ-ṭair, ed. Garcin de Tassy (Paris, 1857), pp. 35-36.

[46] Ritter, Meer, p. 629 (where references).

[47] Cf. J. Berque, Les Arabes d'hier à demain (Paris, 1960), p. 251.

market be moved to a more convenient place that the French *administrateur* had suggested.⁴⁸

4. *The dream bears on politics.*—ʿAlqama an-Nakhaʿī was told in a dream by his brother, killed in the battle of Ṣiffīn (657) that the slain Syrians (adherents of Muʿāwiya) and Iraqis (adherents of ʿAlī) had argued in heaven whose cause had been the just, and God had declared for the Iraqi.⁴⁹ The approval by the community of Saladin's policies is reflected in a dream in which the Prophet is seen visiting the prince's tomb with some of his Companions.⁵⁰ When Saladin died someone heard a voice in his dream announcing: "This night Joseph left his prison."⁵¹ Fully to appreciate this episode it must be recalled that Yūsuf (Joseph) was Saladin's given name, that Yūsuf, the Biblical Joseph, has become, in mystical thought, the symbol of divine beauty and even of the divinity dwelling in the heart of the believer, and that the liberation of the soul from the prison of the body is a favorite Sufi interpretation of death. By contrast, political action is criticized when Ibrāhīm b. Maimūn aṣ-Ṣāʾigh, after his execution by Abū Muslim, whose fellow *dāʿī*, or propagandist, in the service of the Abbasids he had been, and whom he had caused difficulties by insisting on carrying out the letter of the religious law, the *sharīʿa*, is seen in "exalted dwellings," *manāzil ʿāliya,* in Paradise, whither he has been raised because of his perseverance in the Muslim duty of "enjoining the good and inhibiting the bad," *al-amr biʾl-maʿrūf waʾn-nahy ʿan al-munkar.*⁵² In like fashion, after the execution of Aḥmad b. Naṣr in 231/845–846, the Prophet is seen in a dream ashamed that a member of his House, namely the caliph al-Wāthiq (842–847), should have perpetrated such a crime.⁵³

A dream may suggest a specific political action. The Prophet's expedition in 628, undertaken to force the pilgrimage to Mecca which led to the famous treaty of al-Ḥudaibiya, was decided on the impulse of a dream.⁵⁴ Al-Mahdī (775–785) saw Yaʿqūb b. Dāʾūd in a dream, and the caliph was advised to appoint this personage to the vizierate. When Yaʿqūb was later presented to al-Mahdī, the prince is reported to have

---

⁴⁸ Cf. J. H. Servier, "Essai sur les bases de l'économie traditionelle chez les Berbérophones d'Algérie," *Institut de science économique appliquée. Cahiers,* 106 (1960), 87–103, at pp. 102–103.
⁴⁹ Cf. J. Wellhausen, *Das arabische Reich und sein Sturz* (2d ed.; Berlin, 1960), p. 52 n. 2.
⁵⁰ Abū Shāma, *op. cit.,* II, 97.
⁵¹ *Ibid.*
⁵² Koran 3:100; Ibn Kathīr, *op. cit.,* X, 68¹⁻⁷, s.a. 137/754–755.
⁵³ *Ibid.,* X, 306⁶⁻⁹.
⁵⁴ For references to the sources, cf. W. M. Watt, *Muhammad at Medina* (Oxford, 1956), p. 46.

exclaimed: "This is the man who appeared in my dream!" and immediately named him vizier.[55] Conversely, ʿUmar b. al-Khaṭṭāb is said to have dismissed an official because of a dream.[56] Aḥmad b. Ṭūlūn, the governor and, in fact, independent ruler of Egypt from 868 to 884, is made aware by a dream of the arrival of spies sent by the caliph.[57] Another dream counsels Ibn Ṭūlūn to abolish certain "illegal" taxes against the advice of his financial secretary.[58] At one point, a certain Maʿmar b. Muḥammad al-Jauharī induced Ibn Ṭūlūn to become his associate in the flax trade. After a while Ibn Ṭūlūn saw himself in a dream sucking the marrow out of some bones. The well-known interpreter, Ibn al-ʿAssāl, explained: "The *amīr* is running after a profit of little value not worthy of him." Thereupon Ibn Ṭūlūn withdrew his investment and distributed it to the poor.[59] The caliph al-Muʿtaḍid (892–902) told his entourage that certain dreams he had seen in his youth had persuaded him never to do damage to any descendant of ʿAlī.[60]

5. *The dream is used as a tool of political prophecy.*—Particularly numerous are the instances in which the death of a ruler is foretold by a dream. Thus we learn that Saʿīd b. al-Musayyab (d. *ca.* 718/719) is visited by a man who tells him that he saw in a dream the Prophet standing on the shore of the sea. He was seizing a man by his foot and spinning him around three times as the washer spins around a garment, after which he pushed him out into the ocean. Saʿīd said: "If your dream vision comes true [or: if you have seized your dream correctly], ʿAbdalmalik [685–705] will die within three days." And in fact, the caliph did die in three days. On being asked the rationale of his interpretation Saʿīd said: Moses drowned Pharaoh; and the Pharaoh of our time was none other than ʿAbdalmalik.[61] On his deathbed, the caliph al-Manṣūr (754–775) tells of a dream he had before his family came to power. First his brother, then himself received a banner from the Prophet and while carrying it made a number of steps before falling to the ground. The number of steps proved to be the number of regnal years. Manṣūr, recalling the dream, realizes that his death is at hand.[62] Another type of

---

[55] Köcher, *op. cit.*, p. 387 n. 35.
[56] Cf. Z. M. Hassan, *Les Tulunides* (Paris, 1933), p. 203 n. 4.
[57] *Ibid.*, p. 203.
[58] Cf. C. H. Becker, *Beiträge zur Geschichte Ägyptens unter dem Islam* (Strasbourg, 1902–1903), II, 196; Hassan, *op. cit.*, pp. 53–54.
[59] *Ibid.*, p. 181.
[60] Cf. Sourdel, *op. cit.*, I, 343–344.
[61] Yaʿqūbī (d. 897), *Taʾrīkh* (Beirut, 1379/1960), II, 281$^{10-15}$. Saʿīd, who, incidentally, uses *gharraqa* where the Koran employs *aghraqa,* does not refer to a particular passage but to the Koranic tale as a whole.
[62] *Ibid.*, II, 388^{18}–389^{1}.

event is foretold when in 1160 someone dreams in Mosul of the exploits against the Christians which, some day, Saladin would accomplish;[63] or again in the dream in which ʿUmar I announces to Abū Shāma in 1228 that he would personally lead an expedition against the Syrian coast, then held by the Crusaders, and give its rule to a noble and brave prince.[64] With this vision may be compared the dream of Shaikh ʿAlī as-Sakhāwī who, on June 8, 1229, during the siege of Damascus by al-Malik an-Nāṣir, hears a voice crying: "After a month Damascus will be like unto Paradise." The forecast comes true when peace between the warring Muslim factions is restored on July 9.[65]

For the use of the dream as a political weapon the Holy Book itself had set the precedent. After the Muslim victory at Badr (March 15, 624), where some 350 believers vanquished close to a thousand heathen, Muhammad received a revelation in which God claims the merit of having brought to pass the encounter which, without His contriving, neither of the parties would have sought. In this context the Prophet is told: "[Recall] when Allah caused thee to see them in thy dream as few in number; if He had caused thee to see them as numerous ye would have been faint-hearted and vied with each other in withdrawing from the affair, but Allah kept [you] sound [in heart]. He knoweth what is in the breasts."[66] In describing the flare-up of Shiʿite activity after the death of Zaid b. ʿAlī in 121/739, Yaʿqūbī says: "Propagandists appeared, dream visions were seen and apocalyptic books circulated," *wa-ẓaharat ad-duʿāt wa-ruʾiyat al-manāmāt wa-tuduwwirat kutub al-malāḥim*.[67] The general confidence in the dream led to a good deal of "fraudulent dreaming"; obviously this could not be prevented; but it is only fair to note that the Muslims were aware of this danger, witness the story in which the qadi Abū Muḥriz observes that Abū Shaikh al-Mufassir is lying when he tells Ziyādat Allāh I, the Aghlabid ruler of the Ifrīqiya (817–838), of a dream in which he saw Gabriel kiss the hand of the *amīr*.[68]

As recently as 1902, when the request for a loan from Russia was uppermost in his mind, did Muẓaffar ad-Dīn, Shah of Persia from 1896 to 1906, ask a leading divine to interpret a dream in which he himself

---

[63] Abū Shāma, *op. cit.*, I, 292.
[64] Abū Shāma, *adh-Dhail ʿalā 'r-Rauḍatain*, ed. Barbier de Meynard (Paris, 1898–1906), II, 185, s.a. 625/1227–1228.
[65] *Ibid.*, pp. 189–190.
[66] Koran 8:45; the passage extends from verse 43 through verse 46.
[67] Yaʿqūbī, *op. cit.*, 326^{16}; cf. also Fahd's reminder (*op. cit.*, p. 156 n. 44), that Abbasid propaganda operated with dreams in which the Prophet confers the power on al-ʿAbbās (with reference to Abū Bakr al-Baihaqī [d. 1066], *al-Maḥāsin wa'l-masāwī*, ed. F. Schwally [Giessen, 1902], p. 345).
[68] Idris, *REI* (1935), 166.

had appeared to the ruler. The theologian explained: "Whereas Your Majesty saw me in the primitive Moslem garb throw a sack at your feet whence flowed gold and silver, this means that my ancestor the Prophet bids you to make no fresh loans from unbelievers, but to trust for the restoration of your finances to your subjects and fellow servants of the faith." There was some disagreement at the time whether the dream had been invented by the Shah to test the feelings of the clergy.[69] (When Polybius tells of the elder Scipio, in 212 B.C., relating to his mother that in a dream he had seen both himself and his brother elected to the aedileship, and when the same Scipio, two years later, encourages his soldiers by presenting his plans of attack on Cartagena as inspired by a dream vision of Neptune, the historian, at least, is convinced that the Roman invented those apparitions; the success of the pretense is, however, predicated on the prevalence of an attitude similar to that of Muslim society.)[70]

The difference between the Muslim outlook on the dream and our own is not discussed here in detail, especially as our attitude is implicit in the communications made to this Colloquium. Two observations are, however, in order.

1. In a sense, we have less need of our dreams than had the Muslims and our forefathers. For one thing, we are no longer so deeply concerned with the Hereafter and the supernatural; better put, the borders of the "natural" have been pushed out, and with this expansion of the rationally, even experimentally, accessible, the importance of the dream, the vision, the revelatory communication has shrunk within our daily lives and our intellectual life as well. Better knowledge and wider control of our universe have relieved us of anxieties and fears which, in many cases, the *Wahrtraum* was destined to allay. It is important to recall that as late as three and certainly four centuries ago, our psychological situation was not yet such that the dream could be dispensed with, and that the deficiencies of our scientific methods entailed more than a little uncertainty as to what could and what could not be accepted as real and as true.

2. As a result of our scientific advancement we have become able to afford a renunciation long overdue; we have been able to yield the idea that the dream is symptomatic of a reality divorced from the psychological reality of the dreamer and his society. (The progress of investigations into the paranormal stimulation of dreams does not contradict this

---

[69] Great Britain, Public Record Office 070, F.O. 60/660; A. Hardinge to the Marquess of Lansdowne, Tehran, Feb. 27, 1902, No. 32, Secret. The writer owes knowledge of this document to Professor N. R. Keddie, University of California, Los Angeles; the microfilm was loaned by Professor F. Kazemzadeh, Yale University.
[70] Polybius, *Historiae* X.3, 5–6; 11, 7.

statement.) To us, the symptomatic, revelatory, "prophetic" significance of the dream points inward to the dreamer (and to his society), not outward into areas of reality inaccessible by rational or "natural" means. (In fact, to many of us the existence of such areas of reality has become quite doubtful.) The dream explains and reflects, not the mind of the Prophet or the caliph 'Umar, but our own mind; its source is personal or (in the view of some) transpersonal, but, in any event, human.

To restate my conclusion: The great change that has made the dream an instrument for introspection and (collective) self-cognition, rather than an instrument for cognition of "outside reality," has in some ways detracted, in other ways added, to its significance within our own culture. Though it is true that our concern for the dream has lessened, we have developed, beyond our interest in its medical and analytical significance, a sense of the heuristic value of the dream in cultural and cross-cultural research. Our present attitude toward ourselves and toward civilization tends to heighten our perceptiveness of the functional differentiation of common, of universal, of human phenomena in different historical and cultural contexts. To me, the favorableness of the psychological moment implies an obligation and holds the promise of sharpened insight which, to us, is its own reward.

2

Logical and Philosophical Problems of the Dream

ROGER CAILLOIS

There are two problems concerning dreams which have always puzzled men. One concerns the actual meaning or significance of the dream; the other, the relationship between the dream and the waking world or, one might say, the degree of reality one may attribute to the dream.

The first problem centers on the meaning of the dream. Since time immemorial, visions in dreams have seemed to man to conceal a meaning that is mysterious, yet open to understanding, so that a competent interpreter should be capable of elucidating them. From this have stemmed innumerable "dream books" whose purpose is to decipher the strange and disconcerting messages of the dreams. One of the earliest of these collections dates back to ancient Egypt of the period of the Twelfth Dynasty (eighteenth or twentieth century B.C.). In the Indian *Atharva-Veda,* which is usually attributed to the fifth century B.C., the Pariśishtas of the sixty-eighth verse chapter is called "Treatise of Dreams." This is based on a more ancient work that bears the same title and catalogues the various omens foretold in dreams. A. Leo Oppenheim has translated and published a neo-Babylonian dream guide that was discovered at Nineveh among the tablets known as the library of Assurbanipal

(669–626 B.C.). Another dream guide, by Artemidorus of Daldis, has frequently been reissued and adapted. This literature is strangely monotonous.

A dream is teeming in images, confused and inextricable. Of necessity the dream guides retain only isolated acts, individual elements from the dreams. They immediately become interminable litanies. From the Babylonian dream guide, opened at random: "If he eat of the flesh of a bear, rebellion; if he eat of the flesh of an ape, he will acquire something by the use of force; if he eat of more common meat, peace of mind; if he eat asphalt, sorrow; if he eat naphtha, anxiety. . . ." And so ad infinitum. Then come further listings: "If he be given. . . . If he should cut. . . . If he should seize. . . . If he should carry. . . ." Once the principle is adopted, why stop?

Other dream guides, whatever their place and time, hardly deviate either in inspiration or presentation from a tradition that may be considered immutable. I give one more example, this time taken from the Indian *Suśruta Saṃhita* before the fourth century A.D. An extract from a voluminous medical work, it bears more resemblance to psychoanalytic material than to the long subject lists that make up the dream guides peddled by hawkers.

Dreams That Portend Death

I shall speak of dreams that have a bearing on death and on health, of dreams of a friend of the sick man as well as those of the sick man himself: The one who, with his body smeared with oil, turns southward with elephants or beasts of prey, asses, wild boars, or buffaloes,

The one who, tied up, is dragged away southward by a black woman, dressed in red, snickering, disheveled, and jerky,

The one who is lured away southward by his friends or is surrounded by dead persons while walking about,

The one who is roughly seized by men with disfigured faces and the feet of dogs, the one who drinks honey or oil, the one who is sitting in a puddle or the one who, with his body spattered with mud, gesticulates or breaks into laughter,

The one who, without any clothes, wears on his head a red garland, or the one from whose belly sprouts a reed, a bamboo shoot, or a palm tree,

The one who is swallowed by a fish or who enters into his mother, the one who falls from a mountain or into a gloomy ravine,

The one who is carried away by a water course, the one who loses his Brahman cord, the one who is surrounded and tied up by these crows or other birds of misfortune, all these are lost.

The one who sees the falling of stars or other heavenly bodies, sees a lamp going out or an eye torn out, the one who sees the images of the gods or the ground tremble,

The one who vomits, who is purged, or whose teeth fall out, the one who climbs into a cotton tree or into various other trees in full bloom, who climbs on an anthill, on a funeral pyre, or on a sacrificial stake,

The one who receives or eats cotton, oil, cake, iron, salt, sesame, or cooked foods, or drinks alcohol, all these if they are well, fall ill; if ill, die.[1]

The human mind seems strangely conservative on these topics. I suppose it is so of necessity for human nature in its essential difficulties allows for very little modification. There is nothing that is too absurd, too miraculous, or too contradictory of which one may not dream, and it is almost impossible that any more than the very smallest portion of these marvels could ever be realized. The interpreter must therefore reduce their infinite multitude to the small number of events that are almost certain to occur to everyone in the course of his brief life: a meeting, an illness, a loss or a gain, success or failure, riches or ruin, a voyage, falling in love, and the inevitable *par excellence*—death. Neither palmistry, astrology, nor any other science of divination one may imagine, can avoid, any more than can the interpretation of dreams, passing through this narrow gate: to reduce the countless data in their unlimited whimsicality to the sober dozen of dramatic incidents that everybody does cross almost obligatorily during his lifetime. This procedure is bound to succeed for, at the first coincidence, everyone is dazzled by the skill of the interpreter who has been able to read into a discouraging puzzle the forecast of an unexpected event that nothing, except the law of averages, has enabled him to foresee. For approximately four thousand years, in any case, lists of the relationship between dream images and their meaning have met with resounding success. In our own days, in a rather more flexible form and with the help of scientific terminology, the interpretations of psychoanalysis continue the tradition, satisfying the same immemorial need.

The Bible is full of dreams that are explained by the prophets. Thus

---

[1] A.-M. Esnoul, "Les Songes et leur interprétation dans l'Inde," in A.-M. Esnoul, P. Garelli, *et al.*, eds., *Les Songes et leur interprétation*, Sources orientales, Vol. II (Paris, 1959), pp. 223-224.

the dreams of Nebuchadnezzar and Pharaoh. In postbiblical literature the idea was put forward that the dream itself was unimportant and that it was the interpretation that counted, becoming itself the effective forecast, and thereby forcing reality to follow suit. "There were twenty-four interpreters of dreams in Jerusalem. Once I had a dream and went to everyone of them and what any one interpreted, none of the others interpreted in the same way, and yet all of them were fulfilled. This is in pursuance of the saying: *The dream follows the mouth* [of the one who interprets it]."[2]

Certain stories exemplify the truth of this doctrine and suggest its theoretical basis.

The Dream of the Cracked Granary

A certain woman came to Rabbi Eliezer and said to him: "I saw in a dream that the granary of my house came open in a crack." He answered: "You will conceive a son." She went away, and that is what happened.

She dreamed again the same dream and told it to Rabbi Eliezer who gave the same interpretation, and that is what happened.

She dreamed the same dream a third time and looked for Rabbi Eliezer. Not finding him, she said to his disciples: "I saw in a dream that the granary of my house came open in a crack."

They answered her: "You will bury your husband." And that is what happened.

Rabbi Eliezer, surprised by the lamentations, inquired what had gone wrong? His disciples told him what had happened. He cried out, "Wretched fools! You have killed that man. Is it not written: 'As he interpreted to us, so it was'? (Gen. 41:13). And Rabbi Yohannan concludes: "Every dream becomes valid only by its interpretation."[3]

If we believe that fleeting, incoherent dream visions may come true, then we must suppose that they can either announce or compel the unforeseeable future. If, however, we believe that it is the interpretation that eventually comes true, then, in order to admit and understand this, it is enough to remember that men are credulous and easily influenced; furthermore, men are vain, for it is flattering to imagine oneself the object of prophecy or supernatural warnings. It is probable that in our time the

---

[2] Georges Levitte and Guy Casaril, "Les rêves et leurs interprétations dans les textes post-bibliques," *Evidences*, 11 (March, 1960), 18–30, at p. 20, quoting Berakhot 55 B.
[3] *Ibid.*, quoting Gen. R. 89:8.

revelations of psychoanalytical treatments profit by the same privilege and impose themselves in like fashion on the analyzed.

The second type of problem deals with the interference of the waking and dreaming states, their opposition, the order of their importance, and the possibility of their working together. The question to be asked here relates not only to the significance of the vision seen in the dream, but also to the significance of the act of dreaming itself. The world of the dream is another universe. Is it then more real, equally real, or less real than that of the waking state?

It has been frequently maintained that the so-called primitive peoples do not distinguish the dream from the waking state. I think that this idea has to be modified somewhat. They know perfectly well what a dream is and what it is to be awake, but they attribute no lesser degree of reality to the dream than to the waking experience. Sometimes, rather more impressed by dreams, they accord them greater weight than they do a simple, banal perception, and they are convinced that the dreams bear witness to a superior reality. In other words, the distinction is made, but it does not follow, that the dream seems illusory or the waking world incontestable. The dream may even be thought to be more real than reality.

It is the impression that a dream makes which determines its value and gives it persuasive force. A dream that fails to excite is immediately forgotten; it is a futile, empty phantasmagoria that dissolves as soon as it appears, falling away without a trace no matter how rich and swirling. But once a feeling of anxiety or fulfillment fastens consciousness to images that may in themselves be insignificant, then the mind never ceases to search for the secret behind its agitation. It senses a danger signal, a revelation as yet ambiguous and unintelligible, a summons indicating imminent misfortune or a promise of a matchless destiny.

The most remarkable thing about the emotion thus felt is its independence of the image that seemed to be its cause. A certain scene that in the waking state appears merely indifferent, pleasant, or comical, in the dream gives the inert dreamer a shudder he cannot stop. At once he must learn the reason for this fright, the cause remains in hiding as though in deliberate sarcasm. The subject, left without any explanation, remains upset. Conversely, it happens that a normally repugnant, horrifying, or scandalizing spectacle comes associated with a state of bliss and delight, which indicates that it is not to be taken literally but rather signifies some triumph, or some strange and precious favor of fate.

The contrast, or at least the separation, between the image and the emotion accompanying it makes the difference between the dream and the waking world where they are always in accord because the emotion comes from the spectacle and is not something added to it by some obscure, capricious, formidable power. The impact of the dream is that it demands an explanation, a sequel, and, almost, a realization. Whenever it enters competition with reality, it is the dream that wins, and it is with the dream that man is first led to struggle, because the lackluster, orderly continuity of the real is less striking to him than the wonders of the dream, at least whenever its hypnotic spell has aroused in the mind uneasiness and stubborn expectancy.

I do not believe that there is any other secret to the dream's authority. From this authority several consequences derive, the first of which is that the events in a dream do not seem less true than those of the waking state. Everything seen in a dream is held believable. The dreamer, on awakening, finds it natural to demand an explanation from a friend or neighbor whom he has seen, in his dream, to be hostile or threatening, to do him wrong, or to benefit him in some way. The victim knows nothing about it, but has to admit that he has in fact, during his sleep and all unknowingly, become guilty of whatever he is being accused of. Denials are of no use. What evidence can you present against what has been seen?

In a dream an Indian in Paraguay saw a missionary, W. B. Grubb, stealing pumpkins from his garden. Grubb was a hundred miles away from the dreamer's village that night. But no argument could influence the Indian because he had *seen* the missionary picking the pumpkins and carrying them away. Another one dreamed that this same missionary shot at him while accusing him of some fault. The next morning, happy because he was still alive but fearful of another attempt, he tried to kill Grubb.

In the same way a native of Borneo dreams that his wife has been unfaithful. Her father takes her away in order to avoid having to pay the penalty normally due from an adulterous wife. The testimony of a dream easily outweighs a debatable denial. A man dreams that a man he knows and names has struck his father-in-law with a lance. The father-in-law was, in fact, sick, but not at all from a blow by a lance; at least no wound was visible. No matter; a lance in a dream, it goes without saying, effects invisible wounds. The accused individual has no recourse but to seek the protection of the authorities.[4] He himself does not deny his guilt; he has no assurance that his "soul" did not act while he was asleep during a dream he does not remember.

The explanation, very widely accepted, was already well understood in the seventeenth century by the missionaries to the Indians in Canada: "Having no concept of how the soul acts during sleep, they believe that when presenting to them objects absent and far away, the soul leaves the

[4] Henry Ling Roth, *The Natives of Sarawak and British North Borneo* (London, 1896), I, 232.

body while it sleeps, and that it goes by itself to seek things dreamed of or places seen, and that it returns to the body toward the end of the night when all dreams vanish." [5]

Analogous concepts have been noted among the Eskimo of Hudson's Bay, in Africa, and in Australia. When there is a contradiction between them, the dream is deemed more trustworthy than the waking state. H. Callaway reports the case of a Zulu who dreamed that his friend meant to do him harm. Thereafter he acted accordingly. He had more confidence in the dream's revelation than in the experience of friendship.[6] The Iroquois did not stop at half measures: "Their punctiliousness in this matter was scrupulous. Whatever it was they believed they had done while dreaming, they thought it absolutely obligatory to carry out as soon as possible."[7] Father Lalement noted in 1626 that if one of them dreamed in this fashion that he had killed a Frenchman, the first straggler he met ran the greatest risk of being murdered. It was not even necessary for the dreamer himself to have been involved. It was enough that he had witnessed such an act by others in his dream. No effort was spared in duplicating the dream exactly:

> One night not long ago a man from the village of Oiogoen while sleeping saw ten men diving into the frozen river, going in one hole in the ice and coming out by another. When he awoke he immediately prepared a great feast and sent invitations to ten of his friends. They all came happily and rejoicing. When they arrived he told them about his dream, without dismaying them apparently, since all ten immediately offered to carry it out. They went to the river, broke through the ice in two places about fifteen feet apart. The divers stripped, and the first man led the way; leaping into the first hole, he very fortunately came up through the second; the second did the same and so did the others until the tenth man who paid for all of them since he was not able to pull himself out and perished miserably beneath the ice.[8]

It appears from these examples that the dream does not only presage reality, but is a kind of lien on it which has to be redeemed quickly, lest

---

[5] *Relations des Jésuites dans la Nouvelle-France* (1669–1670), LIV, 66, cited by L. Lévy-Bruhl, *La mentalité primitive* (Paris, 1933), p. 104. I have taken most of the examples used here from this book and from others by the same author (*La mythologie primitive* [Paris, 1935]; *L'expérience mystique et les symboles chez les primitifs* [Paris, 1938]).
[6] H. Callaway, *The Religious System of the Amazulu* (Natal, 1868), p. 164.
[7] *Relations des Jésuites*, LIV, 96; "Tout ce qu'ils songent doit être accompli," in *ibid.* (1666–1668), LI, 124.
[8] *Ibid.* (1655–1656), XLII, 150–152.

some irremediable split appear in the tissue of events capable of causing the dreamer's death. Anticipating psychoanalysis, the Hurons believed that dreams manifest secret desires, and that an unsatisfied desire is no less injurious than a poison or acid implacably doing its work beneath the surface: "Now they believe that our soul makes its desires known by dreams as much as by words. So far as its desires are fulfilled, it is content. But, on the contrary, if its desires are not acceded to, it is affronted. Not only does it not then procure for the body the happiness and wellbeing it wished to bring, but it even reacts against the body causing it various illnesses and even death." [9]

There is the temptation to abuse this kind of excuse and, rather than follow through with great trouble on an actual dream that affords little satisfaction, it is profitable to pretend to have dreamed something actually desired but forbidden in order to be absolved in advance for a fault or crime one is burning to commit. The Kurds of Asia Minor, dreaming of something valuable, consider themselves immediately constrained thereby to take it "by force of arms, murder or pillage," and if they dream of an enemy, it is a sign that he should be hurriedly done away with and his goods carried off.[10]

In the most extreme cases, the person dreamed about is held responsible for its realization. According to G. W. Steller, in Kamchatka, to obtain a young girl's favor, it is enough to pretend to have dreamed of obtaining it. She would die if she failed to have reality make good on the debt incurred in the dream.[11]

It is noteworthy that in these various examples, there is never a question of interpreting the dream, of looking for hidden significance beyond the images of which it is composed. The dream is taken literally. Arrangements must be made for it to be canceled or fulfilled (the operation is the same) so that there remains no inactive prediction, no futile threat, no wish floating in the void, no image charged with a dangerous and overriding power whose strength has not been drawn off by its fulfillment of reality.

A dream under such conditions is not prophecy, but a sentence, not a message, but a coercive foreshadowing. Not only the dreamer, but the whole world, must conform to the wondrous phantasmagoria. Hence it is important to dream of victory before the war, of game before the hunt,

---

[9] *Ibid.* (1648–1649), XXXVII, 188–190, cf. "Ils sont convaincus qu'il n'y a pas de remède plus souverain pour guérir (leur mal) et pour leur sauver la vie que de faire tout ce qu'ils ont rêvé," in *ibid.* (1669–1670), LIV, 100.
[10] Abbé J. Tfinkdji, "Essai sur les songes et l'art de les interpréter en Mésopotamiè," *Anthropos,* VIII (1913), 506–507.
[11] G. W. Steller, *Beschreibung von dem Lande Kamtschatka* (Frankfort and Leipzig, 1774), p. 279; Lévy-Bruhl, *Mentalité primitive,* p. 116.

of the prize before the contest. The person concerned will fast and stay awake until hallucination takes over as the next stage in the projection of his desires. The visions crowding the sleep, to which exhaustion finally makes the obstinate seeker succumb, cannot but keep alive the images of his aspirations. The dream also brings him the assurances that he needs. He has no idea that the shadows visiting him are produced by the very fervor of his hopes. He is certain that these new images, over which he has no power, come from somewhere beyond, independent of him, but come for him, and carry a promise on which he can depend. The dream is a guarantee for the future while appearing simultaneously as a reward for merit, sacrifice, piety, or zeal. There is nothing about it, in fact, of passively acquired luck, but an expected, if not forced, evocation, the subsequent fulfillment of which will seem mere duplication, delayed but inevitable.

In the darkness of the inscrutable, a dream becomes an imperious vision invested with supernatural authority by its mysterious origins. The revelation that comes from a dream is a double that precedes and shackles reality. Dream fixes reality as it ought to take place. The future is unknown, diverse, indeterminate. Once dreamed, it becomes immutable. This is the power of the dream: to twist reality after itself. Its weakness is that the first impostor who comes along can, at leisure, preempt a very precious investiture that rises from the heart of an inaccessible secret, that of a consciousness gone to sleep. One ought to be able to control, to record, the images of the dream. In fact—even though suspect by nature, fleeting, fantastic, and absolutely unverifiable—it tends to become institutionalized whenever it contributes to the basis of practical policy, its use regulated, and its area of competency carefully outlined.

Wherever it has been observed, the practice of incubation is accompanied by a precise ritual. From the moment he enters the sanctuary, the candidate is guided, purified, and watched over by someone who reserves for himself the privilege of authenticating dreams sent by the god. Moreover, all dreams are not equally important. Eminent value is attached to those that repeat themselves, visit several sleepers at the same time, or leave behind some significant souvenir. These seem to have been confirmed, attested, ratified. They introduce the elect into a social function, they confer the power to cure, to punish, to nourish, to celebrate a dance or a liturgy, to bring a myth to life, or to recite the sacred genealogies.[12]

---

[12] Lévy-Bruhl, *Mythologie primitive,* pp. xxiii–xxv. E. W. Gifford's regular informant explained that a fellow tribesman incorrectly reported a myth by the fact that he really had not dreamed it ("Yuma Dreams and Omens," *Journal of American Folklore,* XXXIX [1926], 58–69); cf. Lévy-Bruhl, *L'expérience mystique,* pp. 11–133, on the political or social responsibilities having their source in dreams as much among the Australians as among the Yumas of California. New officials for

They form part of a heritage; from generation to generation, the dreams revitalize and perpetuate the bonds with the invisible from which a family derives its title and the inner force of its supremacy.

From this moment the dream is a factor of legitimation. But no longer does it have anything of the character of inconsistent, unheralded, and unforeseen images to which their maker falls victim. Rather does it fill the function of an inherited talisman, a coveted power one may buy or sell, win or lose in a bet, or gain by higher bid, or in battle.

As we have seen, the need to interpret dreams, to uncover their symbolic meaning, and the inclination to regard them as enigmas, is remarkably constant. It is present in every culture, adapted to the style, ambitions, and fancies of each of them. It reappears age after age in new forms, always seductive, as if men were exceedingly reluctant to recognize that there is decidedly no meaning in images that seem to have so strong a need to make themselves understood.

In the same way, there is a similar and no less obstinate uneasiness about the relationship of dreams to waking life, an uneasiness that demands comparisons between their levels or perhaps their ontological densities. It is not a matter here of decoding a secret message, but of distinguishing with certitude the real from the imaginary, the decisive from the insignificant. Almost inevitably, under these circumstances, the dreams that so easily bewilder take precedence over the monotonies of daily living. As literal reflections and photographs of scenes to come, dreams bewitch reality, so to speak, and force it to coincide at the right moment with the inescapable scenario they have revealed to the sleeper, a scenario that is its cause and consequence, model and copy.

The competition—always threatening, sometimes actual—between the perceptions of the waking state and the images of the dream is a source of confusion for the dreamer who does not know which to trust. The most striking image is not necessarily the most solid or the most truthful, and he knows that some that flash like lightning are neither more solid nor more enduring than the dazzlement surrounding them. On the other hand, why should not the force of shock, the sudden and unexplained illumination, give the dream, at least temporarily, a sort of princely privilege in this domain, a position that eclipses the timid claims of trivial reality which can in the end assert itself only by its steady wear and tear.

Whenever the facts of a dream and those of the waking state are placed in balance and the frightened conscience is unable to choose between them, a certain number of difficulties are born of the impossible

---

the Huichols of Mexico are chosen by a designated dreamer. The Tupa-Inbà of Brazil never undertake war unless there have been favorable dreams.

dilemma. The most sophisticated literature echoes strangely the troubles of the mind (as we suppose it to have been) at the dawn of history, poised between the wonderful fantasies of dreams and the insipid stability of the scenery rediscovered at each awakening. The fabrications of our writers seem to rejuvenate the uncertainties of our ancestors. In any case, they are strikingly similar. Anguish frequently gives way to play, the delights of a free imagination to haunting obsessions. The problems are the same, but the key is different. I will try to enumerate the principal of these perpetual inquiries.

First of all, who really acts in a dream? The sleeper's personality is usurped by a double, which he sees living withdrawn from his own control, in complete independence, but in a way that is bound to involve him to a certain extent. At times this actor steps into the dreamer's role, extending his personality, partaking of his sorrows, his fancies, and his desires, baffling and sometimes dumbfounding him. Then again, he is in the skin of his nocturnal double; he sees with the eyes of his counterpart and touches with *his* hands the other personages of the dream. Sometimes he watches this reflection of himself developing among the others, watching—with horror or perhaps indifference—his gestures, which are being performed outside himself, as if they were being shown on a screen or happening on the other side of a mirror.

Another approach involves the possibility of bringing back from the world of dreams some object—a scar, a mark, a token—which will be proof of the dream's reality, something solid and tangible which will survive after the illusions of the dream have faded away to attest to the unimpeachable existence of the world from which it has been brought.

Someone, in a dream, wakes up—or rather believes that he has awakened, although he continues to dream—and now lies expecting another awakening, which this time may be real but may also be as illusionary as the first. In this way he will be transported from one dream to another, from one awakening to another, without ever being absolutely certain whether he has finally arrived at the true awakening, the one that will restore him to the world of reality.

The universe of the daytime existence sometimes appears simply to be a duplication of the world of dreams. The sleeper who arrives in the realm of truthful premonitory images will see in them the unfolding of events that reality will soon be obliged to reproduce or to imitate. After a delay of shorter or longer duration, the waking world will follow, obey, and conform. Inexplicably, inevitably, implacably, it will faithfully repeat the scenes that were earlier observed in the course of the dreams, as if it were nothing but those images, temporarily but compulsorily postponed, to reappear in their own good time on a reflecting, vainly rebellious surface. At times, it is necessary to wait so long for the dream's realization that it is almost forgotten. Reality even seems definitely to take a different turn, and then, at the most unexpected moment, everything assembles, falls into place, and resurrects to the smallest detail the episode that had been revealed earlier in a universe of fantasy—but this time in the world of reality.

Here we can judge clearly this transformation. What was thought to be fate is now presented as no more than a monstrous, thoroughly unsettling exception. What was formerly inexorable law has become simple literary conjecture. For the primitive, everything happened as if the future scene, having once been reflected in the mirror of the dream, had, in a sense, already taken place so that it all had to recur sooner or later exactly as dreamed. The dream was thought to be of such importance that we have seen the dreamer strive after its fulfillment, even at the risk of his life. Henceforth, the opposite is true: the revealing dream is at first neglected or scorned by a skeptical hero who, to his amazement, perceives little by little reality coming gradually closer to it (the dream) and reconstituting it in the end.

There are other themes that have undergone an analogous evolution like the recurrent need that several dreams should mutually substantiate or verify one another. When the dream is no longer the source of political power and ceases to be the authorized witness commanding instant faith, it is no longer embarrassing that nothing but a merely reverential fear should prevent the invention of profitable specimens or a lighthearted challenge of those specimens invoked by a rival.

A comparable nostalgia persists in a world that no longer grants to the dream this inordinate influence. Everyone continues to experience, as a kind of failure, irritating and sad in turn, that there is nothing more personal than a dream, nothing else so imprisons a person in irremediable solitude, nothing else is as stubbornly resistant to being shared. In the world of reality everything is experienced in common. The dream, on the other hand, is an adventure that only the dreamer himself lived and only he can remember; it is a watertight, impenetrable world that precludes the least cross-checking. Hence the temptation to imagine two or more persons (or even a multitude) having the same dream, or dreams that are equivalent or complementary. The dreams thus corroborate one another, fitting together like the pieces of a puzzle and, by acquiring in this way the solidity and stability possessed by the perceptions of the waking world, they become verifiable like them; even better, they create bonds between the dreamers—rare, secret, narrow, and imperious.

The final problem is the most abstract, also the most fundamental and not the least tenacious. Since, at every moment of the dream, the sleeper is unaware of the fact that he is dreaming, and is even convinced that he is awake, it is clear that there can never be a moment in which a person who believes himself to be awake does not have to entertain the suspicion of a doubt that he might perhaps at that time actually be dreaming. This problem has benefited by a long and complex philosophical history.

Mankind had hardly left those first ages, in which dreams could have the force of law and frequently prevailed over reality, when these recurring questions furnished the learned with the elements of a problem complex that soon proved disquieting to discerning minds. In fact, theological systems have been inclined to confirm the view that the dream gives access to the world of the divine or, in any case, a world more meaningful, if not more real, than that of the waking state. Hence, the precocious success of oneiromancy and the oracular theory of dreams.

In a papyrus of the fourth century B.C., the Pharaoh Nectanabis (378–360) witnesses in a dream a scene in the course of which the god Onuris complains to Isis that his temple stands uncompleted. Nectanabis orders an inquiry and learns that no inscription has yet been carved on it. He asks for the best sculptor of hieroglyphics to be brought and orders him to finish the work in the shortest possible time. And Artemidorus (Oneirocritica I.1) mentions dreams that he calls "politic"—those that occur on the same night to all the inhabitants of a city and deal with events that concern that town. The Babylonian Talmud (Ta'anith, 21 B) also alludes to this type of dream. In Mesopotamia, Assurbanipal recounts:

The Dream of Assurbanipal

The army saw the river Idid'e (which was at that moment) a raging torrent, and was afraid of the crossing. (But) the goddess Ishtar who dwells in Arbela let my army have a dream in the midst of the night (addressing them) as follows: "I shall go in front of Aššurbanipal, the king whom I have created myself!" The army relied upon this dream and crossed safely the river Idid'e.[13]

This dream is authenticated because it was experienced simultaneously by many sleepers. It may be authenticated also when its revelation is found to be accurate, that is to say, if reality confirms the message of the dream, as it does in the following example, reported by Plutarch and Tacitus.[14]

---

[13] Quoted by A. Leo Oppenheim, *Le rêve et son interprétation dans le Proche-Orient ancien* (Paris, 1959), p. 99 (trans. from *The Interpretation of Dreams in the Ancient Near East with a Translation of an Assyrian Dream-Book*, Transactions of the American Philosophical Society, n.s., vol. 46, part 3 [Philadelphia, 1956], p. 249).

[14] Plutarch, *De Iside et de Osiride* 28; Tacitus, *Historiae* IV.83–84; cf. Oppenheim, *op. cit.*

The Dream of Ptolemy

Ptolemy Soter saw in a dream the colossus of the god Pluto that stood at Sinope; but since he had never seen the statue, he did not recognize it; it ordered him to transport it as quickly as possible to Alexandria. Not knowing whom it represented nor where it was, the king spoke of his vision to his familiars; they found for him a certain Sosibius who had travelled much and who said he had seen at Sinope a colossus such as the king had dreamt of. Ptolemy sent Soteles and Dionysius thither, who after a long time and with much difficulty, and not without divine help, possessed themselves of it and brought it to Alexandria. When it had arrived at its destination it was examined; the scholars of the circle of Timotheus the Exegete and Manetho of Sebennytus agreed that it was the image of Pluto, concluding from the presence on the statue of Cerberus, the snake; they convinced Ptolemy it was the statue of the god Serapis, and not of any other.

Classical antiquity knew of one proof that was even more convincing of the truth of a dream: the token, received in the course of a dream, which the sleeper finds beside him on awakening. In Pindar, Bellerophon dreams that Pallas brings him a magic bridle resembling a golden diadem, with the help of which Bellerophon will be able to subdue Pegasus. Bellerophon wakes up and immediately grasps the "excess" object, a bridle, which is not of the world and which a god has laid next to him.[15] This theme recurs frequently, notably in ancient Nordic literature.

More subtly, the proof left behind by the vanishing dream is at times not material, but as volatile, ambiguous, and intangible as the dream itself. A short Chinese tale tells of the young Liu of P'eng-ch'eng who dreams of going to a brothel where he and the girls become intoxicated. Each dream takes him back to the same scene of debauchery. He wonders, perhaps, if his dreams are real, for the perfumes of the women continue to permeate his clothes even when he is awake.[16]

In other cases, the dream precedes reality; it announces or foreshadows it with supernatural precision. It is insistent and meticulous, while reality, coming later, docile and servile, is only a hallucinated repetition of the earlier dream. I give two examples of this new theme, one ancient and one modern, both distinguished by the fact that they have been offered as authentic. Worlds separate them—time, distance, differ-

---

[15] Pindar, *Olympian Odes* XIII.65 ff.
[16] "Mong Yeou-lou," in *T'ang Kien Wen Tse*, trans. Bruno Belpaire (1ᵉ sér.; Paris, 1957), p. 262.

ences of tradition and culture. Nevertheless, each affirms in almost identical fashion that life is sometimes only a reproduction of the vision of dreams, the newly arrived present being a delayed and perhaps obscured reflection of the dream. The first account is taken from a Chinese collection that relates the strange events that happened during the T'ang dynasty. It tells of a young scholar, Liu Tao-chi, who, while staying at the monastery of Kuo-ching on Mount T'ien T'ai about the year A.D. 899, dreamed of a young girl in a garden, under a window, near a leaning cypress surrounded by sunflowers. He dreamed of going through the marriage ceremony with her and frequently he came back to see her—always in his dreams. Time passed. One day, in another monastery, the young scholar recognized the garden, the window, the cypress, and the sunflowers. There was a passing guest at the monastery whose daughter, poor, beautiful, still single, had recently fallen ill. She was the girl whom the young scholar had married and had regularly gone to visit—in his dreams.[17]

J. O. Austin, a justice of the peace from Middletown, New York, in a letter to Camille Flammarion dated June 25, 1909, tells of an adventure—similar in a way to the previous account—which happened to him in his youth. Flammarion accepted this account unhesitatingly, even respectfully. He used it later in the second edition of one of his works to replace another story, by Alexandre Bérard, which he had learned from the authors to be purely fictitious.

The Dream of the American Schoolmaster

I was about twenty years old and principal of a public school. Being very absorbed in my duties, I thought of them at night in my dreams no less than by day during my hours of work. One night I dreamed that I was in the classroom and had just finished the opening exercises, when I heard taps on the door. I open the door and see a man with two children, a girl of eleven and a boy of eight years. The visitor comes in and explains to me that, as a result of the Civil War, he had left his home in New Orleans and had brought his family to the district where my school was. He wished to entrust his children to my care for their education and their instruction. He further asked me which books were necessary and I gave him a list which he took with him. The next day the children were accepted as my pupils.

The dream stopped there but it impressed me vividly and the picture of this father and these two children was so strongly photographed on my mind that I should have been able to recog-

[17] *Ibid.*

nize them anywhere, even in the population of Paris or London.

How great was my astonishment when the day after my dream I heard the same knocks on the door that I had heard in the dream and, going to open it, I saw before me this same visitor and his two children. The rest followed: we held the same conversation that we had held in my dream.

I will add that this man was an absolute stranger to me. New Orleans is 1,350 miles, or more than 2,000 kilometers, from here and I have never been further than 100 miles or 160 kilometers from my home.[18]

It also happens that a dream is experienced, told, and interpreted within the dream. The dream of the neo-Babylonian King Nabonidus (556–539 B.C.) has been carved on a stele. (The most indestructible stone was used to record the most fleeting of visions!) The monarch sees in his dream a disturbing conjunction of stars. But a man rises by his side and tells the king: "This conjunction does not hold any evil portents." Then, still in the same dream, as the inscription relates in precise detail, Nebuchadnezzar appears to him, accompanied by a servant. The servant says to Nebuchadnezzar: "Speak to Nabonidus so that he may tell you the dream that he has dreamed." Nebuchadnezzar orders Nabonidus to tell him the dream and Nabonidus does so. No doubt his royal predecessor thereupon interpreted the dream for him but unfortunately the stele is damaged at this point.

The case of a dream related and then interpreted in the same dream is dealt with in the Talmud (Berakhot 55 B). It is similarly mentioned in the *Book of Dreams* of the library of Assurbanipal. "If he should dream a dream inside a dream and (in his dream) he relates his dream. . . ."

Ancient Indians knew the mystery of parallel dreams in which two persons, unaware of each other, have a common destiny announced to them. In the *Kathāsaritsagara (Ocean of the Streams of Story)*, Somadeva, a twelfth-century author, tells how King Vikrāmāditya saw in a dream, in a country unknown, a girl with whom he fell in love. He dreamed that he was embracing her, when his happiness was suddenly interrupted by the cry of the night watchman. At the same time, in a distant country, Princess Malayavatī, who had a horror of men, dreamed that she saw a great personage emerging from a monastery. She married him and was tasting with him the joys of love on the nuptial couch when she was awakened by her chambermaid. After many vicissitudes the king

---

[18] Camille Flammarion, *L'Inconnu et les problèmes psychiques* (2d ed.; Paris: Flammarion, 1929), II, 520–521.

and princess meet, recognize each other, and are united in real life as they had been earlier in their dreams.

Complementary dreams represent a higher degree of complexity. Now it is no longer a matter of simple symmetry, but of a more delicate relation that causes a second dream to become the clue to the first. The most striking example of this is perhaps to be found in *The Arabian Nights.*

The Ruined Man Who Became Rich Again through a Dream

There lived once in Baghdad a wealthy man and made of money, who lost all his substance and became so destitute that he could earn his living only by hard labour. One night he lay down to sleep, dejected and heavy hearted, and saw in a dream a Speaker who said to him, "Verily thy fortune is in Cairo; go thither and seek it." So he set out for Cairo; but when he arrived there, evening overtook him and he lay down to sleep in a mosque. Presently, by decree of Allah Almighty, a band of bandits entered the mosque and made their way thence into an adjoining house; but the owners, being aroused by the noise of the thieves, awoke and cried out; whereupon the Chief of Police came to their aid with his officers. The robbers made off; but the Wali entered the mosque and, finding the man from Baghdad asleep there, laid hold of him and beat him with palm-rods so grievous a beating that he was well-nigh dead. Then they cast him into jail, where he abode three days; after which the Chief of Police sent for him and asked him, "Whence art thou?"; and he answered, "From Baghdad." Quoth the Wali, "And what brought thee to Cairo?" and quoth the Baghdadi, "I saw in a dream One who said to me, Thy fortune is in Cairo; go thither to it. But when I came to Cairo the fortune which he promised me proved to be the palm-rods thou so generously gavest to me." The Wali laughed till he showed his wisdom-teeth and said, "O man of little wit, thrice have I seen in a dream one who said to me:—There is in Baghdad a house in such a district and of such a fashion and its courtyard is laid out garden-wise, at the lower end whereof is a jetting-fountain and under the same a great sum of money lieth buried. Go thither and take it. Yet I went not; but thou, of the briefness of thy wit, hast journeyed from place to place, on the faith of a dream, which was but an idle galimatias of sleep." Then he gave him money saying, "Help thee back herewith to thine own country." . . . [The Baghdadi] took the money and set out upon his homewards march. Now the house the Wali had described was the man's own house in Baghdad; so the wayfarer returned thither and, digging underneath the fountain in his garden, discovered a great treasure. And thus Allah gave him abundant fortune. . . .[19]

A Hasidic folktale gives a less elaborate version of the same story.

Two Others Who Dreamed
A man one day went to consult the Rabbi of Kotzk to ask him if he should leave his native town, where nothing had gone right for him, in order to try his fortune elsewhere. The Rabbi replied with the following tale: A Jew from Cracow had dreamed repeatedly that a treasure had been buried near a certain mill. He got up one fine morning, went to the mill and started to dig all around it; but in vain. The miller asked him what he was digging for and the man explained his purpose. The miller, fully astonished, then related that he himself had repeatedly dreamed that a treasure had been buried in the courtyard of a certain man in Cracow and he mentioned the name of the man—who happened to be none other than our treasure-seeker himself. The man from Cracow went straight home, dug up his courtyard, and found a treasure.[20]

In these two stories, a man discovers a treasure as a result of a dream that has been dreamed by another but which he himself can better interpret. Japanese folklore has a curious variation on the same theme: the hero buys or steals the revealing dream. In one such story, a man sees a gadfly flying away from the nostril of his sleeping friend, then entering it again some time later. The sleeper recounts his dream: a gadfly came to rest in the garden of a very rich man of the Island of Sado, under a camellia bush laden with white blossoms. The gadfly told the dreamer to dig, which he did, finding there a vessel full of gold coins. The hero immediately begs his friend to sell him his dream and the friend agrees. The buyer then goes to the Island of Sado, takes up service in the household of the rich man, digs up the treasure from under the white camellia, and requests his discharge. After this he lives happily ever after in his own village.[21]

Another Hasidic tale with numerous variations in the folklore of

---

[19] Richard Burton, *Book of the Thousand Nights and a Night* (Burton Club, n.d.), IV, 289–290.
[20] Levitte and Casaril, *op. cit.*, p. 27, quoting Kotzker Maasiyoth 105.
[21] R. Sieffert, "Les Songes et leur interprétation au Japon," in Esnoul, Garelli, *et al.*, *op. cit.*, pp. 311–312.

several countries shows how many different episodes of a life can be unfolded in the short duration of one dream.

A Destiny in a Dream

There was once a very hospitable man who never stopped asking: "Oh, my worthy guest, am I not the most hospitable of men?" The Baal Shem-Tov sent one of his disciples to him, Rabbi Ze'ev Kitzez. The man having once more asked his customary question, Rabbi Ze'ev said to him: "We shall see," and the man fell asleep. Rabbi Ze'ev pressed a finger on the man's forehead and the man started dreaming. He dreamed that a great noble had stopped at his house and, after drinking some wine, had fallen down dead at a stroke. The most hospitable of all men thereupon fled the scene and became a carrier of water. The buckets were heavy, he stumbled and fell and broke his leg. The broken leg gave him so much pain that he woke up. He related his dream to Rabbi Ze'ev who told him: "You have been given the privilege of contemplating what will be your lot if you continue to sustain Satan with the arrogance which compels you to solicit compliments for your hospitality." And the man promised to return to the paths of humility.[22]

The most remarkable dream of this type is the one related by Don Juan Manuel, the Infante of Castile (1284-1348), a dream probably inspired by an earlier Arab tale. In this, the whole of a possible destiny, encompassing an entire career, is telescoped into a few hallucinated minutes.

The Sorcerer Whose Reward Was Not Forthcoming

There was a Dean of Santiago who had a great desire to be initiated in the art of necromancy; and, hearing that Don Illan of Toledo knew more of this art than any other person in that country, came to Toledo with a view of studying under him. On the day of his arrival he proceeded to the house of Don Illan, whom he found reading in a retired chamber, and who received him very graciously, desiring him not to inform him of the motive of his visit until he had first partaken of his repast, which was found excellent, and consisted of every delicacy that could be desired.

Now, when the repast was concluded, the dean took the magician aside and told him the motive of his visit, urging him very earnestly to instruct him in the art in which he was so great an

---

[22] Levitte and Casaril, *op. cit.*, quoting Maasiyoth ha-Gedolim he-Hadash 44.

adept, and which he, the dean, desired so anxiously to be made acquainted with.

When Don Illan told him that he was a dean and, consequently, a man of great influence, and that he would attain a high position, saying, at the same time, that men, generally speaking, when they reach an elevated position and attain the objects of their ambition, forget easily what others have previously done for them, as also all past obligations and those from whom they received them—failing generally in the performance of their former promises, the dean assured him such should not be the case with him; saying, no matter to what eminence he might attain, he would not fail to do everything in his power to help his former friends, and the magician in particular.

In this way they conversed until supper-time approached; and now, the covenant between them being completed, Don Illan said to the dean, that, in teaching him the art he desired to learn, it would be necessary for them to retire to some distant apartment, and, taking him by the hand, led him to a chamber. As they were quitting the dining-room, he called his housekeeper, desiring her to procure some partridges for their supper that night, but not to cook them until she had his special commands. Having said this, he sought the dean and conducted him to the entrance of a beautifully carved stone staircase, by which they descended a considerable distance, appearing as if they had passed under the river Tagus, and, arriving at the bottom of the steps, they found a suite of rooms and a very elegant chamber, where were arranged the books and instruments of study; and, having here seated themselves, they were debating which should be the first books to read, when two men entered by the door and gave the dean a letter which had been sent to him by his uncle the archbishop, informing him that he was dangerously ill, and that if he wished to see him alive it would be requisite for him to come immediately. The dean was much moved by this news—partly on account of the illness of his uncle, but more through the fear of being obliged to abandon his favourite study, just commenced—so he wrote a respectful letter to his uncle the archbishop, which he sent by the same messengers. At the end of four days, other men arrived on foot bringing fresh letters to the dean, informing him that the archbishop was dead, and that all those interested in the welfare of the Church were desirous that he should succeed to his late uncle's dignity, telling him, at the same time, it was quite unnecessary for him to inconvenience himself by returning immediately, as his nomination would be better secured were he not

Logical and Philosophical Problems 43

present in the church. At the end of seven or eight days, two squires arrived, very richly dressed and accoutred, who, after kissing his hand, delivered to him the letters informing him that he had been appointed archbishop.

When Don Illan heard this he told him he was much pleased that this good news had arrived during his stay in his house; and, as God had been so gracious to him, begged that the deanery now vacant might be given to his son.

The archbishop elect replied, that he hoped Don Illan would allow him to name to the vacancy his own brother, saying, at the same time, that he would present him with some office in his own church with which his son would be contented, inviting, at the same time, both father and son to accompany him to Santiago.

To this they consented; and all three departed for the city, where they were received with much honour. After they had resided there some time, there arrived one day messengers from the Pope bearing letters naming the former dean Bishop of Tolosa, permitting him at the same time to name whom he pleased to succeed him in his vacant see.

When Don Illan heard this he reminded him of his promise, urging him to confer the appointment on his son. But the archbishop again desired that he would allow him to name one of his paternal uncles to succeed him. Don Illan replied, that, although he felt he was unjustly treated, still, relying on the future accomplishment of his promise, he should let it be. The archbishop thanked him, again renewed his promise of future services, and, inviting Don Illan and his son to accompany him, they all set out for Tolosa, where they were well received by the counts and great men of the country.

They had resided there about two years when messengers again came from the Pope with letters in which he announced to the archbishop that he had named him cardinal, allowing him, as before, to name his successor.

On this occasion Don Illan went to him, and again urging that many vacancies had taken place, to none of which he had named his son, so that now he could plead no excuse, and he hoped the cardinal would confer this last dignity on his son. But once more the cardinal requested Don Illan would forgive his having bestowed the vacant see on one of his maternal uncles; saying he was a very good old man, and proposing they should now depart for Rome, where undoubtedly he would do for them all they could desire. Don Illan complained very much; nevertheless, he consented to accompany the cardinal to Rome. On their arrival they were very well received by the other cardinals and the entire court, and they lived there a long time. Don Illan daily importuned the cardinal to confer some appointment on his son, but he always found some excuse for not doing so.

While they were yet at Rome, the pope died, and all the cardinals assembled in conclave elected our cardinal pope.

Then Don Illan came to him, saying, "You have now no excuse to offer for not fulfilling the promises you have hitherto made me."

But the new pope told him not to importune him so much, as there was still time to think of him and his son.

Don Illan now began to complain in earnest. "You have," said he, "made me very many promises, not one of which you have performed." He then recalled to his mind how earnestly he had pledged his word at their first interview to do all he could to help him, and never as yet had he done anything. "I have no longer any faith in your words," said Don Illan, "nor do I now expect anything from you."

These expressions very much angered the pope, who replied, tartly, "If I am again annoyed in this manner I will have you thrown into prison as a heretic and a sorcerer, for I know well that in Toledo, where you lived, you had no other means of support but by practising the art of necromancy."

When Don Illan saw how ill the pope had requited him for what he had done, he prepared to depart, the pope refusing to grant him wherewith to support himself on the road. "Then," said he to the pope, "since I have nothing to eat, I must needs fall back upon the partridges I ordered for to-night's supper." He then called out to his housekeeper, and ordered her to cook the birds for his supper.

No sooner had he spoken, than the dean found himself again in Toledo, still dean of Santiago, as on his arrival, but so overwhelmed with shame that he knew not what to say.[23]

It may happen that one dreams in a dream that one has wakened from a dream while in actual fact the same dream continues to unfold. The sleeper draws from this peripety but a misleading assurance that he is now awake. He generally passes through a state in which his reason so mingles with illusion that both soon become inextricable from each

---

[23] "Of that which happened to a dean of Santiago, with Don Illan the magician, who lived at Toledo," in Don Juan Manuel, *Count Lucanor,* English trans., James York, 1868 (Alhambra, Calif.: Carl F. Braun, 1953), pp. 72–77.

other. An historical example of this is furnished by the *Memoirs* of Shah Ṭahmāsp I (1514-1576) who dreamed on the nineteenth of Ṣafar in the year 961 of the Hijra (January 23, 1554, of the Christian era) that he saw a verse of the Koran written in the sky. It was 2:131, "Allah will provide for you against them. *He understands and He knows.*" After this he dreamed that he awakened and found himself in his summer encampment at Khoy, fearing the approach of a storm and taking the necessary steps to evacuate his household in case the tents should be carried away. The wind, however, turned aside at the last moment, but in the cloud of dust that it raised could be seen a herd of rams and antelopes.

Then, still in the dream, Ṭahmāsp saw his sister arranging cushions on which fine ladies reclined. They wore neither ornament nor finery and were Georgian women of perfect beauty. Among them was the sister of the vizier whom, however, he could not recognize, her features having changed. He woke up for a moment (or dreamed he had) while he recited the verse from the Koran that he had seen written in the sky. He then fell asleep once more (or dreamed that he did) into the same dream reciting the same verse. Now suddenly he realized that the verse had signified the defeat of his enemies.[24]

India, which may well be considered the center of asceticism and mental discipline, has invested the dream with other powers again. The recluse, carried away by his meditation, gives a material existence to the images of his dreams, if he can only succeed in sustaining them with sufficient intensity. The dream then becomes lucid, deliberate, and creative; it becomes, in fact, a consciously willed effort that will be realized provided only that it is pursued sufficiently long and with sufficient vigor. The poet Tulsidas had composed an epic devoted to Hanuman and his army of apes. Years passed. A despot imprisoned Tulsidas in a tower of stone. The poet set himself to dream, to meditate, to dream again, to put to work all the resources of a mind straining to empty himself of all distracting content. Then from the dream arose Hanuman and his army of apes who overran the kingdom, seized the tower, and set the poet free.

All, or nearly all, these themes are to be found in the inexhaustible literature of China, which seems to have explored in a systematic manner the problems posed by the dream. By carefully choosing stories to illustrate these problems, it would be possible no doubt to outline a kind of casuistry of the dream. Some of them illustrate familiar problems; others refine and invent hitherto unknown complications with extravagant and tyrannical logic. Examples might include the cyclical dream of Pao-Yu; the story of the man who in his dream becomes part of a real

---

[24] Shāh Ṭahmāsp, *Tadhkira* (Berlin, 1923), p. 65; H. Massé, *Anthologie Persane* (Paris: Payot, 1950), pp. 349-350.

fresco; the story where the hero, awake, witnesses a scene someone else is dreaming which he interrupts by a brutal action that enters and ends the sleeper's dream; and lastly, the story of the legal impasse that occurs when the hide is discovered of a deer that a peasant believes to have killed in a dream.

Such confabulations deal genuinely with the powers of the dream and contrast interestingly with the way in which the dream is ordinarily used by Occidental writers. Some of them resort to it as to a convenient method of exposition: thus Plato in the dream of Er the Pamphylian, and Cicero in the dream of Scipio: these are metaphysical hypotheses in disguise. Others send edifying dreams to profligate sinners to make them repent of their ways or to announce the punishments of the Hereafter. (It must be admitted that Buddhism, too, is not ignorant of this use of the dream.)

Romanticism has tended to transform the dream into a literary device in which lyricism finds easy scope. Jean Paul Richter, whose novels are liberally sprinkled with wholly rhetorical dreams, offers perhaps the most drastic example. Later writers were satisfied to set forth their dreams and present them as poetic material in the rough, destined to beguile waking readers after overcoming a sleeping author.

Very frequently the dream remains a fairy tale that is dispelled by the awakening and to which at times a cumbersome allegorical value is attributed; it has nothing in common with the intellectual complications of the Oriental dreams. "It was only a dream," the sleeper cries out upon awakening, occasionally disappointed, occasionally relieved, all according to whether the dream gratified or oppressed him. It is never more than an illusion, which may have been pleasing or distressing, but which the opening of the eyelids suffices to send back into nothingness.

Descartes wondered what would happen to a sleeper who had continuous coherent dreams, if he were transported in dream to varying and dissimilar locations, waking each time in a bewildering environment without links to either the preceding environment or the following. The dream might well acquire the permanence of reality, while reality would acquire the improbability, the instability, the evanescence, and the kaleidoscopic character of the dream.

The founder of the Ismaili (Ismāʿīlī) sect, Ḥasan-i Ṣabbāḥ is traditionally credited with having used the philosopher's theoretical conjecture centuries before him, employing it in the gardens of Alamūt to fanaticize the Assassins. Ḥasan gathered his youngest and most ardent disciples in his inaccessible retreat, the Eagle's Nest, a precipitous and arid stronghold in the heart of the desert where it seemed impossible that the least vegetation might flourish. A secret spring, however, transformed a hidden ravine into a remarkable orchard that abounded with fruit and flowers.

Ḥasan plied his guests with Indian hemp and while they were under the influence of the drug he had them brought into his incredible garden. They woke up there in a bewildering setting where ravishing young creatures, perfumed and dressed in transparent veils, invited the young men to pick the flowers and fruit for themselves. They offered them refreshing drinks and invited them to the pleasures of love. Then, satiated and drowsy, the young men were taken back to their dusty, stifling cells. Awakening, they could glimpse through narrow slits only the endless sand and stone of an inhospitable region. They were told that they had been dreaming and that their dreams had given them a foretaste of Paradise to which they would be admitted if they died in carrying out the orders of the Prophet. As many times as was considered necessary, they were led back between two periods of sleep into the unsuspected garden of delights: each time they regained consciousness they were more convinced that they had been dreaming.

Marco Polo and a manuscript of the fourteenth century now kept in the Vienna Library[25] both attest to this frightening subterfuge. The ruse runs directly counter to the accepted opinions on the subject of dreams which consider it perfectly normal that a dream may—just for a moment—be taken for reality but that reality is never—certainly not for any length of time—taken for a dream. So much so in fact that tradition soon found itself altered and the "hallucinations" were attributed to hashish. Old Ḥasan-i Ṣabbāḥ, more realistically, did not think that he could rely entirely on drug-induced hallucinations and thought it wise to confirm their effects with real fruit, authentic flowers, and young girls who were anything but immaterial.

There is also a Christian version of this Oriental tale of fantasy, *Life Is a Dream,* a play by Pedro Calderón de la Barca (1600–1681). The plot is familiar: since childhood, Sigismond has been imprisoned by his father, the king of Poland, in an isolated tower. His father makes him drink a certain drug which puts him to sleep. He is then carried into the royal palace where he wakes up luxuriously dressed, and, by order of his father who wishes to put him to the test, is treated like a sovereign by all the courtiers. Sigismond at first wonders if he is not perhaps dreaming; then, taking confidence, he quickly shows himself to be brutal and headstrong, cruel and tyrannical. The test is conclusive: the young man —being given once more the same narcotic—finds himself that same day in his prison, dressed in his accustomed rags. His warder has no difficulty in persuading him that he has only dreamed the miraculous interlude. A

---

[25] Marco Polo, chaps. xli–xlii, Vienna MS 107, is quoted after J. von Hammer-Purgstall by Jacques Bolle, *Les séductions du communisme de la Bible à nos jours* (Paris: Morgan, 1957), pp. 186–187.

popular uprising later sets him free and for the second time he is given unlimited power. He believes, however, that he is for the second time experiencing only a dream, that the glittering show will vanish, and he will find himself once more in his dungeon. This time, of course, nothing of the sort is true, but Sigismond now knows that all life is a dream and dreams themselves are also dreams. The lesson to be learned here is metaphysical rather than religious. I do not know to what extent the Polish ruse as dramatized by Calderón was inspired by the Persian stratagem as described by the Venetian traveler. Possibly there was no influence at all, which would make the coincidence even more remarkable.

Studies on dreams multiplied from the second half of the nineteenth century onward. It is perhaps not by chance if among the most remarkable of these studies were those of two scholars who were almost exact contemporaries, both professors at the College of France. One, the historian and archaeologist Alfred Maury (1817–1892), published his work, *Le sommeil et les rêves (Slumber and Dreams)*, in 1861. The other, the Marquis d'Hervey de Saint-Denis (1823–1892), in 1867 published a more ambitious and more significant work whose title, *Les rêves et les moyens de les diriger (Dreams and Means of Controlling Them)*, reveals its basic conception. Under the double influence of classical antiquity and of China (so one may presume) the systematic study of dreams began. The powers of the dream are measured, its delusions submitted to or extolled, its pitfalls charted.

No longer does the dream appear in literature only as an edifying fable, a rhetorical device, or a fantasy deliberately freed from having to conform to the laws of logic and reality. It now becomes a motivating element of the plot, complicating or resolving it. It transforms the personality of the hero, troubles his reasoning, modifies his conduct. At times it is presented as an omen or the announcement of an extraordinary destiny; it heralds the disclosure of an implacable fate. Charles Nodier's *Smarra* remains a learned exercise—to my mind a detestable one—of ridiculous pomposity. Intended to give the impression of a nightmare, its pedantry represents an absurdity that is almost grotesque. *Aurélia,* the disclosure of the agonies and obsessions that were to destroy the sanity of Gérard de Nerval, goes beyond a literary game: it is an upsetting and confusing document rather than the calculated construction that this work is in other respects. In fact, in this domain in which the dream displays redoubtable reversals and sets snares and ambushes, madness takes on the precision and skill of an architectural system even as mastery may hide its speculations under the obliging mask of panic-stricken frenzy. At any rate these stories of uneven literary value have at least endowed the dream with a new importance and, so to speak, with the stamp of literary nobility; they have started the dream off on an extraordinary career.

At bottom it is the old problematics of the dream that reappears—not, however, under the schematic aspect that in the past had invested its unresolved enigmas with the elusive allure of the axiom or of mathematical paradox. Now the problematics fosters a psychology delighting in depicting the human mind as lying in wait for premonitions, responsive to the coincidences and the ambiguous persistence of chance, vulnerable to the assaults of the unseen—an alert recipient of messages and warnings from the Beyond, whose privileged carrier the dream is held to be.

The collusion of dreams and fantasy is inevitable, for the dream—mysterious at all times—readily becomes terrifying. By it, the dreamer can imagine himself introduced into a supernatural world, or, conversely, something from a forbidden world may seem to him to be forcing its way into his consciousness. Hence many stories that build up—in the best of cases, with clockwork precision—a delicate structure in which the dream furnishes the decisive "spring" in one way or another.

At times, these tales elaborate an age-old notion illustrating timeless cares. The bridle that Bellerophon finds beside him on awakening is a token of the same kind as the poem found in the sleeve of the hero of a Chinese tale of the T'ang period, as the cursed opal of Leslie Charteris' hero in *Aurora,* or as the key to the tomb in *Véra,* a story by Villiers de l'Isle-Adam.

The sudden tragedy in the *Pale Blue Nightgown* by Louis Golding, the obsessive warnings imagined by Ksaver Sandor Gjalski in *The Dream of Doctor Mišić,* and by W. Somerset Maugham in *Lord Mountdrago,* extend and romanticize the long-held conviction—or perhaps the occasional experience, generally explicable by the illusion of *déjà vu*—that dreams have the power to "create" the future with frightening vividness by anticipating it.

This type of story replays, so to speak, the adventures that long since befell the young scholar, Liu, at the monastery of Kuo-ching or, in the past century, J. O. Austin, the American justice of the peace. These two reports have the terseness of the documents they are, but the "spring" is provided. To draw dramatic effects from them needs only the skill and inventiveness of a writer.

Rudyard Kipling's *The Brushwood Boy,* a story of parallel dreams experienced independently of each other by a young Englishwoman and a soldier in the Indian army before they meet, recognize each other, and finally marry, furnishes a modern version of the parallel dreams of King Vikramāditya and Princess Malayavatī.

Tulsidas, in giving body to an army of apes which sets him free, foreshadows the ascetic who, in *The Circular Ruins* by Jorge Luis Borges, solely by the power of his dream creates a being indistinguishable from a living person except for the fact that neither fire nor water has any effect on him. Absorbed in concentration, the ascetic suddenly finds his retreat on fire, but the flames do not harm him; he realizes then that he himself is a fictitious creature in someone else's dream. A moving variant of the same theme inspired a short story by Giovanni Papini, *The Last Visit of the Sick Cavalier,* in which the hero defines his precarious state in the following terms:

> I exist because there is a man who dreams me, a man who sleeps and dreams and sees me acting and living and moving and who is dreaming at this moment that I am speaking to you just as I am doing. When he started to dream, my existence began. When he wakes up I shall cease to be. I am a figment of his imagination, a creation of his mind, a guest of his long nocturnal fantasies. The dream of this someone has so much stability and duration that I have become visible even to those who are awake.

Even Chuang-tzu, driven to despair by the debate within himself as to whether he is a philosopher who has dreamed that he is a butterfly or whether he is a butterfly dreaming that he is a philosopher, has his Occidental counterpart in the novella by Théophile Gautier, *The Dead Leman.* The story ends disappointingly as the banal tale of a vampire, but the beginning augured better when Romuald declares at the outset: "Sometimes I fancied myself a priest who dreamed every night he was a gentleman, and at other times a gentleman who dreamed he was a priest. I could no longer distinguish between dreaming and waking, and I knew not where reality began and illusion ended." Despite this ambiguity, the story still deals with one man, the same man, living alternately in two different environments, by turns pious and debauched.

But the contrast between insect and man is drawn in a science-fiction story, *A Wild Surmise,* told with singular daring by Henry Kuttner and Catherine L. Moore. In clinics on two distant planets, a man and an insect dream lives and live dreams that are complementary and inextricable. The contrast between the two stories on a single theme is striking and shows admirably how the given data of a problem can be ramified to produce divergent solutions. In Gautier the perplexed hero living a split life no longer can tell the dream from reality. In the tale by Kuttner and Moore an insect in its dream lives a human existence; the man in his dreams lives the life of an insect, complete with faceted eyes, six legs, and an annulated abdomen. It is no longer the question of a single consciousness powerless to distinguish between illusion and reality, but of two beings from two different realms: while asleep each dreams the daytime life of the other, owing to daily transpositions that recur endlessly.

This list of divergencies or persisting elements is certainly not complete, but I imagine the examples are sufficient to provide a glimpse of the powers a dream may possess to seduce the mind or lead it astray, a dream that is but an orderless sequence of empty images. It is convenient to conclude here with a word to explain the probable origin of the powers that are so obstinately attributed to something that is, after all, only a disordered succession of empty images.

The mystery of the dream originates in the fact that this phantasmagoria over which the sleeper has no control is at the same time entirely a product of his imagination. When it is unfolded before him without his consent, he can hardly believe himself responsible. On the other hand, it is difficult for him not to persuade himself that this shifting series of images is addressed to him. He postulates a meaning for this rarely explicit message, which would not be so troubling if it were not so enigmatic. The sleeper likes to flatter himself by believing that the dream does not come from himself, but rather from some external power that is superior, inaccessible, auspicious, or ominous—it does not really matter which. At the same time he does not doubt that he is the privileged recipient of something solemn and occult. He experiences the dream as a dictation in which the one who dictates (perhaps knowing neither that he is dictating nor what he is dictating), the one who (like a scribe with neither initiative nor control) docilely takes down those despotic words he hears, and the one who, quite astonished, reads the text back (a text he does not know but which seems nevertheless to bring back memories) are all one person: he himself. Throughout his dream, as principal or witness, he participates or looks on by proxy. A fraternal effigy takes his place, an agent without instructions, but for whom he nevertheless must answer, somewhat like the novelist who remains responsible for the characters he has sent out into the world, although their sayings and actions should not honestly be imputed to him.

The marvel of dreams stems on the one hand from the closely related phenomena inherent in them: the feeling of obsession, of being possessed, of the change of personality, of the expectation of a sign from the Beyond, and of the hope for an unimpeachable revelation. On the other hand, it is also because dreams assume a literary form even though literary creation requires the highest degree of vigilance and care, both of which are incompatible with the surrender and passivity of the dream.

The dream remains the common property of the sleeper who has dreamed it and of the waking person who remembers it; in an analogous sense the novel fulfills itself with a mediation between the writer who has created it and the reader who is introduced for a brief instant, for an interlude, as a supernumerary character into a fictional world, no doubt a deceptive and inconsistent world, but a world to which one must resort so long as one delights in literature.

I go further: Is it possible that without fantasies, visions, and dreams, an individual could emerge or exist—I mean a being who is someone without being Everything?

The inference is so commanding that the most rugged of theologians, in every period and of every persuasion, those who have dared to venture to the brink of the dizzy precipice of metaphysics, those who are mathematically cool and precise, have all agreed in assuming (one might say unanimously) that the relation between God and the world is like that which an all-powerful Spirit—a spirit that has no need to use its power, that scorns to impose its will, absentminded, impish, overgenerous—has with its Dream (solely through an excess of excellence), without even being aware of it. The Dream is the unfathomable, the inscrutable Universe that He lets emanate from Himself, a heedless and needless fantasy, perhaps.

While engaged in the collection of material for a problematics of the dream, I have been guided in my choice by a very precise criterion.

I have established that only recently has the dream been used in the literary process.

Recorded dreams and interpreted dreams are both old and plentiful; invented dreams are relatively recent. Narratives in which one discovers at the end that the events recounted were dreams and not real, or narratives told in certain dreams so as to give the reader the same feeling of reality that the dream gives to the dreamer, are rare and date only from yesterday, if not from today. Only they can make me experience the impression of dreaming, that is to say, when I close a volume of such stories or otherwise interrupt my reading, I experience an impression analogous to that which I feel on waking from a dream. Most of the other stories of dreams have the serious fault of being presented as such at the outset, thereby spoiling everything.[26] Can it still be a dream if one has been warned in advance that it is one? It will lack the particular attribute of a dream which is to persuade.

---

[26] See R. Caillois, *L'Incertitude qui vient des rêves* (*The Doubt That Stems from Dreams*) (Paris, 1956), especially the section "Rhétorique du rêve" ("The Rhetoric of the Dream"), pp. 132–149.

3

The Neurophysiological Problem of Sleep

FRÉDÉRIC BREMER

THE HISTORY

A periodical, easily reversible time of suspension for the nervous activities that control *la vie de relation* is a phenomenon common to all superior metazoa. It is debatable whether this suspension is a general physiological necessity rising from a need, resulting in a recuperative rest period for the central neural machinery that controls behavior, or only the expression of a reduction, either fortuitous or cyclical, of sensory stimulation, particularly visual. This sensory factor is certainly important in determining what can be called "sleep" in the invertebrates and the poikilotherm vertebrates. But among birds and mammalia, sleep has all the characteristics of a function, involving the many different activities in the complex organization of postural control. In this regard the combination of attitudes that characterize the hypnoid pause in the activities of communication is very significant. The attitudes differ according to the species and according to the situation of the animal in his surroundings.

All nervous control implies a centralization of the neurological apparatus by which it is accomplished. We know that the first indications of this central localization were obtained by the anatomical study in man of pathological hypersomnias of various origins. This study revealed the usual existence of lesions on the brainstem and in the neighboring subthalamic structures. Already known in the nineteenth century, this topographical relationship was forcefully confirmed during the epidemic of viral encephalitis which raged throughout 1919 and 1920.

Experimentation with animals inspired by these observations soon succeeded in the experimental reproduction of the hypersomnia syndrome, but the significance of these anatomoclinical and experimental data remained very uncertain. Ranson (1939) attributed the hypnogenetic effect of diencephalic lesions in his experiments to disturbances of dynamogenetic descending efferences of hypothalamic origin. A vague notion of a "center of sleep" had been set forth as well. This interpretation remained purely verbal, until W. R. Hess published in 1929 the results of his experiments with electrical stimulation of the median region of the cat's thalamus. The animals carried thin implanted electrodes, but were otherwise free to move about. Sleep provoked in this way had all the characteristics of a natural sleep, which the cat could resist if it found its bed uncomfortable. But sleep did come after delays that were variable and always long. Moreover, the peculiarities of the electrical currents used for stimulation raised some doubts about the excitatory or paralytic nature of the process by which they finally allowed sleep. In fact, it was difficult to explain how destructive lesions and electrical stimulation of the same diencephalic structures had similarly hypnogenetic effects.

Meanwhile Kleitman (1939) gathered together the data of clinical literature and added his personal observations to point out the importance of the part sensory afferences play in maintaining a state of wakefulness. This importance was not contested. But the notion had begun to emerge of the existence of a continuous, spontaneous activity in many of the peripheral receptors, which casts doubt on the importance of the role of overt stimulation of these receptors for the neurophysiological determinism of vigilance.

Experiments of transection of the cat's brainstem (Bremer, 1935, 1937a) demonstrated that a functional state very similar to a deep sleep is produced whenever the continuous corticipetal ascension is interrupted of impulses, supporting what can be called, by analogy with the bulbar-spinal centers, a cerebral or cortical "tonus." While the spontaneous electrical activity of the cerebral cortex of the awake and alert animal can be described as a rapid succession of low-voltage bioelectrical potentials showing no amplitude modulation, the electrocorticogram of the "cerveau isolé" cat is characterized by a monotonous succession of potential waves of great amplitude, with a frequency of about 10 per second, and a spindle-like voltage modulation. There is a striking similarity between this electrocorticogram and that of sleep under barbiturates. Besides, the eyes have the look of deep sleep: globes rolled back and immobile, tight myosis. The illustration (fig. 1) shows this contrast between the tracing of the waking state (*A*) and the tracing of the same cortical region taken after an intercollicular transection of the brainstem (*C*).

At the time of the first researches it was not possible to determine precisely the nature of these ascending impulses, the interruption of which had a hypnogenetic effect. The experiments by section or by anesthesia of the optic nerves, conducted in my laboratory by Elsa Claes (1939), seemed to favor the idea that it was a matter of sensory impulse transmitted by the corticipetal channels of the neuraxis. She found that a section of the optic nerve, made on an animal already deprived of spinal afferences by a high division of the spinal cord ("encéphale isolé" preparation), produced an electrocorticographic syndrome of sleep limited to the visual and paravisual areas. Moreover, I had observed myself (1938) that a complete suppression of corticipetal afferences by a section of the thalamocorti-

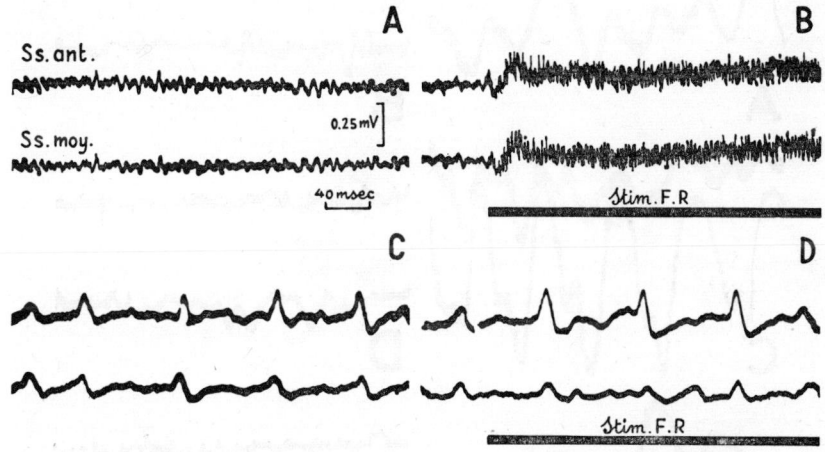

Fig. 1. The effects of electrical stimulation of the ascending reticular formation and of the mesencephalic transection of the brainstem. Cat, "encéphale isolé" preparation (spinal section at C_1). Electrocorticograms (monopolar leads) taken on the anterior and middle suprasylvian gyrus; negativity of the cortical electrode indicated by an upward deflection. (*A*) Awake animal; (*B*) strong activating effect of electrical stimulation of the mesencephalic reticular formation (marked by the block signal at the base of the tracing); (*C*) same animal after a transection of the brainstem above the stimulating electrodes; (*D*) complete absence of effects from the same reticular stimulation used in *B* (Bremer, 1961).

cal radiations resulted in the reception area thus "deafferented" in a functional depression much more marked, although of the same type, than that which followed the mesencephalic transection. Everything seemed then to indicate that the depth of the fall in the tonus of the brain was a function of the degree of its deafferentation. After a mesencephalic transection, the olfactory and visual sensory impulses were apparently not sufficient to maintain a state of vigilant dynamogenesis of the diencephalon and brain cortex.

As is well known, it was left to Moruzzi and Magoun to discover in 1949 that the corticipetal impulses interrupted by a mesencephalic transection are essentially those that emit the reticular formation of the

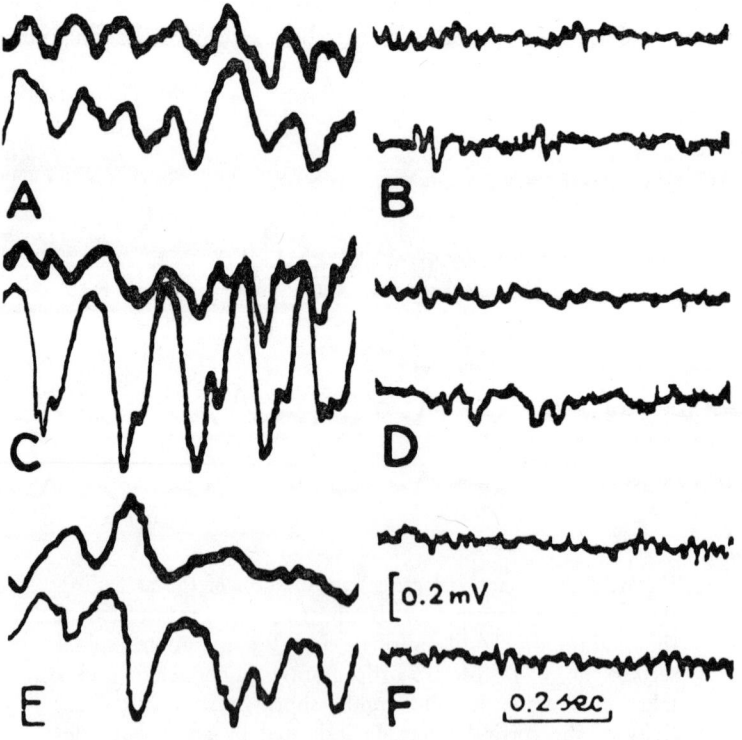

Fig. 2. Identity of the electrocorticographic aspect of reticular arousal and sensory arousal. Cat, "encéphale isolé." Monopolar leads from middle ectosylvian and suprasylvian gyri. Tracings reproduced in the order of their recording. (*A, C, E*) Spontaneous sleep; (*B*) arousal following a brief electrical stimulation of the mesencephalic reticular formation; (*D, F*) sensory arousals (Bremer and Terzuolo, 1954).

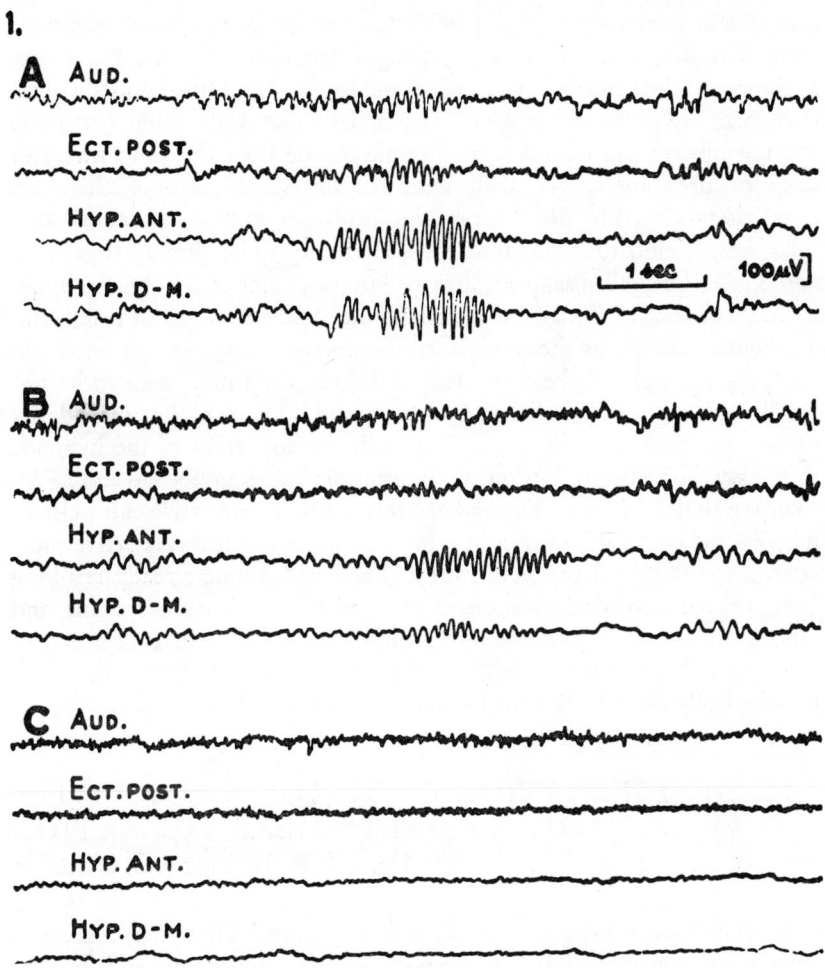

Fig. 3. Sleep, somnolence, and arousal. Cat, "encéphale isolé." Leads from anterior (*Aud*) and posterior ectosylvian gyri (*Ect. post*), and from points in the anterior (*Hyp. ant*) and posterior hypothalamus (*Hyp. d-m*). (*A*) Deep sleep; (*B*) somnolence; (*C*) complete arousal.

brainstem. They demonstrated that, for the lethargic state of a "cerveau isolé" preparation, it was necessary only to suppress these ascending reticular impulses, while a bilateral interruption of the large lemniscal sensory channels is compatible with a maintenance of wakefulness. Moreover, the electrical stimulation of the pontomesencephalic reticular formation has an effect of immediate awakening of the sleeping animal and of intensifying a preexistent vigilant condition. Figures 2 and 3 show that this arousal by electrical stimulation of the mesencephalic reticular formation has, as its electroencephalographic characteristics, the disappearance of slow waves, grouped or not in the "spindles," and their replacement by a scattering of rapid and irregular waves that generally, but not always, are of much smaller amplitude than the slow waves of sleep or drowsiness. We shall soon see the significance of this fact. Arousals produced by direct reticular stimulation and by sensory stimulations were found to be electrocorticographically quite similar (figs. 2, 3, and 8, A). They all disappear after an intercollicular section of the brainstem. Note that in figure 3 a hypothalamic structure reacts to a reticular awakening exactly as the cerebral cortex does.

In the light of these experimental data, sleep may seem to be primarily a functionally deficient nervous condition, involving secondarily various postural adjustments aiming at the prolongation of the hypnotic state as well as the reduction of the thermic losses of the creature. We shall see that we can no longer hold this concept, which we can perhaps describe as "passivist," of the sleep mechanism. Sleep involves active processes, some of which precipitate the fall of cortical tone already resulting from the functional depression of the reticular activating system; and others, much harder to define, which have as an effect the production of short periods of mesencephalic and cortical reticular activation, which paradoxically coexist with the behavioral signs of a deep sleep.

THE PRESERVATION OF THE TONIC ACTIVITY OF THE RETICULAR FORMATION IN THE WAKING STATE

The tonic character of reticular activity in the waking state has been shown experimentally by transections of the brainstem and by the destruction of its central core. The term tonic is preferable to autochthon because its acception includes not only the humoral conditions but the neural factors—sensory and endogenous—of a continually functioning apparatus. The humoral factors are not distinguishable from those long known to be responsible for the respiratory and vasomotor activities of the medullar centers: the pH, pO_2, pCO_2, and adrenalin concentration in blood plasma are the best known (fig. 4). They act on reticular neurons both directly and indirectly, by means of peripheral chemoreceptors, some of which are known, others are yet to be identified. Neurogenic factors are represented by the ensemble of impulses that converge on the reticular neurons. The most important of these are transmitted by collaterals of the great sensory neuraxis channels. There are others of more recent discovery emitted by telencephalic structures, particularly by the

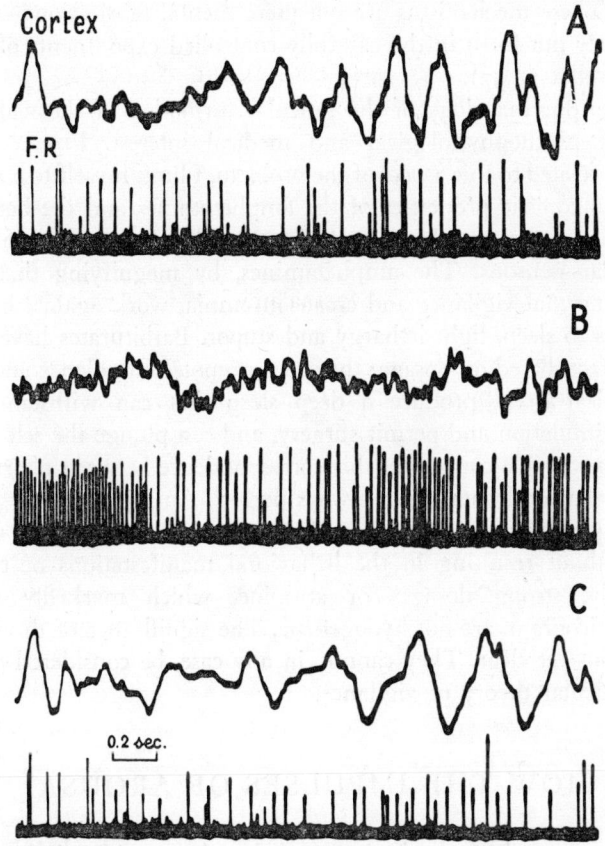

Fig. 4. Arousal by the chemical stimulation of the reticular formation. Cat, "encéphale isolé." Upper tracing of each pair (*Cortex*): electrocorticogram; lower tracing (*F.R.*): unitary neuronal activity in the mesencephalic reticular formation. (*A*) Sleep; (*B*) arousal by the inhalation of carbonic acid (10 percent); (*C*) sleep (Desmedt and Schlag, 1957).

cerebral cortex, which participates thereby in the maintenance of its own tonic activities. As the cortex undergoes the continuous impact of ascending reticular impulses, these impulses are supposed to put into play the reverberative reticulocortical circuit schematized in figure 5. This process of positive feedback, by which reticular activity tends to grow, is probably opposed by the modulating control of a negative feedback, by which any too great an intensification of reticular activity in the awakened state automatically calls for the emission of an inhibitory corticoreticular impulse. These mechanisms are not mere mental fabrications—they have been clearly put forth in the carefully controlled experiments of Hugelin and Bonvallet (1957).

The pharmacology of the reticular formation of the waking state has great psychophysiological and medical interest. From the many questions related to this aspect of the problem, I limit myself to a discussion of the antagonistic properties of the amphetamines and the barbiturates. These two categories of drugs have a predictable effect on the tonic activity of reticular neurons. The amphetamines, by magnifying that activity, intensify normal vigilance and create insomnia, work against narcoleptic tendencies to sleep, fight lethargy and stupor. Barbiturates have a gradation of effects based on dosage: they can promote somnolence and prolong physiological sleep, produce a deep sleep that can withstand painful sensory stimulation and permit surgery, and can plunge the self-murderer into an irreversible coma. But this correspondence between pharmacological and behavioral data is not always perfect. An injection of eserine, for instance, produces a tracing very similar to that of a waking state (fig. 8, *B*) without resulting in the behavioral manifestations of that state. Conversely, strong dosages of atropine, which markedly slow the electrocorticogram, are not hypogenetic. The significance of these discordances is not yet clear. They cannot, in any case, be considered objections to the reticular theory of vigilance.

HOW THE IMPULSES OF AROUSAL WORK

The arousal of the brain must then be considered the result of incessant impact on its neuronal networks of ascendant impulses continually emitted by the brainstem reticular formation. These impulses come in many ways. The greater part pass through the thalamus (fig. 5), whence they are relayed by neurons distinct from those that constitute the sensory and associative nuclei. The cortical projection of this thalamic reticular system is characterized by spatial diffusion (Jasper, 1954).

As far as the visual areas and their neighboring areas are concerned, direct stimulation by impulses originating in the retina (a neural structure itself endowed with autonomous activity) must be added to reticular stimulation so widely distributed by the thalamus. This idea was clearly confirmed by the microphysiological observations made on the "cerveau isolé" preparation in Jung's laboratory (Jung, 1961). Moreover, there is reason to believe that corticipetal impulses that are the result of the incessant stimulation of other sensory receptors also participate in this direct cortical dynamogenesis (Andersson and Wolpow, 1964). Doubtlessly, it is to these direct, extrareticular, impulses that the receptive areas of the cortex owe the peculiar waking activity revealed by electrocorticographic registrations. This direct cortical projection may account for the well-known arousal power of the sensory stimulations that have associative significance or possess an inborn or acquired emotional charge.

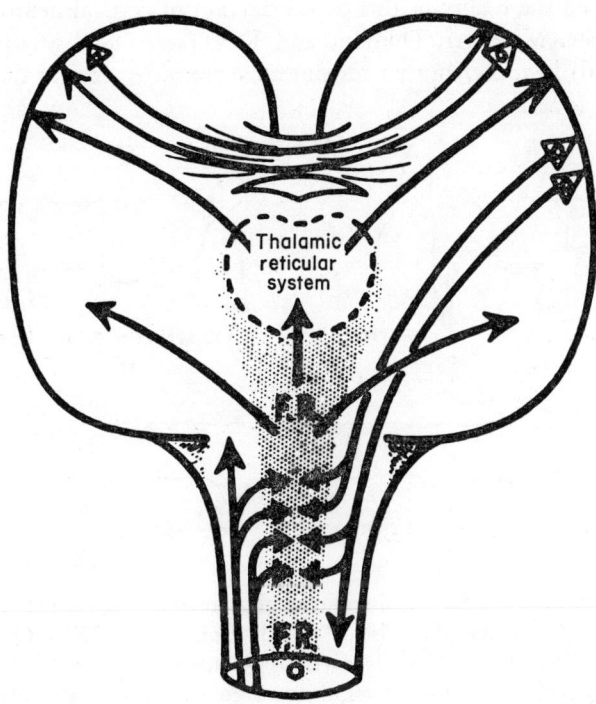

Fig. 5. Diagram indicating the probable pathways of ascending impulses in the brainstem reticular formation and the convergence of its afferences of sensory and cortical origins (Bremer and Terzuolo, 1954).

How does this continuous bombardment by corticipetal—and, more generally, ascending—impulses sustain the brain in a waking state? We have to say ascending because we know that an animal without a cerebral cortex still exhibits alternations of sleep and waking states. The general physiology of the nervous system offers a possible answer to this question. This explanation is based on the fact that a discharge of centrifugal impulses by a neuronal population is conditioned by the state of the cell-membrane polarization (or more precisely by the degree of its reactive depolarization). When this depolarization attains a critical level, the nerve cell emits one or several impulses. The continuous impact of ascending reticular impulses maintains a depolarization of the cerebral neurons which is close to this critical level. This subliminal depolarization, indicated by figure 1, *B*, facilitates the action of the sensory and specific associative impulses. The experiments of Moruzzi and his collaborators (Brookhart *et al.*, 1958), of Bonnet (1962), and of Caspers (1961) have demonstrated the reality of this depolarization of cortical neurons in the waking state. Moreover, Dumont and Dell (1960) and Stoupel and I (1959, fig. 6) have shown that responses by receptive areas of the cerebral

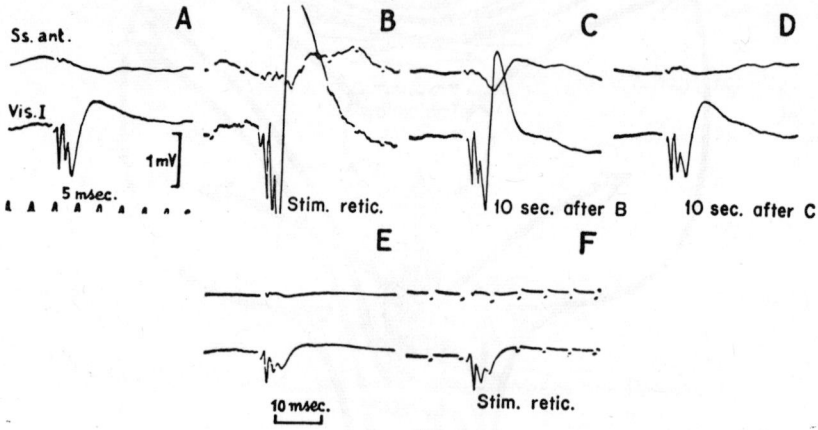

Fig. 6. Reticular facilitation of the cortical evoked potential. Cat, "encéphale isolé." Leads from suprasylvian (*Ss. ant.*) and lateral (*Vis. I*) gyri. (*A*) Control response; (*B, C, D*) responses recorded within 10 seconds, then 20 seconds, after a brief stimulation (200 shocks a second) of the mesencephalic reticular formation; (*E, F*) disappearance of the arousal effects, and of the facilitation of the cortical evoked potential after an intraperitoneal injection of 30 mg of pentobarbital (Bremer and Stouple, 1959).

cortex to an exploratory stimulus applied to the sensory channel corresponding to each of the areas, are greatly facilitated when the testing shock is combined with a reticular stimulation of moderate intensity. Bonnet's microphysiological recordings (1962) have provided proof that the immediate cause of the facilitating effect is indeed the membrane depolarization of the nerve cell created by ascending reticular impulses.

Corresponding to these experimental data confirming the concept of the dynamogenetic action of reticular impulses, we have from Lindsley (1958) and Fuster (1958), psychophysiological data indicating that, with man and with monkeys, perceptive recognition and motor reaction are

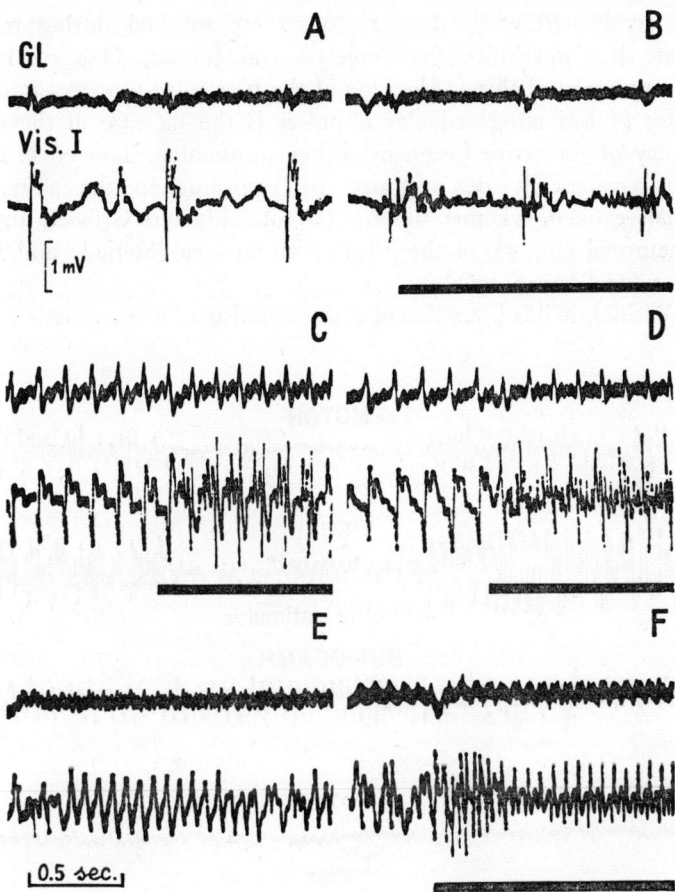

Fig. 7. Effect of reticular arousal on the critical flicker fusion frequency in the cat's visual area. Cat, "encéphale isolé." Upper tracing of each pair (*Gl.*): focal potentials of the lateral geniculate body; lower tracing (*Vis.*): evoked potentials of the cortical visual area. (*C, D, F*) Effect of a mesencephalic reticular stimulation (200 shocks a second), marked by the block signal at the bottom of the tracings. Note, particularly in *F* by comparison with *E*, the fidelity with which the cortical potentials follow the frequency of flicker during the reticular activation of arousal: the electrophysiological aspect of flicker frequency fusion (Bremer, 1961).

clearly accelerated when these responses are solicited during reticular reaction that intensifies the subject's wakefulness. One particularly significant aspect of this acceleration of the perceptive processes under the influence of activating reticular impulses is the increase in the critical frequency of subjective fusion by flicker stimulation. This effect can be electrophysiologically demonstrated by recording in the animal the potentials evoked, whether unitary (Creutzfeldt and Grüsser, 1959) or multineuronal (fig. 7), of the primary visual area (Stériade and Demetrescu, 1961; Bremer, 1961).

Besides, it has been shown that arousal or the accentuation of the

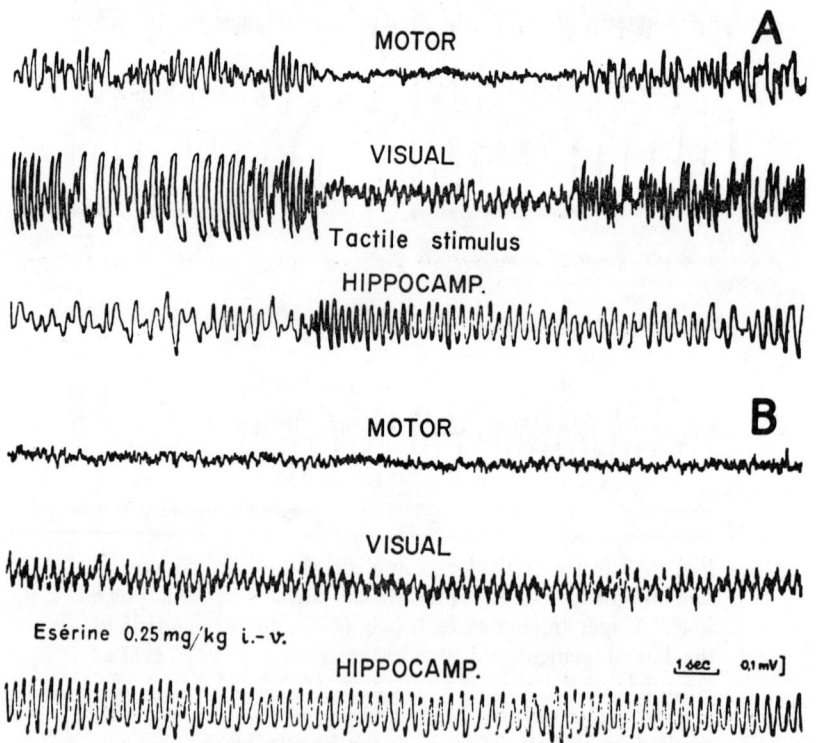

Fig. 8. The effects of arousal and of the injection of eserine on the electrocorticogram of two neocortical areas and of the hippocampal archicortex. Intact rabbit immobilized by an injection of Flaxedil. Note the electrocorticographic similarities in the effects of sensory arousal (*A*) and the eserine injection (*B*), and the contrasting modes of reaction of the neocortex and the hippocampal archicortex. (Unpublished tracings of Dr. P. Ch. Van Reeth).

waking state results in an intensification of "spontaneous" cortico-electrogenesis. In the case of the neocortex, this activation is habitually accompanied by a process of desynchronization of the neuronal unitary potentials, with the effect, as the tracings of sensory visual attention in man show, of reducing the voltage of potential waves, giving the impression of a central inhibition. But, lacking this factor of neuronal desynchronization, arousal is marked by a regularization and an augmentation in the voltage of spontaneous potentials. This is particularly the case with the hippocampal archicortex and the rhinencephalic structures associated with it (fig. 8).

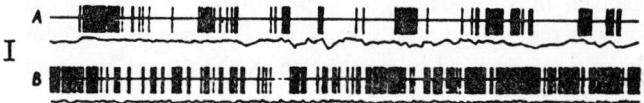

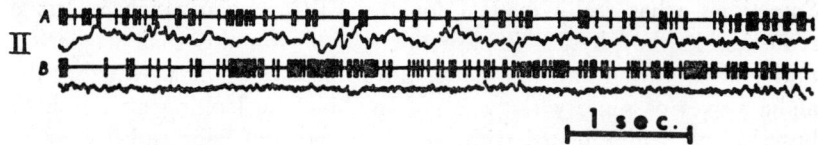

Fig. 9. Unitary cortical activity during sleep and arousal. Cats, carrying implanted electrodes. In the two figures I and II, *A* reproduces the record of unitary activity (visual area) and the surface electrocorticogram during a phase of sleep; *B* shows the activity of the same neuronal unit and the electrocorticogram during arousal. Note the tendency of the spikes to grouping during sleep and their more regular dispersion during arousal (Hubel, 1959).

This interpretation of the electroencephalograms of arousal has been confirmed by the microphysiological recording of unitary neuronal activity. In arousal, the discharge frequency of the already active neocortical neuronal units is accelerated, and units then at rest enter the picture. At the same time, the tendency toward grouping on the part of unitary neuronal discharges in the cortex and the diencephalic nuclei, groupings that constitute volleys corresponding to the slow waves of macroelectrode records, give way to a more uniform time succession without frequency modulation (fig. 9). These electrocorticographic features characterize arousal as opposed to peaceful awakening. In the case of the latter, there is still an observable suppression of the grouping of the unitary potentials, but since the potentials constituting each of the bursts are of a high frequency, the global frequency of the cortical impulses is found to be less than in the relatively deep sleep. Though paradoxical, this change has suggested, wrongly in my opinion, the participation of a process of cortical inhibition in awakening.

THE PROCESS OF GOING TO SLEEP

Why and how do we go to sleep? The factors other than physical or mental fatigue which facilitate falling asleep are well known. Some can be resolved into a lessening of the sensory stimulations that help to keep active the reticular system of arousal. By revealing the slowing and the regularization procured in an electroencephalogram by simply closing the eyes, Berger (1929) demonstrated the particular importance of vision among these physiological sensory stimulations. Darkness has the same effect, but only if it is complete and does not solicit an effort of attention. Sometimes what really matters for the EEG regularization is less a reduction in the physical intensity of a light stimulus than its perfect uniformity. Adrian and Matthews (1934) have, in fact, shown that the alpha waves of sensory rest are not inhibited by looking at a dish of lusterless glass illuminated with absolutely uniform light and occupying the whole visual field. The slightest irregularity detected by the observer in the opalescent dish, however, suffices to instantly dissipate the waves of rest and replace them by a scattering of rapid oscillation (the so-called beta waves).

But sleep can occur without any reduction of sensory impulses—at least primarily.

Two hypnogenetic mechanisms, not necessarily mutually exclusive, can then be imagined. One is based on a plausible hypothesis according to which vigilant activity must in the end involve a state of cumulative fatigue for the cerebral neuronal networks, in particular the cortical ones —a state that makes more and more difficult and contingent neuronal synaptic transmission and the exchange of the intercenter impulses that are necessary for the operational activities of the brain. According to this hypothesis, sleep could be precipitated by an avalanche process, the reduction of activity through nervous fatigue of a cerebral area producing in turn the same effect in areas subordinate to it and receiving from it a continuous dynamogenetic influence. A functional depression of those structures that have an energizing action on the whole brain ought to be of particular importance in determining sleep. This is clearly the case with the reticular activating system (Bremer, 1954; Dell, 1961).

Doubtlessly the central organization of the hypnoid function—

justly insisted upon by Hess (1929, 1949)—finds its most notable expression in the characteristic postures taken in sleep by birds and mammalia, postures that imply a tonic activity by the caudal parts of the reticular formation. For the most part, their functional signification is obvious. A closing of the eyes (which a bird makes complete by inserting his head under a wing) reduces in intensity the stimulation from light. A retraction of the body and its members reduces cutaneous thermolysis. The perching bird and the hanging bat are secure from predators and ready to fly from danger. The firmness of these grips in the air is assured by peculiar anatomical devices. In man and the cat, however, deep sleep is accompanied by a complete muscular relaxation, implying a functional depression of the reticular structure controlling the postural spinal activities. Related to this muscular relaxation is a depression of the neurovegetative activities controlled by specialized regions of the bulbar reticular formation, notably those whose tonic activity is necessary for the maintenance of high blood pressure. Noticeable low blood pressure is a constant symptom of a very deep sleep (Candia et al., 1962).

Such, in rather schematic simplicity, is the concept that tends to make sleep in higher mammalia an essentially passive affair. Clearly, this interpretation now seems inadequate. There is, in fact, a body of experimental data that suggest the active intervention of an inhibitory process in bringing about sleep. First of all, there is the familiar enough notion that sleep can be induced by a rhythmic, monotonous repetition of sensory or central stimulation. Moreover, the physiological stimulation of special receptors like the baroreceptors of the carotid sinus of the dog (Koch, 1932; Bonvallet, Dell, and Hiebel, 1954) and, in rabbits, the facial and laryngeal receptors dependent on the facial, glossopharyngeal and pneumogastric nerves (Van Reeth and Capon, 1962), shows itself to be directly hypnogenetic. Even slow rhythmical stimulation of cutaneous nerves can produce sleep (Pompeiano and Swett, 1962). The suddenness with which an infant or a narcoleptic patient falls asleep also constitutes a positive argument for the intervention of a central hypnogenetic device in the physiological process of falling asleep, a device that can produce its effect, according to the principle of reciprocal innervation, by inhibiting the tonic activity of the waking state's activating system.

All these disparate data actually have the support of more direct experimental argument—thanks to Moruzzi and his associates (see Moruzzi, 1963). Their work has established the fact that the tonic activity of a bulbopontine structure exerts on the telencephalon an influence directly opposed to the influence of the reticular system of awakening. In the cat, the electrical stimulation of a bulbar reticular region near the nucleus of the solitary tract produces a relaxation and a regularization of the cortical electrogenesis which resembles that of drowsiness or light sleep

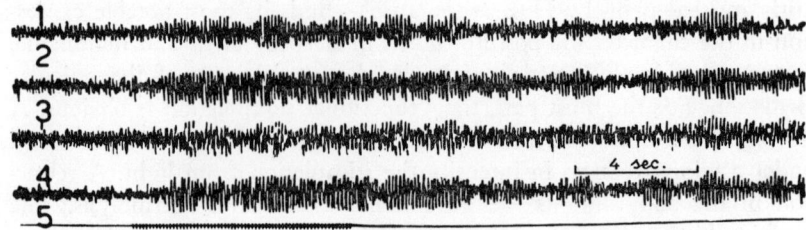

Fig. 10. EEG synchronization by a low-frequency stimulation of region of nucleus of solitary tract. Cat, "encéphale isolé." (*1, 2, 3, 4*) bipolar records of the electrocorticogram of four cortical areas right and left. Note that the hypnogenetic effect (EEG synchronization) outlasts the stimulus, the duration of which is indicated by the signal line on bottom (*5*) (Magnes, Moruzzi, and Pompeiano, 1961).

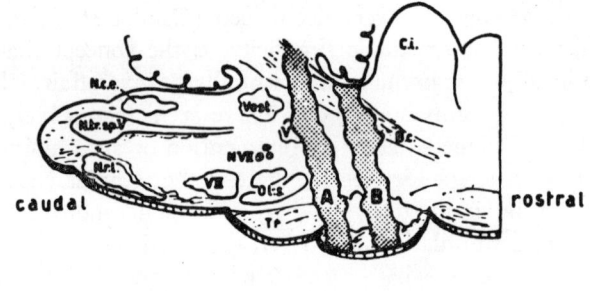

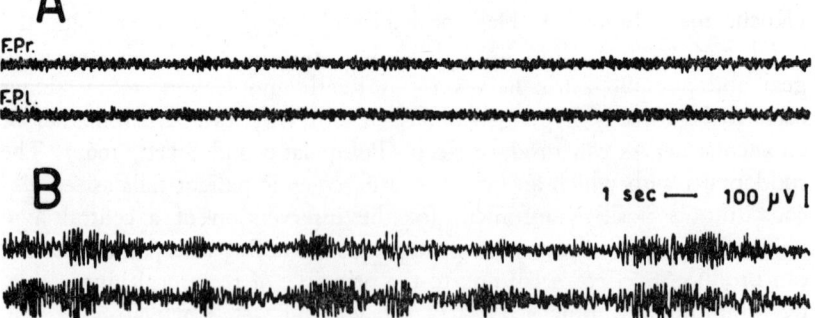

Fig. 11. Permanent cortical arousal determined in the cat by a mediopontine section of the brainstem. The drawing shows, on a sagittal plane, two transections made successively in the course of the same experiment. (*A*) Electrocorticographic records of continuous arousal (frontoparietal leads right and left), corresponding to the posterior section; (*B*) tracings of sleep corresponding to the anterior section (Batini *et al.*, 1959a, b).

(fig. 10). Conversely, disconnecting this region from the mesencephalic apparatus of arousal in the "encéphale isolé" preparation has the effect of a state of continuous vigilance in the animal (fig. 11). This lasting insomnia can also be produced by the anesthesia of the same bulbo-pontine area. Very likely it is by such an intermediary that the hypnogenetic reflexes just mentioned operate. On the clinical level, stubborn insomnia of the belated aftereffects of Economo's (1929) encephalitis find a plausible explanation in these observations of animals.

"ACTIVATED" SLEEP AND DREAMS

The development of this experimental approach, which had such mind-satisfying logical cohesion, had, until very recently, created for all who study the physiology of sleep the comfortable impression that we were on the road toward solving the problem within the premises of the general physiology of the nervous system. This happy repose was destroyed when Dement and Kleitman (1957), and Dement (1958), followed quickly by Jouvet (1962), and by Rossi et al. (1961), demonstrated the existence in man and the cat of brief recurring phases of sleep, which seem to have all the behavioral accompaniments of deep sleep, in particular a generalized relaxation of the postural tone (fig. 12, B) and a notable rise in the electric and sensory excitatory threshold of arousal in the mesencephalic reticular formation, but which at the same time paradoxically and strangely presented the cortical and reticular electrophysiological characteristics of waking activity (fig. 12, B).

Interest in this "activated" or "paradoxical" phase of sleep heightened when it appeared that in man it was closely associated with the phenomenon of dreams (Kleitman, 1961). I do not comment at any great length on this matter because it is the theme of Dr. Dement's paper (chap. 4). I will limit myself to pointing out that the homology of observations in man and the experimental data are not absolutely certain so far as it concerns the place of activated sleep in the chronological succession of the stages of sleep as well as the visual oneiric signification of the rapid ocular movement that accompanies them. Besides, the neurophysiological determinants of activated sleep, the objects of very detailed studies by Jouvet (1962) and by Rossi et al. (1961), are still far from being clearly defined. Absent in reptiles, barely discernible in birds, this phase of sleep is only clearly apparent in superior mammalia (Hermann, Jouvet, and Klein, 1964).

Whatever the answer eventually given these questions, the activated sleep phase reveals a break in the congruence of the electrophysiological processes associated with higher nervous activities in the waking state,

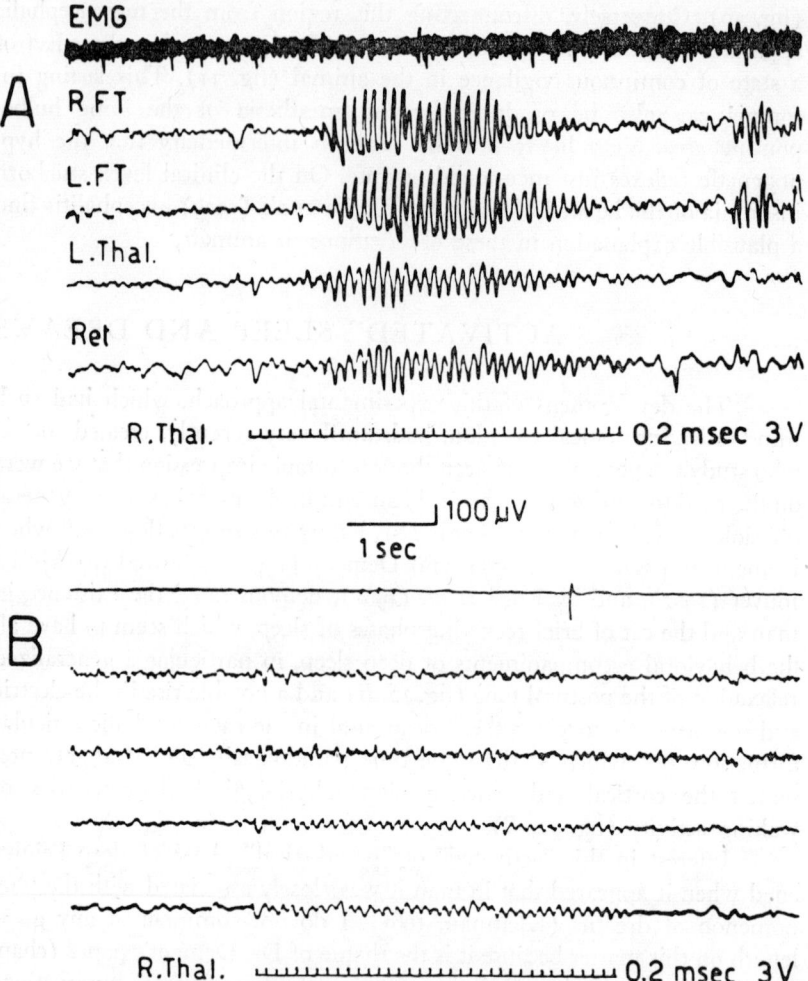

Fig. 12. Two types of sleep. Intact cat carrying implanted electrodes. Oscillogram of the cervical muscles (*EMG*), of the left and right frontoparietal cortex (*R. FT., L. FT.*), of a thalamic nucleus (n. centralis lateralis left [*L. Thal.*]), of the mesencephalic reticular formation (*Ret.*): (*R. Thal.*) signal of the low frequency stimulation of the right n. centralis lateralis. (*A*) Light sleep; (*B*) activated (deep) sleep. Note the complete relaxation of the cervical muscles and the absence of synchronizing effect from the thalamic stimulation, during activated sleep (Rossi et al., 1961).

and of the behavioral manifestations of these processes. When the cerebral cortex emerges periodically from the functional depression of the phase of sleep with slowed electrogenesis, it might be asked if it is not the interruption or the slackening of its connections with its sensory informers and motor commands which permits the activities creative of imagery and myths, which are dream, to develop freely.

The mechanics of sleep appears as the handily arranged interplay of the actions and reactions of reciprocally subordinated central structures. But while in all the great central nervous regulations that assure physiological homeostasis, the reaction tends automatically to correct quickly a functional alteration resulting from the initial trouble, in the case of hypnogenetic mechanisms the reaction seems on the contrary to accentuate and prolong the initial disturbance and to sanction the imbalance. This, obviously, is only a surface impression because sleep will, in the end, result in the restoration of those delicate nervous mechanisms whose alteration was required for its procurement. This restoration of the cortical neuronal networks could be endangered by a functional depression that is too deep or too greatly prolonged. Such may be the physiological signification and the actual goal—Dr. Dement gives you the experimental data suggesting the existence of this goal—of these paradoxical phases of reticulocortical activation which periodically interrupt sleep of slowed electrogenesis.

References

Adrian, E. D., and B. H. C. Matthews. 1934. "The Berger rhythm potential changes from the occipital lobe in man," *Brain*, 57:355–385.

Andersson, S. A., and E. R. Wolpow. 1964. "Localized slow wave activity in the somatosensory cortex of the cat," *Acta Physiologica Scandinavica*, 61:130–140.

Batini, C., G. Moruzzi, M. Palestini, G. F. Rossi, and A. Zanchetti. 1959a. "Effects of complete pontine transections on the sleep-wakefulness rhythm: the midpontine pretrigeminal preparation," *Archives italiennes de biologie*, 97:1–12.

———. 1959b. "Neural mechanisms underlying the enduring EEG and behavioral activation in the midpontine pretrigeminal cat," *Archives italiennes de biologie*, 97:13–25.

Berger, H. 1929. "Über das Elektrenkephalogram des Menschen," *Archiv für Psychiatrie und Nervenkrankheiten*, 87:527–570.

———. 1930. "Über das Elektrenkephalogram des Menschen," *Journal für Psychologie und Neurologie*, 40:160–179.

Bonnet, V. 1962. "Mécanisme d'action de la formation réticulaire sur l'activité réactionnelle de l'écorce cérébrale," *Compte rendu hebdomadaire des séances de l'Académie des Sciences* (Paris), 254:2081–2083.

Bonvallet, M., P. Dell, and G. Hiebel. 1954. "Tonus sympathique et activité électrique corticale," *Electroencephalography and Clinical Neurophysiology* (Amsterdam), 6:119–143.

Bremer, F. 1935. "Cerveau isolé et physiologie du sommeil," *Compte rendu hebdomadaire des séances et mémoires de la Société de Biologie* (Paris), 118:1235–1242.

———. 1937a. "L'activité cérébrale au cours du sommeil et de la narcose: Contribution à l'étude du mécanisme du sommeil," *Bulletin de l'Academie Royale de Médecine de Belgique*, 4:68–86.

———. 1937b. "Différence d'action de la narcose éthérique et du sommeil barbiturique sur les réactions sensorielles acoustiques du cortex cérébral," *Compte rendu hebdomadaire des séances et mémoires de la Société de Biologie* (Paris), 124:848–852.

———. 1938. "Effets de la déafférentation complète d'une région de l'écorce cérébrale sur son activité électrique spontanée," *Compte rendu hebdomadaire des séances et mémoires de la Société de Biologie* (Paris), 127: 355–358.

———. 1954. "The neurophysiological problem of sleep," in *Brain Mechanisms and Consciousness*. A Symposium. Oxford: Blackwell. Pp. 137–162.

———. 1961. "Neurophysiological mechanisms of cerebral arousal," in *The Nature of Sleep*. A Ciba Foundation Symposium. London: J. and D. Churchill. Pp. 30–156.

Bremer, F., and N. Stoupel. 1959. "Facilitation et inhibition des potentiels évoqués corticaux dans l'éveil cérébral," *Archives internationales de physiologie et de biochemie,* 67:240–275.

Bremer, F., and C. Terzuolo. 1954. "Contribution à l'étude des mécanismes physiologiques du maintien de l'activité vigile du cerveau: Interaction de la formation réticulée et de l'écorce cérébrale dans le processus du réveil," *Archives internationales de physiologie et de biochemie,* 62: 157–178.

Brookhart, J. M., A. Arduini, M. Mancia, and G. Moruzzi. 1958. "Thalamocortical relations as revealed by induced slow potential changes," *Journal of Neurophysiology,* 21:499–525.

Candia, O., E. Favale, A. Guissani, and G. F. Rossi. 1962. "Blood pressure during natural sleep and during sleep induced by electrical stimulation of the brain stem reticular formation," *Archives italiennes de biologie,* 100:217–247.

Caspers, H. 1961. "Changes of cortical d.c. potentials in the sleep-wakefulness cycle," in *The Nature of Sleep*. A Ciba Foundation Symposium. London: J. and D. Churchill. Pp. 237–259.

Claes, E. 1939. "Analyse oscillographique de l'activité spontanée et sensorielle de l'aire visuelle corticale chez le chat non anesthésié," *Archives internationales de physiologie et de biochemie,* 48:181–237.

Creutzfeldt, O., and O. J. Grüsser. 1959. "Veränderung der Flimmerreaktion corticaler Neurone durch Reize unspecifischer Thalamuskerne," in *Compte rendu. Ier Congrès International des Sciences Neurologiques,* Brussels.

Dell, P., M. Bonvallet, and A. Hugelin. 1961. "Mechanisms of reticular deactivation," in *The Nature of Sleep*. A Ciba Foundation Symposium. London: J. and D. Churchill. Pp. 86–107.

Dement, W. 1958. "The occurrence of low voltage fast electroencephalogram patterns during behavioral sleep in the cat," *Electroencephalography and Clinical Neurophysiology* (Amsterdam), 10:291–296.

Dement, W., and N. Kleitman. 1957. "Cyclic variations in EEG during sleep and their relation to eye movements, body motility and dreaming," *Electroencephalography and Clinical Neurophysiology* (Amsterdam), 9:673–690.

Desmedt, J. E., and J. Schlag. 1957. "Mise en évidence d'éléments cholinergiques dans la formation réticulée mésencéphalique," *Journal de physiologie* (Paris), 49:136–138.

Dumont, S., and P. Dell. 1960. "Facilitation réticulaire des mécanismes visuels corticaux," *Electroencephalography and Clinical Neurophysiology* (Amsterdam), 12:769–796.

Economo, C. von. 1929. "Schlaftheorie," *Ergebnisse der Physiologie, biologischen chemie und experimentellen Pharmakologie*, 28:312–339.

Fuster, J. M. 1958. "Effects of stimulation of brainstem on tachistoscopie perception," *Science*, 127:150.

Hermann, H., M. Jouvet, and M. Klein. 1964. "Analyse polygraphique du sommeil de la tortue," *Compte rendu hebdomadaire des séances de l'Académie des Sciences* (Paris), 258:2175–2178.

Hess, W. R. 1929a. "Lokalisatorische Ergebnisse der Hirnreizversuche mit Schlafeffekt," *Archiv für Psychiatrie und Nervenkrankheiten*, 88:813–816.

———. 1929b. "Hirnreizversuche über den Mechanismus des Schlafes," *Archiv für Psychiatrie und Nervenkrankheiten*, 86:287–292.

———. 1949. *Das Zwischenhirn: Syndrom, Lokalisationen, Funktionen*. Bâle: Bruno Schwabe.

Hubel, D. H. 1959. "Single unit activity in striate cortex of unrestrained cats," *Journal of Physiology*, 147:226–238.

Hugelin, A., and M. Bonvallet. 1957. "Tonus cortical et contrôle de la facilitation motrice d'origine réticulaire," *Journal de physiologie* (Paris), 49:1171–1223.

Jasper, H. H. 1954. "Functional properties of the thalamic reticular system," in *Brain Mechanisms and Consciousness*. A Symposium. Oxford: Blackwell. Pp. 374–401.

Jouvet, M. 1962. "Recherches sur les structures nerveuses et les mécanismes responsables de différentes phases du sommeil physiologique," *Archives italiennes de biologie*, 106:125–206.

Jung, R. 1961. "Discussion of the report by Bremer," in *The Nature of Sleep*. A Ciba Foundation Symposium. London: J. and D. Churchill. Pp. 51–52.

Kleitman, N. 1939. *Sleep and Wakefulness*. Chicago.

———. 1961. "The nature of dreaming," in *The Nature of Sleep*. A Ciba Foundation Symposium. London: J. and D. Churchill. Pp. 349-374.

Koch, E., 1932. "Die Irradiation der pressoreazeptorischen Kreislaufreflexe," *Klinische Wochenschrift*, 2:225-227.

Lindsley, D. B. 1958. "The reticular system and perceptual discrimination," in *Reticular Formation of the Brain*. Boston: Little, Brown. Pp. 513-534.

Magnes, J., G. Moruzzi, and O. Pompeiano. 1961. "Synchronization of the EEG produced by low-frequency electrical stimulation of the region of the solitary tract," *Archives italiennes de biologie*, 99:33-67.

Magoun, H. W. 1958. *The Waking Brain*. Springfield: Charles C Thomas.

Moruzzi, G. 1963. "Active processes in the brain during sleep," *The Harvey Lectures*. (New York and London), 58:233-297.

Moruzzi, G., A. Fessard, and H. Jasper, eds. 1963. *Brain Mechanisms*. Pisa Symposium. Amsterdam: Elsevier.

Moruzzi, G., and H. W. Magoun. 1949. "Brainstem reticular formation and activation of the E. E. G.," *Electroencephalography and Clinical Neurophysiology* (Amsterdam), 1:455-473.

Pompeiano, O., and J. E. Swett. 1962a. "EEG and behavioral manifestations of sleep induced by cutaneous nerve stimulations in normal cats," *Archives italiennes de biologie*, 100:311-342.

———. 1962b. "Identification of cutaneous and muscular afferent fibers producing EEG synchronization on arousal in normal cats," *Archives italiennes de biologie*, 100:342-389.

Ranson, S. W. 1939. "Somnolence caused by hypothalamic lesions in the monkey," *Archives of Neurology and Psychiatry* (London and Chicago), 41:1-23.

Rossi, G. F., E. Favale, T. Hara, A. Guissani, and G. Sacco. 1961. "Researches in the nervous mechanisms underlying deep sleep in the cat," *Archives italiennes de biologie*, 99:270-292.

Stériade, M., and M. Demetrescu. 1961. "Unspecific systems of inhibition and facilitation of potentials evoked by intermittent light," *Journal of Neurophysiology*, 23:602-617.

Van Reeth, J. Ch., and A. Capon. 1962. "Sommeil provoqué chez le lapin par des stimulations profondes, céphaliques et cervicales," *Compte rendu hebdomadaire des séances de l'Académie des Sciences* (Paris), 255:3050-3052.

4

The Psychophysiology of Dreaming[1]

WILLIAM C. DEMENT

It seems to be a standard practice to begin an article on the subject of dreams by reminding the reader that these nocturnal visitations have intrigued and baffled mankind since time immemorial. In the past, such a reminder would serve to take the writer off the hook by implying that he was at least no more in the dark than anyone else if his theories seemed a little inadequate. It is now possible, however—and in this case the introductory reminder to the reader may serve to emphasize the contrast—to heave a somewhat contented sigh and announce that some of the age-old questions regarding dreams appear finally to have been answered satisfactorily.

Although it is virtually axiomatic that dream experiences occur during sleep (a point that some philosophers have debated strenuously), nonetheless the problem of sleep and the problem of dreams for the most part were dealt with as separate entities. For example, Freud wrote in *The Interpretation of Dreams,* "I have had little occasion to deal with the problem of sleep, for that is essentially a problem of physiology [28]." And certainly, even Freud's emphasis on the clinical im-

---

[1] The research studies conducted by the author and his colleagues were supported by research grants MY-3267 and MH-08185 from the National Institute of Mental Health.

portance of dreams did little to change the traditional conception of dreaming as an occasional, unpredictable, fleeting, and mysterious psychic anomaly. It has turned out, however, that the physiology of sleep and the problem of dreaming are much more intimately entwined than anyone could have imagined, and the physiological pathway has proven to be the shortest route to an understanding of some of the fundamental properties of dreams.

TWO KINDS OF SLEEP

Within the past few years, it has been established that there are actually two kinds of sleep which possess markedly contrasting physiological characteristics and mechanisms, both of which occur normally in any extended period of somnolence. One of these is the recently elucidated "paradoxical" phase of sleep, to use the apt terminology of Jouvet [40], otherwise known as "activated" sleep [15], or "rapid eye movement" (REM) sleep [21], which may also be referred to as "dreaming" sleep because it does, in fact, seem to be the state in which dreaming takes place. Thus, the dream state has its own special attributes and mechanisms, which are nothing more than those of paradoxical sleep. Of course, when a psychological dimension is added to the physiological, there are further problems and complexities, but this does not alter the fundamental concept.

Lest we sound too ambitious, it should be admitted that we are dealing here more with the process of dreaming, and less with the instigation and meaning of its content. Even these latter aspects may yield some of their secrets to investigators utilizing, in part at least, a physiological approach; and it seems inevitable that knowledge of the process of dreaming will exert some influence on theories of the function and meaning of dreams.

A detailed review of the physiology of paradoxical sleep, together with a description of the various experimental approaches, may be found elsewhere [17, 18]. In the interests of brevity, I confine myself mainly to the area of psychophysiological correlation, that is, the evidence for equating the dream state with rapid eye movement (REM) sleep in humans, and, because the existence of dreaming cannot be established in subhuman species, to some of the evidence for equating paradoxical sleep as described in animals, particularly the cat, with REM or dreaming sleep in humans. The latter point is important because we would like to apply the knowledge gained from neurophysiological experimentation in our attempt to further understand the phenomenon of dreaming.

It is perhaps more convenient to deal with the comparative physiology at the outset. Actually, the first hints of the dichotomous nature of sleep were obtained from human studies. In 1953, Aserinsky and Kleitman [5] published the first description of a peculiar type of ocular motility that occurred during sleep. Contrary to the familiar phenomenon of slow, rolling, to-and-fro deviations of the eyeballs seen at the onset of sleep [56, 64, 66], the movements described by these authors were rapid, jerky, and binocularly synchronous. A subsequent study [21] showed that the rapid eye movements (REM's) appeared only during discrete periods of the night and that these periods were precisely defined by a specific stage of the electroencephalogram (EEG). The EEG patterns were divided into four convenient stages[2] and it was found that in all-night undisturbed recordings, a regular, cyclic alternation of these stages occurred. Individual cycles were defined by the repetitive reappearance of lengthy periods of the low-voltage stage 1 EEG and it was only during these periods that REM's were seen. Figure 1 shows the EEG plots from several typical examples of such all-night recordings. A tendency may be seen for the REM periods to increase in length as the night wears on and for most of the stage 4 patterns to occur early in the night, while later, the change is mainly limited to an alternation between stages 1 and 2.

A number of other physiological variables have since been studied in conjunction with EEG and eye-movement recordings. Nearly all have shown some kind of unique behavior during the REM (stage 1) periods as opposed to the remainder of sleep. For example, heart and respiratory rates are accelerated and more irregular [17, 46, 82], finger-pulse volume is constricted [90], tonic electromyographic (EMG) potentials are suppressed [6], and there is an abolition of reflex responses to electrical stimulation of peripheral nerves [32]. Some of these relationships are illustrated in figure 2.

Because of the experimental limitations in studying human subjects, it was natural to turn to the cat for confirmation of the presence of an EEG sleep cycle and REM periods in another species [15], and it was indeed found that, during lengthy intervals of feline sleep, there was a rhythmic succession of EEG stages. Periods of high voltage, slow EEG patterns alternated with periods of EEG activation, and the latter were accompanied by REM's and twitching movements of the limbs, ears, tail, and vibrissae. Although the EEG patterns during this latter phase seemed indistinguishable from those ordinarily associated with behavioral wake-

---

[2] The system that was used, which is quite similar to most others, is as follows: stage 1, a low-voltage, irregularly mixed fast and slow pattern; stage 2, characterized by the presence of 12–14/sec sleep spindles with a low-voltage background; stage 3, an intermediate amount of high amplitude, slow activity with some spindling; stage 4, a predominance of high amplitude, slow activity.

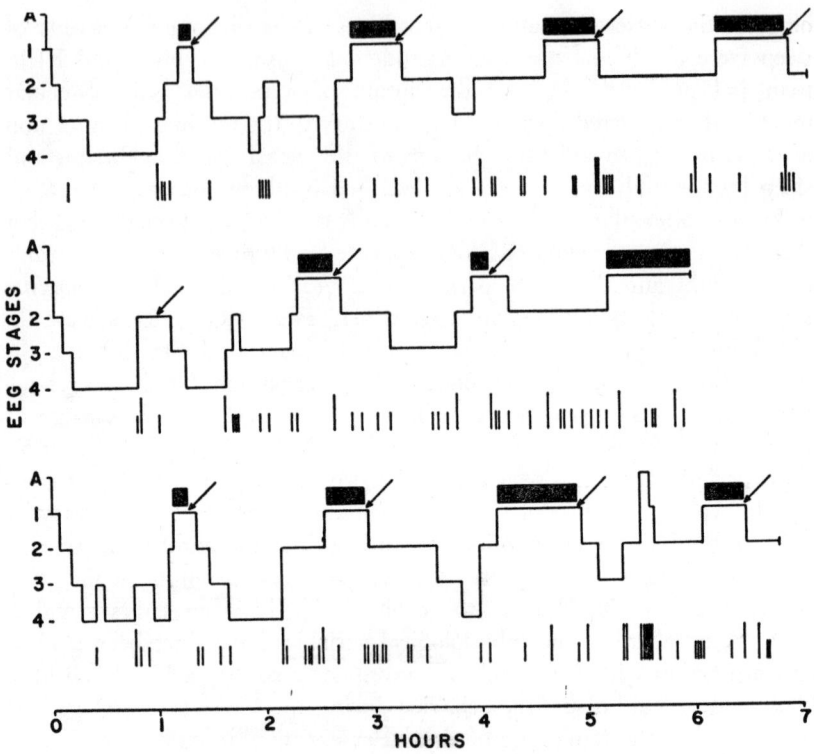

Fig. 1. Continuous plotting of EEG patterns for three representative nights. The thick bars immediately above the EEG lines indicate periods during which rapid eye movements were seen. The vertical lines below stand for body movements. The longer vertical lines indicate major movements, changes in position of the whole body, and the shorter lines represent minor movements. The arrows indicate both the end of one EEG cycle and the beginning of the next (reprinted by permission from W. Dement and N. Kleitman, "Cyclic variations in EEG during sleep and their relation to eye movements, body motility, and dreaming," *Electroencephalography and Clinical Neurophysiology* [Amsterdam] 9[1957], 673-690).

fulness, direct observation and the presence of elevated sensory thresholds clearly established that the animals were asleep.

This area of investigation was carried much further by Jouvet and his colleagues [37-44]. Along with their independent discovery of "activated" sleep, they also demonstrated that the phase was associated with a continuous hippocampal theta rhythm, pontine "spindling," complete loss of muscle tone, and characteristic cardiorespiratory variations. They further showed that the appearance of "paradoxical" sleep was dependent upon a triggering mechanism situated in the medial pontine reticular formation.

Other investigators have taken up the problem and have demonstrated additional remarkable features of paradoxical sleep. To mention a few, microelectrode studies in the unrestrained cat by Evarts [25, 26]

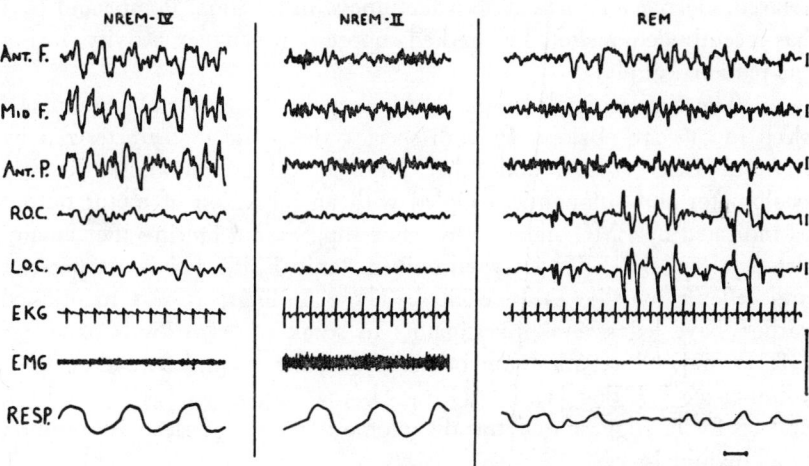

Fig. 2. Polygraphic tracings from different stages of sleep on the same night from the same subject. *NREM–IV*, non-REM sleep, stage 4 EEG pattern; *NREM–II*, non-REM sleep, stage 2 EEG pattern; *REM*, rapid eye movement sleep; *Ant. F.*, anterior frontal monopolar EEG; *Mid F.*, mid-frontal monopolar EEG; *Ant. P.*, anterior parietal monopolar; *ROC*, tracing from right outer canthus with reference to both ears; *LOC*, tracing from left outer canthus, monopolar. Calibration: 50 uV and one second. Note the qualitative differences between REM and non-REM sleep. In stages 2 and 4, tonic EMG potentials are present, in REM they are absent. The fact that there is less EMG in stage 4 is fortuitous. Respiration is smooth and regular in stages 2 and 4. In REM, the irregularity and shallowness are striking. No REM's are seen in stages 2 and 4 (the waves in the outer canthi tracings are EEG artifacts). Although it is not obvious, the heart rate is accelerated in REM sleep. Finally, the EEG in stages 2 and 4 is more synchronized. The sleep spindles in stage 2 cannot be seen at this magnification. Also, the slow waves in the *Ant. F.* lead during REM sleep are eye-movement artifacts.

and Huttenlocher [33] have shown that paradoxical sleep is associated with unusually high rates of unit discharge in the mesencephalic reticular formation, visual and somatosensory cortex. Arduini has reported a heightened activity in the pyramidal tract [4]. Kanzow, Krause, and Kühnel [47] have observed a marked increase in cortical blood flow. Of particular relevance to the possible presence of dreaming is the fact that these increases in neuronal activity and blood flow seem to reach levels that are comparable to those seen in the *active* waking state as opposed to relaxed, inactive, or inattentive wakefulness. In addition, Pompeiano [65] has recently demonstrated a marked suppression of reflex activity during the paradoxical phase.

The similarities between REM sleep in humans and paradoxical sleep in cats are obvious. In both species, the phase is characterized by signs of EEG arousal and other physiological activation, particularly oculomotor and autonomic, coupled with an inhibition of motor output as indicated by EMG silence and reflex suppression. During the remainder of sleep, the EEG is synchronized, tonic EMG activity is present, and reflexes may be easily elicited. These findings, as was mentioned earlier, have led several investigators to speak of "two kinds of sleep" [18, 37, 61]. Observations on other species, for example, monkey [88], chimpanzee [1], dog [1, 11, 81], rat [53, 72, 86], sheep [35], goat [73], and so forth, suggest that the dichotomous nature of sleep is common to all mammals.

Returning for a moment to the human, there were several stumbling blocks that delayed the early recognition of the existence of two kinds of sleep. For one thing, it was assumed that a stage 1 EEG pattern invariably indicated the presence of "light sleep." The position of stage 1 in the EEG sleep cycle (see fig. 1) seemed perfectly compatible with the notion of a cyclic variation in depth of sleep in which the occurrence of the REM period would represent only a quantitative change in an essentially unitary process. Although not associated with REM's, a low-voltage stage 1 EEG also appeared at the onset of sleep. Accordingly, the sleep onset or drowsy period and the REM period seemed to be electroencephalographically identical. One of the early findings of Dement and Kleitman [21] was that the arousal threshold during REM sleep was much higher than during the sleep-onset stage 1. Kleitman attempted to resolve this problem by calling the REM-sleep EEG "emergent stage 1," to distinguish it from the stage 1 EEG at the sleep onset, and perhaps implying that reaching the same level from a different direction could explain the contrasting physiological relationships [48]. Further resolution came, however, with the demonstration that the EEG during REM sleep actually possessed a certain uniqueness by virtue of the presence of the so-called saw-toothed waves in tracings from anterior regions of the scalp [7, 17, 36,

77]. These are illustrated in figure 3. Thus, although the sleep onset and the REM period are both included within the overly general categorization of stage 1, the EEG patterns are not really identical.

A similar difficulty seemed to complicate the early studies of the EEG and arousal thresholds in human subjects. These studies unanimously equated a low-voltage, nonspindling EEG with light sleep [10,

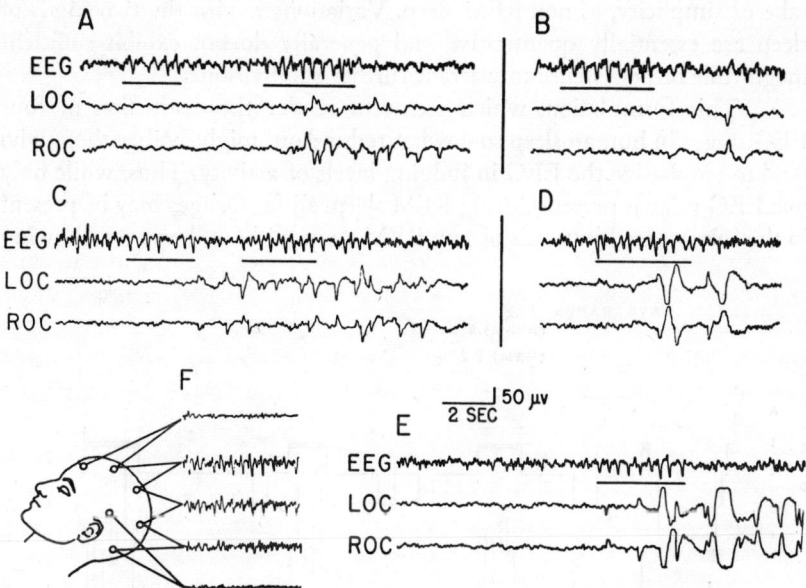

Fig. 3. Sample tracing showing the sharp (sawtooth) waves that precede bursts of rapid eye movement. In *F*, bipolar derivations show the sharp waves to be localized centrally in this subject. In *A–D* and *E*, EEG is recorded monopolarly from the central electrode. *LOC*, left outer canthus to ears; *ROC*, right outer canthus to ears (reprinted by permission from W. Dement, "Eye movements during sleep," in M. Bender, ed., *The Oculomotor System* [New York: Paul B. Hoeber, 1964], p. 383).

12, 51]. It is now clear that such a result, in the absence of measurements to distinguish REM stage 1 and sleep-onset stage 1 (the latter undoubtedly greatly increased as a consequence of numerous arousals to the testing stimuli), is due to the confounding of the two categories of low-voltage patterns. Williams *et al.* [90] carefully made the distinction in their correlations of EEG and arousal threshold, and found, by their technique of measurement, that REM sleep represented a deep stage of sleep comparable to stage 4 of the EEG and certainly much deeper than stage 2.

With these apparent discrepancies cleared up, it became obvious that REM sleep with its low-voltage EEG could not be placed in a depth-of-sleep continuum with the other EEG stages of sleep. REM periods with their unique constellation of physiological attributes thus constituted one kind of sleep; and the interspersed periods containing stages 2, 3, and 4 constituted the other kind, which will hereafter be referred to, for the sake of simplicity, as non-REM sleep. Variations *within* the two kinds of sleep are essentially quantitative and generally do not exhibit sufficient magnitude or persistence to warrant further subdivision.

This formulation, which seems to render the distinction of four EEG stages in human sleep somewhat redundant, might bother those who tend to emphasize the EEG in judging levels of activity. Thus, while only one EEG stage is present during REM sleep, all four stages may be present in the interspersed intervals of non-REM sleep without, however, showing

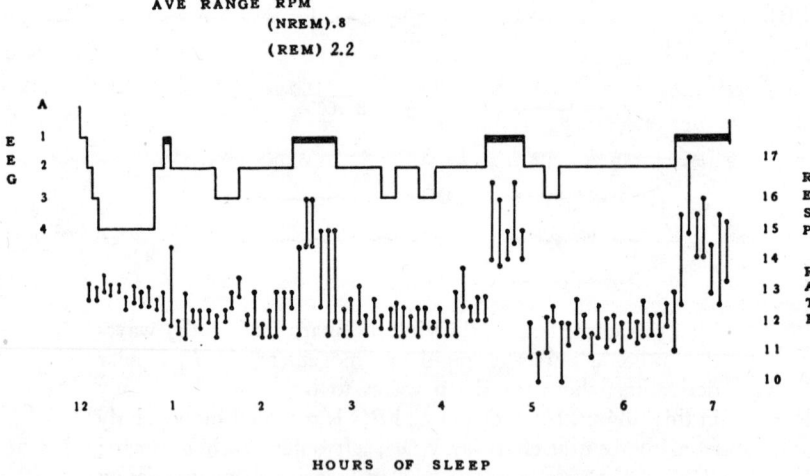

Fig. 4. Variations in respiratory rate during an entire night of sleep. The top line is a continuous plotting of the EEG in terms of the four stages, and the dark bars indicate the eye-movement periods. The number of respirations in each successive minute were counted and each vertical line represents the range of minute counts for each successive five-minute period. It can be seen that during rapid-eye-movement periods there is an overall increase in both range and rate (reprinted by permission from W. Dement, "Eye movements during sleep," in M. Bender, ed., *The Oculomotor System* [New York: Paul B. Hoeber, 1964]).

significant covariance with other physiological measurements. Figure 4, a plot of the data from an all-night recording of EEG and respiration, may be used as an example to clarify this point. The figure illustrating the relationship between EEG and blood pressure in the recent study of Snyder, Hobson, and Goldfrank [84] could similarly be used. A glance at figure 4 reveals that increases in both rate and variability of respiratory rate during REM sleep stand out rather sharply against a rather stable respiratory background. In the first EEG cycle, there is a complete swing from stage 1 at the sleep onset, through stages 2 and 3 to stage 4, and back to stage 2. Almost no change in respiration is associated, though, with this wide EEG fluctuation. The same is true for succeeding cycles, although this cannot be accorded equal significance because the EEG changes are less marked.

Looking at figure 4, it would be only a very slight exaggeration to say that all EEG stages outside REM periods are associated with a uniform rate and regularity of respiration. We have additional evidence suggesting that heart rate, muscle tone, body temperature, and electrically induced reflexes, similarly do not co-vary with the EEG. This is not to say that EEG shifts in non-REM sleep are entirely without significance (for example, they *do* reflect changes in arousal threshold); merely that they are not associated with changes of a degree or kind that would warrant further *qualitative* separation.

RELATIONS TO DREAMING

The starting point for what Snyder [83] has termed "the new biology of dreaming" was Aserinsky and Kleitman's discovery of the occurrence of rapid eye movements and their recognition that this activity might be associated with dreaming. They conducted a series of awakenings and found that if subjects were aroused when REM's were present, they were able to recall dream content on most occasions. When REM's were not present, the incidence of dream recall was low [5].

Subsequent studies of this relationship have dealt, directly or indirectly, with two related problems. First, does the process of dreaming actually occur as an ongoing phenomenon during REM sleep? Second, is REM sleep the only time of dreaming, and if not, how much and what kind of dream activity occurs at other times? Although it is somewhat arbitrary, I have decided to organize my remarks in terms of these two questions, both for the sake of clarity and because the result will be essentially a comparison of REM and non-REM sleep in terms of mental activity, which is more in line with the concept of two distinct sleep states.

DREAMING DURING REM SLEEP

Dream recall.—One method of establishing a relationship between REM sleep and dreaming has been essentially a repetition of Aserinsky and Kleitman's study of awakenings during the two phases, with the addition of a variety of controls and precautions to minimize false positive dream reports and other sources of contamination. There are at least fifteen reports in the literature which contain data related to the responses elicited from REM awakenings [5, 8, 14, 20, 29, 30, 42, 45, 46, 71, 82, 85, 89, 91, 92]. A pooling of the data from these fifteen reports yields a rather impressive set of figures. The various studies utilized a total of 214 subjects and contained a large enough proportion of females so that the findings may be validly applied to both sexes. Eye movements and brain waves were recorded from these subjects throughout a total of 885 nights of sleep, or about 4 nights per subject. On 2,240 occasions distributed among the 885 nights, sleep was interrupted during the REM phase to elicit 1,864 instances of what was usually described as "vivid dream recall." This is a recall rate of 83.3 percent which, when compared to the overall non-REM results to be discussed later, unquestionably establishes REM sleep as the time at which the probability of being able to recall a dream is maximal. It does not, however, provide crucial evidence that the dream experience is actually ongoing during REM sleep. Another possibility is that there is something about the nature of this state which allows whole dream episodes to be conjured up with great ease in the moment of arousal.

At any rate, these results indicate that dream memories are not as highly evanescent as is commonly thought, particularly if recall is tested at the optimal time. On the other hand, the memories of dream experiences are clearly not as persistent as those of waking events since only a small fraction of the apparently possible recall is obtained on the morning following a night of *undisturbed* sleep [2, 49].

Dream duration and length of REM period.—A second demonstration of the correspondence between REM periods and dreaming is the finding that the subjective duration of the dream experience is proportional to the length of the REM period just prior to the awakening at which the recall is elicited [20, 22]. In one series of tests, subjects were awakened either five minutes or fifteen minutes after the onset of an REM period and were asked to choose the correct interval on the basis of the apparent duration of whatever dream events they remembered. A correct choice was made in 92 out of 111 instances. In another series, high correlation coefficients were obtained between the number of words in the dream narratives and the length in minutes of the associated REM periods. Finally, using the method of introducing an external subawakening stimulus into the ongoing dream [22], a precise amount of dream content between the appearance of the stimulus and the subsequent awakening could be delimited and later compared to the actual duration of the corresponding segment of REM sleep. When the delimited portion of the dream story was acted out, the time required was almost exactly the same as the duration of the objective record (i.e., the time between the subthreshold stimulation and the later awakening that terminated the REM period). These data, of course, strongly oppose any notion that dreams occur instantaneously as was suggested by Maury [52] to explain his famous guillotine dream.[3]

REM patterns and dream imagery.—Perhaps the most conclusive evidence that the dream experience actually takes place during the REM period, and further, that it is an ongoing psychic phenomenon, is the demonstrable correspondence between the specific directional patterns of REM's and the spatial orientation of events in the dream. In other words, the sleeping human seems to move his eyes to "watch" or "scan" the hallucinatory dream images more or less as he would if he were really seeing them in the waking state.

Before proceeding further, it will be helpful to give a little additional information about the nature of the eye movements. It must be remembered that the presence and duration of the REM period is actually defined by the occurrence of a stage 1 EEG pattern and the disappearance of tonic EMG potentials. The specific amount of oculomotor activity is immaterial, and, in the strictest sense, it is possible to have a period of REM sleep which contains no eye movement whatsoever, although in practice this occurs rarely, if ever. There is some tendency for the move-

---

[3] In this dream Maury found himself in Paris during the Reign of Terror. After witnessing a number of frightful scenes of murder, he was finally himself brought before the revolutionary tribunal. There he saw Robespierre, Marat, and other prominent figures of those terrible days. He was questioned, condemned, and led to the place of execution surrounded by an immense mob. He climbed onto the scaffold and was bound to the plank by the executioner. The blade of the guillotine fell. He felt his head being separated from his body, woke up in extreme anxiety—and found that the top of the bed had fallen down and struck his cervical vertebrae just in the way in which the blade of the guillotine would actually have struck. Since the lengthy events of the dream were so appropriate to the awakening stimulus (being struck by the bed board), Maury reasoned that the stimulus must have initiated the dream and that all the dream imagery was compressed into the brief interval between the initial perception of the stimulus and the awakening. Ellis [24] has pointed out, however, that Maury did not record this dream until ten years after it had occurred and that he may have embellished it considerably. The best explanation would seem to be that Maury was already dreaming about the French Revolution when the bed board fell, and that only the final specifically appropriate images occurred after the perception of the stimulus.

ment to appear in clusters or bursts, but it may be virtually continuous for fairly long durations or exceedingly sparse. Thus, a comparison of short epochs within the overall REM period may show extreme variability in the actual number of individual movements and in their size and direction. This is illustrated in figures 5 and 6. Antrobus, Dement, and

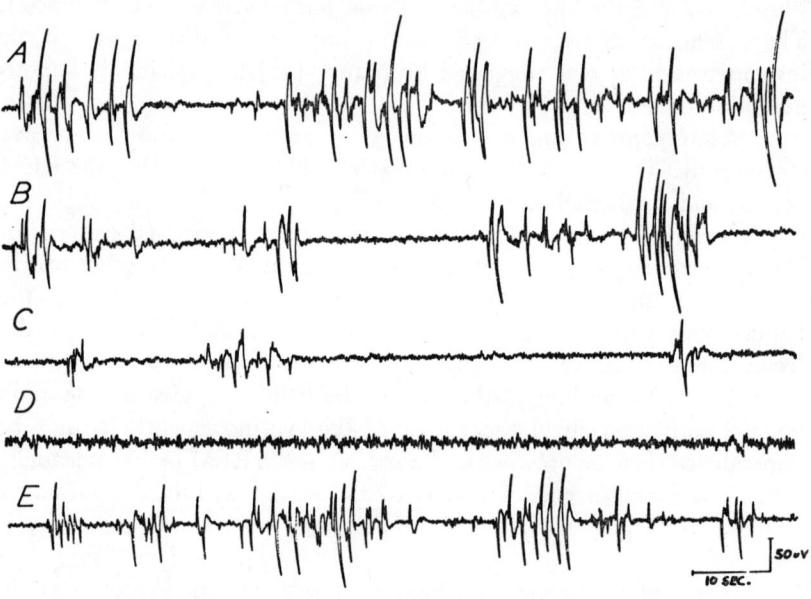

Fig. 5. Sample tracings of eye-movement potentials. *A–C* are bipolar records from the outer canthi of one subject on a single night. *D* is the monopolar occipital EEG coincident with *B* illustrating the low-voltage EEG. *E* is a sample of eye-movement potentials from the same subject after awakening in the morning (reprinted by permission from W. Dement and N. Kleitman, "Cyclic variations in EEG during sleep and their relation to eye movements, body motility, and dreaming," *Electroencephalography and Clinical Neurophysiology* [Amsterdam] 9[1957], 673–690).

Fisher [3] scored successive two-second intervals from the beginning to the end of a large number of REM periods in terms of the presence or absence of ocular motility, and they found that one or more REM's were present in around 15 to 20 percent of all such intervals and that the mean percentage tended to characterize individual subjects.

The first data supporting a correspondence between dream content and eye-movement patterns consisted of a number of anecdotal instances in which the awakenings were immediately preceded by bursts of REM's that were either exclusively vertical or exclusively horizontal. In every instance, the action in the dream was in the same plane. For example, a dream associated with several minutes of vertical movements had to do with watching a small boy repeatedly tossing a ball into the air. A statistical study by Dement and Wolpert [22] showed that REM periods containing many individual deviations were associated with active dreams (running, searching, fighting, and the like), while REM periods in which

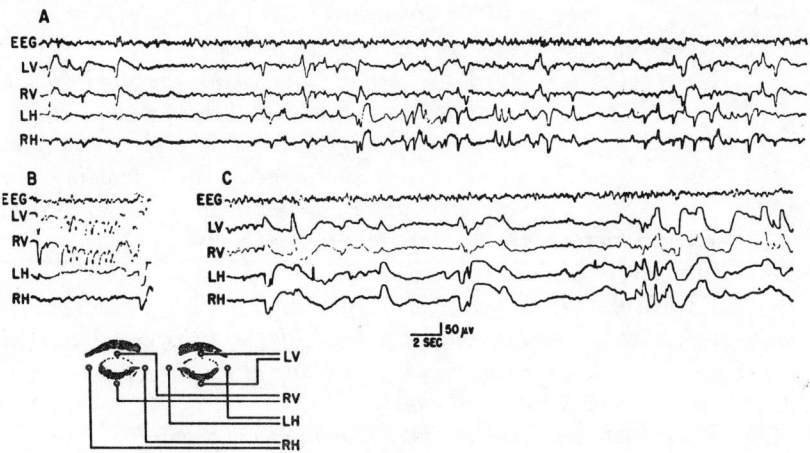

Fig. 6. Sample tracings of rapid eye movements showing that they are binocularly synchronous. The concomitant EEG is low voltage, nonspindling. The four eye-movement pens give the left and right vertical and horizontal derivations as shown in the diagram (reprinted by permission from W. Dement, "Eye movements during sleep," in M. Bender, ed., *The Oculomotor System* [New York: Paul B. Hoeber, 1964], p. 374).

individual movements were relatively sparse were associated with inactive dreams (staring at a distant object, watching television, and so on). A confirmatory study was carried out by Berger and Oswald [8] with nearly identical results.

A much more detailed analysis of the relationship has been accomplished by Roffwarg et al. [71]. In this study, subjects were awakened immediately after or during the occurrence of a wide variety of spatiotemporal REM sequences by an experimenter who continuously monitored the write-out of the electrooculogram (EOG). A second experimenter, who had no knowledge of the EOG, as he was stationed in another room, interrogated the subjects. From the details of their subjective dream experiences, the interrogator derived a verbal description of the eye-movement sequence that he felt must have occurred just prior to the awakening. An example will clarify the procedure and the nature of the results.

Dream

SUBJECT: *Right near the end of the dream, I was walking up the back stairs of an old house. I was holding a cat in my arms.*

EXPERIMENTER: *Were you looking at the cat?*

SUBJECT: *No, I was being followed up the steps by the Spanish dancer, Escudero. I was annoyed at him and refused to look back at him or talk to him. I walked up, as a dancer would, holding my head high, and I glanced up at every step I took.*

EXPERIMENTER: *How many steps were there?*

SUBJECT: *Five or six.*

EXPERIMENTER: *Then what happened?*

SUBJECT: *I reached the head of the stairs and I walked straight over to a group of people about to begin a circle dance.*

EXPERIMENTER: *Did you look around at the people?*

SUBJECT: *I don't believe so. I looked straight ahead at the person across from me. Then I woke up.*

EXPERIMENTER: *How long was it from the time you reached the top of the stairs to the end of the dream?*

SUBJECT: *Just a few seconds.*

Interrogator's prediction

There should be a series of five vertical upward movements as she holds her head high and walks up the steps. Then there should be a few seconds with only some horizontal movement just before the awakening.

The EOG associated with this dream is shown in figure 7. It can be seen that the interrogator's predictive verbal description almost exactly specifies the temporal sequence and direction of the eye movements.

In the overall results of this study, 77 of 121 dreams were recalled with 3+ clarity. In the hands of two independent judges, the correspondence between the predictions derived from the high-clarity dreams and their associated EOG's was rated as "good" (the prediction is an exact or nearly exact description of the directions, timing, and sequence of the actual movements recorded on the EOG) in 80.5 percent of cases by one judge, and in 75.3 percent of cases by the other. The percentage of "good" correspondences was somewhat lower in the remaining 44 dreams where clarity of recall was rated by the subjects as only 2+ or 1+.

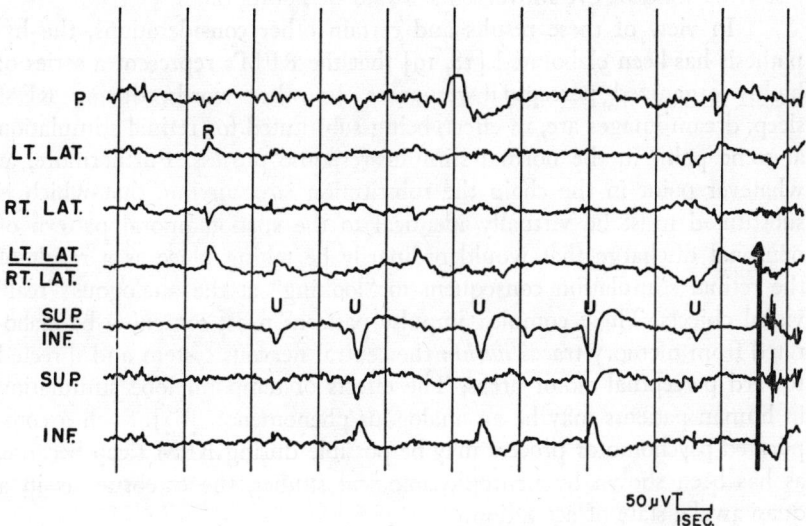

Fig. 7. An a.c. electrooculogram showing the eye movements during the last 20 seconds before the awakening (arrow). Electrode positions: *P.*, parietal (EEG); *Lt. Lat.*, left lateral canthus; *Rt. Lat.*, right lateral canthus; *Lt. Lat./Rt. Lat.*, same leads in bipolar arrangement; *Sup.*, supraorbital; *Inf.*, infraorbital; *Sup./Inf.*, same leads in bipolar arrangement. REM's: *R*, right; *U*, up. Note the five distinct upward deflections recorded in the vertical leads corresponding to the interrogator's prediction of five upward movements. The EEG pattern throughout the record was low-voltage, fast, and nonspindling (stage 1 sleep) (reprinted by permission from H. Roffwarg, W. Dement, J. Muzio, and C. Fisher, "Dream imagery: relationship to rapid eye movements of sleep," *Archives of General Psychiatry*, 7[1962], 235-258).

It was tentatively concluded from these results that there exists a one-to-one correspondence between eye movements and dream imagery, as if the dreamer were seeing and doing exactly the same thing in the waking state. The failure to obtain good correspondence in all instances was explained by assuming that the dreamer forgot a crucial dream image, or gave an inaccurate account of the spatial relationships upon which the interrogator's inference was based. This assumption was supported by the fact that the low-clarity dreams gave poorer results. In addition, judgments were difficult to make for certain dreams, particularly when bizarre events occurred, because the interrogator could not be sure just what kind of eye movements would be appropriate.

In view of these results and certain other considerations, the hypothesis has been elaborated [18, 19] that the REM's represent a series of highly organized perceptual responses. In other words, during REM sleep, dream images are, in effect, being substituted for retinal stimulation at some point in the normal stimulus-response process. Furthermore, at whatever point in the chain the substitution is occurring, that which is substituted must be virtually identical to the spatiotemporal pattern of neuronal discharge that would ordinarily be taking place as a result of the retinal stimulation consequent to "looking" at the analogous "real" visual objects. These complex impulse patterns must somehow be elaborated from memory traces *within* the central nervous system and directed toward perceptual-motor areas. The effects of temporal lobe stimulation in human patients may be an analogous phenomenon [63]. Such a complicated psychomotor process may be possible during REM sleep because, as has been shown by neurophysiological studies, the cerebrum is in a quasi-awake state of activation.

All this is tantamount to saying that the REM's are "caused" by the dream imagery. Indirect support for this notion may be seen in the fact that the REM's closely resemble fixation shifts in the waking state in terms of their binocular synchronicity (see fig. 6) and of their velocity [17, 34]. Also, their very appearance is suggestive. Using Oswald's technique of taping the eyelids [60], Rechtschaffen has been able to observe REM's with the eyes open. He states [personal communication] that although the subjects were unquestionably asleep, as determined by their EEG's, they gave the uncanny appearance of being wide awake and looking about. But the objection can be raised that binocularly synchronous REM's occur during sleep in situations where the presence of dreaming and visual imagery is extremely unlikely, for example, in newborn infants [70], decorticate humans [44], decorticate and decerebrate cats [37], and very young kittens [36]. Furthermore, at least in decorticate cats, a thorough analysis of the ocular motility by Jeannerod and Mouret [personal communication] has failed to show any departure from the norm in terms of organization, amount, pattern, velocity, and so on. While such findings are difficult to reconcile with the hypothesis, the only thing that can be said with absolute certainty is that dreaming is not the only "cause" of REM's. It may be assumed that REM's occur as a nonspecific motor discharge when the neocortex is immature or absent, but, with growth and development, there is a suppression of nonspecific activity and the oculomotor apparatus is only utilized for the quasi-voluntary deviations related to the dream imagery. In favor of this point is the finding that individuals who have been blind from birth show no REM's during sleep, although the other attributes of paradoxical sleep are present, and dream imagery in other sensory modalities occurs during this phase [7, 59]. Even so, a critical demonstration that the REM's occur specifically in response to the dream imagery does not appear to be possible. The notion that dream imagery occurs during REM sleep and is actually, to some extent, guided by the independent and fortuitous occurrence of nonspecific REM's is not completely untenable. It is quite unlikely that the REM's are a necessary condition for the occurrence of dream imagery because, in addition to the findings with blind subjects, dream recall is obtained routinely from the REM phases even during transient intervals of ocular quiescence and very early in the period after EEG activation has taken place, but *before* any REM's have appeared. As already mentioned, however, the possibility that dream content is modified in terms of "feedback" information from the eye muscles, or that eye movements and modification of dream content occur independently in response to some other neural event, cannot be rejected out of hand. Along this line, the spike discharges that occur in the visual system of the cat during paradoxical sleep are worth mentioning. First described by Mikiten, Niebyl, and Hendley in the lateral geniculate nucleus [55], it is now apparent that these spikes arise in the area of the nucleus pontis caudalis, and after a slight delay, synchronous discharges appear successively in the lateral geniculate, oculomotor nucleus, visual cortex, and finally simultaneous EMG bursts appear in the extraocular muscles apparently giving rise to the REM's [9, 31, 54].

Such activity (an example from the lateral geniculate nucleus is shown in fig. 8), which is very dramatic in the cat, has not been specifically described in studies of human patients and its presence is therefore uncertain.

Other correlations with dream imagery.—Contrary to the common notion that dreaming is accompanied by a great deal of thrashing about, there appears to be a relative diminution of body movement during REM sleep [21]. In fact, it is difficult to demonstrate that a gross body movement ever occurs during this phase because at the precise moment of the movement, EMG suppression and stage 1 EEG are no longer present. A gross body movement in the human usually signifies a transient interruption of the REM period. In the cat, although tonic EMG potentials are completely abolished, phasic activity in the form of exaggerated twitches of the limbs, tail, ears, facial muscles, and vibrissae is quite prominent. With the exception of some fine digital movements, however, there appears to be very little activity of the skeletal muscles in the human. We have recently made some preliminary observations in our laboratory with multiple simultaneous electromyographic records from arm and leg flexors and extensors both above and below the knee and elbow. EMG silence during REM sleep was so pervasive that our intent to correlate specific movements in the dream with EMG activity in the limbs could

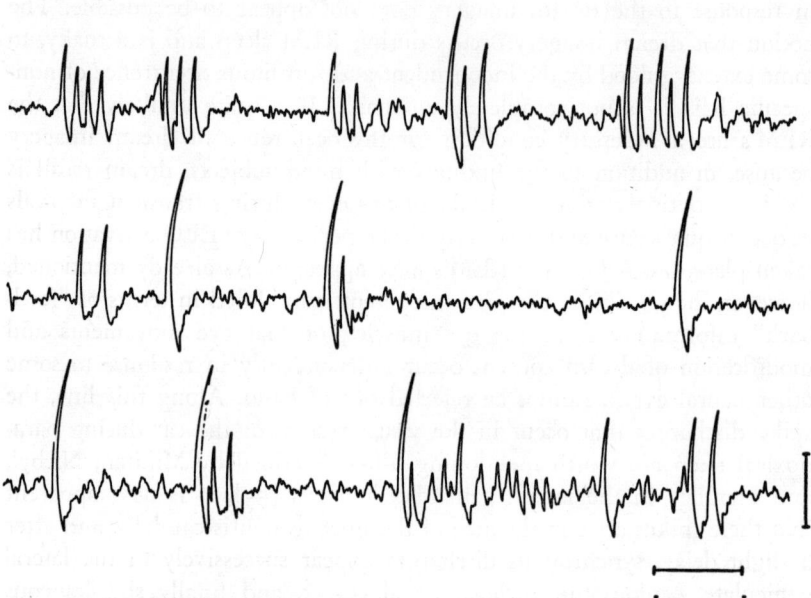

Fig. 8. Sample tracings from lateral geniculate nucleus during paradoxical sleep in the cat. The tracings are from the same period of paradoxical sleep, selected to illustrate the typical variability of the spike activity. Calibration: 50 uV and one second.

not be carried out. On the other hand, Wolpert [91] claims a significant, albeit not very close, association between the site of the small limb movement immediately preceding an REM arousal and the "action" in the dream as narrated by the subject.

Cardiorespiratory variations are a prominent feature of the REM phase, but, as yet, there has been little effort to relate these to specific dream content. We have found an association between the degree of irregularity in respiratory patterns and the amount of "activity" in the dream, but whether or not other variables may be related to dream content with the precision of REM's is a question for the future.

DREAMING DURING NON-REM SLEEP

Non-REM recall.—As has been mentioned, when subjects are awakened during REM sleep, there is an excellent probability that they will recall an experience that they are willing to call a dream. The results from individual investigations have been remarkably consistent, with recall rates closely approximating 80 percent. On the other hand, in ten studies that included awakenings during non-REM periods, the dream-recall rates varied from zero percent [14, 92] to 54 [29] and 57 percent [46] for this phase. This would suggest, depending on which reports are emphasized, that (*a*) dreaming occurs only during REM periods, or (*b*) substantial dreaming occurs in all phases of sleep. Although the marked physiological divergence in the two kinds of sleep favors an equal disparity in psychic activity, the recall studies favoring the other possibility are among the most carefully controlled and cannot be completely ignored. The reason for the wide variation in non-REM recall seems to lie in the methodology. Different investigators have used different criteria for the presence of dream recall and have posed somewhat different recall tasks upon the subjects. It should be remembered that the recall of dreams from awakenings during REM periods seems to be relatively immune to the influence of this kind of methodological variation and fails to show any practice effect [20].

In the study of Dement and Kleitman [20], the task imposed upon the subjects was to state, immediately upon being awakened, whether or not they had been dreaming, and if they answered in the affirmative, "to describe the content of the dream." In judging the responses, our published criteria were that subjects "were considered to have been dreaming only if they could relate a coherent, fairly detailed description of dream content. Assertions that they had dreamed without recall of content, or vague, fragmentary impressions of content, were considered negative." In spite of the inadequate precision and detail in these criteria, at the time they seemed very easy to apply to the responses of the subjects. In all, 191 REM awakenings elicited 152 (80 percent) affirmative replies followed by descriptions of content. The vast majority of these REM responses were long, detailed "adventures" which included a wide variety of characters, events, and emotions. Indeed, the length and detail were very impressive and greatly exceeded those of ordinary spontaneous morning recall. Only 11 of the responses from 160 non-REM awakenings (7 percent) met our criteria. In addition, five of these positive non-REM responses were elicited from the 17 awakenings that were done within eight minutes of the spontaneous termination of an REM period. The interpretation of these results was that dreaming occurred only during REM sleep, and that occasional instances of non-REM recall occurred when the memory of the dream persisted long enough into non-REM sleep to be recalled after it had actually ended. In addition, it was felt that a zero recall rate should never be obtained since the general confusion of being abruptly aroused from sleep would predispose to an occasional confabulatory report. Thus, even when a rare positive non-REM response was *not* preceded by an *uninterrupted* REM period, it would not undermine the basic hypothesis.

The other methodological extreme is well represented by the study of Foulkes [29], whose definition of a dream was "any occurrence with visual, auditory, or kinesthetic imagery" or "any phenomenon lacking such imagery but in which the subject either assumed another identity than his own or felt that he was thinking in a physical setting other than that in which he actually was." In addition, if a subject gave an initial negative response, Foulkes continued to ask if "anything was going through his mind." Not surprisingly, a 54 percent non-REM recall rate was obtained.

The critical nature of the criteria of dream recall is exemplified in the unpublished study of Orlinsky cited by Kamiya [46]. Orlinsky rated subject responses on an eight-point scale as follows: (O) Subject cannot remember dreaming; nothing is reported upon awakening. (I) Subject remembers having dreamed, or thinks he may have been dreaming, but cannot remember any specific content. (II) Subject remembers a specific topic, but in isolation: for example, a fragmentary action, scene, object, word, or idea unrelated to anything else. (III) Subject remembers several such disconnected thoughts, scenes, or actions. (IV) Subject remembers a short but coherent dream, the parts of which seem related to one another: for example, a conversation rather than a word, a problem worked through rather than an idea, a purposeful rather than a fragmentary action, and so on. (V) Subject remembers a detailed dream sequence, in which something happens, followed by some consequence, or in which one scene, mood, or main interacting character is replaced by another (different from III either in coherence of change or in the development of the several parts of the sequence). (VI) Subject remembers a long, detailed dream sequence involving three or four discernible stages of development. (VII) Subject remembers an extremely long and detailed dream sequence of five or more stages; or more than one dream (at least one of which is rated V) for a single awakening.

Of 400 non-REM responses, Orlinsky found that 57 percent fell in the categories I through VII. Combining only categories II through VII, the percent of "dream recall" was 46. The categories II through VII would more or less correspond to a definition of a dream as "any mental activity occurring during sleep, or, any report containing content regardless of how labeled." The percentages declined progressively as fewer categories were combined. For example, combining categories IV through VII gave 27 percent, and combining only categories VI and VII yielded a mere 7 percent.

"Thinking" reports.—Foulkes also obtained reports of mental activity that did not fall within his broad criteria of dreaming and were labeled as "thoughts" or "thinking" by the subjects and usually consisted of what would be called "abstract" material. This occurred in 20 percent of his non-REM awakenings so that the total incidence in which non-REM awakenings elicited reports of mental activity of some kind was 74 percent. Rechtschaffen, Verdone, and Wheaton also conducted a study [68] in which an interest in more than just mental activity labeled as dreaming was communicated to the subjects. They, too, obtained reports of "thinking" from non-REM awakenings, but at a lower rate (7 percent) than Foulkes.

Evaluation.—It is obvious that an understanding of the problem of non-REM dreaming depends almost entirely upon what one chooses to call a dream, and how much faith one has in the veridicality of the subjects' reports. One dictionary definition of a dream is a "train of thoughts or images passing through the mind in sleep." Since thoughts and images in their varying complexity include just about everything ordinarily relegated to the mental sphere, this is tantamount to saying that *any* mental activity occurring in sleep is a dream. But for most people, a dream is generally thought to be an elaborate hallucinatory episode. When one considers the various studies, one finds that the latter kind of report is most often obtained from REM sleep, while non-REM reports are usually much briefer, often involving abstract thoughts, and vague, static, or fragmentary images. Furthermore, while the mental activity occurring during REM sleep can be correlated with specific eye-movement patterns, thereby establishing it as an ongoing process during sleep, there is no such temporal landmark for non-REM mentation. Thus, there is no way of refuting the objection that non-REM reports may be arousal artifacts, compliance phenomena, or mental activity not possessing a temporal dimension. Kremen has gone into this problem at great length [50], and has concluded that dreaming may be assigned solely to REM sleep.

On the other hand, there is not the slightest bit of conclusive evidence that mental activity *cannot* occur in the presence of the neurophysiological concomitants that characterize non-REM sleep, particularly the slow-wave EEG patterns. Furthermore, the difference in amount and content of recall may be a function of memory processes. It is possible to assume that identical experiences are occurring all during sleep, but only in REM sleep are the memory processes operating at a high level. Thus, the reports that characterize non-REM responses may represent what is left after decimation by forgetting or nonrecording of the actual experience.

The current consensus of opinion is to accept the REM period as the time of dreaming with the stipulation that dreaming is defined as an experience that involves vivid and complex multimodal imagery, a progression of events, and sense of reality. Rechtschaffen, Verdone, and Wheaton [68] have likened the non-REM mentation to "background thoughts" that occur during the day; activity that is more or less continuous, usually trivial and nondescript, and often not easily recalled. Thus, while there can be no doubt that dreaming occurs during REM sleep, a similar position with regard to non-REM sleep becomes a matter of the exclusiveness of one's definition of dream recall, and whether or not one feels that the evidence is sufficient for concluding that non-REM reports represent mentation that actually occurred during sleep. Even if one adopts the position that dreaming occurs equally in both kinds of sleep, one must recognize that there are substantial differences in the nature of the experiences as reported by the subjects, and that dream reports from the two phases are easily discriminated [57].

SOME PROPERTIES OF DREAMING

If the REM definition of dreaming is accepted, several aspects of dream activity may be objectively measured, that is, length, amount, frequency, and so on. The physiological state during REM sleep seems particularly congenial to such a definition. As was previously pointed out, the level of brain activity approaches that of the alert waking state. Consequently, it is much more plausible to assume the presence of the complicated and vivid sensory imagery of dreaming. Because of the inhibitory influences that seem to operate at the spinal level, it is also possible to assume the participation of motor functions at higher levels. Thus, a person who is dreaming that he is running may be elaborating the appropriate motor impulses at the level of the cortex, but he will remain in bed asleep because the impulses are blocked at lower levels. This may account for the common experience, in certain stressful dreams, of the extreme difficulty and slowness of body movement.

Although it is very rare to elicit 100 percent dream recall in a series of REM awakenings (except in occasional highly motivated subjects), it is assumed that dreaming is always present, and that forgetting accounts for the overall 20 percent of recall failures.

Studies of undisturbed sleep have shown that REM periods always occur in a regular and predictable fashion [16, 18, 21]. Their mean length is around 20 minutes, and four to six periods usually occur in an average night of sleep. The overall amount of the REM phase tends to be relatively constant in normal sleep. Therefore, it is possible to say that most people spend about 20 to 25 percent of their total sleep time in dreaming. The amount of REM sleep seems to vary somewhat with age [70], but substantial amounts are present from birth to senescence.

There is some confusion in the literature about the number of "dreams" that take place in a single night. Often, a single REM period has been referred to as a dream, leading to the statement that four to six dreams occur in a single night. Actually, it has been shown that several distinct dream episodes usually occur successively within single REM periods [22]. Accordingly, there may be as many as 10 to 20 dream episodes in a single night. I believe that a distinct, self-contained episode is what most people would call a single dream. Thus, in the usually accepted connotation, it would be more accurate to say that we ordinarily have 10 to 20 dreams in a single night, rather than four to six.

The propensity to recall dreams spontaneously in ordinary life is a highly individual characteristic. There are even some individuals who claim that they never or almost never dream. But when such "non-recallers" are studied in the laboratory, they show the usual amounts of REM sleep [3, 30]. It is likely that these people have a more or less normal amount of dream experience, but that other factors interfere with recall. Along this line, it has been shown that people who do not remember dreams have certain characteristic psychometric response patterns [74, 75].

Dream content may be modified by the incorporation of an external stimulus *during* the REM period, but no amount of stimulation will actually initiate REM sleep [22]. Several studies have demonstrated a variety of relationships among dream episodes in a single night [23, 87]. Such things as repetitive dreams and recurrent nightmares have not been studied extensively in the laboratory. Contrary to expectations, sleep talking has not been exclusively associated with REM sleep [46, 67]. In fact, most episodes appear to occur during the partial awakenings associated with gross body movements. Finally, there are a few studies that suggest that dreaming and/or REM sleep may have some important function in maintaining the optimal well-being of humans and animals [16, 27, 37].

Of specific clinical interest are sleep studies that indicate there is a modification of epileptic discharge during REM sleep [13, 62, 78], elevation of blood pressure which may have some bearing upon the occurrence of nocturnal cardiovascular accidents [79, 84], and a certain peculiarity in the nocturnal sleep of narcoleptics which suggests that an abnormality in the REM sleep mechanism may play a role in the pathogenesis of narcolepsy [69].

SUMMARY

In human sleep, and more or less paralleled in all mammals that have been studied, there exists a rhythmic alternation of two distinct physiological states. One state, called the rapid eye movement period after its most dramatic attribute, is characterized by a high degree of central nervous system (CNS) activity, a suppression of peripheral motor activity, and a temporal association with the vivid, hallucinatory experiences we call dreams. The evidence for the latter association is a high incidence of dream recall from awakenings during REM sleep, a correlation between the subjective duration of a dream experience and the length of the associated REM period, and a close correspondence between the spatiotemporal patterns of the REM's and the specific events in the dream.

The other state has been called non-REM sleep and is the state during which the brain-wave patterns show synchronization with the presence of slow waves and/or sleep spindles. There are no REM's, the CNS seems to be relatively at rest, and there is no evidence of an active suppression of motor output. The evidence seems to suggest that a low-grade psychic activity can occur at this time, but it does not warrant the assumption that dreams are at any time associated with non-REM sleep.

References

1. Adey, W., R. Kado, and J. Rhodes. 1963. "Sleep: cortical and subcortical recordings in the chimpanzee," *Science*, 141:932–933.
2. Andress, J. 1911. "An investigation of the sleep of normal school children," *Journal of Educational Psychology*, 2:153–156.
3. Antrobus, J., W. Dement, and C. Fisher. 1964. "Patterns of dreaming and dream recall: an EEG study," *Journal of Abnormal and Social Psychology*, 69:341–344.
4. Arduini, A., G. Berlucchi, and P. Strata. 1963. "Pyramidal activity during sleep and wakefulness," *Archives italiennes de biologie*, 101:530–544.
5. Aserinsky, E., and N. Kleitman. 1953. "Regularly occurring periods of eye motility, and concomitant phenomena during sleep," *Science*, 118:273–279.
6. Berger, R. 1961. "Tonus of extrinsic laryngeal muscles during sleep and dreaming," *Science*, 134:840.
7. Berger, R., P. Olley, and I. Oswald. 1962. "The EEG, eye movements and dreams of the blind," *Quarterly Journal of Experimental Psychology* (Cambridge), 14:183–186.
8. Berger, R., and I. Oswald. 1962. "Eye movements during active and passive dreams," *Science*, 137:601.
9. Bizzi, E., and D. Brooks. 1963. "Pontine reticular formation: relation to lateral geniculate nucleus during deep sleep," *Science*, 141:270–272.
10. Blake, H., and R. Gerard. 1937. "Brain potentials during sleep," *American Journal of Physiology*, 119:692–703.
11. Bonamini, F., V. de Carolis, P. Pastorino, and G. Rossi. 1962. "Sonno superficiale e sonno profondo nel cane," *Bollettino della Società italiana di biologia sperimentale* (Naples), 38:1298–1300.
12. Coleman, P., F. Gray, and K. Watanabe. 1959. "EEG amplitude and reaction time during sleep," *Journal of Applied Physiology*, 14:397–400.

13. Delange, M., Ph. Castan, J. Cadilhac, and P. Passouant. 1962. "Étude du sommeil de nuit au cours d'epilepsies centrencéphaliques et temporales," *Revue neurologique* (Paris), 106:106–112.

14. Dement, W. 1955. "Dream recall and eye movements during sleep in schizophrenics and normals," *Journal of Nervous and Mental Disease*, 122:263–269.

15. ———. 1958. "The occurrence of low voltage, fast, electroencephalogram patterns during behavioral sleep in the cat," *Electroencephalography and Clinical Neurophysiology* (Amsterdam), 10:291–296.

16. ———. 1960. "The effect of dream deprivation," *Science*, 131:1705–1707.

17. ———. 1964. "Eye movements during sleep," in M. B. Bender, ed., *The Oculomotor System*. New York: Paul B. Hoeber.

18. ———. 1965. "An essay on dreams: the role of physiology in understanding their nature," in T. Newcomb, ed., *New Directions in Psychology*. Vol. II. New York: Holt, Rinehart, and Winston.

19. ———. 1965. "Perception during sleep," in *The Psychopathology of Perception*. American Psychopathological Association. Proceedings. New York: Grune Stratton.

20. Dement, W., and N. Kleitman. 1957. "The relation of eye movements during sleep to dream activity: an objective method for the study of dreaming," *Journal of Experimental Psychology*, 53:339–346.

21. ———. 1957. "Cyclic variations of EEG during sleep and their relation to eye movements, body motility, and dreaming," *Electroencephalography and Clinical Neurophysiology* (Amsterdam), 9:673–690.

22. Dement, W., and E. Wolpert. 1958. "The relation of eye movements, body motility, and external stimuli to dream content," *Journal of Experimental Psychology*, 55:543–553.

23. ———. 1958. "Relationships in the manifest content of dreams occurring on the same night," *Journal of Nervous and Mental Disease*, 126:568–578.

24. Ellis, H. 1922. *The World of Dreams*. New York: Houghton Mifflin.

25. Evarts, E. 1962. "Activity of neurons in visual cortex of cat during sleep with low voltage fast EEG activity," *Journal of Neurophysiology*, 25:812–816.

26. ———. 1963. "Neuronal activity in sensorimotor cortex during sleep and waking," *Federation Proceedings*, 22:637.

27. Fisher, C., and W. Dement. 1963. "Studies on the psychopathology of sleep and dreams," *American Journal of Psychiatry*, 119:1160–1168.

28. Freud, S. 1955. *The Interpretation of Dreams*. New York: Basic Books.

29. Foulkes, W. 1962. "Dream reports from different stages of sleep," *Journal of Abnormal and Social Psychology*, 65:14–25.

30. Goodenough, D., A. Shapiro, M. Holden, and L. Steinschriber. 1959. "A comparison of 'dreamers' and 'nondreamers': eye movements, electroencephalograms, and the recall of dreams," *Journal of Abnormal and Social Psychology*, 59:295–302.

31. Hendley, C. 1963. "Sharp waves in lateral geniculate of cat with eye movements during low-voltage sleep," *Federation Proceedings*, 22:637.

32. Hodes, R., and W. Dement. 1964. "Depression of electrically induced reflexes ('H-reflexes') in man during low voltage EEG 'sleep,'" *Electroencephalography and Clinical Neurophysiology* (Amsterdam), 17:617–629.

33. Huttenlocher, P. 1961. "Evoked and spontaneous activity in single units of medial brain stem during natural sleep and waking," *Journal of Neurophysiology*, 24:451–468.

34. Jeannerod, M., and J. Mouret. 1962. "Étude des mouvements oculaires observés chez l'homme au cours de la veille et du sommeil," *Compte rendu hebdomadaire des séances et mémoires de la Société de Biologie* (Paris), 156:1407–1410.

35. Jouvet, D., and J. Valatx. 1962. "Étude polygraphique du sommeil chez l'agneau," *Compte rendu hebdomadaire des séances et mémoires de la Société de Biologie* (Paris), 156:1411–1414.

36. Jouvet, D., J. Valatx, and M. Jouvet. 1961. "Étude polygraphique du sommeil du chaton," *Compte rendu hebdomadaire des séances et mémoires de la Société de Biologie* (Paris), 155:1660–1664.

37. Jouvet, M. 1962. "Recherches sur les structures nerveuses et les mécanismes responsables des différentes phases du sommeil physiologique," *Archives italiennes de biologie*, 100:125–206.

38. Jouvet, M., and F. Michel. 1959. "Correlations électromyographique du sommeil chez le chat decortiqué et mésencéphalique chronique," *Compte rendu hebdomadaire des séances et mémoires de la Société de Biologie* (Paris), 153:422–425.

39. ———. 1960. "Sur les voies nerveuses responsables de l'activité rapide corticale au cours du sommeil physiologique chez le chat (phase paradoxale)," *Compte rendu hebdomadaire des séances et mémoires de la Société de Biologie* (Paris), 154:995–998.

40. ———. 1960. "Nouvelles recherches sur les structures responsables de la 'phase paradoxale' du sommeil," *Journal de physiologie* (Paris), 52:130–131.

41. Jouvet, M., F. Michel, and J. Courjon. 1959. "Sur un stade d'activité électrique cérébrale rapide au cours du sommeil physiologique," *Compte rendu hebdomadaire des séances et mémoires de la Société de Biologie* (Paris), 153:1024–1028.

42. Jouvet, M., F. Michel, and D. Mounier. 1960. "Analyse électroencéphalo-

graphique comparée du sommeil physiologique chez le chat et chez l'homme," *Revue neurologique,* 108:189–205.

43. Jouvet, M., and D. Mounier. 1960. "Effets des lésions de la formation réticulée pontique sur le sommeil du chat," *Compte rendu hebdomadaire des séances et mémoires de la Société de Biologie* (Paris), 154:2301–2303.

44. Jouvet, M., B. Pellin, and D. Mounier. 1961. "Étude polygraphique des différentes phases du sommeil au cours des troubles de conscience chroniques (comas prolongés)," *Revue neurologique,* 105:181–186.

45. Kahn, E., W. Dement, C. Fisher, and J. Barmack. 1962. "Incidence of color in immediately recalled dreams," *Science,* 137:1054–1055.

46. Kamiya, J. 1961. "Behavioral, subjective, and physiological aspects of drowsiness and sleep," in D. W. Fiske and S. R. Maddi, eds., *Functions of Varied Experience.* Homewood, Ill.: Dorsey.

47. Kanzow, E., D. Krause, and H. Kühnel. 1962. "Die Vasomotorik der Hirnrinde in den Phasen desynchronisierter EEG-Aktivität im natürlichen Schlaf der Katze," *Pflügers Archiv für die gesamte Physiologie* (Bonn), 274:593–607.

48. Kleitman, N. 1960. "Patterns of dreaming," *Scientific American,* 203:82–88.

49. Kleitman, N., F. Mullin, N. Cooperman, and S. Titelbaum. 1937. *Sleep Characteristics.* Chicago: University of Chicago Press.

50. Kremen, I. 1961. "Dream reports and rapid eye movements: an appraisal." Unpublished Ph.D. dissertation. Harvard.

51. Loomis, A., E. Harvey, and G. Hobert. 1937. "Cerebral states during sleep as studied by human brain potentials," *Journal of Experimental Psychology,* 21:127–144.

52. Maury, A. 1861. *Le Sommeil et les rêves.* Paris: Didier.

53. Michel, F., M. Klein, D. Jouvet, and J. Valatx. 1961. "Étude polygraphique du sommeil chez le rat," *Compte rendu hebdomadaire des séances et mémoires de la Société de Biologie* (Paris), 155:2389–2392.

54. Michel, F., M. Jeannerod, J. Mouret, A. Rechtschaffen, and M. Jouvet. 1964. "Sur les mécanismes de l'activité de pointes au niveau du système visuel au cours de la phase paradoxale du sommeil," *Compte rendu hebdomadaire des séances et mémoires de la Société de Biologie* (Paris), 158:103–106.

55. Mikiten, T., P. Niebyl, and C. Hendley. 1961. "EEG desynchronization of behavioral sleep associated with spike discharges from the thalamus of the cat," *Federation Proceedings,* 20:327.

56. Miles, W. 1929. "Horizontal eye movements at the onset of sleep," *Psychological Review,* 36:122–141.

57. Monroe, L., A. Rechtschaffen, and W. Foulkes. "The discriminability of re-

ports elicited from different stages of sleep." Reported at Third Annual Meeting of Association for the Psychophysiological Study of Sleep. New York, March, 1963.
58. Offenkrantz, W., and A. Rechtschaffen. 1963. "Clinical studies of sequential dreams," *Archives of General Psychiatry,* 8:497–508.
59. Offenkrantz, W., and E. Wolpert. 1963. "The detection of dreaming in a congenitally blind subject," *Journal of Nervous and Mental Disease,* 136:88–90.
60. Oswald, I. 1960. "Falling asleep open-eyed during intense rhythmic stimulation," *British Medical Journal* (London), 1:1450–1455.
61. ———. 1962. "Sleep mechanisms: recent advances," *Proceedings of the Royal Society of Medicine* (London), 55:910–912.
62. Penfield, W., and H. Jasper. 1954. *Epilepsy and the Functional Anatomy of the Human Brain.* Boston: Little, Brown.
63. Passouant, P., J. Cadilhac, M. Delange, and Ph. Castan. 1962. "Indications apportées par l'étude des divers stades du sommeil sur la physiopathologie du petit mal," *Archives françaises de pédiatrie* (Paris), 19:1389–1397.
64. Pietrusky, F. 1922. "Das verhalten der augen im schlafe," *Klinische Monatsblätter für Augenheilkunde* (Stuttgart), 68:355–360.
65. Pompeiano, O. 1965. "Supraspinal control of reflexes during sleep and wakefulness," in M. Jouvet, ed., *Aspects anatomo-fonctionnels de la Physiologie du Sommeil, Lyon, 9–11 Septembre 1963.* Paris: Centre National de la Recherche Scientifique.
66. Raehlmann, E., and L. Witkowski. 1877. "Ueber atypische Augenbewegungen," *Archiv für Anatomie und Physiologie. Physiologische Abteilung.* Leipzig. Pp. 454–471.
67. Rechtschaffen, A., D. Goodenough, and A. Shapiro. 1962. "Patterns of sleep talking," *Archives of General Psychiatry,* 7:418–426.
68. Rechtschaffen, A., P. Verdone, and J. Wheaton. 1963. "Reports of mental activity during sleep," *Canadian Psychiatric Association Journal,* 8:409–414.
69. Rechtschaffen, A., E. Wolpert, W. Dement, S. Mitchell, and C. Fisher. 1963. "Nocturnal sleep of narcoleptics," *Electroencephalography and Clinical Neurophysiology* (Amsterdam), 15:599–609.
70. Roffwarg, H., W. Dement, and C. Fisher. 1964. "Observations on the sleep-dream pattern in neonates, infants, children and adults," in E. Harms, ed., *Problems of Sleep and Dream in Children.* New York: Macmillan. Pp. 60–72.
71. Roffwarg, H., W. Dement, J. Muzio, and C. Fisher. 1962. "Dream imagery: relationship to rapid eye movements of sleep," *Archives of General Psychiatry,* 7:235–258.

72. Roldan, E., and T. Weiss. 1962. "The cycle of sleep in the rat (preliminary report)." *Boletín del Instituto (Laboratorio) de estúdios médicos y biológicos* (Mexico City), 20:155–164.

73. Ruckebusch, Y. 1962. "Activité corticale au cours du sommeil chez la chèvre." *Compte rendu hebdomadaire des séances et mémoires de la Société de Biologie* (Paris), 156:867–870.

74. Schonbar, R. 1959. "Some manifest characteristics of recallers and non-recallers of dreams," *Journal of Consulting Psychology,* 23:414–418.

75. ———. 1961. "Temporal and emotional factors in the selective recall of dreams," *Journal of Consulting Psychology,* 25:67–73.

76. Schwartz, R. 1962. "EEG et mouvements oculaires dans le sommeil de nuit," *Electroencephalography and Clinical Neurophysiology* (Amsterdam), 14:126–128.

77. Schwartz, B., and H. Fischgold. 1960. "Introduction à l'étude polygraphique du sommeil de nuit (mouvements oculaires et cycles de sommeil)," *Vie médicale,* 41:39–46.

78. Schwartz, B., and G. Guilbaud. 1962. "Étude electroclinique de crises B.-J.: enregistrement d'une nuit de sommeil," *Revue neurologique* (Paris), 106:126–128.

79. Shapiro, A. 1962. "Observations on some periodic and non-periodic phenomena in normal human sleep," *Annals of the New York Academy of Sciences,* 98:1139–1143.

80. Shapiro, A., D. Goodenough, and R. Gryler. 1963. "Dream recall as a function of method of awakening," *Psychosomatic Medicine,* 25:174–180.

81. Shimazono, Y., T. Horie, Y. Yanagisawa, N. Hori, S. Chikazawa, and K. Shozuka. 1960. "The correlation of the rhythmic waves of the hippocampus with the behaviors of dogs," *Neurologia Medico-Chirurgica,* 2:82–88.

82. Snyder, F. "Dream recall, respiratory variability and depth of sleep," Symposium on dreams. American Psychiatric Association. Atlantic City, N. J., April, 1960.

83. ———. 1963. "The new biology of dreaming," *Archives of General Psychiatry,* 8:381–391.

84. Snyder, F., J. Hobson, and F. Goldfrank. 1963. "Blood pressure changes during human sleep," *Science,* 142:1313–1314.

85. Stoyva, J. 1961. "The effect of suggested dreams on the length of rapid eye movement periods." Unpublished Ph.D. dissertation. University of Chicago.

86. Swisher, J. 1962. "Manifestations of 'activated' sleep in the rat," *Science,* 138:1110.

87. Trosman, H., A. Rechtschaffen, W. Offenkrantz, and E. Wolpert. 1960.

"Studies in psychophysiology of dreams. IV. Relations among dreams in sequence," *Archives of General Psychiatry,* 3:602–607.

88. Weitzman, E. 1961. "A note on the EEG and eye movements during behavioral sleep in monkeys," *Electroencephalography and Clinical Neurophysiology* (Amsterdam), 13:790–794.

89. Whitman, R., C. Pierce, J. Maas, and B. Baldridge. 1962. "The dreams of the experimental subject," *Journal of Nervous and Mental Disease,* 134:431–439.

90. Williams, H., J. Hammack, R. Daly, W. Dement, and A. Lubin. 1964. "Responses to auditory stimulation, sleep loss and the EEG stages of sleep," *Electroencephalography and Clinical Neurophysiology* (Amsterdam), 16:269–279.

91. Wolpert, E. 1960. "Studies in psychophysiology of dreams. II. An electromyographic study of dreaming," *Archives of General Psychiatry,* 2:231–241.

92. Wolpert, E., and H. Trosman. 1958. "Studies in psychophysiology of dreams. I. The evocation of sequential dream episodes," *Archives of Neurology and Psychiatry* (London and Chicago), 79:603–606.

5

The Dynamics of So-Called Paranormal Dreams

EMILIO SERVADIO

Studies of the psychologically abnormal, or extranormal, or paranormal, require adequate knowledge of what we usually call "normal," just as knowledge of the normal human body is the necessary basis for our studies of pathological anatomy or of physiopathology. This does not contradict the fact that, in turn, extranormality or pathology can teach us a great deal about normality, and can make our concepts about it more precise. Unfortunately these basic scientific tenets have been, and still are, very often forgotten or neglected by those who want to explore that particular realm of psychological "exceptions," or "curiosities," that now go under the name of parapsychology. It is self-evident that the knowledge of psychological mechanisms and theories for studying an alleged parapsychological phenomenon is not exclusive of other approaches or disciplines. The term "parapsychology" should certainly not be taken in any restrictive sense. In this Colloquium, we have a fine instance of a manifold approach to a problem—the dream —which, though essentially psychological, is by no means a hunting preserve of the psychological squad.

It is traditionally known that dreams—in ancient as well as in modern times—have been supposed by many people every now and then to transcend the boundaries of what is normally knowable, and to convey to the dreamer some true information through unknown and hardly comprehensible channels. Modern studies, however, have usually neglected this purported aspect of the dream phenomenon, and have built up theories that give a more or less satisfactory account of the dream as of a natural, normal manifestation of the mind. These theories usually also discard such allegedly extranormal or paranormal dreams, stating or implying that they are nonexistent, or at any rate unproven.

Other serious students of the subject, as we know, think otherwise, and base their conclusions on a large number of well-substantiated examples of paranormal dreams which have been published and classified since the nineteenth century, and also at times on their own direct, personal experience. I have no hesitation whatsoever in stating that I am firmly persuaded of the existence of certain kinds of psychological experiences during sleep—let us call them dreams, for the present—which imply an extranormal or paranormal cognition of thoughts or events external to the subject. This assumption I take as proven, and what I am going to say starts from this as a premise, a premise it is not my present purpose or intention to demonstrate or to discuss.

What, in my opinion, should the student do when he proposes to investigate a dream that is presented to his attention as paranormal, that is, as implying an extrasensory, telepathic, or perhaps precognitive piece of information? Briefly, he must first examine the object of the investigation and decide if it is, or is not, a dream in the usual psychological sense. The event in question can actually be one of the following:

a. An invention.—It is the easiest thing in the world to invent an apparently paranormal dream from a wide variety of conscious or unconscious motives.

b. A delusion.—I think that in many cases—in the majority of cases, perhaps—the person who relates an allegedly paranormal dream is simply the victim of a delusion. The wish to be the hero of something exceptional and fascinating may easily lure anybody into distorting and embellishing a very commonplace dream experience, and the latter is finally thought to be, and described as, a "case" of telepathy or precognition in a dream. One of the first cases studied by Freud belonged precisely to this class.

c. "Psychagogic images."—Under this term I describe a particular series of images that can come to one's mind during twilight mental states, or just before actual sleep, and seem to convey some kind of mes-
or teaching, or warning. In some instances the subject of such an
ience may have the idea that a paranormal phenomenon has oc-
and may hasten to relate it, always in good faith, and with the
istortions—not realizing that the images in question are almost

always part and parcel of his own deeper mental processes, and have no paranormal value whatever.

d. A normal psychological event during sleep, different from a dream.—As we all know, not everything that happens during sleep is actually a dream. Faint perceptual impressions (auditive or tactile) may be recalled afterward in a very distorted fashion, and believed to have been paranormal dream elements. A feminine acquaintance of mine had vaguely perceived, while she was asleep, the faint noise her daughter made in the adjoining bathroom while taking a shower at a very unusual time, early in the morning. She thought that she had dreamed about the whole performance. On awakening, and on being told what had actually happened, she was convinced that she had had a paranormal dream!

e. Just a real dream.—Almost everyone knows that dreams can sometimes be very vivid, and can impress the dreamer to such an extent that only some seconds after awakening does he realize "that it was only a dream." Some people—not necessarily uncultivated or naïve—can be misled by this particular quality of some dreams, and believe that the event was no "ordinary" dream at all: nay, that it was a sort of out-of-the-body traveling, in space, or in time. I suspect that some instances of what is nowadays called "traveling clairvoyance" by some students are nothing more than particularly impressive dreams that have not been taken for what they really were. Every psychoanalyst has met many examples of these allegedly extraordinary dreams, and has been able to explore and utilize them according to the well-established, regular laws and rules of dream interpretation.

Now there is no doubt that all the examples and classes of experiences mentioned have a psychological interest. The psychologists among us have certainly had many occasions to study the inner motives that may prompt a person to make up a false dream; or the subtle interplays of perception and imagination in dreamlike states; or the process of wishful thinking which lures so many people into the fantastic mazes and snares of the pseudoparanormal. Here, however, we are committed to examine those psychological phenomena which can be of importance for the dream theory. In my opinion, these phenomena are the following:

1. *Dreams that the dreamer thinks to be paranormal, but that cannot be evidenced or accepted as such.*—As we just said, these dreams can usually be assessed and interpreted according to the customary analytical technique. In several cases, however, the subjective belief by a person undergoing analysis that he has had a paranormal dream gives the dream itself a peculiar importance, and deserves special attention. From my own observations I would be inclined to say that in these cases the supposed paranormal quality of the dream is a specific defense, whereby the dreamer tries to cope with some strongly repressed, strongly ego-alien

material—mainly of a scoptophilic (voyeuristic) kind—pretending, as it were, that the material has presented itself without any possible involvement on his part, as a bolt from the blue. A general tendency to consider one's own dreams as paranormal reveals particular personality traits, ranging from narcissistic lack of sensitivity to one's real psychological problems, up to megalomanic or paranoid substructures.

2. *Presumptive telepathic or precognitive events that may occur during sleep but are not real dreams.*—This is a distinction submitted by Freud in a paper "Traum und Telepathie" ("Dreams and Telepathy"), which appeared in 1922 [9]. In this connection, may I briefly recall that according to psychoanalytic theory, the dream is a sign, or a group of signs, containing a meaning. This meaning, however, has to be discovered, because the manifest aspect of a dream is merely the final issue of a conspicuous inner elaboration, which Freud called the *Traumarbeit,* the dreamwork. The operations of the dreamwork are instrumental in distorting the latent ideas—that is, the true significance—of the dream, and in presenting the result to the dreamer's consciousness in a form that should not cause him too much disturbance. I need not enter into a description of the various mechanisms of the dreamwork, such as condensation, displacement, inversion, symbolism, and so on, which anybody can find in the psychoanalytic literature. The point I wish to stress is the following. In his essay on "Dreams and Telepathy," as in subsequent writings on the same subject, Freud contended that the dreamwork may deal with a telepathic stimulus, or element, just as it deals with any other element of the dream material, that is to say, submitting such an element to any kind of distortion. The result, as we shall see presently, could very well be as little recognizable as are often the latent ideas of a dream when the dream is still uninterpreted. In other words, Freud's contention was that it might be possible to discover paranormal elements—if such elements do exist—not in the manifest content of a dream, but in its latent content, after straightening out the distortions of the dreamwork.

Freud, however, did not dismiss the idea that a telepathic stimulus could hit a sleeping person, and provoke a clear-cut image in his mind—that is, an image that would be as undistorted and true to life as a well-taken photograph. On awakening, the subject would certainly say that he had had a most impressive *dream:* but according to Freud he would be mistaken. His experience, Freud states, would be no dream at all: it would be a telepathic experience during sleep, just as one might have a telepathic experience during hypnosis, or in a twilight mental state, or even when fully awake. Such experiences, Freud says, have nothing to do with dream problems. If they occur, they belong to another set of natural phenomena.

As we shall see, this does not mean that such telepathic pseudo-dreams are "just so" events without any psychological background or conditioning. But we have certainly to keep in mind the difference that seems to exist between these phenomena and those real dreams that may contain some paranormal data. We now turn our attention to the latter phenomena.

3. *Actual dreams that have manifest or latent paranormal elements as structural factors.*—Of such dreams, Freud gave a classical example [9]. One of his correspondents dreamed that his second wife had had twins and a day later found out that at the time of the dream his daughter by his first wife, who lived some distance away, had given birth to twins, the confinement occurring about a month earlier than the expected date. Freud's contention was that if one made the assumption of telepathy, then an acceptable interpretation of the dream could be given. The unconscious wish that the daughter replace the wife could have combined with the telepathic communication to produce a "manifest dream content" altered by the "censorship" in the dreamwork. Psychoanalysis would thus have discovered a possible telepathic event that otherwise might have escaped attention.

In my own psychoanalytic practice, I have come across several dreams of this nature; and I was able to verify that the presence of paranormal elements in them was either in the manifest or in the latent content, or in both; moreover, that the dreams in question could be interpreted in the most minute and satisfactory fashion only if any such paranormal elements were duly accepted and taken into account. Otherwise, those dreams could have appeared somewhat unjustified, and to some extent incomprehensible.

The ways and means whereby a possible paranormal element is included in a dream, and manipulated in the dreamwork, may be very different. The element in question may be openly shown, or hinted at, or symbolized. It may be highly condensed, or appear in a misleading form. In one particular dream, in which my patient was lending a man a fountain pen and not getting it back from him, the pen—which appeared as a telepathic element—was the meeting point of a whole range of problems concerning the patient's psychosexual difficulties, and a crisis in the analyst's life having mainly to do with writing and publishing. Needless to add, the fountain pen was also a phallic symbol!

On a different occasion, another patient of mine produced a dream in which he distinctly saw my wife at the seashore, with three little girls of whom he correctly assessed the age, although, consciously, he knew that we had only one daughter, and he could not have known that my wife had gone there with our daughter and two little nieces! All these details were absolutely correct. In the same dream, the appearance of a bowl of noodles had a direct connection with an impending event in the analyst's life, the bowl itself being the symbol of a breast that had been taken away from the subject by a negligent and egoistic father figure. In two separate articles [18, 21] published in the *International Journal of Psycho-Analysis,* I give the full history of these two dreams.

Now what can be the actual dynamic reasons, if any, which may be promoting and conditioning a paranormal dream? This is probably the main point of interest in our case, and it is the point where psychoanalysis can give its best contribution to a very ancient problem. In fact the question boils down to whether we should go on considering alleged or actual paranormal dreams as occurring for no conceivable reason and without any particular motivation—that is, in a noncausal, timeless, spaceless, "synchronistic" setting (as the late Professor Jung would have put it)—or whether we can justify their occurrence to some extent from a psychological and a psychodynamic angle. In my opinion, this justification is possible, and I have tried for many years, and in several papers, to show how and why this is so [16, 18–21].

The key concepts to understanding the dynamics of paranormal dreams are frustration and transference. By frustration, I mean any kind of physical or psychological obstacle that can prevent or hinder expression or communication. By transference, I mean—following Freud's concept—the emotional, unexpressed accompaniment of practically all human attempts to communicate: an accompaniment that is part and parcel of one of the most primitive needs of the individual, that which seeks to reinstate a lost primordial unity through bridging "distances," and filling gaps between the "self" and the "whole." This is the kind of transference which Freud called "a universal phenomenon of the human mind," a phenomenon that "in fact dominates the whole of each person's relations to his human environment," and "is merely uncovered and isolated by analysis" [13].

If transference in this broader sense is a primitive emotional mechanism intended to bridge "distances" (physical as well as mental) between people (because of obstacles and frustrations that are felt to be insuperable by more advanced means), it is almost natural that it should be accompanied by attempts to express in images, signs, and symbols its particular sense or significance. It is also understandable that such images, signs, and symbols should be part and parcel of a crude, primitive, regressive language: a "forgotten language," as Erich Fromm would call it. In fact, it is not forgotten; it is obsolete. But in some particular occasions and under certain mental conditions, we are all bound to use it again. The most frequent and most widely known of these occasions and mental states occur when we sleep, and dream.

In 1933 [12], Freud contended that telepathy "may be the original archaic method by which individuals understood one another, and which has been pushed into the background in the course of phylogenetic development by the better method of communication by means of signs apprehended by the sense organs." I in turn contend that whenever "distance" between people is felt as unbearably frustrating because of the urgency of some kind of communication which "must" be carried out anyway, individuals may recur to that "original archaic method" of mutual understanding—crude and limited as it may be—and revert to a more immediate kind of communication, or, better still, to a "communion" of some sort, that is, to a telepathic, paranormal contact. The condition of sleep, and the regressive quality of dreaming, make dreams and dreamlike phenomena the most suitable vehicles for this kind of event.

In a typical telepathic dream, or in a telepathic event during sleep, we usually find an emotional (transferential) tie between two people; a singular emotional event of an objective or subjective sort; conditions adverse to better communication (distance, helplessness, inhibitions, repression); the necessity of defeating them; and finally, the condition of sleep, which is regressive and which favors the reinstatement of archaic means of thought expression, such as dreams.

These, briefly, are the general dynamics of a paranormal dream as I studied and assessed them in the psychoanalytic setting where the mainsprings of such dreams—frustration and transference—can be closely and minutely investigated. The interpersonal problems of the dreamer seem to have a direct bearing on these dynamic processes. In my opinion, based on my own analytical experience, a patient is apt to produce a "paranormal" dream (usually about an occurrence in the analyst's life) in specific transference-countertransference situations, for example, when the patient seems to feel (unconsciously) that the analyst neglects him and his problems, because he (the analyst) is emotionally preoccupied with other people's or his own problems of the same order. Dr. István Hollós [15] in Hungary and I [16] in Italy simultaneously discovered this mechanism. It is a sort of unmasking by the patient of emotional psychological material pertaining to the analyst's mind, a material thrown in the analyst's face. Considered from this angle, the occurrence challenges the analyst's attempt to conceal or repress something from the negative side of the analyst's countertransference that appeared, and perhaps was, unfriendly to the patient.

Jan Ehrenwald [2, 3], Jules Eisenbud [4, 5], and I [16–21], among others, have described the analytic subtleties of such situations *à deux*. We all agree that the "dovetailing" of the analyst's emotional patterns with the patient's in a specific phase of the analysis is a typical and unmistakable binomial configuration that seems to be a strong precondition for the occurrence of a telepathic dream or other paranormal phenomenon.

Recent studies have gone still further. Some researchers, following a working hypothesis that I first put forward in 1955, have started to ask themselves whether particular *complementary,* unconscious situations, attitudes, and configurations of two and perhaps more persons do not take part regularly in the formation of a paranormal (telepathic) dream (see, e.g., Eisenbud [5]). In other words, they have begun to wonder whether the telepathic communication discernible in a dream is not in some way conditioned by a not necessarily conscious correlation of the affective relations and needs—let us suppose—of the dreamer and of the person or persons appearing with him in the total context of the communication. At the conscious level this connection has always been more or less known: in fact, we all know that telepathic dreams are supposed to take place (truly or allegedly) between persons closely bound to each other by strong affective ties. But may there not be also some particular, mutual, unconscious problematics between the persons involved?

In more than one instance, co-workers and I have held it possible to reach the conclusion that it was so, naturally without being able thus far to generalize such conclusions, which were reached on the basis of very few investigated and analyzed cases. Research, however, is going on also in these pioneering areas, seeking in the specific binomial unconscious configurations of the protagonists of a paranormal communication an effective correlation that might, to a certain extent, condition and justify this particular kind of phenomenon, and thus definitely enlarge our theoretical comprehension of the dreamworld.

References

1. Ehrenwald, J. 1942. "Telepathy in dreams," *British Journal of Medical Psychology*, 19:313–323.
2. ———. 1948. *Telepathy and Medical Psychology*. New York: Norton.
3. ———. 1954. *New Dimensions of Deep Analysis*. London: George Allen & Unwin.
4. Eisenbud, J. 1946. "Telepathy and problems of psychoanalysis," *Psychoanalytic Quarterly*, 15:32–87.
5. ———. 1947. "The dreams of two patients in analysis interpreted as a telepathic 'rêve à deux,' " *Psychoanalytic Quarterly*, 16:39–60.
6. ———. 1948. "Analysis of a presumptively telepathic dream," *Psychiatric Quarterly*, 22:103–135.
7. Fodor, N. 1942. "Telepathic dreams," *American Imago*, 3:61–83.
8. Freud, S. 1900. *Die Traumdeutung* (*Gesammelte Werke*, II, III [London: Imago], hereafter cited as *Ges. W.*; *Standard Edition of the Complete Psychological Works of Sigmund Freud*, IV, V [London: Hogarth], hereafter cited as *Stand. Ed.*).
9. ———. 1922. *Traum und Telepathie* (*Ges. W.*, XIII; *Stand. Ed.*, XVIII).
10. ———. 1925. "Die okkulte Bedeutung des Traumes," *Einige Nachträge zum Ganzen der Traumdeutung* (*Ges. W.*, I; *Stand. Ed.*, XIX).
11. ———. 1926. *Hemmung, Symptom und Angst* (*Ges. W.*, XIV; *Stand. Ed.*, XX).
12. ———. 1933. *Neue Folge der Vorlesungen zur Einführung in die Psychoanalyse* (*Ges. W.*, XV; *Stand. Ed.*, XXII). Vorlesung XXX, "Traum und Okkultismus."
13. ———. 1934. *Selbstdarstellung*. Vienna: Internationaler Psychoanalytischer Verlag (*Ges. W.*, XIV; *Stand. Ed.*, XIX).
14. Gillespie, W. H. 1953. "Extra-sensory elements in dream interpretation," in

G. Devereux, ed., *Psychoanalysis and the Occult*. New York: International Universities Press. Pp. 373–382.

15. Hollós, I. 1933. "Psychopathologie alltäglicher telepathischer Erscheinungen," *Imago*, 19:529–546.

16. Servadio, E. 1935. "Psychoanalyse und Telepathie," *Imago*, 21:489–497.

17. ———. 1950. "La percezione extra sensoriale," *Nuovi problemi di metapsichica*. Roma: Edizioni Società Italiana di Metapsichica.

18. ———. 1955. "A presumptively telepathic-precognitive dream during analysis," *International Journal of Psycho-Analysis*, 36:27–30.

19. ———. 1956. "Transference and thought-transference," *International Journal of Psycho-Analysis*, 37:392–395.

20. ———. 1958. "Telepathy and psychoanalysis," *Journal of the American Society for Psychical Research*, 52:125–132.

21. ———. 1958. "Magic and the castration complex," *International Journal of Psycho-Analysis*, 39:147–150.

6

The Psychology of the Dream

Its Instructive and Therapeutic Uses

ROLAND CAHEN

Faced with the fascinating richness and the baffling ambiguities of oneiric phenomena, I have had to shape and trim on all sides trying to summarize my findings in fifteen points. These fifteen points summarize the leading ideas about the interpretation of dreams which are currently used in the West and which we owe to the genius of Freud and Jung.

1. THE PHENOMENOLOGY OF THE DREAM AND A PROVISIONAL DEFINITION

What is a dream? A definition is not necessary. Everyone knows about it: it belongs to the realm of fact, it is a matter of experience. The dream is part of a scheme of existence that imposes itself to a greater or lesser degree on all of us, involving us in a reality—a peculiar human and mental reality—in which we are made to participate. It may seem paradoxical to speak of the dream as involving us in reality, but this very paradox is the mainspring of our interest in dreams. The role played by the dream in our inner world is equivalent to that held by the object in the external world. We see objects in the external world just as we see dreams in the inner world. I would even go so far as to say that dreams have an even greater immediacy than perceptions because they are within us from the start and do not require the intervention of the senses. Since dreams often deal with external objects, they introduce them, make them live interiorly.

When I say "dream," everyone knows immediately what I am saying, just as when I say "day" or "night." A dream is an irrational *datum* no different from that of external or inner perception. It is a succession of images, most often without continuity, which unfolds within and imposes itself upon our mental being. I say "mental being" because a dream is a sort of inexportable commodity. Often difficult to remember, a dream is likely to be badly described. Put into words, it is no longer what it was. A dream is a mountain of irrational and incoherent images, which, more or less every night, mocks our rationality and sweeps aside the most deeply rooted structures, each time plunging even the most balanced, the most solid, and the most reasonable of us into a world of unreason. The phenomenon is so unsettling that the first reaction upon awakening is to call it absurd, or delirious, and to reject it.

Such are, at first sight, the uncomprehending and defensive attitudes that a rationally brought up individual will oppose to protect himself from this multiform world of images out of which he has had to emerge as a rational being and from which he must again, day after day, tear himself away.

For the analyst, a dream wells up within a twofold silence: the silence of night, and the silence of that very special human situation, unique in the history of man and human relations, known as the analytic confrontation. This confrontation has great and creative originality thanks to the analytic silence, a silence emphasized by the analyst's presence, detached yet watchful. In this silent, protective, and catalytic presence, we allow, and cause to emerge, the imagination of those who have endowed us with the formidable honor of their trust; a little like the magician pulling the rabbit from the hat. But just as the rabbit was already in the hat, hidden by a double bottom unknown to the onlookers, so these tons of psychic matter, which will need three years to be poured out and formulated, were already in the unfathomable double bottom unknown to the conscious personality, called, for the want of a better term, the unconscious. It is from this double bottom, unfathomable and unknown to the conscious personality of the dreamer, that little by little, his oneiric material emerges.

Although reason and consciousness, to gain authority in an age of rationalism, have tried to minimize the importance of the dream, innumerable authors have stressed its importance. For Aristotle the dream was the mental activity of the sleeping man's soul. For Jacques-Joseph Moreau de Tours the mental activity of the dream when exaggerated is responsible for madness. For Freud the dream is a confidential statement, but a veiled statement made in improper terms. For Jung the dream is a specific exteriorization of the unconscious rising into the conscious.

Today it is well established, and it is my personal position, that a dream is the expression of a living, thinking, feeling, speculating activity within us, coexisting with our diurnal activity and on all levels—from the purely biological to the most spiritual—without our knowing it. The dream, which reveals an underlying psychic current and the imperatives of a vital pattern engraved in the deepest layers of our being, is the expression of the individual's most profound aspirations and, as such, provides us with infinitely precious information.

Such appears to me the basic phenomenology of the dream.[1]

2. THE POSITIONS OF FREUD AND JUNG

Let us pause a moment at the very outset. What does it mean: to interpret dreams? It is an attempt at understanding them. Should we not therefore ask ourselves what it is to "understand"? Kant defined understanding as a knowledge adequate to our intentions. "Our intentions" introduces into the *processus* of understanding the subjectivity as well as the idiosyncrasies of mental functions peculiar to the one seeking to understand.

Understanding, then, cannot but be subjective and interrelational, as between two individuals such as doctor and patient, or between the intellect of a scientist and the phenomenon to be understood.

---

[1] Let me show by as brief and concise an example as possible the practical utilization of the fifteen sections, each of which serves as a point of reflection. The example I have chosen and propose is this: one of my patients reported the following dream to me: "I am standing in a room, and I have to swallow a raw fish."

Let us apply successively the fifteen methodological points of view I set forth. As far as section 1 is concerned, it is certain that the dream rising out of the silence of night defies reason, understanding, and all the theories—sexual desire, will to power, repression. It is not apparent at first sight how any theory at all could adequately label and explain this example, an example I nevertheless chose because it was particularly brief and simple.

Freud said that the dream was a *via regia* to the unconscious. At first glance this royal road seems to be a rather tortuous labyrinth of small promise and little interest. We shall see, in fact, that we need all this demonstration to provide a satisfactory explanation of this dream.

If "our intentions" vary, that is, if the suppositions, the references, and the goals of those who seek differ, what they understand will be different.

Hence also, in part, the quarrels between the schools of thought which have occurred in our field of study, quarrels that we shall try to set aside here.

Jung observes:

> Nothing would be more fallacious than to pretend to explain dreams with the help of categories and a psychology derived from consciousness. The dream reflects a certain functioning which is independent of the conscious aims of the ego, of its will, of its desires, and of its intentions. On occasion the dream even opposes them. This functioning presents itself—and thereby establishes its title to fame—as a "development" devoid of any appearance of intentionality, similar, in this, to all natural phenomenon. Consequently it is in the psychology of the dream that theoretical prejudices undergo their most violent denials and where they are the least appropriate.[2]

Freud (with regard to whom I shall be very brief, and for this I apologize to my Freudian fellow practitioners) looked upon the dream as an already somewhat disturbed form of mental activity, or as a form of psychic activity that, if it worsens, would tend to become pathological —symptoms of hysteria, obsessive or delirious ideas—an activity that is not significant in itself and at the very most manifests a more or less infantile desire. Jung completely abandoned such residual prejudices against the dream. He sees the dream as a spontaneous, normal, creative expression of the unconscious in the form of images and symbols.

Freud, therefore, was particularly concerned with finding within dreams—but *outside* them, in a sense, because he regarded them only as means—whatever complexes or pathological disturbances they were concealing. Jung, on the contrary, concerned himself with their meaning.

In the matter of the psychology of dreams, as in so many other fields, Jung criticized and continued the work of his great predecessor. In order to make my position clear, I should state as my opinion that the work of Jung is a successful attempt not to bypass or oppose the work of Freud, but to go beyond it.

Although Jung considered as basically valid certain principles of Freud's oneiric psychology (I am supposing that the phenomena of condensation, agglutination, and so on, are well known), he rejected its nar-

---

[2] C. G. Jung, *L'homme à la découverte de son âme* (6th ed.; Geneva: Mont-Blanc, 1962; Paris: Société des Livres Français), p. 201.

rowness and one-sidedness, especially the intention of attaching all dreams to a vague kind of monism, be it sexual like Freud's, or voluntaristic like Alfred Adler's. A monistic explanation by desire, for example, is absolutely unacceptable to him, however important sex or volition may be to existence.

For Jung the dreamworld was just as rich, as diversified, and as polymorphic as the conscious world. Since it can touch upon all the structures of the self and the conscious, not only the affective (pleasure and displeasure) but also the ideational, perceptive, and sensorial, the dream presents a diversity and a richness potentially even greater than those of consciousness. For the dream can draw on all the subliminal psychic materials: memories, perceptions, and apperceptions, cryptomnesia, suppression, and all endogenous elaborations, all psychic contents in process of becoming, none of which ever finds its way into the conscious. For Jung the dream possesses, in this dreamworld of limitless possibilities, a value impossible to overestimate. The dream for him—and for those of us following him—is the spontaneous autorepresentation and autodescription of the situation as it is in fact crystallized and as it exists within the unconscious. The dream draws up a sort of interior balance, that of the actual intrapsychic situation.

We ask our patients to record their dreams because the dreams of the patient, whom so far we know only superficially, lead us at once into that dark garden, that secret garden whence spring all the drives that are meaningful, especially from the therapeutic point of view. Experience shows that dreams can be either a simple reaction to a situation where conscious behavior is the governing element, or the product of spontaneous, endogenous activities of the unconscious, almost without conscious stimulation. Between these two poles range every possible variation and combination.

A dream seems to me a geometric point, a place where experiences intersect and are stored, as in a property room—the living memories, from which the dreamer can choose, subject to a double law of (1) what is found there and (2) selection.

When the unconscious has something to say it goes to find, with a sleepwalker's self-assurance, the most exact and expressive image. This image is often striking, pertinent, and impertinent; it says in a condensed form, which is often extraordinary and arresting, what otherwise requires many phrases, and even many paraphrases.

Therefore Jung could not accept the generalized notion of the dream as a façade. Far from being "nothing but" . . . the dream is often precisely what it is—that is to say, a genuine expression of the inner life, as it is momentarily crystallized, which is to be taken quasi-literally and not fitted into any theory whatever. A dream's façade is its unintelligibility, that is, the projection of our uncomprehension.[3]

3. THE ANALYST'S BASIC ATTITUDE

In his practice, what ought to be the analyst's attitude? Faced with such a complex phenomenon, the analyst should know how to forget all his knowledge except to keep in mind certain working theories, like the notion of the existence of the unconscious, and that there are several things important to the dreamer's life, his equilibrium and health, stirring and working in his unconscious. These working theories ought to be managed in each particular case with tact, a sense for the nuance, and discretion.[4]

4. THE NECESSITY TO KNOW THE BIOGRAPHY OF THE DREAMER

An indispensable first condition to any oneiric interpretation is as thorough, detailed, and meticulous a biographical knowledge of the dreamer as possible: family history, medical profile, kind of education, intellectual background, scientific and religious formation, profession, loves, marriage, past and present environments and involvements, all the external, group, intimate, and general dramas that can be brought to light; to have been deported, for example, is not the same as not to have been deported.

Before undertaking any oneiric interpretation it is necessary to learn from the dreamer's medical condition something about the subject's relations with his body, his body profile, static and dynamic. We must learn from his social condition about his social relations; it is not the same to be poor as to be rich. From his sexual condition we will learn about his relation to the world of temptations and the world of desires and obsessions; his emotional condition will tell of his relations to the "other"; his spiritual condition will tell of his relationship with the sacred

---

[3] With reference to my example, let us beware of hasty conclusions but continue to be motivated by the working hypothesis that my patient's unconscious wants to tell us something by this message.

[4] Do you not have the impression that my example represents an unintelligible and undecipherable text? Façade or not, the problem of this dream has to be seen in its fullness. If we do this from the outset we will see that the explanations in the following sections will permit a step-by-step elucidation of the riddle.

and divine; his "educational" condition will tell of his relationship with the concrete; his professional condition will reveal something of his activities.⁵

5. ASSOCIATIONS AND INDIVIDUAL UNCONSCIOUS

Things are much easier for the analyst once these biographical facts have been acquired. But the question is how to proceed, since the practitioner has had to set aside all procedural assumptions and theoretical baggage.

As the exteriorization of a hidden psyche that expresses itself in the only vocabulary available to it—images that are more or less archaic and crude, personal or collective—the dream generally constitutes at first sight a message just as hermetically closed and incomprehensible to the dreamer as to the analyst. The analyst is on each occasion like Champollion faced with the first hieroglyphs.

Both with Jung and with Freud, associations must be brought to the rescue. They can provide the key to decoding these perfectly incomprehensible messages. In each instance they are the means for decoding a language unknown to all, including the dreamer. Associations provide the vocabulary, the personal and topical lexicon of the oneiric language. For instance, we may have dreamed of Royaumont (the place of our present conference) eight days ago. If we dream of it again in two weeks, Royaumont will not have the same associative and emotional value. Thus associations permit us to "decode" a message formulated in a very personal and also variable language. You can see that these modern conclusions signal the end of those inflexible and banal "keys to dreams."

But, here again, while accepting associations and attributing to them all the importance they deserve, Jung has taught us to handle the

---

⁵ In my example these are the elements we have: the man is thirty years old, married, father of a family. He came for consultations because of timidity, stifled mannerisms, rigidity, apraxia, and a totally inadequate rate of efficiency. Altogether, it seemed a diffuse and slight neurosis at first, but it revealed itself to be much deeper and more serious.

He was in good health generally, had considerable social standing for his age, and a great deal of ambition. His sexual life with his wife was normal. He had married for love. He had completed higher education at the cost of great effort because he came from modest circumstances, and, moderately endowed, he had had to apply himself seriously to his studies in order to realize his ambitions.

associative process with certain essential refinements. From him we have learned not to lose ourselves in certain rigid lines of associative thought which end, whatever the point of their departure, in complexes only momentarily crystallized and active in the dreamer, complexes whose presence no longer needs to be demonstrated or proven: the existence of complexes has long been established scientifically and empirically.

Whoever does get lost in these rigid associative lines necessarily hits upon complexes that are shared by everyone. It must ever again be repeated that complexes are a necessary normal element in the normal psyche. The "psyche" deep within us is made up of personal or inherited complexes fundamentally present in each human being. These complexes are just as indispensable to a human being with a mind as a normal anatomy and physiology. The bad reputation complexes have with the public is highly unjust.

From the point of view of mental hygiene the very term "complex," as denoting an indispensable constituent of psychic life, must be rehabilitated; an individual deprived of complexes would be intellectually and affectively debilitated. But, by losing ourselves in these complexes, the meaning of a dream could be completely lost. So, if one of us should dream tonight about this conference table he would have to be asked about his associations with the word "table" and those with the word "conference" because this table is not just any table. It is a very particular table and if the dream is so precise this fact must be taken into consideration.

Attention must be paid in a sort of concentric manner to the specific details of the dream if one is to discover its meaning and not lose oneself in an endless flight of ideas.

This method of association is of capital importance for everything that is "personally thematic" for the dreamer, but it does sometimes happen that the dreamer finds himself absolutely incapable of making associations. We have here one of the points of departure in the diverging ideas of Jung and Freud. Rather than dogmatically insisting, like the latter, on the idea of resistance or protest (notions that of course are fundamentally valid in a great many cases), Jung believed this "drought of ideas and associations" in the person under analysis was a sign that the element involved had perhaps never been related to the ego and its consciousness.

It could be an endogenous factor emanating from basic psychic levels, be it as an element of personal synthesis, or, on the contrary, as an element that even though lying within the subject, is in no way an acquisition of his individual life, but an element of the unconscious predating the levels of personality—an element therefore of the collective unconsciousness.

This "associative drought" in the patient has been a stumbling block between Freud and Jung and one of the points of departure for Jung in developing the famous idea of the collective unconscious.[6]

6. THE METHOD OF AMPLIFICATION AND THE COLLECTIVE UNCONSCIOUS

What is to be done when there are no associations? We come to the celebrated method of amplification. When associations have been solicited and every associative resource stubbornly looked into and exhausted without success, Jung thinks that the practitioner can rightfully make a personal associative effort in order to provide the patient with elements for a new start, taken from an historic, an ethnographic, or some other parallelism; it is here that the sciences and the findings of neighboring disciplines are so useful to us, and it is here that we are so grateful to our colleagues in these neighboring disciplines for bringing us their knowledge and contributions.

These ethnographic, sociological, and other such parallelisms, stemming from the history of religions, enable us to place the contents of a dream that lacks associations of its own into a relationship with the general psychic and human patrimony.

The school of Jung is perfectly aware that this intervention by the analyst is to be classed in the general category of countertransference. This notion is well known and I shall not insist upon it. When I am present in the patient's "vital field" there is already transference and countertransference. Beyond the spontaneous countertransference assured by my presence, and beyond the elements of emotional countertransference of sympathy and of devotion, Jung thinks I have the right to contribute an intellectual countertransference by putting what I know at the patient's disposal.

In this way the idea of amplification enters into the most general category of human relationships which is, as you know, inseparable from the ideas of transference and countertransference.

This method of amplification must be handled with the utmost reserve and prudence. Otherwise it opens the door to all types of abuse and to the worst, most unspeakable kinds of proselytism. Handled

---

[6] In my example, these are the associations the dreamer had with regard to his dream: "I am standing" evokes "not sitting." "In the middle of a room" evokes "the room reminded me of the analyst's office where I receive treatment." "I had to swallow a raw fish" evokes "fish live in the depth of the sea. Their rawness disgusts me." Associations were limited to these and all my solicitations produced no echo.

competently, this method allows us a practical way out of many an impasse. It allows the subject to confront problems common to humanity which greatly surpass the range of his conscious ego and individual personality. These are problems that he often carries unawares within himself, whereas they have been ripening there for years if not for decades.

When we have come this far we are much better equipped to attempt the interpretation of a dream. We have set aside our theories; we have a thorough biographical history of the dreamer; his associations have given us the associative context; the method of amplification attempts to give us whatever data may exist on the level of the collective unconscious.

This method of amplification, which is one of the basic original contributions of Jung and his school, appears to be a procedure permitting a new start that is both fortuitous and geared to the occasion. It is, moreover, a method *sui generis* made necessary by the existence of problems tied to the collective unconscious. It is a method that brings us back to certain theoretical data and to a theory of knowledge, but it has to be practiced with the utmost prudence. If an analyst lightly embarks thereon, without exhausting the associative material, without delivering the patient from his unsuspected taboos, the unknown searing matter that he cannot formulate, if the analyst suggests just any historical parallel, he creates, or risks creating, some form of mental sequestration in his patient. Despite and even because of all the analyst's beautiful oratory, the patient would find himself less able to bring out or disentangle all the personal mental material he cannot formulate. If the analyst lightly brings forth ethnographic, religious, and general philosophical considerations and suggests symbols, he is in danger of bypassing the real experience. Certainly one point most apt to bring discredit to the school of Jung is too ready a recourse to this method of amplification.[7]

---

[7] In my example, the elements we had at our disposal thus far allowed us to look at the dream in the following way. The dream has some obvious relationship to the subject's psychoanalytic treatment, because the dreamer was standing in a room reminding him of the analyst's office. The dream then was part of the regular course of the treatment. Nevertheless—and note at this point the extraordinary finesse of the unconscious—the dreamer is standing. He associates this with "not sitting." Since analytic treatment occurs seated (Jung) or lying down (Freud), but certainly never standing, this seems to mean that the subject had not yet truly entered into treatment. Everything occurs as though he were still on the outside, as though he were not taking part in the analytic dialogue (we were at about the tenth session).

Now, in this situation, he has to swallow a raw fish. One might say that because he has not yet swallowed this raw fish, the analysis has not yet really begun.

It is necessary to discover what this fish means. Here the dreamer's associations leave the dreamer and the analyst totally up in the air. The dreamer's sole association for the fish is that it is an inhabitant of the deep sea. We brought the dreamer

7. THE GATHERING OF ASSOCIATIONS

All dream interpretation has three phases: in phase (1) the dream is dreamed, and in phase (3) the analyst and the dreamer attempt an interpretation. But to go from (1) to (3) it is necessary to undertake phase (2), the indispensable link that is the gathering of associations. The most delicate of the three is obviously the second.

---

back to this fish again and again, but no associations were obtained. At this point we were tempted to have recourse to the method of amplification and to look for light in the general symbolism of fish. But which way to take? (*a*) Should the fish be regarded as a phallic symbol? Fish would then connote sexuality, and this dream would somehow compel the dreamer to swallow, that is, accept or integrate, his sexuality. Or (*b*) perhaps, recalling the expression "to be like a fish in water," it ought rather to bespeak the ideas of adaptation and ambition dear to Adler. (*c*) But he had indeed said that this fish was raw. Perhaps, then, this sensation of disgust indicates a pleasure-displeasure point of view. Or (*d*) finally, should it perhaps represent the general symbol of Christ who was designated in primitive Christianity by the term *ikhthys,* the fish?

You know that for Jung, Christ symbolizes self, totality, the complete perfection of being. My patient ought certainly to realize this wholeness, but every analyst knows that it is a long way from cup to lip and that long work with oneself is necessary to get there.

You see the danger of inculcating in the subject a psychology that cannot be his own, a danger so much the greater since in psychotherapy, as in dentistry, what counts above all is what one takes out, before even dreaming of putting anything whatever in.

I was greatly puzzled, and, seeing that my patient was also slightly embarrassed, I insisted once more. The dreamer ended by telling me: "Listen, Doctor, there is something here which hurts me very much to tell you because it embarrasses me, and I am ashamed of myself. Moreover, I hide it from everyone, you are the first person I have told. My parents-in-law are fishmongers."

In other words, his parents-in-law were fish peddlers. His wife was the daughter of a fish peddler and he had married her because there was a baby coming.

Now, while honorable, this is a much demeaned profession, socially speaking, and it was evidently a fact that embarrassed our dreamer a great deal so that he carefully hid it, and personally avoided thinking of it himself. He hid it from others and repressed it for himself.

Needless to say, if the analyst had set out lightly upon sexual or voluntaristic considerations—Freudian, Adlerian, or Jungian—or into ethnographic, philosophical, general, or religious considerations on the overall symbolism of the fish, but bypassing the major fact that was very important for the internal economy of the dreamer, namely, that his wife was a fish peddler's daughter, the door to misunderstanding would naturally have been opened. My patient would never have been able to admit this fact after such high-flown speeches by me. I would then have helped involuntarily to create a mental sequester in the patient's interior world, which would have had, structurally and dynamically, the role and importance we might compare to a foreign body in a joint.

The ease with which appeal is made to this method of amplification, with

The first step is quite simple; the dream is a mental automatism; a dream is dreamed or is not, it is more or less clear, more or less well defined, more or less blurred. It is remembered more or less clearly, more or less hazily, but it either is or is not. The change a dream undergoes during the transition between sleep and consciousness ought to be included in the dream's working imagery.

During the third phase, the patient can be helped, to a certain extent, by the analyst, and the two together work toward an interpretation on which they can agree if all goes well.

Practically speaking, however, the reverse is true with regard to gathering associations. Here the analyst cannot help the patient, as both analyst and patient depend on the good graces of the subject's associative and underlying psychism to produce the associations, and both also depend on the receptive ability of the patient's consciousness, which must know or learn to know during the course of the analysis how to embrace and assimilate these associations with a kind of maternal instinct since they are often very fragile and tenuous as they emerge. Associations are of primary importance because without them in the majority of cases the

---

insufficient recourse to the person's associative alphabet and its verbalization, is, to repeat, one of the things most likely to bring criticism on the school of Jung. But note well what follows: enlightened by the biographical revelation and the great resistance the dreamer had to making it—a circumstance that had frustrated the whole analysis and after which the patient had had finally to sit down in his chair—we know now that to swallow the fish was (*a*) to swallow, to accept his sexuality and the painful situation into which it had placed him (Freudian point of view), (*b*) to dominate the same painful social situation (Adlerian point of view). In both perspectives, it was a matter of accepting the mother-in-law and accepting himself, this self that had chosen a "bad" mother-in-law. It was to show Christian charity as far as he and others were concerned. (*c*) Now, on the other hand, if the patient had not given us his associations, and if I had held onto the amplifying perspective of the fish, symbol of Christ, to swallow the fish would have meant to accept his Christianity, and in this way the subject would have been led to ask himself what he had not yet accepted in himself and in the world. This means that very quickly we would have discovered the mother-in-law problem at the bottom of the woodpile. What seems fundamental to me, considering the means we actually have at our disposal for the interpretation of dreams, is this convergence of interpretative efforts.

If an amplification is successful it ought to merge with the results obtained from associations, if there were associations to be had, and the lack of which it compensates.

As popular wisdom has it, "All roads lead to Rome."

Whatever road thinking takes, it ought to arrive at Rome, at the dreamer's truth that is expressed—with extraordinary pertinency, not to say impertinency—in the image of the dream.

meaning of a dream is and will remain forever in the dark, at least as far at it bears on the sphere of his personal unconscious.[8]

8. A DREAM IS LIKE A PLAY IN FOUR ACTS

Jung counsels as a help in clarification and analysis to consider the dream as an abridged play in four acts in which Act I contains exposition, characters, place, time, and decor; Act II announces and ties the plot; Act III is the drama's peripety; and Act IV finds the drama working toward its termination, its solution, its "lysis," suggestion, or conclusion. This four-part outline is generally very enlightening and valid. Jung thinks that some dreams—in particular those ending with the dreamer's sudden awakening—because they have succeeded in breaking through all the psychological and psychophysiological mechanisms that protect sleep, have a psychological content of such magnitude and such urgency that the unconscious allows them to pass directly into consciousness in order to make sure that the matter is not lost to the dreamer's consciousness and ego.[9]

---

[8] We have just seen in my example the difficulties of gathering associations. A great deal depends on a biographical detail, or on an association uncovered or held on to! The difficulty comes precisely from the dialectic of resistances.

I do not like the word "resistance" which always implies the idea of resisting "against," against the hold of consciousness or against the analyst who is its catalyst and promoter. What I mean is that to my mind the word "resistance" places the analyst and his narcissism too much in the foreground. More often, it is less resistance to the analyst than a kind of inertia or of conservatism that marks all mental structures. A consciously existing, acting, living, mental structure offers as much resistance to being replaced by another, as any government does. If bodies have a quality of inertia, so, equally, do mental structures, an inertia strengthened by laziness, stubbornness, and conventions. In my own experience, mental inertia is just as often involved as unconscious resistance and just as active. The term "inertia" ought, it seems to me, to be introduced into analytic terminology because it has the immense advantage of de-intoxicating, in part at least, the confrontation of analyst and analyzed in the mind of the patient and the uninitiated.

However that may be, and as we might have seen in my example, the gathering of associations proceeds from beginning to end in the analysis via the dialogue between the progressive conquest of consciousness and the difficulties (resistances, inertia, and the like), which make it so hard.

[9] In my example: Act I. The character—all alone—is the dreamer, who is in a very particular place of his interior geography, his analyst's office. Act II. The dreamer is standing. We saw what this revealed about the temporary paralysis in the progress of his analysis. Act III. The climax is contained in the fact that he has to swallow the raw fish. Act IV. Our dream is so very short that there is

9. THE CONCEPT OF COMPENSATION

One of the approaches most useful for the practitioner involves the concept of compensation. I have no desire to get lost in the byways of biology but, as you know, the sphere of the biological is composed of self-regulated systems, and the psychological sphere, which depends on it to a degree I do not propose to discuss here, is subject to the same rule. According to Jung, in man psychological balance is achieved between the levels of his conscious and unconscious.

If the minute biographical knowledge of which I spoke earlier is necessary, it is because, thanks to it, we can search out the complementary relationship between the dreamer's consciously experienced, objective state and the images of the dream. There exists a complementary relationship, a dynamic equilibrium between the conscious and the unconscious, concretized in the dream.

And, thanks to the contribution of the subconscious material brought out by dreams, compensations occur, which widen the conscious subjectivity. The one-sided orientations, the desires, the anguishes, the defenses, and the aspirations of the conscious find salutary compensation in correctly understood oneiric images.

The concept of compensation has thus a very great practical use: it is truly one criterion that, with the hypothesis of the unconscious, has to be kept in mind in practical work.

One of several hypotheses to remember is to ask oneself, whenever confronted with a somewhat obscure dream: what conscious attitude does this dream compensate? This concept of compensation is easily managed as long as it has a connection with the subject's personal problems. In a case of conflict or in a case of aroused emotion—and it is in cases of aroused emotion that we are consulted—one can often see with great accuracy for what element of the conscious a particular dream is compensating. This concept of compensation is like the beam in a balance joining the conscious and the unconscious. Faced with an aroused emotion, this concept of liaison by compensation is very easy to use in principle, but actually the compensations that originate in a brain of ten billion cells, a symphony of innumerable voices connecting conscious and unconscious, are practically infinite in number.

The limitless complexity of possible human compensations, beyond interpretative paradigms, beyond monisms, is such that the idea of com-

---

nothing to add here, but the very absence of this act opens the door to interpretative solutions with which we can experiment.

This point of view is not essential in so short a dream, but it is very useful in longer dreams and especially in those that are similar to long, drawn-out sagas.

pensation becomes a matter for very delicate handling when it does not occur in response to an immediately practical or personal problem, but, for example, to a social or cultural situation or to a spiritual problem.

Spontaneous compensations that occur are very useful. But unfortunately the corrective faculties of compensations are not unlimited. When things have gone awry seriously enough, it can be that an attempt at compensation may be just as off-balance and off-balancing as the initial factor for which balance is being sought.

In addition to the limitations imposed by the infinity of possible compensations, the concept of compensations also finds itself limited by the autonomy of the unconscious. The autonomous activity of the unconscious gives rise to data with signification derived from another level, another dimension of thought.[10]

10. PERSPECTIVES OF INTERPRETATION

Another working hypothesis that must be kept in mind is the notion of the perspective of interpretation.

Freud, guided by his basic principles of reference, places dreams at the service of the study of those grand determinants of human comportment—instincts and impulses. His interpretative method is essentially reductive and causal. Jung, recognizing fully that this way of looking at things is fundamentally and essentially valid, has demonstrated its limitations and deficiencies—and the dangers—if handled dogmatically and onesidedly. He has shown the necessity of adding (it is not a question of excluding but adding) a prospective, synthetic and final point of view—prospective and anticipatory, not in a prophetic sense but in the sense of a search for the "energetic gradient" affective and libidinal, which may show in the dream by way of a preliminary sketch.

There is need for a synthetic interpretation side by side with the need for analysis because the mind proceeds by a series of necessary and unavoidable syntheses more or less fragmentary, more or less successive, more or less general. From this point of view it must be said that the very word psychoanalysis is unfortunate; if psychoanalysis were only to analyze and not to synthesize it would become an enterprise doomed to failure. Whether wished for or not, resynthesis follows implicitly and automatically every analysis and every analytic effort. (Often an analyst has very little desire for this process; any temporary synthesis, hastily and prematurely formed, must in turn be dissolved and so will originate by

---

[10] It seems clear enough that in my example the dream was to compensate for the refusal within which the dreamer had thus far locked himself.

its own inertia new obstacles and new resistance.) If dreams, in their associative context, make major contributions to the reductive and causal analysis of a past situation or a past life, they bring at the same time, and whenever necessary, with an unparalleled pertinence and finesse, in an almost organic manner, and with incorruptible consistency, the elements necessary for the process of synthesizing analytical and mental efforts.

And, at last, the final interpretation: no interpretation can do without the dimension of finality which relates to science with the same justification as the dimension of causality. The dimension of finality cannot be separated from biological, psychological, and mental life.

Jung, after many others, has demonstrated that finality is a magnitude, a dimension inherent in all biological life, that it is equally inherent in all mental evolution, in all psychological life, and that causes are often only a means toward an end.

To sum up, if Freud asks himself: What causes a dream? or: Of what is it a symptom? Jung asks himself: What is its goal? or: Of what is it the symbol or the sign? and: What is it aiming at?

It is very evident that this prospective, synthetic, and final point of view, added to the reductive and causal point of view, often leads to discovery of the dynamic tendencies inherent in the autoregulation and the autoevolution of a subject.

Psychotherapy tries to leave operative or to make operative, by catalytic presence of the analyst, this autoregulation and autoevolution, important vital powers of a properly functioning person which work beyond all our analytic clumsiness.

So, we can now state with precision that for Jung dreams can be, at the same time: (1) an expression of past life, whether this past has been actually lived or is purely imaginary, (2) a balance sheet of the present situation and its compromises between behavioristic and intrapsychic tendencies, and (3) the expression of a subliminal determination of the future as it is being formed.

Let me repeat, in order to avoid all misunderstanding, analytic psychology tries in each case to reconcile the reductive-causal method and the prospective-synthetic method: it is a matter of joining two perspectives of a single unitary whole.[11]

---

[11] In my example, in a reductive perspective, the dream leads back to the mother-in-law problem and we may guess that she is its cause. But from a prospective point of view, if the mother-in-law is behind the story of the fish, the solution proposed by the subject to resolve the impasse is to swallow the thing, to cover it up, and not to continue to make it into an illness of pride and self-esteem, a dissociation of *persona* and *shadow,* that is, a social mask coexisting with contents that have been more or less repressed and stained with guilt feelings.

Note carefully that this prospective, synthetic, and final resolution is not a

11. SUBJECT LEVEL—OBJECT LEVEL

We have here a point where the disagreement between Freud and Jung breaks out with great force and also in the most enlightening way. In certain cases we must say: long live differences! We should not try to create a weak unanimity wherein no one can recognize what is his own. Each should hoist his own standard loyally.

When a dreamer dreams of one of his kin, or of someone with whom he maintains a vital relationship, common sense suggests that he recognize in the person of the dream the flesh-and-bone person of daily life. The dream, then, deals with this vital relationship between the dreamer and the person he knows. Understood in the perspective of the object level, the dream can then reflect a worry, a relational disharmony, a problem of reciprocal adaptation, projections. In short, it can express a concrete problem of behavior or of interpersonal tension. This is the level of the object: I take my friend, my child, my employer such as they are, inasmuch as they are beings or existent objects.

It must be admitted that this spontaneous, commonsense point of view becomes sterile when the dreamer has no important relationship or no relationship at all with the dreamed about, or, indeed, when it is a wholly imaginary or a historic or fictional person.

Jung has demonstrated that whenever the dreamer dreams about Pope Pius XII, Napoleon, or Genghis Khan, these figures must be considered the incarnations of one aspect of the dreamer's personality; the incarnation of a fraction and a "faction" of himself appropriately disguised and expressed by the chosen figure.

Thus, if I dreamed tonight of Genghis Khan, Genghis Khan will express the invading, destructive, conquering part of my personality; it is

---

matter of course. Although the mother-in-law cause is precise and univocal, the prospective perspective is not so by any means. Faced with the same difficulty or the same cause, the dreamer could just as well have dreamed that he left for America with his wife and child, or had gone to Australia alone, or was divorcing, or was still an adolescent celibate, or what have you? Here finality could have been of any kind whatever, and unpredictable. The dream is interesting precisely because it proposes an answer made to order, extremely personal, very finely drawn, matching exactly what there is of irreducible originality in the subject, and matching the level of his evolution and maturation at the time of the dream.

You see that a simple dream can illuminate thoroughly and decisively a situation that is certainly commonplace enough in itself, but is the occasion, for reasons we shall soon see, for a pathologically neurotic reaction on the part of the subject. For the moment, let us content ourselves with the fact that the mother-in-law is the cause of the dream and the desirable inclination, or the inclination desired by the subject's mental being, is that it be accepted in a Christian manner.

as if the unconscious went looking in a costume room, a little like the opera's, for the personality that is the most natural and at the same time the most relevant for the expression of that fraction of myself which is involved.

Here, as in the preceding paragraph, there is no question of mutually exclusive perspectives; interpretation on the level of the object and interpretation on the level of the subject are often difficult to separate. In medical practice, it is often only gropingly and by using the associations of the dreamer that we can decide where the separation of the levels is to be sought, and which is the level of interpretation most appropriate to exterior circumstances, to the image dreamed, and to the intrapsychic situation of the dreamer. Sometimes it is one, sometimes the other, sometimes both at the same time, in proportions that are infinitely subtle and variable.

Both levels of interpretation are productive. Interpretation on the objective level affords certain indications about objective behavior. Interpretation on the subjective level will help with the introspective, reflective —and intrapsychic elaboration of current problems.

The overlapping, in practice, of these two levels of interpretation can be followed right into the consideration of their results; behavioral readjustment can lead to new reflection and to new and useful elaborations for the maturation of the subject, and, on the other hand, intrapsychic elaboration of problems on the subjective level can contribute strongly to determination and decision in behavioral change.

Connected with these two kinds of interpretation, we find again the great problems inherent in the cooperation of what one can call the two realities—the exterior reality, extroversion, and the interior reality, introversion, of which the two levels of interpretation, the object level and the subject level, are only the extension in the domain of dream psychology.

This dream psychology must necessarily reflect in some way the fundamental fact that the exterior world is only one of the two sources of impressions that assail us. The other source is the inner world, which is at the same time a receptacle and a basis for all our intimate elaborations that in turn will burst forth into the outer world. The dialectics between the two worlds, exterior and interior, is found again on the level of interpretation.

In practice, and as a general rule, it is the objective level that dominates, at the beginning of an analysis, especially with young subjects, to give way little by little and more and more to interpretation on the subject level and to the intrapsychic elaboration of problems. Naturally this indication needs to be taken with a great deal of flexibility. The older the person under analysis, the more one can expect to find it inadequate.

You have certainly perceived that there is a relationship between the reductive and causal interpretation, which is situated essentially on the object level—since we seek a cause, we seek to assign it in a concrete fashion—and the prospective, synthetic interpretation, which is principally situated on the subject level. This is a matter of prime importance. I believe that subject level and object level are at the origin of much of the theoretical discussions between the schools at Freud and Jung. It is because the Freudian school ignores the subject level that it finds fault with the carefully differentiating attitude we Jungians take toward the phenomenon of transference. Since our Freudian colleagues ignore this dimension of the subject level, everything for them must come to pass on the level of the object. They must incarnate everything with equal felicity, Lucifer as well as God the Father, and all within a short time span—a rather difficult feat. With the help of an interpretation on the subject level, one can, however, help a patient to understand that there are many things that involve his interior ideality. There will be no need, as with the Freudians, to transfer his entire experience onto the personality of the analyst.

I think once our Freudian colleagues have accepted this concept of the subject level, the greater part of the otherwise rather pointless discussions between the schools and the greater part of our theoretical differences will disappear.

If they reproach us for handling transference in a less absolute manner and with greater pliability than they do themselves, it is because we have, thanks to the subject level, an instrument that they ignore, or pretend to ignore. I have never understood why.[12]

---

[12] In my example, the object level associated with the causal level is the mother-in-law who is designated bodily by the dream. But why does the dreamer consider her so very important? Suppose, in order to make myself better understood, that the mother-in-law and all the circumstances of reality do not exist at all. All the circumstances are invented by the dreamer and are the product of his imagination. This being the case, we would be on the subject level, and the mother-in-law and the circumstances involved with her would be manifestations of the subject's personal problem—his social position which he judges as much too modest. Described in another way, the mother-in-law would embody the dreamer's feelings of inferiority. It seems that this is the reason, this projection of the inferiority feelings of his own shadow onto his mother-in-law, that the dreamer attributed to her so much negative libido. In his contact with her he lives his interior problem as if it were an exterior problem of relationship. He has "externalized" the drama and the neurotic tensions present within him.

This is doubtlessly why the patient makes such an important affair out of all this and why his mother-in-law, through a sad and not at all infrequent misunderstanding, has become the scapegoat for his intrapsychic problems.

As we can see, the object level often provides a camouflage for the subject

12. DREAMS IN SERIES

What solidity and validity this dream analysis has in psychotherapy does not come from the interpretation of bits of dreams, but from the study and interpretation of a subject's consecutive dream material extending over a more or less long slice of life. If all we had were scraps of dreams, it would be best to change our profession, for it would become a rather chancy activity far too redolent of fortune-telling.

---

level. The mother-in-law problem became a serious emotional problem that seriously disturbed the subject's behavior, going as far as to put the subject's home in danger. The subject, simply in meeting his mother-in-law (which was but a propitious opportunity—and if this occasion had not arisen, others would have presented themselves later) experienced all the problems of lower-class birth and inferiority, a deep torment for someone dreaming of being a grand personality.

This affords me an opportunity, in passing, to establish the fact that there is no such thing as an inferiority complex. What is often called such is always an infero-superiority complex (or, inversely, a supero-inferiority complex), inferiority being bitterly resented always in reference to and in comparison with dreamed-of superiority. The interlocking of the two levels of interpretation shows clearly in my example.

On the object level, set free by the acceptance of his mother-in-law as she is, the subject can experience and meditate on the efficacy of the Christian virtues of acceptance and forgiveness. At peace on the object level with the relationship of his life, he will be enriched on the subjective and intrapsychic levels. There will be progressive interior maturation that began exteriorly. Conversely, if, bypassing the object level, a beginning is made on the subject level, the dreamer will come to understand intellectually and emotionally what of himself and which of his inadequacies he has projected onto his in every respect innocent mother-in-law. His relationship with her will then be smoothed and sobered as if by magic. This change will be felt in the dreamer's home in numerous ways. His wife, for example, will no longer find herself torn between her husband and her mother.

As you can see, this concept of an object level and a subject level permits the discussion and the careful differentiation of the dependent effects. Things become so evident and clear in a report of this kind that the reader doubtlessly has the impression that I spend my time breaking down open doors during practical analysis. In actuality it is not at all like this. There is in life such a fine interlacing and meshing of objective reality and subjective projection, that even a highly intelligent subject like our dreamer is incapable of taking his bearings by himself. Faced with so much blinding pseudo-objectivity, the mind rejects the intrapsychic projection. This common attitude seems to me a response to three motivations: (1) the rule of specific blindness which I have described elsewhere (*Cahiers Laënnec*, X [Dec., 1950], 3–29); (2) the fact that projection modifies, disguises and stifles perception—the complex "projection-perception" becoming an indecipherable mass; (3) the fact that there are emotional resistances which spring from the narcissism inherent in every ego which always prefers to incriminate a third party rather than himself.

Errors are always possible during the interpretation of one dream. Dream analysis will be carried out with greater assurance when the study bears upon a series of dreams by the same subject. By studying a sequence of dreams over a prolonged period, we encounter thematic repetitions that demonstrate in a fundamental way, and under forms slightly modified each time, the subject's "gradient of evolution"—the larger themes of his personality, his philosophy, even his personal and collective myths, and "personal mythologems."

If errors do occur as work progresses—and they sometimes do— the later dreams come in, somehow, to comment on previously formulated interpretations, confirming what is pertinent, pointing out what is erroneous, thus allowing for the a posteriori rectification of a lingering doubt or an affirmation too categorically advanced; all of this thanks to the mechanism of compensation which we already discussed, and thanks, too, to subtle interactions between the conscious and the aroused unconscious.

The study of a dream series may perhaps allow us to compare the process of analysis to a sinusoid dwindling away by oscillation on its axis.

In medical practice, these series of dreams are comparable to a film with numerous episodes, something like the motion-picture serials of the silent era in 1925, like Georges Ohnet's "Maître de Forges" or "The Perils of Pauline," where something new was added each week.

It is a matter of no little surprise or wonder for the practitioner to find this inner cohesion and extraordinary coherence. Until Freud and Jung, no one expected to find in this material anything but incoherence, disorder, and alogical confusion, whereas dreams in series are the expression of a wondrous vital stream, constructive and dynamic, if one knows how to make use of it.

Generally there is such abundant dream material supplied by a subject under analysis that lack of time often prohibits the exhaustive examination of it all. For the same reason, an interpretation in practice rarely seeks out all the significant meanings and implications in a dream, but limits itself to what seems of practical use.

There is no reason to regret this, as it does not constitute a major inconvenience. Experience shows that anything of importance which is neglected will appear again in subsequent material.

Thoroughly understood and thoroughly assimilated, a dream can afford such progress to the dreamer and open so many horizons for him that there is no great harm in neglecting other dreams for lack of time.[13]

---

[13] I have chosen an excessively short dream as an example. We cannot in this compass fully exemplify the concept of dreams in series, but every analyst has an abundance of such materials.

13. THE ANALYST'S ATTITUDE

To repeat, the most desirable attitude to have, for the analyst involved in dream analysis and confronted with the fascinating, many-faceted world alluded to above, is that which Freud defined as an attitude of diffused, rather than concentrated, attention. Things must be left to unfold. I think the analyst is best compared to a good midwife, a good radiologist, or a good catalyzer, especially in regard to gathering associations.

The successful interpretation of dreams represents an agreement between analyst and patient. It is not an intellectual fencing match; the two participants must be able to adhere honestly to an interpretation found and proposed together. Neither the one nor the other must, I repeat, conduct himself like an intellectual contestant. When it comes to treatment, particularly, it would be unfortunate—even dangerous—for the analyst to be found "right" in contradiction to his patient. The great turning point, the great psychiatric revolution, came at the beginning of the century and with the early works of Freud when it became the psychiatrist's place to know no better than his patient. From that time on, the psychiatrist became the confidant of his patient rather than some sort of autocratic paterfamilias; he was to follow his natural sympathy. The analyst must not be proven correct against his patient; this can only arouse feelings of reticence and resistance which in such cases would only be too well founded. The patient must, however, be helped toward an understanding that is much more than purely intellectual. If, for us, analysis is the art of an inhabited and creative silence, this silence must provide that critical moment of "ideational metabolism," if you will allow me the image, which permits the subject to feel deeply the psychological countdown for which he is providing the stage, and to participate emotionally in this process for which the dream, as a detached piece of an unconscious and doubtlessly much longer sequence, represents only a fragmentary index.

The dreamer must, therefore, be led into living emotionally the passions and conflicts of the dreams.[14]

---

[14] In my example, the analyst enters only with great delicacy, virtually and functionally. No personal relationship of transference seems established as yet. One of the difficulties of the whole treatment has been that the subject never passed through the classic transference phase.

14. PRACTICAL INTEREST

The practical interest of all this dreamwork comes from the fact that the dream supplies the perspective of the unconscious. Its interpretation, whether expressed verbally or implicit, makes known the point of view of the unconscious and progressively gives the patient access to the deepest part of his psyche. It is as if the analyst, in interpreting the dream —which, moreover, he does not always do—slid gently into the point of view of the subject's unconscious in order to help him discover and experience, or even spell out loudly to his conscious self, what the unconscious expresses in images.

This is why the patient is tempted to attribute to the analyst "supernatural" powers, those which belong to his own unconscious. Hence, in part, that famous phenomenon, transference.

Let it be understood that during analysis the greatest attention must equally be given to the point of view of consciousness. Only so can progress be made toward confrontation, the tackling and, therefore, toward the harmonization of these two major levels of personality: the conscious and the unconscious, which must arrive at an ideo-emotional harmonization.

Because the patients' conscious is weak, it is often necessary to treat conscious values with the utmost care. If the conscious is treated roughly or destroyed, nothing is left with which the emerging material can be integrated.

Successive and progressive conscious insights will result from this procedure of agglomeration; these insights are accompanied as by a rebound by action on the unconscious. Conscious insight seems to us now— one of Freud's greatest historical merits was to have called attention to the idea of conscious insight—like the detonator for a whole chain reaction that takes form and happens in the innermost depths of the person, finally "to lose itself" through link after link, only a few of which we know, "in the silent intimacy of the tissues," to use René Leriche's beautiful phrase.[15] Here we come in contact with all of psychosomatic medicine.

In this manner, the analysis of dreams, by bringing about interaction between conscious and unconscious, mobilizes psychic energy, liberates it from the symptoms, and, to a large extent, achieves its transfer from the unconscious to the conscious.

That a patient "understands," not only intellectually but in a broad sense, that a patient feels—"pinpoints"—the meaning new to him of a

---

[15] René Leriche, *La Chirurgie de la douleur* (2d ed.; Paris: Masson, 1940).

dream, means that a new perspective on this or that problem of life, or on life itself, has unfolded: this enlargement of the area of consciousness constitutes a major event in every mental life. But for those neurotics in our charge whose area of consciousness has been strangled and held in by their neuroses, this enlargement is doubly important. By virtue of the dreams a new level of consciousness will have been reached that will make possible new syntheses.

Jung has demonstrated that this is the road to an integrated personality. From a certain point of view, it is giving back life to the human person legitimately defined as an integrating integration. The whole *processus* is what Jung calls "individuation."

All analysis, then, organizes itself on four levels: (1) a level of disclosure, wherein the patient unburdens himself; (2) a level for the analysis of the transference formed during the period of confession; (3) a level of education and self-education, the patient being forced to face what he has discovered of himself; and (4) a level of metamorphosis and "moulting" of the personality in which the activities of the first three levels converge and reinforce each other.

These four levels are constantly overlapping and I am separating them only for didactic purposes.[16]

15. GENERAL AND CULTURAL POINTS OF VIEW

From a general point of view, dream analysis is a thing of the highest importance for civilization and its spirit. That civilization should even accept the principle of dream analysis suffices to lift the condemnation of centuries from the irrational potentialities of a being and of beings. Civilization must accept the principle of dream analysis as a matter of

---

[16] Cf. C. G. Jung, *La Guérison psychologique* (Geneva: Georg, 1953; Paris: Buchet-Chastel). In my example, the dreamer consciously repudiated his mother-in-law. His unconscious proposed acceptance of the self-same mother-in-law was an action beneficial to his relationships, to his integration in the world, and to his personal maturing. This dream and its comprehension permitted the subject, by recognizing this tendency in himself, to appreciate its point, and to put this sector of his personality in order: not because of any imperatives, external and therefore arbitrary, but because of a tendency that was completely personal, entirely and intimately his own.

This is all-important, since the procedure suggested to him a solution that was acceptable and necessary, a solution of conciliation and synthesis between his own diverse and opposed tendencies, and a balance between the aftertaste of his ill-digested past and his development in the future. This procedure being *his own* inclination, he could accept it without surrender.

importance, even of major importance; henceforth irrationality is admitted by rationality—a rationality knowledgeable enough to surpass itself and to recognize its own limitations and restrictions—as the necessary transition between logical knowledge on the one hand, and life and living flesh on the other.

So you see, the dialectic becomes a triangular relationship. I do not think that we can overevaluate this fact. All this work liberates extraordinary forces. "The synthesis of conscious psychic activity and the psychic activity of the unconscious constitute the very essence of creative mental work." [17]

A man is like an arch; since the beginning of the century it becomes ever more evident that the keystone of the arch is the psyche. Dream and the study of dreams can open unexpected horizons; the eruption of the idea of the unconscious into our lives through our dreams constrains us to create new designs for life and thought.[18]

---

[17] C. A. Meier, *Antike Inkubation und Moderne Psychotherapie* (Zurich: Rascher, 1949).

[18] Finally, my example helps to remind that the disassociation-conflict, which constituted the neurosis of my patient, as it does all neuroses, was as alienating as a disassociation-scission or psychosis would have been. If the first is less drastically apparent than the second, because it does not entail the social isolation behind the walls of a clinic, it is no less troublesome in its consequences for the affected subject's group and family unit. And who in our errant century is not the bearer of some neurotic manifestation?

In my example, my dreamer understood—what still remains to be understood by twentieth-century man—that he had within the depths of his own irrationality a food that nourished him in spite of the distaste its crudity aroused.

In the same way, it seems that if contemporary man accepts (despite his distaste) to examine his own neurosis with understanding, he would find therein that builder of inner substance for which our century seems to be so passionately looking through many a labyrinth and in many an avatar.

7

On the Dream Psychology of C. G. Jung

SONJA MARJASCH

Before going into the dream psychology of C. G. Jung we must clarify what we understand by a dream. A dream is first of all an individual experience of the dreamer which at the time of the experience he cannot share with anybody else. Therefore the dream as an immediate experience can never be the object of psychology. Dream psychology can focus its attention only on the remembered dream. A fair number of people can remember their dreams or parts of their dreams, often knowing that there was more to it but unable to recall the rest. Many remember that they dreamed without being able to recall the content matter. Some people claim that they do not dream at all, but the recent experimental investigations of Nathaniel Kleitman and William Dement have proved this claim to be a fallacy: They nevertheless dream several times a night.[1] In his essay "On the Nature of Dreams" (1945), Jung defines the dream as follows: "A dream is a fragment of involuntary psychic activity, just conscious enough to be reproducible in the waking state."[2]

---

[1] Compare Nathaniel Kleitman, *Sleep and Wakefulness* (rev. ed.; University of Chicago Press, 1963), which contains an extensive bibliography; cf: also chapter 4, above, by William Dement, "The Psychophysiology of Dreaming."
[2] Carl Gustave Jung, *Collected Works,* ed. Herbert Read, Michael Fordham, Gerhard Adler (London: Routledge and Kegan Paul, 1953——), VIII, 282.

Dream interpretation may be compared to the effort of deciphering that fragment by relating it and enlarging it with contiguous material. But we have to bear in mind that dreams are not dead things, say broken bits of a vase. Truly there are lifeless dreams (from now on we speak only of remembered dreams) and they are almost useless to work with. Yet there are many others that have at least as much life in them as caught fish gasping and writhing on the dry land. Some dreams are quite restless. They change form. In retelling accents are shifted, a new part is added. If written down some dreams shrink surprisingly to a meager two lines, others, to the amazement of the dreamer, expand to several pages. Some dreams are remembered a lifetime, others forgotten in a moment. On occasion a dream persecutes the dreamer until he has written it down or told it to somebody. In other words: Dreams are carriers of emotion. They can change the mood of the dreamer, fill him with joy, sadness, anxiety, or anticipation, even when he does not recall them. Strictly speaking the carriers of emotion are not the dreams but the complexes revealed in them. A dream may be compared to a play, and the complexes to the actors.

C. G. Jung started his research into the human psyche by investigating a normal phenomenon: the distractability of perceptions and the subsequent inrush of nonconscious material. It may happen to all of us to misread a word, to misunderstand what is said, or to mistake an unknown person for an acquaintance. On some occasions we act more violently than is our custom, say words we afterward regret, and wonder, after having regained our composure, what got into us and made us behave in such a strange way. Or we act on a sudden hunch, we have a lucky thought or an inspiration that makes us see everything in a new light. All these phenomena point to a momentary loss of control over ourselves: Instead of sitting at the wheel of our car we are suddenly driven. Jung termed such an autonomous impulse that alters consciousness a feeling-toned complex. He later stipulated that the complexes are the nuclei of all psychic activity and that the course of our life is the resultant of the interplay between conscious and unconscious complexes.

In his first psychiatric study "On the Psychology and Pathology of So-Called Occult Phenomenas" (1902),[3] Jung made it clear that the same psychic process is at work whether we deal with a simple misreading or with such an inrush of unconscious material that the observer diagnoses a somnambulistic dream state. On the basis of his findings Jung developed the word-association experiment.[4] In this experiment a hun-

---

[3] C. G. Jung, *Collected Papers on Analytical Psychology*, ed. C. E. Long (London: Baillière, Tindall and Cox, 1917), pp. 1–93.
[4] Jung published the results of his experimental research in *Studies in Word-Association* (London: Heinemann, 1918), to be reprinted as Vol. II in *Collected Works*.

dred words are used as stimuli and the experimenter asks the person being tested to respond with the first word coming to his mind. In each case the experiment shows the existence of some disturbing factors; that is, it registers the disturbance but not the precise reason for it. This is done by measuring the time between stimulus and reaction: A deviation from the probable reaction time indicates a complex. The method is naturally more refined, but in our context it is not necessary to go into further details. On the grounds of comparative studies between the results of the word-association experiment and the dreams of the same person, Jung came to the conclusion that the unconscious complexes are the roots of our dreams. In "The Psychology of Dementia Praecox" (1907) he says:

> Over the gate-way of sleep there stands the imperative "you wish to sleep, you don't wish to be disturbed by anything." The suggestive force of this acts as absolute command for the ego-complex and checks all its associations. But the autonomous complexes are no longer under the direct control of the ego-complex. They allow themselves to be pushed back only so far, but not completely lulled to sleep. They are like little secondary psyches having their affective roots in the body, by means of which they always keep awake. During sleep they are perhaps just as inhibited as in the waking state, because the imperative command to sleep inhibits all subsidiary thought. Yet from time to time they succeed in presenting their blurred, apparently senseless subsidiary associations to the sleeping ego, just as they do during the noise of the day in the waking state.[5]

Jung maintains here the thesis that we dream continuously, that is, that the "little secondary psyches" are always at work, but that the "noise of the day" and the conscious willing of the ego-complex are so strong that the persistent murmuring of the complexes is usually unheard.

In our present civilization a dream is interpreted only in the confines of an analyst's consulting room. The therapeutic motivation is an enlargement of the patient's consciousness by a confrontation and eventual reconciliation with his unconscious drives and tendencies. As such this is not the only profit we may draw from our dreams. Jung has made the observation that whenever his patient was in a conflict situation reflecting, on an individual level, a general human conflict, the dream motives also have a general aspect for which parallels may be found in mythology and fairy tales. On the ground of their timelessness and ubiquity, Jung has called these dream motives "archetypal patterns" and the layer of the

---

[5] Jung, *Collected Works*, III, 65–66.

unconscious from which they are welling up "the collective unconscious." In order to distinguish them from purely personal complexes Jung has called them "archetypes." In "Psychology of the Transference" (1946), he defines the archetypes as follows:

> The archetypes do not represent anything external, nonpsychic, although they do of course owe the concreteness of their imagery to impressions received from without. Rather, independently of, and sometimes in direct contrast to, the outward forms they may take, they represent the life and essence of a nonindividual psyche. Although this psyche is innate in every individual it can neither be modified nor possessed by him personally. It is the same in the individual as it is in the crowd and ultimately in everybody. It is the precondition of each individual psyche, just as the sea is the carrier of the individual wave.[6]

A close observation of these archetypal patterns in a number of dream series revealed a process aimed at a fuller self-realization of the dreamer, which Jung termed "the individuation process." His great discovery was to find parallel psychic developments in the intiation rites of primitive tribes and of ancient mystery cults, in Eastern religions, and in the opus of the alchemists. They helped him to a better understanding of the dreams of modern man, which in turn gave him the key to almost unintelligible ancient texts. Thus one of Jung's great aims was with the aid of dreams "to open the way to a general comparative psychology from which we may hope to gain the same understanding of the development and structure of the human psyche as comparative anatomy has given us concerning the body."[7] A great part of his work is devoted to this task; the landmarks on this road are "Symbols of Transformation" (1912),[8] "Psychology and Alchemy" (1944),[9] and "Psychology of the Transference" (1946).[10]

The practical interpretation of a dream cannot be separated from its specific human situation. It is not a detached scientific investigation but the fulfillment of an immediate need. The dreamer has exhausted all the conscious possibilities of solving his particular conflict. He is at his wit's end and therefore wants additional information. The analyst acts as mediator between the dreamer and his dream. A dream interpreta-

[6] *Ibid.,* XVI, 169.
[7] *Ibid.,* VIII, 248.
[8] *Ibid.,* V.
[9] *Ibid.,* XII.
[10] *Ibid.,* XVI,

tion is the result of a joint effort of both the dreamer and the analyst, and it comes to an end when a dream content that is meaningful for the dreamer emerges. Then the interpretation leads to a discussion of the problem, to a critical reappraisal of the conscious situation in the light of this new knowledge, and to a search for the best way of expressing it. The discussion terminates in a conscious act of the dreamer, and the pragmatic value of this act finally determines for the dreamer and the analyst whether their interpretation was adequate or not.

There are various ways of enlarging a remembered dream fragment with auxiliary associations. Some practical examples may illustrate this.

A middle-aged woman consulted me because she was suffering from a tenacious skin rash for which she was also treated by a dermatologist. Her whole being was full of subdued irritability. In the first weeks of analysis she had the following dream: "In a train my mother and I meet Sarah and Ann Thompson. They are sisters. Sarah is standing with us, Ann is approaching us, bustling through the coach and pushing people out of her way. Her sister whispers to us: 'She is rather rude.'" The dream brings a latent conflict between the two sisters to light. Sarah is suffering from the aggressiveness of Ann but does not or cannot defend herself. Instead she complains to the dreamer and her mother, and even this she does not dare to do aloud. The dreamer and her mother are spectators of the conflict but they are in the same train. As they are now let into the secret they get entangled in the problem and are forced either to take sides or to mediate.

This dream is clearly a fragment: it does not offer a solution. In order to understand its meaning for the dreamer additional information is needed. The presence of the mother pointed to the fact that they were inseparable and shared everything together. I asked: "Who are those two ladies?" They were very good friends of the dreamer and her mother. They knew hardly anybody who was as well educated, nice, and sweet as those two sisters. The dream statement that Ann was reckless and rude came as a shock to the dreamer. She could not accept it at first because it was quite incompatible with her conscious experience. The dreamer herself was very well educated and well mannered. She lived in "a nice world," was "very nice" herself and expected everybody else to be so. In fact it was a world much too good to be true. The dream was interpreted as a statement concerning the character of Ann Thompson, that is, the aggressive dream complex "Ann Thompson" was by association referred to the real person. It appeared in the dream because the dreamer had repressed some observations to that point. This method of associatively linking dream complexes to real people (or objects) is called the interpretation on the objective level. It can also be said that the dream tended to modify the dreamer's conscious evaluation of her friend. Its prospective tendency is expressed by the moving train. This dream interpretation started a discussion about the relationship of the dreamer to Sarah and Ann Thompson and of her ability in general to size up people.

The next example shows that only a certain number of dreams can be meaningfully interpreted on the objective level. A man in his middle forties came for treatment for no specific conscious reasons. He complained of migraines (also was medically treated for them) and of a general lack of enthusiasm. Life was just going by. After a while he dreamed: "Somehow I have made Fleshman so angry that he is constantly following me around, trying to beat me up. I am not in a fighting mood and give him ample opportunity to get rid of his anger, restricting myself to fending off his worst blows with my arm. After this has gone on for quite a while, he cools off." The dreamer added a question to his report: "Why is he so angry with me?" We first tried to interpret the dream on the objective level. The dreamer did know a man by the name of Fleshman but he was an indifferent acquaintance whom he had not seen for quite a time. He had had no quarrels with him. The effort to enlarge the dream fragment with meaningful associations to the real Mr. Fleshman proved to be unfruitful and was therefore abandoned. What next? Apart from the dreamer's conscious recollections we had another source of information, namely the patient's earlier dreams. Mr. Fleshman had popped up in other dreams, and in one in particular he had a little hut attached to the back of his house overlooking a rural countryside that in Swiss dialect is called the "pig-county." The figure of "Mr. Fleshman" was therefore considered to be a dream motive, or a recurrent complex having its own biography that does not tally with the facts known about the real person. The main point about Mr. Fleshman seemed to be his allegorical name. The dream interpretation started anew, this time on the subjective level; that is, "Mr. Fleshman" was considered to be an autonomous complex at work in the dreamer's unconscious, representing his own earthbound and lusty side. The complex had the vigor the dreamer was lacking in reality. The dream showed that the dreamer was at odds with his more primitive and instinctual side and also that his dream ego tried to evade a conflict at all costs. What did the aggressive "Mr. Fleshman" want? Obviously to pound some energy into the all too complacent dream ego. The dream revealed a compensatory effort of the unconscious to overcome the dryness and staleness of the conscious situation: It told of an upsurging of vital energy that, unresponded to, ebbed back again. The question added to the dream report ("Why is Fleshman so angry with me?") was misleading, as it tended to replace an emotional engagement by an intellectual discussion. Who should know the answer better than "Fleshman"? Why had he not asked him in the dream? The problem brought to light was the *belle in-*

différence of the dream ego which frustrated the conscious effort to remedy the situation. The dream diagnosed a hidden streak of self-complacency or hybris in the dreamer. It was not so much that he was afraid of the "natural man" in himself, but that he did not take him seriously enough. His attitude in the dream showed that he rather despised his instinctual side as below himself and not really worthy of attention. In his youth the dreamer had had strong ascetic tendencies, which in middle age he had thought to have overcome but evidently he had repressed. The dream interpretation led to the conscious task of reviewing his former moralistic and strongly ascetic attitudes of which his dream ego had become the advocate.

The dream interpretation on the subjective level approximates the examination of conscience as practiced in various religious systems. It can also give rise to a problem that has a highly theoretical aspect but which is at the same time eminently practical, namely the relationship between the conscious ego and the dream ego.

In this context I deal only with its main practical consequence: the responsibility of the dreamer for his dream. This moral aspect of the problem was first taken up by St. Augustine, who, after his conversion, was still troubled by sensuous dreams. In his *Confessiones* (X.30) he wrote:[11]

> But yet there still live in my memory (which I have now spoken so much of) the images of such things as my ill custom had there fixed; and they rush into my thoughts (though wanting in strength) even whilst I am broad waking: but in sleep they come upon me, not to delight only, but even so far as consent, and most like to the deed doing. Yea, so far prevails the illusion of that image, both in my soul and my flesh as that these false visions persuade me unto that when I am asleep, which true visions cannot do when I am awake. Am I not myself at that time, O Lord my God? And yet is so much dif-

---

[11] English translation by William Watts (1631). The passage reads: "Sed adhuc vivunt in memoria mea, de qua multa locutus sum, talium rerum imagines, quas ibi consuetudo mea fixit; et occursantur mihi vigilanti quidem carentes viribus, in somnis autem non solum usque ad delectationem sed etiam usque ad consensionem factumque simillimum. et tantum valet imaginis illius illusio in anima mea in carne mea, ut dormienti falsa visa persuadeant quod vigilianti vere non possunt, numquid tunc ego non sum, domine deus meus? et tamen tantum interest inter me ipsum et me ipsum, intra momentum, quo hinc ad soporem transeo vel huc retranseo! ubi est tunc ratio, qua talibus suggestionibus resistit vigilans, et si res ipsae ingerantur, inconcussus manet? numquid clauditur cum oculis? numquid sopitur cum sensibus corporis? et unde saepe etiam in somnis resistimus, nostrique propositi memores atque in eo castissime permanentes nullum talibus inlecebris adhibemus adsensum? et tamen tantum interest, ut, cum aliter accedit, evigilantes ad conscientiae requiem redeamus; ipsaque distantia reperiamus nos non fecisse, quod tamen in nobis quoquo modo factum esse doleamus."

ference betwixt myself and myself, in that moment wherein I pass from waking to sleeping, or return from sleeping unto waking! Where is my reason at that time, by which my mind when it is awake resisteth such suggestions as these? At which time, should the things themselves press in upon me, yet would my resolution remain unshaken. Is my reason closed up together with mine eyes? Is it lulled asleep with the senses of my body? And whence comes it to pass, that we so often even in our sleep make such resistance; and being mindful of our purpose, and remaining most chastely in it, we yield no assent unto such enticements? And yet so much difference is there, as that when anything hath otherwise happened in our sleep, we upon our waking return to peace of conscience: by the distance of time discovering that it was not we that did it, notwithstanding we be sorry that there is something some way or other done in us.

St. Augustine came to the conclusion that there was a difference between the waking ego and the dream ego and that therefore he was not responsible for his actions in his dreams, yet he suffered that he could not change them. He prayed to God to cure the diseases of his soul (Numquid non potens est manus tua, deus omnipotens, sanare omnes languroes animae meae . . . ?) hoping for an eventual reconciliation between the outer and the inner man (sperans perfecturum te misericordias tuas usque ad pacem plenariam, quam tecum habebunt interiora et exteriora mea, cum absorpta fuerit mors in victoriam [St. Augustine, *Confessions* X. 30]).

There is a group of dreamers who have a natural inclination to interpret their dreams on the subjective level, that is, to accept all complexes revealed in them as tendencies of their own, even if they might be referred to outside events or people. Yet even among those dreamers there is a noticeable difference of reaction, if, for example, the dream ego kills a person in a dream or if the deed is done by somebody else. The moment the dream ego is concerned, the problem of responsibility looms. As far as it can be experienced as a moral suffering, the reality of the problem cannot be denied. But it is possible to shift it back to the conscious level. Let us assume that in reality a young man was bullied by his superior and that he cringed without defending himself. In his dream his repressed aggression manifests itself: He tries to kill his superior. Is he responsible for his dream deed? Directly, certainly not. But indirectly, to the extent that he did not take his stand in reality? Yes. To some degree our dreams are influenced by our conscious attitudes and therefore we have a certain amount of responsibility for them. This responsibility pertains only to the dream ego acting as a bridge between the conscious and the unconscious, not to the other dream complexes. Accepting a grain of indirect responsibility prevents the dreamer from identification with the dream ego, which in some cases could lead to a depression or an inflation. If the dream ego roughly equals the waking ego, or surpasses it, mastering a problem that the dreamer is not yet capable of handling in reality, this is an indication that the psychic process can freely unfold itself. But what about the dilemma of St. Augustine who first raised the question? He was torn between two kinds of conscience: his waking ego responding to his religious conscience and his dream ego obeying the laws of nature. His ascetic conscience forced a part of the natural man into a dream existence, yet he did not deny him, suffering the tension between himself and himself in the hope to be cured.

The moral question cannot be kept out of dream interpretation, but not all dreams open up a conflict; many of them point to a way of overcoming it. Those dreams have a marked prospective tendency and happen when a conflict has been consciously experienced. While the waking ego is still wavering, the dream ego makes a decision and leads the way out of a difficulty. This is another aspect of the compensatory function of the dream: outbalancing an uncertainty or reluctance of the waking ego. To give an example:

A man in his early thirties was in a conflict whether to pursue his personal inclinations, especially his interest in psychology, or to accept a breadwinning job. He dreamed:

> There is a thunderstorm in the air. I am in a lonely place in the mountains. At my feet a calm lake is inviting me to bathe. But the water is too cold and too pure. On the water I see the reflection of my dark figure surrounded by a glimmering flickering aura. I should like to remain here in this quiet of nature. But the family-chorus calls: "Come back, we need you!" And with heavy heart I decide to cross the mountain, following one of the dangerous passways that leads through dark, gloomy woods and past craggy rocks.

The dream tended to overcome the conscious ambivalence whether at the moment the outer or the inner world should be given preference. It revealed that the dreamer's psychological studies could end in a fatal kind of self-fascination and stressed his obligation toward his family. The moment had come for the patient to give his full attention to exterior tasks and the dream encouraged him that this was possible, although it meant a sacrifice for him and he started his journey with a heavy heart. Soon afterward the analysis came to an end and the patient got a job that allowed him to support his family and to a certain extent also corresponded with his interests.

In the dream the mountain lake invited the dreamer to take a bath yet he refrained from it because the water was too cool and too pure. He remained on shore staring into the water and becoming fascinated with his own image. It was dark yet had an aura, a dream image that could mean he was inclined to see himself either in too dark or too bright a light: He was wavering between self-dejection and self-idealization. The main point of this part of the dream was the purely reflective relation to the unconscious. How dangerous this could become was seen clearer when this dream fragment was enlarged.

The dreamer had written down his dream and spontaneously used the word "family-chorus": "The family-chorus calls: Come back, we need you!" This word "chorus," out of place as it might be in the rather prosaic rendering, nevertheless opens the gate to a deeper layer of the dream. The dream is a paraphrase of the Greek myth of Narcissus. With the chorus we enter the world of the antique stage and the world of symbols. At the height of a personal crisis the dream used imagery from the large treasure-house of the human soul:

> When the water nymph Liriope had given birth to Narcissus, her son by the river-god Cephisus, she went to the seer Tiresias asking him, whether her boy would live to an old age. "If he does not come to see himself" (*si non se noverit*), answered Tiresias. Narcissus grew up into a beautiful youth, loved by many, most so by the nymph Echo but scorning them all. Hunting alone he rested by a mountain-spring—and suddenly saw his own image in the water. Mistaking it at first for a beautiful boy he immediately fell in love with him, then realized that it was his own reflection. But the spell could not be broken: He had fallen in love with himself and, unconsoled, he pined away because only death could unite him on land with himself in the water (*nunc duo concordes anima moriemur in una*). He died and when the nymphs came to mourn him they found a flower, the narcissus, instead.[12]

This is a mythological story, meaning that it is an approximation of human experience that can be told only in images because in its full depth it cannot be made entirely conscious. It is open to many interpretations and has a specific meaning only when it is related to a particular human situation. Dreams of this kind are like plays acted on a double stage: In the foreground we see the dreamer contemplating his own image in the water, called back by the family-chorus, voicing the will of destiny. At the back of the stage we see Narcissus bending over his own reflection in the spring and the nymph Echo vainly appealing to him. The dream portrays the conflict between self-love and love for others. It is in these terms that it expresses the dreamer's dilemma whether to pursue his studies or take a job. The dream shows the general human aspect of the

---

[12] See Ovid, *Metamorphoses* III. 340–510.

problem and, using the myth of Narcissus, it tells the dreamer that he is making a choice toward life or death and, more than that, it weighs the scale in favor of choosing the hazardous path forward into life.

The method of enlarging a fragmentary aspect of the dream with the help of material gathered from folklore, fairy tales, mythology, or religious symbolism is called "amplification." It is a specific Jungian contribution to dream interpretation. A most careful description of this method can be found in the third chapter of *Jung and Analytical Psychology* by C. A. Meier wherein he illustrates the interpretation of dreams.[13] *Antike Inkubation und moderne Psychotherapie*[14] by the same author can be called the prototype of the amplification method; it consists of material gathered and interpreted in order to explain one single dream. By amplification the emotional charge of the dream has a chance to enrich and express itself in further images. It makes an instinctive choice of the material and discards many intellectually possible and meaningful associations as worthless to its own purpose of self-revelation. As this method asks for considerable knowledge and skill to find contiguous material it is more often used by the analyst than by the dreamer. But the analyst's contribution is only valid if he or she is caught by the emotion of the dream and personally engaged in the basic human problem it contains. To give a further example: A young woman was engaged in rebuilding her life which also included the choice of a new profession. After a year of analysis we both felt that now the ground was cleared for further development. At this moment she had the following dream: "I am in a dark room dressed in a long robe. A man comes towards me with a burning torch to set me on fire. He is also dressed in a long robe. I evade him for a while and then almost voluntarily let him set the edge of my robe on fire. I can feel the heat. On awakening I felt no fear—only curiosity."

This dream was emotionally accepted as being very significant. Neither the dreamer nor I made an attempt to rationalize it by looking for associations that might relate it to the dreamer's past or present biography. The prospective tendency of the dream was underlined; for the time being its essential meaning consisted in the fact that it had changed the mood of the dreamer. It had filled her with curiosity and with anticipation. Further development showed this dream to be the first of a series that continued to heighten the mood of anticipation, until there came a dream in which the dream ego clearly and with new-found

---

[13] Carl Alfred Meier, *Jung and Analytical Psychology* (Newton Center, Mass.: Andover Newton Theological School, 1959).
[14] C. A. Meier, *Antike Inkubation und moderne Psychotherapie,* Studien aus dem C. G. Jung Institut, Bd. I (Zurich, 1949).

determination made her professional choice. This last dream was intensively discussed as to how the dream decision could be realized in practice. As the new professional plans stimulated the patient's interests in adolescent psychology, I gave her the book by Margaret Mead, *Growing Up in New Guinea,* to read. I did this on a spontaneous impulse with no specific intention. In the next session the patient reported that she had found a passage in the book which had vividly reminded her of the dream where she was pursued with a burning torch. It referred to a part of the initiation ceremonies of the girls of the Manus tribe on the Admiralty Islands, north of New Guinea. The dreamer was very impressed by this coincidence and so was I. I had read the book rather carefully some months before but had forgotten this description. My sudden impulse may have been stimulated by a preconscious memory. This incident shows how the unconscious of the analyst can be affected by the emotional charge of the dream urging for further expression. The passage from *Growing Up in New Guinea* reads:

> At the end of five days the first feast for relieving the girl Kiteni of her tabus was held. This was a feast looked forward to by all the girls and regarded by the men as particularly daring and spectacular behaviour on the part of woman-kind. It was held after nightfall. A great quantity of bamboo torches and large lumps of raw sago were prepared. The house was crowded with women and girls and brightly lit by the torches piled in each of the four fireplaces. On this particular occasion the last to arrive was Kiteni's paternal grandmother. Kiteni, who giggled and held back, was bidden to stand up and run the length of the house pursued by her grandmother, waving a burning torch over her. But Kiteni ran without conviction and the whole party laughed as the grandmother perfunctorily pursued the girl. The torch was held overhead as the grandmother pronounced an incantation over her.
> Meanwhile the girls seized the bowls of raw sago and the bundles of burning torches, loaded them upon a large canoe and set off through the village. As they went they waved the torches and showered sparks into the sea. Three small girls encountered on the way were bidden to splash vigorously as the canoe passed. At the house of brothers, grandparents, uncles a cake of sago and a torch were left on the platform. The village streets were empty of canoes. Attracted by the shouting or by the gleam of the torches reflected through the floor slats, people came to the doors and peered out, shouting hilarious greeting. The last sago distributed, the last glowing torch laid quickly on a doorstep, the party returned only slightly sobered, to the house of Kiteni where a feast was spread.
> Kiteni was now free to walk about in the house and to go out on the platform or into the sea near by, in the dark or in the rain.

She still was not allowed to go about the village or leave the house when the sun was shining.[15]

With the help of this amplification the meaning of the dream emerged. It celebrated the transition of the dreamer to a more advanced stage of consciousness and psychic maturity. The amplification enriched the feeling of anticipation with many new images: To the pursuit with the burning torch were added the incantation, the distribution of fire and food, the vigorous splashing of water. The theme of handing the torch of life from one generation to another was taken up by a subsequent dream, in which the dreamer attended the ceremonial funeral of her grandmother and afterward enjoyed a new feeling of femininity. The symbolism of the burning torch and the pursuit by the torchbearer is surely not exhausted by the one comparison. On the contrary it unlocks a flood of images—from hymeneal processions to the kindling of the new fire in Easter night—but for practical purposes the point was achieved: The dream rooted the woman who was about to fashion her own life in the experience of her sex and it told her that, in spite of all the differences, she and the Manus girl Kiteni were sisters. At the moment on the threshold—between "no more" and "not yet"—she was given the assurance by her unconscious that she was not alone. Dreams like this one are like wells: They cannot be exhausted and after many years a new bucketful of meaning can be drawn up to light. In their individual formation, they are a unique experience of the dreamer, yet it is the experience of a relatedness between one's own existence and human fate.

Dreams that have an immediate healing effect are rare. Although they impress both the dreamer and the observer as the sudden and apparently completely autonomous effect of a numinous healing factor, they nevertheless seem to be at least partly conditioned by outer circumstances, for example, the genius loci, and by inner circumstances, such as the readiness of the dreamer. Most of the pioneer research concerning this kind of dreams has been done by C. A. Meier. I refer again to *Antike Inkubation und moderne Psychotherapie* and to *Jung and Analytical Psychology*. In the latter he describes such a dream that happened in analysis,[16] and also to the more theoretical paper, "Projektion, Uebertragung und Subjekt-Objektrelation in der Psychologie." [17] Another paper

---

[15] Margaret Mead, *Growing Up in New Guinea* (London: Pelican Books, 1930), pp. 35–36.
[16] Meier, *Jung and Analytical Psychology*, pp. 44, 57–63.
[17] C. A. Meier, "Projektion, Uebertragung und Subjekt-Objektrelation in der Psychologie," *Dialectica*, 8 (Dec. 15, 1954), 302–321 (English trans., "Projection, Transference and the Subject-Object Relation in Psychology," *Journal of Analytical Psychology*, 4 [1959], 21–34.)

on the same topic by the Jungian analyst Rev. James Aylward, "Lourdes and Its Mysteries," is not yet published.[18]

Until now the dream contents have either been referred by associations to the biography of the dreamer or to his outside world, or they have been understood as tendencies at work in his own psyche. Yet in the great healing dreams there are at work factors that cannot be integrated within the dreamer's own psyche without dangerous inflation.

As an example of a dream in this category I quote the dream experience of Thérèse of Lisieux as she recorded it in her autobiographical statements published as *The Story of a Soul*.[19] The dream is the core of her second letter written, "in obedience," to her sister Marie of the Sacred Heart. But the passage in question is directly addressed to Jesus as he was understood to be the emissary of the dream. The letter was written in September, 1896, when Thérèse was 23 years old, eight years after she had entered the Carmel of Lisieux and a year before her death. It can be assumed that the dream happened in May, 1896, and was written down four months afterward, as the first recollections of Thérèse went up to January, 1896. I quote in extenso to demonstrate not only the dream but also the emotional climate in which it originated and the impact it had. The passage reads:

> Jesus, my well-beloved, how considerate you are in your treatment of my worthless soul; storms all around me, and suddenly the sunshine of your grace peeps out! Easter Day had come and gone, the day of your splendid triumph, and it was a Saturday in May; my soul was still storm-tossed. I remember thinking about the wonderful dreams which certain souls have been privileged to experience, and how consoling an experience it would be; but I didn't pray for anything of the kind. When I went to bed, my sky was still overcast, and I told myself that dreams weren't for unimportant souls like mine; it was a storm that rocked me to sleep. Next day was Sunday, the second Sunday of May, and I'm not sure it wasn't actually the anniversary of the day when our Lady did me the grace to smile on me. As the first rays of dawn came, I went to sleep again and dreamed.
>
> I was standing in a sort of gallery where several other people were present, but our Mother was the only person near me. Suddenly, without seeing how they got there, I was conscious of the presence of three Carmelite sisters. I had the impression that they'd

---

[18] James Aylward, "Lourdes and Its Mysteries," Diploma thesis for graduation, C. G. Jung Institute, Zurich.

[19] Thérèse of Lisieux, *Autobiography of a Saint: The Story of a Soul*, trans. Ronald Knox (London: Fontana Books, 1958), pp. 182-183.

come to see our Mother; what was borne in upon me with certainty was that they came from heaven. I found myself crying out (but of course it was only in the silence of my heart): "O, how I would love to see the face of one of these Carmelites!" Upon which, as if granting my request, the tallest of the three saintly figures moved towards me, and, as I sank to my knees, lifted her veil, lifted it right up, I mean, and threw it over me. I recognized her without the slightest difficulty; the face was that of our Venerable Mother Anne of Jesus, who brought the reformed Carmelite order into France. There was a kind of ethereal beauty about her features, which were not radiant but transfused with light—the light seemed to come from her without being communicated to her, so that the heavenly face was fully visible to me in spite of the veil which surrounded both of us. I can't describe what a weight was taken off my mind; an experience like that can't be put down on paper. Months have passed by now since I had this reassuring dream, but the memory of it is as fresh as ever, as delightful as ever. I can still see the look on Mother Anne's face, her loving smile; I can still feel the touch of the kisses she gave me. And now, treated with all this tenderness, I plucked up my courage: "Please, Mother," I said, "tell me whether God means to leave me much longer on earth? Or will he come and fetch me soon?" And, she, with a most gracious smile, answered: "Yes, soon, very soon, I promise you." Then I added: "Mother, answer me one other question; does God really ask no more of me than these unimportant little sacrifices I offer him, these desires to do something better? Is he really content with me as I am?" That brought into the Saint's face an expression far more loving than I'd seen there yet; and the embrace she gave me was all the answer I needed. But she did speak too: "God asks no more," she said. "He is content with you, well content." And so she embraced me as lovingly as ever mother embraced her child, and then I saw her withdraw. In the midst of that happiness, I remembered my sisters, and some favours I wanted to ask for them; but it was too late, I'd woken up. And now the storm no longer raged, all my sky was calm and serene. I didn't merely believe, I felt certain that there was a heaven, and that the souls who were its citizens looked after me, thought of me as their child. What gave more strength to this impression was the fact that, up till then, Mother Anne of Jesus meant nothing to me; I'd never asked for her prayers or even thought about her except on rare occasions when her name came up in conversation. So when I realized how she loved me, and how much I meant to her, my heart melted towards her in love and gratitude; and for that matter towards all the Blessed in heaven.

Jesus, my Beloved, this was only a prelude to greater graces still with which you'd determined to enrich me. . . .

This report may be divided into an introduction, in which Thérèse gave the conditions of the dream, and a description of the dream itself including the immediate impact it made on her. At the time of the dream she was in conflict. The "storms" mentioned are later explained as clashes between her conscious will to adapt to the restricted life of a Carmelite and the upsurgings from her unconscious: her desires to become a priest, a missionary, or a martyr. These tendencies she also called her "dreams": strictly speaking they may have been daydreams that distracted her. She was at least partially hoping that her conflict might be solved by a dream. She further stated that the dream probably happened on the anniversary of her first visionary experience. This can be understood as an attempt to link associatively both the vision and the dream, which might lead to a better understanding of both. As our interest is focused on the dream, and not on the psychology, of Thérèse of Lisieux, we do not pursue this further. The fact, that a certain periodicity in the course of events is felt by the dreamer is an interesting point of research.

The dream itself has the characteristics of a great initiation: In dream literature the classic example for dreams of this category is Cicero's *Somnium Scipionis*. In Thérèse's experience the dreamer is liberated from her earthly ties—her filial bonds to her own mother—and is received as a child by a new mother, the founder of her order in France, whose objective nature is stressed by the fact that she had until now played no part whatsoever in the dreamer's life. The motive of "lifting the veil," which has many parallels in the mystery cults, notably of Isis, prepares for the revelation of a life beyond. "Mother Anne of Jesus," who from another point of view can be understood as a personification of the dreamer's conscience, acts as mediator between the dreamer and her God, revealing her approaching death and giving her at the same time confidence in herself and assurance of an afterlife.

The effect of this dream was immediate: When Thérèse woke up "the storm no longer raged, all [her] sky was calm and serene." Her belief in a beyond had become a certainty. She considered her dream experience as a prelude or preparation for her subsequent spiritual developments, which after another stormy period culminated in her vocation of love. In 1925 Thérèse of Lisieux became a canonized saint of the Catholic Church. Lisieux is today a shrine of pilgrimage where her help is invoked.

The Story of a Soul was first published in 1898, two years before Freud's *The Interpretation of Dreams* and four years before Jung's "On the Psychology and Pathology of So-Called Occult Phenomena." It became a religious best seller, which means that it encompassed and expressed psychic problems and aspirations that—in individual variations —were and still are shared by a great number of people. As the dream was a landmark in the spiritual process of the saint, it had a message not only for Thérèse but also of a general nature: It compensated most effectually for the materialistic tendencies of her period.

As we have seen happen in the case of Thérèse, a great religious dream transforms the belief of a dreamer into a certainty. The receiver of such a dream has no doubts that his experience was a "somnium a deo missum." The dream manifestations of the divinity vary according to the religious background of the dreamer, but it can also happen that the God believed in and the God revealed in the dream are not one and the same, which tension may lead to a conversion. We are facing in this realm all the "varieties of religious experience." [20] Great dreams draw the dreamer into a personal I-Thou relationship with his God, while in the interest of science the psychologist observes the phenomena in terms of a subject-object relation and with the hypothesis of an "objective psyche." The target of pilot research including experimental work is a closer investigation of the conditions under which the essentially undefined factors or arrangers of the objective psyche come into operation. For the practical analyst who works close to the fire it is wise to remember what Jung wrote in "General Aspects of Dream Psychology" (1916): "Everyone who analyses the dreams of others should constantly bear in mind that there is no simple and generally known theory of psychic phenomena, neither with regard to their nature, nor to their causes, nor to their purpose. We therefore possess no general criterion of judgment. We know that there are all kinds of psychic phenomena, but we know nothing certain about their essential nature." [21]

---

[20] William James, *Varieties of Religious Experience* (New York and London: Longmans, Green, 1902).
[21] Jung, *Collected Works*, VIII, 259.

8

Parapsychological Dream Studies

MARTIN EBON

In dealing with the subject of parapsychological dream studies, it is essential to define the concept of parapsychology, to delineate the areas of its current research, and to examine the specific scope of dream research within the parapsychological framework, its history, and its present achievements, limitations, and prospects.

Modern parapsychology has its origins in ancient and primitive occult beliefs and practices, just as the modern sciences are indebted to the alchemists, just as medicine, specifically, acknowledges the allegedly magical or miraculous healing powers of saints and witch doctors. Parapsychology has remained close to traditions of the supernatural which remain as a strong but mostly unacknowledged residue within our own materialistic society. It has tried to apply up-to-date scientific methods to verify, record, and analyze phenomena that do not seem to fit into the pattern of known scientific laws.

Modern parapsychology, just because it has as its subject matter what may be termed the supernatural, paranormal, magical, or pseudomagical, is intent upon applying the most rigid standards of documentation, experimental control, and statistical evaluation available to current scientific research. Aside from criticism that it entertains and requests from nonparapsychologists, parapsychology generally is much concerned with self-criticism and subsequent refinement of its own methodology. This very tendency toward high standards of evidence and experimentation may, however, endanger the delicate fiber of the phenomena that modern parapsychology seeks to record, study, and, if possible, repeat.

Parapsychological dream studies cannot be entirely separated from the general mass of research in parapsychology or, as it has often been called, psychical research. Parapsychology owes a heavy debt to British researchers active during the second half of the nineteenth century. Often they were men of distinction in such diverse areas as public affairs, literature, theology, and the sciences. Their original research, undertaken through the London Society for Psychical Research, received its main stimulus from a desire to study the possibility of the survival of the human personality after bodily death. The leading researchers of the British Society hoped to apply new methods of documentation to the ancient concept of man's immortality in order to achieve a union of science and faith.

Much material of varied quality, but of undoubted originality and sincerity, emerged from these studies. As a by-product, so to speak, other areas of more or less "occult" phenomena were made the subject of investigations. There thus exists, accumulated during the past eight decades, a considerable body of data concerning dreams in categories such as these:

1. the dream as omen, as a more or less supernatural indication of certain critical events, present or future;

2. the dream as part of initiatory rituals, notably those of shamanism;

3. a telepathic or precognitive quality of the dream, which has been the subject of current research;

4. other areas in which the dream plays a major or minor part linking it with the magical, supernormal, metaphysical, or extrasensory.

It is specifically in the third category that modern parapsychologists seek to apply various scientific criteria to the dream. They are aware, of course, that these very criteria are continuously undergoing tests concerning their general validity and their applicability to the phenomena with which they are concerned. In dream studies, as in various other parapsychological research areas, the relative values of qualitative and quantitative studies are constantly being tested and examined.

The dilemma of parapsychological dream studies, and, indeed, of virtually all other parapsychological studies, centers on the problem of capturing, so to speak, highly elusive (and presumably subjective) phenomena with the still rather limited scientific tools at hand. By its very nature, the parapsychological phenomenon depends on a constellation of factors that are exceedingly difficult to anticipate or control, and virtually impossible to adapt to laboratory conditions. Indeed, the verification of these phenomena often proves so difficult that I am tempted, at the cost of sounding flippant, to use a somewhat primitive parable to illustrate this point.

The parapsychological researcher all too frequently faces a situation that resembles the hunt for a mythical animal, whose presence has long been "known," and which has just been reported, once again, by a rather excited (and therefore, of course, not entirely trustworthy) witness. Let us assume that a boy has just come into a remote, forest-ringed Asian village, shouting that he has positively seen the famed and fabled purple tiger. This animal, for our purposes, might be a telepathic or precognitive dream. Naturally, the villagers are much excited: at last, they feel, the elusive beast may be encircled, hunted down, trapped, and finally exhibited to prove to all doubters that it does, indeed, exist.

Teams of skilled hunters are assembled, wielding special traps perfected in their trade; statisticians bearing computers, as if they were lighted torches; anthropologists, equipped with data of similar cases; psychologists, loaded down with Rorschach, Thematic Apperception, and Rosenzweig test materials; physicists with delicate instruments and charts; theologians, bearing the wisdom and doubt of the ages; even psychopharmacologists, with the more esoteric products of Swiss pharmaceutical firms; and physiologists with highly specialized electroencephalographic equipment. Thus, with drumbeating and shouting, a ring is completed, and everyone is in high spirits, temporarily convinced that this time, surely, the purple tiger will be trapped, caged, and suitably exhibited before learned societies. The hunting party at last converges upon the center of the forest. But, behold, their precious prey has, once again, vanished.

To finish the parable appropriately, the assembled scientists have little more to show for their pursuit than more or less painful scratches on their academic reputation, and possibly the makings of a learned paper, "Some Preliminary Observations on the Trapping of Alleged Purple Tigers"; plus a great deal of controversy as to whether it might not be more significant, statistically, to trap several purple tigers instead of only one inconclusive specimen.

And that, essentially, is the dilemma of the parapsychological researcher who seeks to observe and verify such phenomena as telepathic or precognitive dreams, or who endeavors to develop experiments and perfect methods of evaluation. The very attempt to "trap" the phenomenon, to measure or verify it, may destroy it, may "scare it away." Indeed, the high emotional content of most "paranormal" dreams, the deep involvement of the dreamer, tend to make scientific appraisal extraordinarily difficult.

During the past few years, various associations in Europe and the

United States have sought to screen, verify, and evaluate thousands of what parapsychologists call spontaneous phenomena (apparitions, hunches, telepathic and precognitive experiences, or similar unplanned, nonlaboratory phenomena), but they have found it virtually impossible to establish a fully proven, airtight case in the category of the precognitive, or even the telepathic, dream. That, on the surface, seems unlikely; virtually everyone has experienced, or heard of, a startling experience in this area. But parapsychologists admit that anthropologists and psychologists can find good raw material in subjectively reported, anecdotal material; they consider it their special task, however, to give documentation and verification the highest priority.

Let me give you an example. Let us suppose that a newspaper reports on the case of a New York housewife who awoke her husband at 2 o'clock one morning, violent with fright, to tell him that she had dreamed their son had crashed in a flaming aircraft near the U.S. Air Force base at San Diego, California, where he was stationed. Early next morning, she related this same dream to two other people, perhaps to the mailman and to a neighbor. Later in the day, or perhaps a day or two after, she received official notification that her son had, indeed, been involved in an air crash; he may, however, have escaped the accident with no more than relatively mild injuries. The accident had taken place at 2 A.M. on the very morning that she had dreamed her frightening dream.

One would think that it should be relatively easy to document such a chain of events; that the woman's and husband's testimony could be tape-recorded; that the mailman and the neighbor could sign appropriate statements; and that the Air Force notification, the official record of the accident, and the attending physician's diagnosis of the son's condition could be made part of a conclusive case history. But as parapsychologists specializing in the verification of spontaneous phenomena will attest, it is highly unlikely that all such documentation can be obtained—mind you, not what the legal profession calls circumstantial evidence but actual airtight verification. The time element may not check out; one or the other of the witnesses will be vague in his recollection; or, quite simply, the husband will not want his wife's psychic peculiarities to become a matter of public record. For one reason or another, our mythical purple tiger will remain untrapped and uncaged.

These difficulties are not new. They were encountered by the thorough and conscientious British researchers who originally established standards for what should be regarded as veridical in the documentation of psychic phenomena. These traditions, I can assure you, are so ingrained that at least one leading member of the London Society for Psychical Research carried his skeptical attitude over into a dream itself! Professor C. D. Broad, a former president of the society and a distinguished philosopher at Trinity College, Oxford, recalls that he once dreamed of levitation, of floating within a room and close to a fireplace. Within this very dream, he urged himself to be thorough at all cost, and so he proceeded to float up to the fireplace, to take a heavy glass vase from a shelf above it and to place it on the floor as "evidence."

Professor Broad's scholarly predecessors included Edmund Gurney, F. W. H. Myers, and Frank Podmore, whose classic in the field of spontaneous phenomena, *Phantasms of the Living,* was published in 1866. From this volume comes one of the most frequently cited, because one of the most incongruous, dream anecdotes on record. It is so odd, and so trivial, that it is difficult to ignore. Mrs. Atlay, wife of the Bishop of Hereford, dreamed that after reading morning prayers in the hall of the palace, she went into the dining room and found an enormous pig standing between the sideboard and the table. She was so amused at this dream that she told it to the children and their governess before prayers began. After prayers, she went into the dining room and there she found a pig standing, just as she had seen one in her dream. It had escaped from its sty while prayers were being read. In 1913, Dr. Frederik van Eeden, developed nine dream classifications based on 500 of his own recorded dreams; he reported on his research in a lecture to the Society for Psychical Research.

Much case material concerning apparent telepathic and precognitive dreams was published in the *Proceedings* of the British Society, as well as in certain volumes of the *Journal of the American Society for Psychical Research.* Mrs. Henry Sidgwick published a long paper in the British publication, in 1922, bringing the 1886 volume of *Phantasms of the Living* up to date.

Recently, fresh impetus to related studies was given by the Conference on Spontaneous Phenomena (Cambridge, England), organized by the London Society for Psychical Research and sponsored by the Parapsychology Foundation, New York. From this meeting, several regional studies emerged, including surveys either completed or in progress in the United States, Great Britain, several Scandinavian countries, the Netherlands, Germany, Finland, and Austria. The work in the United States was carried out by the American Society for Psychical Research, under the direction of Dr. Gardner Murphy, now the Society's president, a former president of the American Psychological Association, and director of research of the Menninger Clinic, Topeka, Kansas.

In all these, and in other studies, the methodological development of parapsychology plays a significant part. The work of the early British group and of Mrs. Sidgwick, for instance, was largely qualitative in nature. In other words, it centered around the collection of anecdotal material, strengthened by the apparent quality of each case to those experiencing it, and to the researcher weighing it against similar data. Efforts to design quantitatively oriented experiments were made in France by the physiologist and Nobel Prize winner Charles Richet. In the nineteen-thirties, however, parapsychology received new impetus from the work of Dr. J. B. Rhine, director of the Parapsychology Laboratory, Duke University, Durham, North Carolina. Dr. Rhine developed means and techniques that lent themselves to the carrying out of laboratory experiments in extrasensory perception which could be evaluated in a statistical, or quantitative, way. This involved, for the most part, experiments with five cards, known as Zener cards, to establish extrasensory perception (ESP). At present, there is a certain amount of reevaluation of parapsychological methods, and this has a specific impact upon current and future dream studies. Such studies are now largely in the category of telepathic dreams (the dream incorporating apparent transfer of thought or impressions of information from another person to the dreamer); the clairvoyant dream (in which the dreamer apparently observes an image or situation directly by extrasensory means); the precognitive or prophetic dream (in which the dreamer seems to observe an event that will occur in the future). Dreams make up a large segment of the phenomena classified as "spontaneous," although experiments are now under way in the United States to study or induce such dreams under laboratory conditions. Telepathic and precognitive dreams are among the relatively most frequent and colorful case material now being studied in parapsychology.

It is probably fair to say that the accumulated evidence in favor of precognitive dreams is much less voluminous, much less commanding, much less convincing than material concerning telepathic dreams. It is self-evident that a simultaneous event is much easier to check than a subsequent event that may be subject to retrospective falsification of the original precognitive dream or consciously or unconsciously manipulated. On the other hand, precognized events may be anticipated and recorded quite accurately in many cases. For the remainder of this exposition, we mostly limit ourselves to a discussion of the allegedly telepathic dream.

At the Cambridge Conference on Spontaneous Phenomena, which tried to establish certain international criteria of recording and evaluation, emphasis was placed on two aspects: more stringent verification than had been possible or attempted in the past; and an effort to elicit psychological aspects that might help researchers to gain some understanding of the underlying psychodynamic elements, or interpersonal relations that may favor the happening—the outburst, so to speak—of telepathic dream phenomena, as well as of other spontaneous cases. But case histories that are sufficiently well recorded to permit psychological evaluation are rare. One of these has been reported by Dr. Emilio Servadio (Rome), whose account may be summarized as follows:

On the night between the 23rd and 24th of April, 1955, a sixteen-year-old girl, whom I shall call Luisa, dreamed that the mother of her fiancé, Guido, had on her finger a strange silver ring. On the ring's surface were unusual signs, resembling hieroglyphics. The ring itself could be opened, and she thought that it contained a scent. On awakening, Luisa related her dream to her mother. A few hours later, she telephoned Guido and began to tell him of her dream. The fiancé, in great excitement, said that he had just returned to Rome from Milan, where he had bought a silver ring for his mother. He had purchased it at the Somali Pavilion of the International Fair. The ring, he added, had a surface that could be opened, and strange writings were engraved on it. Hearing this, Luisa dropped the telephone and frantically called her mother to confirm that all of these details had appeared in her dream.

Dr. Servadio's comments are as follows:

> Luisa and Guido are well known to me. All details were related to me immediately after the telephone call, and I recorded them carefully. I asked Luisa and Guido to read over my notes and they found them correct in every detail. Let us now reflect on the psychological setting for this apparent telepathic dream. Luisa and Guido were engaged to be married and very much in love. Their engagement was still unofficial, but Luisa was eager to become formally and publicly engaged to Guido. She looked forward to the day when he would present her with an engagement ring. Luisa's father had died when she was still an infant. She was brought up by her mother and also cared for by her mother's three sisters. No male figure played any prominent role in her childhood. Her mother remarried in 1951, when Luisa was eleven years old. In psychoanalytic terms, it is quite obvious that her Oedipus complex was quite notable. Luisa still had strong enthusiasms and passive-masochistic phantasies about outstanding men, and unfriendly attitudes toward her mother and maternal figures. She was aware of Guido's attachment to, and respect for, his own mother. She also knew that he would visit the Milan Fair. Possibly, she expected that Guido would bring her a present, which he actually did—although it was not a ring for her finger, but a pair of earrings. Probably because of oedipal attachment of his own, he selected a ring for his mother and not for Luisa. . . .
>
> One might say that, being emotionally attached to two women at the same time, Guido showed a preference for his mother, by bringing her a ring, while selecting for Luisa a nice, but much less significant present. He probably had no intention of concealing from Luisa the fact that he had bought a ring for his mother. At this point, the interweaving in the pattern of relations between Luisa and Guido represented a very ambiguous ethical situation. The ring had become a focus of this very relationship, which had not become concrete (the engagement had not been publicized by an

engagement ring), because of psychological obstacles. Luisa broke through this obstacle by means of telepathy. She was able to establish a temporary symbolism between Guido and herself, and to merge in an unconscious psychic world, which comprised them both. She was thus able to express, in a dream, her insurmountable rivalry toward the mother figure, including her hostility based on the fact that her own mother, and not she, had been subject to an experience involving engagement and marriage. Through the dream, she could tell her own mother of Guido's preference for his mother, and of the wrong he had thus done his sweetheart. . . .

The case presented by Dr. Servadio, as happens often in dream telepathy and nondream telepathy, involves a crisis situation. Much anecdotal material collected by anthropological and ethnological researchers is also in the crisis category. We must acknowledge that there seems to be a pattern to this type of telepathic material, which points toward a piercing of the barriers restricting "normal" sensory communication: the crisis-induced need seems to bring about extrasensory communication.

Dr. Servadio's case was subjected to a Freudian interpretation. Other psychological analysis may be possible. One work devoted to the recording and evaluation of spontaneous case material from the Freudian point of view is *Geistererscheinungen und Vorzeichen (Apparitions and Omens)* by Mrs. Aniela Jaffé, who analyzed more than one thousand cases that had been made available to Dr. C. G. Jung by a popular magazine. All these were cases sent in by individuals who had either experienced these phenomena or had heard of them more or less directly. While this work does not attempt to verify the data, it is nevertheless a unique effort of applying psychological criteria to this type of evidence.

As noted, the American Society for Psychical Research has engaged in an extensive study of such case material. As a result of magazine publicity, it obtained a large number of cases, from which Dr. Murphy, Mrs. Laura Dale, and Miss Rhea White have selected seventeen cases for presentation in the American Society's *Journal*. At about the same time, Mrs. Louisa Rhine, wife of Dr. Rhine, published a book, *Hidden Channels of the Mind*. The research team of the American Society compares its own selected cases—which it described as meeting "the three minimum criteria of authentication"—with the much larger, but unselected group of cases reported by Mrs. Rhine. The three criteria referred to had been established originally by a widely experienced parapsychologist, Mr. Fraser Nicol. He suggested that such an experience should be veridical in that it "related to an actual event that is occurring, had occurred, or would occur," that there be "an independent witness who testifies that the percipient related his experience to him before he came to know, by normal means, that the experience had been veridical," and that the experience should not be more than five years old, between the time of the experience and the reporting of it. The American Society, in developing the data it had recorded, sought to employ the services of a psychologist for interview and evaluation purposes.

In England, the Society for Psychical Research had reported the results of its own survey in a volume of its *Proceedings*. This issue is entitled "Report (1959) on Enquiry into Spontaneous Cases." In line with Mrs. Rhine's approach, the survey included the following two categories: the "unrealistic dream" symbolic in content, and the "realistic dream" which, "like a photograph of the actual event or fact, shows true detail, with no imaginative or embroidered addition." Some statistical conclusions were reached in this survey, but their numerical bases were narrow. It was found difficult to engage in psychological interviews. The report was compiled by the Society's then research secretary, Miss Celia Green.

A comparatively ambitious survey was undertaken in Germany, under the auspices of the Institute for Border Areas of Psychology and Mental Hygiene, University of Freiburg im Breisgau. The material was similar in quality and quantity to the data collected in the United States and Great Britain. Here, too, letters had been sent in by correspondence responding to news of the Institute's interest, conveyed by radio, a newspaper, and magazine articles. The Freiburg Institute investigated more than a thousand allegedly paranormal spontaneous cases, including much dream material. The results, divided by psychological and statistical aspects, were compiled by Dr. Gerhard Sannwald and published in the Institute's quarterly journal, the *Zeitschrift für Parapsychologie und Grenzgebiete der Psychologie*. Experiences in the waking and dreaming state were evenly divided: 50.1 percent were dreams, while 49.9 percent were waking experiences. Half the reported material was of a "realistic" rather than "symbolic" nature. Dr. Sannwald observed:

> The picture language of the dream, because it is a product of the unconscious, is often symbolic in nature. The surprising division of the dream data may be attributed to two reasons. To begin with the relationship between a symbolically disguised dream and an actual event is not always recognized. That is to say, the symbolism is often elusive and the case is therefore not regarded as paranormal in nature. On the other hand, many of the experiences that are regarded as symbolically significant by the person reporting them, are not so considered by the evaluator. These cases have thus only a limited chance of being incorporated into the case collection. In fact, among cases that are rejected, symbolic cases greatly outnumber realistic cases.

172   *The Dream and Human Societies*

The German study also attempted to analyze the material in terms of "conviction" or "nonconviction" of those reporting the cases. Dr. Sannwald wrote that "a certain group of people know immediately, with varying feelings of conviction, that an experience is related to a specific realistic event, that it is 'meaningful.'" Very often, he continues, the original experience creates a tension of expectation which is released when the expected event takes place; this, of course, refers to a precognitive dream. This feeling is more in the nature of "relief or release than a feeling of surprise." A second group of people do not attribute any particular significance to an experience of a precognitive nature. These are then truly surprised or even shocked, particularly if they had previously doubted or denied what they regarded as a "supernormal" experience.

Among the total number of cases recorded at Freiburg, those reported as having been experienced with a feeling of conviction, which included the telepathic and precognitive dreams, made up about 62 percent, while those reported without a feeling of conviction came to about 38 percent. It may be interpolated here that a feeling of conviction and expectation probably tends toward an evaluation of a subsequent event in paranormal terms, although the oversimilarity of the event to the original precognitive dream may be relatively slight. Furthermore, behind a professed feeling of "nonconviction" may well lie a hidden desire to experience the functioning of paranormal faculties. The surprise or shock may, in such a case, be in the nature of unconscious camouflage of the recorder's basic attitudes.

Speaking specifically of precognitive experiences, the Freiburg study noted that 31.5 percent of such experiences are reported as originating in dreams, while 20.6 percent are reported to occur during the waking state.

Dr. Sannwald's effort to establish a psychological evaluation of the reported spontaneous cases was based on the utilization of depth psychological criteria, designed to separate paranormal, or a-causal, phenomena from events that were causal in origin. The writer cited the case of a woman who dreamed of an appendectomy which, in fact, was performed on her a few days later. He also refers to a woman who dreams of a motorcycle accident, a dream ignored by her son with laughter and derision, but nevertheless suffered by him that very day. Dr. Sannwald notes that, in the first case, the woman may have been subconsciously aware that the appendix was inflamed at the time of the dream; and in the second case, the son's very defiance of his mother's warnings may have created a psychodynamic situation that caused the accident anticipated in the dream. He adds that such cases are notable because of a possible psychological bias, or unconscious communication of feelings, experiences, and stimuli that may "help to create an apparently precognitive dream."

From the German material, the following dream may also be cited:

We did not receive news from my youngest brother for quite some time during the war. I then dreamed as follows: I stood before a high painting that was hidden by a curtain. I opened the curtain by pulling a cord. There, life-size, was a picture of my brother in full uniform. A delicate cloud of smoke rose from his left hand. The next morning, I told my mother, "Willy has probably suffered a slight wound in his left hand." Shortly afterwards, we received a postal card from my brother. He had scribbled on the margin, "I have been slightly wounded in the left hand."

Dr. Sannwald's interpretation of the factors contributing to this particular dream refers to an underlying affective condition, based on the fact that the girl was worried about her brother, and that lack of news presumably deepened this anxiety. Under these conditions, the evaluation continues, the object of her concern could well appear in a dream, and she might also draw some parallel between her dream experience and the possible link with actual fact. Even the interpretation of the cloud of smoke in terms of a wound should be ascribed to affect and anxiety. Nevertheless, Dr. Sannwald observed that "a telepathic element would seem to be indicated," adding, however, that the brother-sister relationship may encompass elements that would allow for a depth psychological or psychoanalytic explanation; he wonders why she sees her brother as a painting that she "unveils," or why she should see a "cloud of smoke," rather than an actual wound, blood, or a surgical dressing. His observations illustrate that dreams apparently telepathic may be approached from a variety of psychological viewpoints.

A step in the direction of controlling dreams by experimentation has been made at the suggestion of Dr. Montague Ullman (Maimonides Hospital, New York.) In 1961, the Research Division of the Parapsychology Foundation began a pilot study in New York, designed to explore the possibility of inducing telepathic elements in dreams. It was attempted to create laboratory conditions and to record phenomena, which until then had apparently appeared only quite spontaneously. Dr. Ullman designed experiments that combined electroencephalographic recording with the rapid eye movement (REM) technique. The experimental design was the following:

The subject (dreamer) spent a night in the laboratory, attached to an electroencephalograph (EEG). Electrodes were attached to different parts of the skull and to the outer canthus in order to register electric potentials of the brain and the movement of the eyes. When the subject was asleep, the experimenter or another participant tried to communicate a certain stimulus from another soundproof room, or perhaps even from another part of town. This might be done by opening an envelope containing a picture of specific factual or emotional content. The picture was selected at random from a collection built up for this purpose. It was unknown to both participants.

When the rapid eye movement and a certain stage of brain waves indicated a dream, the subject was awakened through an intercom system, asked to tell his dream, and his statements were tape-recorded. About four dreams were recorded nightly in this way. It was assumed that the subject's dream might contain some elements of the target picture that had been used in the experiment. The EEG methods made it relatively easy to indicate the actual moment of dreaming.

Two levels of evaluation were used: (*a*) The data can be qualitatively evaluated in case studies; psychological evaluation can examine the relationship between telepathic stimuli and actual dream content. (*b*) A quantitative rating method can be applied: an independent judge receives the dreams of each night, together with ten different illustrations, only one of which is the picture actually used as the target picture; the judge does not know which of the ten was the target and thus must rate the individual illustration against apparent similarities to dream content. Ideally the target picture would receive the highest rate on the established scale. A variety of subjects were used in these experiments, and, in a new series undertaken in New York by Dr. Inge Strauch (Freiburg) during a stay in New York in 1962, various refinements in techniques, in the selection of subjects, and in evaluation methods were introduced, including biographic-psychological information on subjects and further psychological interviews after each night's session. This work is continuing; it will require further refinements, repetitions by other researchers, and the integration of new findings in psychology, physiology, and other scientific areas.

Such dream experiments illustrate both the dilemma and the challenge that parapsychological studies face today. They are conscious of the strict requirements of experimental controls, the need for repetition, careful design, and execution. At the same time, the fabric of parapsychological phenomena is a good deal more delicate than are the phenomena examined in the natural sciences. Parapsychologists must, for instance, be aware that the experimenter himself may play a subtle but influential role in the experiment he conducts.

Beyond this, however, man's dreams have retained, even in our supposedly rational civilization, an aura of the otherworldly; man, dreaming, is somehow believed to be in touch with worlds outside his daily ken, even if these be the worlds of his own unconscious. In dreams, we meet the archaic language of symbols; we are in touch with our ancient traditions of myth, or with our childhood wishes and fears; our dreams reflect the pressures and hopes of our daily lives, and are thus peculiarly sensitive to manipulation and observation.

Parapsychological dream studies call for these unusual qualities of research: detached, scientific, cerebral preparation and execution of investigation or experiment; sensitive understanding of the delicate, the deeply emotion-laden, traditionally magical that may lie at the root of not yet understood phenomena. To strike a balance between detachment and understanding, between the scholar's role as outsider and as participant—that is the challenge that gives this work its unique, demanding quality.

Bibliography

Bender, Hans, and John Mischo. 1961. " 'Praekognition' in Traumserien," *Zeitschrift für Parapsychologie und Grenzgebiete der Psychologie* (Freiburg im Breisgau, Institut für Grenzgebiete der Psychologie und Psychohygiene), 5 (no. 1):114–201.

Broad, C. D. 1959. "Dreaming, and some of its implications," *Proceedings of the Society for Psychical Research* (London), 52 (part 188):53–78.

"Conference on spontaneous phenomena, July 11 to 17, 1955." 1957. *Proceedings of Four Conferences of Parapsychological Studies*. New York: Parapsychology Foundation. Pp. 101–103.

Dale, Laura A., Rhea White, and Gardner Murphy. 1962. "A selection of cases from a recent survey of spontaneous ESP phenomena," *Journal of the American Society for Psychical Research* (New York), 56 (no. 1):3–47.

Gurney, E., F. W. H. Myers, and F. Podmore. 1886. *Phantasms of the Living*. 2 vols. London: Trubner.

Jaffé, Aniela. 1958. *Geistererscheinungen und Vorzeichen*. Introduction by C. G. Jung. Zurich: Rascher.

Myers, F. W. H. 1895. "The subliminal self," *Proceedings of the Society for Psychical Research* (London), 11:487 ff.

"Report (1959) on enquiry into spontaneous cases." 1960. *Proceedings of the Society for Psychical Research* (London), 53 (part 191):83–194.

Rhine, Louisa E. 1961. *Hidden Channels of the Mind*. New York: William Sloane.

Richet, Charles. 1923. *Thirty Years of Psychical Research*. London: Macmillan.

Saltmarsh, H. E. 1938. *Foreknowledge*. London: G. Bell & Sons.

Sannwald, Gerhard. 1959. "Statistische Untersuchungen an Spontanphänomenen," *Zeitschrift für Parapsychologie und Grenzgebiete der Psy-*

chologie. (Freiburg im Breisgau, Institut für Grenzgebiete der Psychologie und Psychohygiene), 3 (no. 1):59–119.

———. 1960. "Zur Psychologie paranormaler Spontanphänomene," *Zeitschrift für Parapsychologie und Grenzgebiete der Psychologie* (Freiburg im Breisgau, Institut für Grenzgebiete der Psychologie und Psychohygiene), 3 (nos. 2, 3):149–191.

Servadio, Emilio. 1956. "Telepathy: a psychoanalytic view," *Tomorrow,* 4 (no. 2):35–41.

Sidgwick, Eleanor Mildred. 1961. *Phantasms of the Living: Cases of Telepathy Printed in the Journal of the Society for Psychical Research during Thirty-five years.* Bound in one volume with *Phantasms of the Living* by E. Gurney, F. W. H. Myers, and Frank Podmore. Abridged and edited by E. M. Sidgwick. Introduction by Gardner Murphy. New Hyde Park, N.Y.: University Books.

Van Eeden, Frederik. 1913. "A study of dreams," *Proceedings of the Society for Psychical Research* (London), 26 (part 67):437–461.

9

Toward a Phenomenological Analysis of Sleep and the Dream

ENZO PACI

In an essay entitled "Réflexions sur une problématique husserlienne de l'inconscient, Husserl et Hegel," Adolphe de Waelhens observed that "we are witnessing an ever growing rapprochement between theoreticians of anthropology with an authentic psychoanalytic inspiration and phenomenologists concerned both with remaining faithful to the Husserlian spirit and with extending its reign to the human sciences, particularly those related to psychology in its broadest sense."[1]

I think de Waelhens is right, although I cannot go along with his interpretations of particulars. Nevertheless, I must say that generally phenomenology tends inevitably to develop as anthropology. In *Krisis*[2] Husserl affirms that psychology is the "science of decisions." At

---

[1] *Edmund Husserl: 1859–1959. Recueil commémoratif* (The Hague: Martinus Nijhoff, 1959), pp. 221–237, at p. 221.
[2] Edmund Husserl, *Die Krisis der europäischen Wissenschaften und die transzendentale Phänomenologie,* ed. Walter Biemel, Husserliana, Vol. VI (The Hague: Martinus Nijhoff, 1954) cited in the text as *Krisis.*

the same time, it should be recalled that in *Ideen II*³ Husserl had already analyzed the indissoluble relationship between the three rules: of the body (*Leib*), of the soul (*Seele*), and of the spirit (*Geist,* which more or less corresponds to Hegel's "objective spirit").

Leib is rooted in the *Erlebnis* of this material life, in the precategorical causality of this life, and in the "circumstantiality" of the *Lebenswelt* which precedes all scientific elaboration.

Lebenswelt, basically explained in the first section of the third part of *Krisis,* is not a map, but the landscape without which it is impossible to construct the map (according to an example Merleau-Ponty derived from Husserl).⁴

Lebenswelt is whole and complete, whereas the fields of all the sciences are specialized. *Lebenswelt* is original while the scientific domains are derived. Generally speaking, we may say that the *Lebenswelt* is the world as it presents itself in its diverse modalities to the subject and to the intersubjectivity, that is to say, to the dialectical relationships among the subjects.

Lebenswelt is not created by the subject (Husserl is not, as a matter of fact, an idealist). Rather it must be understood as a world "pregiven" from all time, the *vorgegebene Welt* of Husserl. For this reason, Husserl, in *Krisis,* criticizes Kant's transcendental "ego" and argues for a concrete "ego," a concrete monad that is always a psychophysical unity, a unity of soul and body (*Leib*).

Concrete monads, as Husserl explains, particularly in *Manuskript E,*⁵ are bound together by genetic concatenation. A concrete subject is therefore someone who is in contact with how-he-came-to-be, and in contact with how-the-past-has-formed-him. In the present, he "lives" in the first person (*erlebt*), and it should be emphasized that in phenomenology one must always start from the present and consciousness of the present. Care, however, must be taken; this consciousness is never something set apart—never, then, the occasion for a philosophy of consciousness—and

---

³ Edmund Husserl, *Ideen zu einer reinen Phänomenologie und phänomenologischen Philosophie* (Book II), ed. Marly Biemel, Husserliana, Vol. IV (The Hague: Martinus Nijhoff, 1952), cited in text as *Ideen II.*
⁴ Maurice Merleau-Ponty, *Phénoménologie de la perception* (Paris: Gallimard, 1945), p. iii.
⁵ The letters *E, K, D, A* refer to the subdivision of the *Manuskripts* by Husserl which can be found at the Archives Husserl in Louvain. This denomination was arranged by L. Landgrebe and Eugen Fink. Under letter *A* are collected manuscripts referring to "worldly phenomenology"; under *D* those referring to "primordial constitution" (of which "transcendental aesthetic" is part); under *E* those referring to "intersubjective constitution"; *K* refers to the manuscripts concerning the problems studied in the *Krisis.* The Arabic or Roman numerals are used to list the manuscripts of a same group.

Husserl conceives of it always as situated in time and incarnate in the world. We can add, parenthetically, that this position disavows much of the criticism existentialists have directed at Husserl.

One of Husserl's fundamental conditions is that the beginning must always be in the present. The present is origin and reflection; consciousness is always consciousness in which what is happening is retained by *retention* and the future is awaited by *protention*.

In retention, the present becomes the past and is eventually lost in oblivion. In order to find the forgotten present, it must be rediscovered and uncovered. This is accomplished by means of a phenomenological analysis of the past, or more precisely, by means of genetic phenomenology that intentionally turns its attention toward the structure of time by which it is possible to understand the present through the past.

The past is covered: it must be uncovered. This uncovering is possible if phenomenological analysis uncovers the subject's, the monad's, forgotten history. This history has its beginning in a birth that I can never recall and make re-present (i.e., reconstitute as the present). I cannot recall my birth and consequently I cannot recall the first bonds between my *own "ego"* with *the "other,"* what Husserl, in *Manuskript K III* (July 11, 1935), calls the *"first Einfühlung."* Origin, then—and this ought to be remembered always, even though phenomenologists sometimes do not—has two aspects: (1) it is primordially and above all the present wherein everything has its origin because it is only in the present that I have awareness, and because from the present alone lines can be sent out to the past and to the future; (2) it is the precise and individual temporal origin in which the monad, by being born, begins in time.

Birth binds a man to his parents. For instance, it gives the hidden *Einfühlung* into the mother. But by means of this *Einfühlung*, birth also binds a man to his parents' parents, to all past history, so to speak. The phenomenologist's task consists in re-presenting this past in the present "ego," although this task appears to be infinite and can therefore never be entirely achieved. The greatest part of the past remains in shadow, in oblivion, in darkness, and even the past that is not truly forgotten is often hidden for various reasons. Phenomenology has the task of uncovering the past, bringing it into the light, and transforming it into phenomenon.

Looked at from this angle, phenomenological method appears related to psychoanalytic method. As Eugen Fink has clearly explained in Beilage XXXI of the *Krisis*,[6] however, the phenomenologist knows very well that one cannot start with the unconscious, and that the beginning must necessarily always and solely be made from consciousness.

---

[6] Husserl, *Krisis*, pp. 514–516.

Consciousness for phenomenology, as we know it, is always "intentional," which means that it is always "consciousness of something." This consciousness may be awareness of some small part of the past, perhaps even something forgotten but linked to the present by a very thin thread, like Proust's *madeleine*. If I analyze the *madeleine* phenomenologically, I will find the past in it. The *sedimentation* of the forgotten or hidden past is to be found in the perception of the present. Intentionality that looks toward the hidden past in the sedimentation that we find in actual perception is an *intentionality toward the sediment* and permits the discovery and evoking into the present of what is hidden in the actual perception. Thus Proust finds his whole life beginning with Combray in the *madeleine*;[7] he rediscovers the maternal kiss with which his work begins and this leads him finally to transform time lost into rediscovered time.

It can be said that something comparable happens in the memory we have of a dream. It is by starting from what we have retained in the state of wakefulness that we can reconstruct in the present the dream that is past. If we claim that the dream preserves past experiences, it amounts to saying that the individual is uncovering what he has forgotten, or wants to forget and hide, of the past experiences of his own life.

I have already said that past experiences can never be re-presented completely and wholly. Deep down they are bound to parents and to the whole history of humanity. We can then come to this conclusion: the study of dreams is part of humanity's great study of the past, part of the reconstruction of an unfolded history.

The dream leads us back to the mother, much as we see it in Proust's *Remembrance of Things Past*. It leads us back to the *"first Einfühlung,"* to the first experience of the other, that is to say, to all the problems of the relationship between the ego and the other.

Since the *first Einfühlung* cannot be re-presented, we look in the present for the relationship with the other, just as Proust, for example, sought it in Gilberte and Albertine. We look for the *Einfühlung* in the opposite sex before anything else. But this is only a beginning. In reality the *Einfühlung* sought for in the present leads, by a complicated constitutive process, to the formation of groups and communities oriented toward the future, toward the horizon of the future.

To repeat, the study of dreams becomes fundamental for anthropology and all the human sciences. Because in the dream the past is deposited to be rediscovered in the present, the phenomenology of the dream is analogous to the activity of history. Moreover, as far as the phenomenology of the dream is a waiting, a preparation, an intention, and an

---

[7] Marcel Proust, *Swann's Way* (New York: Modern Library, 1928), p. 54.

activity for the future, in the present it is analogous to the construction of a history of humanity according to a finality, a *telos*.

The elements of the past which are necessary to the *praxis* of the present to build a directed, teleological future, are to be found in the dream that starts from the present. This is why comparative anthropology finds that in all civilizations the dream has two characteristics: it appears (1) as a search for a forgotten past, for the origin, for the connection with divine creation or with the gods; and (2) as the expectation, the hope, and the preparation for the future.[8] It is in this second sense that the dream is closely bound to prophetism, as is very clearly seen in Jewish and Islamic civilizations.

As indicated, the dream is also closely tied to the problem of the ego and the other, to the problem of the others, to the dialectical problem of subjects, of groups, and of communities. We say dialectical here because an ego does not and cannot understand completely another ego, just as one group is never identical with another group.

Each community and each group has its function in the history of humanity, in the ongoing history or, as Sartre says, in the "ongoing totalization."

Dialectics becomes a battle to the extent that one group seeks to reduce the other to a thing (I am referring to the "reduction to a thing," or *Verdinglichung*, of Marx), and from this point of view consciousness is a "becoming conscious" that begins with the fact that as an individual I am, or my group is, or my people are, reduced to things: from subjects we have been reduced to objects. Becoming conscious has its beginnings, then, in the objectivization I have undergone. In phenomenological psychoanalysis this situation gives rise to sadistic or masochistic behavior, behavior that is to be found not only in individuals but also in groups and communities. Phenomenology fights against this reduction to a thing, this objectivization, and this sadistic or masochistic behavior. It fights all this through inducing awareness, with its *praxis* oriented toward the future.

What has preceded is related to the psychiatric study of dreams. But there is more here than a psychiatry for the individual. There is a psychiatry that must look to humanity's crises and can use for this the analysis of all the dreams of humanity's past, and of the manner in which dreams have influenced the history of all people. This psychiatry of crisis is an anthropology and a sociology as well, but not a neutral anthropology, nor a neutral sociology. These sciences must be oriented, must be directed

---

[8] See Henry Corbin, "The Visionary Dream in Islamic Spirituality," pp. 381 ff., below, and Fazlur Rahman, "Dream Imagination and ʿĀlam al-mithāl," pp. 409 ff., below.

toward a *telos,* they must try to bring about the constitution of a human society wherein the relationships exist between subjects, and where groups, communities, and peoples are never reduced to objects.

This is the teleological society of which Husserl speaks: a society that appears to us today as a never-ending task demanding a synthesis of the sciences in the sense that the foundation of all the sciences begins in the *Lebenswelt,* begins, that is to say, in experience of the subjects as first persons.

From the phenomenological point of view, anthropology is the "science of the *Lebenswelt*" of subjects whose task is the constitution of a society for which, as Husserl says, it is possible to conquer naturalism, objectivization, and oblivion.

The study of dreams is a fundamental aspect of this anthropology understood as science of the *Lebenswelt.* The dream lends itself to such a study. It presents two aspects: from one point of view the dream is absolutely individual and incommunicable. As Roger Caillois said, "there is nothing more personal than a dream, nothing else so imprisons a person in irremediable solitude, nothing else is as stubbornly resistant to being shared." [9]

It is then an experience of solipsism. We know that for Husserl phenomenological methodology not only had to begin with consciousness and the present, but it had also to be in the beginning, by way of an experimentation, solipsistic.

Roger Caillois also speaks, however, of the temptation of imagining two or more people, or even a multitude (of people), having the same dream, or parallel dreams, or complementary dreams.[10] James Joyce has given in to this temptation in *Finnegans Wake.* *Ulysses* is the story of one day. *Finnegans Wake* is the story of one night. It is the description of the dreams in the night of one man, be he Finnegan from the Irish ballad, or Humphrey Chimpden Earwicker, Joyce himself, Joyce's reader, or Here Comes Everybody, that is, Everyman.

As María Zambrano says,[11] poetry, literature, and the myths of humanity in humanity's history are born of dreams, of images, and of the *phantom beings* of dreams. Giambatista Vico has said the same in his *Scienza Nuova,* and Joyce evokes Vico in *Finnegans Wake* as he evoked the *Odyssey* in *Ulysses.* It must be remembered that Vico's *Scienza Nuova* is the first great work in which an attempt was made to treat anthropology as a phenomenology of humanity, wherein dreams, myths, language,

---

[9] See Roger Caillois, "Logical and Philosophical Problems of the Dream," pp. 23 ff., above.
[10] *Ibid.*
[11] See "The Dream and Literary Creation," pp. 189 ff., below.

symbols, and culture as a whole are studied with fantasy and imagery as the starting points.

Here we broach the great problem of the relationship among *phantasm,* myth, image, and dream. The problem of phantasms was studied by Husserl in the very rich analyses of *Manuskript D,* which gives us Husserl's *transcendental aesthetics.* It is helpful to remember here that phantasms also play an essential part in the state of wakefulness. Phantasms are also studied by *Gestalt psychology.*

A visual phantasm is the perspective view we have of an object so that the phantasm changes in relation to its closeness or its distance. There are not only visual, but auditory and tactile phantasms as well.

Phantasms are not real things. They are only aspects and perspectives of real things, and not bound together by what Husserl calls the precategorical and circumstantial causalities that bind real things together. For phenomenology, phantasms belong outside the storehouse of real things because they are not real like my subject of the first person which is rooted in the *Lebenswelt* or in the *vorgegebene Welt.* They are "representations" of things: visions, anticipations, presumptions. They are not at the center where the subject or the subjects live; they are peripheral. They are far from the center light, or *Kern.* They are things slipped away, or, as Husserl calls them, the *Abschattungen.* These are, for example, the modalities by means of which things far away are close to me when I am looking at them. In this sense phantasms are symbols of things, if it is true that the symbol is above all the way in which the distant and the absent are present in me. Although we cannot accept the basic argument in Merleau-Ponty's last essay "L'oeil et l'esprit" [12] he deserves the credit for analyzing this situation as far as it concerns painting. What he says is valid for all the human arts and it holds in a very particular way, to begin with, for language.

Language has its origin in the concretization of the ego, in the concrete monad situated in time. It originates in the behavior and the gestures of the ego; in this sense its origins are "gesticular." Language is possible because it is expression by symbols, images, and phantasms. This is why it can communicate, bring the far and near together, and it can be representational (not *specular* as Wittgenstein understood it, but *intentional*) of world, life, and history. This means that language is a fundamental factor in the making of history, and that a summation at any point in history's course is made possible by language, that is to say, by culture.

We should bear in mind that we are never wholly awake just as we are never wholly asleep. During sleep, language "speaks" in dreams.

---

[12] Maurice Merleau-Ponty, "L'oeil et l'esprit," *Les Temps modernes,* 184–185 (1961) 194–227.

When we are awake language "speaks" with words of a culture, in aesthetic images, in myths, symbols, and the linguistic techniques of science. In sleep, we are free from the cares of the present and consequently the past and the future break into sleep in a seemingly disorderly way. In the waking state the past and the future are organized for the *praxis* of the present. It is precisely this organization that provides the basis for culture and allows us to attribute meaning to life and to history.

The task of determining history's significance is a continuing battle between what is hidden by distance and what is hidden by being forgotten. It is a battle against a negative past, against heredity and error, and against evil. It is an attempt as positive transformation of the world, of man, and of society. The interpretation of dreams, the study of myths and their meanings are very important factors in transforming humanity's history into the *praxis* of the present. This takes place in the continuous confrontations between "the dreamer's time of fantasy" and the time of wakefulness, between irreversible time and that temporalization wherein significant time is realized, time that, despite irreversibility and the inevitability of death, gives continuity and meaning to the history of individuals and of humanity.

Just as a dream preserves the continuity between my ego before sleep and my awakened ego, so dreams analyzed, by use of comparative anthropology and history, connect for us the various phases of humanity's history. The study of dreams can also be seen as a study of the continuity of civilizations and cultures: it partakes of the dialectics of history. Man sleeps and awakens; the continuity of his ego remains in the dream. Husserl came to this conclusion in the analysis he devoted in *Manuskript A IV 14* (1930–1932) to birth, death, sleep, and the unconscious.[13]

In mentioning the unconscious, it ought to be reaffirmed that the unconscious for Husserl depends always on presence and consciousness. The center, the *Kern,* is always presence. The unconscious coincides with what becomes remote from presence, with the *Abschattungen*. It is inherent especially in time, but it is necessarily linked to space. In the final analysis, it can be said that for phenomenology the unconscious is also what is becoming, what is called the external, material world.[14] From this point of view the unconscious is the modality by which external matter is made present in the subject. Understood in this way, the unconscious is never entirely "presentable" to consciousness. It is for this

---

[13] Cf. Ida Bona, "L'interesse e la fenomenologia del sonno," *Aut Aut: Rivista di filosofia e di cultura,* 64 (1961), 362–365.

[14] See my essay, "La psicologia fenomenologica e il problema della relazione tra inconscio e mondo esterno," *Aut Aut: Rivista di filosofia e di cultura,* 64 (1961), 314–334.

reason that man has his roots in unconscious matter or, better, in inert matter, which means that the task of transforming the unconscious into consciousness is originally entrusted to a working with matter, a working to conquer inertia, or as Sartre calls it, the *practico-inert praxis*. The history of humanity can be looked upon as a constant interpretation of dreams, as a continual psychoanalysis, and as a transformation of the hidden into the revealed, of obscurity into phenomenon. But the historical process is *praxis* and work. It is a perpetual battle against inert matter. It is a technique for transforming matter into matter formed by man, into the tools for the life of human society. As far as this *praxis* in its concrete form contains a psychoanalysis, an analysis of what is hidden and an analysis of man's dreams, it is not a blind *praxis,* but a conscious, seeing *praxis*. It is, in brief, the transformation of a dream into significant truth.

10

Dreams and Literary Creation

MARÍA ZAMBRANO

Dreams come from a waking state. They are in fact a state of waking. If this were not so, wakefulness could not capture them. This is especially true for dreams arising from a poetic impulse, which confers on them a greater degree of validity. In contrast, consciousness can grasp purely psychophysiological dreams only as simple facts.

Creative dreams, the nature of which we propose to define here, do indeed possess an obsessive character. They are what they are, so to speak, suggesting a conflict without apparent solution, an aporia. They enclose the individual within a magical circle, as does the concept of the totality of life. And thus, the individual who experiences them finds himself as if confronted by this totality of life, as if life were a magical circle to transcend, and furthermore, to transcend by living.

Confronted by this totality, the individual feels and even sees himself as if before an unscalable mountain, a limitless desert, or an inert expanse. He does this in dreams symbolically, and in waking by virtue of those moments when time seems to stand still. Such images reveal to the individual a dichotomized situation in which life has undergone a schism: on one side is the individual alone, the totality of life as something to be explored, to attempt to grasp, but in vain. The person who experiences such a confrontation will necessarily find it impossible to retain his identity intact.

To the image of the mountain that occurs in this situation, there corresponds, without a doubt, the pyramid into which conscience, through rationalization, transforms it. And when this dream image is subjected to reason, it then acquires its full symbolism.

The symbol, then, is a product of reason. An image charged with significance realizes the full potential of its symbolism only after having been subjected to the process of reason, because only then is its significance fully accepted consciously, and extended to all regions of the soul. Until this has taken place, it is only a fetish, a magical figure that resists exposure to reason or remains at the threshold of a reason that rejects it. It cannot be deciphered; it floats about uncontrolled.

To decipher an oneiric image, a dreamed story, cannot therefore be to analyze it, for to analyze it is to subject it to waking conscience which rejects it, to confront two mutually exclusive worlds. On the contrary, to decipher it is to guide it toward the clarity of conscience and of reason, extracting it from the obscure, timeless limbo in which it lies. This may happen only if clarity arises out of a reason that accepts the image because it is capable of incorporating it: a broad, total reason, a poetic reason, both metaphysical and religious.

It is true that in modern postrationalist civilization the conscience of the "normal" man has lost contact with the rest of his being. His body and his soul are as strange "phenomena" to him. With this besieged conscience, and by virtue of tenets that will not be examined here, he thinks that analysis is the only method of acquiring an understanding of himself and of that obscure zone of dreams within himself—dreams that are the dawn of conscience.

It has been discovered, nevertheless, that the mythical content of religions is the very manifestation of the life of the soul, a type of procession of objectivized dreams in which the human being is revealed to himself, while at the same time seeking his place in the universe.

Man's search for his place in the universe consists of his passing through various zones, of journeying, in the sense of having to cross numerous thresholds; and this is possible only through a very profound transformation, one that must come from the very center of his being.

Independent of the various religions, and with autonomous existence, there have appeared the great genres of verbal creation, which are like steps in the procession of dreams, activation of the human being's irrepressible drive to transcend.

Dreams have often been known to come true. One of the two ways in which they may do this is without suffering any transformation at all, that is to say, by passing over the threshold between sleep and waking without undergoing any transformation, imposing their timelessness on time. These are the tormenting obsessions that are sometimes acted out: misdeeds, crime, violence. The application is not only to an individual life, but also to the collective. The other way in which dreams pass over the threshold that separates them from waking—from reality—is to realize themselves through transformation, or reexpression. The dream is by nature an inmost recess, a quantum of the depths of the soul. When poetically realized, it enters into the realm of freedom and time, in which the individual more easily recognizes and rescues himself. Through such a transformation the dream emerges from its previous obscurity, and its significance is brought to light.

It is a question, then, of trying to know a dream by taking its elements in their elementary sense, not by analyzing, but rather by simply telling. But how is this possible? One may dream of being king through having killed his father and married his mother; or one may dream of being king of a city ravaged by a plague, and then awaken just as he is about to learn the reason and the cure. Even more deeply entangled, one may dream of killing his father and subsequently finding himself married to his mother; or simply the latter. The simple act of recounting the dream would have a liberating effect not achievable in the act of dreaming itself. Or perhaps only through dreaming it in another form would exorcism be achieved, the exorcism being, in this case, the simple story.

THE ORIGIN OF TRAGEDY: OEDIPUS

At a certain level in the development of conscience and the activation of the concept of freedom in history, tragedy no longer exists. One might say it has been surpassed.

The explanation may be the following: the specifically tragic situation is no longer valid. The suffering that previously served the cause of transcendence and freedom is nothing more than an anomalous suffering, or even a lingering illness, if indeed all illnesses of "being" are not always so. Certain religions, philosophy since its birth in Greece up until recently, and entire periods of music and even of poetry appear as having surpassed the concept of tragic knowledge, that which is acquired through suffering the conflict through to the point of purification. But this declaration of having surpassed tragedy has almost always occurred a little hastily, in the desire to take advantage of that glimpse of freedom and the brief respite it permits, as happened with philosophy in Greece.

Recognition of the tragic situation, be it in an author or simply in an individual who awakens, occurs at a certain level of freedom, in an awakening of that freedom in a not unrooted conscience. Such a conscience is not alienated from the subconscious, but rather recognizes its inmost recesses. It is a conscience that has not constituted itself in an instrument of power over reality, nor denied the existence of other manifestations of temporality. It respects those feelings which, like drifting islands or obscure mists, cannot come to have conscious content, those feelings which are the obscure seeds of dreams, for that which is devoid of time is equally devoid of light.

The awakening of the conscience, which may assume the dimensions of tragic suffering, can occur only in an innocent conscience, which precedes the "pure conscience" of philosophy. Tragic awakening is an awakening from the depths of being. The conscience in which this awakening is kindled is an innocent conscience that does not impose its own law. It is a mediating conscience that does not fear a descent into the depths of the subconscious.

Since atemporality does admit varying degrees, tragic conflict may be more appropriately designated a question of infratemporality. It originates in the depths or recesses of time, from which all that is imprisoned struggles to escape. The term infratemporality suggests impending time and a suffering owing to privation of it.

The content of the tragic dream may possibly have no determined conflict, although of course the latter will always be somewhat determined by the situation and circumstances of the individual in whom it occurs. Therefore the *obstacle* dream is especially well suited to recognize the tragic conflict, owing to the representation of the barrier that reality poses to man, to the inexorable need to overcome it, and to the element of finality which seeks freedom. All these are elements that reveal the inexorable process of birth.

To be born is to have to emerge from an enclosure in which the individual cannot remain, and not at the risk of his existence, but rather of his essence. It means having to abandon a place in which the being is enveloped in himself, submerged in darkness. To be born, in the primary sense, and actually in all other possible senses, is to take on the autonomy of one's own being and, therefore, to confront light and what it signifies: to see and be seen. Light is the atmosphere of supreme exposure for man, one in which he must allow himself to be seen before he himself sees. Feeling and knowing oneself to be the object of another's sight is a subject for philosophers, for those who have surpassed, or believe they have surpassed, the concept of tragedy. If Oedipus had been granted a second life after his purifying blindness, he would have had no choice but to dedicate himself completely to seeing, according to the belief of the first Greek philosophers, the founders of that discipline.

The protagonist of the tragedy may achieve vision, as does

Antigone, who occupies the highest step in the tragic scale, and is a victim of sacrifice rather than a protagonist of tragedy.

The anguish the tragic protagonist suffers is born of knowing himself to be seen, and furthermore, of having to actively expose himself to view. In the corresponding dream it is caused by having put himself into a position in which he will be visible. "Threshold" dreams in which there appears a clear empty space are not tragic, since the emptiness represents freedom, and the threshold to be crossed symbolizes the last stronghold of a situation that was tragic, its termination, and an entrance into personal history.

Every poetic tragedy bears within itself a dream that is slowly and laboriously brought to light. Visibility is the action peculiar to the tragic author and to the tragic dream itself. It is, in essence, a question of something being brought to light. And therefore it is the revelation of a moment, a single instant, in which the depths in which it is buried are penetrated and exposed. Thus the protagonist of tragedy is tied to what happens, captive to his dream; for it is indeed a dream, although it occurs in waking.

Something has happened to him, a vision. He has seen something he cannot dismiss from his mind, and the act of seeing is also an act of happening.

To see is in itself awesome. The light in which we see is kindled with the participation of the human being, for there is no sight that does not imply acceptance of being seen, a willing appearance. Man suffers a passion for light, and in it, seeing and allowing himself to be seen, he continues to be born; he re-creates himself.

At birth, the being goes beyond the boundaries that encircle the situation in which he finds himself, goes beyond its horizon. At the moment of being born, there is no horizon, just as there is none when one crosses a threshold. Movement consumes vision; births are always blind.

But it is not fatalistically that one is born blind. Blindness occurs because of a failure of the individual at the decisive moment, through a hesitation or an error in direction. Then comes the tragic situation as *fatum;* the magical circle is created.

This is the situation in *Oedipus Rex*. Oedipus was to be born; it was a matter of an instant. He did not achieve it and thus remained tied to the womb, an idea the author of the fable could not express in any way other than to have him marry his mother, which in the reality of history can happen, and which, moreover, may be a psychological reality, according to the well-known Oedipus complex. But in reality, it is a question of inertia; the inhibition of an essential, existential, or essential-existential movement; an inertia that diverts *eros* from its transcendent direction.

The individual's failure to act bears with it the consolidation of the initial blindness. And thus Oedipus does not see that he must be born, above all, as a man and not as a king, nor as anything else. He becomes like a character who hides his identity behind a mask, the person without pores in a dream, even more hermetic than the initial dream.

And thus the dream of a real Oedipus could consist in simply seeing himself king, or in seeing the figure of a king as a vision that never leaves him and obliterates all else.

The errors committed by one who is blinded by a vision are fatal; they are consequences of having been born without fulfilling the movement appropriate to birth, without having truly been born.

Thus we see ourselves confronted with birth and death taken as fatalistic acts, not lived intimately, as is required of man, as the being who suffers his own transcendence.

Then the *nemesis* begins to operate with an implacable revenge. Being itself takes revenge. The sphinx is almost a mockery, since it is the figure of Oedipus himself who does not recognize himself in her, and, more precisely, misses the invitation to anagnorisis while there is still time. The *nemesis* is the justice sought by simple being, when it has been mocked. And all that it gives rise to is blind fatality.

"Who has not wanted to kill his father?" asks Dostoyevsky. Everyone who failed at birth and who is not disposed to continue being born endlessly.

Killing one's father always occurs at the crossroads. In collective history also, when pushed fatally by the unavoidable necessity of re-forming and of re-creating himself in history, man has delusions, dreaming of himself as a character, the mask of a blinded power. Oedipus dreamed of nothing more than of crowning himself, as does the beggar quite often. For man is the beggar for his own being.

If Oedipus dreamed about his mother, it was because he was already irrevocably tied to her. It was one of those dreams that reveal a real situation, a nightmare of the past, and not a desire. There may certainly be in it a degree of libidinal drive, the paradoxical pleasure in inertia, the attachment to the womb in which the soul tends to assimilate itself to matter, assuming a supreme passivity in which only a dreamed or dreamlike activity is possible. In short, the inability to let go of the past may be seen as the expression of a failure truly to emerge from the womb.

The conscience of the tragic author captures the instant not lived by the protagonist as it ought to have been. He lives it for him. But in order for the author to fulfill his role as author, and in order that he may capture that single instant, he will have to offer time in several of its dimensions. First of all, he must offer chronological time, in order to transform the conflict into fable, or the fable into a story. Just as the infratemporality, in which the larvate character and his dream were enclosed, has opened itself up to the author's view, chronological time, a product of the conscience of the author, must also open up. And there must follow a kind of supratemporality peculiar to lucidity. Only from that vantage point is infratemporality visible.

In chronological time, the case of Oedipus is simply monstrous. The story told and seen from that point of view, as if Oedipus had already been born, and, having been born, conducted himself as he did, causes Oedipus to cease to be the "guilty-innocent," and he becomes simply a man condemned to death, just as the guilty-innocent of today are condemned.

Only from a superior vantage point in time, in which conscience presents what it captures without occupying all of time, does such an event become visible. It must be approached from a time that assumes different levels of temporality without confusing them and without mutually canceling them out, without any abstraction or omission of any aspect. It is in much the same way that one may see the bottom of the sea, from the heights, without succumbing to dizziness. Supratemporality is a unity that embraces the multiple dimensions of time and permits the existence of history-fable. It contains within itself that unlived instant of being born, and the depths in which the creature remains.

The author thus effects a sacrifice, as does anyone who retrieves another who has gone astray. This is the act of an innocent conscience. The *pure* conscience of philosophy has, of course, fulfilled some sacrifice, but it is not discussed here. The difference lies in the fact that innocence is fulfilled and utilized in sacrifice; purity is acquired.

Innocence cannot be acquired. There is, therefore, a certain affinity between the author and the classical character. They may sacrifice themselves mutually, one allowing himself to be seen, and the other disposing himself to see. In this respect every tragedy is a sacrifice to the light in which man recreates himself. And the spectator participates in this recreation. The light of tragedy is not an impassive light, but rather the light of the passion of man, that being who must continue to be born. It is the light that undoes the fatalism of birth and penetrates the abyss of time. "I will wound with light your sad, dark prisons," says Celestina, exorcising the devil.

THE AUTHOR-CHARACTER: ANTIGONE

There exists, then, through time, a symbiosis between author and protagonist: the author offers the chronological time in which the story may develop, the history that originates in the loss of an instant—error, simple vacillation, or abstention. It arises from not having made the decisive move, much the same as original sin, which gave birth to human history. History arises from an initial error; but its existence is a gift of time which permits purification and salvation of the error. "Time," said E. Mounier, "is the patience of God."

In this symbiosis between character and author, it happens that the character, according to the degree in which his initial dream approaches freedom, participates in the condition of author and comes to be author of himself, coauthor. This is the difference that separates Oedipus and Antigone into two different types of characters within the tragedy. They are prototypes of species, which might be designated by their respective names. The reason for this is found in that transcendent movement that we have proposed as the real element of the creative dream. Creative dream means the dream of the author who creates, as well as the dream that needs creating; and the latter means that the character needs to re-create himself or to be re-created.

Oedipus was never born, and neither was Antigone, though in a different sense, since Antigone fulfilled true action. She was a girl who had her own life, and by fulfilling the action her own being demanded, by offering herself, rather than accepting the end offered her, she never developed into a woman. Marriage, and even life, were denied her. This was her conflict, her crossroads. Either she rejected her own being, her transcendent being, or she rejected the fulfillment of her femininity, on the verge of realization. For Oedipus the question was that of being a man, since he had no obligation to be king, unless one considers the desire to crown oneself—the superman urge—as an inherent fatality in human history. And in that case Oedipus would be the character who assumes the tragedy of having to be king, with all that it symbolizes, without having been completely born as a man; of having to be wise while submerged in blindness; of having to discover the nature of things, without knowing his own identity.

What destiny proposed to Antigone was the fulfillment of a very simple act: to rescue the body of her brother, killed in a civil war, in order to give him an honorable burial. But in order to do this, she had to surmount an obstacle: the law of a people, a human law. She was flung out to interweave life and death like a loom. She was motivated by love, not by the orexis that would have submerged her in one of those dreams that dominate a life. A dream of the libido would have loosed in her the appetite for death through the image of her brother; she would have been converted into a living dead, immobilized, and as if enshrouded. Hers was a dream of love, of knowledge and lucidity that sees its own inevitable doom, its own death, and accepts it, since it is situated in the point of time in which life and death converge. It occurs in a moment of pure transcendence in which being absorbs life and death within itself, transmuting both. She was the weaver who in an instant joins the threads of life and death, those of guilt and of unrealized justice, an act that may be performed only by love. This was her act; the rest are reasons her antagonist obliges her to give, reasons of love and of piety.

Thus she was born in a pure form, re-creating herself in sacrifice. She saves her whole line from the remote ancestral guilt that had weighed upon them like a nightmare of existence. And thus is untangled the thread of her anomalous birth, doubtless symbolized by the cord with which Jocasta strangles herself.

Antigone could be represented bearing a thread in her hands, which, like the spider, she has extracted from her own entrails. She has re-created herself in the most transcendent act of all, an inevitable sacrifice fulfilled with the lucidity in which dream and waking unite. But sacrifice is not inevitably chosen. Therefore, when it is, the victim is deprived of the innocence that characterizes the authentic victim, and represents a source of fertility.

Her sacrifice, then, resolved the guilt of her father Oedipus, the guilty-innocent who was father but not author, and who left the task of being author to his daughter, to the mediator. In Antigone the passion of the daughter is humanely fulfilled.

In this type of sacrifice the mediator must cross a deserted space, a no-man's-land, an abandoned battleground where no one dares to set foot. One must overstep one law in order to obey a new and just law.

The femininity of Antigone is revealed in the way in which she acted out that passion; in her virgin figure bearing the jug of water, symbol of virginity, of contained water that will be poured out in its entirety without having previously released a single drop. And thus Antigone is the image, in the fullness of its significance, of this ancient figure of the virgin who comes and goes to the fountain with the water jug. She is indeed herself a fountain, since life is poured from her without dispersing itself, in a transcendent form. It is a life given not for a specific human being, but rather in behalf of the conscience of every man; a life that vitalizes, frees, and saves.

She bears a remote symbol, and therefore a dream: a sacrificial dream. The virgin who comes and goes to the fountain never marries, as some cultures know. But she is not lost either. She is the sacrificed virgin that every culture needs at some time, when the threads of history have become entangled, when the riverbed threatens to run dry, or when upon the threshold of a unity to be achieved. She is the virgin sacrificed in every historical advance. Such was Joan of Arc.

But in order to fulfill the total significance of her symbolic figure, Antigone had to speak, to display conscience and thought. And for this, the innocence of her perfect virginity did not suffice. She had to acquire pure conscience, not only innocence. She had to know, to achieve that knowledge which is not sought after, but which opens up like the clear space that appears beyond certain threshold dreams, the symbol of freedom, which does not deny the fact that upon crossing that threshold, life is lost. This cannot be changed by the pure conscience of the author, by the word. The word frees because it reveals the truth of the situation, and therefore its only real solution. But it cannot avoid the consequences, for that would be to change the situation.

The word of the author has been given to the protagonist within the limits of her situation, without breaking the magical circle of her dream. To transcend is not to break through or destroy, but rather to extract from the conflict a universally valid truth needful of being revealed to the conscience.

The poet here, like the character, has fulfilled his transcendent action: he has poured forth his conscience intact—time, light—in a way that we might call transsubjective. He has converted himself, just as did Antigone, into a life beyond death. Thus emerges the life of the conscience, or what has sometimes been called spirit, the living conscience.

Sophocles could have said "I am Antigone," which is not the same as saying "Antigone is I." Antigone and he have fulfilled the same action on different levels.

II

The Sociology of the Dream

ROGER BASTIDE

For sociology, interested only in man awake, the sleeper might as well be dead. Sociology leaves it to anthropology to study the dream's place in the traditional civilizations, and to psychology to discover in the web of our dreams the profound motivations of our actions. Following the dictates of our culture, which, on each side of any curtain—iron or bamboo—is a culture of productivity, sociology pushes into the foreground the act that presupposes the tension of man awake fighting against his physical and social environment with the intention of changing it. It feels certain that work will exorcise the phantasms born of the long night whenever they threaten to interfere with Promethean deed.

The question I have asked myself is whether the sociologist is right to ignore the other half of our life, to envisage man standing and sitting, but never asleep and adream. Both starting from Bergson, and approximately at the same time, Dr. Charles Blondel defined an unhealthy consciousness as a consciousness not socialized, or ill socialized,[1] and Maurice Halbwachs ejected dream memories from the social framework of memory.[2] For Halbwachs the dream was pure memory, not social

---
[1] Charles Blondel, *La Conscience morbide* (Paris: Alcan, 1914).
[2] Maurice Halbwachs, *Les Cadres sociaux de la mémoire* (Paris: Alcan, 1914).

memory, just as for Blondel insanity was pure coenesthesia and not socialized emotionality.

How well founded is this radical division between the psychic and the social, which is like a reflection, at the scientific level, of the division in man between work and dream? Is it not about time to reestablish channels of communication between these two worlds? To see how the twilight states of our life, how the dark and obscure half of man, extends the social half exactly as the social half feeds on our dreams? In short, is it not time to attempt a sociology of the dream?

Precisely this, based on my past work, is my subject. Hence the sociology of the dream must contain two parts: the first to study the function of the dream in society; the second, the social framework of oneiric thought. Two problems, tightly tied together, for it may be that society provides a framework for oneiric thought to make it socially usable.

For the Indian or the African to consider his dreams as premonitions, these dreams must consist of images corresponding to those basic to his "waking" civilization; or at least, there must exist a system of easy translation from collective to individual representations; or, perhaps better said, the umbilical cord that ties the world of dreams to the world of myths must not have been cut by cultural norms.

For some time now anthropological studies have provided conclusive evidence for the two facts just mentioned. First there are the many social functions of the dream in primitive societies, from medical diagnosis to receiving messages from the Great Beyond, in the most diverse circumstances, in everyday life as well as in the moments of transition, in the institutions of initiation, and even in the dynamics of cultural change, from the creation of a new song, an original step in a dance, to the emergence of certain messianic movements like those born in America fifty or a hundred years ago. Second, anthropologists have brought to light what may be termed "the backstage of the dreams": the dreamer looks for the apparatus of his dreams in the vast panoply of collective representations which his civilization provides for him. Thus the door is always open between the two halves of man's life; there is a constant exchange between dream and myth, between individual fictions and social constraints; culture permeates the psychic and the psychic leaves its imprint on culture.

In our Western civilization, however, the bridges between the diurnal and nocturnal halves of man have been cut. Of course, people can always be found—and not only in the lower classes of society—who consult dream books, or who at least examine their dreams and assign to them a role in their lives. But such vital functions of the dream remain personal and never become institutionalized. On the contrary, far from constituting regularized norms of conduct they are considered aberrant; they are classed as "superstitions"; sometimes it is even suggested that people who look for significance or direction in dreams are not entirely all there.

There do exist certain places like Brazil—to limit myself to a single example—where the function of dreams has been institutionalized: the game of *bichos* is the most popular form of lottery although forbidden by law. It is based on a code that links certain numbers with certain animals, and the choice of numbers depends on the appearance of one or another of the animals in the buyer's most recent dream. A reading of sociologists who have noted this Brazilian phenomenon allows it to be considered the result of a cultural hybridization of the nation's three races—European, Indian, and African—and, consequently, the survival of a persistent primitive mentality, Indian or African, behind the Occidental façade. A discussion of the validity of this hypothesis does not interest us. What does is the hypothesis itself. In itself it expresses precisely the refusal of contemporary civilization to accept any institutionalization whatever of the dream's social function, considering such an institution a "waste product" not within the competence of a sociology worthy of its name—a kind of social sewer service.

Since Descartes we have closed the doors between night and day. We have devalued the nocturnal half of our life. Naturally, this does not mean that phantasms cannot penetrate the barrier. Psychology bears witness to the contrary; but phantasms only appear singly, always in disguise or, as the doctors say, as fantasies and by remaining part of the unconscious. I am more and more convinced that the greatest number of our mental illnesses are the result of our refusing free passage to all these phantasms and to all these desires that exist deep down in every one of us.

I have tried to expound the importance of this sociology of the dream in a series of radio broadcasts made this year: the more one puts a stop to contacts with the dead, the more one penetrates into the world of boredom, of moral suffering; and in the last analysis, productivity and mental illness may well be twins absolutely impossible to separate.

For the moment it is not the psychology that interests us but the fact that society today refuses to allow oneiric images the passport and visa necessary for entry into everyday social activity. On the other hand, we can ask ourselves if this dichotomy prevents the intrusion of society into the dream, and if we cannot talk about the social framework of our imagination within sleep itself. I have always thought that we could not, and that we have to react against the Bergsonian line of thought to which I alluded in the beginning. I would like to devote this study to an explication of this latter point.

Certain authors like Foucault have tried to show that a dream is a chaos of disjointed images, and that the link we establish between these disordered images is made only after our awakening. In fact, the more time has passed after our awakening when we take note of our dreams, the more logical a character they will offer.[3] But it matters little whether this coherence is imposed during sleep or immediately on awakening, because in attempting to construct a sociology of the dream, I wish to include the whole of man's other half, its twilight phases as well as its fully nocturnal states. Psychoanalysis has taught us that these disjointed images, even when they cannot be translated into coherent terms, are not the product of chance, and that dreams do have a structure. Freud looks for the meaning of this structure on the personal level. He wanted to show that even the seemingly most absurd dream is integrated in a personality's innermost framework. What we would like to do is to extend this structural definition to another level and to show that a similar interpretation exists also within the framework of a given civilization and of a given social system. Freud repersonalized the dream; now we must resocialize it.

Understand me well; this is not to remind you that the images of our sleep are furnished by the experiences of our waking day, experiences that are perforce social, thereby making these images social. Obviously a professor is more likely to dream of his students or of his colleagues than of a box factory. We would be simply repeating banalities like these that leave the basic problem untouched. For example, when I read in the diary I kept of my trip to Nigeria: "I am beginning to become African, last night I dreamed of 'Ogoun'" (Ogoun is the Yoruba god of iron and blacksmiths), the phrase may have a sentimental value for me, but it has no scientific value. A psychoanalyst could easily prove to me that I had only changed symbols, that Ogoun played the same role in my African dreams that someone else played in my European dreams. The analyst would see one structure beneath this diversity of content. I will therefore put aside the material involved in these dream images in order to go below the surface, to the structure that gives them form.

Nevertheless, I shall begin with that little phrase taken from my diary because this dream about Ogoun appeared to me like a first moment of marginality. I think the most effective perspective for ascertaining the social framework of oneiric thought consists in taking one's study materials from societies or groups in the process of acculturation, and in looking for examples among marginal man. We have opportunities to find together in these places two heterogeneous cultures, two different social systems each of which operates in relation to the other. A study made in France, and only among Frenchmen, would be particularly

---

[3] M. Foucault, *Le Rêve* (Paris: Alcan, 1906).

difficult since we share this Occidental civilization as a starting point, and we lack the perspective necessary to judge it. But by choosing marginal groups, the degradation or modification of two confronting civilizations will make stand out in bold relief the differences in their social structures, and more clearly reveal their importance.

I take as example the collection of dreams I once made among the lower-class Negroes and middle-class mulattoes of São Paulo in Brazil.[4] I have drawn on this material in a previous article, but contented myself therein with the subject matter of the images involved and their manifest content, being interested only in the differential psychology of the classes in a multiracial society. I had put aside the structural problems of oneiric thought. Now I refer to the same material, but from another angle; and finally, I compare the data I gathered there with the results of a Rorschach testing of members of an African religious confraternity conducted by my friend Dr. René Ribeiro.[5] His first objective in this study was to determine the level of anxiety among the Xango faithful in Pernambuco in an effort to reach conclusions about the social functions of pagan sects in a Catholic society. He wanted to see if a Rorschach would reveal feelings of security or of anxiety among the faithful.

But the test provided richer results than those he had aimed for, and we may gather from them a set of data comparable in my mind to what I had found for dreams. I do recognize definitely a certain heterogeneity between the images of a dream and the results of a Rorschach, and I know that my comparison is not absolutely satisfactory, but neither do I think it may be rejected.

I made allusion a moment ago to the Foucault theory that a dream acquires its structure not during sleep but at the moment of awakening. Does the Rorschach test not place the mind in a similar situation? A person finds himself faced with blots in much the same way he is faced with absurd images created in the shadows of night, and with the necessity of making sense out of them. I think there is a certain homology between the two positions. Moreover, there is a sense in which the images found in a Rorschach come from the perception of dreams and from memory, but this contrast between external and internal, between perception and memory, between true and, as French psychologists say, false images, no longer seems very important. It is precisely the purpose of a Rorschach to desocialize sensations and fasten on them as much as pos-

[4] R. Bastide, "Rêves de Noirs," *Psyche* (Paris), 49 (1950), 802–811.
[5] R. Ribeiro, "O Teste de Rorschach no estudo da 'aculturação' e da 'possessão fetichista' dos negros do Brasil," *Boletim do Instituto Joaquim Nabuco* (Recife), I (1952), 44–50; "Projective mechanisms and the structuralization of perception in Afrobrazilian divination," *Revue internationale d'ethnopsychologie normale et pathologique* (Tangier), I/2 (1956), 161–181.

sible the form of dream images. The comparison is therefore appropriate.

The persons tested belong to three different groups which I shall describe briefly. Group A is a largely feminine group of devotees belonging to the African Xango sects of black or mulatto members of the lower class: domestics, cooks, laundresses, vegetable-sellers in the street, and so on, who have submitted to the test of initiation, and consequently show signs of a mystic trance during the sacred dances. They are possessed by the god to whom they have been dedicated, and who has been replanted in their body during the course of the initiation rites.

Group B is another largely feminine group, also recruited from the lower classes, composed only of domestics, but living in highly industrialized São Paulo—a city where organized African cults did not exist at the time the study was made—rather than in Recife. (Since then, those cults have rapidly spread throughout Brazil under the form of a spiritualism called Ubanda. At the time of our researches two or three attempts to establish it were made. I was even a kind of "pope" for one of them, but unsuccessfully.) The people of this group are totally assimilated to Brazilian culture and in no way African, except that their skin is black.

Unlike the two others, group C is exclusively masculine. With regard to color it is recruited from the colored middle class, or in American terms, the lower middle class, that is in process of formation in São Paulo. It consists of minor employees, the small printer, or underpaid professor (of which there are many in South America because they must work in secondary schools that are commercial or in schools where benefices are provided for the director of the schools but not for the professors). It is also exclusively mulatto, for in Brazilian society vertical mobility is based on color: the clearer the shade of skin the easier it is to be accepted into the upper classes.

Now for the result of the studies made of these three groups.

Group A is distinguished by the African structure of perception and significance of its images. This does not mean that the Negroes of Recife were not part of Occidental civilization or that they were totally outside the Brazilian social system. On the contrary, they were politically very proudly Brazilian and very nationalistic. Economically they were an integral part of a capitalistic society's class system. But thanks to what I have sometimes called the principle of severance—a principle found, individually, also among cultivated Negroes in Africa—they live in two separate worlds, an African religious world and a Brazilian social world. They are not marginal, if marginality is defined as the conflict between two civilizations or two social systems face to face in one soul. The two systems merely coexist. Borrowing a phrase from Pasteur who said that when he entered his laboratory he closed the doors of his chapel, it can be said that when they enter the world of the Xango, they close the door on Brazil.

When priestesses or initiates, as part of an African rite of divination, were confronted with the absurd, strange, and, let me repeat, oneiric characters of the Rorschach figures, these people immediately reentered their world of African myths and the whole associative world of ideas almost automatically took on mythical form. In short, they denied that the figures were absurd. Their strangeness, in relation to figures taken from Brazilian reality, came as no surprise. Instead, they were a natural signal for entry into the world of Negro Africa. There is nothing astonishing here. This is a tradition-maintaining group, a world in which, I can assure you, dreams are not considered isolated realities, but messages, divine messages to be interpreted by the religious specialists for whom they have meaning. If the message foretells some evil, a change of behavior will take place or food sacrifices be made to the gods.

If I may be allowed a digression, I would like to see this discovery of René Ribeiro applied.[6]

When given Rorschachs those Africans revealed myths they concealed from anthropologists. In pointing to a blot, they would say, this is Ogoun, because there is a serpent and the myths say that so and so, and so on. Africans, and I think Indians as well, often refuse to give away their myths, but their Rorschachs in some way suspend their will to keep the secret.

Let us turn now to group C, the group most unlike the preceding: mulattoes rather than Negroes, men rather than women, middle class rather than lower class, urban São Paulites rather than Africans in culture. One essential problem appeared in almost all the dreams collected: the problem of money. Money is the great means of social ascent. It is money problems that push middle-class individuals toward the lower class, and money problems that determine their social place in a capitalistic society like ours.

A mulatto wants to have money because according to the proverb, "A rich Negro is white, and a poor white is black."

In addition to their poverty these people of color face another obstacle in rising vertically—their dark skin—and in their dreams we also find that "in the élan that pushed them higher there is the desire to destroy all witnesses of their *négritude*." To use an expression of Sartre, it is a matter of "killing the reflection of their blackness in the eyes of others."[7]

---

[6] Ribeiro, "Projective mechanisms."
[7] J. P. Sartre, "Orphée noir," in L. S. Senghor, *Anthologie de la nouvelle poésie nègre et malgache* (Paris, 1948).

This dream found in a mulatto illustrates my point.[8] "I am a passenger in an overcrowded bus which gathers far more than normal speed. Panicked by the vehicle's speed, the passengers one after the other hurl themselves out of the moving vehicle. But when they jump, they fall dead on the ground, and I am left alone in the bus, because fear prevents me from jumping." It is not arbitrary that we connect the two phenomena of *négritude* and vertical mobility in a society where the lighter the skin, the easier the rise, and where the positions of authority belong to the whites.

This agony of color is expressed very well in dreams, but it is distinctly Brazilian to be so constantly bound up with vertical mobility. "They have stolen my yellow shoes and put them by the chimney to make them black." This anxiety over the passing from the yellow to the black, which incidentally I am observing in a sick French Negro obsessed by the question of color, stands most clearly revealed in all his designs and paintings. Now, however, he is healed, because, as he says, he can paint people in black, in green, in red: color no longer counts. But this fear of the color, this obsession exists because the color prevents rising and not because one is ashamed of his color.

Dreams, then, show themselves to be part of the characteristic structure of our capitalistic and competitive society, which is the exact opposite of the precapitalist and community-like society of traditional Africa. Dreams of this kind obsess only people of color who are now caught up not in closed but open classes. Culturally they have assimilated Occidental values: individualism, struggle for social status, and money as the symbol of social position. Oneiric thought has detached itself completely from the mythical structures only to express the problem posed by skin color in Occidental social structure.

But what is there between the two opposite poles? This question brings us to group B, which is feminine and low class, but like group C made up of Negroes living in a city without African institutions. The striking feature here is the lack of dream structure, not, certainly, that there is no psychological structure, but that there is no sociological structure, no collective problem.

In the article I wrote about the dreams of Negroes, I wrote that there is in this group "desire to have little things [toys, pets], desire to attend a ball, to have lovers, and good drink, sexual desires, and finally desire for money." [9] But money does not have here the significance it has in the dreams of the mulattoes, as manifestation of social status. It is, on the contrary, always bound to consumption. It is a means to buy pretty

---

[8] Bastide, *op. cit.*, p. 804.
[9] *Ibid.*, p. 807.

clothes or to pay for an elegant meal, it is a means to pay for amusements, to afford a woman, and so on.

In these dreams it is money for consumption and not a symbol in a class struggle.

These results come as no surprise to our American Negro colleagues since American Negro psychoanalysts have shown in several articles that among Negroes in the lower classes of the United States the dream translates equally elementary desires, very simple desires, much as our children dream before they are socialized. It is interesting to find in the network of oneiric images an idea gathered by Claude Lévi-Strauss from his readings in the life histories of North American anthropologists, that sleep is only the reverse side of man's waking world.

Acculturation studies, he writes, do not get through to social systems, because these systems have already collapsed, but only to symptoms, which, incidentally, are very few. For our dreams, we could repeat word by word the sentences of Lévi-Strauss: the old social and cultural system has collapsed without as yet being replaced by something else, and only attitudes are left.[10] We find from their dreams that for these people the African social system has fallen apart. They are domestics, and in Brazil the system of domestic service is still close to slavery. The appropriate term to use is paternalism. They are part of the family. It was my own experience when I was in Brazil. There were tears and kisses for all the family among our servants. When we left for France they wanted to go with us.

This paternalistic regime makes impossible, or in any case impedes, any return to competitive society, and the domestic has only attitudes or symptoms. That is to say, a dream is doubtlessly an expression of their personality, but not an expression of a social system.

A study of pathological cases confirms these conclusions.

Dr. René Ribeiro found that in group A certain responses to a Rorschach showed states of anxiety which came to the surface through mythical interpretations of given figures, and, further, that precisely because of these mythical interpretations, these states of anxiety were never more than slight. They were slight precisely because they were immediately caught up in a collective structure that somehow softened their sharp edges and so exerted a "securing" effect.

It seemed to me that the dreams of group C generally manifest a more acute anxiety. Dreams of the dead, of assassinations, of fleeing in terror, and the like, are not rare. But here, too, there is no opposition to the sociological structure of the dream, because this anxiety is in a certain

---

[10] C. Lévi-Strauss, review of M. E. Opler, *An Apache Life-Way* in *L'Année sociologique*, 3ᵉ série, 1940–1948 (Paris: Presses Universitaires, 1949), p. 335.

sense an element in defining the situation of the Negro in a multiracial society where shades of color, from deep black to white, correspond *grosso modo* to the divisions of the social classes.

The neuropathic dreams of group B are equally clear-cut. They, too, are reflections of particular social situations and not of a collective social situation. There are, for example, people born of an unknown father, or of a prostitute mother, or those who have suffered from an uncle or an aunt during vacation. These people will have pathological dreams that fall in the usual social structure because the pathological person is not against the normal, but is at the periphery of the normal.

These are the facts as they appear. Can we go further in the interpretation of the data which I just summarized? I think we can.

A first point: We have underlined the infantile character of the dreams of people in group B. We have said that the oneiric thought of the child must take form at the same time that his thought becomes socialized. There are many collections of dreams, but all taken in a horizontal cross section, from one group to the other, as I myself have just done. But has one ever made a vertical cross section which permits following a person from infancy to adolescence and to see the transformation of his dreams? Personally I don't know any, but it would be a worthwhile undertaking.

The second point requires more attention. What is the nature of that inversion of the communication network between diurnal and nocturnal life which occurs on passage from a traditional society to a society of an Occidental cast?

In the former, the social factor works its way more easily into oneiric thought to orient, direct, and form it, in proportion to the dream fulfilling useful functions governed by the norms of that civilization. If passage occurred in both directions, the dominant direction was from inside to outside. In our society, on the other hand, the door of communication with the waking state is closed. Whatever few exceptions exist are individual, and often considered as vaguely somewhat neuropathic symptoms. Passage is limited to a one-way street going from outside to inside. Society furnishes the social framework for oneiric thought.

I have presented this confrontation by means of a functionalist theory, and have pointed briefly to some of the roles played by dreams in traditional societies. Let me take up once again this theme, but this time from a structuralist point of view. If dreams have functions, it is because society is organized in such a way that these functions can be fulfilled. Institutions exist which serve as relay stations between day and night. Some are privileged places, like the grove or temple, some are meaningful moments, like rituals of initiation or seasonal dances.

Sickness also must be considered to be more than a simple organic disturbance. It becomes an authentic institution for the same reasons as an initiation despite the differences between them. And since the cure for a sickness is carried out within this institution, it falls under the same system controlled by collective representation. In societies called primitive, a certain number of stations have been established which hold tightly together the lines that cross between the two worlds.

A dream is taken in by the nets of social organization, and a real unity results between man's two halves just as it does between the world of myth or the sacred, with which the dream is associated, and the social world in which the individual lives in a waking state. The sociological structure of the dream is then, not as with us, a reflection, or the obverse of social structure; it is an integral part of it.

There is actually no passing from one world to another because it is always the same world—the world of night and the world of day.

The extension of night into day, or day into night, is not a matter for astonishment or skepticism, any more than one is astonished or has doubt about the religious basis for a place to live, or about the metaphysical foundations of customs, or about the religious roots of tradition.

We are dealing in each of these cases with one whole: the dream is part of one all-embracing structure. Is the psychoanalyst about to institutionalize the dream? Possibly, and in fifty years it could be considered a true institution. But at the moment this is not happening. On the contrary, with the secularization of culture, the growing emphasis on producing, on *praxis,* on work, and on class stratification, all the relay stations of communication are being torn down. The dream ceases, in this case, to have an objective existence, an institutionalized place. It is consigned to the imagination. But then, something strange and paradoxical happens. When the dream is thus consigned to the imagination because it is not mythical, it becomes magical; that is, the minute that it is no longer considered sacred by most people, it becomes so strange that it becomes the occasion for fear.

Freud explained the sacred and magical character of the dream by narcissism and other theories, but as far as I am concerned, there exists alongside the Freudian explanation this sociological one, which I shall demonstrate by returning to our group. The solution that the dreamer of this group finds for the problem involved in his social ascent—a rising in a capitalistic society which depends on money, and the color of his skin which interferes with the means of getting this money—is magically applied: he kills all his white competitors in the labor market.

The example I cited of the runaway bus is significant in this regard, but the example could be multiplied: ". . . fights with fellow workers which ends with many dead, whose bodies were then thrown outside into a driving rain. I was waiting with some of them for the train to come in order to run away, when I woke up." [11]

One wonders whether this magic solution is not a survival of African man. I think not. This theory might find support in a number of remarks made by John Dollard about the Negro in the United States, who emphasized that superstitious dreams are found as much in middle-class as in lower-class Negroes, but that in the rural lower class, the magic is above all defensive, and in the middle class of the northern cities, above all, aggressive.[12]

I know, too, that the Negroes I analyzed in São Paulo, and whose dreams I studied, have an aggressive magic. But Freud was right, I think, provided he is supplemented by sociology. There is a narcissistic explanation for the magic character of dreams, but it is also true that the dreams seem magical to us because we have lost all knowledge of the sacred, we no longer know what is the religious; I could say that all our religions themselves are, at heart, secularizations. We have heard of Sunday religion; it would be better to talk about religion from eleven to noon.

Consequently we no longer know, nor any longer understand, what the sacred is. In our banal, day-to-day life, everything is determined by something other than the sacred, so when we are confronted with the jarring images of the dream, we are startled at their absurdity and we relegate them to magic, myth, the sacred; it is supernatural but supernatural in the objective of the real supernatural, if I may say so. Now then, with us the dream's images have no relay line in which to join; its institutions are relegated outside reality and are considered to be a troubling thing called magic.

To summarize, I should say that with us as with the traditional societies, the dream always takes its place in a social framework. But the anthropologist is able to achieve for the primitive a direct reading of the sleeping world from his observations of the waking world, because with him whether he sleep or work, he is the same man, and one continues in the same myth-based world.

But as far as we are concerned the sociologist must make an inverse reading because sociological structure does indeed find its place in oneiric images, but in a somehow inverted form. It is for this reason that the sociologist must at any price uncover this social structure. It is per-

---

[11] Bastide, *op. cit.*, p. 803 n. 2.
[12] John Dollard, *Caste and Class in a Southern Town* (New Haven: Yale University Press, 1937); cf. J. E. Lind, "The Dream as a Simple Wish Fulfillment in the Negro," *Psychoanalytic Review*, I (1913–1914), 295–300; and "The Color Complex in the Negro," *ibid.*, pp. 404–414; C. F. Gibson, "Concerning Color," *ibid.*, XVIII (1931), 413–425.

haps precisely because the sociologist must make such an effort that some people, like Charles Blondel and Maurice Halbwachs, have said, "There is no sociology of the dream yet,"[13] but I am convinced that there is one.

[13] Blondel, *op. cit.;* Halbwachs, *op. cit.*

12

Pathogenic Dreams in Non-Western Societies

GEORGE DEVEREUX

1. CAUSALITY AND THE PATHOGENIC DREAM

The history of anthropology reveals that a great many concepts that seemed singularly clear and precise when first introduced into anthropological discourse, tend to become vaguer and more evanescent when, with the increase of factual knowledge, they are subjected to a more careful scrutiny. The history of the concept of totemism is an example of this process.

The first part of this essay seeks to demonstrate that the seemingly very precise concept of pathogenic dreams is actually far from precise, and appears precise only because it has not been carefully scrutinized, and also because most data pertaining to dreams commonly thought to be pathogenic are incomplete.

The central difficulty in the anthropological, psychoanalytic, and phenomenological study of so-called pathogenic dreams is the fact that the term "pathogenic" clearly implies causality. Now, it is well known that the definition of causality, both in theory and in practice, has been one of the most vexing problems of science and of the philosophy of science. To take a famous example, many scientists and logicians hold that the Heisenberg indeterminacy principle actually undermines, at least in part, the concept of causality, whereas Einstein, Bertrand

Russell, and some other authorities feel that the Heinsenberg indeterminacy principle does not defy the laws of causality for the simple reason that it has no bearing whatever upon the problem of causality. If difficulties and controversies of this kind can arise in the exact sciences, then the student of cultural and behavioral phenomena may be excused for experiencing difficulties in connection with concepts that imply causality.

Superficially, the definition of the pathogenic dream is quite simple: Any dream that causes an illness is a pathogenic dream. Unfortunately, as soon as this simple definition, and the data from which it is derived, are subjected to closer scrutiny, we realize that—in Henri Poincaré's words—we have been guilty of labeling the problem, instead of solving it. The first section of this essay seeks to remedy this scientifically untenable and intolerable situation.

The starting points in any situation in which a pathogenic dream is said to have occurred are two empirical data: (1) a dream, and (2) an illness. It cannot be sufficiently stressed that at this juncture the two phenomena must be treated as discrete phenomena, as two isolated items on a trait list including all known phenomena on earth.

Next, we may, or may not, observe a third phenomenon, which is of an entirely different order; it belongs, in Bertrand Russell's terminology, to a different "mathematical type" in that it is a statement about two empirical phenomena: "a dream" and "an illness." This statement—which can be either an individual, idiosyncratic assertion or a cultural tenet, or both—asserts that the two phenomena under consideration are *somehow* connected. In other words, the existence of *a* nexus is predicated, but the *nature* of this nexus remains *unspecified*. In particular, at this point it is not even asserted that the (unspecified) nexus between "dream" and "illness" is a *causal* one. What is more, at this stage of reasoning, not even the concept of a temporal *sequence* is introduced into our informants' discourses. This means, in practice, that, at this point, the two phenomena our informants have—legitimately or illegitimately—conjoined, by the imputation of some unspecified nexus, can also occur simultaneously, perhaps in the form of having a dream and falling ill simultaneously; or else the illness may precede the dream, in which case the latter may be viewed not as a pathogenic dream, but as a symptomatic or pathognomonic one. In brief, in such cases we surreptitiously introduce a special type of causality, which Petzoldt calls "simultaneous causality" and utilizes as an explanation of the coherence of spatial (simultaneous) structures, rather than of the coherence of temporal (sequential) structures. Since we have done so surreptitiously, we must discard this inference at once, at least at this stage of our reasoning.

In principle, our position, and that of our informants, with regard to the predication of an *unspecified* nexus between a dream and an illness, is comparable to the position of a statistician who finds that there is a high degree of correlation between two phenomena, without being able to explain the actual connection between the two phenomena in a causal way. This fact is so well known that statisticians sometimes amuse themselves with thinking up pairs of phenomena between which a statistically highly significant correlation exists, and which are, nonetheless, not causally connected. One well-known "correlation" of this type is the birth of babies and the coincident appearance of the doctors' black bags at the time and place of the birth. I have pointed out elsewhere (Devereux, 1953) that nearly all experimental studies in parapsychology are of this type. Indeed, in strictly logical terms, even if a given experimental subject in a clairvoyance study guessed right every time, as long as we are unable to suggest any *clearly specified mechanism* connecting the appearance of a certain card and the ("correct") utterance of the subject, we simply impute an *unspecified* nexus to these two discrete phenomena. And we do so not because logic obliges us to do so, but because of a subjective need to impute an order to nature and its phenomena. It may be objected that, according to Mach, there are no laws *in* nature . . . that we *put* laws into nature. I feel, however, that *at this point* we have not even operated in accordance with Mach's principle. Even less have we operated in terms of the type of reasoning propounded by St. Thomas Aquinas ("by the conformity between intellect and things we define truth"), by Spinoza ("the order and connection of ideas is the same as the order and connection of things"), or by James Clark Maxwell (mathematical physics is possible because the laws of numbers happen to parallel the laws of bodies). Rather have we—or our informants—satisfied a purely emotionally determined Sumnerian "strain toward consistency" which, as psychoanalysis has shown, is not the mother of rationality, but of rationalizations.

In brief, at this stage of our inquiry, we have simply discovered that the native informant chooses to assert that a nexus, as yet unspecified, exists between a dream and an illness. It cannot be stressed sufficiently that, strictly speaking, our informant is not (yet?) speaking of *pathogenic* dreams, since he has not (yet?) specified that the imputed nexus is a causal one. Even less has he specified the *mechanism* whereby this causal connection comes into being and becomes operative. To take, for a moment, only the special case of the actual sequence "antecedent dream, subsequent illness," when we predicate a nexus between the two and possibly also assert that the nexus is a causal one, the logical status of our statement is strictly that of the well-known "post hoc ergo propter hoc" fallacy.

Turning for a moment to empirical field data, a careful scrutiny suggests that available data seldom go beyond this point, and that, quite illegitimately, the concept of "pathogenic dreams" is introduced at this point. At the risk of seeming critical of fieldworkers, I must confess that in many cases the actual published data cause me to wonder (1) whether, at this point, it is the fieldworker or the native informant who introduces the concept of a (causally) pathogenic dream; (2) whether the fieldworker stopped his inquiry too soon, and therefore failed to obtain precise and specific information about native beliefs concerning the *nature* of the causal nexus between the antecedent dream and the subsequent illness.

The first of these questions I cannot answer with any degree of certainty. Indeed, most of us go into the field so eager to discover the exotic, we seduce our informants so consistently to elaborate the unfamiliar and the strange, that sometimes a kind of *folie à deux* comes into being between informant and fieldworker—a tacit and unconscious contract to ignore all practicality and logic. This collusion is amusingly epitomized by Róheim's quip that, quite often, the only savage in the field is the visiting anthropologist.

With respect to the second question, I feel I can speak with a little more assurance. I am practically certain that there exists no truly exhaustive investigation of native dream theory, not even for the dream-oriented and dream-obsessed River Yumans—and this despite the fact that both conventional anthropologists (Kroeber, 1925; Gifford, 1926; W. J. Wallace, 1947) and psychoanalytic anthropologists (Róheim, 1932; Devereux, 1957a, 1961, and elsewhere) have specifically studied their dream life. The simple fact is that each new investigation discloses that River Yuman dream theory is far more complex than it previously appeared to be.

On a worldwide scale, it is evident that our information concerning the range and variety of primitive dream theories is fragmentary, and that, in this respect, we are not much better off than we were when Lincoln (1935) wrote his book on primitive dreams. This is partly because of the general tendency to expect very little in the way of theoretical complexity and of multiple or variegated types of explanations from our primitive informants. In addition, when the anthropologist hears of one, officially emphasized and functionally important, dream theory, he is quasi-hypnotized by it and calls off any search for other, less prominent but equally traditional dream theories of a different type. Thus, while it is quite certain that the theory of the "soul–wish–manifesting" dream is the most striking and socially most important Iroquois dream theory (A. F. C. Wallace, 1958), I cannot help harboring the conviction that there exist also a number of additional Iroquois tenets pertaining to dreams, which have not hitherto been recorded and/or adequately exploited.

This point is, methodologically, of some importance, and should be substantiated at least by means of a parallel example. Without exception, all earlier published data concerning the River Yumans have described only the official, and functionally and behaviorally important, theory that twins are heavenly visitors who are welcomed with joy and are gladly granted special privileges. Not until relatively recently did we discover (Devereux, 1941) the existence of a second, completely different, and emotionally rather than behaviorally important, theory concerning twins: this second theory views twins as contemptibly acquisitive ghosts who return to earth only in order to obtain a second set of funeral gifts from the living. The official emphasizing of the first theory and its extreme elaboration simply diverted anthropologists from the task of exploring further the range of Mohave beliefs concerning twins.

I strongly suspect that something of this order occurred also in connection with the Iroquois, in whose case the functionally important "wish-of-the-soul" dream theory short-circuited interest in supplementary, or possibly even contradictory, dream theories. A hint of this may be found in an incident, cited without any indication of its source by Linton (1956). An Iroquois extorted a gift from a white officer on the grounds that he had dreamed having received such a gift. When, subsequently, the white officer turned the tables on the Iroquois and, also on the basis of an (alleged) dream, extracted a countergift from the latter, the Iroquois did give the desired gift, but informed the officer that from that day forward neither he nor the officer would have any further (wish-of-the-soul) dreams.

As regards the Mohave in particular, the more data I have accumulated regarding Mohave dreams, and the more I have analyzed them, the more I have been impressed by the range, scope, and variety of Mohave dream theories. Hence, on the basis of the preceding considerations, I am inclined to believe that the logical incompleteness or arbitrariness of the connections that natives allegedly believe to exist between an antecedent dream and a subsequent illness may be more the result of an incomplete inquiry in the field than of a distressing fragmentariness of native dream theory.

Returning now to the problem of the logical aspects of so-called pathogenic dreams, the postulation (or imputation) of an unspecified nexus between dream and illness next demands that the *nature* of this nexus be specified and be shown to be of a causal nature. At this point what we meet with is utter chaos. In many cases we simply have no information. In other cases, the fieldworker applies to all dreams that portion of native dream theory which is known to him. This latter state of affairs may explain, in some small measure, why, in discussing the general problem of such sequences as "antecedent dream, subsequent event," Lévy-Bruhl (an unjustly neglected genius) found that, in many cases, one could not determine whether the antecedent dream was the efficient cause, or else simply the prophetic intimation (omen) of some subsequent event (Lévy-Bruhl, 1922).

Lévy-Bruhl therefore concluded that, in a genuine though complex sense, the omen dream actually also "causes" the event it foretells. We might perhaps amend this formulation somewhat and suggest that the haziness of the boundary line between omen dream and causal dream is often due more to the fact that both occurrences are part of a rigidly deterministic (kismet-type) conception of the order of events in time, than to a direct causation of the event (or illness) by the dream.

There is a broad range of phenomena in which an antecedent dream is linked to a subsequent illness in some manner only remotely connected with causality, even if one conceives of causality in the most elastic sense possible. A good example of this is one aspect of the Iroquois-type soul-wish dream. If Kamchadal A dreams that B is doing something for him, and B fails to comply with this demand in reality, then not only the frustrated dreamer, but also the frustrating and uncooperative person dreamed about will fall ill (Steller, 1774). I think it requires further study to determine whether A's wish dream should be viewed as a *pathogenic* dream with regard to B's illness, even though there is said to exist a clear-cut—though not explicitly specified (pathogenic)—nexus between A's dream and B's illness.

A similar difficulty arises when A dreams that B will fall ill, and B does, in fact, fall ill, with or without B having learned that A had dreamed that B will become ill. We can, of course, seek to dispose of the matter by asserting that, in such instances, A's dream is not pathogenic within the primitive meaning of that term, and should therefore be considered as an omen dream rather than as a causal one. I am inclined to question this simple-seeming explanation, quite apart from Lévy-Bruhl's cogent argument that the omen dream is, in a sense, also a causal dream, at least within the purview of native logic. Indeed, Lévy-Bruhl (1922) himself cites the following case: A Lengua man dreams that he ate a tabooed bird and, on arising, confidently declares that his (absent) child had a fretful (sick?) night as a result of this dream (Grubb, 1911). In this case a true (native-type) causal nexus is predicated between the father's dream and the child's (a priori inferred illness). The argument runs as follows: if fathers eat this tabooed bird, their children will become ill. The father dreamed of having violated this taboo. Dreams being real experiences of the soul, the taboo had been actually violated, which necessarily calls for the child's illness. *Ergo:* Individual A can have a "genuinely" pathogenic dream causing the illness of B.

Instead of rambling all over the ethnological map of the world, I limit myself in the second part of this study to an exploration of the various types of connections believed to exist between dream and illness in Mohave culture. I do so partly because, as stated above, the whole problem of pathogenic dreams is so complex and so poorly documented that the exploration in depth of the problem in a culture whose dream theories are relatively well understood is likely to clarify matters more than would a poorly documented comparative approach. This, however, is not all. I postulated elsewhere (Devereux, 1955) that something resembling the mathematician's ergodic hypothesis also exists in social and behavioral science, so that at least the range and meaning of phenomena, typology, and patterns of connections between phenomena, can be ascertained with equal precision by four means:

1. the study of a single individual in depth (e.g., through psychoanalysis);
2. the cross-sectional study of many individuals (e.g., through Rorschach tests);
3. the study of a single culture in depth (intensive fieldwork);
4. the study of a large number of cultures cross-sectionally (comparative method).

Part 2 of this study represents the third of these four approaches. It is presented without further justification, since empirical proof of the validity of this social ergodic hypothesis was already presented in the work just cited (Devereux, 1955).

2. DREAM AND ILLNESS IN MOHAVE CULTURE

The first point to be discussed is that the very existence of illnesses of various types—for example, the existence of a gastrointestinal disorder, as distinct from the concrete gastrointestinal illness of a given Mohave individual, here and now—is, in a sense, derived from a pathogenic dream, in the broadest sense of the term. All illnesses were foreordained, established, and created at the time of creation. The event of creation included (in principle) at least one such concrete case of illness (e.g., gastroenteritis) and at least one actual cure of this illness. The illness "gastroenteritis" exists because there was a case of such an illness during creation, which was both a precedent and a "prophecy" that such illnesses would occur subsequently. Each case of this illness—a hundred years ago, today, and a hundred years hence—is thus a duplication of the mythical precedent and an implementation of the "prophecy" that that prototypal illness represented.

The creation myth is, moreover, not a finished product. The creation myth, as recorded, let us say in 1900, simply records those portions of the creation myth which had been revealed in dream up to that time.

Thus, when firearms were introduced and bullet wounds became known, a shaman promptly dreamed of having witnessed that portion of the creation event which pertained to the primordial, prototypal, and precedent-setting bullet wound and its cure. In principle, tomorrow or the next day a Mohave shaman may dream of the creation of radiation burns or space sickness, and of its healing. These new dreams automatically call for the completion of previously known versions of the creation myth, in the sense in which the discovery of a new fossil demands that last year's handbook of paleontology be brought up to date.

Of course, the Mohave do not explicitly affirm that the original act of creation was a dream, in the sense in which some Australians speak of the time of creation as "dream time." But the Mohave do hold certain beliefs concerning creation, which cause creation as an act and the creation myth as a dream to differ no more than Tweedledum differs from Tweedledee. Indeed, the future Mohave shaman witnesses in his mother's womb those portions of the creation which pertain to his therapeutic specialty. He even specifies that he had witnessed the actual act of creation, saying: "I know it, I was there." At the same time, he insists that the creators repeated or reenacted the creation for his benefit while he was still in the womb. Now, there is a basic paradox in this latter statement: All the gods of the Mohave are dead and have been dead since creation, while the culture-hero or quasi-god Mastamho, exhausted by his labors, became a (catatonic?) osprey, or fish eagle, and no longer intervenes in human affairs (Kroeber, 1925, 1948; Devereux, 1961). Now, the gods being dead, they cannot possibly reenact creation anew for the unborn shaman. Hence, his statement "I know it, I was there" necessarily predicates that the shamanistic dream can move backward in time. This implies that in his intrauterine dream, he witnessed the *true, original* illness-event and recreated it. This event serves as the prototype of the illness that he will later cure, and is the nucleus of his intrauterine experience. In this very definite sense, his intrauterine dream is an act of creation; his dream is pathogenic with regard to the occurrence of a type or category of illness (e.g., the clinical entity: gastroenteritis), though not pathogenic, *at that time,* with regard to the gastroenteritis of a concrete Mohave individual A, on June 1, 1962, which he may subsequently cause through witchcraft, by inducing a pathogenic dream in the victim.

Later on, in adolescence, he will once more—and this time explicitly—dream of this part of creation and will experience a double sense of *déjà vu:* he will remember having witnessed the same scene already in the womb, and will feel that what he witnessed in the womb was the act of creation itself.

Sometimes, later in life, under the impetus of some strong stimulus, he may have further dreams, also accompanied by a sense of *déjà vu,* of having also witnessed already *in utero* some other illness and its cure. Ahma Huma : re, a nonobstetrical shaman, saw his unborn child die in his dead parturient wife's womb. Shortly thereafter, he had the proper obstetrical dreams and became also an obsteterical shaman (Devereux, 1948). We must assume that the same thing took place also when the first Mohave shaman had the necessary dreams, enabling him to heal bullet wounds.

In brief, all knowledge about creation is acquired in dream, and the creation myth is held to be a dream-revealed guide to reality. Moreover, the nature of shamanistic intrauterine experiences seems to imply that reality is a product of dream, a reality that necessarily includes also the various illness categories represented by precedent-making illnesses. Needless to say, the Mohave are not alone in feeling that reality, or portions of reality, are the products of dreaming. In some other groups there are explicit statements that the gods and even the ancestors create portions of reality by dreaming about them. In Hindu theology, a certain tenet clearly suggests that the world is a dream of Brahma. Even the Old Testament conception that the world was created through or from the Word (Logos) serves to underscore that man, in one way or another, tends to see reality as a projection of psychic forces and materials. This principle is applied by the Mohave also to cultural reality. The dream alone validates learning culturally: anyone can learn to sing a medicine song, but its singing is therapeutically ineffective and remains a purely extracultural, individual act, unless it is backed and validated by the proper shamanistic dreams. Likewise, in theory, a newly introduced item or fact becomes a Mohave *cultural* item only if someone can dream of that fact being present already at the time of creation. Dream is both the funnel that admits and the sieve that rejects facts and events in regard to Mohave culture. It is the sole legitimate means whereby new elements can be culturally "naturalized."

I might add, in passing, a theoretical point of some importance. Anthropologists have carefully explored the value-meaning-affect matrix of cultures, as well as the trait-item content of cultures. It seems necessary to add to these two levels of culture a third one: the standard mechanism whereby a new item—an invention, a borrowed trait or attitude, an individual's subjective experience, and so on—acquires the status of a cultural item and becomes, so to speak, culturally "naturalized." I suggest that in Mohave culture this role is assigned to dream, and that *the Mohave interpret their culture in terms of dreams, rather than dreams in terms of their culture,* at least in theory.

To sum up our findings, with special reference to pathogenic dreams creating illness *categories* in Mohave culture, it seems fairly clear that nosological entities (as distinct from individual cases of illness) are "caused" by dreams, and that these "pathogenic" dreams form that portion of the creation myth which pertains to the coming into being of illnesses through precedent-setting events, which play both a causal and a prophetic role with regard to individual cases of illness occurring in the future.

All this should not surprise us in the least, since, as psychoanalytic findings show, all theories of genesis, creation, and the like are the intellectual consequences of the child's curiosity about birth in general and its own coming into being in particular. To cite only a limited case, Abraham (1927) has shown that a certain competent chemist's decision to specialize in the study of the state called "status nascendi" was ultimately rooted in his infantile interest in the origin of babies and, we suspect, of his own origin.

Having demonstrated that a stylized "pathogenic" dream (the creation myth) accounts for the existence of illness in general, and of all clinical entities in particular, our next objective is the scrutiny of pathogenic dreams related to the concrete illness of a given person, at a given time. At this point, we are struggling not with a paucity of data, but with a veritable embarrassment of riches. All of Mohave life and culture unfolds itself in an atmosphere of dreams; Kroeber (1925) called Mohave culture a dream culture. Dreams literally crowd around every salient event of life, as well as around every important cultural item. Just as nothing good can happen, and no capacity or power to be successful can be acquired, without an appropriate dream (Kroeber, 1925; W. J. Wallace, 1947; Devereux, 1937, 1956, 1957a, 1961, and elsewhere), so no calamity, no illness, can occur without appropriate dreams (*ibid.*). Bad dreams are called either *sumatc itcem* (Wallace's spelling is *achemk*) or *sumatc alayk;* Wallace states that the first of these terms is applied specifically to dreams related to failures in undertakings and the second to dreams of illness and death. My own informants definitely did not follow, in practice, this terminological distinction, which does not necessarily imply that Wallace is wrong, or was misinformed: the difference between his informants' views and my informants' practice may reflect nothing more than the extreme elasticity of Mohave culture. Wallace also specifies that *sumatc alayk* dreams are omens of illness. As will be seen, this latter specification is somewhat narrow, and quite debatable.

Every dream related in any way to illness is held to be pathognomonic and to possess diagnostic value. In brief, from the native diagnostician's point of view, any dream related to illness can, functionally, be treated as a symptom. Indeed, in every illness the diagnostician promptly investigates the patient's dreams, so as to make the proper diagnosis and prognosis. Admittedly, we possess no date concerning the diagnostic and prognostic use of dreams in the treatment of such obvious accidents as injuries resulting from horse kicks and the like. On the basis of the general pattern of Mohave healing sciences, however, I am inclined to suspect that even in such cases an inquiry may be made into dreams, albeit probably only for prognostic purposes, and/or in order to ascertain whether or not the injury (a "straight" or natural illness, like a "straight" gastroenteritis) is complicated (made "not straight") by an admixture of witchcraft, viewed as a "secondary invader," which makes the illness "not straight" (Devereux, 1961). This, however, is admittedly a speculation and need concern us no further in the present context.

The fact that any dream—whatever its ultimate relationship to the illness may be—is used for diagnostic and prognostic purposes necessarily implies that even pathogenic dreams, in the strict sense of the term, as well as omen dreams, are also viewed, apart from their causative or prophetic function, as symptoms of the illness and as (prognostically important) indicators of its gravity. Now, it is obvious that dreams can be exploited diagnostically and/or prognostically only if there is a body of theory concerning the meaning of various kinds of manifest dream content, that is, if there exists an oneirocritic science.

Oneirocritic interpretations can be of three types: paralleling the manifest content (e.g., coitus with a woman means good luck), running counter to the manifest content (e.g., luck in a love intrigue is foretold among the Malays by dreams of being bitten by a snake), and symbolic. The last is so rare that, according to Hundt (1935), the only symbolically interpreted dream in Homer is that of Penelope, which, as I have shown elsewhere, happens to be the key to the latent content of much of the *Odyssey* (Devereux, 1957*b*).

Broadly speaking, much of Mohave dreaming in connection with illness—and also much general dreaming—is interpreted parallel to the dream content. Unpleasant dreams, experienced as such *regardless of their manifest content,* dreams whose manifest content is unpleasant, and dreams that contain some element which, by definition, pertains to illness (e.g., dreams about ghosts) would all be interpreted as bad dreams. Since illness-and-death is practically the prototype of "badness," unpleasant dreams are sometimes interpreted as heralding sickness, even if they contain no specific element *traditionally* associated with a certain illness. Moreover, some dreams are held to foretell illness or trouble even when they contain nothing specifically unpleasant: on narrating a dream of mine to the Mohave, I received from one informant a favorable interpretation; a second informant declared that the first informant must have been too tactful to tell me its real meaning and asserted that it foretold some bad luck or illness (Devereux, 1961).

In view of the well-known influence of culture and of culturally and subjectively determined expectations upon dreamwork (Devereux, 1951), it is fairly certain that a person who more or less consciously suspects that he has a certain illness will, sooner or later, produce the type of dream which, in his culture, is habitually correlated with that type of illness. This process is further facilitated by the fact that many "classical" diagnostic dreams do, in fact, pertain to quite basic fears, repressed wishes, and anxieties; among the Mohave, they are exemplified by dreams of incestuous coitus with the dead. In such instances the cultural tenet that illness X presupposes a certain type of dreams is, to all practical purposes, a self-fulfilling prophecy.

Such pathognomonic dreams can also be scrutinized from the opposite point of view, that is, as the products of unconscious autoscopy, or self-diagnosis, in dream. The dynamics of such dreams were already clearly understood in classical Greece (Hippocrates, Aristotle). They were held to reveal a latent illness, because in dreams one's attention is entirely focused on oneself, and is withdrawn from distracting external reality. This point of view fully dovetails with the findings of Ferenczi (1927) and Bartemeier (1950). It implies that, both in psychoanalytic theory and in Mohave belief, such dreams are neither pathogenic nor omen dreams: they are self-diagnostic dreams and the products of autoscopy in dream.

A closely related group of dreams can be viewed, without unduly stretching the meaning of Mohave dream theory and medicine, as manifestations of an internal struggle involving the instincts or such entities as health and illness, whose battleground the organism as a whole has become and which manifest themselves also in dream. Again, we are dealing largely with pathognomonic and symptomatic dreams rather than with strictly pathogenic or omen dreams. It is hardly necessary to add that whenever such autoscopic or symptomatic dreams precede in time the obvious onset of illness a certain laxity of speech and thought habit tends to view these dreams as pathogenic or as omen dreams. Yet, even a brief supplementary inquiry usually reveals that no such meaning is actually implied by the Mohave themselves.

In the strictest sense of the term there are, then, only two types of pathogenic dreams in Mohave culture:

1. Dreams in the course of which the organism falls ill because of certain harmful adventures the soul experiences in dream. These experiences may include also the invasion of the psyche by an alien power, such as that of a witch, of an enemy, or of a ghost.

2. Dreams that are so upsetting that the patient reacts to them by illness.

Actually, the distinction between category (1) and category (2) is far from sharp. A dream that seriously upsets the dreamer is almost always one that involves a pathogenically dangerous adventure of the soul. Thus, the Mohave report that a woman became upset, anoretic, and severely depressed after dreaming that a dead relative cooked and served her a fish, and that after beginning to eat the fish, the dreamer realized that the head of the fish was the head of her dead mother. Since dreams about ghosts, and especially about the ghosts of relatives, are known to cause illness, and are particularly dangerous if they involve being fed by, or engaging in coitus with, the ghosts of the dead, the dream in question—though said to have "caused" the woman's illness, because it was upsetting—was actually a pathogenic dream of the "illness bringing adventures of the soul" type; in fact, it proved so upsetting precisely because it was quite obviously a pathogenic dream of this type.

Strictly speaking, the only truly pathogenic Mohave dreams are those in which the soul undergoes illness-causing adventures (visit to the land of the dead, for example), or else in which the soul (and the dream) is invaded by a malignant adversary, such as a witch.

A subspecies of this type of pathogenic dream is the dream that both causes and reveals the nature of the impending illness but does not lead to the proper type of activity on awakening. In some such instances, it is the dream itself that prevents the patient from taking the proper action on awakening: the fact that one is being bewitched is revealed to one in dreams. Sometimes, the evil witch disguises his identity by borrowing the shadow soul of another shaman, or else assumes an entirely different type of disguise, so that he appears in his victim's dream in an impenetrable disguise. By these means, he simultaneously achieves his aim of bewitching the victim and prevents the latter from knowing and revealing his magical assailant's name. In other instances, the witch simply "closes the lips" of the prospective victim, making the victim actually desirous of succumbing to witchcraft, and therefore inducing him not to reveal the identity of the witch, though only such a revelation can save him.

In such instances the dream is doubly pathogenic, albeit on two distinct levels. The dream itself is, and portrays, the invasion of the victim by the power of the witch. Simultaneously, the victim is prevented, in some way, from saving himself on awakening, by not recognizing his assailant, or by being unable to utter his name, if he did recognize him, or by remaining silent because he is unwilling to be saved.

This, then, is the sum total of what exists in the way of *genuine* pathogenic dreams in Mohave society. Of course, grouped around this nucleus, are pathogenic dreams such as those of people who become insane because they dreamed of Mastamho in his final insane avatar. These, however, again represent little more than bona fide pathogenic adventures of the soul, albeit of a somewhat special kind.

As regards omen dreams, we have indicated above that, on closer scrutiny, the dream is linked to the illness by altogether nonprophetic mechanisms, even in Mohave thought, if one but takes the trouble to study the matter carefully enough. I suspect that the same will prove true of many other omen dreams pertaining to illness, if one but takes the trouble to reinvestigate with some measure of psychological sophistication reported illness omen dreams in the field. I would even venture to suggest that, if we but knew enough about dream theory in the ancient Near East, the many illness omen dreams listed in Oppenheim's (1956) monumental work would be recognized as either pathogenic, or else as symptomatic-autoscopic dreams, at least initially, though there can be no doubt that, as oneirocritic science snowballed, *omina* of illness were ground out by oneirocritic craftsmen as fugues once emerged by the yard from the contrapuntal sausage machines of the Baroque masters, Bach himself often not excluded.

CONCLUSIONS

In the study of primitive medicine, one often meets with reports that a dream is believed to be connected in some way or other with an illness. The dream and the illness between which native informants postulate a nexus may occur either in sequence or simultaneously. Unless the scholar is able to demonstrate that native dream theory itself specifies the *nature* of the nexus between dream and illness, and further specifies that this nexus is a *causal* one, he is not entitled to speak of genuinely pathogenic dreams. He can only speak of omen dreams, generalized fate-foretelling dreams, symptomatic, pathognomonic, or autoscopic dreams. Only where the nature of the nexus is specified and also explicitly stated to be *causal* is it legitimate to speak of pathogenic dreams. It is suggested that, owing to defective data, many nonpathogenic dreams have been misidentified as pathogenic, and that, conversely, owing to lack of adequate information about native dream theory, some definitely pathogenic dreams were mistakenly believed to be omen dreams and the like. A more thorough exploration, not only of native dreaming and dreams, but also of native dream theory and of its influence upon both dreaming and waking thought, is one of the most urgent tasks of psychologically oriented anthropology.

References

Abraham, Karl. 1927. *Selected Papers of Karl Abraham, M.D.* London.
Aquinas, Thomas. *Summa contra gentes.*
Aristotle. *De divinatione per somnum.* 463a.
Bartemeier, L. H. 1950. "Illness following dreams," *International Journal of Psycho-Analysis*, 31:8–11.
Devereux, George. 1937. "L'Envoûtement chez les Indiens Mohave," *Journal de la Société des Américanistes de Paris*, n.s., 29:405–412.
———. 1941. "Mohave beliefs concerning Twins," *American Anthropologist*, n.s., 43:573–592.
———. 1948. "Mohave Indian obstetrics," *American Imago*, 5:95–139.
———. 1951. *Reality and Dream.* New York.
———. 1953. (Ed. and contrib.) *Psychoanalysis and the Occult.* New York.
———. 1955. *A Study of Abortion in Primitive Societies.* New York.
———. 1956. "Mohave dreams of omen and power," *Tomorrow*, 4 (no. 3): 17–24.
———. 1957a. "Dream learning and individual ritual differences in Mohave shamanism," *American Anthropologist*, n.s., 59:1036–1045.
———. 1957b. "Penelope's character," *Psychoanalytic Quarterly*, 26:378–386.
———. 1961. *Mohave Ethnopsychiatry and Suicide.* Bureau of American Ethnology. Bulletin 175. Washington.
Ferenczi, Sándor. 1927. *Further Contributions to the Theory and Technique of Psycho-Analysis.* London.
Gifford, E. W. 1926. "Yuma dreams and omens," *Journal of American Folklore*, 39:39–66.
Grubb, W. B. 1911. *An Unknown People in an Unknown Land.* London.
Hippocrates. *Peri enhypnion* 86.

Hundt, Joachim. 1935. *Der Traumglaube bei Homer*. Greifswald.

Kroeber, A. L. 1925. *Handbook of the Indians of California*. Bureau of American Ethnology. Bulletin 78. Washington.

———. 1948. *Seven Mohave myths*. Anthropological Records. Vol. 11, no. 1. Berkeley, Calif.

Lévy-Bruhl, Lucien. 1922. *La Mentalité Primitive*. Paris.

Lincoln, J. S. 1935. *The Dream in Primitive Cultures*. London.

Linton, Ralph. 1956. *Culture and Mental Disorders*. Springfield, Ill.

Oppenheim, A. L. 1956. "The interpretation of dreams in the ancient Near East," *Transactions of the American Philosophical Society*, n.s., 46 (pt. 3):177–373.

Róheim, Géza. 1932. "Psychoanalysis of primitive cultural types," *International Journal of Psycho-Analysis*, 13:1–224.

Russell, Bertrand. 1903. *Principles of Mathematics*. London.

Steller, G. W. 1774. *Beschreibung von dem Lande Kamtschatka*. Frankfurt and Leipzig.

Wallace, A. F. C. 1958 "Dreams and the wishes of the soul," *American Anthropologist*, n.s., 60:234–248.

Wallace, W. J. 1947. "The dream in Mohave life," *Journal of American Folklore*, 60:252–258.

13

The Dream, Charisma, and the Culture-Hero

WESTON LA BARRE

The dream, in Freud's conception, is a homeostatic mechanism that serves to preserve sleep—certainly a finalistic notion. Classic analytic theory supposes that dreaming is continuous and that the remembered dream is merely that one in which anxiety has partly aroused the conscious ego. Recent experimental evidence of Dr. Dement[1] has shown this temporal discontinuity of dreaming, hence the neurological and the psychoanalytic evidence are not inconsistent. Day-residue tensions in the mind are released by wish-discharges in the "dream-work," and a compromise between organism and environment (physical and social) is partly achieved.

The means used is that of symbolism: in dream-work, the id-wish is disguised in symbolism in order to evade the dream-censor, which is the representative during sleep of the superego. Psychoanalysis considers that partial awakening (and memory of the dream, and

[1] William Dement and Nathaniel Kleitman, "The Relation of Eye Movements during Sleep to Dream Activity: An Objective Method for the Study of Dreaming," *Journal of Experimental Psychology*, 53 (1957), 339-346; "Cyclic Variations in EEG during Sleep and Their Relation to Eye Movements, Body Motility, and Dreaming," *Electroencephalography and Clinical Neurophysiology*, 9 (1957), 673-690.

hence awareness of one's having had a dream) occurs only when repressed wishes threaten to break through too massively; anxiety is aroused and the ego is called upon for help. Neurological evidence is that marked differences in electrical potential as well as eye movements and other phenomena occur only in connection with these rememberable dreams. In any case, probably only those dreams that are, so to speak, "important" in libidinal economy are ever remembered.

Dreamwork is therefore one method the individual person has of handling unresolved conflicts between the organic id and either the moral superego or physical reality. Small wonder, then, that the dream so closely resembles in symbolic content and defensive purpose the similarly disguised conflicts found in the neuroses and psychoses. In this sense, dreams are the temporary psychoses that "normal" people have when the reality-testing function of the ego is in abeyance during sleep. Similarly, neurosis can be viewed as only partly conscious and incomplete ego-work. And again, the psychosis can be seen as a fixed nightmare, or life-residue dream, without contemporary reality testing. The psychosis is a nightmare that persists while we are otherwise wide awake.

Modern psychiatry has shown us the many and varied defense mechanisms of the ego. The characteristic use of these mechanisms is a major component of both normal and neurotic personality. Róheim,[2] further, has shown that, in part, the *culture* of a society can be viewed as *its peculiar set* of defense mechanisms. French scholars, especially, have deepened our understanding of the differences between sacred culture and secular culture. Considered as an ideal type (in the sense of Max Weber) secular culture is ego-oriented and reality-adapted. Therefore adaptive technology doubtless undergoes a cumulative evolution through time: the giant automatic fender presses of Detroit are a more specialized and immensely more effective tool than the Abbevillean flint hand ax. But both are examples of secular culture. Human cultures are man's adaptive speciations; and these cultures vary competitively in their ecologic or adaptive potential; and hence, historically, some societies prevail over others. But technological culture is probably more easily borrowed than nonmaterial or ideological culture is. On secular culture, different societies tend to agree; secular culture tends to become intertribal and, like the science upon which it is based, secular culture tends to become international. It snowballs historically; it survives, and procures the survival of those societies that possess it preeminently. Secular, technological, reality-adaptive culture has a low emotional potential and is highly accessible to feedback from experience.

---

[2] Géza Róheim, *The Origin and Function of Culture* (New York: Nervous and Mental Disease Monographs, 1943).

Sacred culture, on the other hand, is of high emotional potential. Sacred culture is relatively inaccessible to feedback, and undergoes not evolution (ecological adaptation) but only change (psychological adaptation)—change "adaptive" to the *inner* tensions and *residual unresolved problems* of a *society* of persons. "Culture is man's ecology," then, in a double sense. In the secular realm, culture is in part ego-oriented adaptation to the environment. But culture also constitutes or is an important part of the human individual's "environment"; and not all of culture is adaptive to the outer world. Some culture is "adaptive," so to speak, only to the inner anxieties of persons (some of these anxieties being themselves culture-engendered!); and hence sacred culture partakes so conspicuously of the nature of the dream. In neurosis, the individual strives to cope with the unresolved problems (sexuality, aggression, and so on) of his ontogenetic past. Sacred culture is the "phylogenetic neurosis" of the society, a "sociosis" that, for a group of persons, strives to cope with the unresolved problems and anxieties (death, for instance) from the phylogenetic past of the society. "History is a nightmare from which I am trying to awake," as James Joyce has written.[3]

There are further concepts that we need for a fuller understanding of the dream and its role in the innovation of new sacred culture. Durkheim[4] has shown us that the sacred culture of a society must be "tailor-made" to the specific tensions of a historic society of persons: that is to say, people suffering from a common and group-characteristic unresolved need or tension (Lévy-Bruhl)[5] will mutually support one another in a common "will to believe" (William James).[6] The product of this group autism is not new technologic-secular culture, but new autistic-sacred culture. Just as the neurotic elaborates new defenses when his earlier defenses are threatened, so also a society elaborates new defensive sacred culture when the old autisms are threatened. Religion is one way men have of bearing one another's emotional burdens. But sacred culture is *not* an evolving adaptation to a physical environment, ecologically; it is adaptive to an irrational cultural past, primarily. Stubborn faith in the old autistic "solution" as well as new "liberal" theologizing are equally necessary for all historic religions, if they are to perdure through historic technological changes in culture. There must be a legitimizing contact with eternal verities of the past for the infantile authoritarian personality to depend upon; fundamentalist minds need, like children, to depend on the cate-

---

[3] James Joyce, *Ulysses* (New York: Random House, 1934), p. 35.
[4] Emile Durkheim, *Elementary Forms of the Religious Life* (New York: Macmillan, 1915).
[5] Lucien Lévy-Bruhl, *Primitives and the Supernatural* (New York: Dutton, 1935).
[6] William James, *Principles of Psychology* (2 vols.; New York: Holt, 1890), II, 230–232.

gorical rightness of the parental past, the cultural ancestors, the "fathers" of each church. But technologic evolution forces change in sacred culture, because secular culture constitutes a real change in the environing conditions socially. The epistemologically ambidextrous religionist deals with both hands: it always has been and still is true (fundamentalism and faith), but it means something entirely different now (liberal theologizing).

A nice balance must be preserved by any paranoid prophet who speaks with the voice of God (his authority being his own infantile omniscience; his god being himself speaking, from a childlike view, with his father's voice). For, just as the neurotic becomes very combative when his defense mechanisms are threatened on tender issues, so also a society becomes very punitive when its sacred-culture defenses are threatened. Men fear to acknowledge their existentialist predicament. They insist that they be loved by a supernatural father who is as omnipotent and as omniscient as the culture that shaped them as children—and children, authoritarian personalities will emotionally and intellectually remain. French sociologists, I think, have been particularly sensitive to the group-psychological aspects of sacred culture. We need a Durkheimian view to bridge the understanding of the dream Freud has given us. And we need the understanding of culture as a group defense-mechanism, which Róheim has given us.

A further insight is available through a dynamic understanding of Weber's term "charisma."[7] And here I remind you of the Jungian term of the numinous figure of the dream. Charisma is the compelling (seemingly reality-originated), seemingly outside, "supernatural" *authority* of the culture-hero and his visionary new culture. Quite as the just awakened dreamer may have for a while a compelling conviction of the authority of his dreamwork product (although an awakened critique will show the "profundity" as either trivial or absurd) so also a society under duress may have a compelling conviction of the authority of the charismatic culture-hero's innovation. But here, however, a functional distinction must be made between the psychotic and the culture-hero. As Devereux[8] has pointed out, the acceptable shaman must have less "social negativism" than the person recognized as psychotic. To the observer from outside the culture, both shaman and psychotic may seem to be objectively the same.

---

[7] Max Weber, *The Theory of Social and Economic Organization,* ed. Talcott Parsons (Glencoe: Free Press, 1964), pp. 358–392 [= *Wirtschaft und Gesellschaft,* Part I, vol. 3 of *Grundriss der Sozialoekonomik*].

[8] George Devereux, "Charismatic Leadership and Crisis," in Warner Muensterberger, ed., *Psychoanalysis and the Social Sciences,* Vol. IV (New York: International Universities Press, 1955).

The *society* takes differing attitudes toward them, however, and this is important. The reason for this is that the shaman uses defenses that are relatively *more* sanctioned culturally, and he uses culture traits more *in proper context* than, in both cases, does the socially recognized psychotic. The psychotic has failed to become the emotional lightning rod for his society, whereas the shaman has succeeded in this function. Devereux has also illuminatingly shown how charismatic behavior conforms to the "ideal image of the adult" as formulated by the child. The success of the shaman socially must be also viewed in this light, because the psychotic is too threateningly *like the child,* whereas a frightened clientele is seeking a *father* in the shaman.

The most notable quality of the charismatic message is its compelling authority. This compelling authority comes, however, not from the external supernatural but from the internal subconscious: the "authority" is not that of external physical reality but of the imperiously wishful internal id. Charisma is the emotionally *déjà vu*. The "charisma" of the culture-hero is the measure of the appetizingness and appositeness of his dream message to the unconscious minds of his fellows. The culture-hero does the dreamwork for his society. But we insist upon a distinction. If the autistic new sacred culture is too anxiety-arousing, the religious paranoid is adjudged "psychotic" by his fellows; if the new sacred culture is anxiety-allaying, he is charismatic culture-hero to his communicants. In the same way as the ego of the awakening individual may destroy the authority of his dream upon reflection and reality testing, so also the authority of the charismatic culture-hero may be destroyed by the reality testing of some reluctant individuals in the society (less pressed by anxiety, or with other or better defense mechanisms available) who do not join in the cult. Only thus can we explain the savage *odium theologicum* that ardent religionists have for the scientist or the freethinker. It is the same as the neurotic's hatred that flares when the psychiatrist tampers with defense mechanisms or fails to acknowledge their blessedness or necessity.

For the source of the "compelling authority" of the charismatic message is the same as that of the dream or of the neurosis: the human unconscious, not the cosmic supernatural. The psychotic is the shaman *manqué,* whose emotional message frightens because it ignores or destroys too much culture at a blow; the shaman reassures in communicating that the collective unconscious is, after all, in conformity with contemporary social "truth." New sacred culture is the *accepted* dreamwork of the charismatic. Psychosis is the *rejected* autism of the unsuccessful culture-hero. Thus, historically, secular technological culture tends to be universalistic and international because the same outside world is being viewed through a common language of hypothesis. But sacred culture tends to as many disputatious fragmentations into sects as there are subcultures (or even individuals!) in the society, because it is differing social and individual internalized and irrational pasts that are being attended to.

The Ghost Dance of the Plains Indians is illustrative of all these concepts. Under the competitively powerful pressure of a technologically, politically, and economically superior (that is to say, more adaptive) culture of Europeans, Indian cultures suffered a trauma, or, more exactly, all the individuals in Plains society suffered a collective threat to their traditional cultural defenses. Plains Indians believed, in a situation that saw the disappearance of the buffalo and of Indian prestige-warfare culture, that by dancing the Ghost Dance (ritual is the compulsive-neurotic act of a society, theology its obsessional neurosis concerned with wrongly defined and hence insoluble problems) they could bring about a new supernatural dispensation: the overwhelming of the whites by a new skin rolling over the old earth, with the dwindling buffalo now to become plentiful on the new earth, and the ghosts of the old warriors and shamans (secular and sacred protectors) reborn as helpmates in the new world. Sometimes, as with the Sioux tribes, technical culture of the ego and the strong right arm was added; but guns were technologically better adapted to war than bows and arrows, and the Sioux uprisings failed on the battlefield. But because other tribes had much the same will to believe, Ghost Dance theology, with tribal variations, spread like wildfire to other Plains groups. In some of them a compulsive fundamentalist loyalty reaffirmed old (but outmoded) cultural defenses; these were "revivalistic-nativistic" phrasings of the cult. In others, there was a selective borrowing of white culture traits; these were "acculturational-adaptive" movements. But in many of the Ghost Dance theologies there was an incorporation into native culture of only the *sacred* culture of the whites (or its most superficial aspects), and many Indian culture-heroes subsequently partook of the nature of the Messiah of Christianity and colored their theologies with the Christian eschatology of the prestigeful whites. If its sacred culture is presumed to be the basis of the more powerful society, why not try to borrow it too? In the New Guinea "cargo cults," which dreamed of ghost ancestors returning with argosies of white trade goods, we have a curious mixture: massive rejection of the old native culture, both sacred and secular, and ready acceptance of new white material culture, *but* with an autistic explanation of its basis. Whites were thought to have intercepted the boats sent by native spirit ancestors who labored to produce goods for their descendants, but now the cargoes could come in unobstructed, together with the spirit ancestors.

In summary, probably every "new" religion arises out of a crisis cult—a crisis of the society's cultural defense mechanisms, both technological (when feeble technology is overwhelmed) and sacred-autistic (when these defense mechanisms are discovered to be ineffectual). Messiahs are individuals who, for reasons of personality, feel most acutely acculturational stresses. Their fantasied autistic omnipotence (which is a paranoid reaction-formation to helplessness) finds a ready buyer in the society of those consciously feeling their cultural impotence in dealing with new predicaments. Paranoia and anomie become bedfellows and a new cult is born. The culture-hero's dreamwork (Freud) thus has charisma (Weber) for the collective wishfulness of other members of the society (Durkheim, Lévy-Bruhl, Marcel Mauss), and hence the crisis cult (Devereux) erects new autistic defense mechanisms in that society's culture (Róheim). Just as the dream preserves sleep in the individual and holds the real world at arm's length, so also sacred culture preserves the intellectual sleep of the society. Each crisis in life requires dreamwork; each crisis that epistemologically threatens faith in sacred culture, requires new theologizing. The dream vision of the culture-hero is the source of this new sacred culture: the "supernatural" is the shaman-messiah's own unconscious.

14

Hopi Dreams in Cultural Perspective[1]

DOROTHY EGGAN

INTRODUCTION

This study is concerned with the Hopi Indians, a small sedentary, agricultural pueblo tribe in the southwestern desert plateau of the United States. It must be emphasized that "Hopi" in this or other papers by the writer refers to those individuals who had attained maturity and full tribal responsibility before 1939, when my research among them began. Much of it would apply less strongly to their children and grandchildren, who, particularly since World War II, have been subjected more positively to white pressures. It discusses certain religious beliefs and ceremonies, particularly those that feature Palulukon, the Water Serpent, and a number of Hopi dreams related to them. We shall see that Hopi culture not only stressed the importance of

[1] My obligation to Hopi informant-friends cannot be adequately acknowledged because they wish to remain anonymous. I wish particularly to express my gratitude to Milton Singer, who is familiar with various fields that are relevant to this paper, and who has been kind enough to read several versions of it; Dr. Montague Ullman and Fred Eggan have also read preliminary drafts. It has been impossible, however, to incorporate many of the suggestions made by these readers. Fred and Alice Kabotie, close Hopi friends for several decades, have refused to act as "informants," but have tried to further my understanding of Hopi psychology.

dreams, but that their religious ceremonies provided a rich source of imagery, which was present from infancy to death, and which served both the purposes of the dreamer and the interests of the society. We suggest that dreams may be thought of as a triangular production involving (1) the latent content that is said to appear in universal symbols, and represents material not accessible to consciousness; (2) the dreamer's personality organization, and his personal situation at the time of the dream; and (3) the *relation of the dreams to cultural provision,* with which this paper is directly concerned.

In order to understand the vitality of Hopi social structure and religion, and its impact on the individuals who maintained it, one should first examine the educational system through which it was instilled, and consider also the harsh physical environment into which successive generations of this farming people have been born. For they, or groups ancestral to them, have occupied for more than a thousand years villages on or near the three arid mesas of sand and rock on which they now live. Surrounded by nomadic enemies, at the mercy of the always fickle and frequently destructive elements, strongly conditioned interdependence was their only hope for survival. A relentless environment thus became the ultimate axis around which an all-inclusive, thoroughly interconnected social and religious structure was built. In fact, these united into a system of thought and action which, as we shall see below, was so demanding, that it was in a sense as coercive as the environment itself.

It was, however, more rewarding. A strongly functioning maternal household, with extended matrilocal residence, surrounded the individual and gave him support against those outside the clan; and a dramatic, colorful kaleidoscope of religious ceremonies built on Hopi mythology wove the beauty of extraordinary theater through all of the years of a Hopi life-span. From the moment an infant's eyes could follow moving objects, beautiful masked gods—Kachinas—danced into and out of his awareness as he lay comfortably in his mother's lap. The color, the singing, and the drums that accompanied the dance, the graceful rhythm and intense concentration of the dancers, all combined into a superb artistry that is a hypnotic and impressive form of prayer. And as soon as an infant could sense moods in those around him, he must have been aware of the at once happy and absorbed attitude that pervaded the entire group on dance days. As the child grew, his participation increased, and understanding became inextricably interwoven with affect, each constantly reinforcing the other, as need patterns became organized through social process around specific ways of satisfying them.[2]

---

[2] For the discussion in the following pages see Murphy, 1947, particularly chapters 8, 9, 11, 12 and 14; see also Asch, 1952.

For the purposes of this discussion, then, we are interested in those aspects of integrated perception which are *learned,* and which are thus modified and eventually canalized through socially defined experiences. All facets of these experiences among the Hopi were consistent, and this consistency, plus affect in teaching, was combined with the fact that their language made exchange of ideas with other groups difficult, so that the whole created a situation in which psychological anchorage occurred in a much less diffuse field than in our society. The resulting reaction patterns became deeply ingrained and resistant to change, and the individual then responded to incoming stimuli with selective attention depending partly upon whether they aroused confusion or antagonism, or whether they were congenial enough to the perceptual structure so that motivation was aroused to try to integrate them with what had gone before. With ourselves the learning process calls to mind the ever widening waves produced by a pebble dropped into still water; but the Hopi *speak* of their social and religious organization as "concentric walls." Thus their learning process is not so much wide as deep.

Elsewhere we have discussed the role of the Hopi educational system in the continuity of their culture,[3] but we must briefly describe it here in order to provide a framework into which the dream action can be placed. The instruction through which a Hopi acquired the personality organization that made him so consistently and determinedly Hopi was deliberate and systematic. The early and continued conditioning of the individual in the Hopi maternal extended family was, on every level, an inculcation of interdependence as contrasted with our striving for independence. At the same time, and never separated from it, there was an emphasis on religious observance and beliefs, also stressing interdependence, a constant preoccupation with the ceremonial cycle, and frequent reference to myth and dreams, for storytelling and dreams played an important role in the Hopi world.

If we examine the pattern of integration through which the Hopi erected a communal wall around their children, we find that their maternal kinship system, with matrilocal residence and an extended household, was the foundation of it. From birth the young of the household were attended by a wide variety of relatives in addition to the mother. These attentions came both from household members and from visitors in it. In no way was a baby ever as dependent upon his physical mother as are children in our culture. Weaning, of course, when discussed in personality contexts, means more than a transition from milk to solid food. It is also a gradual process of achieving independence from the comfort of a mother's body and care, of transferring affections to other persons,

[3] Eggan, 1956.

and of finding satisfactions within oneself and in the outside world. Most people learn to eat solid food; many of us are never weaned, which has unfortunate consequences in a society where *individual* effort and competitive independence are stressed. The Hopi child, on the other hand, from the day of his birth was being "weaned" from his biological mother. Many arms gave him comfort, many faces smiled or frowned at him, and from a very early age he was given bits of food which were chewed by various members of the family and placed in his mouth. So, for a Hopi, the outside world in which he needed to find satisfaction was never far away. He was not put in a room by himself and told to go to sleep; every room was crowded with sleepers of all ages, and he normally slept with a mother, a grandmother, or another adult. He was in no way forced to find satisfaction within himself; rather, in infancy these were provided for him, if possible, by his household and clan group. His weaning, then, was from the breast only, and as he was being weaned from his biological mother, he was at the same time in a situation that increased his emotional orientation toward the intimate ingroup of the extended family, which was consistent with the interests of Hopi social structure. Thus, considering "weaning" in its wider implications, a Hopi was never "weaned"; it was not intended that he should be.

For, as *self* emerged for the Hopi, he was at the same time being taught to deny it, rather than to exercise it; he was taught that this emerging entity was an important part of the *group-self,* past, present, and future.[4] In other words, he was taught to achieve self-fulfillment only in group-fulfillment, in contrast to our creed of reveling in selfhood, of exercising it, and striving to reach self-fulfillment through competitive independence. He was not merely told that Hopi beliefs were right or wise; he lived them as he grew, and in his *total environment* (as contrasted with our separation of teaching at home, in school, and in Sunday school), until these responses on the overt behavior level became largely automatic. Within these "concentric walls" of "Hopi-ness" then, each individual was first a learner and then a teacher, in an atmosphere conducive to conviction rather than doubt.

We can now examine the hypotheses that are central to this discussion: (*a*) that the conceptual universe of the Hopi (described in the section on concepts and values) was not delimited, as ours is, by notions of time and space which made of dreams an experience apart from reality; and (*b*) that much of the learning process among the Hopi, especially with reference to religion, involved perception through *imagery derived*

---

[4] Compare Hallowell, 1955, chap. iv, on the positive role anxiety may play in a society, and on theories of self; see also Murphy, 1947, p. 855, and Asch, 1952, pp. 334–335, 605 ff.

from dramatic rituals enacted over and over again before learners, and that this imagery later, according to individual need patterns, could easily be, and frequently was, translated directly into dreams. For as memory, thought, and even perception can be trained by repetitive response to needs through consistent opportunities to satisfy the needs by specific responses, it would seem that, as Murphy suggests, the richness and form of imagery available to a dreamer would depend in part "upon the specific way in which training and broader cultural emphasis have enriched, intensified, or inhibited the imaginal processes of the individual." [5] We have suggested that a tightly structured society such as the Hopi tends to yield a uniform continuity of needs, and a consistent satisfaction of these needs, from birth to death; and that experience is limited in Hopi culture, both because of an isolated environment and because the society deliberately channeled experience in patterned ways for all members of it.

It would thus seem to follow that when such a society conveys much religious and recreational experience through dramatic and richly satisfying "images," as Hopi society does, the self-world of individuals would be richly endowed with images, particularly since these images were consistently presented long before conscious thought began to catalogue the world of experience, and continued to be presented throughout one's lifetime. This cataloguing is obviously always done largely below the level of awareness, and experimental evidence seems to indicate that much of what has been registered on the edge of consciousness, or just below it, is a particularly rich source of imagery.[6] But, in any event, it is evident that not only imaginative experience but logical thought draws upon this inner source, since no form of mentation could function without it. Logical thought, however, also depends upon the *outer* world's verbalized definitions of experience, and a Hopi, like the rest of us, soon learns that one's subjective experience, and another's definition of it, may be radically different.

No matter how tightly the society is structured, nor how thoroughly individuals in it are integrated with the society, there is always an insistent whisper from self, a point beyond which an entity that the Hopi call *hikwsi*—the Spirit of the Breath or Breath Body—resists what they sometimes call *himu*,[7] the Mighty Something, which may be thought of not as a god, but rather as their composite concept of divinity. But

---

[5] Murphy, 1947, p. 397.
[6] *Ibid.*, chap. xvi; Tauber and Green, 1959; cf., for instance, Fisher and Paul, 1959.
[7] Whorf, 1956, p. 60, translates *'a'ne himu* as "the Mighty Something"; cf. Voegelin and Voegelin, 1957: *'a'ani*, "very or intensely so," and *himu*, "tribes or persons, things or belongings"; Stephen, 1936, p. 1203: *a'ni*, "very much, intense, powerful."

when Hopi *hikwsi* resists *himu,* self-awareness in this interdependent household and society then becomes far more of a threat than it does among ourselves. Here a confused, unhappy, or guilty Hopi self searches for familiar anchors in the field of his inner world, so that often for a time dream fantasy carries the burden of self. And the Hopi, with a wisdom often shown by nonliterate groups,[8] acknowledges the dream as a type of thought-action in which *hikwsi* explores the world within and the world without, often bringing the two into closer alignment, through images and experiences provided by Hopi religion. In fact, the importance attached to a dream is indicated by the Hopi term for it, *dimoki,* which one Hopi "philosopher" translated in the following way: "It means a bundle of the dead body prepared for burial; it means a bundle of corn [corn being *literally* the staff of life for the Hopi] ready to carry on your back; and it means dream—maybe you could think of it as a bundle of thoughts. But anyway, all three have a *deep meaning.*" A bad dream, in fact, was considered so important that one must immediately arouse a sleeping partner and report it, after which one must go outside and spit four times, in order to complete the elimination of bad thoughts. A good dream, however, had to be "held in the heart" and not told until after it had been fulfilled.

SELECTED DREAMS

We now present brief versions of several Hopi dreams, and subsequently consider the religious background to which they are related before we examine them further.

The first dream is prefaced by a long discussion in which the dreamer relates what his father has told him: that people with good hearts have nothing to fear from Palulukon, the Water Serpent, and that if one is brave enough to take prayer objects to this serpent, the reward will be sufficient water for good crops.

Dream 1

In the dream, the dreamer has crossed a sacred cornmeal path laid down by the Hopi Snake Society, whose members are out gathering snakes for the famous Hopi Snake Dance. [This is a relatively small society which is said to have no direct connection

---

[8] Cf. Devereux, 1951, in which he demonstrates the use of dreams as a defense mechanism in "Wolf" Indian culture; Eggan, 1955; French, 1937; Wallace, 1958; and further bibliography on this subject in Eggan, 1961.

with Palulukon.]⁹ Having thus trespassed upon the Society, he knows he can be forcibly initiated into it. He remembers that he would then have to dance with live snakes in his mouth and is afraid he would get bitten and die. But the Snake Priests give him a choice *between joining the Society and taking sacred prayer objects to Palulukon, the Water Serpent, in a sacred spring.* [The Snake Priests may either initiate a male trespasser or impose a heavy fine unless the offender can join a woman or women before he is caught. The Priests may not approach women during the ceremony.] *After much self-doubt, and much advice from the Snake Priests, he goes to the spring where the Water Serpent emerges. The dreamer finds that the Serpent is indeed beautiful, as the old people have said, colored like a rainbow. Although frightened, he gives the prayer objects to Palulukon and says:* "The serpent's eyes are so bright, kind of yellowish red and he look very colored and nice—he look like a tame serpent and I wish I could catch him for a pet." *After a long prayer, the dreamer deposits his sacred gifts and says,* "I'm afraid to turn around; that powerful snake may catch hold of my legs and hold me tight. But I look on myself and found I'm a middle-age man and have to put all those childish thoughts away and act like a man."

After the dreamer leaves the spring, he looks back and finds the snake gone and: "I make my lively steps away from there." *A terrific storm comes up. The lightning flashes, there is roaring thunder, and the dreamer is knocked down by the lightning which strikes the edge of the mesa.* "I hear a wall of the mesa fall down to the bottom and this scare me and I woke up suddenly, so I didn't get back to tell the Priests I had seen the snake."

Having been sent on legitimate business, even though in penalty for wrongdoing, the dreamer proves his bravery and says it was a good dream, although he felt frightened after he woke up.

In a second dream, this same dreamer is less fortunate.

---

⁹ I do not agree, as is sometimes stated, that there is no direct connection between the two; it would seem that this conclusion depends upon what is meant by direct connection. Much evidence seems to indicate that there *is* a *conceptual* connection. The use of the same black paint—so sacred it can cause death if a young man touches it—in both ceremonies, the use of Palulukon figures on the Snake dancers' kilts, and the swelling and curing aspects among others of both Palulukon and live snakes indicate a connection among all aspects of the Snake-spirit-substance (see Parsons, 1939, I, 185 n).

Dream 2

He finds a hole like the sipapu [*the hole through which the Hopi emerged from the Lowerworld*] *in which yellowish water is boiling up and coming toward the top. He is afraid that the Water Serpent may rise up, and he is shaking with fear. The creature does appear, and is described typically as brightly colored, red and green, with white belly and with a head like a cat, and fur along its body. The dreamer says:* "What shall I do to get away from that terrible Serpent? But I thought of my Grandfather's story. He say a brave person can pull fur from the Serpent's body to make prayer-sticks for the Cloud People and that Serpent will not harm him."

The dreamer looks guiltily around to see if anyone is near and says "I don't want to be seen." *The Serpent then commands the dreamer to put his arms around its neck:* no one is watching *so the dreamer then breathes his prayer on his sacred cornmeal and goes to the Serpent.* "I was kinda scared but the Serpent told me to obey. Down into the water we go. I woke up with a scream, finding myself in bed and I tell my dream out right away."

This whole dream is charged with guilt. The dreamer is *not* on sacred tribal business, but he is snooping around a sacred spot where he should not be. At the time of the dream he had been discharged from a sacred office where a large part of his duties was the making of prayer sticks in a traditional way—not with fur from the Water Serpent's body. In other dreams he has been praised for his refusal to learn special magic from an uncle.

At another time, when he was in great conflict with his people, he records a third dream about Palulukon.

Dream 3

"I come toward my home village. People are frightened. Children run toward where I am and tell me there is a big Water Serpent in the pond [*where there is in fact no pond*] standing out of it four feet high, making an awful noise." *When the dreamer nears the pond the Water Serpent is looking at him* "sharply . . . as if he is thinking he has seen me before. It look like one I have seen before. The people are all frighten . . . and ask me what can be done to make the Serpent go away." *The dreamer reminds his neighbors that they all dislike him and deride him, and that they cannot expect help from him. By the time he reaches his house the village is shaking in an earthquake.*

He is hungry but his wife begs him to prevent destruction of the village. The dreamer eats, then makes prayer-sticks, and takes these with sacred cornmeal to the water. People cry and beg him to save them. The Serpent now stands eight feet high and is shining like a star.

The dreamer [who cannot swim] strips, swims to Palulukon, and tells the serpent to go back where he belongs. The Serpent lowers his head and is given the sacred objects while the dreamer breathes a prayer.

The creature disappears, and the dreamer lectures his neighbors about their bad habits (particularly gossip about the dreamer), and returns home.

Soon a station wagon arrives bringing the writer and her husband [who have never arrived in one], and then he sees Greyhound Buses coming toward his village, bringing more white friends. He wakes in surprise "feeling good."

This dreamer is very unpopular in his village, and prominent among the many causes of his difficulties is his work with whites. He is also said to be a coward. He desires companionship with white people, but shows guilt over his desire. He also shows constant need in his dreams to identify with his culture's heroes and to prove himself brave and of good heart, both necessary qualifications if one is to approach Palulukon.

Here is a fourth dream by this man.

Dream 4

He is carried in his bed toward the west ["west" being the direction of the land of the dead] by five men who are wearing Kachina masks. They have tried to put a mask on him but he has said that he could not wear a mask because he has been incontinent. The men throw him in a pond. He has felt numb with fear, but regains his strength, climbs out, and throws all five men in the water. They sink, and as he looks back he sees five Water Serpents standing out of the water, beautifully colored.

He tries to go home and is lost in a narrow canyon. His strength is gone. The Sun is coming up out of the west; he sees a river running east where there is no river. He wakes sweating, and calls it a bad dream.

This dreamer dreams frequently of incontinence in connection with Kachina dancing, often being assured by people who want him to dance that "it is all right anyway." The dreamer lost all five of his babies, and one of these was said to have died because he was incontinent before taking part in a Kachina dance. In his life history he mentions only four children, and when asked about this he said he forgot the fifth. In discussing another dream he "remembered" the accusations of incontinence connected with the death of one of them.

A second dreamer from a different village, who takes life much less seriously, records the following dream of trespass.

Dream 5

He is taking a walk and his attention is diverted by a car accident in which a small white girl is killed. He finds that he and his companion have trespassed across the sacred cornmeal path of the snake-gatherers before a Snake Dance. They run away from the Snake Priests and take refuge with some women, and he then finds himself in the peculiar situation of helping them with their washing; but as long as he is with women he is safe from the Snake Priests. There is a heavy rain and the dreamer finds shelter in bed with two women, both of whom are holding him "tight around the waist and neck." He awakens and comments regretfully that "this sure didn't seem like a dream but it was anyway."

Awake or dreaming, this solution to the problem of trespass upon Snake Priests is more pleasantly typical for the Hopi male than the one recorded in the preceding dream. In fact this form of protection becomes a game, and many humorous stories are told about it.

This is a second dream recorded by the same man.

Dream 6

Some men and girls are swimming nude in a government dam near a sheep corral. Someone pushed the dreamer in and he came up with a bleeding nose "looking like a Mud Head." [This Kachina often acts as a drummer in Palulukon ceremonies.] He then asks a girl to go away with him (romance in mind) and they become aware that the others are all running, clothes in hand, looking back at "something in the water." The girl screams for help, saying "There is something looking at us from the water." The dreamer puts her on his back; they run, he with one leg in his trousers, leaving the rest of his clothes behind. They laugh at their predicament, find a deserted house, and try again, but are again interrupted. The girl jumps from a ledge and lands in the dreamer's arms with her legs "tight around my hips." But he wakes up, and says it was a bad time to wake up.

The dreamer awoke laughing after both of these dreams, and when asked what it was in the water which frightened the swimmers, he said he was in too much of a hurry to look, but "it must have been the Water Serpent because we were behaving that way." At the time this dream was recorded nudity was said to be a rare favor bestowed on few lovers. Both of these dreams and the dreamer's comments on them have a humorous quality that is characteristic of his waking behavior, and he usually manages to find an audience that includes his hapless companions in his dreams.

The following dream concerns a spring in which a famous Palulukon lives, and is from a male dreamer who was under much family pressure to become Christian.

Dream 7

"I was walking toward the spring in the old village. I have been told that evening that the village is going to be flooded because of some kind of mistake the people have made. In this dream an earthquake started, and it have already made large cracks in the earth so I couldn't turn back. Everywhere the water is flowing and great streams of water were coming down from the mesas on all sides. People were drowning one after another when they fall into cracks trying to run some place. I was trying to run but I couldn't run far. Then I saw something in the water. It was all white. Its feet are not in the water. As it came closer I recognized Jesus Christ. I was waiting to see what He would do or say to the people around there when I woke up before he got to the village. Awful dream!"

This dream plainly states the confusion between two ways of life which plagues this dreamer in waking life, but punishment—a flood—still comes from Palulukon.

A woman dreams the following.

Dream 8

The woman and her husband's deceased mother are cleaning sand from a spring. Two Water Serpents are standing out from the spring. The dreamer is afraid but the older woman says these are good serpents and will not harm the workers, so they keep at their task. There is only a narrow passage with little steps leading out from the spring, and the dreamer wonders how they are going to get out of it, but the older woman assures her that they can do so. And, "the passage sure gets larger as we are going out so that we come out all right. Then on the way home I see my old uncle asleep in another spring, and there are two Water

> Serpents sticking out of it and they might harm him. But when I wake him up he say that the Serpent won't harm him but they might harm the ladies. I didn't get home when I wake up but I didn't feel scared when I wake up."

We shall find later that women do, indeed, have more to fear from Palulukon than do men, and the dreamer's dead mother-in-law and dead uncle are not reassuring companions in a dream. This is particularly true when one remembers that among the Hopi discipline is in the hands of one's uncles, and that *this* uncle reminds his niece—who at the time was involved in several affairs—that Palulukon can harm women of careless virtue.

The next dream was recorded from a younger woman who was a recent and seemingly ardent convert to Christianity. Her mother and grandmother had also been "converted," but in conversation and in dreams they expressed as much respect for the old Hopi gods as they had had before their conversion.

Dream 9

> *In this dream the young woman and a companion go to the village spring for water. Her grandmother has told her about seeing a snake in agitated water in the spring and has said that now no one wants to go there for water. But the dreamer and her companion ignore the warning and when they arrive at the spring, a little girl tells them that the water won't get still, but just keeps going round and round. They then see a black and white Water Serpent and it is bigger than a horse. They start running away, but the water catches up with them, and even though they were holding on to each other in order to stand up, they kept slipping on something. They finally realize that they are slipping on the snake, although it is now much smaller, and they don't know what to do. "I woke up half crying, my heart just jumping so hard I was glad I was only dreaming this awful dream."*

Here a recent report by the dreamer's grandmother of a water serpent in a specific spring, plus the dreamer's guilt over a current disgraceful affair with a clan relative—*a brother of her companion in this dream*—combined to produce a dream of sheer terror in which the snake is unquestionably a sexual symbol.

This is a second dream recorded from this woman.

Dream 10

> *The dreamer is wandering around an ancient deserted village populated with spirit people. She went into the house of an aunt*

long dead who recognized her. Numb with fright, the dreamer tried to leave. She found a snake in her shoe. She killed it and threw it over the cliff. It had been raining but had cleared. Looking down the dreamer suddenly sees a great flood and people are trying to climb up the cliff to get away from their flooded homes. The dreamer sits crying and hoping that her family will be among those who come, *but they are not. She awakens in fright.*

It was through the pressure from her family that this woman joined a Christian church. One does not kill a snake carelessly among the Hopi, and the violence implied in killing one and throwing it over the cliff is a very un-Hopi-like gesture. Although Palulukon is not specifically mentioned in the dream, the connection (see no. 9) between an earthly snake and the mythical one is plainly indicated by a great flood that destroys the people, including the dreamer's family.

HOPI CONCEPTS AND VALUES

The symbolism in these dreams is in one sense too obvious to require comment, particularly since the maleness of Palulukon is consciously verbalized in Hopi tales. But if we consider the symbolism only, we neglect many aspects of the personal situation drawn sharply in the dreams, and we would also lose the richness of an added dimension of the dream triangle: that of the relation of these dreams to what may be thought of as a culturally conditioned and very consistent "tribal Super-Ego," [10] which was "internalized" by these older Hopi to a very remarkable degree, for each dream given calls attention to personal infringement of the tribal code through the use of imagery drawn from the dramatization of an important figure in it. In contrast, the average person in Western society does not make recognizable contact with a God in a dream, possibly because our religion is not taught as intensely, nor pictured and dramatized so vividly, nor absorbed into our lives with the same conviction. Instead, our symbolism of authority in dreams—whether snake or another—is usually uniquely tailored to our own personal experiences with it and symbolized ambiguously.

And, since we cannot divide ourselves between two worlds and

---

[10] See Piers and Singer, 1953, p. 6, where Dr. Piers defines "Super-Ego" as stemming from the internalization of the punishing, restrictive aspects of parental images, real or projected. Hopi society does not have a primary family in our sense, but extends relationships widely within the household and clan (children have many "mothers" around them from birth), so that "punishment" is more of a societal function than purely parental, as it is among ourselves (see Eggan, 1956).

expect to find each equally intelligible, if we are to understand the deep conviction that stemmed from the religious mosaic built into the concentric walls of "Hopi-ness" mentioned above, and its relation to imagery in their dreams, we shall have to attempt to cross a bridge of language and live for a time in the Hopi Indian universe where reality does not dwell exclusively in propositions that can be examined through mathematical equations and scientific experiment, as it does in our intellectual world. In doing so we shall frequently find that this bridge of language affords at best a precarious passage, and that if we do not leave behind much of the intellectual luggage we have acquired in our own world we cannot cross it at all. For we, no less than the Hopi, have a perceptual structure engineered by language.[11] The requirements of communication thus direct those aspects of perception which can be verbally symbolized into concepts provided by language, and by the time one has acquired the verbal system of his culture, he has also, without being aware of the process, created a situation that serves as a context in which subsequent stimuli are interpreted.

Much in human experience, however, defies verbal projection in any microcosm. Experience more convincing than any mathematical equation forces upon intellectual man, as upon nonliterate man, an awareness of something that our language calls "psyche" and the Hopi call *hikwsi*. Certain nondiscursive aspects of existence are thus conceptually objectivized, and in order to further examine this objectivized "psyche" we abstract layers of it so as to deal more intellectually with it. But most of our intellectual world does not accept "being" in any but its physical aspects. We thus study "psyche"—a nonknowable phenomenon—in a manifestation that many investigators are convinced is a concept rather than a reality, and we do so through techniques designed only for *knowing*. The Hopi rightly say that intellectual man stands embarrassed on the threshold of a mystery which he carries within himself, and which is therefore thrust upon him; that this mystery does not fit intelligibly into the web of scientific propositions from which he has created a surrealistic God of geometric space and time, held together by a tension system so tightly anchored in our own linguistically structured perception that there is no escape from it. They may well be right that the ultimate paradox of intellectual man is that he can understand atomic energy and cosmic space more easily than this enigma within himself.

To the extent, then, that we are able to travel without familiar mental luggage, we may perhaps cross the bridge about which I spoke and briefly escape the boundaries of our linguistic perception. We shall

---

[11] Cf. the discussion in the following pages with Boss, 1958; Tauber and Green, 1959; Whorf, 1956.

then find that while we use different terms for similar patterns or concepts in dealing with experience, the approach is comparable, for if, as Professor Eliade says, religion begins where man's relation to the sacred is assumed by him in his entire being, and if it is an experience of existing in its totality,[12] then the Hopi know religion in its essence. For the Hopi *hikwsi,* Breath Body, as the vital aspect of their being, is not confined within the mortal manifestation that is an individual Hopi, even during its sojourn in the Upperworld. It can be projected through thought, prayer, and dreams, and can thus, in one sense, interact with distant people and things. It is at once personal and universal; in some contexts it is a part of *'a'ne himu* (the Mighty Something). [Our informants, when questioned about *'a'ne himu,* said in "certain ways of talking" this has "deep meaning" and that in this case "it could mean all Hopi, past and present (tribe), or even be applied to one Hopi, but only to very extraordinary or sacred persons, things, or events." They were reluctant to discuss it and were annoyed at our questions.]

But the Hopi are not "embarrassed" by *hikwsi,* as we are by "psyche." And the intensity factor, the action, and above all the thought with which Hopi religious concepts were implemented and retained are radically different from those of intellectual man. Different, too, and perhaps most important in the "reality" of their dream experience, is their concept of existence as timeless in our sense, for they do not measure time as a linear band stretching behind and ahead of them. Rather, as Titiev has stressed in his work on Hopi religion, the day and the year have duality,[13] as do all aspects of being, including a duality of Spirit. When the sun shines in the Upperworld, it is dark in the Lowerworld; when it is summer "here" it is winter "there." When *hikwsi* occupies its human body, this duality lives in the Upperworld; after death the Breath Body goes alone to the Lowerworld, where it continues the same pattern of existence it knew in the Upperworld. But having merged with, or perhaps because it is now closer to, the Mighty Something, it can work more effectively for the welfare of the tribe, both past and present, in its dual capacity of Kachina and Clouds. The universe for the Hopi may be described, then, as divided into the Upperworld, which we all know through objective experience, and the Lowerworld, which we have called a vast and inexhaustible reservoir of universal being, of male- and femaleness, and of Spirit, the Mighty Something that every Hopi knows through his *hikwsi,* his own Breath Body. Its existence is confirmed in every ceremony, of which it is invariably a part; in fact, without the Lowerworld, the Hopi in the Upperworld would be helpless in their environment. This

---

[12] Eliade, 1960, pp. 17, 18.
[13] Titiev, 1944, chap. xiv.

reservoir of being, however, imposes heavy responsibilities upon the living Hopi, for the *hikwsi*'s of living and dead Hopi must unite in, or with, the Mighty Something—which is accomplished through the unity of thought involved in their central religious concept of the Good Heart—so that the available potential of their spiritual reservoir can be fully realized.

As Kennard has said, the abundant literature describing Hopi ritual has concentrated so much on the magical devices that produce automatic results, that the psychological concomitants have been largely neglected.[14] Ceremonies may be observed and accurately recorded, but both concepts and subjective experience are frequently impossible to translate from one language into another, even in the rare instances where the sacred may be discussed without fear or embarrassment, and with no sense of betrayal in talking to those of another faith.[15] The average Christian, no less than the average Hopi, would find it difficult or impossible to describe to an anthropologist either the concepts of Christianity, or the subjective experience involved in his religion, even in his own language. This seems an obvious truism, but precisely because our intellectual tool *is* language we sometimes assume that conceptual thought is absent rather than untranslatable or withheld.

Whorf[16] has attempted to correct this tendency toward ethnocentric bias, and to hurdle the inarticulate barrier that stands between the student of Hopi and understanding, by contrasting certain aspects of our linguistically conceived universe with that of the Hopi. He describes our two cosmic forms as "static, three-dimensional, infinite space, and kinetic, one-dimensional time." As with our concept of the psyche, we also objectivize time, and divide it into measurable parts; and we conceive of space as measurable in light-years of time. We thus tend to "feel" about and to verbalize these cosmic "somethings" as a reality comparable to objects which we can hold in our hands, although we also speak of time and space as "infinite," which has nonmeasurable and even nonknowable implications.

But the Hopi have no linguistic terms for what we call time; no

---

[14] Kennard, 1937.
[15] This is far from the situation workers have found among the Hopi. All investigators have recorded Hopi reluctance to discuss any esoteric aspect of ceremony or belief, although their ever-present preoccupation with a Good Heart has been universally recorded. And it is not intended to imply, as the summary in this paper may seem to suggest, that each Hopi possesses a unified and articulate body of philosophy. Such explicit codification depends upon written, rather than oral inheritance. But through ceremonies, tales, and dreams, as well as in the occasional discussions with Hopi where "explanations" of sacred concepts were attempted, a remarkably interconnected picture of Hopi "philosophy" has emerged, however illogical the components may seem to us.
[16] Whorf, 1941, 1956.

past, present, or future tenses of verbs; nor do they have a term for space as we know it. Whorf divides the Hopi macrocosm into two entities, which he calls *objective* or *manifested,* and *subjective* or *manifesting.* "The objective or manifested comprises all that is or has been accessible to the senses," including the "historical physical universe, in fact, with no attempt to distinguish between the present and past...."[17] It excludes, however, all that we call future. We see, then, that for the Hopi the *objective* or *manifested*—that which we call the past and present—is already fulfilled, although it continues to influence being, through an accumulation of what one Hopi tried to express to us as "power or force, or maybe just what you might call conscience." For the Hopi, and particularly as it influences their behavior, "time" seems to be that aspect of being which is the knife-edge of now as it is in the process of becoming both "past" and "future." Viewed thus, we have no present either, but our linguistic habits make us feel as if we had.

The Hopi are well aware of the difference between our concept of space and time and their own. With regard to space, one Hopi informant said: "Close your eyes and tell me what you see from Hopi House at the Grand Canyon." With enthusiasm I described the brilliantly colored walls of the canyon, the trail that winds over the edge of it reappearing and crossing a lower mesa, and so on. He smiled and said: "I see the colored walls too, and I know what you mean all right, but your words are wrong. The trail does not cross, nor disappear, nor do anything. It is only where the mesa has been changed by feet. The trail is still there even when you do not see it, because *I can see all of it.* My feet have walked on the trail all the way down. And another thing, did you go to the Grand Canyon when you described it?" I said, "No, of course I didn't!" His answer to that was, "Part of you was there or part of it was here." Then with a broader smile: "It is easier for me to move you than to move any part of the Grand Canyon."

Similarly, the Hopi are aware of the burden that our concept of time imposes on us. They call us "hurry-up people," and say, "You are running around in circles trying to get nowhere in particular in a hurry." Another said, "You are running down a long road trying to catch up with something but it always keeps ahead of you." For people for whom time is an unceasing process in which everything is predetermined, rather than something that, through measurement, regulates behavior, our approach to time naturally seems demented. They further say, "When you ask a *bahana* [white] if he is hungry or sleepy he looks at his watch; you wear your God on your wrists."

And we can now understand that this Hopi feeling of timelessness

---

[17] Whorf, 1956, p. 59.

in our sense, of the continuity, or more exactly the coexistence of events (the *manifesting* and *manifested*) through time, and the nonrestrictive aspects of their concept of space, give a validity to Hopi dream experience which we, with our linguistically circumscribed concepts of time and space, cannot know. For neither time nor space exists in dreams. Dream action for all men unites past and future in the present, and in dreams space is absent.

It is the cosmic entity of the *subjective* or *manifesting* that each Hopi, in spite of his studied calm, stands in his human condition, face to face with the Mighty Something, and is obliged to interact with it, both awake and asleep. It is *here* that he experiences religion in its essence, seldom if ever in exaltation, for Hopi religion contains no quality of ecstasy, either priestly or secular; but certainly a Hopi here experiences what Eliade calls a total revelation of reality, which regulates every aspect of life, both physical and mental, through the Hopian Good Heart. For this subjective or manifesting aspect of Hopi being—this knife-edge of now which is at once the past and the future—includes not only action but all that we call mental, everything that exists in the mind, that the Hopi speak of as the heart. The need that is prayer may be transferred from the heart by means of *hikwsi*—the Breath Body—to a prayer object with the same effect as spoken prayer. It is no more necessary to speak one's prayer than it is possible to hide a "bad" heart.[18]

We thus see that, for the Hopi, thought is not merely energy expended through electrical impulses, either turned inward upon self, or dissipated into the surrounding atmosphere; instead thought is a form of energy that acts upon anything with which it comes in contact, either in waking life or in sleep, and this desiring-praying energy may be said not only to be "organized" in ritual, but it *must* at the same time be "organized" in each Hopi's heart, for each Hopi is responsible *to* and *for* everyone in the community; even one heart burdened with malice, worry, or doubt, although it might not be visible to a mortal observer, could defeat the entire community's interaction with life-giving forces. In such a situation, since the Hopian concept of a Good Heart was impossible of attainment, and since one can tolerate only a certain amount of guilt, there was a great game of blame shifting among the Hopi and this added a further burden of guilt through constant gossip and suspicion. This concept of a good heart, in conscious contradistinction to a bad heart (*kahopi:* not Hopi and therefore not good), has been recorded by every observer of the Hopi since the early days of white contact, and is of greatest importance, not only in understanding Hopi philosophy but as the major factor in their deep sense of cultural continuity and their re-

---

[18] Kennard, 1937, p. 492.

sistance to change. A good heart included conformity to all rules of Hopi good conduct, both external and internal; it was a positive thing. If a Hopi did not keep a good heart, he, or his children, might fall ill and die, or the ceremonies—and thus the vital crops—might fail, for, as has been said, only those with good hearts were effective in prayer. Doubt was *kahopi;* and through reiteration and drama, the dreamlike Lowerworld with its spirit inhabitants became as "real" as the Upperworld.

WATER SERPENT BELIEFS AND RITUALS

In order to relate the dreams given above to concepts provided by Hopi culture, and accepted as reality by the people, we now turn briefly to the religious background of the dreams in which Palulukon appears. Space requires belief and ceremony be shorn of their dramatic beauty, separated from the entity of related parts through which all these are united into a religion, and be merely summarized. Unfortunately, this is comparable to describing an abstract painting by referring to a fragment torn from it, and the Hopi justifiably resent such desecration of the tapestry of their lives.

It must therefore be stressed that neither the Palulukon ceremony, which is one of a number of winter-night *kiva* (ceremonial chamber) dances in the Kachina cycle, nor the famous Snake Dance, which is performed in August in the village plazas, is of special importance in the total ceremonial cycle. Rather, each has its part in a related whole, and although both are particularly spectacular—and thus have a rich potential yield for imagery—they are chosen here only because their themes are easily identifiable in Hopi dreams, and *not* because mythical snakes occur more often than do other religious images. Rather they are scattered through Hopi dreams along with other dramatic characters.

Although the Water Serpent concept is widespread in American Indian cultures, the Hopi, in particular, gave Palulukon a definite place in their ceremonial cycle. For them he was a flexible deity, at once a collective and a singular personage. As a specific deity he was spoken of as Palulukon who lives in the interior of the earth, controlling all the waters of the universe, including the large bodies of water on which we are floating. If displeased by the misconduct of humanity, particularly family, village, and tribal discord, and by sexual misconduct, he might turn over, thus causing earthquakes, landslides, and floods. The older Hopi were unanimous in saying that he is also associated with agitated water, whirlpools, flooding waves, foaming water, and water bubbling up from the ground or bursting from cliff walls. Hopi tales about this serpent include some or all of the above items, and often the following as well: persons who go into the springs ceremonially, sometimes in punishment, sometimes voluntarily, sometimes turning into Water Serpents, sometimes returning in human form, but always carrying prayer objects to Palulukon. When any of these items are mentioned in a dream, particularly one in which intense affectual discomfort is reported, the Water Serpent is usually overtly or covertly present. The creature is also said to impregnate careless women, but in only one tale known to the writer does this happen, and there are no dreams reported where he does so. There are also female Palulukonti, as we shall find in the Palulukon ceremony. There is no doubt as to his general maleness, however, nor that he is a greater threat to women than to men.[19]

Palulukon also supplies the life-giving sap to plants, and blood to animals, as well as water for all purposes, and in this sense, is all-important to desert dwellers. Collectively—sometimes immense, and sometimes "just small"—he lives in his "house" in all springs, pools, and bodies of water. From these he is watching the affairs of men, judging not only their actions but the condition of their hearts.

It must be remembered in this connection that the same bodies of water that are inhabited by the conceptually collective Palulukonti are, by the same sort of extension, symbolic *sipapus,* which are entrances to what I have described as a reservoir of universal being; thus Kachinas and Clouds, which are also the Hopi dead, and other spirit people, as well as the Water Serpent, all have "houses" in these places of water, and it is evident from ceremony and tale that he can intercede effectively with these Cloud-Spirits-Dead to bring rain. Thus the Water Serpent, as deity of the fertilizing waters on the earth and a god of the Lowerworld, conceptualized by the Hopi as a place of germination, was normally a giver of life rather than a destroyer of life. But here, as in all facets of Hopi philosophy, the role that Palulukon might choose to play was the direct responsibility of the Hopi, individually and collectively. Prayer sticks, carrying, as we have seen, the powerful Breath-Spirit-Desiring-Prayer quality of the Hopian Good Heart, were made for this deity on all important ceremonial occasions. He was so sacred, in fact, that most of my informants were reluctant to discuss him, and Parsons reports that one of her informants refused to draw a picture of Palulukon for this reason.[20] If approached with reverence, however, and given prayer objects by persons with good hearts, he watched quietly, eventually disappearing with these into agitated water. Only those with bad hearts need fear Palulukon.

[19] Cf. La Barre, 1962, p. 60.
[20] Parsons, 1939, p. 186 n.

THE PALULUKON CEREMONY

The vital problem for the Hopi in their arid land was an uncertain water supply, and the outward expression of their deep need for the power available in their macrocosm was arranged in a cycle of ceremonies, the most impressive of which, at least among the exoteric rituals, were the Kachina dances mentioned above. These were colorful pageants in which meticulously trained dancers performed on winter evenings in underground ceremonial *kivas,* and often during the spring and summer in the village plazas from sunrise to sunset, with short intermissions for food and rest. Their bodies were ceremonially painted, and brilliant costumes were worn, along with beautifully carved and painted masks which identified the particular gods who were taking part in the ceremony.

In the religious context, also, we must remember the intimate atmosphere that surrounded a Hopi child in the learning situation. Here children were taught that if *all* Hopi kept good hearts, the dancing gods would send rain. There was a holiday atmosphere throughout a village on dance days, but while each dance was being performed, there was the quiet of profound concentration. As the children grew older, carved likenesses of these gods, as well as other presents, were given to them by the gods themselves. These Kachina dolls were objects of instruction, and as a child grew in understanding, he could not fail to realize that the dancers were part of a religious ceremony of utmost importance in his world, that they were rain-bringing and thus life-giving gods, as well as the focus of communal release from a drab workaday world. Of the winter *kiva* dances Kennard writes as follows:

> The dance steps, the songs, and the Kachinas are the same that are used in the large dances in the plaza, but the effects are all intensified by the setting. Within that small enclosed space the gods seem to dominate. Nothing else matters. As a Hopi once remarked when we were watching a particularly colorful and vigorous dance, "You don't care about the outside world at all." The pounding of their feet on the floor reverberates, the song fills the *kiva* with music. The always pronounced rhythm becomes more pronounced. The flickering of the fire creates lighting effects impossible in a modern theatre as it flashes on silver bow guards, on shining black hair, on brightly painted mask, on glistening body paint. Each detail is accentuated for a moment and dropped into shadow again. The Kachinas turn and new colors, new feathers stand out for a moment and recede to mingle their individual beauty with that of the whole. For it is the whole line performing, the merging of so many

details of costume, dance and song, in synchronous movement that creates such an effective performance. Their numbers seem doubled and trebled by the shadows on the walls and ceiling, which assume fantastic forms.[21]

It was during this series of night *kiva* dances, in this period of the year when freedom from fields meant freedom to unite worship and drama so richly on an inside stage, that the ceremony featuring Palulukon puppets was performed.[22] All observers agree that this ceremony is an intricate and magnificently staged drama. The Palulukonti "house" (see pl. 1) is an elaborately painted screen on which are depicted human and

Plate 1. Palulukon screen from Third Mesa (H. R. Voth Collection, Mennonite Historical Library, Bethel College, North Newton, Kan.).

supernatural figures, among them Clouds, Corn, and Lightning—itself the acme of fertilization—and Snake, Sun, and Moon symbols. The Sun

---

[21] Kennard, 1938, pp. 17–18.
[22] Cf. the following account of the Palulukon ceremony with Titiev, 1944; Stephen, 1936; Hough, 1915.

and Moon symbols are on hinged disks through which the Palulukonti are thrust during the dance. These effigies are cleverly constructed of a spine and a series of hoops, over which cured skin is tightly stretched and then painted. The serpents vary from 1 foot for the young Palulukonhoyas to 4 feet for the adults. The gourd heads have prominent eyes, and a horn of wood, white teeth, and a red leather tongue. The whole results in exceedingly realistic-looking serpents which are very flexible. There is always one large male and one large female serpent, the latter having prominent seed-filled skin udders, and there are at least two young Palulukonhoyas.

On the night of the ceremony, while esoteric rites are being performed by the Kachinas at the village spring, villagers gather in the *kiva* for the exoteric performance, and a fire is built in the fireplace. The return of the Kachinas carrying the serpent effigies from the spring is announced outside the *kiva* by the hoarse roar of gourd trumpets or drums, this being the voice of Palulukon. The Hopis say that the trumpeting during the course of the dance is the "voice of the water, or water talk." When the trumpet is first heard, the *kiva* is darkened so that the scenery can be arranged. In preparation for the ceremony, members of the sponsoring *kiva* plant corn which is forced-grown in the *kiva*. On the night of the ceremony the young plants are arranged in small clay supports, which are invisible in the dimly lit *kiva*, and when the blankets are withdrawn from the front of the fireplace, the screen—which is described above—is in place, the field of growing corn is seen on what minutes before was a bare *kiva* floor, and small birds run back and forth on top of the screen. Then, as the songs of the Kachinas and the roar of the trumpet mingle and increase in volume, the Sun and Moon flaps suddenly spring open, and the Palulukonti, with fierce teeth and red tongue glinting in the firelight, come through them. The serpents struggle with one another and with the actors, they writhe and bite, until having emerged full length into the room, they finally bend down and "harvest" the corn in the simulated field. At this point the central Serpent is seen to have udders, and she suckles the other serpents. Then, amid great excitement and a terrific sound of mingled "voice of the water," and Kachina voices, Hahai, the Mother of the Kachinas—and in this capacity also the ancestress of the Palulukonti—comes forward and presents her breasts to each of them, and each serpent goes through the motions of suckling from them.

After the performance the fire is again covered, so that the Kachinas may take the Palulukonti and the screen out of the *kiva* in darkness. The blankets are then removed from the fireplace and the "harvested corn" is given to the girls and women in the audience.

This *kiva* performance is deeply etched in the memory of all who have seen it, and for the Hopi, who know its sacred implications, and particularly for the uninitiated children, who, in the dimly lit *kiva* must certainly have believed that these were actually supernatural serpents, the impact of the entire ceremony must have been tremendous. And we again repeat that this was not an isolated, once-in-a-lifetime experience, but something these older Hopi have experienced repeatedly from infancy.

SUMMARY

We can now return with greater understanding to the dreams reported above. We have suggested that dreams may be thought of as a triangular production: (1) the latent content that is said to appear in universal symbols, and represents material not accessible to consciousness; (2) the dreamer's personality organization, and his personal situation at the time of the dream; and (3) the relation of the dreams to cultural provision.

With reference to latent content and universal symbols, we do not have the kind of data that can legitimately be used for depth analysis of specific dreams. We can, however, make certain general suggestions with regard to the symbolic implications of Palulukon. First, we have in Hopi individuals a strongly controlled ego structure, and throughout the society what we have called a culturally conditioned superego that was remarkably consistent among these older Hopi. As far as the writer has been able to determine through personal investigation and from the rich literature on the Hopi, there was strong overt control in *all* emotional situations: anger, physical aggression, joy—in fact, in everything except verbal aggression through gossip, and in sexual activity, but even here orgiastic group aspects that are present in many nonliterate groups were absent. Much evidence suggests that sexual activity early comes to be positively valued for reasons of intrigue, boasting, and joking, in addition to the physical act itself. Nor was sexual activity romanticized as it is in Western society. Rather sexuality was *assumed,* at both the personal and societal level, from childhood on, in a highly realistic and matter-of-fact fashion. In this situation sexual repression was a less serious problem than among ourselves, and sexuality in dreams, as in waking life, was more directly expressed. Having separated sex from sin in all but certain specific categories, the Hopi have in one sense defanged the "snake."

We find, however, that Palulukon, as well as other fertility figures (for instance, Muingwa who grows heavy with seeds that grow on his body, and then thin when he shaves them off), remains a *conscious* sexual symbol in the culture, and as such is sometimes overt, or on the edge of awareness in Hopi dreams. But Palulukon, along with other deities, objects to *all kahopi* behavior, including sexual misconduct, gossip, quarrels, and physical aggression. Thus we find that Palulukon, as a completely overt cultural concept, is taken over in individual dreams, as are other dramatic cultural characters, *not in the sense of sought visions* that are so frequently important in nonliterate cultures, but simply as everyday, culturally defined symbols that are applicable to personal situations in the dreamer's life situation at the time of the dream. When Palulukon appears in a Hopi dream, it indicates that the dreamer or his dream companions are *kahopi* and the dream usually indicates in what way this is so. Even though the dream may support the dreamer at the moment, we see that it is seldom completely satisfying, and Hopi rules about dream discussion thus start a frequently successful probing of the dreamer's situation. By contrast, in our culture, which does not stress dreaming, nor prescribe ways of dealing with dreams, nor define its symbols so plainly, an individual may awaken in fright from a dream in which he was in mortal danger from a mortal snake, but unless he is psychoanalytically oriented, he is unlikely to connect the dream with transgression accomplished or desired.

The problem-solving dimensions of Hopi dreams, which have been discussed elsewhere,[23] have great importance in a culture where ego is in the hands of a doubly reinforced superego—personal and societal. (It is not suggested that the larger but more diffuse society in which we live does not contribute to our own superegos; obviously it does, but by the very nature of its diffusion it cannot do so as effectively as does the closely knit and consistently conditioned Hopi society.) The personal factor, or state of being at the time of the dream, of course determines the specific use both of cultural and of "personally invented" symbols, as well as the use of culturally prescribed ways of dealing with the dream. We find that the Hopi Water Serpent is firmly imprinted upon Hopi minds through ceremony and tale, both as a possible punishing and a possible supportive agent. He may appear in dreams charged with guilt or fear, as in dreams 2 and 4 above, or in dreams that give ego-support through making the dreamer feel brave or good of heart and his enemies wicked, as in dream 3; occasionally he appears in dreams where the dreamer is somewhat humorously involved with his culturally constituted self.

If a man trespasses across a sacred cornmeal path (dream 1) he may pay the penalty imposed by the Snake Priests, who are known to have scorned this particular dreamer by refusing to utilize a socially recognized mechanism to initiate him into their society. The dreamer thus partially reassures his ego by going to Palulukon and proving in the dream that he is brave and good of heart, but he is not fully reassured; he awakens in fright after a narrow escape from lightning before he can report his suc-

[23] Eggan, 1955.

cess to them. In the second man's dream of trespass, his fear of *living* snakes is frankly admitted by running away from the Snake Priests and taking refuge with women so that the Snake Priests cannot capture him; and he indicates his laughing acceptance of sexuality as the possible result of such refuge by ending the dream in bed with two possessive women, but awakens with regret that it was only a dream. It is, after all, impossible for him to cross a sacred cornmeal path with *complete* disregard of its significance. This form of escape is as logical a solution for this dreamer as it would have been illogical for the first dreamer, who shows in many dreams that he is not sure of his welcome with women.

Again, if one approaches a sacred spring with selfish motives, or on unauthorized business, as indicated by the desire not to be seen (dream 2) one has reason to be afraid, and is vividly reminded of the questionable state of one's heart by being taken by Palulukon down through the water into the Lowerworld. Even in a dream where a nominal Christian sees Christ walking on a Water Serpent flood—in effect replacing the Palulukon of Hopi dreams—the dreamer is not reassured and he calls it an "awful dream"! Christ evidently has not supplanted Palulukon effectively in his life. Nor does a second recently converted Christian (dream 9) find her new religion adequate protection against this *kiva* visitor of her childhood. Here a recent report by her grandmother of a Water Serpent in a specific spring, plus the dreamer's guilt over a current disgraceful affair with a clan relative—*a brother of her companion in this dream*—combine to produce a dream of sheer terror in which the snake is unquestionably a sexual symbol. This relationship is incestuous for a Hopi, even though Christian. And in addition, one does not ignore the warning of a strong old Hopi grandmother who is head of one's clan and who disapproves of the woman's shocking behavior. In dream 10, while in a spirit village, which is a dangerous situation in Hopi dreams, this same dreamer finds that her family, who exerted pressure to convert her to Christianity, has no protection from Palulukon. They are destroyed in the flood. Although Palulukon is not specifically mentioned in this dream, his attributes as given in the summary of beliefs regarding him, are present in it and in all the Christian dreams given. In this desert country, only Palulukon could cause a flood of such proportions.

As for the third aspect of the dream triangle, the cultural provisions, it is obvious that a cultural stress on dreams, and definite rules for dealing with them, must have important implications for an individual dreamer, if only because they emphasize recall and "confession" of the bad thoughts in a dream, a practice that results in a discussion of dreams and a tendency to further work out problems in them through "confession" of questionable behavior. That this practice contributes to secondary elaboration in frequently producing what is more properly termed a "dream story" than a *dream* cannot be denied; but it is almost always possible to distinguish clearly between the characteristically illogical dream and the culturally available associations with it.[24] Also the cultural elaborations chosen can usually be related to the known past and present problems of the dreamer, if one is familiar with both the dreamer and his culture. And it must be emphasized that the Hopi are perfectly well aware that any dream is an attempt by self (*hikwsi*) to make a statement about the dreamer's present situation and cultural integration. This is a conscious, culturally specific belief, otherwise dreams would not require specific treatment. A Hopi dreamer who wears his culture as easily as he wears his clothes, with satisfaction, with deep emotional commitment, or with humor, and is at the time of the dream more or less at peace with self, neither "begs" from his culture and its heroes, nor "questions" it in his dreams, as do the first male dreamer and the Christian dreamers above. Rather he simply *experiences* it as a continuation of his waking life, as does the second male dreamer discussed. But guilt, fear, and doubt make different demands upon self, upon cultural provisions, and upon dreams, and all these demands are clearly reflected in the manifest content of Hopi dreams.

We have long emphasized both the positive individual and social aspects of dreams as manipulated by the Hopi,[25] and their pertinence in the study of Hopi society and culture. And while neither the conceptual nor the therapeutic utility of examining *hikwsi*-psyche in its many-faceted parts can be questioned, the two are, after all, related wholes. For when a Hopi *hikwsi* searches through *dimoki*—the "bundle" of his dream thoughts—he finds it richly populated with cultural images that act as a rudder to push a demanding self back into the coercive tide of social process.

[24] Cf. Devereux, 1957; Opler, 1942; Wallace, 1947; Hallowell, 1948.
[25] Eggan, 1949, 1952, 1955.

References

Asch, Solomon E. 1952. *Social Psychology.* New York: Prentice-Hall.

Boss, Medard. 1958. *The Analysis of Dreams.* New York: Philosophical Library.

Devereux, George. 1951. *Reality and Dream: Psychotherapy of a Plains Indian.* New York: International Universities Press.

———. 1957. "Dream learning and individual ritual differences in Mohave shamanism," *American Anthropologist,* 59:1036–1045.

Eggan, Dorothy. 1949. "The significance of dreams for anthropological research," *American Anthropologist,* 51:177–198.

———. 1952. "The manifest content of dreams: A challenge to social science," *American Anthropologist,* 54:469–485.

———. 1955. "The personal use of myth in dreams," in T. Sebeok, "Myth: A symposium," *Journal of American Folklore,* 68:445–453.

———. 1956. "Instruction and affect in Hopi cultural continuity," *Southwestern Journal of Anthropology* (Albuquerque: University of New Mexico Press), 12:347–370.

———. 1961. "Dream analysis," in B. Kaplan, ed., *Studying Personality Cross-Culturally.* Evanston, Ill.: Row, Peterson. Pp. 551–577.

Eliade, Mircea. 1960. *Myths, Dreams and Mysteries.* New York: Harper.

Fisher, Charles, and I. H. Paul. 1959. "The effects of subliminal visual stimulation on images and dreams: A validation study," *Journal of American Psychoanalytic Association,* VII, no. 1.

French, Thomas. 1937. "Reality testing in dreams," *Psychoanalytic Quarterly,* 6:62–77.

Hallowell, A. Irving. 1948. "Acculturation processes and personality changes," in Clyde Kluckhohn and Henry A. Murray, eds., *Personality in Nature, Society and Culture.* New York: A. A. Knopf. Pp. 340–346.

―――. 1955. *Culture and Experience*. Philadelphia: University of Pennsylvania Press.

Hough, Walter. 1915. *The Hopi Indians*. Cedar Rapids, Iowa: Torch Press.

Kennard, Edward A. 1937. "Hopi reactions to death," *American Anthropologist,* 39:491–496.

―――. 1938. "Introduction," in Edward Earle and Edward A. Kennard, *Hopi Kachinas*. New York: J. J. Augustin.

La Barre, Weston. 1962. *They Shall Take Up Serpents*. Minneapolis: University of Minnesota Press.

Murphy, Gardner. 1947. *Personality: A Biosocial Approach to Origins and Structure*. New York and London: Harper.

Opler, Marvin K. 1942. "Techniques in social analysis," *Journal of Social Psychology,* 15:91–127.

Parsons, Elsie Clews. 1939. *Pueblo Indian Religion*. Chicago: University of Chicago Press. 2 vols.

Piers, Gerhart, and Milton B. Singer. 1953. *Shame and Guilt: A Psychoanalytic and a Cultural Study*. Springfield, Ill.: Charles C. Thomas.

Stephen, A. M. 1936. *Hopi Journal,* ed. Elsie Clews Parsons. New York: Columbia University Press.

Tauber, Edward S., and Maurice R. Green. 1959. *Prelogical Experience*. New York: Basic Books.

Titiev, Mischa. 1944. *Old Oraibi.* Papers of the Peabody Museum of American Archaeology and Ethnology, XXII, no. 1. Cambridge, Mass.: Harvard University Press.

Voegelin, Carl, and Florence Voegelin. 1957. *Hopi Domains*. Indiana University Publications in Anthropology and Linguistics. Memoir 17. Bloomington, Ind.: Indiana University Press.

Wallace, Anthony F. C. 1958. "Dreams and wishes of the soul," *American Anthropologist,* 60:234–248.

Whorf, B. L. 1941. "The relation of habitual thought to language," in Leslie Spier, A. Irving Hallowell, and Stanley S. Newman, eds., *Language, Culture and Personality: Essays in Memory of Edward Sapir*. Menasha, Wisc.: Sapir Memorial Publication Fund. Pp. 75–93.

―――. 1956. *Language, Thought and Reality: Selected Writings of Benjamin Lee Whorf,* ed. J. B. Caroll. Cambridge, Mass.: Technology Press; and New York: John Wiley and Sons.

15

The Role of Dreams in Ojibwa Culture

A. IRVING HALLOWELL

While dreaming has long been taken for granted as a commonplace human phenomenon, recent experimental observations in the laboratory have supplied firmer empirical evidence of its universality, particularly since objective quantitative measures of the frequency and amount of time consumed by dreaming in laboratory subjects are now available. Among other things, it has been demonstrated that the total amount of time devoted to dreaming during any single night is much greater than previously realized. Dreams reported following a night of sleep offer no precise measure of dreaming time since most of the dreams experienced of individuals are never recalled.[1] On the other hand, a high percentage of dream recall is possible when subjects under experimental observation are awakened. Dement, moreover, has advanced the hypothesis that since experimental curtailment produces such phenomena as anxiety, irritability, and so on, "a certain amount of dreaming each night is a necessity."[2] If this hypothesis is substantiated, it may turn out that we can assume

---

[1] See Dement and Kleitman, 1957; Kleitman, 1960; Wolpert and Trosman, 1958.
[2] Dement, 1960.

that dreaming is not only a universal human experience but that it is vitally linked with man's psychobiological functioning and his distinctive level, perhaps, of behavioral adaptation.[3]

Since *Homo sapiens,* as contemporarily observed, is the end product of a long process of hominid evolution, it may be possible in the future to consider the phenomenon of dreaming in this wider evolutionary perspective. Although direct observations of early hominids can never be made, it would be interesting to know whether systematic observations on living infrahuman primates would yield any of the objective indicators of dreaming which have been observed in man. I should like to suggest, speculative though it may be, that a consideration of dreams in an evolutionary frame of reference has important anthropological implications that are closely related to a revitalization of interest in man's behavioral evolution. For it is becoming increasingly clear that the problems presented by hominid evolution no longer can be focused exclusively in the area concerned with the study of the structural changes that occurred. It is necessary to take into account all the complex and interrelated variables that made possible not only the emergence of *Homo sapiens* considered as a zoological species, but concomitantly to consider the development of language and the cultural mode of adaptation which distinguish the behavior of the euhominids (i.e., the subfamily Hominidae) from earlier hominid species and other primates. Linguistic communication and cultural adaptation may be interpreted as the culminating stage of anciently established modes of organized social living in which protolinguistic and protocultural levels of social organization represent earlier evolutionary levels. A fact often overlooked is that structural changes, such as the erect posture that distinguishes the earliest hominids from related primate groups, and the expansion of the brain that characterizes the later hominids, occurred in animals typified by the fact that they lived in discretely organized social groups. Consequently the interplay and cumulative effects of such structural changes must have been fed back into the systems of social action that existed and, in time, modified social behavior and prepared the way for later developments.[4]

---

[3] In the course of the Fifth Conference on Problems of Consciousness, held in 1954, Kleitman said at one point in the discussion (1955, p. 114): "I am quite sure you need a cortex for dreaming." If this is so, the question may be asked whether the *expansion* of the cortex in the course of hominid evolution did not introduce a differential factor of importance with respect to the level of dream functioning that we find in the later and more evolved hominids. Early hominids, or other primates, may have experienced dreaming but, if the cortex is given special emphasis, it would be interesting to know how its expansion influenced dreaming.

[4] For a more detailed discussion of the behavioral evolution of man, see Hallowell, 1960.

I have made this brief excursion into the behavioral evolution of man because it seems to me that the same condition that made possible the development of a new behavioral plateau, characterized by language and fully developed forms of cultural adaptation, was also that which enabled dreams, visions, and products of imaginative processes to be articulated, and thus to assume the social significance we find in *Homo sapiens*.[5] Dreaming may have occurred in the early hominids, but, without the psychological potentialities fully released only with the expansion of the hominid brain, it would not have been possible for the content of dreams or the products of imaginative processes to have been communicated to others. It will be recalled that Mrs. Hayes observed the homebred Viki playing with an imaginary pull toy. This was inferred from Viki's overt behavior. "Viki was at the pull-toy stage when a child is forever trailing some toy on a string . . . dragging wagons, shoes, dolls . . . [Viki's] body assumed just this angle." Viki herself had no means of representing and articulating the content of her imaginative processes and communicating them to Mrs. Hayes.[6]

The development and elaboration of cultural adaptation in the hominids implies a psychological restructuralization. It led to the development of a personality structure in which ego-centered processes and self-awareness became prime characteristics. Until this psychological level was reached memories of dreams could not be recalled and integrated with other self-related experiences. But, once in possession of psychological capacities, which made symbolic modes of personal expression and communication possible, the inner life of individuals could take on a new personal significance and be communicated to others through verbal and graphic means. The inner world of private experience and the outer world of publicly shared experience now became intricately meshed through symbolic representation. Unconscious psychological forces, hitherto latent in hominid evolution, but now mediated through dreams, visions, and other imaginative processes, intruded themselves upon man, because of

---

[5] Beres (1960), departing from the everyday usage "which makes imagination a phenomenon associated with creativity and unreality, beyond the realm of ordinary thought processes," defines it as a "process whose *products* are images, symbols, fantasies, dreams, ideas, thoughts, and concepts." He considers imagination to be "a ubiquitous component of human psychic activity unique to man. . . ." He views it as "a complex psychic function, itself the resultant of a group of ego functions, that enters into all aspects of human psychic activity—normal mentation, pathological processes, and artistic creativity. . . . Reality is a relative, indeterminate concept, influenced by the imaginative processes in man." Thus "imagination is not opposed to reality, but has as one of its most important applications, adaptation to reality."

[6] See Hayes, 1951, chap. 11, p. 81, and comments in Hallowell, 1960, p. 354.

his evolving capacity for self-awareness and the knowledge he could acquire of the inner life of other persons. Dream experiences could become the object of reflective thought and become socially significant. Varied interpretations of the meaning of dreams could become an integral part of the diversified world views that arose and became embedded in traditional cultural systems.

When we assume that contemporary individuals in our society are able to recall and report dreams, we are postulating psychological capacities and an evolutionary level of communication and cultural adaptation that did not exist at the earliest levels of hominid evolution. The capacity for recalling, communicating, and identifying "more or less coherent imagery sequences during sleep" as a "dream" not only implies complex psychological functions, but a culturally defined attitude toward a particular kind of subjective experience. We assume the existence of a sense of the continuity of a self in time and a capacity for objectifying self-related experience. We take it for granted that the subject associates memory images recalled from his period of sleep with a continuing self in the same way that memory images from past experience when awake can be recalled and self-related.

While dreams in our culture are recognized as self-related, the manifest content of dream experiences is not fully integrated with memories of past experiences while awake. Dream experiences are not considered to be of the same order. A dichotomy exists in our thinking. The world of dreams is considered to be a world of unreality, imagery, and fantasy, as compared with the "real" world of perception. The dreams I report are recognized as mine, but they are not considered the equivalent of other personal experiences. In the cognitive orientation of individuals in other cultures, however, such a sharp dichotomy may not exist, or may exist only to a lesser degree. Dream experiences may be interpreted, in some cases, as the literal equivalent of the experiences of individuals when fully awake. Indeed, the psychological depth of this attitude is attested by the fact that even in acculturated individuals, the "reality" of dreams may persist.

Devereux, for example, refers to the case of a highly educated Plains Indian who was once a patient of his. When this man "realized that the florist's delivery wagon of which he had dreamed represented the counselor, he quite spontaneously, though with an air of half-humorous shamefacedness, asked the counselor where he went after he disappeared from the patient's dream." Devereux also mentions a group of Papuan natives who, having been converted to the Catholic faith, were "sufficiently well indoctrinated to know that they were not 'morally' responsible for the content of their dreams." Nevertheless, their priest discovered that when they frequently confessed adultery, "the adultery occurred merely in dream."[7]

Dorothy Eggan has pointed out that, viewed in cross-cultural perspective, dreams "can be considered both a projection of the personality and a reflection of the culture," so that in this frame of reference depth analysis of dreams is only a single facet of the area of dream study. Dreams may "not only [be] remembered and told," she says, but likewise may become "an active force in cultural conditioning and personality expression." And, functioning in response to varying cultural concepts, they "can operate in one direction as a sanction for witchcraft, murder and cannibalism, and in the opposite direction to maintain group unity and individual equilibrium. . . ."[8]

What I wish to do here is to show how the dream experience of a group of North American Indians, the Ojibwa, interpreted as actual experiences of the self, functioned as a positive factor in the operation of their aboriginal sociocultural system. In this case we have an interesting example of a mode of cultural adaptation in which man's capacity for dreaming has been made an integral part of the life adjustment of a people who faced the harsh realities of a northern environment in which subsistence depended upon hunting, fishing, and gathering. If dreaming may be considered to be a necessity at the individual level of psychobiological adjustment, here, at the level of group adaptation, the Ojibwa interpretation of dreams may be seen as a positive and necessary factor in the maintenance of the sociocultural system that gives meaning to their lives. Imaginative processes linked with traditional values play a vital role in psychocultural adaptation.

The northern Ojibwa represent a regional branch of a widely distributed group of Algonquin-speaking Indians in the United States and Canada, perhaps numbering 50,000 in all. When first reported in the Jesuit *Relations* of 1640, they appear to have occupied a much more restricted area in the region north of the Great Lakes. Their association with the Sault Sainte Marie led to their designation as Saulteurs by the French fur-traders, a name which, in its Anglicized form, Salteaux, is still applied to them in Canada. A form of the term Ojibwa is an equally early name for them. In the United States their designation as Chippewa is derived from the fact that the Bureau of American Ethnology officially adopted this term, a corruption of Ojibwa.

What I say here applies primarily to the northern group of Ojibwa I have studied at first hand. Located east of Lake Winnipeg along the

[7] Devereux, 1951, p. 86.
[8] Eggan, 1961, pp. 552, 554.

Berens River in the eastern part of the province of Manitoba and western Ontario, at approximately 52° N. Lat., these Ojibwa retained much of their aboriginal system of beliefs until recent years. During the period of my fieldwork (1930–1940) for example, there was one band that had not yet become entirely Christianized. The relative conservatism of the Ojibwa east of Lake Winnipeg is partly the result of the fact that, unlike many other North American Indians, they were able to retain their native ecological adjustment as hunters and fishermen. The physical environment inhabited by them was not fitted for agriculture or settlement, and the white population has remained extremely sparse.

I shall not deal with the changing aspects of their culture here but endeavor rather to present the substantive aspects of their outlook upon the world as it was constituted for them by their aboriginal culture.[9]

Man's cultural adaptation everywhere embodies a cognitive orientation that makes life meaningful and establishes a blueprint for action. A psychological field, or behavioral environment, is structured for the individual. Traditional beliefs, knowledge, concepts, and values mediate personal adjustment to a culturally defined world.[10] It is in these terms that events become intelligible to human individuals. A world view is created which establishes the ultimate premises for all that is involved in any comprehensive explanation of the nature of events in the universe and man's relation to them. "Of all that is connoted by 'culture,'" says Redfield, "'world view' attends especially to the way a man, in a particular society, sees himself in relation to all else. It is the properties of existence as distinguished from and related to the self. It is, in short, a man's idea of the universe. It is that organization of ideas which answer to a man the questions: Where am I? Among whom do I move? What are my relations to things?"[11]

The culturally defined attitude toward dreams which we find among different peoples is often a direct clue to the basic premises of their world view. Among other things, it provides insight into how what we are accustomed to designate as "objective" and "subjective" phenomena are sharply differentiated, fused, or blurred. It will be recalled that Tylor, in his *Researches into the Early History of Mankind* spoke of the life of primitive man as resembling "a long dream."[12] And, in his *Primitive Culture,* he referred to the "vivid and intense belief in the objective reality of the human spectres" which peoples at lower levels of culture "see in sickness, exhaustion, or excitement. . . . Even in healthy waking

---

[9] See Hallowell, 1955, chap. 5, "The Northern Ojibwa."
[10] See Hallowell, 1955, chap. 4, "The Self and Its Behavioral Environment."
[11] Redfield, 1952, p. 30.
[12] Tylor, 1878, p. 137.

life," he says, "the savage or barbarian has never learned to make that rigid distinction between imagination and reality, to enforce which is one of the main results of scientific education." [13]

What I should like to emphasize here is the fact that it is inconceivable that man could have evolved without making *some* distinction between dreams, or visions, and the objective realities of his actual physical environment. Man could not have developed the tools and techniques for which we have ample evidence in the archaeological record if this were not so. What should not be overlooked is that the intrusion of dreams upon man's consciousness and the exercise of imaginative processes of all kinds did not overwhelm him or submerge him in a totally subjective world. Early man became endowed with capacities that enabled him to absorb such experiences and, through his creative imagination, to integrate them with an apprehension of the actual properties of the objects in his actual environment. This human capacity is reflected in the world view of different peoples when we examine and compare the cultural patterning of the polarity we characterize as "objective-subjective." Too often conceived as a simple linear continuum, I believe that the basic principle involved has been stated by MacLeod. He points out that "subjectivity and objectivity are properties of an organized perceptual field in which points of reference are selves (subjects) and objects, and the degree of articulation in this dimension may vary greatly." [14] This variation is a function, in part, of the outlook upon the world provided the individual by his culture. It is through concepts pertaining to the nature of the self, and to the nature of the objects in the universe other than self, that the individual receives his basic psychological orientation.

Ojibwa culture defines a psychological field of conduct for individuals in which their cognitive orientation—in the dimension of self to other—is elaborated with particular emphasis upon the interaction of "persons" in a "society" that is cosmic in scope. The participating individuals of this "great society" manifest differential personal characteristics and play various roles, but they are unified by traditionally established rights and obligations. There are two categories of the "person" class which can be differentiated: human beings and other-than-human persons. While animals, plants, and inanimate objects constitute other classes of being in the Ojibwa world, "persons" are the focal point of their ontology and the key to the psychological unity and dynamics of their outlook. This aspect of their metaphysics of being permeates the content of their cognitive processes; perceiving, remembering, imagining, conceiving, judging, and reasoning. Nor can the motivation of much of

---

[13] Tylor, 1874, I, 445.
[14] MacLeod, 1947.

their conduct be thoroughly understood without taking into account the relation of their central values and goals to the constant awareness they have of the existence of other-than-human as well as human persons in their world. "Persons," too, are so inextricably associated with notions of causality that, in order to understand their appraisal of events and the kind of behavior demanded in situations as they define them, we are constantly confronted with the role of "persons" as loci of causality in the dynamics of their universe. For, by and large, the Ojibwa make no cardinal use of any of the concepts of impersonal forces as major determinants of events. Thus it is within an intricate web of social relations with other-than-human, as well as human persons, that the Ojibwa individual strives for *pīmädazīwin,* life in the fullest sense.[15]

Whereas social relations with human beings belong to the sphere of waking life, the most intimate social interaction with other-than-human persons is experienced chiefly, but not exclusively, by the self in dream. Social interaction in terms of the Ojibwa outlook involves no vital distinction between self-related experience when awake and experiences during sleep which are recalled and self-related. There is no sharply defined differentiation between subjectivity and objectivity here. The culturally accepted patterning overrides any such polarity. At the same time, dream experiences are not confused with events when awake. Qualitative differences are recognized as well as the fact that the kind of persons who play the major role in dreams are not those with whom the individual is most concerned in waking life. On the other hand, it should be noted that the Ojibwa are expert hunters whose reliable knowledge of the "real" properties of the fauna of their physical environment, as well as other resources, is highly impressive. Important as dreams are when considered with reference to their world view and the functioning of their sociocultural system, the Ojibwa cannot actually be said to live in a world of dreams.

What kind of entities, then, comprise the other-than-human class of persons of the Ojibwa world? I have used this somewhat awkward term in order to avoid applying the label "supernatural" to them. The concept of the "natural," ambiguous as it often is when used in Western culture,[16] is certainly not indigenous to Ojibwa thought. Consequently, the use of the term "supernatural" doubly distorts their outlook. Supernatural is an easily applied cliché but its descriptive accuracy, when introduced into discussion of the cognitive orientation of non-Western peoples, is highly

---

[15] Cf. Hallowell, 1961.
[16] Many years ago Lovejoy observed that the "word 'nature' is probably the most equivocal in the vocabulary of the European peoples . . ." (see Lovejoy and Boas, 1935, p. 12; Lovejoy, 1948, p. 69).

questionable.[17] Bidney, among others, has pointed out that "the dichotomy of the natural and supernatural implies a scientific epistemology and critical, metaphysical sophistication which must not be assumed without reliable evidence." [18]

A few selected examples must suffice to illustrate the *types* of *other-than-human* objects or personified natural objects. They are thought of as persons; they may be addressed as such, and interaction with them is cast in a personal mode. In an anecdote I recorded, it is recounted how two old men at dawn vied with each other in influencing the sun's movements:

> The first old man said to his companion: "It is about sunrise now and there is a clear sky. You tell Sun to rise at once." So the other old man said to Sun: "My grandfather, come up quickly." As soon as he had said this, Sun came up into the sky like a shot. "Now you try something," he said to his companion. "See if you can send it down." So the other man said to Sun: "My grandfather, put your face down again." When he said this, Sun went down again. "I have more power than you," he said to his companion, "Sun never goes down once it comes up."

In a myth, an other-than-human person once set a snare in the path that Sun regularly traveled. Sun was caught and could not move; darkness continued until Sun was released by an animal sent by human persons who could not carry on their daily activities in the darkness. In this myth, the movements of Sun are those of a person, not a natural object subject to impersonal forces. In the anecdote, the "natural" movement of the sun is reversed by the command of a human being. When Sun appears in the dream of a human person he addresses the dreamer by the reciprocal term used by the old men, that is, my grandchild. These brief examples give the flavor of the Ojibwa outlook; they illustrate the occurrence of "social" interaction between the "persons" of the Ojibwa universe,"[19]

---

[17] With respect to the general applicability of the natural-supernatural dichotomy to primitive cultures see van der Leeuw, 1938, pp. 544–545. Ackerknecht (1958, p. 53) says: "'Supernaturalistic,' though often used by the best authorities, is quite obviously a misnomer for these primitive representations, as it presupposes the notion of the predictable natural which primitives characteristically do not have. This notion of natural is a much later invention. I have been as prone to use 'supernatural' in some of my earlier writings as others have."

[18] Bidney, 1953, p. 166.

[19] Radin (1924, p. 518) records an anecdote that refers to a man who had dreamed of the "thunder-spirit." "When he wanted to make lightning he used to sing a song praising the thunder-spirit. Then when he had finished singing, he would cut up some tobacco, put some into the fire and some into his pipe. Then he would shout in the direction of the south, 'Let thunder come!' The next day there would be a tremendous thunder storm."

and they demonstrate the unity in thought which prevails in anecdote, myth, and dream.

The Winds are conceptualized as siblings, and there is a myth referring to their birth from an anthropomorphic mother. The directions of the Ojibwa cosmos are defined by their dwelling places, that is, the homes of these other-than-human persons. Another typical subcategory of other-than-human person comprises the "owners" or "masters" of what we term natural species of plants and animals. There is a "master" of birch trees, and of bears. If animals, like the bear, are not treated properly after being killed, the master may take offense and retaliate by withholding members of the species from the hunter.

The Thunderbirds represent another type of personage. They live in a land above the flat earth that is the dwelling place of human persons, that is, *änicinabék* (the Ojibwa). The Thunderbirds are classified with the hawks, of which there are several natural species known to the Ojibwa. In a myth, a human being reaches Thunderbird Land where he immediately finds himself at home. These creatures hunt and talk and dance. Besides this, the young man is enabled to find his place in their kinship system at once because it is precisely the same as that of the Ojibwa. He marries a Thunderbird girl. Later she and her sisters return to earth with him and her sisters marry his brothers, a pattern that often occurs among the Ojibwa. In one case in my genealogies six blood brothers were married to a sorority of six sisters.

Although the Thunderbirds are primarily conceived as avian in form, their outward appearance is not constant. In the myth, metamorphosis occurs as part of the plot. Some of them become anthropomorphic in appearance. Here we come close to the metaphysical core of the Ojibwa conception of being. Outward appearance is actually superficial. Although the Thunderbirds, like other entities of the other-than-human category, have distinctive attributes of their own, they have the same basic, enduring essence as do human persons. It is this vital core that is constant in both categories of persons. Human persons, too, have a constant and enduring essence (*òtcatcákwin*) and a bodily form (*miyó*) which, under most circumstances, is an identifying characteristic. But in neither category of the person class is the inner essence accessible to *visual* perception under any conditions. What can be perceived visually is only the aspect of being that has form. As we shall see later, metamorphosis, under certain conditions, is also possible for human beings. Change in outward appearance is potentially inherent in individuals belonging to both categories of persons. Consequently, the metamorphosis of the Thunderbird girls in the myth, and their marriage to human beings, can be accepted by the Ojibwa as an actual event in the kind of world to which they are culturally oriented. It is not a fanciful event attributable only to fictitious characters in an alien world of myth. I was once told of an Ojibwa woman (identifiable in my genealogies) who claimed that North Wind was the father of one of her children. My informant said he did not believe this; nevertheless, he thought it would have been accepted as a possibility in the past.[20]

The kind of social interaction possible between human and other-than-human persons in the context of daily life is illustrated by another anecdote. An informant told me that once on a summer afternoon during a storm he was sitting in a tent with a very old man and his wife. There was one clap of thunder after another. Suddenly, the old man turned to his wife and asked, "Did you hear what was said?" "No," she replied, "I didn't catch it." My informant, an acculturated Indian, told me that at first he did not know what the old man and his wife referred to. It was, of course, the thunder. The old man thought that one of the Thunderbirds had said something to him. He was reacting to this sound in the same way as he would respond to a human being whose words he did not at once understand. The casualness of the remark demonstrates the psychological reality of the social relations with other-than-human persons that may become explicit in the behavior of the Ojibwa as a consequence of the cognitive "set" induced by their culture. I may add that, implicit in this anecdote is the assumption that the old man must have had previous contact with a Thunderbird in the dreams of his puberty fast. This explains why he thought he was addressed. By and large, the Ojibwa do not attune themselves to receiving messages every time a thunderstorm occurs!

Another occasion when social interaction becomes possible between human and other-than-human persons is at a conjuring performance (*ķosábandamowin*). Its purpose is to secure help from other-than-human persons by invoking their presence and communicating human desires to them. A barrel-like framework of poles is built and covered with birchbark or canvas. The conjurer enters the structure after dark; the audience gathers outside. The conjurer invokes his particular benefactors among the host of other-than-human persons. They manifest themselves vocally, the voices issuing from the lodge being distinguishable from each other and from the voice of the conjurer who kneels within. These invoked entities may sometimes sing a song and name themselves. The Master of the moose may say: "Moose I am called." The lodge is in almost constant movement from the time the conjurer enters it. The Winds are responsi-

---

[20] This may have been a rationalization of mother-son incest. But, if so, the woman's "bad conduct" was never punished by sickness, nor did she ever confess her wrongdoing. These circumstances may have lent credence to her claim, when considered in the context of the Ojibwa world view.

ble for this. Direct communication sometimes takes place between members of the audience and some of the other-than-human persons present. At one performance I attended several members of the audience called for Mikīnák, the Great Turtle. Anyone may speak to Mikīnák and he always has a witty answer ready. He talks in a throaty nasal voice not unlike that of Donald Duck. His popularity with the audience was manifested throughout the evening by the intermittent stream of repartee that took place between Mikīnák and members of the audience. He strikes a note of levity in performances that are basically very serious in purpose.

One of the major sources of information about other-than-human persons, both to the Ojibwa themselves and to the investigator, are the myths. From the Ojibwa point of view they are not fiction. On the contrary, they narrate the past activities of well-known other-than-human persons who are their chief characters. The attitude toward myth exemplified in Ojibwa culture is essentially generalized by Eliade when he says that "it is the foundation of a structure of reality as well as a kind of human behavior. A myth always narrates something as having *really happened,* as an event that took place, in the plain sense of the term. . . . Myths reveal the structure of reality, and the multiple modalities of being in the world. . . . They disclose the *true* stories, concern themselves with the *realities.*" [21] In the context of their aboriginal culture, myths among the Ojibwa were only told during the long winter evenings by a narrator who dramatized them by gestures and other appropriate actions. These occasions were, in fact, a kind of invocation. The characters of myth, immortal living persons, were thought to come and listen to what was being said. In ancient times, one of these entities (Wisekedjak) is reputed to have said to the others: "We'll try to make everything to suit the *änicinabék* as long as any of them exist, so that they will never forget us and will always talk about us." Whereas we are inclined to think of myths as a special class of stories, the Ojibwa term for them—*ätisokának*—has no such connotation. It refers, rather, to the characters themselves, so that as William Jones said many years ago, "Myths are thought of as conscious beings, with powers of thought and action." [22] Consequently there is conclusive linguistic evidence of the category to which the characters in these belong. Along with other persons of the other-than-human category they are collectively referred to by the Ojibwa as "our grandfathers." This attests both to their psychological status as persons while, at the same time, it brings them within the boundaries of a social system in which everyone is given a kinship status. On account of the repeated recitation of myths winter after winter, children growing up in Ojibwa society be-

---

[21] Eliade, 1960, pp. 14–15.
[22] W. Jones, 1919, Part II, p. 574 n.

came almost as familiar with their other-than-human grandfathers as they did with their human grandfathers.[23] They also heard the voices of the former at conjuring performances.[24] Furthermore, the individuality of other-than-human beings became reinforced by the fact that a character like Mikīnák always was heard to speak in the same characteristic manner whether in the narration of myths or in the shaking tent. Thus the reality of these characters did not depend upon conceptualization alone; their image was strongly reinforced by actual perceptual experience.

Any members of the other-than-human category of persons might appear in the dreams of Ojibwa individuals. In this context they were usually referred to as *pawáganak*, which may be rendered "dream visitors." Their appearance in the dreams was, of course, not as strangers or unfamiliar figures but as well-known living entities of the Ojibwa world. It is scarcely to be expected, then, that interpersonal relations with them in dreams could be dissociated from the knowledge of them which already existed in other contexts. Such relations could not be interpreted as other than experiences of the self. But dream experiences brought the individual into intimate personal contact with particular other-than-human persons. Besides this, the role that this category of persons played in those experiences was culturally defined as immensely vital to the welfare of the individual.

DREAMS, MOTIVATION, AND THE SOCIOCULTURAL SYSTEM

Having considered the world view of the Ojibwa, I now analyze the relations between dreams, the motivation of individuals, and the functioning of their sociocultural system. I already have indicated that, for the Ojibwa, social relations with other-than-human persons are not metaphorical but intimately meshed in their thought and experience with interrelationships between human beings. I have referred to a few examples which show how social relations with other-than-human persons

---

[23] I was told that on the winter evenings when myths were narrated children were encouraged to dream about their other-than-human grandfathers. That they may well have done so is suggested by the fact that C. W. Kimmis has called attention to the influence of stories read to children before going to sleep upon the content of their dreams. See quotations from Kimmis in Woods, 1947.

[24] I once asked an informant who was about seventy years old to name all the other-than-human persons he had heard speak, or sing, in conjuring performances (see Hallowell, 1942, for the list). They included five characters who play a prominent role in myth; four other personages semihuman in form; and almost two dozen of the "masters" of various animal species.

may enter the waking consciousness of human beings. Dreams, however, assume a special significance in any analysis of the functioning of the Ojibwa sociocultural system because the dream imagery that is interpreted as bringing the individual into direct face-to-face contact with other-than-human persons becomes so intimately linked with the motivation of individuals, traditional values, and social behavior. Contacts with other-than-human entities are highly motivated and sought by individuals as a means of achieving a personal life adjustment consonant with the characteristic values of the Ojibwa world. At the same time, dream experiences have significance with relation to the social system and community life because they are not only influential components of actual conduct but because they validate specialized services, like curing, which become available to other persons.

It must likewise be noted that interpersonal relations between human and other-than-human beings involve reciprocal rights and obligations, in the same way that social relations between human persons do. And these obligations are reinforced by the same sanctions that apply to social relations between human beings. Failure to fulfill them, in either case, is one variety of "bad conduct," bad conduct being culturally defined as any unpredictable or deviant conduct that fails to conform with the traditional normative standards of interpersonal relations. The penalty for bad conduct is illness. Any kind of bad conduct on my part is said to "follow me." I will inevitably become ill, or my children may get sick, or my wife may die. The fear of becoming ill and the anxiety engendered by any serious sickness is the major sanction of the Ojibwa sociocultural system. What is particularly characteristic is the fact that the bad conduct of human beings is believed to be the major source of illness. Consequently in every case of serious sickness an individual must reflect upon what kind of misdeeds he may have been responsible for in the past. Even in cases of sorcery the reputed act of the sorcerer is interpreted as retaliation for some previous bad conduct on the part of the *victim* in his interpersonal relations with the sorcerer.[25]

In this society no institutionalized means exist for the public adjudication of disputes or personal conflicts of any kind. There is no way in which publicly sanctioned punishments can be initiated in cases of incest, murder, or other offenses. For adults there are no superordinate modes of social control. Nor do other-than-human persons, any more than human beings, sit in judgment upon the acts of the latter and initiate punishment. Other-than-human entities exercise no punishing role; their relations to man are benevolent. If a human being fails to fulfill any obligation to them, sickness "follows him" as a matter of course. Social control

---

[25] For a detailed discussion of Ojibwa world view and disease, see Hallowell, 1963.

in Ojibwa society conforms to the type that Whiting describes as operating through the mechanism of conscience or superego.[26] It involves a highly developed sense of personal responsibility for one's own conduct, sensitivity to guilt, and readiness to accept blame for one's actions. Consequently, it is necessary that the Ojibwa individual be groomed for independent action, associated with the capacity for bearing a heavy burden of moral responsibility, acquired through self-discipline. At the same time he needs to develop an inner sense of personal security in order to face the vicissitudes of life. This applies particularly to males who, being the hunters, are responsible for supplying the daily needs of their families.

A central value correlative with the Ojibwa food-gathering economy is the emphasis laid upon what may be called "equalitarian" values; these serve to equilibrate the distribution and consumption of goods in a system where purchase in a market is absent. They are expressed through sharing, borrowing, and mutual exchange. Dependence upon hunting, trapping, and fishing for a living is precarious at best and, even though the individual hunter may exercise his best skills, it is impossible to accumulate food for the inevitable rainy day. As a result, if I have more than I need today, I share it with you because I know that you, in turn, will share what you have with me tomorrow. In Ojibwa society there are no culturally structured incentives that induce individuals to surpass their fellows in the accumulation of material goods. No one is expected to have much more than anyone else, except temporarily.

It is particularly important to recognize that sharing what one has with others is a value that permeates the "great society" in which the Ojibwa live. This is the reason why the Ojibwa expect that powers possessed by other-than-human persons will be shared with them. Beings of the other-than-human category, considered as persons, are believed to be oriented to the same values and to be motivated like themselves. Other-than-human beings have more power than they need. From the Ojibwa point of view they may be said to have a surplus of power, so that it is legitimate to induce them to share it with human beings in order to meet the latter's needs.

The Ojibwa believe that a good life, free from illness, hunger, and misfortune (i.e., *pīmädazīwin*) cannot be achieved through relations with other human beings alone, cooperative as they may be. The help of powerful persons of the other-than-human category is a necessity, especially for

---

[26] On the basis of systematic cross-cultural sampling, Whiting (1959) has discriminated three types of social control, which he related to three independent motivational systems and the child-rearing practices and conditions required to produce and maintain them. Although he did not include the Ojibwa in his study, they would appear to conform to Whiting's Type 3.

men. Women may obtain such help but men cannot get along without it. Since the Masters of the game animals, for instance, control the most vital source of food supply, a man needs contact with them. His own acquired skill as a hunter and trapper is not all that is required. With the help of powerful other-than-human persons a man can also defend himself against human beings hostile to him. Besides this, every special aptitude—such as curing and conjuring—exercised by men, depends upon the help of other-than-human entities, rather than upon their own individual talents or efforts. Furthermore, other-than-human persons of any functional significance were males, a fact correlative with patrilineal descent in Ojibwa culture and the subordinate role that women played in ceremonial life, and in such specialized activities as conjuring and curing.

THE DREAM FAST

The help that men needed from males of the other-than-human category was primarily obtained in a lonely vigil through personal face-to-face contact with them in dreams. The grandfather of one of my informants said to him: "You will have a long and good life if you dream well." In aboriginal days it was customary to send boys between the ages of ten and fifteen out to fast for six or seven nights. They became suppliants in need of help; they were said to provoke the "pity" of their other-than-human grandfathers.[27] Coming to their aid these *pawáganak* "blessed" them, as English-speaking informants phrase it, by offering to share their knowledge and power.

A boy undergoing a dream fast was called *kīgúsämo*. The essential condition for this experience was that he be *pékize,* that is, pure, clean. He must never have had sexual intercourse. Even less intimate relations with women before, during, and immediately after fasting were considered contaminating and were to be avoided. If he had not met these conditions

---

[27] Blumensohn, in his survey, points out that "the use of fasting in a personal relation with the supernatural was peculiar to the Central Algonkian" (1933, p. 468). "They believed that by fasting the suppliant underwent such suffering, made himself so weak, that the spirits were overcome with pity, and so granted him whatever he desired" (p. 451). Kohl, visiting the Lake Superior Ojibwa over a century ago, was fascinated with the dream fast. "I found this subject most remarkable," he writes (1860, p. 228), "in fact, could it be possible to hear any thing stronger, or, I might say, more wonderful, than these stories of unheard of castigations and torments, to which young boys of thirteen or fourteen subject themselves, merely for the sake of an idea, a dream, or the fulfillment of a religious duty, or to ask a question of fate. . . . What courage! What self control! What power of enduring privation does this presuppose!"

no other-than-human person would bless him or even approach him. Anecdotes are told to illustrate the importance of keeping such taboos. Boys were sent out in the spring to some distance from the camp. One informant said he was about thirteen years old at the time. A boy's clothes were carefully washed beforehand and he was provided with a new blanket. A moose or caribou skin, dyed with red ochre or sometimes painted with pictographs, was given him to lie on. Prior to his departure the boy slept in the "cleanest" place in the dwelling, that is, toward the rear, in the area reserved for the men. Before this he had slept nearer the front with his mother and other prepuberal children. This shift in sleeping quarters symbolized his segregation from the women and his approach to manhood.

When a boy is ready to depart for his dream fast he is accompanied into the bush by his father, grandfather, or other male relatives. When they arrive at a desirable spot a "nest" (*wázisan*) is built. In the case of the informant mentioned, an older brother built it. The *wázisan* is a platform made by laying poles across the branches of a tree, about 15 feet from the ground. The *kīgúsämo* climbs the tree and seats himself, or stretches out, on this platform. It was forbidden to descend to the ground during the dream fast except to urinate and defecate. No food or drink must pass his lips. My informant said that his dream fast had lasted ten nights. "While I was there," he said, "I only thought of the good things I wanted for myself. I thought of nothing evil."

During the period when a boy was fasting alone in the forest, his father or grandfather might drum and sing continually in order to strengthen and help him. It may be mentioned in passing that many songs of the Ojibwa are not composed in the ordinary sense, but are the consequences of dream experiences.[28] Thus, older male relatives of the *kīgúsämo* may invoke, or communicate with, their own other-than-human tutelaries at the same time that the boy is undergoing his first personal contacts with such entities. When the fast is ended the *kīgúsämo* usually returns to camp shortly after daybreak. He hides in the bushes nearby and signals his presence by a whistle, or call, his father knows. The latter goes immediately to him and brings him to camp. The purpose of this procedure is to avoid being seen by a woman first. This would endanger the boy's blessings.

Many years ago Paul Radin published a sample of dreams from the dream fasts of Ojibwa boys. It should be emphasized, as Radin pointed out, that all the dreams of this type which we have on record were told by adults in later life, in some cases, filtered through another person. We

---

[28] Densmore, 1910, p. 118.

have no information whatever on dreams obtained immediately or even a short time after the dream fast itself.[29] I believe, nevertheless, that the general outlines of the basic cultural patterning of such dreams is known to us. Since recounting experiences in a dream fast violated an obligation to *pawáganak,* no investigator who had been present when aboriginal culture was flourishing could have obtained such material. Although I was not able to add very much to the scanty corpus of published examples, discussion with informants confirmed the general pattern exhibited by Radin's sample. There are, however, a few points with regard to the content of dream experience on which I wish to comment.

In one dream I collected, a *pawágan* first appeared to a boy in anthropomorphic guise. Later, this being said, "Grandchild, I think you are strong enough now to go with me." Then the *pawágan* began dancing and, as he danced, he turned into what looked like a golden eagle, that is, the Master of this species. Glancing down at his own body, the boy noticed that it was covered with feathers. The Great Eagle spread its wings and flew off toward the south. The *kigúsämo* then spread his wings and followed.[30] In this case we find the instability of outward form in both human and other-than-human persons succinctly dramatized. Individuals of both categories undergo metamorphosis. In later life the boy will recall that in his dream fast he himself became transformed into a bird. This does not imply that subsequent to his dream fast the boy can transform himself into a golden eagle at will. But it does demonstrate by personal experience that such a metamorphosis is possible for a human being. In this instance, the dream itself does not inform us whether the boy's blessing included power to transform himself. There are, however, many anecdotes told where it is believed that a human individual has appeared in the guise of a bear.[31] The assumption is that power to do this does exist in exceptional cases and that it was obtained in a dream fast. In the

---

[29] See Radin's discussion (1914, pp. 7-10) regarding the transmission of the patterns of the dreams reported. Not all of the Ojibwa material in Radin (1936) is new. Dreams to be found in the earlier article are republished in a different wording but with no reference to previous publication. Lincoln (1935, pp. 271-293) gives a selection from Radin's material.

[30] For a fuller account of this dream see Hallowell, 1955, p. 178.

[31] For a more detailed discussion of this kind of metamorphosis see Hallowell, 1961, pp. 36-38. Peter Jones, a converted Ojibwa, who became famous as a preacher and author says (1861, pp. 145-146) that "sorcerers can turn themselves into bears, wolves, foxes, owls, bats, and snakes. . . . Several of our people have informed me that they have seen and heard witches in the shape of these animals, especially the bear and the fox. They say that when a witch in the shape of a bear is being chased all at once she will run around a tree or hill, so as to be lost sight of for a time. . . . Then, instead of seeing a bear they behold an old woman walking quietly along or digging up roots, and looking as innocent as a lamb."

dream cited what we do know is that the Master of the Golden Eagles became one of the boy's tutelaries, or "guardian spirits," for life.

Even in the dreams of acculturated individuals who never underwent a dream fast, we find a manifest content that is interpreted as a great blessing, so that the significance of certain dream experiences remained the same for individuals long after the period when the aboriginal culture flourished. An example of this is a dream of my friend W. B. He entered a house and there he found a small boy wearing a red toque. This boy had a bow and two arrows, one red and the other black. "I'm going to find out how strong you are," he said to the dreamer. The latter took up a position in the middle of the room and when the boy shot his arrows he managed to dodge them. Then the boy exchanged places with the dreamer. My friend managed to hit the boy with the second (red) arrow, but it did not kill him. He said it was difficult because the boy seemed to be constantly moving, yet remaining in the same place, which was about a foot above the floor. The boy acknowledged that he had been beaten in the contest. The *pawágan* identified himself as an insect, "one of those which are so quick in their movements that they never seem to be at rest." The narrator called them "flies." [32] They have a yellow body and red marks on the head. The latter feature he associated with the red toque worn by the boy in his dream. Finally, this boy said to the dreamer: "If at any time in your life you are in a fight, think of me. Your body will always be quivering like mine." The dreamer was then directed to enter the next wigwam he came to on the trail. The moment he did so a man pointed a gun at him and fired. But W. B. felt no bullet enter his body. "This proved to me," he said, "how I had been blessed. Later I told my wife I would not be killed if I went to war. She asked me how I knew that, I told her it was none of her business." W. B. recognized this dream as a very special kind of dream. And it was. It falls within the type that is traditional in the dream fast. Other dreams of this man, of which I have more than a dozen, were not all of this type. W. B. was absolutely confident with respect to his invulnerability to bullets and if he had gone to war I am sure this would have given him unusual courage.

Another dream of this same man likewise illustrates the kind of manifest content associated with the dream fast. W. B. said it would have enabled him to become a *manáo* if he had so desired. A *manáo* is a doctor who dispenses medicine, which he obtains from the *memengwécīwak*. The latter look very much like human beings, but they belong to the other-than-human category. They travel in canoes and make their home in the rocky escarpments that border some of the lakes. W. B. dreamed that

---

[32] He said they did not sting. But I never was able to make a positive identification of the species.

he was out hunting and met one of the *memengwécī*. He asked W. B. to visit his home. "On the northwest side of the lake there was a very high steep rock. He headed directly for this rock. With one stroke of the paddle we were across the lake. The fellow threw his paddle down as we landed on a flat shelf of rock about level with the water. Behind this the rest of the rock rose steeply before us. But when his paddle touched the rock this part opened up. He pulled the canoe in and we entered a room in the rock." In this dream the geographical details are extremely precise. W. B. said that some time later, when *awake* and out hunting, he recognized the exact spot he had visited in his dream. He could go back any time in the future and obtain the special kind of medicine for which the *memengwécīwak* are famous.[33] The fact that W. B. said he could act this way in the future with reference to a dream experience of the past indicates clearly enough that in the Ojibwa world there is a unified spatiotemporal frame of reference for *all* self-related experience.

While the personal motivation of the boy who undergoes a dream fast is to secure "blessings" that will augment his limited human powers and enable him to achieve *pimădazīwin,* exceptional powers can be obtained which may be exercised for the benefit of other human beings. If W. B. had been a pagan instead of a Christian, he would have become a *manăo*. All specialized forms of curing, such as the ability to remove from the body lethal objects that have been projected there by sorcery,[34] depend upon dream revelation. The boy destined by his dream fast to become a conjurer is blessed by the Master of conjuring who lives in the West, but not on earth; he also must dream of the Winds, who are responsible for the movements exhibited by the conjuring lodge, and the Great Turtle, who acts as a messenger. I was told that four dreams are required before the instructions of the neophyte are completed. In the last dream he is told what kind of wood to select for the poles of the conjuring tent, which differs from conjurer to conjurer. The Master also designates the "moon" in which his initial performance must take place. The neophyte is told that he must not conjure too frequently, or to show off. There must be a real need for his services. In practice the occasions when there is a resort to conjuring are quite varied. If game is scarce and famine threatens, a conjurer, with the aid of his other-than-human helpers, may be able to direct hunters to the place where game can be found. By similar means it is possible for him to receive news about the health or circumstances of absent persons which will alleviate apprehension. A powerful conjurer is also able to protect a whole community for malevo-

---

[33] For the full text of this dream, see Hallowell, 1955, p. 97.
[34] See Densmore, 1910, pp. 119 ff., where the songs used by this type of doctor, as well as other details, are recorded.

lent influences, such as the approach of a cannibal monster (*windīgo*).

The knowledge and power acquired by human individuals in their dream experiences vary greatly. One man may acquire a great many more tutelaries than another, but only a relatively few individuals acquire exceptional powers. In these cases, there is no sharp line that divides human from other-than-human persons. Exceptional men may be able to make inanimate objects behave as if they were animate.[35] They are able to transform one substance into another, such as ashes into gunpowder, or a handful of goose feathers into birds or insects. In such manifestations they are elevated to the same level of power as that displayed by other-than-human persons. We can, in fact, find comparable episodes in the myths. It must also be observed, however, that despite wide variation in the powers obtained from other-than-human sources, "equalitarian" values prevail in this sphere, too. Although other-than-human persons are willing to share their knowledge and power with human persons, greediness is discountenanced, as is the hoarding of material goods among human beings. I was once told about the dream fast of a boy who was not satisfied with his initial blessing. He wanted to dream of all the leaves of all the trees in the world so that absolutely nothing would be hidden from him. This was considered greedy and, while the *pawágan* who appeared in his dream granted his desire, the boy was told that "as soon as the leaves start to fall you'll get sick and when all the leaves drop to the ground that is the end of your life." Overfasting is considered as greedy as hoarding. It violates a basic moral value of the Ojibwa world and is subject to a punitive sanction.

The knowledge and power that other-than-human persons share with the suppliant who seeks their help is not a free gift. The dream fast introduced a boy to a new set of moral obligations. The full benefit of the power and knowledge obtained was made contingent upon the fulfillment of obligations to other-than-human entities that assumed a primary moral force in his life. A reciprocal principle, equivalent to the basic patterning of social interaction between human persons, where rights and duties obtain, was operative. Besides this, the commands of *pawáganak* were considered absolute. The obligations they imposed took various forms. There might be a food taboo in the case of relations with the Masters of game animals. One man was forbidden to kill or eat porcupine by the Master of the porcupines.[36] In another case a man was commanded to wear the kind of headgear attributed to the mythical character who had blessed him in a dream. Another man was forbidden to speak to, or to

---

[35] For example, the animation of a string of wooden beads, or animal skins (Hoffman, 1891, pp. 205–206).
[36] This is an example of what was called "individual totemism" by older writers.

have sexual intercourse with, his wife for a defined period after marriage.

Such obligations are never talked about because there is a general taboo directed against any reference to the relations of a man and his *pawáganak*, except in a highly allusive manner or under unusual circumstances. It is equivalent to the taboo against narrating myths in summer, which is not considered the proper time to talk about "our grandfather." All children are given a personal name by a human grandfather and this name contains an allusion to some dream event in the namer's experience. But no one is given further information. We can see, then, that the obligations imposed by the *pawáganak*, which individuals must fulfill in order to obtain great blessings, often involve firm self-discipline, because the behavior they involve cannot be explained to anyone. The man who was not permitted to sleep with his wife, or even talk to her, did not succeed in fulfilling his obligation. She did not understand his conduct and left him after one winter of married life. He married again and this time he broke the taboo. One of his children became sick and died; later his new wife died. He married a third time and the same thing happened. It was useless for him to expect *pīmǎdazīwin*. He had received a blessing, but had not been able to exercise sufficient self-control to benefit by it. Food taboos were interpreted so rigidly that inadvertent or unconscious violations did not modify the penalty for their infraction. The linguistic term for such infractions means "failure to observe an obligation earnestly entered into."

The seriousness of the failure to fulfill obligations to *pawáganak* is exemplified by the belief that the sickness that inevitably follows as a penalty cannot be cured. Other-than-human persons have done what they could for me; they have fulfilled their role. If I have been unable to fulfill my obligations to them it is my own fault, and I can only blame myself. The severity of the disease sanction in such cases is psychologically sound if it is interpreted as a means of strongly reinforcing self-discipline and personal independence among a people for whom life is fraught with objective hazards that are inescapable. At the same time the sanction lends support, in principle, to a readiness to accept personal responsibility for one's conduct in all interpersonal relations in a society where any organized superordinate forms of authority are absent.

The existence of the dream fast undertaken by boys in aboriginal days receives explanation as a necessary institution when considered in the perspective of the world view of the Ojibwa. It served to validate, through direct personal experience, the existence of other-than-human persons. It served to engender, at an early age, self-confidence in meeting the vicissitudes of life as defined by Ojibwa values. The dream fast was the most crucial experience of a man's life: the personal relations he established with his *pawáganak* determined a great deal of his destiny as an individual. He met the "persons" on whom he could most firmly depend in the future. He also acquired knowledge of the specialized powers that would be of potential benefit to his fellow human beings. The dream fast was recognized as the ultimate source of their validation. If a doctor or a conjurer offered his services without dream validation, this was considered "deceit" and illness would surely follow. One such conjurer began to suffer from acute insomnia and a phobia. He found he could not go into the woods alone, not even for 200 yards. He confessed "deceit" and recovered from his phobia. Finally I believe we can say that the obligations, imposed in the dream fast, were the source of psychological effects which were of characterological importance. They reinforced a type of personality structure that, functioning primarily with emphasis upon inner control rather than outward coercion, was a necessary psychological component in the operation of the Ojibwa sociocultural system.

This system exploited a generic human experience—man's capacity for dreaming. Individuals, through appropriate socialization processes and institutions, were given a cognitive orientation toward the universe and themselves which required participation in a greater-than-human society in order to fulfill their personal needs. Dreaming was a means to this end. But dreaming was always linked to conduct. Thus, the role that dreaming played in the sociocultural system of the Ojibwa exemplifies the complex, coordinate, yet variable factors that may become structurally and functionally related in man's adjustment to a world in which his own imaginative interpretation of it is fed back into his adaptation to it.

References

Ackerknecht, Erwin H. 1958. "Primitive medicine's social function," in *Miscellanea Paul Rivet Octogenario Diata*. Mexico City: Universidad Nacional Autónoma de México. I, 3–7.

Beres, David. 1960. "Perception, imagination, and reality," *International Journal of Psycho-Analysis*, 41:327–334.

Bidney, David. 1953. *Theoretical Anthropology*. New York: Columbia University Press.

Blumensohn, Jules. 1933. "The fast among North American Indians," *American Anthropologist*, 35:451–469.

Dement, William. 1960. "The effect of dream deprivation," *Science*, 131: 1705–1707.

Dement, William, and Nathaniel Kleitman. 1957. "Cyclic variations in EEG during sleep and their relation to eye movements, body motility, and dreaming," *Electroencephalography and Clinical Neurophysiology* (Amsterdam), 9:673–690.

———. 1957. "The relation of eye movements during sleep to dream activity: An objective method for the study of dreaming," *Journal of Experimental Psychology*, 53:339–346.

Densmore, Frances. 1910. *Chippewa Music*. Bureau of American Ethnology. Bulletin 45. Washington.

Devereux, George. 1951. *Reality and Dream*. New York: International Universities Press.

Eggan, Dorothy. 1961. "Dream analysis," in Bert Kaplan, ed., *Studying Personality Cross-Culturally*. Evanston: Row, Peterson.

Eliade, Mircea. 1960. *Myths, Dreams and Mysteries*. Trans. Philip Mairet. London: Harvill.

English, Horace B., and Ava Champney. 1958. *A Comprehensive Dictionary of Psychological and Psychoanalytical Terms*. New York: Longmans, Green.

Hallowell, A. Irving. 1942. *The Role of Conjuring in Saulteaux Society*. Philadelphia: University of Pennsylvania Press.

———. 1955. *Culture and Experience*. Philadelphia: University of Pennsylvania Press.

———. 1960. "Self, society, and culture in phylogenetic perspective," in *Evolution after Darwin*, vol. 2 of *The Evolution of Man*, ed. Sol Tax. Chicago: University of Chicago Press.

———. 1961. "Ojibwa ontology, behavior, and world view," in *Culture in History: Essays in Honor of Paul Radin*. New York: Columbia University Press.

———. 1963. "Ojibwa world view and disease," in Iago Galdston, *Man's Image in Medicine and Anthropology*. New York: International Universities Press.

Hayes, Cathy. 1951. *The Ape in Our House*. New York: Harper and Brothers.

Hoffman, W. J. 1891. *The Midēwiwin or "Grand Medicine Society" of the Ojibwa*. Bureau of American Ethnology. Seventh Annual Report. Washington.

Jones, Peter. 1861. *History of the Ojibwa Indians*. London.

Jones, William. 1919. *Ojibwa Texts*. Publication of the American Ethnological Society. Vol. 7, Part II. New York.

Kimmis, Charles W. 1920. *Children's Dreams*. New York: Longmans, Green.

Kleitman, Nathaniel. 1960. "Patterns of dreaming," Scientific *American*, 203:82–88.

———. 1955. "The role of the cerebral cortex in the development and maintenance of consciousness," in *Problems of Consciousness*. Transactions of the Fifth Conference sponsored by Josiah Macy, Jr., Foundation, 1950–1954. New York.

Kohl, J. B. 1860. *Kitchi-Gami: Wanderings Round Lake Superior*. London: Chapman and Hall.

Leeuw, G. van der. 1938. *Religion in Essence and Manifestation*. London: Allen and Unwin.

Lincoln, Jackson Steward. 1935. *The Dream in Primitive Cultures*. London: Cresset.

Lovejoy, Arthur O. 1948. *Essays in the History of Ideas*. Baltimore: Johns Hopkins Press.

Lovejoy, Arthur O., and George Boas. 1935. *Primitivism and Related Ideas in Antiquity*, vol. 1 of *A Documentary History of Primitivism and Related Ideas*. Baltimore: Johns Hopkins Press.

MacLeod, Robert B. 1947. "The phenomenological approach to social psychology," *Psychological Review*, 44:193–210.

Radin, P. 1914. *Some Aspects of Puberty Fasting among the Ojibwa.* Canada Department Mines. Museum Bulletin no. 2, Ottawa.

———. 1924. "Ojibwa ethnological chit-chat," *American Anthropologist,* 26: 491–530.

———. 1936. "Ojibwa and Ottawa puberty dreams," in *Essays in Anthropology Presented to A. L. Kroeber . . . June 11.* Berkeley: University of California Press. Pp. 233–264.

Redfield, R. 1952. "The primitive world view," *Proceedings of the American Philosophical Society,* 96:30–36.

Tylor, E. B. 1878. *Researches into the Early History of Mankind.* New York. (1st ed., 1865.)

———. 1874. *Primitive Culture.* 2 vols. New York. (1st ed., 1871.)

Whiting, John W. M. 1959. "Sorcery, sin and the superego: A cross-cultural study of some mechanisms of social control," in *Nebraska Symposium on Motivation.* Lincoln: University of Nebraska Press. VII, 174–195.

Wolpert, Edward A., and Harry Trosman. 1958. "Studies in the psychophysiology of dreams. I. Experimental evocation of sequential dream episodes," *American Medical Association Archives of Neurology and Psychiatry,* 79:603–606.

Woods, Ralph L. 1947. *The World of Dreams: An Anthology.* New York: Random House.

16

The Place of Dreams in the Religious World Concept of the Greeks

ANGELO BRELICH

In a complex civilization like that of ancient Greece which developed, and therefore stratified, with extraordinary rapidity, no one expects to find just one attitude toward any phenomenon or a simple answer to any problem. In each particular case there is inevitably an extended range of subtle differences of opinion which leads from one position to its opposite. The historian's task is to understand thoroughly and to evaluate the relative importance of these different ideas as related to the general dynamics of a civilization: for example, he must not take as characteristic what is exceptional or overestimate what is only about to be left behind while passing lightly over what determines the specific and creative orientation of a culture, nor should he confound the various layers that do indeed make up the totality of a culture, yet do not within this totality possess the same historical value.

It is easy to see that it is not possible to talk of a general Hellenic attitude toward dreams without differentiating among epochs, locales, and cultural or social environments. Disparate attitudes are encountered even in so archaic an era as that of the Homeric epics, and even within those poems themselves: the *Iliad* mentions only the dreams of men, the *Odyssey* only the dreams of women. It is hard to believe that this is just pure chance, although it is equally difficult to find a convincing explanation. There is a well-known verse of the *Iliad* (I.63) according to which the dream comes from Zeus. The same poet, however, calls a dream both *theios,* divine (II.56), and *oulos,* baneful (II.6), and the *Odyssey* makes it plain (XIX.560 ff.) that not all dreams are truthful. Later, contradictory evaluations about dreams are also to be found within the work of individual poets. Pindar, for example, viewed the dream as the very symbol of all that is meaningless—we, men, are the dream of a shadow— but he does not hesitate to say that the soul (*eidolon*), which is divine and sleeps while we are awake, makes its correct judgments known in dreams while we are asleep.[1] There is nothing surprising in this state of affairs, especially for us moderns who have become used to contradictory opinions in the course of our civilization.

What I attempt to show in this short paper is but one of the attitudes with regard to dreams which one may distinguish in the total Hellenic tradition. It seems to me that it, more than all the others, expresses a specifically Greek cultural orientation.

Everyone knows the books of dreams that even today circulate in European villages and countrysides, and even in the culturally backward classes of the city population. They are concise and laconic, like the works of the Byzantine lexicographers: in one word or two, the subject of the dream (in alphabetical order), and then in two or three words its explanation, an explanation that is naturally more divinatory than psychological. The probable result of thumbing through one of these books is astonishment at the extreme variety of criteria—if criteria they are—for the interpretations: one might even think it is only the purest whim or unrestrained folly that determines the oracular "answers" found in these works of popular literature. In fact, painstaking philological research would permit us to reconstruct the history of the oneirocritic tradition running largely in like channels, to determine its direct sources (almost invariably similar compilations that immediately preceded them), and to uncover its indirect sources, the search for which through the humanist literature leads very easily back to Artemidorus. Even without such philological efforts, after becoming familiar with the chaos of absurdities which, at first glance, one finds in these books, one becomes aware, among others, of two totally contradictory types of interpretation frequently used side by side. In certain cases, what is seen in a dream is, in effect, considered to presage a happening, similar or symbolically equivalent, which is about

---

[1] Pindar, *Fragment* 131.

to become reality. As an example, here are a few excerpts from a single page taken from a Hungarian dream book: to see a fortress means that one will be protected; to have a velvet robe means riches, and so on. In other cases, on the contrary, a dream predicts that an event of contrasting meaning will come true. For example, to clink glasses as a sign of reconciliation means a quarrel; courage signifies the necessity of prudence; a peace treaty signifies threat of war.

This very coexistence of the two types of contrasting interpretations is to be found in Artemidorus' book of dreams, *Oneirocritica*. But there is a difference. The Greek author—and probably also his predecessors—in each case explains why a dream presages an event of contradictory character, or rather *seemingly* contradictory. A sick man asked Zeus in a dream if he could recover. The god signified yes, but the sick man died. Was the dream false? No, because in signifying yes, the god lowered his head and looked toward the earth, the dwelling place of the dead. A man sees in a dream that his son is about to be buried in Olympia. Actually his son wins an agonistic contest. Certainly, because Olympic winners, precisely like the dead, receive honor, commemorative inscriptions, and so on. To dream of riches presages misfortune. Why? Because riches are in actuality not a good, but give worries. And so forth. Sorrow, suffering in a dream: joy in reality, because we know very well in our hearts that sorrow and joy alternate in such a way that heralded joy can only follow a dream's suffering.

It might perhaps be thought that it is precisely this difference between the popular modern book of dreams and the ancient erudite work which would supply a key to our theme. One might say that by dropping the complicated explanations, popular literature evidently preserves only the skeleton of ancient oneiromantic tradition—the contents of dreams and what they mean for the future. Artemidorus and his predecessors would never have proceeded from the idea that a dream can symbolize an event of contrasting character; they merely observed that in certain cases this was what came true, but explained correctly, these instances proved illusory: the dream always told the truth. The impression given us by modern popular dream books (that there exists a role parallel and contrasting to that which would make a good dream a good omen and a bad dream a bad omen) would therefore be false, and the source of the error would be in the impoverishment suffered by oneiromancy as a consequence of its descent to the popular level.

Such philological reasoning seems plausible, but it is abstract and refuted by more concrete philological tools. If one compares explanations given by Artemidorus to justify those dreams that, instead of finding straightforward fulfillment, are followed by seemingly contrary events, they will be found to be heterogeneous. I have cited only a very few of many more cases, but they are sufficient to support my thesis. That riches in dreams are a bad omen can be explained by the fact that riches in themselves truly are not a good thing, or so philosophy says—at least that philosophy followed by Artemidorus, the philosophy tinged with Stoicism, which pervaded the Hellenistic milieu. But that the sign given by Zeus to the sick man should mean the opposite of what one might have thought has nothing to do with philosophy. More probably, it ties in with the Greek tradition about the ambiguity of oracles. In the case of the Olympic athlete seen by his father buried in Olympia, Artemidorus appeals neither to philosophy nor to the ambiguity of oracles, but to a symbolism widely used in his time wherein the emblems of death coincide with those of triumph. There are as many criteria for explanation as there are cases.

What then are we to conclude from the heterogeneity of expedients employed by the ancient author to explain apparently misleading dreams? I think there is but one possibility: that explanations are *secondary* to a tradition according to which dreams could announce events exactly contrary to their context. The misleading dream sent by Zeus to Agamemnon in the *Iliad,* the fallacious dreams that, according to the *Odyssey,* rise from the Gate of Ivory, prove to us that this was a very old tradition in the Hellenic world. I leave to my colleagues who concentrate in other areas of philology the question how characteristically Greek this tradition is. Personally I only know a few scattered examples in the *Atharva-Veda* and only one in Assyro-Babylonian oneiromantic tradition. What interests us at the moment is that there was in Greece an ancient and widespread belief that dreams could mean the opposite of what they said. This belief was preserved throughout all classical antiquity. We find one piece of evidence of it in the letter of Pliny the Younger to Suetonius on the question of "eventura . . . an contraria somniare" (dreaming of things which will come to pass . . . or their opposite). Another illustration appears in the late Byzantine period to which goes back the little oneiromantic tract of a certain Blaisos published by A. Delatte, where to dream of clothes signifies nudity and poverty; of tears, happiness; to see a corpse, a cure; and so forth.[2] In his commentary the learned editor observes: "One does not see for what reason certain presages conform to natural symbolism, while others obey the law of antithesis." The idea became part of modern popular beliefs, as we have seen from the contemporary dream books and as it appears in the French saying *"songe, mensonge."*

---

[2] A. Delatte, *Anecdota Atheniensia et alia* (Paris, 1927), I, 184–204; and "La Méthode oniromantique de Blaise l'Athénien," in *Mélanges offerts a M. Octave Navarre* (Toulouse, 1935), pp. 115–122.

We now face the problem: why did this "law of antithesis" play so considerable a role in Greek oneiromancy?

First of all we should remember that oneiromancy was not too important an element in the Greek religion, especially not in that religion's archaic period. Although it had been practiced from pre-Homeric times, its prestige was inferior to that of other divinatory practices, as for example the observation of objective signs, such as the flight of birds, the condition of the viscera of sacrificial victims, and, later, to that of inspired mantics that determined the sublime destiny of Delphi. As a marginal phenomenon, oneiromancy seems to have given way to directional influences more decisively Greek in spirit than to have imposed its own laws on religious ideas, adapting itself to the valuation that Greek civilization allowed the dream. Consequently, we must try to define the place occupied by dreams—independently of oneiromancy—in the organic unity of the Hellenic world concept. Now, as it happens, on oneiromancy we can follow only recent developments, but in respect to the place that Greek mentality allotted to the dreams, we possess a rich and varied documentation beginning with the most archaic period.

The expression "the place of dreams" is not as metaphoric as it may seem. The Greek *cosmos* was organized in space. In space, and, we might add, in time; but space and time are not abstract categories as they are with us. They are expressions homologous to a human experience. It is, besides, not a matter of something exclusively Greek; there are analogies —sometimes even more precise—among various archaic peoples, but what matters to us is that also according to the Greek concept, the world is situated within a framework both temporal and spatial; its center is always normal existence, the city or country lived in, *here and now*. Farther back in time, farther back in space, the organized order of here and now disappears. In the dimension of time, there were times when humanity was ignorant of the civilized forms of existence, ignorant of fire, the gift of Prometheus, and of wheat, the gift of Triptolemus. Men lived in caves. Farther back was the time of the Giants, the Titans, the Cyclopes, and the Hundred Hands—the sovereignty of the gods was not yet established. Beyond that, there was a time in which the gods did not exist, when Kronos ate his sons, when Uranus and Gaea in embrace blocked all attempt at movement, all birth of life, and still beyond that there existed only Chaos, Night, and Erebus. It should be added that from another point of view, this fabulous past can take on the aspects of a vanished and regretted golden age.

We find the same stages in the dimension of space, where, in proportion to our distance from the organized world of society, we are led back to nonorder, to spatial chaos. In the first place there were the countries situated on the edge of the Greek world, barbarous countries with strange and paradoxical customs; then came imaginary countries with imaginary people, monsters and cannibals like the Lestrigons or the Cyclopes; of course, there were also the Isles of the Blessed where, in a precise coincidence of time and space, rules Kronos, the god of the golden age; beyond that was the outermost edge of the cosmos, the Okeanos itself, besides, in a temporal sense, the origin of things. Beyond the Okeanos, outside the cosmos, there was only the world—or rather, the antiworld—of nonexistence, the realm of the dead. In the middle of these concentric circles of time and space, the normal world finds itself: the normal world, founded on the laws of Zeus, the world of human values, social norms, good and evil, joy and suffering—in short, reality.

To the question then, which we can take in its literal sense—what is the *place* dreams occupy in a cosmos thus organized in space—Greek documents answer with striking unanimity. The first explicit answer is given to us in the twenty-fourth song of the *Odyssey*. The god Hermes is conducting the souls of the dead suitors toward the other world; the group is traveling, skirting the Okeanos, the frontier of the real world; they arrive at the White Rock (*leukas petrē*), at the Gates of the Sun, and there is the village of dreams (*dēmos oneirōn*), after which they *quickly* (*aipsa*) arrive at the mead of asphodele where dwell "the souls, images of the dead." Dreams, then, inhabit a region outside the real cosmos, in immediate proximity to the world of nonexistence, the other world, that of the dead.

This passage from Homer has certainly given direction to a long literary tradition on infernal regions, but his location of the world of dreams has given rise to more and more explicit developments. In the sixth song of the *Aeneid,* Virgil gathers in the vestibule of the *inania regna* (*Ditis*) all that is odious to men: sorrow, anguish, sickness, old age, fear, hunger, poverty, fatigue, war. In the middle of the dwelling place for these terrifying personages, there is a tree that is the home of the *somnia vana* that are attached to its leaves. Around the tree are to be seen that great flock of mythical beings in which the Greek imagination projected the reverse side of the cosmic order, monsters like the Gorgons, the Harpies, the Hydra of Lerna, the Chimera, and so on.

But these infernal regions are not the only possible expression of the anticosmos. Classic tradition had others. We find in Ovid a description of the house of Somnus who is personified as a god and attended by *somnia vana*.[3] The house is a cave near the country of the Cimmerians who, even in the *Odyssey,* were a people living in the neighborhood of the Okeanos, not far therefore from the infernal regions. The Cim-

---

[3] *Metamorphoses* XI. 592 ff.

merians, in the Nekyia, live covered by clouds and mists. The rays of the sun never touched them. Ovid made use of the Homeric expressions, but he developed them by insisting on the negative characteristics of the place. There were no birds there to awaken the dawn. Silence is not broken by the voices of animals or men, *muta quies habitat*.

Lucian, in turn, knew of an Isle of Dreams (*oneirōn nesos*) in the extreme west of the world and beyond the Okeanos. The sight of this island is indistinct and confused, like dreams.

Since we noted the parallelism between the organization of space and time in Greek mythical thought, it seems worthwhile to inquire if dreams too have a determined place in the temporal framework of the cosmos, and whether or not this place corresponds in some way to the place it occupies in space.

As time in mythology is often measured by genealogy, we can begin by asking who in Greek mythology are the *parents* of dreams. Tradition gives us two or three answers to this question, different but equivalent in the same measure that the different localizations in space may be considered equivalent (at the entrance to the infernal regions, near the Cimmerians, or an island beyond the Okeanos). When we first hear that the "people of dreams" were brought forth by Night—as is said in Hesiod's *Theogony* (212)—our usual way of thinking in abstractions and allegories immediately offers us a banal interpretation: one dreams when one sleeps, normally one sleeps at night, therefore dreams are the children of the night. This interpretation is false: the Nyx in the *Theogony* is not the night of our daily rest. The Nyx *oloē* is one of the most serious and formidable powers the Hellenic imagination was capable of creating. The daughter of Chaos, impregnated by Erebus, gives birth—according to the same Hesiodic passage—to Moros (odious destiny), to ominous Ker (archaic demon associated with inexorable doom), to Thanatos (death), to Hypnos (sleep), and to the people of dreams. As you can see, in defining the genealogical position of the dream amid the dark powers that precede in order of time the birth of the Olympic gods, the series excludes any allusion to ordinary nighttime.

According to a different tradition, documented for us by Euripides, among others, dreams are children of the Earth.[4] This Earth is not the goddess Ge, but Chthon—"sovereign Chthon, mother of black-winged dreams." On the other hand, the underground origin of dreams can be more closely defined to mean an emerging of the Lowerworld. We are always dealing with variants of the same idea: the genealogical linking of dreams with primordial powers of darkness. In *The Frogs* of Aristophanes, a dream is said to be sent by Night and the Servant of Hades.

[4] *Hecuba* 71 ff.; *Iphigenia in Tauris* 1263.

The conclusion to be drawn from this is quite clear, at least at first glance. To archaic Greek consciousness, dreams belonged to the spatial and temporal peripheries of the cosmos, to the antiworld that surrounds the world, to the antireality that is found outside real time and real space. From the point of view of the profoundly realistic culture of Greece the position assigned to dreams implies a decidedly negative judgment. This negative judgment was to express itself in early Greek thought in the well-known Heraclitean fragment about the "one and common" world of the awake as opposed to the particular—and therefore false—worlds of the asleep. This negative judgment is also reflected by the fact that, unlike other civilizations, Greek culture never created important institutions for exploiting dreams.

In spite of this, the picture we have drawn would be too one-sided if we did not add a few words to place the facts in focus. We know that oneiromancy existed in Greece in pre-Homeric times although it had no great importance. Later, in Greece too, rites of incubation were to develop and to occupy a considerable place in religious life, especially when, from the sixth century, the Cult of Asklepios flowered. Is there a contradiction between these facts and the negative judgments on dreams which we deduced from the place assigned them in the mythical thought of the Greeks?

This question may be answered from two points of view. First, it should be noted that oneiromancy and the rites of incubation were practiced throughout the entire Mediterranean region long before the formation of Greek civilization, which inevitably inherited them; their existence in Greece presents no difficult historical problems. It is much more important to note that as soon as Greece presents an autonomous cultural *morphē,* the Mediterranean heritage gives way to a typically Greek orientation that tends to deny the dream a positive valuation.

There is another answer, more complex but more exact. It must be given because otherwise the existence of oneiromantic practices in Greece, in contrast with the prevailing antioneiric tendencies of Hellenic culture, could be explained only by the mechanics of "survivals." Now, nothing "survives" without a function to fulfill. Cultural heritages are only preserved so far as they are usable. In other words, if, despite its fundamentally negative approach toward dreams, Greek culture preserved and developed certain institutions based on their positive valuation, we have an indication that Greek culture has succeeded in integrating those institutions organically. As we have seen, the space and time peripheries of the cosmos have, for the Greeks, as for other archaic peoples, an ambivalent position. They are the antiworld, the antireal, but they are this in two opposing senses: the golden age and the Isles of the Blessed prove that those regions are also the antipode of reality inasmuch as they are more perfect than reality. Moreover, the temporal anticosmos is always the origin of the cosmos, and as such, it has a supernatural value: Chaos is not only the reverse of cosmos, it is also its condition and foundation. In relegating dreams to a place outside the confines of the real, organized world, Greek civilization preserved the possibility of attributing a positive function to dreams.

17

The Dream in Ancient Greece and Its Use in Temple Cures (Incubation)

CARL ALFRED MEIER

How the dream was viewed in ancient Greece has a long history: at the beginning, as far as we know, the attitude was purely religious, whereas in the end the dream had become a prey to cheap impostors found by the dozen in every marketplace, at every festival or country fair. Incidentally, the wide diversity of esteem accorded the dream is manifest in many other cultures so that it might almost appear to be either a culture pattern or the result of something inherent in the phenomenon itself. But the wide variety of meanings attributed to dreams has not only been a function of the dreamer's lifetime but also demonstrably of his social standing, education, or philosophy. And here the correlation may have been direct or inverse, just as it is in our day. If we try to find a *constant,* it consists most probably in the dreamer's attitude toward the *irrational.* Interestingly enough, one phenomenon connected with dreams has survived the tides of changing opinion for several thousand years; incubation was practiced in the most archaic spelaea, for example, of Amphiaraus at Oropus or Trophonius at Lebadeia and is still flourishing at many

Christian shrines today, and not only in Greece.¹ I point out later some of the reasons for this striking fact.

Here I select, in chronological order, some of the more important things that Greek poets, philosophers, and medical men had to say about the dream.

In Homer *oneiros* is always a personified and at the same time divine (*theios*) and winged being that appears to the dreamer *hyper kephalēs* (at the head of his bed) and disappears again, being independent of time and space! Nestor, for instance, visiting Agamemnon in a dream, calls himself "Dios de toi angelos eimi" ² ("I am a messenger of Zeus"), and his task is to tell Agamemnon the will of God. This example may be taken as a model for almost all Homeric dreams, and they all come from Zeus. In the so-called Homeric hymn of Hermes this god is called the *hēgētor oneirōn,* the guide or mediator of dreams. It certainly strikes us as significant that the gods, as a rule, appear in person and speak directly to the dreamer ("quod ipsi di cum dormientibus colloquantur").³ From innumerable dreams related in ancient literature it is apparent that everybody was convinced that dreams were messages from the gods. More theoretically, and theologically or philosophically, this may be explained by the Orphic idea of *sōma-sēma* (which we find again in Plato's *Phaedrus* 250 C), since in sleep the soul is freed from its tomb (the body) whereby it is sensitized and so is able to perceive and converse with the higher beings, a thought that was also held by the Pythagoreans. This idea can be found in Aeschylus and Euripides still, as well as in Pindar⁴ and Xenophon.⁵ It goes without saying that dreams of such dignity must be carefully observed and interpreted, an attitude that is reflected in Aeschylus' *Prometheus Bound,* where it is said that dream interpretation is one of the most important inventions of Prometheus.⁶ The high dignity of dreams also made it imperative to go to any length in order to avert the evil that, according to the dream, was impending. Either such a dream had to be told to Helios whose bright daylight would frighten away its dangerous implications,⁷ or sacrifices had to be made to the apotropaic gods.⁸ In minor cases lustration with water seems to have been sufficient.⁹

---

¹ Mary Hamilton, *Incubation* (London, 1906).
² Homer, *Iliad* II. 26.
³ Cicero, *De divinatione* I.64; Homer, *Iliad* X.496; *Odyssey* XVI.21–24; XX.32.
⁴ Pindar, *Fragment* 131 S.
⁵ Xenophon, *Cyropaedia* VIII.7, 21.
⁶ Aeschylus, *Prometheus Bound* 486.
⁷ Sophocles, *Electra* 424 and scholia; Euripides, *Iphigenia in Tauris* 42.
⁸ Xenophon, *Symposium* IV.33; Hippocrates, *Peri enypniōn* II.10 (ed. D. C. G. Kühn [Lipsiae, 1826]).
⁹ Aeschylus, *Persians* 200; Aristophanes, *Frogs* 1339; Apollonius Rhodius, *Argonautica*

In Euripides we find another interesting aspect of dreams when he calls Lady Earth "ō potnia Chthōn, melanopterygōn mēter oneirōn," "Mother of black-winged Dreams."[10] It is this chthonic origin of dreams which has survived down to our time in the practice of incubation. More about this presently.

Plato did not create a theory of dreams except that in his psychology it becomes clear that the content of a dream is determined by the particular part of the psyche that is active, namely the *logistikon,* the *thēriōdes,* or the *thymoeides.* If the *logistikon* prevails, however, we may have a dream that reveals to us the all-important truth.[11] In regard to such dreams, Xenophon, in his *Commentary,* clearly advocates interpretation, as ordinary knowledge may not suffice for their understanding. In the *Symposium*,[12] moreover, Plato calls a man who knows how to judge dreams a *daimonios anēr* as opposed to the *banausos.* But these are the words of Diotima, his specialist on Eros, and according to her, demons are the originators of dreams and oracles, and one of these demons is Eros. It should be noted that Plato attributes this view to a woman.

We deal briefly now with the most powerful authority on dreams, Aristotle. Two opuscula contained in the *Parva Naturalia* are in relatively good condition: (1) "peri enypniōn" and (2) "peri tēs kath' hypnon mantikēs" (especially 464b). According to these, the dream is the result of the affection of the *koinon aisthētērion,* that is, the heart as the central seat of representations, by those minimal movements during sleep left over from the waking activities of the senses. These residual movements are, of course, present in the waking state, too, but remain unperceived—unheard, as it were—because of the violent movements of the senses, that is, because of the far greater noise they make. This is how veridical dreams are possible because during sleep the dreamer is much more sensitive to small disturbances of an organic nature. A skilled doctor can therefore predict illness, cure, or death from such dreams.

Dreams about people we know well can, according to Aristotle, also be veridical or precognitive, because we know these people's motivations well and are consciously deeply involved with them, so that from such knowledge we can reach certain conclusions concerning their future actions.

Also, according to Aristotle, the dream is an incentive to future actions of the dreamer. Concerning the diagnostic and prognostic use of

---

IV.662; for further examples, see B. Büchsenschütz, *Traum und Traumdeutung im Alterthume* (Berlin, 1868).
[10] Euripides, *Hecuba* 70.
[11] Plato, *Republic* IX.571 C ff.
[12] Plato, *Symposium* 203 A.

dreams, Aristotle closes his treatise "On Prophecy in Sleep" with an interesting simile by which he shows how dreams can and should be understood and interpreted:

> The most skilful judge of dreams is the man who possesses the ability to detect likenesses; for anyone can judge the vivid dream. By likenesses I mean that the mental pictures are like reflections in water, as we have said before. In the latter case, if there is such movement, the reflection is not like the original, nor the images like the real object. Thus *he* would indeed be a clever interpreter of reflections who could quickly discriminate, and envisage these scattered and distorted fragments of the images as representing a man, say, or a horse or any other object. Now in the other case too the dream has a somewhat similar result; for the movement destroys the clarity of the dream.[13]

Generally speaking, Aristotle paradoxically sides with Diotima when he attributes *demonic* origin to dreams. Were they sent by God, he argues, they would only be bestowed on the best and wisest men, which is most obviously not so. This sweeping devaluation of the dream has had a lasting effect. For example, the Epicureans, as well as the New Academy philosophers like Carneades, naturally had as little use for dreams as did the Cynics. But in the Stoa, dreams again play a prominent part. The ancient Stoics seem to have been the first to classify dreams[14] by their sources: they come either from God or from demons or from the activity of the soul itself. Apart from this, the Stoics allow for prognostication through dreams by virtue of the interrelation of the human soul with the soul of the universe. Because of these correspondencies man is aware of the coherence of all things when his senses are at rest—that is, in his sleep—and thus he is able to know the future.[15] Posidonius[16] claims that the *divine* has three ways of acting upon man in dreams: (1) the soul may see the future by virtue of its own godlike nature; (2) the air is full of immortal souls carrying obvious signs of truth, who penetrate the sleeper's system through the channels (*poroi*) of the senses;[17] and (3) the gods themselves talk to the sleepers.[18]

---

[13] Aristotle, "On Prophecy in Sleep" in *Parva Naturalia* (trans. W. S. Hett, *On the Soul; Parva Naturalia, On Breath* [Cambridge: Harvard University Press, 1936] p. 385).
[14] *Stoicorum Veterum Fragmenta* III.605.
[15] *Ibid.* II.1198.
[16] Cicero, *De Divinatione* I.30.
[17] Plutarch, *De placitis philosophorum* V.2; *Quaestiones conviviales* VIII.10. 2.
[18] Karl Reinhardt, *Poseidonios über Ursprung und Entartung* (Heidelberg: Carl Winters Universitätsbuchhandlung, 1928), pp. 457-459.

These thoughts, together with the idea of the macrocosm-microcosm relation, seem to give almost a causal explanation for all mantic belief: the order of the universe consists of the concatenation of causes and effects. Certain signs let us perceive certain causes that will lead to certain effects. In turn, these signs are perceived in certain dreams: "Poseidonius esse censet in natura signa quadam rerum futurarum." [19]

This theory, in my opinion, certainly allows for precognitive or veridical dreams, or rather dreams to be so interpreted, whereas for the possibility of so-called telepathic dreams one must resort to a theory that had already been proposed by Democritus, astonishingly enough. His atoms or *eidōla* have all the qualities of an individuum, the Latin word created by Cicero in translating the Greek *hē atomos* of Democritus. The air is full of atoms-individuals that offer themselves as carriers of messages from one person to another, which should indeed make it easy to transmit telepathic effects.[20] As I have already committed an anachronism by going back to Democritus, let me do so again by calling your attention to the well-known *Fragment* 89 D of Heraclitus "tois egrēgorosin hena kai koinon kosmon einai, tōn de koimōmenōn hekaston eis idion apostrephesthai" (the waking are having one world and a common one, but when asleep everyone turns away from it into his own one). His *own one* therefore must be his dreamworld, where he is all by himself, in a primordial condition; in other words, the dreamer finds himself in a mythological realm and what happens there is actually cosmogony. In this sense Heraclitus' saying corresponds exactly with Jung's concept of the meaning of dreams "on the subjective level."

Now to outline the medical approach to dreams in Greece. We go back to the fifth century B.C. where we find a Hippocratic writer dealing with the problem in *Peri enypniōn*.[21] According to this treatise, the soul is preoccupied with bodily functions during the waking state, whereas in sleep she is the unrestricted ruler of the house, since the sleeping body has no perception. While the body sleeps, the soul, which is always awake, has all the psychological and physiological functions at her disposal, so that he who is able to judge this relationship correctly possesses a good deal of wisdom. Hippocrates also admits that there can be divine influences in dreams through which we can know things otherwise unknowable. Regarding the diagnostic value of dreams, he thinks the soul can perceive the causes of illness in *images* during sleep. Here we see for the first time that a symbolic quality of the psyche is assumed. When Hippocrates is particularly interested in the medical aspect, he shows very

---

[19] Cicero, *op. cit.* I.52–57.
[20] *Ibid.* I.43; II.67.
[21] Hippocrates, *op. cit.* II.1–16.

clearly that the health of the dreamer is reflected in his dream. There are, of course, *divinely* inspired dreams, interpretation of which he leaves entirely to the dream specialist. But then there are the *natural* influences whereby the soul perceives the bodily condition and thus becomes a hygienic system. As long as the dreams simply repeat what has happened during the day the body is obviously in order. But when the dream pictures strife, war, and the like, this means disorder in the body. When we, for instance, dream of the sun and the moon as they appear in nature, this is a sign of good health, but when something is wrong with these planets in our dream, then there must be something the matter with those systems in us which correspond to sun and moon according to the macrocosm-microcosm relation. Springs and wells correspond to the uropoietic system, rivers to the circulatory system where flood or drought would be the same, for example, as hypertonia or anemia.[22] Galen had little more to say about this problem. The diagnosis, as the examples have shown, was reached exclusively from the dream text by what we might call "thinking in analogies." And this technique has been called by several authors the only significant point in the art of dream interpretation.[23]

It is evident that there is hardly anything new in the dream theories of Hippocrates and Galen as compared with those of Plato, Aristotle, and Democritus. Plato already had the conception that dreams were the perception of residual movements in sleep ("tas entos kinēseis") and Aristotle the "kinēseis phantastikai en tois aisthētēriois." Those inner movements are the dream images that are exclusively based on an inner faculty of perception—*phantasia*. Aristotle's psychology could be called a differential computation of the mutual inhibitions, stimulations, and superpositions of those inner movements. But medical men could apply this dream theory to therapy only by cutting out all extraneous sources for dreams. The "somnia a deo missa" had to be excluded. And here we touch upon a decisive distinction regarding the immanence or transcendence of the source. Medical and rationalistic influence became very strong and almost replaced the purely religious attitude of the earlier days. It is clear that the transcendent source had been the only one that interested the Greek peoples earlier. Dreams were considered to be objective facts, things that happened to you. The Greek was "visited" by a dream (*episkopein*), at best he "saw" a dream (*enypnion idein*). They would never have dreamed of saying as the French do nowadays, "J'ai fait un rêve," or the Italians, "Ho fatto un sogno." We could therefore predict that after

---

[22] Hippocrates, *Peri diaitēs* IV.88 ff. (English trans. W. H. S. Jones [London and New York, 1931], IV, 421–447).
[23] Aristotle, "On Prophecy in Sleep" 464^{b}5; Artemidorus, *Oneirocritica* II.25.

this rationalistic period the pendulum would swing again in the other direction. We have but to look at the Hellenistic period of which I take Philo as an example. To him the most important organ is the *pneuma*. It is the *psychē psychēs,* the soul of the soul, that has the cleanest and best *ousia,* substance, namely a divine one. The dream is to him a phenomenon in which the pneuma is the protagonist. Therefore all dreams are interesting mainly for their prophetic quality. He has three categories of dreams: (1) dreams prophetic by direct divine influence; (2) dreams prophetic by virtue of the movement of the *ratio* inasmuch as it is in symphony with the general divine movement; and (3) dreams that spring from purely psychic emotion because of the powers of enthusiasm. Only dreams in the last category need interpretation, though here too, the enthusiastic powers point to divine origin, and generally speaking, *all* is irrational again. This trend prevailed to Roman times.

This lopsided enthusiastic view is of course as unsavory as the purely rationalistic one. The early Homeric distinction should never be forgotten.[24] There will always be confused, relatively unimportant dreams that penetrate the Gate of Ivory, and clear and very significant dreams that come through the Gate of Horn (Penelope's dream of the geese and the eagle, by the way, is interpreted purely allegorically and not symbolically in Jung's terminology). It is rather on the strength of such a dichotomy that dreams can be taken seriously at all, as is shown very impressively by Greek dreamers who had temples built, sacrifices performed, and so on, because of dreams.[25]

I am strongly disposed to believe that almost all the observations of the Greeks on dreams still hold good. There are a few obvious exceptions owing to changes in condition: for instance, with everything so utterly secularized with us, there are rarely any divine epiphanies in our dreams. And, for the same reason, it is no longer true nowadays that only kings, priests, or medical men have dreams of great import.

So far the scanty sources about dreams in ancient literature have had to be carefully and painstakingly collected, a task carried out mainly by B. Büchsenschütz[26] and to some extent by E. R. Dodds.[27] Unfortunately all the important books on dreams written in antiquity have been lost and for synopses of them we must look to authors of the second and fourth centuries A.D., namely Artemidorus (who calls himself of Daldis, although he was born in Ephesus), and Macrobius and Synesius of

---

[24] Homer, *Odyssey* XIX.560 ff.
[25] Aelius Aristides (A.D. 117 or 129–189).
[26] Büchsenschütz, *Op. cit.*
[27] E. R. Dodds, *The Greeks and the Irrational* (Berkeley and Los Angeles, 1956).

Cyrene. Artemidorus has the advantage of having known all the antique literature on dreams as well as having been in practice for a lifetime. He not only collected more than 3,000 dreams but also took a good look at the dreamers themselves, their history, and the outcome of their dreams. Compared to him, Macrobius and Synesius were highly educated men, much less influenced by the earlier dream literature, and much more scholarly. Macrobius was an initiate into the neoplatonic mysteries, and Synesius became a Christian bishop (with wife and children!) though he had never been baptized, a fact that testifies to his scholarly merits and prestige. Contrary to Artemidorus, who is an eclectic, Macrobius and Synesius are both true to their neoplatonic convictions. Briefly, Synesius' book *Peri enypniōn* was written in one night, at God's command. With him dreams are prophetic inasmuch as through and in them we practice what will, according to cosmic harmony, happen to us later anyhow. They are the preludes to the events and they may tune us into them. They are the best kind of prophecy because they come to all men, poor and rich. Dreams arise from the soul which contains the images of things to come. These images are reflected in "phantasy" which is a kind of life on a deeper level. Its sense organs are finer, more divine, hence more reliable than ours, but its perceptions are blurred, which is a wise limitation and accounts for the need for interpretation. Synesius gives no general rule for interpretation but strongly recommends that we keep "nightbooks" instead of silly diaries. Macrobius' "Commentariorum ex Cicerone in Somnium Scipionis libri duo"[28] first gives a classification of dreams closely resembling that of Artemidorus. Then he gives a long and exhaustive context to Scipio's dream text and goes to great lengths to give exactly what we would today call an amplification of the material according to C. G. Jung. In this way we learn that the dreamer by means of his dream was not only given a thorough lecture on contemporary psychology but was truly initiated into the mysteries of his soul, an initiation that winds up with the mystagogue's assertion "deum te esse scito." Toward the end of the book, Macrobius also presents a very useful and reliable synopsis of most of the Greek philosophers' ideas about the nature of the psyche. Macrobius' interesting classification has been available since 1952 in a good annotated English translation.[29]

I point out some of the more unusual qualities of Artemidorus' five books of *Oneirocritica* because his views give us a chance to compare ancient ideas with modern ones. I skip over his classification, which as you already know is in Macrobius in translation, but keep in mind that

---

[28] In Cicero, *De Republica* VI.
[29] W. H. Stahl, *Macrobius' Commentary on the Dream of Scipio* (New York: Columbia University Press, 1952).

he scrutinized 3,000 dreams and carefully investigated the dreamers' personal circumstances as well as the outcome (anamnesis, catamnesis, and epicrisis).

(1) What stands out as important is the fact that in contradistinction to modern dream material a large proportion of his dreams contain divine epiphanies. Here he knows of one and only one absolutely reliable criterion: that is (2) as long as the god appears true to his attributes and to his cult-image, the dream is favorably interpreted. The slightest flaw in this respect, however, renders its meaning ominous. This conviction clearly reveals a totemistic element. With aborigines of northwestern Australia, odd behavior of the totem animal in dreams is always interpreted unfavorably (personal communication from Rix Weaver, Perth, W. Australia). Gods appearing in a wrong costume may easily lie. It seems that such deviations had the quality of blasphemy, which psychologically meant that the dreamer was in conflict with whatever deeper psychological truth or quality the particular god represented. This would of necessity call down the god's wrath upon the dreamer. Generally speaking we notice here the common features of ancient *oneiromanteia,* namely, that all dreams are mainly judged (3) in terms of future actual events and (4) as to whether they will turn out favorably or unfavorably. (5) The particular dreamer's god also has to obey the rule of *suum cuique,* so that goddesses, for instance, are considered more appropriate for women than for men. (6) Gods may appear only as their attributes (*pars pro toto*) which is another reason why the interpreter (as well as for [2]) had to be very well informed in mythology (trees, and so forth). (7) Gods may make prescriptions, even in the medical sense, in the event of physical illness. These prescriptions are very simple and need no interpretation. A god speaks in riddles only in order to make us ponder the dream (IV.22). (8) There are two kinds of dreams: (*a*) *theorēmatikoi* and (*b*) *allēgorikoi*. The dreams in group (*a*) correspond exactly to reality and very soon after being dreamed are *tale quale* lived out by the dreamer. The dreams in group (*b*) have a deeper meaning, showing *di' ainigmata* (through enigmas) and take a long time to come true, sometimes years. (9) There are dreams that come from within and dreams that come from without. All dreams containing unexpected elements belong to the latter category since they are regarded as being sent by the gods (*theopempton*).

Concerning the principles of interpretation I point out a few peculiarities that compare favorably with modern principles. (1) There are relatively few standard equations for typical dream elements, as for instance:

business = mother, because it is nurturing
business = wife, because of the close connection between a man and his business
head = father
foot = slave
right hand = father, son, friend, brother
left hand = wife, mother, mistress, daughter, sister
pudendum = parents, wife, children

(2) There are six *stoicheia* (elements) to be found in all dreams: nature, law, custom, professional skill, art, and name. Everything in the dream that takes its course in harmony with its nature, law, and the rest, is of good omen; what deviates in one way or another is of bad omen. (3) You must know all about the dreamer's life (anamnesis) and situation; if necessary you must seek information from others (objective anamnesis). (4) You must know the dreamer's character. (5) You must consider the dreamer's actual mood. (6) You must be given the whole dream; fragments must not be interpreted (IV.3). (7) You must be familiar with the customs of the place and of the people in order to judge the dream correctly according to (2). (8) Etymology should always be used, particularly in the case of proper names. (Thus a Greek dreaming of a Eutychos, or a Roman of a Felix, should take this as a good sign because both names mean literally "happy.")

(9) We now dwell a bit on the most prominent feature of Artemidorus' approach, the *polarity* and *ambivalence* of dream motives, of which I give some examples:

a) To have asses' ears is a good omen only for a philosopher because the ass will not listen and give in easily. To all other people it means servitude and misery (I.24).

b) Taking a bath: formerly this was performed after tedious work and would consequently have indicated sweat and tears. Nowadays it is a sign of wealth and luxury and consequently a good omen (I.64).

c) To sleep in the temple indicates a cure to the sick, illness to the healthy (I.79).

d) Gold as such is of good omen, but should a man, for instance, wear a gold necklace it would be the opposite (II.5).

e) Being struck by a flash of lightning takes from you what you possess. As the poor possesses poverty and the rich wealth, the portent of such a dream is accordingly good or bad (II.9).

f) A dolphin *in* water is of good omen, *out of* water of bad omen (II.16).

g) Something bad happening to your enemies is of good omen to you (I.2).

h) If you are happy and are promised happiness in the dream this means bad luck; if you are unhappy, good luck. Conversely, should you be

unhappy and dream that you will be unhappy it means good luck.
i) Simple people dream directly, whereas people who know a lot about dreaming in their dreams translate the crude facts into symbols (IV.Introduction). This is in the genuine Sophoclean tradition: "For wise men author of dark edicts aye, / For dull men a poor teacher, if concise."[30] Generally speaking, people have pleasant dreams when they live under unpleasant conditions. Explaining this ambivalence or multivalence of dream "symbols," Artemidorus simply points out that the facts in life *are* ambivalent.
j) In IV.67 he gives a striking paradigm for seven different meanings of an identical dream dreamed by seven different pregnant women: all dreamed that they had given birth to a dragon. The interpretation had to be adapted to the particular circumstances of the dreamer's life, her anamnesis, for in each case the *apobasis* was actually different.
k) Artemidorus makes allowance for wish fulfillment in dreams by saying that we want the god to help us to see more clearly what is going on in us. In this sense we are *aitēmatikoi,* disposed to ask, and so are our dreams. But, he adds, we should never ask the gods undue questions either! And if the answer has been granted, we must not forget to sacrifice and give thanks (IV.2).
l) In the art of dream interpretation you must skillfully synthesize all these and many more principles and never forget *respicere finem,* to adapt your verdict to the personality of the dreamer before you (III.66). Many a dream may be *akritos* (uninterpretable) before its *apobasis* (IV.24).
m) In IV.20 we find advice for the scribes among analysts. He says in so many words that the analyst should, after due consideration of all the circumstances mentioned above, present his interpretation pure and simple, and not try to justify it by reasoning and quoting authorities, as in doing so he would simply be trying to impress the client with his scholarliness and intelligence. This and other remarks about decorum are often delightful.

There is no end of sound advice, as modern as can be, in Artemidorus' *Oneirocritica,* but it requires close philological scrutiny. Artemidorus makes difficult reading and there are no reliable translations. This may account for the fact that most modern psychologists turn up their noses at him, in spite of the fact that Freud has taken quite some trouble to discuss him. But even with Freud, strangely enough, Artemidorus did not stick. He had apparently to hurry on to develop his own *new* ideas, which were indeed shattering enough, so that we can well understand that he got completely wrapped up in them.

---

[30] Sophocles, *Fragment* 704 (ed. A. Nauck [Leipzig, 1889]).

We have seen that in ancient Greece dreams were thought of as real oracles. But where the many existing techniques for receiving answers to problems, like auguries, haruspicy, and the like, all had fixed systems of reference and only a relatively limited number of possible answers, the dream lacks these points of reference altogether, and is so polymorphous that its proper interpretation either takes a great deal more skill and knowledge or leads to quackery, as in fact it mostly did.

Probably because of this difficulty the Greeks very early limited the scope of dreams to one particular purpose by accepting them exclusively as oracles regarding sickness and cure. It seems that this specialization required two main adaptations: (1) one had to have recourse to a god who specialized as a healer and the appropriate cult had to be established, and (2) one had to resort to the chthonic deities, as "body" and "mother earth" are practically synonymous. Moreover the age-old belief that *potnia Chthōn* is the mother of dreams was helpful. Chthonic gods have their definite abodes to which they are confined so one must make a pilgrimage to the shrine. And in the course of time the shrine will no doubt accumulate an enormous amount of prestige and mana. There were archaic models for the worship of primitive chthonic gods or heroes who had the reputation for answering questions about illness and for working miraculous cures, like Amphiaraus and Trophonius, already mentioned. Moreover there was an old mythical doctor who had later been granted apotheosis, Asklepios. It is not that there had not been many others in many other cultures who also shared the same speciality, but Asklepios' fame knew no boundaries and his cult was certainly the most elaborate. This is an extremely condensed description of the practice of incubation as it was performed at the shrines of Asklepios. A study of the older and contemporary parallels, including the cults of Trophonius, Amphiaraus, Calchas, Faunus, Isis, and more particularly Serapis, as well as many others, which regrettably must be omitted here, would put Asklepios in the right perspective, but we treat him as *partem pro toto,* or better, as a representative sample.[31]

I take Epidaurus to illustrate what went on at an Asklepieion. The place is beautifully situated far out in the country with a *via sacra* five miles long connecting it with the port. Its buildings are world famous for their beauty, particularly the theater and the rotunda called *tholos.* The place swarms with harmless snakes. Lots of trees, predominantly Oriental plane trees, and a plentiful supply of water are found in the sanctuary. Near the entrance are six stone stelae with inscriptions telling the case histories of more than a hundred cures that had become famous.

---

[31] See C. A. Meier, *Antike Inkubation und Moderne Psychotherapie* (Zurich, 1949), for a full account of the sources.

Seventy of them are still extant and are accessible in a fine edition by Rudolf Herzog.[32]

As a patient you would readily be admitted to the sacred precinct unless you were moribund or a pregnant woman near confinement, as the sanctuary had to be kept ritually pure from death and birth. After having performed certain purificatory rites, ablutions, and preliminary sacrifices, you would go to sleep on your *klinē* (clinic!) in the *abaton* or *adyton,* "the place not to be entered by the unbidden." To have to be bidden by the god into his temple is a *locus communis* in many mystery cults (e.g., Isis, cf. Apuleius) and most probably depended on the outcome of your preliminary sacrifice. Once admitted, all will depend upon your having the *right* dream, while sleeping in the *abaton.* This was the actual process of incubation. *Incubare* means "sleeping in the sanctuary," the Greek word being *enkoimēsis.* Whether the dream was the right one was decided by its result, for, if it was the right one, the patient woke cured. Apparently he was always cured if in his dream he experienced an epiphany of Asklepios. The god then appeared to him *onar* "in the dream" to use the technical expression, or else *hypar* "in the waking state" or, as we should say, "in a vision," in case he was too excited to go to sleep. The god came either alone as the bearded man of his cult-image, or as a boy. Or he might be accompanied by his virgin wife or daughter Hygieia and sometimes by Panacea or Iaso. Instead of appearing personally he might delegate one of them or prefer to show himself in his theriomorphic aspect, as dog or snake. In one or another of his aspects he would then touch the stricken part of the patient's body and disappear. In early times the patient was apparently regarded as incurable if he did not experience a dream epiphany on the very first night. He then was probably regarded as "unbidden." Later this decision seems already to have been made as the result of the preliminary sacrifices. Because of this ritual it became customary to stay at the Asklepieion until the sacrifice turned favorable, thus indicating the *kairos oxys,* the decisive moment. The place therefore turned eventually into a thriving hotel.

But this development had another, genuinely religious aspect. The normal situation seems to have been that the former patient became a strong believer in the god's power and kindness, an experience that turned him into what was technically called a "religiosus." This must have been of considerable importance, psychologically speaking, in determining whether the cure was lasting. The patient did not have to become a "fanatic" who could not tear himself away from the *fanum,* the sacred precinct. In other words, he did not have to develop an unsavory transference, but only a healthy one. There are cases on record of patients who

---

[32] *Die Wunderheilungen von Epidauros* (Leipzig, 1931).

spent very long periods in the precinct and who remind us therefore of the institution of *katochē* recognized especially at shrines of the most prominent of Asklepios' colleagues, Serapis. The *katochoi,* temple prisoners, voluntary prisoners of course, must have spent a good deal of time in the ancient theurgic clinics. One of the most famous habitués of many an Asklepieion was the rhetor Aristides of Smyrna. Another famous man, Apuleius, called himself a *desmios* of the goddess Isis.

As can be seen there was no need for dream interpreters in these places. Nor were there any physicians in the sacred precinct and no medical therapy of any kind was practiced.

The applicants were obliged to write down their dreams or have them written down. Aristides tells us that the "prisoners" carefully noted down their dreams until a *symptōma,* a coincidence with the dream of the priest, occurred. Referring to the Asklepieion he says that the priest with whom he lodged outside the Hieron, or else the priest's slave, sometimes dreamed for him. This certainly indicates that the spirit of healing pervaded the whole atmosphere of the place, and if we sought a theoretical concept for such a possibility we would certainly find an answer in the ideas of Democritus, Aristotle, and Hippocrates mentioned above. Apuleius sums up the imprisonment during the Isis mysteries in the apt saying: "Neque vocatus morari nec non jussus festinare" (Do not hesitate when called, nor hasten when not commanded) and the day on which he was bidden to initiation was "divino vadimonio destinatus" (destined for him by divine guarantee). Sometimes a definite vision was required as a sign that the applicant was ready for initiation. This corresponded to what was known in the Asklepian cult as the *enypnion enarges,* the effective dream or healing dream that immediately brought about the cure.

After the cure the former patient was expected to pay certain fees and make thank offerings. We have on record instances in which the god administered a sharp lesson to tardy debtors, or people who regressed after the cure into their earlier rationalistic skepticism, by promptly ordaining a relapse.

You will be able to appreciate the absolute authority these dream decisions possessed from Plato's *Republic*[33] where it is said that Asklepios refused to treat those who had not lived according to the established order as they were of no use to the community. On the other hand, some patients seem to have established a jovial sort of relationship with the divine doctor, reminiscent of the modern dialectical concept in psychotherapy. We hear, for example, the amusing anecdote of a certain Polemon[34] who, being forbidden by Asklepios to drink water, replied, "What

---

[33] III.14, 15.
[34] Philostratus, *Lives of the Sophists* I.25.

would you have prescribed for a cow?" or of a certain Plutarchus who asks, when Asklepios ordered him to eat pork, "What would you have prescribed for a Jew?"[35] Asklepios reacted amiably to these waggish objections and varied the treatment accordingly. But in other cases, when it was necessary to heal by means of paradoxes, and the forbidden thing was at the same time the remedy, the god remained firm ("ho trōsas iasetai") even if a Syrian should have to partake of a roast pig or a Greek Adonis-worshiper eat wild boar's meat. "Contraria contrariis," a principle that you find as frequently as "similia similibus curantur." As you can see from these few examples there are cases where the god makes out actual medical prescriptions. This is an exception, though, and can be found only in relatively late periods. But it has already given rise in antiquity to much conjecture about the origins of the art of medicine. They even went so far as to say that Hippocrates learned his therapy from the temple cures in Cos, although archaeology proves that the famous Asklepieion of Cos was founded after Hippocrates' death. Nevertheless, it was founded by members of his *medical* school, so that we may justifiably say that, sooner or later, even the so-famous rational Hippocratic medicine had to take account of theurgic competition.

The symbolism of healing accruing at these shrines certainly shows striking similarities to that developed at the equally famous centers of the mystery cults. The cure, in effect, was given all the dignity of a rebirth. But it was brought about by contact with the Earth Element in its divine aspect. Demeter and Zeus *katachthonios* therefore were always worshiped in the Asklepieia along with Asklepios and his divine father, Apollo. Many opposites were united in the *cult* as well as in the mythology of Asklepios. Thus Apollo and his arts, music, and theater, held a prominent place in the Epidaurian cult, so that it can be said that what actually was provided for in these clinics of antiquity was the *cura animae* and that it really was a *cult of the psyche,* which in itself should be the object of true therapy. The ensemble of water, snakes, trees, art, music, theater, and a chthonic cult whose acme came about at night in a dream, seems to explain a good deal of the miraculous effects. It is certainly more inclusive than what is offered at healing places these days whether at a university clinic or at Lourdes. The most famous of the approximately 420 Asklepieia in the whole of the ancient world, like Epidaurus, Cos, and Pergamos, are all situated in a natural environment of exquisite beauty; this fact should not be overlooked because it is most conducive to establishing harmony between the inner and outer worlds (macrocosm and microcosm). Nor must it be forgotten that in antiquity illness was equivalent to the lack of something, or poverty (*penia*), which could, under such

---

[35] Damaskios, in *Suidas, s.v. Domnīnos.*

circumstances of plenitude, be converted into health, which in turn, according to ancient thinking, is equivalent to wealth (*ploutos*), which again is equivalent to wholeness, holiness, or health. All these words are etymologically closely connected. This is actually how illness became the remedy. And this remedy was provided by a god who had himself been a patient, and, being a god, had been able to overcome the disease and consequently to know the cure and, by divine intervention, to bestow it on the patient too.

With all this in mind it becomes understandable that Epidaurus jealously guarded the tradition of the cult and saw to it that new foundations of Asklepieia elsewhere had to be closely affiliated with the one at Epidaurus. The mode of *translatio* of the cult from Epidaurus to any other place had to be the strictly ritualistic transportation of one of the holy snakes to the new center. Thus the possession of the true tradition could never give rise to such unpleasant discussions as we now witness, when doctors, analysts, or schools of thought, bogged down by their personal prestige, vainly claim to be the only possessors of the true spirit of the master.

Incubation seems to me to be only one example of something you will notice at once when you go to Greece: the whole country is imbued with myth even today. All the old gods are still alive. And if you take a map of the country in one hand and Pausanias' Baedeker (if possible in Frazer's edition with commentary[36]) in the other, you will soon realize that what you are actually looking at is the geography of the human soul. Not the Greek, not the "Western," but the human soul, *tout court*. Spread over the peninsula and its islands are hundreds of places each of which has its special myth, its cult and cult-legends, and sanctuaries, each of which would take care of one or another of the most basic problems of human life in the most varied, complete, beautiful, and healing way. If you had been in need of help in those days, you would have known exactly where to go to find enacted for you the appropriate archetype. Let me close with a pun: Nomina mutantur, permanent numina.

---

[36] Pausanias, *Description of Greece* (trans. and with commentary, J. G. Frazer [London, 1913]).

Bibliography

Artemidori Daldiani *Oneirocritica*. Ed. Rigaltius. Lutetiae, 1603.
Büchsenschütz, B. *Traum und Traumdeutung im Alterthume*. Berlin, 1868.
Deubner, Ludwig. *De Incubatione*. Leipzig, 1900.
Dodds, E. R. *The Greeks and the Irrational*. Berkeley and Los Angeles, 1956.
Edelstein, Emma J., and Ludwig Edelstein. *Asclepius*. Baltimore, 1945.
Hamilton, Mary. *Incubation*. London, 1906.
Herzog, Rudolf. *Die Wunderheilungen von Epidauros*. Leipzig, 1931.
Macrobii *Opera*. Ed. Societas Bipontina. Biponti, 1788.
Meier, C. A. *Antike Inkubation und moderne Psychotherapie*. Zurich, 1949.
Preuschen, Erwin. *Mönchtum und Sarapiskult*. Giessen, 1903.
Synesii Espiscopi *Opera omnia*. Ed. Dionys. Petavius. Lutetiae, 1612.

18

Dreams and Social Character in Mexico

ALFONSO MILLÁN

MEXICAN SOCIETY

According to Erich Fromm, the creator of humanist psychoanalysis, whose ideas and theories I have followed throughout my work,

Each society is structuralized and operates in certain ways which are necessitated by a number of objective conditions. These conditions include methods of production and distribution which in turn depend on raw materials, industrial techniques, climate, size of population, and political and geographical factors, cultural traditions and influences to which society is exposed. There is no "society" in general, but only specific social structures which operate in different and ascertainable ways. Although these social structures do change in the course of historical development, they are relatively fixed at any given historical period, and society can exist only by operating within the framework of its particular structure.[1]

Mexico can indeed be called a cultural crossroads in the process of passing rapidly from semifeudal organi-

[1] Erich Fromm, *The Sane Society* (New York: Rinehart, 1955), p. 79.

zation to industrialization and mechanization. This evolution is taking place in a land of 761,830 square miles with a wide variety of climates and natural resources. Its population is 35 million (double that of twenty-five years ago). Four million of these are non-Spanish-speaking Indians of many different languages, sociocultural and economic organizations. Certainly this population has an influence on Mexican society as a whole, but in this study I leave the Indian population aside to concentrate on the *mestizo* (half-caste) we now call Mexicans.

The means of production are concentrated in a very few hands. Business enterprises depend in growing numbers on private Mexican capital, or on non-Mexican, that is to say foreign—especially American—capital, or they belong to the government, which owns such industries as oil, electricity, all railroads, and many others of lesser importance. Ownership and cultivation of the land depend on agrarian organizations (*ejidos*) which are utilized individually or collectively by cooperative societies. These may also be communal or national lands. Individuals may possess only limited amounts of land; nevertheless there still exist those who possess large amounts of it. The government gives economic aid to the *ejidos,* and even to individual proprietors, by means of loans payable in kind. In addition to the workers and the peasants, there are many craftsmen and businessmen, not to mention a burgeoning bureaucracy.

Economic development is not totally under overall government planning, but the government has the right to control and direct all the country's economy in such a way that its intervention in this domain is definitive. This supervision is accomplished through the Central Bank, through credit extended to the peasants or to industry, and by control of the prices of different products, especially food. Although monopolies are forbidden by law, some still exist. Enough of the economic and political power is controlled by the clergy and the enriched older revolutionaries as to be concentrated in the hands of a few. Consequently most Mexicans are necessarily dependent on this minority for whom they must work. Certainly, during the past fifty years, thanks to the efforts of the revolutionary government, the economic situation of most Mexicans has been bettered, especially that of the peasants, the workers, the bureaucrats, and the lower middle classes. But this situation is not yet satisfactory. Agrarian and labor laws, social security, the great expansion of public instruction, the intervention and control of government in the country's economic and political life, and the like, all make the government itself paternalistic. It is not composed of peasants, workers, or bureaucrats, but it governs or works for them like a father-protector who punishes and is to be feared. Although the law clearly defines and limits the authority of the federal government, there incontestably is a maximum amount of force and power concentrated in the president of the Republic, even when the president himself does not seek it. Mexico has suffered from avowed and camouflaged dictators in the relatively recent past.

The family is a typical patriarchal complex, the father exercising unlimited power over his wife and children. This authority is in itself irrational, as is nearly all authority exercised in Mexico. Thus authority is exercised by virtue of circumstantial or hierarchical status and not because of competence or capacity, although, of course, all sorts of rationalizations are made. Nevertheless, the Mexican family still functions under certain clan forms; the bonds of blood and land being very powerful, the intra-family psychodynamics thus produced are very complex. The mother's function is one of submission to her husband, but, at the same time, by "handling" her husband, she is a kind of protective advocate between him and her children. Rivalry among children is not rare: on the contrary, each child tries to become the favorite son of his father. There are also rivalries between the families of parents and in particular among the satellites of the family, the grandparents exercising considerable influence. In general, the woman is limited to secondary standing, an inferior position that dates from Aztec through Spanish times and continues in our own day.

As for love, Mexicans prefer the relationship considered by Fromm to belong to a character of the receptive-exploitative type, that is, uniting one more or less passive element, submissive and dependent, to the other "exploitative" element, which is dominant and possessive, jealous and suspicious. The general attitude toward sex is repressive, principally by means of religious education. Virginity is very highly regarded. Men make a great show of virility, called *machismo* (male predominance) in Mexico. This attitude implies an overevaluation of the man who not only can and must conquer women but must also be very "courageous" in the face of death, which he is supposed to accept with ease, be it during a civil war, a revolution, a bullfight, or simply in a state of drunkenness.

As I have indicated, many of these norms or patterns are the results of a fusion of Aztec and Spanish cultures. This union took place without serious difficulties, although it provoked much psychic traumatism during the Spanish Conquest, because, I believe, Spanish culture in that era was similar to Aztec culture. There was in both a concentration of power within the same types of social groups: military, commercial, and clergical. The structure and functioning of the family were similar and, as far as religion is concerned, the Spanish had little trouble substituting their gods and rites for those of the Aztecs because the same psychological and social functions were involved. Except for admirable but isolated examples of devotion and love of a few missionaries for the Indians, the Spanish Christ was in effect a cruel and authoritarian God who, under other rationalizations, was not merciful. The human sacrifices of the Aztecs were followed by the Inquisition, which burned many Indians alive. At the same time, the conquerors were themselves not sufficiently developed to resist in a rational way either the Aztecs' sadomasochism or their faith in magic. This explains why even now religion for so many Mexicans is a complex mixture of fear, guilt, and idolatry, and the cause of quarrels, disputes, and obstinacy which in the past have caused civil wars, and even foreign wars. The political clergy of Mexico, as elsewhere in the world, has always allied itself with regressive and conservative forces. Despite the fact that President Juarez and Mexican liberals have fought against the clergy for more than a century, they still possess very important political and economic power. Important manifestations of belief in magic are still to be found among many Mexicans who not only look for help from certain saints, especially the Virgin of Guadalupe, "mother of all Mexicans," but also from sorcerers, healers, luck, destiny, lotteries, or some specific protector or "godfather."

Another very considerable influence, particularly recently, is the United States of America. It is well known that Mexico was stripped of nearly half its original territory by the North Americans and that they have on occasion made Mexico the victim of military and political intervention. Mexico has also profited from the technical progress and friendly assistance of her good neighbor whenever it wished to be a good neighbor. At the present time the cultural and economic influences are the most important. They are the consequence of the "mercantile" American character, described by Fromm as belonging to the capitalistic industrial society of the Western world. For many Mexicans money is not everything, because for them time is still time and not money. Time is in fact so elastic that neither punctuality nor concentration on work has become habitual. But there are already a goodly number whose ideal is money, because this ideal is thoroughly disseminated by every available means of publicity, such as radio and movies.

The foregoing conditions, described very summarily, correspond to unconscious phenomena such as ambivalence toward authority of all kinds —father, family, government, teacher, law; feelings of insecurity more or less compensated for or rationalized; a lack of self-confidence or of confidence in personal abilities; susceptibility and instability (I have called the Mexican "a provisional man"); a character of the receptive-exploitative type; extreme fixation on family and ambivalence toward it; and certain surviving manifestations of emotional or magic thought. Daydreams, daytime fantasy, or the ideal, then, consists of getting, receiving, being helped or protected by another, or else getting and possessing, thanks to good luck, to cunning or guile, or to cheating. The family is included in all these fantasies. Despite all the improvements developing or already achieved, the basic situation just described remains the same: fantastic hopes, unrealistic or barely realistic, and irrational as well; conformism; fatalism; fear of solitude; lack of faith; fear of being abandoned. There are also, it is true, many Mexicans who are self-confident and determined to transform their country.

DREAMS

In the actual dreams of many Mexicans, which we were able to study in the manner that I outline later, my attention was drawn to the following categories:

1. With many nuances or variations, the essential theme is: "Life is very beautiful, happiness is possible, but not for me." Here is an example: "I dreamed more than three times in my life that I was on a great street, full of trees, lined with beautiful and large houses. Among them there was one with a high gate. Someone told me it was mine; however, I did not enter." Or this other theme: "Life can perhaps be beautiful; but, although help is promised me, I never get it." For example: "Several times I dreamed that I was engaged to a very beautiful young girl richer than I; I have never been able to identify her because I always see her in a confused way. As she lives at a distance, I go to visit her in my car. Her father knows of our relationship and he always promises to help me with my career, but this help never comes."

Frequently these dreams develop in this general tone with many nuances.

2. In another order of ideas, the dreams express clearly that needs or desires, ambitions, even the most irrational, become reality, thanks to the help of someone else, some all-powerful being, or simply by dreaming that one has everything. For example: "I am usually happy in my dreams. A while ago I dreamed that my aunt and I visited a church, but when I made the sign of the cross, someone made fun of me; I do not remember what I asked of the Virgin, who wore a great blue mantle and had two angels at her sides; but I remember only that what I asked was granted by a nod of the head." Or else, the most unreal or fantastic desires are satisfied effortlessly in a dream, as, for example, in the many cases in which the dreamer finishes his studies without obstacle; or is professionally successful, generally in association with his family; or is a great sportsman; or is successful with women; and so on. In this category, passivity predominates, everything comes easily, and there is satisfaction for all sorts of childish or magic desires.

3. There are many dreams in which the family has a part. In these dreams, the family makes the dreamer happy or unhappy, or vice versa; the dreamer is abandoned by his family, or feels superior to them. Some

examples: "I dreamed several times that my brothers and my parents were traveling in a bus. There was an accident and they were all killed. I felt sad and alone in the world, and I had to beg." Or, "I often dream that I am with my own family and that we are extremely happy." And another: "We all go for a walk, my brother, my parents, and I, very happily; suddenly my parents argue and fight, and everything is spoiled."

4. Finally, there are dreams in which, despite every effort, the dreamer does not succeed, or if he does succeed, everything is spoiled later in one way or another; or, there is fear or difficulty in getting what is wanted: conflict. For example: "Very often, I have a rather confused dream. . . . I am working on a musical arrangement, but I can never finish it; then, I am at the gymnasium (practicing boxing); then, I find myself at the racetrack for the horse races; but I never finish whatever it is." In this category of ideas, dreams of climbing, of reaching for something, and then of falling into emptiness also frequently occur.

Relatively frequently there are dreamers who think or believe that dreams become realities or that they presage some event.

The dreams studied are, for the most part, recurrent ones or such as had made a strong impression on the subject. In comparing daydreams or waking fantasies with the categories of true dreams (both are manifestations of the unconscious) a general coincidence becomes obvious. It is equally clear that the dreams were indeed the expression of a state of social and family conflict in Mexico.

I cannot now give definitive numbers. But, out of about 500 dreams taken at random from more than 4,000 gathered up to the present, more than 60 percent can, with their many variations and nuances, be classified in one of the four categories. The character of more than 80 percent of the 500 dreamers studied corresponds to the receptive-exploitative type. The character of the dreamers was studied by different methods, including an educational and socioeconomic questionnaire, a questionnaire on general cultural formation, a questionnaire on the dreamer's interests and the organization of his time, a special questionnaire that explored character traits according to Fromm's typology, an autobiography written by each dreamer in which he classified himself from a characterological point of view. Added to this file were clinical interviews with groups of dreamers who were students of medical psychology at the School of Medicine of Mexico, and who, therefore, already had theoretical knowledge of psychodynamics and characterology. Last, they answered a special questionnaire about the nature of their dreams in general, prepared to reveal the character traits expressed in these dreams. Consequently we know a great deal about the dreamers, and our assertion that about 80 percent of them belong to the receptive-exploiter type of personality is well founded. It is in the dreams of these subjects that one finds the character predominant in

Mexico, as described above, which is the basic personality or social character of the individual Mexican.

I have obviously not made use of the technique of interpretation, nor of association, nor of the theory of Freud. Nor do I content myself with the manifest, simple dream content. Moreover, humanist psychoanalysis does not concern itself with biological aspects nor with the Freudian theories of the libido. As far as the Oedipus complex is concerned, we understand it and explain it as a struggle for power and authority, and not as sexual rivalry. It is true that frequently dreams are realizations of infantile desires, irrational and of sexual content, but it is also true that dreams satisfy other desires as well, desires not necessarily infantile or sexual. Often, too, these dreams are not the expression of a subject's irrationality, but precisely the opposite, that is to say, of what is best and most human in all men. Last, dreams may also be the expression of the dreamer's conflicts. We consider dreams, along with myths and fables, to be a symbolic language that needs understanding rather than a key to its interpretation. Its symbols are universal, conventional, or accidental. But the dream itself, taken as a whole, as a global entity, is in turn symbolic as well as expressive. The universal symbol is the only symbol whose relation to what it represents is intrinsic and not merely coincidental. It has its roots in the experience of affinity existing between an emotion or thought on the one hand and a sensory experience on the other. Every human being who shares with the rest of humanity the essential qualities of a mental and corporeal entity is capable of speaking and understanding this symbolic language, based on these common qualities. These things then are not learned, just as we do not learn to cry when we are sad, or blush when angry. For the same reason, these reactions do not belong to any determined race, the proof being that this symbolic language is found in all cultures. The symbols employed are everywhere similar because they are all derived from basic experiences, as much sensory as sentimental, which are the common lot of all men in all cultures (also verified by experiments in hypnotism). But there are symbols that differ in meaning, according to their actual signification in all the different cultures: thus the function and, therefore, the significance of the sun are different in northern countries, where it provides heat and is protective and loving, than in tropical countries and the desert, where the sun is a dangerous and menacing power. We can, therefore, speak of dialects in the universal symbolic language which are the result of differences in natural conditions which give different meanings to certain symbols in dissimilar parts of the earth. It is not possible in so short a time to discuss more extensively the characteristics of this forgotten language of dreams and myths. I repeat only that the understanding and not the interpretation of the dreams I have studied is based on these ideas.

In other words, I understand these dreams to be expressions of the conditions of existence of the Mexicans as they appear in their social character.

It is also Fromm who, in his books *Escape from Freedom*[2] and *The Sane Society,* brought out clearly in what this social character consists and how it is produced. Social character is the core of the character structure shared by most individuals in the same culture. This concept is not statistical, but functional, the function of social character being that of molding the energies of the individual within his society. Individual behavior, thus molded, is no longer a question of consciously deciding whether or not to follow the social norm, but of the individual's wish to act as *he must act,* and at the same time finding pleasure in behaving as the culture would have him behave. Society succeeds in this function from the individual's childhood by using the family and the school. Social exigencies are transmitted to children by the family in such a way that children want to be, to feel, and to act as they are expected to. That is, it is the *content* of social character which is transmitted and exacted by parents and teachers. The *methods* used by parents and teachers, although important, are not essential because methods change. On the other hand, the character itself of parents and schoolmasters is much more important in well forming the characters of the future men according to the meaning of social exigencies. Also to be counted here are the influences of all the modern means of communication—radio, movies, the press, the markets, publicity, and so on—because these methods constitute an anonymous authority that demands, praises, and transmits social norms desired by the group in possession of and manipulating these methods.

For his part, the individual who has been formed from his childhood as I have just explained must adapt himself dynamically to it all. It is fitting to clarify here the difference between mechanical adaptation and dynamic adaptation. The former implies no change in the individual's character, as in the case of the Oriental woman who can wear Western clothes in place of her own without thereby changing anything in her character. Conversely, dynamic adaptation forcibly modifies the personality. The child interiorizes the ideals and social persons; he acquires interior authorities: conscience, duty, norms. In other words, social character interiorizes exterior needs, channeling human energies in this way toward the tasks demanded by the socioeconomic system.

For humanist psychoanalysis, the essential problem of psychology is the manner—or specific mode—of the individual's relationship with society and with himself. Individual accidents of the libido do not, therefore, determine or form character. On the other hand, it is understandable that a social group that is in the majority but dependent in every sense on

---

[2] Erich Fromm, *Escape from Freedom* (New York: Farrar and Rinehart, 1941).

another group that is in the minority but possesses all the power, can be molded and its character formed in this way. Psychological agents, such as the family or the school, help to transmit and sustain the norms of this society. It is up to the individual, using psychical tools, to resolve the contradictions of human existence, his character being equivalent to the animal's instinct. The dynamics and motivations of character are unconscious and are molded by society. So it is understandable that social character can be expressed in dreams.

In summary, I have presented a working hypothesis asserting that there is a relationship of cause and effect between social character and certain repetitive themes, or rather between social character and certain types or patterns of dreams which, if they are wholly understood, express modalities of social character as well as reactions, conflicts, and desires of dreamers in relation to their society. Finally, the dialectical dynamism of the individual-society (or cultural) relationship, and vice versa, is revealed in dreams.

19

Initiation Dreams and Visions among the Siberian Shamans

MIRCEA ELIADE

Sicknesses, dreams, and ecstasies are but means of reaching the condition of shaman. Sometimes these singular experiences signify no more than a "choice" from above and merely prepare the candidate for new revelations. But usually sicknesses, dreams, and ecstasies are in themselves the initiation; that is, they transform the profane individual into a technician of the sacred. Naturally, this ecstatic kind of experience is always and everywhere followed by theoretical and practical instruction at the hands of the old masters; but that does not make it any less determinative, for it is the ecstatic experience that radically changes the religious status of the "elected" person.

The ecstatic experiences that determine the future shaman's vocation involve the traditional schema of an initiation ceremony: suffering, death, resurrection. Seen from this angle, any "sickness-vocation" fills the role of an initiation, for the suffering that it brings on corresponds to initiatory tortures; the psychic isolation of the "elected" is the counterpart to the isolation and ritual solitude of initiation ceremonies; the imminence of death felt by the sick man recalls the symbolic death represented in almost all initiation ceremonies.

The content of the first ecstatic experiences of the

Siberian shaman, although comparatively rich, almost always includes one or more of the following themes: dismemberment of the body, followed by a renewal of the internal organs and viscera; ascent to the sky and dialogue with the gods or spirits; descent to the Lowerworld and conversations with spirits and the souls of dead shamans; various revelations, both religious and shamanic (secrets of the profession). All these themes are clearly initiatory. In some documents all are attested; in others only one or two are mentioned (bodily dismemberment, celestial ascent). It is possible that the absence of certain initiatory themes is caused, at least in part, by the inadequacy of our information, since the earliest ethnologists were usually content with summary data.

Among the Siberian and Central Asiatic peoples, the shamanic vocation is often manifested in the form of illness. Sometimes there is not exactly an illness but rather a progressive change in behavior. The candidate becomes meditative, seeks solitude, sleeps a great deal, seems absent-minded, has prophetic dreams and sometimes seizures. All these symptoms are only the prelude to the new life that awaits the unwitting candidate. His behavior, we may add, suggests the first signs of a mystical vocation, which are almost the same in all religions.

But there are also sicknesses, attacks, dreams, and hallucinations that determine a shaman's career in a very short time. We are not concerned with whether these pathogenic ecstasies have really been experienced, or have been imagined, or at least later enriched by folkloric motifs, to end by being integrated into the frame of the traditional shamanic mythology. Essential is the fact that these experiences justify the vocation and the magical-religious power of a shaman, that they are invoked as the one possible validation for a radical change in religious practice.

For example, a Yakut shaman, Sofron Zateejev, states that as a rule the shaman dies and lies in the yurt for three days without eating or drinking. Formerly the candidate went through the ceremony three times, during which he was cut to pieces. Another shaman, Pjotr Ivanov, gives further details of the ceremony. The candidate's limbs are removed and disjointed with an iron hook; the bones are cleaned, the flesh is scraped, the body fluids are thrown away, and the eyes are torn from their sockets. After this operation all the bones are gathered up and fastened together with iron. According to another shaman, Timofei Romanov, the ceremony of dismemberment lasts from three to seven days; during all that time the candidate remains like a dead man, scarcely breathing, in a solitary place.

The Yakut Gavriil Alekseev states that each shaman has a Bird-of-Prey Mother, which is like a great bird with an iron beak, hooked claws, and a long tail. This mythical bird shows itself only twice: at the shaman's spiritual birth, and at his death. It takes his soul, carries it to the Lowerworld, and leaves it to ripen on a branch of pitch pine. When the soul has reached maturity, the bird returns to earth, cuts the candidate's body into bits, and distributes them among the evil spirits of disease and death. Each spirit devours the part of the body that is his share; this procedure has the effect of giving the future shaman the power to cure the corresponding diseases. After devouring the whole body, the evil spirits depart. The Bird Mother restores the bones to their places and the candidate wakes as from a deep sleep.

According to another Yakut account, the evil spirits carry the future shaman's soul to the Lowerworld and there shut it up in a house for three years (only one year for those who will become lesser shamans). Here the shaman undergoes his initiation. The spirits cut off his head, which they set aside (for the candidate must watch his dismemberment with his own eyes), and cut him into small pieces, which are then distributed to the spirits of the various diseases. Only on this condition will the future shaman gain the power to cure. His bones are then covered with new flesh, and in some cases he is also given new blood.[1]

According to another Yakut belief, also collected by Ksenofontov, shamans are born in the north. There a giant fir grows, with nests in its branches. The great shamans are in the highest branches, the middling ones in the middle branches, the least are low in the tree. According to some, the Bird-of-Prey Mother, which has the head of an eagle and iron feathers, lights on the tree, lays eggs, and sits on them; great, middling, and lesser shamans are hatched in respectively three years, two years, and one year. When the soul comes out of the egg, the Bird Mother entrusts it to a devil-shamaness—who has only one eye, one arm, and one bone—to be taught. She rocks the future shaman's soul in an iron cradle and feeds him on clotted blood. Then three black "devils" come and cut his body to pieces, thrust a lance into his head, and throw bits of his flesh in different directions as offerings. Three other "devils" cut up his jawbone—a piece for each of the diseases that he will be called on to cure. If one of his bones is missing, a member of his family must die to replace it. Sometimes as many as nine of his relatives die.

In all these examples we find the central theme of an initiation ceremony: dismemberment of the neophyte's body and renewal of his organs; ritual death followed by resurrection. We may also note the motif of the giant bird that hatches shamans in the branches of the world tree; it has wide application in North Asian mythologies, especially in shamanic mythology.

According to T. Lehtisalo's Yurak Samoyed informants, initiation

---

[1] M. Eliade, *Le chamanisme et les techniques archaïques de l'extase* (Paris, 1951), pp. 47 ff., quoting G. W. Ksenofontov.

proper begins with learning to drum; it is on this occasion that the candidate is able to see the spirits. The shaman Ganyakka told Lehtisalo that once when he was beating his drum the spirits came down and cut him in pieces, also chopping off his hands. For seven days and nights he remained unconscious, stretched on the ground. During this time his soul was in the sky, going about with the Spirit of Thunder and visiting the god Mikkulai.

A. A. Popov gives the following account concerning a shaman of the Avam Samoyeds. Sick with smallpox, for three days he remained unconscious and so nearly dead that on the third day he was almost buried. His initiation took place during this time. He remembered having been carried into the middle of a sea. There he heard his Sickness (that is, smallpox) speak, saying to him: "From the Lord of Water you will receive the gift of shamanizing. Your name as a shaman will be *huottarie* [diver]." Then the Sickness troubled the water of the sea. The candidate came out and climbed a mountain. There he met a naked woman and began to suckle at her breasts. The woman, who was probably the Lady of the Waters, said to him: "You are my child; that is why I let you suckle at my breast. You will meet many hardships and be greatly wearied." The husband of the Lady of the Waters, the Lord of the Lowerworld, then gave him two guides, an ermine and a mouse, to lead him to the Lowerworld. When they came to a high place, the guides showed him seven tents with torn roofs. He entered the first and there found the inhabitants of the Lowerworld and the men of the Great Sickness (syphilis). These men tore out his heart and threw it into a pot. In other tents he met the Lord of Madness and the lords of all the nervous disorders, as well as the evil shamans. Thus he learned the various diseases that torment mankind.

Still preceded by his guides, the candidate then came to the Land of the Shamanesses, who strengthened his throat and his voice. He was then carried to the shores of the Nine Seas. In the middle of one of them was an island, and in the middle of the island a young birch rose to the sky. It was the Tree of the Lord of Earth. Beside it grew nine herbs, the ancestors of all the plants on earth. The Tree was surrounded by the seas, and in each of these swam a species of bird with its young. The candidate visited all these seas; some of them were salt, others so hot he could not go near the shore. After visiting the seas, the candidate raised his head and, in the top of the tree, saw men of various nations: Samoyeds, Russians, Dolgans, Yakuts, and Tungus. He heard voices: "It has been decided that you shall have a drum [that is, the body of a drum] from the branches of this Tree." He began to fly with the birds of the seas. As he left the shore, the Lord of the Tree called to him: "My branch has just fallen; take it and make a drum of it that will serve you all your life." The branch had three forks, and the Lord of the Tree bade him make three drums from it, which must be kept by three women, each of the drums being for a special ceremony—one for shamanizing women in childbirth, the second for curing the sick, the third for finding men lost in the snow.

The Lord of the Tree also gave branches to all the men who were in the top of the tree. But, appearing from the tree, in human form down to the waist, he added: "One branch only I give not to the shamans, for I keep it for the rest of mankind. They can make dwellings from it and so use it for their needs. I am the Tree that gives life to all men." Clasping the branch, the candidate was ready to resume his flight when again he heard a human voice, this time revealing to him the medicinal virtues of the seven plants and giving him certain instructions concerning the art of shamanizing. But, the voices added, he must marry three women (which, in fact, he later did by marrying three orphan girls whom he had cured of smallpox).

After that he came to an endless sea and there he found trees and seven stones. The stones spoke to him one after the other. The first had teeth like bears' teeth and a basket-shaped cavity, and it revealed to him that it was the earth's holding stone; it pressed on the fields with its weight, so that they should not be carried away by the wind. The second served to melt iron. He remained with these stones for seven days and so learned how they could be of use to men.

Then his two guides, the ermine and the mouse, led him to a high, rounded mountain. He saw an opening before him and entered a bright cave in the middle of which there was something like a fire. He saw two women, naked but covered with hair, like reindeer. Then he saw that there was no fire burning but that the light came from above, through an opening. One of the women told him that she was pregnant and would give birth to two reindeer; one of them would be the sacrificial animal of the Dolgans and Evenkes, the other that of the Tavghis. She also gave him a hair, which would be useful to him when he shamanized for reindeer. The other woman also gave birth to two reindeer, symbols of the animals that would aid man in his works and also supply his food. The cave had two openings, toward the north and toward the south; through each of them the young women sent a reindeer to serve the forest people (Dolgans and Evenkes). The second woman too, gave him a hair. When he shamanizes, he mentally turns toward that cave.

Then the candidate came to a desert and saw a distant mountain. After three days' travels he reached it, entered an opening, and came upon a naked man working a bellows. On the fire was a cauldron "as big as half the earth." The naked man saw him and caught him with a huge pair of tongs. The novice had time to think, "I am dead!" The man cut off his head, chopped his body into bits, and put the whole in the cauldron. There he boiled his body for three years. There were also three anvils, and the naked man forged his head on the third, which was the one on which the best shamans were forged. Then he threw his head in one of three pots that stood there, the one in which the water was coldest. He now revealed to him that, when he was called to cure someone, if the water in the ritual pot was very hot, it would be useless to shamanize, for the man was already lost; if the water was warm, he was sick but would recover; cold water denoted a healthy man.

The blacksmith then fished his bones out of a river in which they were floating, put them together, and covered them with flesh again. He counted them and told him that he had three too many; so he must procure three shamanic costumes. He forged his head and taught him how to read the letters that are inside it. He changed his eyes; and that is why, when he shamanized, he did not see with his bodily eyes but with these mystical eyes. He pierced his ears, making him able to understand the language of plants. Then the candidate found himself on the summit of a mountain, and finally he woke in the yurt, among his family. Now he can sing and shamanize indefinitely, without ever growing tired.[2]

We have reproduced this account because it is so astonishingly rich mythologically and religiously. If the same care had been taken to collect the confessions of other Siberian shamans, probably no one would ever have been reduced to the meager common formula: the candidate remained unconscious for a certain number of days, dreamed that he was cut to pieces by spirits and carried into the sky, and the rest. It is clearly apparent that the initiatory ecstasy very closely follows certain paradigmatic themes: the novice encounters several divine figures (the Lady of the Waters, the Lord of the Lowerworld, the Lady of the Animals) before being led by his animal guides to the center of the world, on the summit of the cosmic mountain, where are the world tree and the Universal Lord; from the cosmic tree and by the will of the Universal Lord Himself, he receives the wood to make his drum; semidemonic beings teach him the nature of all diseases and their cures; finally, other demonic beings cut his body to pieces, boil it, and exchange it for better organs. Each of these elements in the initiatory dream is consistent and has its place in a symbolic or ritual system well known to the history of religions. Taken together, they represent a well-organized variant of the universal theme of the death and mystical resurrection of the candidate by means of a descent to the underworld and ascent to the sky.

The same initiatory schema is also found among other Siberian

---

[2] *Ibid.*, pp. 50–53, quoting A. A. Popov.

peoples.³ The Tungus shaman Ivan Tscholko states that a future shaman must fall ill, have his body cut in pieces and his blood drunk by the evil spirits (*saargi*). These spirits, which are really the souls of dead shamans, throw his head into a cauldron, where it is forged with other metal pieces that will later form part of his ritual costume. Another Tungus shaman relates that he was sick for a whole year. During that time he sang to feel better. His shaman ancestors came and initiated him. They pierced him with arrows until he lost consciousness and fell to the ground; they cut off his flesh, tore out his bones and counted them; if one had been missing, he could not have become a shaman. During this operation he went for a whole summer without eating or drinking.

Although the Buriats have very complex public ceremonies for consecrating shamans, they also know the "sickness-dream" of the initiatory type. Ksenofontov reports the experience of Michail Stepanov. Stepanov relates that before becoming a shaman the candidate must be sick for a long time; the souls of his shaman ancestors then surround him, torture him, strike him, cut his body with knives, and so on. During this operation the future shaman remains inanimate; his face and hands are blue, his heart scarcely beats. According to another Buriat shaman, the ancestral spirits carry the candidate's soul before the Assembly of the Saaytani in the sky, and there he is taught. After his initiation his flesh is cooked to teach him the art of shamanizing. It is during this initiatory torture that the shaman remains for seven days and nights as if dead. On this occasion his relatives (except women) come to him and sing: "Our shaman is returning to life and he will help us!" While his body is being cut to pieces and cooked by his ancestors, no stranger may touch it.

The same experiences are found elsewhere. A Teleut woman became a shamaness after having a vision in which unknown men cut her body to bits and cooked it in a pot. According to the tradition of the Altaian shamans, the spirits of their ancestors eat their flesh, drink their blood, open their bellies, and so on. The Kazak Kirghiz *baqca* says: "I have five spirits in heaven who cut me with forty knives, prick me with forty nails," and so on.

The ecstatic experience of dismemberment of the body followed by a renewal of the organs is also known to the Eskimo, to some South American and North American tribes (e.g., Araucanians, Coast Pomo, Menominis, and others), in Malekula, among the Kiwai Papuans and the Dyak of Borneo,⁴ and especially among the Australians. I will limit myself to some examples of ecstatic, initiatory dreams of the Australian medicine men.

³ Cf. *ibid.*, pp. 53–55.
⁴ Cf. *ibid.*, pp. 62–70.

The Arunta know three ways of making medicine men: (1) by the Iruntarinia, or "spirits"; (2) by the Eruncha (that is, the spirits of the Eruncha men of the mythical Alchera times); (3) by other medicine men. In the first case the candidate goes to the mouth of a cave and falls asleep. An Iruntarinia comes and "throws an invisible lance at him, which pierces the neck from behind, passes through the tongue, making therein a large hole, and then comes out through the mouth." The candidate's tongue remains perforated; one can easily put one's little finger through it. A second lance cuts off his head, and the victim succumbs. The Iruntarinia carries him into the cave, which is said to be very deep and where it is believed that the Iruntarinia spirits live in perpetual light and near cool springs. In the cave the spirit tears out his internal organs and gives him others, which are completely new. The candidate returns to life but for some time behaves like a lunatic. The Iruntarinia spirits—which are invisible to other human beings, except medicine men—then carry him to his village. Etiquette forbids him to practice for a year; if during that time the opening in his tongue closes, the candidate gives up, for his magical virtues are held to have disappeared. During this year he learns the secrets of the profession from other medicine men, especially the use of the fragments of quartz (*atnongara*) that the Iruntarinia spirits placed in his body.

The second way of making a medicine man resembles the first except that, instead of carrying the candidate into a cave, the Erunchas take him underground with them. Finally, the third method involves a long ritual in a deserted place, where the candidate must silently submit to an operation performed by two old medicine men; they rub his body with rock crystals to the point of abrading the skin, press rock crystals into his scalp, pierce a hole under a fingernail of his right hand, and make an incision in his tongue.[5]

A famous magician of the Unmatjera tribe told Spencer and Gillen that

> . . . when he was made into a medicine man, a very old doctor came one day and threw some of his *atnongara* stones at him with a spear-thrower. Some hit him on the chest, others went right through his head, from ear to ear, killing him. The old man then cut out all of his insides, intestines, liver, heart, lungs—everything in fact—and left him lying all night long on the ground. In the morning the old man came and looked at him and placed some more *atnongara* stones inside his body and in his arms and legs, and covered over his face with leaves. Then he sang over him until his body was all swollen. When it was so he provided him with a complete set of new inside parts, placed a lot more *atnongara* stones in

---

[5] *Ibid.*, pp. 56–57, quoting B. Spencer and F. J. Gillen.

him, and patted him on the head, which caused him to jump up alive. When he awoke he had no idea as to where he was, and said: "I think I am lost." But when he looked round he saw the old medicine man standing beside him, and the old man said: "No, you are not lost; I killed you a long time ago." Ilpailurkna had completely forgotten who he was and all about his past life. After a time the old man led him back to his camp and showed it to him, and told him that the woman there was his lubra, for he had forgotten all about her. His coming back this way and his strange behavior at once showed the other natives that he had been made into a medicine man.[6]

Among the Warramunga, initiation is performed by the puntidir spirits, which are equivalent to the Irantarinia of the Arunta. A medicine man told Spencer and Gillen that he had been pursued for two days by two spirits who told him that they were "his father and his brother." On the second night these spirits came to him again and killed him. "While he was lying dead they cut him open and took all his inside out, providing him, however, with a new set and, finally, they put a little snake inside his body, which endowed him with the powers of a medicine man."[7]

Among the Binbinga, medicine men are believed to be consecrated by the spirits Mundadji and Munkaninji (father and son). A medicine man told how, entering a cave one day, he came upon the old Mundadji, who caught him by the neck and killed him.

> Mundadji cut him open, right down the middle line, took out all of his insides and exchanged them for those of himself, which he placed in the body of Kurkutji. At the same time he put a number of sacred stones in his body. After it was all over the younger spirit, Munkaninji, came up and restored him to life, told him that he was now a medicine man, and showed him how to extract bones and other forms of evil magic out of men. Then he took him away up into the sky and brought him down to the earth close to his own camp, where he heard the natives mourning for him, thinking that he was dead. For a long time he remained in a more or less dazed condition, but gradually he recovered and the natives knew that he had been made into a medicine man.[8]

In the Mara tribe the technique is almost exactly the same. One who wishes to become a medicine man lights a fire and burns fat, thus

---

[6] B. Spencer and F. J. Gillen, *The Northern Tribes of Central Australia* (London, 1904), pp. 480–481.
[7] *Ibid.*, p. 484.
[8] *Ibid.*, pp. 487–488.

attracting two spirits called Minnungarra. These approach and encourage the candidate, assuring him that they will not completely kill him.

> First of all they make him insensible, and in the usual way cut him open and take out all his organs, which are then replaced by those of one of the spirits. Then he is brought to life again, told that he is now a doctor, shown how to take bones and evil magic out of men, and carried up into the sky. Finally he is brought down and placed near to his own camp, where he is found by his friends, who have been mourning for him. . . . Amongst the powers possessed by a Mara medicine man is that of climbing at night-time by means of a rope, invisible to ordinary mortals, into the sky, where he can hold converse with the star people.[9]

As we have just seen, the similarity between the initiations of Siberian shamans and those of Australian medicine men is quite close. In both cases the candidate is subjected to an operation by semidivine beings or ancestors, in which his body is dismembered and his internal organs and bones are renewed. In both cases this operation takes place in an "inferno" or involves a descent to the Lowerworld. As for the pieces of quartz or other magical objects that the spirits are believed to place in the Australian candidate's body, this practice is of little importance among the Siberians. There is only rarely some reference to pieces of iron set to melt in the same cauldron in which the future shaman's flesh and bones have been put. There is a further difference between the two areas: in Siberia the majority of shamans are "chosen" by the spirits and gods, while in Australia the career of medicine men seems to result from a voluntary quest on the candidate's part as well as from a spontaneous "election" by spirits and divine beings.

We must add, too, that the methods of initiating Australian magicians cannot be reduced to the types we have cited. Although the important element of an initiation appears to be the dismemberment of the body and replacing of the internal organs, there are also other ways of consecrating a medicine man, especially the ecstatic experience of an ascent to the sky, including instruction given by celestial beings. Sometimes initiation includes both the candidate's dismemberment and his ascent to the sky. Elsewhere, initiation takes place during a mystical descent to the underworld. All these types of initiation are also found among the Siberian and central Asian shamans. Such parallelism between two groups of mystical techniques belonging to archaic peoples so far removed in space is not without bearing on the place to be accorded to shamanism in the general history of religions.

[9] *Ibid.*, p. 488.

20

Mantic Dreams in the Ancient Near East

A. LEO OPPENHEIM

Among the numerous cuneiform tablets dealing with divination is found a small group that treats dreams. In these texts, predictions are derived from dream contents in the way the future is predicted from other divination media, such as the behavior of certain animals, the movements of planets, the trivia of the daily life, and the like. Hence, in order to evaluate the role assigned to the dream in Mesopotamian civilization, one must, first, place the dream omens in the context of the entire gamut of the diviner's art.

In ancient Mesopotamia, divination was the subject of greater and more sustained interest than in any other known civilization. Although divination was important, even essential, in a number of other civilizations, only in Mesopotamia was it set down in writing quite early (middle of the second millennium B.C.) and did it occupy a predominant position during the entire span of this civilization. Moreover, it served there in many respects as a vehicle for the intellectual aspirations and the speculative interests of the scholars.

When I investigated these texts, the Assyrian dream book and its earlier formulations,[1] some years ago,

[1] A. Leo Oppenheim. *The Interpretation of Dreams in the Ancient Near East with a Translation of an Assyrian Dream-Book,*

I approached the Mesopotamian text material on the interpretation of dreams in the spirit of the essentially Greek interest in the etiology of the dream, utilizing both the dream book and passages from literary and other texts referring to dream incidents. By now, however, I have come to realize that information thus obtained can satisfy our curiosity only on a more or less superficial level, because the text material has been studied under the influence of modern, Western, conceptual patterning. The results, therefore, cannot adequately reflect Mesopotamian views.

The primary task of this presentation, then, is to bring out what the dream was as experience in Mesopotamian terms. This I present on three distinct levels. On the first, I demonstrate the existence of what we would call, in today's civilization, a "scientific" explanation of the dream phenomenon. Second, I discuss the psychological aspect, and, last, I outline the role of the dream in the social context of Mesopotamian civilization, its theological validity, and its role within the literary conventions.

The main accent, however, is on the contrast between the first two levels, the one I call "scientific" and the other for which I choose the term "folklore" in order to accentuate this contrast. I am using these terms deliberately to characterize my approach to Mesopotamian divination, an approach that represents an inversion of the traditional viewpoint of the Assyriologist. I propose to see in the divination aspect of the dream a "scientific" attitude, while I consider as falling under the heading of folklore the aspect that derives no predictions from dreams but accepts them as a psychological phenomenon. To state this view of mine more emphatically, I am prepared to say that predictions derived from such dream contents as, for example, seeing certain animals, eating certain foods, and so forth, are based on a "scientific" attitude of the Mesopotamian interpreters, whereas dreams that the modern psychologist would characterize as nightmares, or as typically symbol-affected dreams, belong in Mesopotamia to an "unscientific" view of the world; they are vestiges of dream explanations on a folklore level.

Let me now explain why I consider it essential for the understanding of Mesopotamian divination—and that includes dream omens—to see in it a "science," that is, a willingness to face reality, a willingness endowed with the same seriousness of intent and the same innate global aspiration that characterize that aspect of our modern relation to reality which we call science.

Mesopotamian divination lore is codified in extensive collections consisting of highly formalized one-sentence units, which we Assyriologists call omens. Each omen consists of a protasis, in which the ominous fea-

---

Transactions of the American Philosophical Society, n.s., vol. 46, part 3 (Philadelphia, 1956), pp. 179–373.

ture or event is described, and an apodosis, which offers a prediction. The protases attempt to observe specific, objective aspects of the reality critically and systematically and to describe them. Both, observation and description, are strikingly devoid of irrational attitudes, of a priori explanations, and of direct references to divine agents. In the readiness to observe reality in this spirit and in the desire to record observations in carefully chosen terms that reduce complex facts to unequivocally statable subunits, these omen texts reflect a consistently rational approach which is hardly paralleled in Mesopotamian literature.[2]

In another civilization of the ancient Near East, and again, only in a special literary context, we come across the same absence of references to specialized divine agents, and the same lack of interest in causality induced again by a restriction of the observer's attention to what can be observed directly and in time and space. In certain parts of the Old Testament, such as in the Book of Job and in sections of Ecclesiastes, a singular interest in the marvels of nature is revealed.[3] The descriptions show a keen power of observation, without any mythological or too obviously theological trappings. In a beautifully simple but forceful language, these passages attest a definitely rationalistic world picture and can, and should, for this reason, be compared with the omen texts of Mesopotamia. In both instances, the attitude revealed is clearly style-bound; in the Bible it appears solely in that genre of literature which we call "Wisdom Literature"[4] and in Mesopotamia in the compendiums of the diviners.

There are, of course, essential differences involved—in fact, a definitely antithetic outlook. In the Bible passages the observations, however factual and purely descriptive, are formulated ultimately to bring to the fore the glory and the power of the Lord and Creator whose very acts these marvels are. The astronomical and meteorological phenomena described are meant to evoke admiration and pious submission in their observer: "The heavens declare the glory of God; and the firmament sheweth his handywork." Mesopotamian man likewise reached toward the deity through the observation of the world around him, but in mood and purpose this took place on a different level. In the planets moving among the fixed stars, in the waters of the rivers swollen and colored by the

---

[2] As an interesting and important sequel of the characteristically scientific endeavor to make and to record observations, there arose in the Babylonia of the first millennium B.C. the realization of the inherent rhythm of recurring events in the sky. Eventually such sequences were expressed in numerical terms, and in this way mathematical astronomy grew out of astrology, that is, out of divination.
[3] Siegfried Hermann, "Die Naturlehre des Schöpfungsberichtes," *Theologische Literaturzeitung,* 86 (1961), 414 ff.
[4] Cf., e.g., O. S. Rankin, *Israel's Wisdom Literature* (Edinburgh: T. and T. Clark, 1936).

spring flood, in plants and animals, and in many other features and happenings, the ancient Mesopotamian saw the manifestations of some anonymous supernatural power. His interest in these manifestations was based principally on the assumption that they represented the expression of that power's care and concern for himself, and his family, his city, and his country. What happened, happened for him. This is the reason that these manifestations were understood as containing warnings or promises for him.

The Mesopotamian observer was as keen with his eyes and precise in his formulations as he was obtuse to the dimension of causality. Causality he replaced by the concept, quite paradoxical to us, of an impersonal divine intent that manipulated reality out of a personal interest for the observer. Only exceptionally are awesome or miraculous events or features mentioned in the protases of these omens. No fear-inspiring apparitions in the sky—*letalia fatalia me nuntiant cometae*—only here and there a rain of blood, a child born bearded and walking and talking, are observed and interpreted. In most instances, the diviner, had, so to speak, to "read" the intentions of that divine power which released the signs in small and apparently insignificant deviations from what was considered normal and expectable.

We then have to realize that both biblical and Mesopotamian men were able to face the world with two diametrically contrasting attitudes: one that dealt with the observable reality in the way just expounded; another—under the stress of misfortune and sickness—when good behavior, prayers, and conjurations were considered the only possible reaction.

Thus, for the Old Testament, on the "Wisdom" level, the observable reality proclaims the acts of the deity and the wise and pious man substituted the divine fiat for a search for causes, whereas for the Mesopotamian diviner this same reality was but a medium of communication for divine expressions. For him the divine desire to communicate with him replaced any notion of causality.

Only with the Ionian thinkers did the search for principles and conceptual tools begin which would explain the reality as observed in time and space in terms of causality. With the introduction of this new approach, the "signs" ceased to be viewed as communicating messages to man, at least on the level of what we call science.

It is probably only an accident that the development from Babylonian astrology to mathematical astronomy took place only a little later than the rise of Ionian natural philosophy. Still, even when sustained recording of observations led in Mesopotamia to the recognition of the periodicity, for example, of the rising of stars and planets, and hence to that of the predictability of such events, the Babylonian diviner did not simply turn from an astrologer into an astronomer as the historians of science often tell us. He remained a diviner at heart, even when the observations had yielded reliable mathematical formulas to predict the events. The causes that underly the erratic, if predictable, movements of the planets did not interest him. Not until the records of these observations became known to Hellenistic astronomy was the traditional, anthropocentric view of the sky abandoned for one that posited independent and regular movements of the several planets and adduced geometric reasons to account for the apparent irregularities.

My foregoing remarks concerning the nature and the purpose of observing and recording as contained in Mesopotamian omen texts should make it evident that the recording of dream omens represents only a special and rather narrow section of the universal interest of the Mesopotamian diviner. What happened in dreams was for him neither more nor less interesting than what happened in the sky, in the fields, or anywhere else around him.

Now to the relationship between omen content and prediction. The essential feature characteristic of all omen texts, and by no means restricted to dreams and their interpretation, is that no obvious connection can be established between an ominous event, encounter, or feature, and the nature of the prediction derived therefrom.[5] This statement is not intended to deny either the existence of a number of paronomastic relations—puns and plays on words—between protasis and apodosis, or the existence of associations that obviously impart to certain words favorable or unfavorable connotations liable to influence the character of the prediction. Still, in the large majority of omens, it is impossible to discover a rational relationship. In this respect, we face a problem to which I can see no solution because of the impossibility of gauging adequately the conscious and subconscious associations inherent in the words of a dead language. Incongruous interpretations are therefore not characteristic of dream omens but are a common trait in all Mesopotamian omens.

In the first part of this paper I have tried to establish the attitude of the professional Mesopotamian diviners toward dreams; now, in the second part, the dream as a specific personal experience is discussed.

As is to be expected, the Mesopotamian sources show several coexisting etiologies of the dream. Such explanations of the phenomenon are recognizable in allusions, in the use of certain terms and phrases, but nowhere is a coherent or systematic statement available. None of these

---

[5] This does not apply to the secondary elaborations through which a given prognostic is altered owing to external circumstances such as direction, timing, and so on, nor to those omens that are enumerated for the sole purpose of covering the entire range of theoretical possibilities.

native "dream theories" is in any way strikingly different from those found in other, or, for that matter, in primitive, civilizations. One of them suggests that the soul, or some part of it, moves out of the body of the sleeping person and actually visits, in some mysterious way, the places and persons the dreamer "sees" in his sleep. Sometimes the god of dreams is said to carry the dreamer—in other passages no reference is made to a divine agent. Some texts indicate that the Mesopotamians were as aware as the Bible and certain Greek sources of the impact of the fears and the hopes of the day on dream contents.

More important than these sparsely attested, and probably more or less vestigial "dream theories," is the massive evidence for an entirely different aspect of the dream as experience. It is offered by texts that speak of untoward, disturbing, and evil dreams. These evil dreams are conceived of as a disease rather than as the symptoms of a disease, or at least as an expression of a poor state of health, caused either by divine wrath or by mischievous machinations of human enemies. In both instances, the evil dreams are conceived of as demonic phenomena and are always referred to in the anonymity of the plural. Their content is never mentioned for fear of causing increased entanglements. Only quite rarely are allusions found to their content, and they suggest that evil dreams are related to the realm of sexual life, and often deal with tabooed relations or exhibit nightmare characteristics. All these dreams are taken as untoward encounters with evil and demonic powers, and, to rid himself of their influence, the dreamer has to undergo cathartic rites. A substantial literature of short and long conjurations and pertinent rituals already existed in Sumerian,[6] which were to be used to ward off the evil consequences of such dreams or, prophylactically, to prevent their occurrence. It should be added here that some texts refer to pleasant dreams as a sign of divine favor and good health and thus corroborate the proposed explanation of the use of the term "evil dreams."

It will be evident from what has been said so far that this type of dream does not predict future events for the dreamer; these dreams are not listed in the dream book; they are not the concern of the interpreter of dreams. Such dreams have to be fought and dispelled by magic means just like any other evil sign; such dreams are in fact indications of the cultic status of the person who experiences them. They are not caused by those unknown powers who manipulate the "signs" and portents, but rather they are the consequence of what we would call today the internal conflicts of the dreamer. This state of mind and of health is in Mesopotamia customarily conceived of as an absence of those pro-

---

[6] Edmond I. Gordon, "A New Look at the Wisdom of Sumer and Akkad," *Bibliotheca Orientalis,* 17 (1960), 127 n. 46, 129 n. 57.

tective spirits who are thought to maintain a person's happiness and well-being. When these spirits abandon their ward for some reason, demonic dreams, ill health, and all sorts of misfortunes begin to plague the person. The unprotected is also a prey to the magic machinations of his enemies who often send evil dreams to torment him.

As an illustration of one of the techniques used to obviate the consequences of evil dreams, I might mention the practice of "telling" the content of such a dream to a lump of clay, which is then dissolved under appropriate prayers and thus clears the dreamer from any contamination. We will come back to the *topos* of telling a dream in a moment.

We may here draw a parallel. In the first part of this presentation I showed that dream omens belong to the large body of divination lore that interprets signs of all kinds as bearing on the future of the person who has observed or experienced them. In the second part I turned to a different aspect of the dream, and here, again, the dream was found to be not a category in itself, but rather a subcategory of Mesopotamian demonology. The concept of demonic powers was very well known in Mesopotamia; they manifest themselves in an array of more or less individualized demonic figures who swarm out from the depth of the Lowerworld to attack and to defile man. Many cuneiform texts provide exorcistic rituals, and the like, to protect the healthy and to help those who suffer from such attacks. The evil dreams belong, therefore, in a much wider context of magic and countermagic, just as do certain diseases dealt with normally in medical texts.

I turn now to the third, and last, part of my presentation. After having pointed out what I call the "scientific" aspect of the dream, and the psychological—not to say the psychosomatic—aspect, let me present now an aspect that relates to such important topics as the theological, social, and literary meanings of the dream in Mesopotamia. The relationship between these three topics might at first seem farfetched, but they are quite intimately linked in the texts from Mesopotamia.

Within the entire ancient Near East only one type of dream was considered theologically acceptable, and this is the dream that I term "message" dream. Of the several characteristics of this type, I here point out only the most salient: the dream is always reported in a strictly conventionalized frame, to be discussed presently; the dreamer is nearly always a man, typically a king, hero, or priest. Accounts of this dream type are found in literary texts, from the Sumerian and Egyptian royal stelae to the Gospel of Matthew, from the *Iliad* to Ptolemaic Egypt, and throughout the literary products of the Western civilizations as far as the classical tradition exercised its sway.

The pattern requires furthermore that the dream happen in a

moment of crisis, even if the dreaming person is not aware of this circumstance, that a deity appear and call the sleeper in order to get his attention, that the message conveyed be termed in clearly understandable words, and that the sleeper awake suddenly after the disappearance of the god or his angelic substitute. I have discussed this frame in extenso in my book, *The Interpretation of Dreams,* and there I analyzed all the meaningful deviations and a number of specific circumstances that are often added by the poet in order to enhance the solemnity of the occasion, the importance of the message conveyed or of the deity appearing in the dream. It should suffice to state that in my opinion the "message" dream as a "theological" event and as a literary *topos* goes back to an age-old dream pattern, that of the incubation dream. Actual incubation dreams are quite rare in the texts of the ancient Near East, but the "message" dream is most easily explained as a literary creation based on transformed actual dream experiences of persons passing the night, after due ritual preparation, in the cella of the god's sanctuary in order to receive his command and advice. Only divine messages obtained under such circumstances are considered theologically—or politically, whatever the context demands—valid and genuine. How far, of course, a literary pattern of such consistency was able to influence decisively actual dream experiences cannot be said. It is well known, however, how culture-conditioned and standardized actual dream experiences can become in certain typical situations.

It is again self-evident that such a message dream does not require interpretation.

This, however, is not the case with dreams of another type which appear quite often in the same literary frame as the "message" dreams and under circumstances that are often quite similar to those just described. The essential difference is that the message these dreams contain is not couched in immediately intelligible terms. Instead, it consists of a sequence of more or less rational activities, gestures, or events that the person sees in his dream. The relation between the rational acts is quite often rather irrational; the protagonists can be anything from gods and stars to normally inanimate objects. Everything, however, that happens in such a dream is endowed with an urgent meaningfulness, an immediate appeal that impresses the dreaming person and instills in him the vivid desire to learn what the dream has been expressing for him. The understanding is, in nearly all instances, that an important message was transmitted but willfully distorted by the substitution of actors, acts, and objects for a set of corresponding elements taken, as a rule, from the world of the dreamer's experiences and expectations.

Some such "symbolic" dreams, as I have dubbed dreams of this type, are self-explanatory, such as the two dreams of Joseph which foretell his supremacy over his brothers: He and his brothers immediately understood that the sheaves and the stars making their obeisances before a solitary sheaf or star "symbolized" his brothers and himself respectively. Other dreams of this type are less transparent. I remind you only of the seven lean and seven fat kine of another dream in the story of Joseph. Normally the services of a dream interpreter are required to decode, so to speak, the manifest dream content in order to reach the underlying message, proceeding, item by item, from the substituted to the original elements. This interpreter of dreams is not a diviner; there are no dream books available, or even conceivable, which could be of assistance in such a decoding operation. The interpretation of "symbolic" dreams is not the domain of the diviner-scientist, but rather that of the inspired interpreter-artist, the wise man whose genius or god enables him to see through the phantasmal disguise into the core of the message.

The raw materials for such dreams are clearly actual dream experiences that the literary conventions of the ancient Near East normally did not admit as a topic. Only when this material was transposed by the poet who reshaped these dreams are such dreams told.

It must have been quite difficult for a person who experienced an evil dream to establish whether the irrelevance, scurrility, and meaningless concatenations of such a dream were to be ignored as parts of an evil dream that only required a purification rite or were to be accepted as a divine message needing interpretation. The Old Testament solves this problem in one way and the Mesopotamian texts in another. In the Bible, "symbolic" dreams are reported solely by gentiles—the Pharaoh of the Exodus and Nebuchadnezzar—for whom the Lord very conveniently provides the services of an interpreter—Joseph and Daniel—who is his pious worshiper. In the cuneiform literature, Sumerian and Akkadian alike, "symbolic" dreams occur only in mythological texts and are interpreted there by gods and heroes.

There nearly always remains a certain uneasiness and more or less voiced feeling of distrust in the texts that contain such dreams and their interpretation. Incidentally, "symbolic" dreams without interpretation do not and cannot occur. A means of adding information and assuring the correct decoding of such dreams is the repetition of the dream. The same message is then coded in two parallel versions whose individual interpretations should corroborate each other. Another way is to have the interpreter communicate directly with the deity who sent the message, either to receive inspiration or to obtain the confirmation of a proposed interpretation by means of an omen, another dream, and so forth.

The need to tell a "symbolic" dream in order to obtain its interpretation is caused at least as much by the necessity of a purification as by the wish for information. As a matter of fact, in the Sumerian and

Akkadian texts the same term is used for the "telling" of an evil dream to a piece of clay, and for the interpretation of a "symbolic" dream. Clearly, the "symbolic" dream is basically an "evil" dream as long as it remains without interpretation. In the need for interpretation, or for a catharsis, we have in ancient Mesopotamia—and to a large extent have even today —the natural reaction to such dreams.

When one searches literary and lexical cuneiform texts for terms denoting the dream interpreter, one comes upon a number of rare Sumerian and Akkadian terms that cannot be analyzed and discussed in this presentation. Dream interpreters in the texts that reflect the daily life, according to the evidence of Old Assyrian and Old Babylonian letters (first half of the second millennium), were of low standing and often were women, who at the same time practiced some forms of necromancy, which reminds one of the Witch of Endor. This is confirmed by the fact that in literary texts from Mesopotamia and Asia Minor the interpretation of dreams is sometimes done by women.

Conversely, the royal correspondence found in the archives of the last Assyrian capital shows that at the Assyrian court, where diviners, soothsayers, physicians, and exorcists were abundantly represented and played an important role, the interpreter of dreams was conspicuously absent.

Generally speaking, it can be stated that professional interpreting of dreams seems to have been as rare in Mesopotamian as it was in classical texts and in the Bible. "Symbolic" dreams, and their ingenious and miraculous interpretation, show the most interesting flowering exclusively in literary texts.

21

The Dream in Medieval Islamic Society

TOUFY FAHD

Oneirocritic literature represents for Islam the most authentic cultural heritage of its Semitic past. In it, we can find a great many ideas, symbols, images as well as an undeniably primitive atmosphere, all reproducing the prototypes of ancient thought. Oneiromancy is still both the oldest and the youngest form of divination and one of the most authentic witnesses to certain of the abiding features of the human spirit—religious restlessness, the desire to know the divine plan, and the tendency to predict the future.

Enriched by a Greek element working within like ferment, Arab-Muslim oneirocriticism reached heights no other civilization seems to have known.[1] From the beginning of the Abbasid epoch several treatises were in circulation which were later incorporated or assimilated into compilations. In addition to these compilations there are innumerable dreams scattered in every literary genre. All together this oneiric material permits us to paint with remarkable precision and color a picture of

---

[1] Greco-Roman civilization seems to have had a vast amount of oneirocritical literature (cf. B. Büchsenschütz, *Traum und Traumdeutung im Alterthume* [Berlin, 1868]). Apart from Artemidorus of Ephesus, however, very little remains.

Abbasid society, a picture showing traits found in no other literary genre of the epoch. The dream serves as a screen on which a past history is projected, a history the chroniclers were unable to write; if they were able to write it, for one reason or another, they used the dream as a subterfuge for telling it.

The history of the dynastic rivalries between Abbasids and Umayyads is well known, but it is only in deftly forged dreams interpreting *ab intra* facts of the everyday chronicle that there appears the underlying psychological need of the former for prophetic investiture, for divine sanction, and for a mysterious voice affirming their vocation to rule and their superiority to the other pretenders to the caliphate.

So it was that, bearing him, the mother of the second Abbasid caliph al-Manṣūr (136/754–158/775) saw in a dream a lion come from her loins, crouch with a roar, and beat the ground with its tail. Other lions arose on all sides and pressed toward him, each coming to prostrate himself.[2] Before his ascension to the caliphate, the same al-Manṣūr saw himself at Mecca. The door of the Kaʿba was open. A man emerged and called, "'Abdallāh b. Muḥammad.' Manṣūr said, "I arose and my brother arose with me. The man then added, 'Ibn al-Ḥārithiyya.' My brother entered and stayed a minute before coming out. Then I saw him come out with a flag in his hand, but he had hardly come five steps when the flag fell from his hands.[3] The same man came out again and called, 'Abdallāh.' I arose and my uncle ʿAbdallāh b. ʿAlī rose with me; he climbed the steps, but I blocked him and entered ahead of him. I found myself before my father and the Prophet. The man told me to begin by saluting the Prophet who had a flag brought and gave it to me saying, 'This flag is for you and your children. . . .' Telling this story to a member of his family, al-Manṣūr said, 'You must record this dream on parchment with a pen of gold, and tell your children and grandchildren.'"[4]

This kind of dream, which consecrates the triumph of the successful pretender in a dispute over succession, occurs rather frequently in Islamic literature. Al-Mahdī (158/775–169/785), al-Manṣūr's successor, owed his accession to the caliphate to the efforts of his father's vizier, al-Faḍl b. ar-Rabīʿ, a fact foreseen in a dream of al-Manṣūr's: the Kaʿba broke open and a man closed it with the aid of a black cord, the man being none other than al-Faḍl b. ar-Rabīʿ.[5]

---

[2] Masʿūdī, *Murūj adh-dhahab,* ed. Barbier de Meynard and Pavet de Courteille (Paris, 1861–1877), VI, 157 f.
[3] An allusion to the brief reign of the first Abbasid caliph, as-Saffāḥ (132/750–136/754), the brother of al-Manṣūr.
[4] Baihaqī, *Kitāb al-maḥāsin wa'l-masāwī,* ed. F. Schwally (Giessen, 1902), p. 345.
[5] Abū 'l-Faraj al-Iṣfahānī, *Kitāb al-aghānī,* Vol. XXI, ed. R. E. Brünnow (Leiden, 1888), p. 123.

At the end of the Umayyad era, one of ʿAlī's descendants, Muḥammad b. ʿAbdallāh, had seen in a dream a descendant of the Banū Hāshim, Muḥammad b. ʿAlī b. ʿAbdallāh b. ʿAbbās, erasing the name of the Umayyad caliph al-Walīd b. ʿAbdalmalik which had been inscribed above the mihrab in the mosque of the Prophet in Medina. Finding himself in the mosque one day, al-Mahdī saw the inscription. He asked for a chair, sat down in the middle of the mosque, and said, "I shall not leave until this name has been erased and replaced by mine." He sent for workmen and ladders and in fact remained until he had seen his own name put in place of al-Walīd's.[6] Al-Mahdī is remembered for his oppression of the Manicheans; he told his son Mūsà, "I saw your forefather al-ʿAbbās in a dream presenting me with two swords and commanding me to kill the dualists."[7] The same al-Mahdī sees the reigns of his two sons in a dream. "I dreamt," he said, "that I offered a staff to Mūsà [the future al-Hādī: 169/785–170/786] and another to Hārūn [the future ar-Rashīd: 170/786–193/809]. Several leaves had sprouted at the tip of Mūsà's staff, whereas Hārūn's was completely covered with foliage." He sent for al-Ḥakam b. Mūsà aḍ-Ḍamrī, known as Abū Sufyān, and asked him for an interpretation of the dream. He answered, "Both will reign but the reign of Mūsà will be brief; as for Hārūn, he will live longer than any other caliph, his days will be the best, and his epoch the most flourishing."[8]

A fratricidal struggle to succeed Hārūn ar-Rashīd erupted between his sons al-Amīn (193/809–198/813) and al-Maʾmūn (198/813–218/833). We have been left a picture of the psychological and moral state of al-Amīn in a dream of Zubaida, his mother. She saw in a dream on the very night of his conception three women enter her apartment and seat themselves, two on her right and a third on her left. One of them came forward, placed her hand on Zubaida's womb, and spoke these words, "He will be a proud king, lavish in his largesse; his burden will be heavy and bad luck will hound him." The second, doing the same, said, "A king lacking in willpower, limited in his means, and little sincere in his friendship, he will reign as a despot and will be betrayed by fortune." The third did the same, and said, "A wasteful and squandering king, quarrelsome and unjust." The same women appeared again to Zubaida when she brought Muḥammad (al-Amīn) into the world. "They appeared to me," she said, "in my sleep just as I had seen them the first time. They sat down by the head of my bed and stared at me. Then one of them said,

---

[6] Ṭabarī, *Annales,* ed. M. J. de Goeje (Leiden, 1879–1901), III (1), 534–535; Baihaqī, *op. cit.,* p. 344.
[7] *Aṣḥāb al-ithnain;* Ṭabarī, *op. cit.,* p. 588.
[8] *Ibid.,* p. 577.

'Your son will be a tree of green, a sweet-smelling plant freshly cut, a flourishing garden.' The second continued, 'An abundant spring, but short of duration, quickly drained and soon gone.' The third continued, 'His own enemy, weak in power, quickly deceived, he will be dethroned.' One night after Muḥammad had been weaned," Zubaida continued, "I was lying on my bed; the cradle in which my child slept was nearby. The three again appeared to me walking toward the cradle. The first spoke these words, 'A despotic king, prodigal, foolish in his language, who has lost his way and runs toward his ruin.' The second added, 'Contradicted in all he says, defeated on the field of battle, frustrated in his desires, unhappy and crushed by cares.' The third finished, 'Dig his grave, prepare his place, unwind his shroud, form his funeral procession. Death will be better for him than life.' I awoke," said Zubaida, "troubled and anxious about the fate of my son. In vain the interpreters of dreams and the astrologers whom I consulted assured me that we would live happily and for long years. My heart rejected their promises. But in the end I reproached myself for weakness and asked myself, 'Can the tenderness of a mother, her solicitude, her prudence, exorcise destiny, and can affection successfully turn back the decrees of fate?' " [9]

Trapped by his implacable fate, cornered by his brother al-Ma'mūn whose victory was assured, al-Amīn, against the advice of his friends, refused to surrender to his brother's general Ṭāhir b. al-Ḥusain, who was then besieging Baghdad. Why? Because he had seen himself in a dream standing on a very high, thick, and solid brick wall dressed in his black robes, belt, sword, cowl, and boots, while Ṭāhir was at the foot of the wall undermining its foundation. "The wall fell," he said, "and I with it, my cowl dropping. So Ṭāhir became for me a bad omen; I distrust him and it is repugnant to me to go to him." For this reason he preferred to surrender to Harthama, a family *mawlà* in whom he had much more confidence.[10]

For his part, al-Ma'mūn denied to the dream any veracity, and said, "The dream is nothing. If it were truthful we should have been able to ascertain it, and nothing about it would fall away. Since we have been able to see only a tiny part (of a dream) come true, we are convinced that it is vain, and that most of them do not come true." He had sent his son al-ʿAbbās into Byzantine territory and news of him was slow in coming. One morning, after prayer, he slept for a short time. When he awoke, he called for his mount. He got up, and said, "I will tell you a miracle; I have just seen in a dream an old man with a beard and white hair, dressed in a skin which he had wound around his neck. He carried

---

[9] Masʿūdī, *op. cit.*, pp. 417–419.
[10] Ṭabarī, *op. cit.*, III (2), 913.

a cane in one hand and a letter in the other." His brother and successor, al-Muʿtaṣim (218/833–227/842), answered: "I hope that God will fulfill this dream of the Prince of Believers and give him joy by (the news) that al-ʿAbbās is safe and well." Al-Maʾmūn set out and, behold, before he had gone far, he saw an old man coming toward him like the one he had seen in the dream. Al-Maʾmūn said, "By God, this is the man I saw in my dream, just as I described him." The man approached, but the guards pushed him away. Al-Maʾmūn sent for him and he came. "Who are you?" asked the caliph. "I am the messenger of al-ʿAbbās. Here is his letter," he answered. "We stood dumbfounded for a long time," concluded the storyteller, "and then I asked, 'O, Prince of Believers, will you henceforth say that dreams are lies?' " "No," he answered.[11]

Al-Muntaṣir (247/861–248/862), another Abbasid caliph whose dreams reflect the state of his soul and his remorse, saw one night in a dream his father al-Mutawakkil (236/847–247/861) whom he had assassinated. His father said to him, "Woe to you, Muḥammad, you killed me. You were unjust to me and you have deceived me (by depriving me) of the caliphate. By God, you will enjoy it only a few days. Then you will go to the Fire. . . ." On another night, al-Muntaṣir saw himself climbing a ladder. At the twentieth rung a voice said to him, "Behold your reign." When his friends came to congratulate him on such a happy dream, he said to them, "You have not been correctly informed. Actually, when I reached the last of the rungs, I was told, 'Stop, this is the end of your days.' " He lived barely a year after that, and died at the age of twenty-five.[12] With regard to the end, which everybody felt coming for such a murderer, ʿAbdalmalik b. Sulaimān b. abī Jaʿfar had the following dream: "I saw in my sleep al-Mutawakkil and al-Fatḥ b. Khāqān surrounded by fire. Then I saw Muḥammad al-Muntaṣir arrive. He asked

---

[11] Baihaqī, *op. cit.*, pp. 343 f. The same caliph saw Aristotle in a dream (al-Qifṭī, *Taʾrīkh al-ḥukamāʾ*, ed. J. Lippert [Leipzig, 1903], p. 29). Some people consider this to be one of the reasons for the favor al-Maʾmūn accorded the translation of Greek philosophical writings.

[12] Ṭabarī, *op. cit.*, III (3), 1497, 1498; cf. Masʿūdī, *op. cit.*, VII, 398 f., who gives a different version of these dreams foretelling the death of al-Muntaṣir. The essential features of this version are: The secretary Ibn al-Furāt slept a moment, then suddenly awakened and said, "I have had a strange dream. I saw the vizier Ibn al-Khaṭīb standing here and telling me, 'The caliph al-Muntaṣir will die in three days.' 'The caliph,' I said to him, 'is at the hippodrome jousting. Your dream is only the effect of your pituitary and bile.' " Fatigued and sweating, al-Muntaṣir took a bath and lay down under the fans. He died later of pneumonia. Reproached by the vizier, al-Muntaṣir answered, "Are you afraid that I shall die? Last night someone came to me in a dream and said, 'You will live for twenty-five years.' In this I saw good news about my future, and that I shall remain caliph for all that time."

if he could go to them, but was held back. Then, al-Mutawakkil came to me and said, ' 'Abdalmalik, tell Muḥammad, "You shall drink of the cup, from which you made us drink."' In the morning, I went to al-Muntaṣir. He had the fever. I cared for him and I heard him say, 'I have shortened a life; for this my own has been shortened.' "[13]

During the life of his father (al-Mustakfī, 530/1136–555/1160), al-Mustanjid (555/1160–565/1170) saw in a dream an angel descending from heaven and writing the letter *khāʾ* four times on the palm of his hand. Immediately on awakening, he sent for the interpreter of dreams and told him his dream. The interpreter said, "You will be Caliph in the year 555 ("fī sanat khams wa-khamsīn wa-khams miʾa")." And so it was.[14]

Ibn Khallikān's grandfather saw in a dream the death of Ibn Hubaira (in 555/1160), the vizier of the caliph al-Mustanjid. He relates: "The night the vizier died, I was sleeping on a terrace with friends. I had a dream in which I saw myself in the reception room of the vizier where he was sitting. A man came in holding a short lance in his hand. He struck the vizier between his testicles. Blood sprang forth like a jet of water and covered the wall. I looked and in front of me I found a gold ring. I picked it up, saying to myself, 'To whom shall I give it? I will wait and give it to a servant.' Then I awoke and told the story to my friends. I had just finished when a man arrived and said, 'The vizier is dead.' One of those present exclaimed: 'Impossible. I left him last evening in perfect health.' Someone else arrived and confirmed the truth of the report. His son said to me, 'You must wash him.' This I began to do. When I raised his arm to wash the armpits, the ring fell from his hand. When I saw the ring, I was amazed at my dream."[15]

These examples, taken from among so many, suffice to demonstrate how firm a grip oneiromancy held on Abbasid society. It was the same before this period, as well as after. The biography of the Prophet of Islam is interwoven with dreams announcing the great events of his life. He conceded to the dream considerable importance. Every morning as he left prayer, he inquired of his Companions whether they had had any dreams during the night. He did so, Ibn Khaldūn tells us, to draw from them portents about events likely to favor the manifestation of the faith and its strengthening.[16]

---

[13] *ʿajjaltu fa-ʿujjiltu*; Masʿūdī, *op. cit.*, VII, 301.
[14] Ibn Khallikān, *Wafayāt al-aʿyān* (Būlāq, 1275/1858), II, 214.
[15] *Ibid.*, p. 372.
[16] Ibn Khaldūn, *The Muqaddimah*, trans. F. Rosenthal (New York: Pantheon, 1958), III, 103–104; see Toufy Fahd, "Les Songes et leur interprétation selon l'Islam," in A.-M. Esnoul, P. Garelli, *et al.*, eds., *Les Songes et leur interprétation*, Sources orientales, Vol. II (Paris, 1959), pp. 127 ff., for a discussion of this period.

In this presentation we limit our interest to the Abbasid epoch during which a previously little-known literary genre developed in an unexpected manner. Dreams had most certainly been interpreted before; the names of some of the interpreters have remained famous, such as, in the Umayyad period, Saʿīd b. al-Musayyab who lived under the caliph ʿAbdalmalik (65/685–86/705), and of whose interpretations Ibn Saʿd preserved a certain number.[17] There was also Ibn Sīrīn (d. 110/728), who was to become the interpreter of dreams *par excellence* and the ultimate authority in oneirocritics. Nevertheless, there are no known collections of dreams and, still less, of oneirocritical treatises dating from this epoch. The oldest treatise of this genre seems to have been the *Dustūr fī 't-taʿbīr* by Abū Isḥāq al-Kirmānī who lived under the caliph al-Mahdī (158/775–169/785). His work was used by later dream interpreters, but it has not come down to us.[18]

Despite the lack of collections dating from this epoch, the dreams scattered through its chronicles allow one to realize the perfection reached by the method of the Arab oneirocritics and the richness of their symbolism. No stronger proof is needed than the few interpretations attributed to Ibn al-Musayyab.

One man told him, "I saw myself seated in a shadow and I rose into the sun." Ibn al-Musayyad said to him, "By God, if your dream is true, you will leave Islam." The man added, "It seemed to me that I was made to go out into the sun and that I was thrown back." The interpreter answered, "You will be compelled to apostatize." The man was taken prisoner under the caliph ʿAbdalmalik and forced to abandon Islam. Later he returned to Medina and enjoyed talking about his dream.[19]

Islam-shadow-freshness and sun-infidelity-fire are symbols suited to the desert. Another dream connects fire and the sea. A man of Fahm told Ibn al-Musayyab that in a dream he had seen himself enter fire. If your dream is true, he was told, you will not die before taking a sea voyage; then you will die a violent death. The man made a sea voyage during which he came to the brink of death; later he died by the sword at the battle of Qudaid.[20]

One dream tells where hens come from: al-Ḥusain b. ʿUbaidallāh wished to no avail for a child. He had a dream which he recounted to Ibn al-Musayyab: "I saw someone had put eggs in my lap." Ibn al-Musayyab answered, "Chickens come from Persia (ʿajamī); look for

---

[17] Ibn Saʿd, *Kitāb al-ṭabaqāt*, ed. E. Sachau (Leiden, 1905–1940), V, 91 ff.
[18] Fahd, *op. cit.*, pp. 131, 154 n. 24.
[19] Ibn Saʿd, *op. cit.*, p. 93.
[20] *Ibid.*, p. 92.

something from that quarter." He took then a (Persian) concubine and had children.[21]

The symbolism of dreams related to married life and descendants proceeds from the same principles one finds in Artemidorus of Ephesus and later Arab treatises. A man in a dream sees the caliph ʿAbdalmalik b. Marwān urinating in the direction of the mosque of the Prophet in Medina. And this four times. "If this dream is true," said Ibn al-Musayyab, "four caliphs of his line will succeed him."[22] Ibn al-Musayyab drew the same portent from another dream concerning ʿAbdalmalik: a man saw himself in a dream stretching this caliph out on the ground and driving four stakes into his back. The interpreter said to him, "This dream is not yours." "It is," asserted the man. "I will give you an interpretation only if you tell me whose dream it is," retorted Ibn al-Musayyab. "It is Ibn az-Zubair's," confessed the man, "and it is he who sends me to you." "If his dream is true," said Ibn al-Musayyab, "he will be killed by ʿAbdalmalik b. Marwān of whose line four caliphs will reign." The man who reported this interpretation to ʿAbdalmalik had debts; the caliph paid them.[23]

For someone to see himself urinating in his hands or into the slashed trunk of an olive tree is the sign of an illicit marriage.[24] The marriage of al-Ḥajjāj with the daughter of ʿAbdallāh b. Jaʿfar b. abī Ṭālib was foreseen by Ibn al-Musayyab from a dream of astonishing simplicity: the man saw a dove land on the minaret of the mosque.[25] In actual fact this marriage was politically very important: it produced a certain amount of peace in the sectarian quarrels then bitterly dividing Islam.

Last, we find in Ibn al-Musayyab the symbolic associations current in oneirocritics: teeth, members of the family; he-goat, informer; vine, firm faith; dates, livelihood.[26]

The impression created by reading this series of interpretations given by Ibn al-Musayyab is that this literary genre was already in existence and that the materials of the oral tradition were in the process of being codified on the model of *ḥadīth* and ancient poetry. Such codification could be justified only by an abundance of material; this would make less likely the existence of the 7,500 dream interpreters enumerated

---

[21] *Ibid.*
[22] *Ibid.*, p. 91.
[23] *Ibid.*
[24] *Ibid.*, p. 92.
[25] *Ibid.*
[26] *Ibid.*, pp. 91–92.

by al-Ḥasan b. Ḥusain al-Khallāl in his *Ṭabaqāt al-Muʿabbirīn,* a work written before 400/1009, which we no longer have.[27]

In any event, language, style, formulas, clichés seem already firmly established when the *taʿbīr* treatises begin to appear; we possess several fragments from about the middle of the third/ninth century.[28] Yet to come were the method of classifying dreams and the organization of oneirocritical materials.

At this point there appeared a work that was to give to the literary genre the framework it lacked and to instill into it new vigor. Ḥunain b. Isḥāq (d. 260/873) translated from the Greek the *Oneirocritica* by Artemidorus of Ephesus, heir to several generations of oneirocritics from whose writings he gathered what is best in his work.[29] Artemidorus' systematization of oneiric material was to serve as a model throughout the Middle Ages both in the East and in the West.[30]

The Arabic translation must have been the response to contemporary preoccupation with classification and codification. The Abbasid caliphs began to give importance to the role of the *muʿabbir*. For having interpreted for him in the reign of Hishām b. ʿAbdalmalik a dream announcing his accession to the caliphate, al-Manṣūr had already asked an interpreter whose home was in Mosul to settle at his court, assuring him and his family a living.[31]

The most important treatise on Arab-Muslim oneirocritics, *al-Qādirī fī 't-taʿbīr* by Abū Saʿīd Naṣr b. Yaʿqūb ad-Dīnawarī, is dedicated (as the title indicates) to the caliph al-Qādir billāh (381/991–422/1031). We have more than twenty-five copies of this book composed in 397/1006, the oldest in its genre to reach us intact. It is an immense compilation

---

[27] A work quoted by Dīnawarī, *al-Qādirī fī 't-taʿbīr,* fol. 44ᵛ-45ʳ; cf. Fahd, *op. cit.,* pp. 130, 153 n. 16.
[28] An example is the *Taʿbīr ar-ruʾyā* attributed to Ibn Qutaiba (213/828-276/889), large parts of which are quoted in the *Muntakhab al-kalām* traditionally but erroneously attributed to Ibn Sīrīn (Būlāq, 1294/1877), I, 11 ff.
[29] See n. 1, above.
[30] I discovered the *unicum* of Ḥunain b. Isḥāq's Arab translation in the library of the University of Istanbul during the summer of 1959. I have prepared a critical edition, which has appeared in the publications of the French Institute of Damascus (cf. Toufic Fahd, *Le Livre des songes* [Damascus, 1964]). Consult my introduction about the importance, characteristics, and author of this translation.
[31] He had dreamed that he had mounted a black donkey carrying a very heavy load of straw. The *muʿabbir* gave the following interpretation: the donkey is the man's good fortune (*jadd-Gad*); the black color (*sawād*) refers to his dignity (*suʾdad*); the straw with which it was loaded symbolizes the wheat and barley that it will bring; to sit on it means to possess it; to control food is to rule over men (cf. Baihaqī, *op. cit.,* pp. 345 f.).

bringing together the oneiric material as a whole, material reflecting all man's activities, his preoccupations, his social milieu, his religious concepts, his hopes and anxieties. The dream is like a screen on which is projected the daily life of every class in the society of tenth-century Baghdad. Obviously influenced by Artemidorus of Ephesus, the thematic classifications developed in this rich compilation came to dominate all later tradition, which introduced only minor variations.[32]

After ad-Dīnawarī, oneirocritical treatises followed one another with increasing rapidity. In the course of our manuscript researches, we ascertained the titles of more than a hundred treatises, some by celebrated oneirocritics, others by unknown authors. Many are anonymous, and a large number are only abridgments, adaptations, or versifications of older treatises prepared for personal use. But there is in each of these treatises something new stemming from the author's experience or from inquiries directed to his contemporaries.

A summation of most of these contributions was made in the *Taʿṭīr al-ānām fī taʿbīr al-manām* by ʿAbdalghanī an-Nābulusī (d. 1144/1731), lithographed in two volumes in Cairo around 1858, and edited and published at Būlāq and at Cairo more than once since.

Between ad-Dīnawarī and an-Nābulusī, several authors deserve our attention.

Among the authorities most frequently invoked in *al-Qādirī fī 't-taʿbīr,* we find the name of Ibn Sīrīn (d. 110/728). According to Ibn Khaldūn, "Muḥammad b. Sīrīn was the most famous of all oneirocritics; rules of his were taken down in writing, rules which were handed on until our own day." [33] This testimony is corroborated by the existence in nearly all Arab, Turkish, and Persian manuscript collections of treatises on *taʿbīr* bearing his name,[34] but there is as yet no study fixing the age of the writings attributed to him. One fact is certain: no evidence exists from before the end of the fourth/tenth century that Ibn Sīrīn left any oneirocritical writing.[35] On the other hand, sources from the third/ninth century attest to the existence of interpretations bearing his name.[36]

---

[32] The rest of these themes appear in Fahd, "Les Songes et leur interprétation selon l' Islam," p. 132.
[33] ". . . wa-kutibat ʿanhu fī dhālika qawānīn wa-tanāqala-hā 'n-nās li-hādhā 'l-ʿahd." *Prolegomena,* ed. É. Quatremère (Paris, 1885), III, 86 (trans. F. Rosenthal, III, 110).
[34] In Istanbul alone, I counted some thirty manuscripts bearing his name. Time did not allow me to determine in what measure these manuscripts resemble or differ from one another.
[35] The *Fihrist* by Ibn an-Nadīm, written in 377/987 (ed. G. Flügel [Leipzig, 1871–1872], p. 316) is the first to note the existence of a *Kitāb taʿbīr ar-ruʾyā* attributed to Ibn Sīrīn.
[36] In particular it is quoted by al-Jāḥiẓ (255/869) in *Kitāb al-ḥayawān* (Cairo, 1357/1938–1366/1947), I, 130 f., and VII, 57; and by Ibn Qutaiba (d. 276/889),

Hence, it is very likely that lists of dreams with interpretations imputed to him had been put together at first for private use. Later these were copied and amplified as the legend of Ibn Sīrīn developed to make him, according to the expression of ʿAbdallāh ʿAbd ad-Dāʾim, "a kind of abstract personage, the very incarnation, as it were, of Arab oneiromancy." [37] This study was based on a compilation entitled *Muntakhab al-kalām fī tafsīr al-aḥlām* which was attributed to Ibn Sīrīn by its first Egyptian editor in 1868, although according to a manuscript in Paris (Ar. 2749) it is a compendium of several famous authors made by al-Ḥusain b. Ḥasan b. Ibrāhīm al-Khalīlī ad-Dārī.[38]

Several other tracts bear the name of Ibn Sīrīn: notably *Kitāb al-Jawāmiʿ*;[39] *Taʿbīr ar-ruʾyā*, which seems to be an abridged *Muntakhab*;[40] *al-Ishāra fī ʿilm al-ʿibāra*;[41] *Tafsīr al-manām*;[42] *Kitāb al-luʾluʾ fī taʿbīr al-manām*;[43] *Kitāb at-tanwīr fī ruʾyā 't-taʿbīr*.[44] These are all late writings; the authenticating manuscripts generally do not go back beyond the eighth/fifteenth century. Ibn Sīrīn's lists of interpretative types, which may have been in existence before ad-Dīnawarī, must have been so absorbed into later writings that they cease to have an independent existence to the point of seeming incomplete and therefore useless.

The Arab translation of Artemidorus of Ephesus' *Oneirocritica* has similarly been discredited, although for different reasons. No longer

---

ʿUyūn al-akhbār (Cairo, 1925–1930), cf. Vol. IV, Index of Proper Names, s.v. Ibn Sīrīn; cf. also C. Brockelmann, *Geschichte der Arabischen Litteratur*, Supplement I (Leiden, 1937), p. 102.

[37] ʿAbdallāh ʿAbd ad-Dāʾim (A. Abdel Daïm), *L'Oneiromancie arabe d'après Ibn Sīrīn*; *thèse complémentaire* defended in Paris in 1956 and published by the University Press of Damascus in 1958; cf. p. 56.

[38] Brockelmann, *op. cit.*, Supplement II (1938), p. 1039.

[39] Used in the printing, Cairo, 1310/1892. Mss. Paris, Ar. 2742, 2743; Istanbul, Laleli 1657.

[40] Edited for the first time at Būlāq in 1281/1864; popular editions appeared several times thereafter (cf. Y. I. Sarkis, *Dictionnaire encyclopédique de bibliographie arabe* [Cairo, 1928–1930], fasc. I, 126). Cf. MS Paris, Ar. 2742, 2743; Istanbul, ʿĀtif Ef. 1924 (156 fols., 17 ll., 21 × 14 *naskhī*), Esat Ef. 1832 (72 fols., 18 ll., 24.5 × 16.7 *naskhī ʿarabī*, of 749 A.H.), Umumi 393, Fatih 3650, Bagdatli Vehbi Ef. 936; Cairo, 4897; Berlin, 4281, 4282; Strasbourg, 4212, fols. 265–287.

[41] Vatican MS Barberini 66 adds *Riwāyat Ibn Sīrīn li-Muḥammad b. Aḥmad as-Sālimī* (ninth/fourteenth century), the name under which the work is most often known (cf. M. Steinschneider, *Zeitschrift der Deutschen Morgenländischen Gesellschaft*, 17 [1863], 234 ff.; MS Paris, Ar. 2744; Istanbul, Velieddin 2296).

[42] Istanbul, Üniv. Kütüphane A 2889, A 6243; cf. Vatican MS 569; Berlin, 4271; Algiers, 1542–1543.

[43] Istanbul, Saray Ah. III 3170 (303 fols., 23/17 ll., 27 × 18.5 *naskhī*).

[44] Istanbul, Üniv. Kütüphane A 6233 (185 fols., 19 ll., 22 × 15 *naskhī*, of 1147 A.H.). I am passing over the Turkish and Persian translations of this work of which there are many under the title of *Taʿbīr Nāmeh*.

adapted to daily usage, being as different in inspiration as the social milieu from which it sprang, it sank into oblivion after being emptied of all the elements that are common to all men wherever and whenever they may live.

After Pseudo-Ibn Sīrīn, several other Arab oneirocritics became famous through their writings. Abū Saʿīd al-Ḥarkūshī al-Wāʿiẓ (d. 407/1016), contemporary of Dīnawarī, wrote a book called *al-Bishāra wa'n-nidhāra fī taʿbīr ar-ru'yā*, many copies of which we still possess.[45] It is not until the seventh/thirteenth century that we see another name arise to eclipse in some way those of his predecessors: Abū Ṭāhir Yaḥyà b. Ghannām al Maqdisī (d. 674/1275 or 698/1294) was the author of *Taʿbīr ar-ru'yā*, which exists in both prose and verse and was very widely known.[46] He was followed by Abū ʿAbdallāh b. ʿUmar as-Sālimī (at the end of the eighth/fourteenth century) who claimed to have gathered together the heritage of Ibn Sīrīn in a treatise entitled *al-Ishāra ilà ʿilm al-ʿibāra*,[47] and by Khalīl b. Shāhīn aẓ-Ẓāhirī (813/1410–873/1468), the author of *al-Ishārāt fī ʿilm al-ʿibārāt*.[48]

This seemingly very rich literature will appear in rather more modest dimension, I think, when all known manuscripts have been collated, all the manuscripts that now carry different titles identified, the authors sorted out, and that part noted which is original with each. On this last point, it would seem that one should expect no big surprises. By its very nature, literary property is foreign to material such as this. A collection of dreams presupposes an accumulation of experiences which allows conclusions drawn from the frequency of occurrences and the diversity of people and situations. Nevertheless, evolution of the level of family and social life brings with it enrichment in the imagery as well as the symbolism of the dream. We may thus believe that, conversely, oneiric imagery and symbolism reflect the dreamer's times, his cultural level, and the currents of thought agitating his period, while at the same time continuing to reflect all that is durable in the ideas, images, and relationships mankind carries with it through the ages. Thus, by transmitting and progressively enriching the heritage of centuries, these documents that embody the permanencies of the past and the reflections of actuality are immensely valuable for studying the history of progress and the evolution of ideas.

---

[45] Fahd, "Les Songes et leur interprétation selon l'Islam," p. 154 n. 27.
[46] *Ibid.*, n. 28.
[47] *Ibid.*, n. 29.
[48] *Ibid.*, p. 155 n. 30. In addition to these famous names, there is between Dīnawarī and ʿAbdalghanī an-Nābulusī a large group whose names are obscure, whose dates cannot be determined, and whose writings rarely appear. A list of them appears in T. Fahd, *La Divination arabe* (Leiden: E. J. Brill, 1966), pp. 330–363.

One example, taken from many, will provide convincing proof. Chapter xii of *al-Qādirī fī 't-ta'bīr* by Dīnawarī,[49] devoted to the crafts, makes it possible for us to paint a picture, both lively and rich, of the position of the arts and crafts in fourth/tenth-century Baghdad. A detailed presentation of the content of this chapter is now available.[50] Here we bring out only the almost universal symbolism that emerges from it: to construct or to sew is to unite; a bird with colored feathers is a pretty woman; household utensils are a wife; the mother is the earth; the midwife is defamation; money is words; to cook is to slander and seduce; the tree is a man; fire is a despotic king; milk is knowledge; plaster (gypsum) is lies; the soul is a jewel; the pearl fisher is a king; thread is the road and the course of life; leather is a woman; iron is power; grain is riches, glory, and dominion; the laborer is a great benefactor; wood is calumny and lies; the serpent is perfidy; bread is happiness and good living; the skin of animals represents inheritance; writing is trickery; the thief is sickness; hair is worry; to buy and sell is to be in need; to dig is to trick or to search for secret knowledge; to demolish is to improve; the butcher is the incarnation of injustice and death; dirt is sin; the shepherd is a leader; the river is a king; a seat is a wife; a bellows is harmony; the lion is a powerful, conquering king; the bird of prey is a cunning, deceitful king; the physician is a benefactor; and many more.

From collections of Arab dreams we could thus reconstruct the full imagery of human thought, particularly that of the Semitic world.

We should not fail to find in those collections confirmations of the tenets developed by both Freud and Jung; and we should rediscover the prominent factors of all human civilizations in their primeval nudity, stripped as they are of the dust of the ages and the varnish of progress.

---

[49] MS Istanbul, Esat Ef. 1833, dated from 599/1202, fols. 117^v–124^v; cf. Köprülü, 1363, written in the seventh century.
[50] Toufy Fahd, "Les Corps de métiers au IV/Xe siècle à Bagdad d'après le chapitre xii d'*al Qādirī-fī-t-Ta'bīr* de Dinawari," *Journal of the Economic and Social History of the Orient*, VIII/2 (1965), 186–212.

22

The Dream in Popular Culture: Arabic and Islamic

JEAN LECERF

It would be futile to claim that anything truly new could be added to the very complete picture of dreams in medieval Islam provided by Toufy Fahd in "Les Songes et leur interprétation selon l'Islam."[1] Consultation of sources in folklore seems to do little beyond confirming, in more or less original forms, the important role dreams played in general popular representation and in Islamic civilization in particular.

This role appears considerable even in the oldest echoes we have of pre-Islamic Arab antiquity, traditional forms that can be traced *grosso modo* as far back as to the fifth, or perhaps even to the fourth, century of our era. Our redaction of these forms is of much more recent date, and bears the marks of much redoing. It is possible that many elements of the traditions can claim even greater antiquity. But aside from this general affirmation of the role of dreams, one may wonder if much is to be learned about this period from popular sources as naïvely tendentious as these are. The general tendency that characterizes this cycle of legends is to serve as a

---

[1] Toufy Fahd, "Les Songes et leur interprétation selon l'Islam," in A.-M. Esnoul, P. Garelli, *et al.*, eds., *Les Songes et leur interprétation,* Sources orientales, Vol. II (Paris, 1959), pp. 125–158.

kind of letter of nobility or ancestral record for the Arabs who, after Islam and the Conquest, found themselves in much the same situation, *mutatis mutandis,* as the Hebrews did more than a thousand years earlier when they depicted for themselves, in a rather romanticized fashion, the golden age of the patriarchs and their own origins as nomad people coming into contact with the great civilizations of Egypt and Mesopotamia. This similarity of attitudes is reemphasized by the Islamic conception of the common origin of the Semitic peoples, a conception, incidentally, not at all at variance with philological data.

According to the Koran, the Arabs and the Israelites represent the senior and junior branches of the descendants of Abraham whose religion the Prophet was sent to revitalize. The Koran itself mentions the prophets who were sent to the Arabs; and punishments were not spared those who disbelieved their message.

Among these accounts, one about a break in the dike of Maʾrib has aroused the imagination of historians and traditionalists. According to the most widespread version, it took place in the reign of King ʿAmr b. ʿĀmir and was announced in a dream to his wife Ṭuraifa, one of the most famous prophetesses of her time. The transparent symbolism of such a dream of divination does not require great clairvoyance. In the dream Ṭuraifa saw the country covered by a great advancing cloud, and there was a crash of thunder, hail, and flashes and bolts of lightning. These manifestations were taken to symbolize a flood. She was sure that a catastrophe was foreshadowed and said so in an oracle of rhymed prose. The simplicity of the case would be surprising, except that it involves a royal dream. Toufy Fahd has said that royal dreams have the privilege of direct interpretation, which dreams of simple mortals lack. Special rules applied to a dream of a member of the royal family, and the dream announced directly future misfortune.

Toufy Fahd's statement is important because it is precisely this dream and this myth (the myth that in this special case relates, paradoxically though truly, to three occurrences) which afford proof that the Arabs had kings. Perhaps they were only petty kings, but the word occurs in all the texts and all the traditions. It reveals that there were important dynasties in South Arabia, which has been confirmed by archaeology. Inscriptions found in South Arabia have proven the existence of a brilliant civilization during this period. That this was a king's dream is not surprising, then, because there were kings. It concerns the famous kingdom of Saba (Sheba) which the Bible has already made renowned and whose existence has been confirmed by South Arabian epigraphy. The episode of the dike is chronologically placed in a period incontestably more recent, as the most ambitious estimates do not place it further back than four centuries before Islam, and the event itself, according to students of South Arabia, is even more recent.[2] Even so, this Arab kingdom and the whole legend are visibly intended to emphasize the past glory of the South Arabian dynasties whose annals can rival those of neighboring countries.

Another aspect of the legend is the mixing of the premonitions communicated in the dream with those of reality, or of those that appeared in the reality of the waking state rather than in the dream. This reality for us is not very clearly distinguished from the reality of the dream by the very singular logic of the events supposed to have occurred therein. When the diviner tells her husband, the king, about her dream, she gives him a series of signs for recognizing the imminence of the event. These signs include a turtle that leaves the water and turns itself over on its back. Unable to right itself, it rowed in the air, as the text says, with its flippers. And there were moles standing on their hind legs. All this clearly is not impossible. Nor is the rat—she told her husband that he was to go to the dike and look for a rat digging at the foundation stones with its teeth and moving them with its hind legs. The king went and, in fact, found a rat moving with its hind legs—according to the legend—blocks that could not have been moved by fifty men. (Here we have the mixture of supposed reality with something that has a tinge of the logic of the dream.)

A similar compound of divinatory dreams and wondrous premonitions of catastrophe can be found in the famous story gathered by several sources, and reported by Ṭabarī, in particular, about the *omina* that announced the birth of the Prophet of Islam. A dream of the Grand Mobed (the Mobed of Mobeds, the high priest of the Iranian ecclesiastical hierarchy) disturbed the king of Persia. The dream itself is not very puzzling; he saw wild horses led by camels crossing the river and invading the country, Persian Iraq. This still is not very puzzling. The dream quite naturally upset the king of Persia, and just as he convened his council in order to discuss its importance—it was important especially because it was the dream of the Grand Mobed—it was learned that an earthquake during the night had toppled a wing of the palace and extinguished the sacred fire. Real omens are again mixed into the dream. The dream is extremely simple, but it involves omens. The omens are not difficult to interpret either, but we shall see nevertheless that the king of Persia, Kisrà Anūshirwān, thought it necessary to consult experts. The legend tells us that for some unaccountable reason he called in Arab experts. He wrote to Nuʿmān, the Arab king of a part of Persian Iraq, asking for someone capable of interpreting the dream to be sent. King

---

[2] Actually the legend condenses three breaks of the dam occurring in 450, 542, and *ca.* 570 respectively, with the last proving irreparable.

Nu'mān sent the expert and we can find here a very curious theme which is to be found in the Old Testament. André Caquot has shown in a study of Old Testament dreams[3] that the two great Hebrew specialists in the interpretation of dreams were the patriarch Joseph and the prophet Daniel. In Joseph, an innovation makes its appearance. Joseph interprets dreams, but not as the Egyptians do. His manner is not science but prophecy—direct communication with God. Joseph's technique involves showing that the religion of the Hebrews is in no way inferior to the religion of the Egyptians and that it too can obtain interpretations of dreams.

There is something analogous in the case of the prophet Daniel. He withdrew to his room and begged Jehovah to send him the interpretation. It is the same thing as before, but, as Caquot says, there is a refinement in the story of Daniel. The King of Kings, the king of Persia, who had had some disquieting dreams and wanted them interpreted, gathered his magi, his Chaldeans, as the text says. The scene in the book of Daniel is vivid, and I would say sarcastic, almost a burlesque, when the King of Kings says to the magi: "Would you like to tell me my dream and then interpret it for me?" The magi answered that such a thing had never been heard of. There is a passage that says: "No honest magian, no honest Chaldean, has ever had to deal with such unreasonable demands." Here we have the corporation, the board of the magi, saying, "It's inconceivable," and only Daniel, with the confidence of the chosen people, recklessly and intrepidly accepting the bargain. Not knowing the answer he is to give the next day, he has to withdraw in order to ask God to interpret the dream. The tendency, as you can see, is to show to just what point the Hebrew religion is superior.

This theme about a dream whose text must be given before an interpretation is made recurs in the Arab sources I have mentioned. But in them it has become a simple stylistic clause. It just occurs; the story cannot be told in any other way. When the king, this time Kisrà, received Nu'mān's envoy, he said, "Now tell me my dream." The envoy answered, "I cannot, but we have among us people who can. We have illustrious diviners"—notably the famous Saṭīḥ who is one of the two legendary diviners of the Arabs. Nu'mān's envoy was then sent to the famous Saṭīḥ who was found on his deathbed. The envoy spoke to him but received no answer. Saṭīḥ did not understand until the envoy began to speak in verse. Verse was the only admissible language among the Arabs of the time. When the envoy spoke in verse, Saṭīḥ answered. He answered in an oracle much less clear than the dream itself, but easily comprehensible to us because we know what followed. He said, "The recitation will

---

[3] André Caquot, "Les Songes et leur interprétation selon Canaan et Israël," in Esnoul, Garelli, et al., op. cit., pp. 99–124.

become abundant"; the reference is to Koranic recitation. We who know, understand, but it would hardly have been very clear to the Persian king. So Saṭīḥ answered and died.

The interpreter of dreams in pre-Islamic Arabia seems to have been the *kāhin* (pl. *kahana* or *kuhhān*). This is etymologically the same word as the Hebrew *kohen,* but for diverse reasons his function is perhaps not exactly the same. Several *kahana* were, it seems, interpreters of various kinds of omens, not only of dreams; in any event, they were diviners. They spoke either in verse or in rhymed prose. For example, in the story I have been discussing, when a diviner was asked, "But is what you have said true [*haqq*]?" he answered, "Khawaq" or "Falaq." You can see the type of words, doggerel.

This presents a problem: in the Koran there are verses of exorcism which are composed in just this style. For example, the last two Suras are in exactly the same style as employed by the diviners, a fact that misled the Quraish into considering the Prophet a *kāhin*. This had the effect of "giving him a toothache," and he vehemently denied being a *kāhin*. We see the importance of this when later he forbids the *kāhin* profession lest he be connected with this race of *kahana,* this impious race of pre-Islamic Arabia. So, as the *Sīra* (biography of the Prophet by Ibn Isḥāq [d. 768]) says, the door was closed to *kahana,* and, therefore, there are no more *kuhhān*. Let us look a little more closely at these *kāhin* or *kohen,* especially at the two *kahana* Saṭīḥ and Shiqq.

"Saṭīḥ" means one who is flat as a pancake laid out on the ground. The legends tell us that Saṭīḥ was boneless except for his head. His head, moreover, was attached to the center of his chest. Whenever he was lying on his bed of dry leaves and had to move, he had to be rolled like a rug—Persian, naturally—all of which is singular enough.

"Shiqq" means half a person: one broken in two. In what way was he broken in two? The explanations are not very clear. Does it refer to height, breadth, or length? I think there is something completely different to be made of this. "Shiqq" could mean hemiplegic, a man who exists only in half the body, a man paralyzed on one side. This leads us to think that there existed in the popular imagination a connection between physical infirmities or disabilities of whatever kind and the possession of superior powers to establish contact with demons, the souls of ancestors, or hidden realities. Later there were no more *kuhhān,* but the interpretation and interpreters of dreams have continued.

In popular circles, even today, there is a continuation of scientific oneiromancy by men who write treatises, such as Ibn Sīrīn, but there are also men who practice dream interpretation. Very often these individuals are heads of brotherhoods, spiritual leaders, intermediaries between the people and higher powers. There are two sources of recruitment, if the term be allowed, for these heads of brotherhoods, these men of God. Some are simply sons of their predecessors, the recipients of a more or less hereditary charge transmitted from father to son. But we notice that the father is himself already regarded as inferior or crazy, marked by some not very clearly defined divine curse or blessing.

Perhaps there is here a bond between modern Arabia and the primitive society of pre-Islamic Arabia. The "officers" of that society were first of all political, the tribe had a sheikh; and then there were the intellectual "officers": the poet who was at the same time a kind of magician, and the diviner who was a kind of shaman. One wonders if they were not the same thing at the same time, for if the poets were not the diviners, the diviners were poets, as they spoke naturally in verse. So, perhaps, a bond did exist, or at least was presumed to exist, between an inability to fulfill a normal function in society and an aptitude for supranormal functions. Finally, let me remind you that all this goes on in civilized societies where the desire not to do manual labor leads to intellectual work.

I have another legend; a legend about a Lakhmid princeling, Rabī'a b. Naṣr, who presented the same problem to the two legendary diviners Saṭīḥ and Shiqq. He consulted them both in order to be sure, wanting to hold all the trumps for his game. Naturally he said, "Tell me my dream. If you cannot, how can I be sure of your interpretation?" (This practice of putting diviners to the test was in vogue, not to the extent previously described, but whenever diviners were consulted as arbitrators in a conflict, they were tested by hiding something from them which they were to guess: "We have concealed something in order to see if you can tell us about it." If they knew, what they had to say thereafter was believed.) The princeling, then, sought out the two divines and told them of his dream. Again, it was a king's dream which was not difficult to understand, although it contained some obscure points. He said, "I saw a burning ember, a live coal emerging from the darkness, and burning as it fell everything that had a soul, everything alive." Another version says, "everything with a skull." In either case all this certainly meant something was about to happen. The king did not understand the coals, the obscurity, or the darkness. We who know the outcome understand well enough, and the diviner understood immediately. The consulted diviner said, "You saw a live coal," and he goes on to relate the dream, "and this means that your country is about to be invaded by the Abyssinians who come from a little-known country in the Sudan, a country of Negroes. Clearly these invaders are a people with darker skins." The king said, "What you tell me is very disturbing. How will it end?" The diviner replied, "It will end because the Persians will help. A certain Saif dhū Yazan will ask the king of Persia for help and will chase the Abyssinians from the country." "And afterward?" "Afterward, a prophet will come and establish his reign." "And afterward?" "Kingship will remain with his people until the end of time." "But will there be an end of time?" The diviner said, "Yes, there will be a Last Judgment to reward the just and punish the guilty."

There is here, you see, a nice catechism lesson to lend a little meaning to the legend. It is intended to show that a royal history existed, a history with worldwide importance, involving the international politics of the Arabian peninsula, and, most of all, that Islam is the consummation of the history of the Arabian peninsula. There is something a little strange and surprising about this, since we are inclined to think of Islam as a great world event, yet this legend treats it as an Arab event. In short, our attitude toward people like Saif dhū Yazan has a very special perspective, which brings us back to what I said at the outset.

This cycle of legends is something of an exaltation of the Arab past, but blended in are traces of reality. We know from the study by Toufy Fahd that Islam preserved the interpretation of dreams despite the revolution it brought about in the ideology and in the moral ideal with which it replaced Bedouin ideals. I said in the beginning that Islam abolished the office of diviner. There is a break with tradition on this point, but Islam continued the interpretation of dreams. There is a question whether from this point of view the Prophet made the break during his lifetime, since as long as he lived he exercised the function if not the profession of interpreting dreams. He "had it both ways"; as chief of state he dispensed justice, but he did not refuse to interpret dreams occasionally and he did so with undeniable competence. What he did, in effect, was to integrate in Islam dreams and their interpretation without integrating the *kāhin* profession.

Sources of information about popular beliefs provide us with abundant documentation on the subject of different kinds of dreams. For reasons of space, I must confine myself to a somewhat arbitrary selection. It would be preferable not to draw our material from that inexhaustible source of information, *The Thousand and One Nights,* so I cite only one example from a study by Victor Chauvin,[4] the great specialist on this work, dealing with "The Dream of Treasure on the Bridge." Victor Chauvin has shown that this story, extant in many countries, has an Eastern origin, and belongs probably to the most ancient core of *The Thousand and One Nights.*

The theme is as follows: A spendthrift of Baghdad, his fortune wasted, dreams that he will recover it in Cairo and goes there. He falls

---

[4] Victor Chauvin, "Le rêve du trésor sur le pont," *Revue des traditions populaires,* XIII (Paris, 1898), 193–196.

asleep in a mosque from which a band of thieves leave to rob a nearby house. He alone is captured by the police, beaten, and jailed. Arraigned, he tells his story to the chief of police who says to him: "How silly you are; for years I have dreamed that my fortune is in Baghdad in a certain man's house." He names the man, describes the tree under which the treasure was buried, adding, "But I am not foolish enough to go there." Freed, the story's hero returns home and, thanks to the instructions he had received in Cairo, finds the treasure.

Chauvin's argument is concerned primarily with attributing the story to the tenth century, where he finds it in the *Kitāb al-faraj ba'd ash-shidda* of Tanūkhī, and secondarily with tracing the source of a Western version discussed by Gaston Paris:[5] "In Balduch, a village near Paris, two brothers lived near a stream," and it continues analogous to the Arab story. Balduch, said Grimm,[6] is doubtless Bailly near Marly-le-Roi. Chauvin has little difficulty in demonstrating that Balduch is an erroneous reading of Baldach, or Baghdad, and that the story's author had before him a version of the Arab text, perhaps a Spanish translation of *The Thousand and One Nights*.

The tale shows that in *The Thousand and One Nights* the dream, among other things, plays a part in the discovery of treasure, a role also attributed to it by the common classes of the Middle Ages. Such a dream was altogether fitting in a society that had no great industry or expanding economy, where the only way to riches semed to be in the discovery of treasure, especially when one had lost a fortune. In such a world without financial prospects the only truly prosperous industry was war, especially holy war. The tales of chivalry painted a picture conforming to the ideas of the time.

In her study of *La Geste de Melik Dānişmend*, Irène Mélikoff notes that the dream held a large part "in the wonder common to all the epics. It is through dreams that the prophet appears to mankind either to effect the conversion of chosen souls by means of prophetic visions, or to communicate his orders to the faithful. Sometimes the epic heroes are also visited by 'Alī, his sons, or by Salmān-i Fārisī. . . ."[7]

We are dealing actually with a Shi'ite epic about which we shall say more later. But it produces a kind of dream which, though rather surprising for us, is quite common in these accounts; it has to do with the appearance of the Prophet in dreams of Christians. From the very beginning of

---

[5] Gaston Paris, *Histoire poétique de Charlemagne* (Paris: Librairie Emile Bouillon, 1905), p. 485.
[6] Jakob Grimm, *Kleinere Schriften,* Vol. III, Abhandlungen zur Litteratur und Grammatik (Berlin: Dümmler, 1866), pp. 414-428, at p. 417.
[7] Irène Mélikoff, *La Geste de Melik Dānişmend* (Paris, 1960), chap. vi ("Epic and Folkloric Themes"), I, 161-170, at p. 163.

Melik Dānishmend's adventures, in the very first episode,[8] dreams are there to aid his education. Every evening, "When night came, Sultan Ṭūrasān remained at Chahār Bāgh, but Melik Aḥmed returned to the city to read, write, and study the sciences until morning." (He led a very full life.) We might say he passed his days in training sessions for tournaments in the hippodrome. He was young and learning to use arms. At night he went home to study, to read, and to write. "When some point in his study of the sciences remained unclear, the Lord Prophet, may God exalt and bless him, appeared in a dream with the correct explanation." Such utilization of the subconscious brings to mind certain pages of Henri Poincaré on his mathematical discoveries, which have only recently been put to use in teaching modern languages, without, however, the benefit of prophetic intervention. On the following page, the dead grandfather Baṭṭāl Ghāzī enters the scene in a dream: "Why are you not pursuing the Holy War? The hour of Islam has come." And the warriors set out to enter the service of the caliph.

In planning the campaign[9] Dānishmend lists the cities about to be conquered. Asked by his companions how he knew them, Melik Dānishmend answered: "Last night, in my dream I saw ʿAbdalwahhāb and his companions coming toward me. They took me by the hand, showed me the cities I have mentioned and said you must conquer these countries."

There are other dreams on succeeding pages, dreams serving continually in the narration of the adventures. In the second episode, Dānishmend converts an adversary named Artuhi with whom he stops at a monastery where he is welcomed by its superior, the ascetic Harkil. As they arrive the monks flee, but the imperturbable Harkil receives them kindly according to traditional hospitality. He bids them welcome and asks, "How are you, Lord Dānishmend and Lord Artuhi?" They asked, "How do you know us?" The monk said, "O Melik Dānishmend, first describe Muḥammad for me so I may see if what you say corresponds with what I have seen in my dream." The Prophet had indeed appeared to him, evidently effecting thereby some degree of welcome for the Muslim conquerors. The historical points of reference are the alliances that quite often during this Holy War against the Arabs bound together Muslims and Christians—sometimes with Armenians, sometimes with Georgians. A rather unexpected type of dream.

Farther along in the story a young girl loved by Artuhi, Efromiya, whose marriage was systematically opposed by her father, joins her fiancé in the middle of a battle. She had been alerted by a dream, in which once again the Prophet had appeared.

[8] *Ibid.*, p. 191.
[9] *Ibid.*, p. 200.

In a second study on the legend of Abū Muslim,[10] Irène Mélikoff uncovered for us an example of another familiar dream, the dream of initiation, but much shorter and not altogether the same as the dreams of the shaman. It is in keeping with the atmosphere peculiar to the epic of Abū Muslim which developed in Shiʿite society. As Mircea Eliade has demonstrated, early society was often rich in professional groups, themselves tied to social movements. The esoteric propaganda of the Bāṭinī appealed to a society of artisans and journeymen, binding together, in particular, the members of those trades considered impure or inferior and suffering, therefore, from the social oppression of elite classes. Caught up in the currents of the extreme Shiʿa and in the movement of Sufism these professional societies assumed social-mystical characteristics. On this subject, Irène Mélikoff has recourse to a study by Louis Massignon.[11] Mrs. Mèlikoff observes:

> Through these esoteric movements the cult of Abū Muslim penetrated the corporations. Epic literature, being an important factor of propagation . . . among the illiterate classes . . . the novel of Abū Muslim entered into the framework of guild literature. This story, with its basis in history, takes place in the circles of the Akhi of Merv and of the towns of Khurasan. Close to the Akhi are the ʿAyyār, bands of mercenaries turned soldiers of fortune, organized in corporations according to the principle of *futuwwet*. . . . The conspiracy of Abū Muslim was prepared in the *tekke* of the Akhi of Merv, after he had been initiated by the Prophet himself as befitted such a superior being. In an other-worldly meeting, in this case a dream, the Prophet, accompanied by the Archangel Gabriel from whom he himself had received the *futuwwet* regalia, invested Abū Muslim with the insignia: crown, robe, and belt. Through the agency of the society's three most important patrons, Gabriel, Muḥammad, and ʿAlī, Abū Muslim received the ax which became his distinctive emblem. Finally he received the accolade and sword from the fourth patron of the Akhi, Salmān-i Fārisī. His closest companions were the forty Akhi of Merv with their chief Akhi, Khurdek the Blacksmith.[12]

Having given this much space to Mrs. Mélikoff's text, we abridge the text of the epic itself, which she later translates: Abū Muslim prayed

---

[10] Irène Mélikoff, *Abū Muslim, le porte-hache du Khorrassan*. (Paris: Adrien-Maisonneuve, 1962).
[11] Louis Massignon, "La 'Futuwwa' ou 'pacte d'honneur artisanal' entre travailleurs musulmans au Moyen Age," *La Nouvelle Clio* (Brussels) IV (1952), 171-198.
[12] Mélikoff, *op. cit.*, pp. 63-64.

forty *rak'a,* then lay down. Suddenly he saw a dazzling light, and before him stood someone encircled by light. The Prophet of God came forward and placed a crown on his head. Then he dressed him in a coat and belted his waist. "O Abū Muslim," he said, "you are the one who must avenge my house. That which I have given you, no mortal has received." "O my Sultan," answered Abū Muslim, "I have no weapons!" "Look behind me," said the Prophet, "and you shall see an ax such as no human has ever seen." Abū Muslim raised his eyes and saw the Archangel Gabriel, wings outstretched, facing the sun, and in his hands shone an ax. "Remember the ax," said the Prophet, "and have one forged like it." Abū Muslim awoke. The vision had disappeared, but the room remained lighted and in his hand he held a paper with the design of the ax seen in the dream. (Note that the dream left its visible and tangible traces in reality.) He ran into the room of his mother, who had recovered her sight through a miraculous intervention of the Prophet who had appeared to her in a dream and announced the mission of her son. Seeing the design of the ax, she told him about the blacksmith he must approach, sending him to a blacksmith friend of Abū Muslim's dead father. When he arrives he finds that the blacksmith is also dead, but his son, the Akhi of the town, receives him cordially and says, "This ax will require a large amount of iron, you will have to wait an entire week." He promised it "for Friday." Meanwhile, the governor, the famous Naṣr b. Sayyār, an adversary of Abū Muslim's, was organizing a tiger hunt. Abū Muslim said, "If only I had my ax. . . ." But he met a young man who sold him wood he had cut, and said to Abū Muslim, "Here is an ax. My father was an ax-bearer. I have seen the Prophet in a dream. He told me to give it to you." You can see that reality here is complemented by a world of dreams, this curious world which reality overlaps to such an extent as to appear partly dreamed itself. Dreams leave behind a glow, or a paper in the hand, or an ax brought by an obliging friend, whose information is provided by ancestors or companions who never stop watching over the living, with whom they still constitute, as phrased by Auguste Comte (1798–1857), that humanity that is composed more of the dead than the living.

As far as modern times are concerned, I have mentioned several texts in my résumé. There is, in Arabic, the *Dictionary of Customs* by Aḥmad Amīn,[13] which offers little in the way of facts, but does offer evidence that Ibn Sīrīn's basic work of interpretation is currently used in popular Egyptian society.

More is to be gained from the curious notes written in Egypt by

---

[13] Aḥmad Amīn, *Qāmūs al-ʿādāt wa't-taqālīd wa't-taʿābīr al-miṣriyya* [*Dictionary of Customs*] (Cairo, 1953), really a dictionary of Egyptian folklore.

Edward William Lane[14] nearly a century earlier than Aḥmad Amīn. The narration of one dream produces the same impression of constant intermingling of dream and reality. During a discussion of a popular belief as to the presence in Cairo's Mosque al-Ḥasanain of the head of ʿAlī's son, Ḥusain, the martyr of Kerbelāʾ, a student of al-Azhar was shocked by the skepticism of his master who told him that it was not true; the head of Ḥusain was not there because, said the master, the traditions contained no mention of it. The student, a sheikh with a reputation for being a saint, was so affected that he wept the whole evening. He begged the Prophet to appear to him and tell him whether or not the head was in the mosque. He begged the Prophet to grant him a dream. He dreamed, after praying the requisite number of *rakʿa*, that he left for a pilgrimage to the sanctuary. He found it bathed in supernatural light, as in the dream related earlier. At the entry to the tomb's rotunda, a *sharīf*, or descendant of the Prophet, invited him to enter and to pay homage to the Apostle of God. He advanced toward the *qibla* and saw the Prophet (God bless and keep him!) sitting on a throne, a man on his right and another on his left. He raised his voice to repeat several times, "Blessing and peace to you, O Apostle of God!"—all the while continuing to weep. Then he heard the Apostle (God bless and keep him!) say: "Come forward, my son Muhammad." The first of the two men attending the Prophet took him by the hand and led him to the Prophet (may God bless and keep him!) and placed him in his noble hands ("in his hands" means "before him" in Arabic). The student saluted him, ritually, and the Prophet returned the greeting, adding: "May God reward your pious visit to the head of my son Ḥusain." "O Apostle of God," said the student then, "the precious head is here?" "It is here." The narrator then asked the Prophet (may benediction be his!) for permission to tell him about the previous day's discussion. He (may benediction be his!) lowered his eyes, then raised his head, saying, "Copyists merit indulgence." Then the narrator awoke, filled with joy, and waited impatiently until he could go and give the great news to his master. They went to the tomb together, and because of the vision and the famous *ḥadīth* by which all visions of the Prophet are held genuine, the master confessed his error. Lane points out that this manner of settling arguments is not at all rare. Since the story is told with proper names, the principals evidently having no objection to the publication of theirs, no effort was made at concealment. On the contrary, quite independently of the method it illustrates, the story affords an interesting and very complete description of the ceremony, the etiquette surrounding a dream appearance of the Prophet with his chief followers, because it is

---

[14] Edward William Lane, *An Account of the Manners and Customs of the Modern Egyptians* (5th ed.; London, 1871), I, 269 f.

pointed out that the personages at his right and left were Abū Bakr and ʿUmar and that ʿAlī b. abī Ṭālib was at the entrance to the tomb.

This text also seems valuable from another point of view. This kind of dream of consultation comes not only when needed in order to designate a battle plan for a warrior like Dānishmend, or to provide a battle-ax for a tiger hunter like Abū Muslim, but also for less important people for whom they seem to come on demand. Taking the initiative seems to be an almost necessary condition for each of these dreams. Antiquity had its technique for inducing dreams; the most widely known involved passing the night in the sanctuary of the god whose oracle was being sought. This is the practice called incubation. As Toufy Fahd has very justly remarked, there are only traces of incubation in orthodox Islam, as in the therapeutic usage of dreams, or medical oneiromancy. The practice called *istikhāra* consists of the recital of a special prayer with the expectation of an answering dream. This practice, says Toufy Fahd, is an Islamic substitute for incubation, a substitute because that element ordinarily thought essential —the all-night vigil in the sanctuary—has been eliminated. You will recall that the dream related by Lane very specifically involved a sanctuary. The dream unfolds in a sanctuary, but because no one spent a night in the sanctuary in order to evoke the dream, it is not a case of incubation. In the tale of the two bridges in *The Thousand and One Nights,* curiously enough, the hero passes a night in a mosque, but not only did he not dream there, it was someone else who dreamed.

In dealing with folklore, it can always be asked whether some seemingly meaningless element is not the relic of something quite meaningful. The result of such deduction may of course be somewhat flimsy. Specifically, the question is whether in the most popular practices of Islam —I have in mind the mystic cults or the mystic brotherhoods—more characteristic traces of this obviously universal rite cannot be found. E. Doutté asserts that incubation is frequently practiced in North Africa, especially in Morocco among the Tuareg, and he says, not very precisely, that "in all of Islamicized North Africa it is a common practice to sleep in the shrine of a Marabout in order to dream there." [15] Nevertheless he comes to the same conclusion as Toufy Fahd, that *istikhāra* is the true canonical form of practicing incubation in Islam, or is the substitute for incubation where the latter does not exist. In the same passage,[16] he says that a similar evolution took place in the East. He offers no references.

There are curious clues to be found in the dream told by Lane dealing directly with a sanctuary, even though it is only in the dream that the person involved goes there. I suggest that an investigation be made to

---

[15] E. Doutté, *Magie et religion dans l'Afrique du Nord* (Algiers, 1909), p. 142.
[16] *Ibid.,* p. 414.

discover, if possible, definite traces of the practice of incubation. I cite the only examples I have been able to gather, which, though not conclusive, may at least serve as a basis for discussion.

The first comes from the autobiography of Ṭāhā Ḥusain, *Al-Ayyām*,[17] in which mention is made of a miracle that took place during a pilgrimage. A grandmother fell from her horse and was hurt. She was cured through the intercession of the sheikh after being left alone with her ancestors in the mosque of Medina, as she was a descendant of the Prophet. I think we have a very clear indication here of the practice of incubation and even of therapeutic oneiromancy. The grandmother was left in the sanctuary so that the Prophet would appear and cure her. The story is told in such a way as to deny incubation. It runs thus: "Her husband had hardly turned his back when she ran after him, cured." Here this is clearly a late reworking of a miracle story. Whenever the story of a miracle is told, we hear, "An appeal had hardly been made to the religious authorities when the miracle occurred," just as it was said when the Prophet had at one time caused it to rain: the Prophet prayed and "he had hardly spoken when a terrifying storm broke," and it was even necessary to add, "around, but not on us." "Hardly" is a characteristic sign that simply indicates that the miracle was so incontestable as to be instantaneous.

On the other hand, incontestable examples are to be found in Central Syria, in the Damascus region. There are sanctuaries there where incubation is practiced. Unfortunately, the most famous of them are Christian, rather than Muslim. There is reference to one Muslim sanctuary in an article by R. Thoumin.[18] Thoumin's theory is that some Christian sanctuaries turned Muslim along with the population. This is not impossible, especially since there exists in popular tradition the famous story of the parish priest of ʿAin at-Tīna (a village near the famous Aramaic-language island of Maʿlūla, 30 miles north of Damascus) who became a Muslim when his parishioners were converted in order to remain the parish priest of the town. There were conversions, certainly, but this explanation alone does not take into consideration that the tradition of incubation was acquired by Christianity itself from an earlier era. If it turns up integrated in Islam, it is by how many detours? Perhaps it is a question of secondary importance. In any event I cite these examples with the greatest reserve,

---

[17] Ṭāhā Ḥusain, *Al-Ayyām* [*The Days*], English trans. of Vol. I, E. H. Paxton, *An Egyptian Childhood* (London, 1932); English trans. of Vol. II, H. Wayment, *The Stream of Days* (London, 1948); see the chapter in Vol. I concerning the sheikhs of traditional brotherhoods.
[18] R. Thoumin, "Le Culte de Sainte Thècle dans le Jebel Qalamun," in *Mélanges de l'Institut français de Damas,* I (1929), 163–180.

especially since these incubations are practiced by Muslims. I know the case of a child, now a grown man, whose mother up to the time of the rite of incubation was barren. But cases involving Europeans are extremely rare. For Muslims, however, these are common incidents, one of the topics of discussion in orthodox circles of Damascus having recently been: how is it that the omnipotent Lord makes many more miracles for Muslims than for Christians? A vexing question.

What we must investigate is to what degree this integration of ancient practices might in certain cases have been done, with pre-Islamic beliefs as the starting point. This is the problem to be faced in a story taken by J. Wellhausen from the *Kitāb al-aṣnām* of Ibn al-Kalbī about the idol of the god Jalsad.[19] The idol's priest who "habitually slept in the sanctuary" did in fact have a vision. He had a vision of the god who appeared to him saying, "All is finished now, the time of idols has ended." That this is incubation is clearly questionable. It is theophany.

The same thing can be said about the famous story of Ḥātim Ṭayy[20] who was invoked by someone in the supposed place of his tomb. Someone came during the night saying, "We have nothing to eat. Bring us something. Provide for us." Ḥātim appeared in a dream, and procured a camel by slaughtering or hamstringing one of the camels belonging to the man who had just arrived—a strange way to treat a guest. But the next morning the son of Ḥātim Ṭayy arrived, out of breath. "My father came to me in a dream, and told me to bring you two camels." Here again we have theophany rather than incubation. But is there a basic difference between theophany and incubation? It is a little like the question of experimentation and observation. Recourse is made to incubation wherever theophany has been experienced. It is a matter of producing at will a phenomenon that ought to have been spontaneous in origin.

This outline of dreams in popular traditions is not intended to be conclusive, but is simply a look at possibilities.

---

[19] J. Wellhausen, *Reste arabischen Heidentums* (2d ed.; Berlin, 1961), p. 55.
[20] Abū 'l-Faraj al-Iṣfahānī, *Kitāb al-aghānī* (Būlāq, 1285/1868–1869), XVI, 101.

23

The Visionary Dream in Islamic Spirituality

HENRY CORBIN

1. MYSTIC ETHOS AND PROPHETOLOGY

The significance of the visionary dream in Islamic spirituality can be understood only as a function of the spiritual ethos that a prophetic religion, such as Islam is in essence, develops for itself. We must then keep in mind the structure of its prophetology. This prophetology was enunciated for the first time in the teachings of the Imams of Shi'ism. It established the essential relationship between the concept of the Prophet and the concept of the Imam. In it the very concept of Shi'ism finds expression.

Unfortunately, the West still knows very little about the theology of Shi'ite Islam as a whole. Some ready-made ideas affixed to the basic concepts of Shi'ism distort it and have nothing whatever in common with the texts that preserve for us the Imams' teachings. Moreover, the concept that organically binds imamology to prophetology is the concept of *walāyat,* the spiritual initiation of the "men of God." This concept is an equally dominant factor in Sufism; whence the important question concerning the Shi'ite presuppositions of non-Shi'ite Sufism, a question familiar to the religious thinkers of

Iran, but far less so to Orientalists in the West, since Shi'ite spiritual life has, in fact, remained hidden and ignored.

To whatever degree a man's hidden consciousness expresses itself in his dreams, and the characteristic archetypes of those dreams match those experienced in dreams by people sharing his faith and aspirations, it is necessary to differentiate between this faith and these aspirations and those of all others. What has to be kept in mind is the spiritual situation peculiar to the faithful of Islam. This spiritual situation is determined and maintained by a prophetology on which are based the various modes of a higher visionary knowledge, a *hierognosis*—a prophetic theory of knowledge which accounts for and distinguishes the visions of dreams as well as the visions of the waking state. The existential situation of the believer is profoundly different from that commonly created for his Christian counterpart. It is only possible to refer very briefly here to the broad lines of this very complex whole.

To proceed as quickly as possible, let me begin by establishing the tonality in which our remarks must be developed. I have chosen two leitmotivs that will bring out certain contrasts.

The koranic Sura of the Dawn (89:27-28) proclaims this invitation: "O soul at peace, return to your lord, accepting and accepted." If we bring closely together the meaning of this verse, as it has been meditated on by Islamic spiritual thinkers, and the motto repeated over and over since the time of the Prophet, "Whoever knows himself [his soul], knows his Lord," these two leitmotivs enable us to understand the underlying ethos that characterizes the mystic of Islam, whatever he may have in common with certain mystics of Christianity, and at the same time what does, in essence, set them apart.

What is called in Islam "esoteric" (*bāṭin,* interior realities), as opposed to "exoteric" (*ẓāhir,* exterior things), has given rise to forms of consciousness, to positions taken, which are only conceivable within the framework of a prophetic religion, that is, a religion essentially based on revelation—the Book—received from a prophet. Commentaries written around the koranic verse and the motto cited provide the best information on the nature of the contrast between the religion of spiritual Islam and its mystic gnosis on the one hand, and the concept of a legalistic religion, commonly called official Islam, on the other. At the same time, this contrast affords some insights into both the affinities and the differences to be found in the situations that had to be faced on the one hand by the esoteric in Islam, and on the other by what in spiritual circles marginal to the official churches appeared as Christian esoterism.

Because these differences seem to me to contain certain presuppositions indispensable to an appreciation of content and meaning of some of the visionary dreams I refer to, I broadly sketch in several of them as they appear to me after many years spent in Iran in constant contact with Shi'ite friends.

This much can be said: the phenomenon of the "unhappy consciousness," to employ the name that Hegel introduced into common usage, is perhaps peculiar to the phenomenology of the Christian conscience. Nevertheless there exists on the horizon of all Sufic spirituality a contradiction to be overcome, a void to be filled, a spiritual combat to be endured. But the terms differ profoundly from the Christian's, at least if the search for the expressions of Christian spirituality is confined to the teaching of the official dogma.

Take, for example, some of the opposites that have become commonplace for us—sin and sanctifying grace, faith and science, believing and knowing—or the kindred opposition trivially formulated as between "mysticism" and "sensuality," because the "love of God" supposedly excludes a certain kind of love of the creature, beauty being the demon's trap, and because traditional asceticism has become accustomed to denounce any hesitation on this point as a reawakening of "paganism." It will take much more than a "post-Christian" state of society to make these oppositions disappear. It is true, there is no more talk of "sin," but there is talk of a "guilt complex." We are always dealing with symptoms of the same disease whether it is laicized or not.

To these contradictions within our secular ethics we can add others of a more specifically intellectual order, like the opposition between the reality of historic fact and interior truth, between the object of historical faith and that spiritual reality which is not conditioned by an event accomplished within chronological time, between the literalism of a revealed dispensation and its spiritual significance, between a dogmatic conscience and a conscience that perceives all exterior revelation as symbols, and so on—these contradictions live on even after the situation that engendered them has been laicized. The burden of a "historical conscience," which has weighed so tragically on Christian consciences since Origen, has never been heavier than in post-Christian sociological philosophies.

Such oppositions and presuppositions are foreign to the spiritual world wherein the verse beginning "O soul at peace . . ." and the motto "Whoever knows himself knows his Lord" resound for the Sufi. The latter motto put into practice leads the mystic to a knowledge and an awareness of the one who, before all "givens" (*data*), is the "giver of givens" (*dator datorum*).

To mark the difference, we can point out that the Sufi has in no regard the consciousness of being a sinner. He is not "diseased." He feels no need of "justification." He is an exile, an expatriate (*gharīb*), and this basic feeling makes him a member of the enduring family of Gnostics. His is not a vague nostalgia; he knows precisely whence he comes and whither to return. Sohrawardī, *shaikh al-ishrāq* (d. 587/1191), writes: "When someone says to you, 'return,' a place of previous presence is implied. And woe to you, if you understand the place of return to be Damascus, Baghdad, or some other earthly fatherland."

What the Sufi prays for from the depth of his being is a messenger, a teacher of truth, a companion and spiritual guide who points out the way home. The meaning of his existence, the only conceivable future of his existence, consists in this recovery of his place of origin, this return home. This sense of return results in a concept of history which is essentially cyclical rather than an irreversible linear evolution; the end meets the beginning (*maʿād* and *mabdaʾ*). This return cannot be accomplished without a guide. We have in this idea of the cycle and the idea of the guide the double theme that informs prophetology as it is meditated and experienced by the *spirituales* of Islam.

More precisely, the reference is to Shiʿite prophetology. It is, as we shall see, the first of the presuppositions necessary for an understanding of visionary dreams, of which I cite certain examples.

We are dealing with prophetology as expounded by the Imams of Shiʿism, primarily the fourth Imam (ʿAlī Zain al-ʿĀbidīn, d. 95/714), the fifth Imam (Muḥammad Bāqir, d. 115/733), and the sixth Imam (Jaʿfar Ṣādiq, d. 148/765). These most ancient sources within our reach are accessible through the monumental collection of Kolainī (d. 329/940). By some as yet not fully determined route, this prophetology has, if at the price of severe mutilation, entered the metaphysics of Sufism.

This prophetology[1] classes the prophets according to a gnoseology whose criteria correspond to the degrees of visionary perception, from the sights and sounds of a dream to the suprasensible perception in the waking state. There is the *nabī,* or simple prophet. There is the envoy (*nabī morsal*) to a more or less numerous group. Finally, among the envoys there are the six great prophets—Adam, Noah, Abraham, Moses, Jesus, Muhammad—who were charged with revealing a *sharīʿat,* a new law. These are the legislator prophets. Prophetic gnoseology has appointed a degree of visionary perception to each of these categories: the simple *nabī* sees or hears the angel in a dream; the envoy sees the angel while awake; the prophet charged with revealing a *sharīʿat* receives, while in a waking state, the dictation of the text from the angel.

[1] Cf. H. Corbin, "De la philosophie prophétique en Islam Shiʿite," *Eranos-Jahrbuch,* XXXI (Zurich, 1962), for the prophetological contents of Imamic traditions as recorded in the great collection by Muḥammad ibn Yaʿqūb Kolainī; "Le combat spirituel du shiʿisme," *Eranos-Jahrbuch,* XXX (Zurich, 1961), on the problem of the relationship between Shiʿism and Sufism as expounded by the Shiʿite theologian Ḥaidar Āmolī (eighth/fourteenth century); *Histoire de la philosophie islamique,* Vol. I, Idées, vol. 38 (Paris: Gallimard, 1964).

The prophet Muhammad is the Seal of the Prophets closing the cycle of the six periods of prophecy. Nevertheless, according to a specifically Shiʿite concept, the religious history of humanity has not been closed. What is closed is legislative prophecy (*nobowwat al-tashrīʿ*); there can be no new *sharīʿat*. Prophecy pure and simple continues but under a new name. Shiʿite authors profess that what before Islam was known as "simple *nobowwat*," * has as the Islamic equivalent, *walāyat*, a term that is not adequately translated by "sanctity"; it signifies a bestowal of divine friendship, the spiritual initiation into the "friends of God." The name has changed, owing to Muhammad's quality as the Seal of the Prophets; but the phenomenon remains, and for this reason our sources in this case use the term "esoteric prophecy" (*nobowwat bāṭinīya*) as well as *walāyat*.

The final point of the prophetic cycle was at the same time the initial point of the cycle of the *walāyat* in its pure form, that is, a *walāyat* that is not paving the way for a new *sharīʿat*. In Twelver Shiʿite terms, it is the Cycle of the Imāmat which is dominated by twelve figures, the twelfth being the Hidden Imam, the Imam of our time, which is the time of his occultation. This figure holds a pivotal position in the spirituality of Shiʿism as well as in the speculations of its theosophists (a better word than "theologian" or "philosopher," *ḥikmat ilāhīya* being the exact equivalent of the Greek *theosophia*). Just as the Prophet of Islam was the Seal of law-giving prophecy, so the Imāmat, the *plērōma* (fullness) of the Twelve, is the Seal of the *walāyat*: the Seal of the universal *walāyat* in the person of the first Imam, ʿAlī ibn Abī Ṭālib; the Seal of the Muhammadan *walāyat* in the person of the Twelfth Imam, Muḥammad al-Mahdī. The *parousia* of the "Imam to come," who is present in both past and future, will announce the end of the cycle of our *aiōn*.

But in Islam, since *walāyat* (the quality of the *auliyāʾ*, the friends or men of God) is the name of what in times preceding the Seal of the Prophets was called simple* prophecy, it goes without saying that any gnoseology concerning this simple* prophecy must refer to *walāyat* as well. It is precisely in these terms that the traditions from which we learn the teachings of the Imams of Shiʿism describe whatever differentiates the knowledge of the envoys from that of the Imam, and therefore from that of all those who participate in the *walāyat* of the Imam. The envoy receives the *vision* of the angel in a waking state, while the Imam *hears* the angel in a dream (which differentiates *waḥy*, divine communication by the angel, from *ilhām*, inspiration). From the point of view of *hierognosis*, our traditional texts treat the case of the Imam (the spiritual guide) in the same category as the *nabī* or simple prophet.

We may say, then, that the spirituality of the cycle of the *walāyat*

---

* So rendered at the express behest of author.

is directed toward a kind of suprasensible knowledge with the Imam as guide, since he is in essence the initiator into the hidden meaning of the divine revelations, and since on understanding this meaning depends the spiritual birth (*wilādat rūḥānīya*) of the adept. We can, therefore, understand how and why the figure of the guide, preeminently one or the other of the twelve Imams, dominates the visionary dreams of our *spirituales,* and why these dreams generally have the character of initiatory dreams. The same fact also affords us an understanding of why this search for and the encounter with the personal guide, with the individuation this implies, resolve some of the contradictions previously discussed.

The currently accepted opposition between prophetic religion and mystic religion does not exist for the Sufi, Shiʿite, or non-Shiʿite. Mystic religion is the truth, the true meaning (*ḥaqīqat*) of prophetic religion, prophetic experience (the *miʿrāj*) being the very prototype of mystic experience. Thereby disappears as well the conflict that in Christianity presents itself as the opposition between historical exegesis, that of the natural sense of scriptural revelation, and the exegesis of the spiritual meaning (which is unfortunately often confused with the allegorical meaning). There is no choice to be made, nor any merely edifying superstructure to be tolerated; there is simply a transition to accomplish, that transition upon which the spiritual birth of the adept depends (*taʾwīl* as spiritual exegesis is *exēgēsis,* exodus, return).

Last, the phenomenon "Church" has remained foreign to Islam. A Sufi could never understand that he was to receive his faith and hence eternal life from anything like a church. Therefore, too, he disposes of resources of his own to face the restrictive norms of the collective conscience. What is essential is the individual, personal bond between the initiate and the initiator, a bond with the guide, *shaikh* or *pīr,* who can be a visible human person like the person he guides, but who can also be, as in the case of the Owaisī order, an invisible personal guide. In Shiʿism, this individual relationship is particularly typified by a bond of personal devotion with one or the other of the twelve Imams, preeminently with the Hidden Imam, "hidden from the world and the senses but present in the hearts of his adepts." Stories of a visionary meeting with the Imam abound in Shiʿite literature. They represent, preeminently, the archetype of an individuated and individuating relationship with a personal heavenly guide. Avicenna calls this guide Ḥayy ibn Yaqẓān.[2] Sohrawardī describes him, with the esotericism of the Arab tongue, as "Perfect Nature," the "angel of the philosopher." Najmoddīn Kobrà calls him the "invisible master" (*shaikh al-ghaib*), the "witness in Heaven" (*shāhid fi ʾs-samāʾ*).

---

[2] H. Corbin, *Avicenna and the Visionary Recital,* trans. Willard K. Trask, Bollingen Series, no. 66 (New York: Pantheon Books, 1961).

Semnānī shows us that the mystic's relationship with him is like that of the Prophet with the angel of revelation, his Holy Spirit, because the guide is "the Gabriel of his being." This is the figure who appears on the horizon of his dreams, be he awake or asleep.

This figure is the guarantee of the final attainment of spiritual individuality. Certainly that individuality has nothing to do with the empiric ego represented by the idea of *nafs ammāra* (the domineering soul in disorder), but with what our sources describe as the Holy Spirit in man, a superior preexistential ego whose closeness must be recaptured. All spiritual combat is directed toward this transformation of *nafs ammāra* into *nafs moṭma'inna,* the quiet "soul at peace" addressed by the koranic verses we cited at the outset, because in it the motto has been realized: "He who knows his soul, knows his Lord." Such a soul engages in a kind of spiritual combat which takes on, especially in Iranian Sufism, a markedly different character than that envisaged by traditional Christian asceticism. We shall find evidence for this in a first series of visionary experiences, chosen in the work of Rūzbehān of Shīrāz.

2. RŪZBEHĀN BAQLĪ of SHĪRĀZ (d. 606/1209)

Rūzbehān is certainly one of Iran's greatest mystics. His doctrine is characterized by a complete asceticism of love which puts an end to the opposition established by traditional asceticism between human love and divine love. For Rūzbehān there is but one love, but one text, the meaning of which must be learned. In his beautiful book, entitled *Jasmin of Love's Faithful*,[3] Rūzbehān expressly distinguishes between those he calls the "pious devotees," whose spiritual experience did not have its origin in human love, and those he calls the "intimates," the faithful of love (*khawāṣṣ al-maḥabbat*), who have been initiated by a human love that was for them the beginning of the spiritual way. Let it be especially noted that no "conversion" is involved here, no passing from a human object to a divine object (God is not an object), but that a transformation takes place within the loving subject: the unity of the Contemplator and the Contemplated announces itself in the ecstatic agitation of the soul when it is exposed to human beauty experienced as the mystery of a supreme theophany, that is to say, in the ecstasy of the soul that perceives the prophetic meaning of beauty.

---

[3] Rūzbehān Baqlī Shīrāzī, *Le Jasmin des fidèles d'amour* (*ʿAbhar al-ʿāshiqīn*), ed. H. Corbin and Moh. Moʿīn, Bibliothèque iranienne, vol. 8 (Tehran and Paris, 1958), a Sufic treatise in Persian; cf. also H. Corbin, "Soufisme de Rūzbehān," *Eranos-Jahrbuch,* XXVII (Zurich, 1958).

We can mention here only one of the other works by Rūzbehān, his voluminous *Commentary of the Paradoxes of the Mystics,* which is a veritable *summa* of the Sufism of his times. Rūzbehān wrote a preliminary sketch in Arabic, then at the request of his disciples he wrote a much expanded Persian version.[4] Last, we should take note of an invaluable work, a unique document called the *Kashf al-asrār* (*Uncovering of Secrets*), Rūzbehān's diary of visions; the only comparable work in the West, I believe, is Swedenborg's *Spiritual Diary.* A friend asked him to put the material together when Rūzbehān was fifty-five years old; his first visionary experiences dated from his fifteenth year. Here we take several of the stories related to events that occurred at about that age. They bear particularly the character of visions or dreams of initiation; they form a series of decisive inner experiences whose narration attests to a personal spiritual initiation that Rūzbehān owed to no earthly master.

At the age of fifteen, then, we can see awakening in his conscience the aspiration characteristic of Sufism: to verify by a personal mystical experience the testimony of prophetic experience, to resolve the contradiction between the refusal given by God to Moses ("Thou wilt not see me" [Koran 7:139]), and the paradoxical attestation of the Prophet ("I have seen my God in the most beautiful of forms"). In Ibn ʿArabī's doctrine of theophany, the paradox is resolved by an assertion that theophany (*tajallī*), divine manifestation, can never occur except when it corresponds to the form of the aptitude of the person to whom it reveals itself.* Otherwise it would be impossible. What the visionary sees (*al-motajallā laho*) is his own form in "the mirror of God." All the mystics held to this, and the thesis was already outlined in a teaching of the eighth Imam, ʿAlī Rezā (d. 203/818).

At this moment, then, in his life, an inner voice tells the adolescent Rūzbehān that he is a *nabī,* a prophet, certainly not a prophet-envoy (*nabī morsal*) and still less a prophet charged with revealing a *sharīʿat,* but a mere *nabī* (that is, a *walī;* see the prophetology sketched in the preceding section). He resists, thinking that the state of *nabī* is incompatible with the weakness of mortal flesh. The decisive inner experience of his entire life is already in evidence. It should be noted that at that age the young Rūzbehān was as yet ignorant of all the theological difficulties that had accumulated around the *tauḥīd,* the profession of faith pronouncing the concept of monotheism. He was as yet incapable of explaining the differences between exoteric *tauḥīd,* the monotheism as understood by

---

[4] Rūzbehān Baqlī Shīrāzī, *Commentaire sur les Paradoxes des Soufis* (*Sharḥ-e Shaṭḥiyāt*), Persian text with introduction and notes ed. H. Corbin, Bibliothèque iranienne, vol. 12 (Tehran and Paris, 1966).

* So rendered at the express behest of author.

official and legalistic religion, and esoteric *tauḥīd,* the "theomonism" as understood experientially by the theosophy of Sufism. Nevertheless, because he had already found the road of his personal secret, his *guide,* the "soul of his soul," the decisive experience presented itself as the first confrontation with this formidable problem.

One evening after dinner he left his home and turned toward a certain place in the desert around Shīrāz with the intention of making his ablution for prayer. He writes: "Suddenly I heard the sound of a sweet voice. My innermost conscience [*sirr*] and an ardent longing [*shauq*] were stirred. I cried: 'Oh, man of the voice, wait for me.' I climbed a nearby hill and found myself in the presence of a person of great beauty who had the appearance of a Sufi sheikh. I was unable to say a word. He spoke several words to me about the *tauḥīd.* I did not understand, but I experienced simultaneously deep distress and an overwhelming love." The young man stayed in the desert part of the night in this enraptured state. Then he went home where he remained "until morning a prey to agitation and disquietude, to sighs and tears . . . then I felt relief. It seemed to have lasted hours and hours." He remained seated for another hour, meditating. Then, giving in to the violence of his emotions, he got up, made a bundle of his effects which he threw into a corner, and went into the desert. "I remained in this state for a year and a half, nostalgic, stupefied, carried away by emotion. Every day was marked by tremendous ecstatic visions, and by sudden visitations from invisible worlds. During these visions, the heavens and the earth, the mountains, the deserts, the plants, everything seemed to me to be pure light. Then, I felt a kind of relief."

In describing the first stages that followed, Rūzbehān's spiritual journal reveals for us the archetypal figures that force themselves on the consciousness of an Iranian Sufi:

> This time, I seemed to be in my vision on the mountain of the east, and I saw there a great group of angels. From the east to the west stretched a vast sea. There was nothing else to be seen. Then the angels said to me, "Enter the sea and swim to the west." I entered the sea and began to swim. When I arrived at the place of the setting sun as it was going down, I saw a group of angels on the mountain of the west; they were illuminated by the light of the setting sun. They called to me, "You, down below, swim and have no fear." When I at last reached the mountain, they said to me, "No one has crossed this sea except ʿAlī ibn Abī Ṭālib and you after him."

There are two striking features in the events of this initiatory vision. First, the reference to the first Imam of Shiʿism who appears here as the exemplary hero of the new initiate. Second, the scene itself. The dangerous crossing to the setting sun, the region of darkness, this is the theme of the Source of Life. Two great archetypal figures dominate the legend: Alexander and Khiḍr, the mysterious prophet who is sometimes associated with Elias and sometimes identified with him. Khiḍr is superior to the lawgiving prophets (he is the initiator of Moses [Sura 18]). He has an extraordinary role in Sufism. Century after century his presence reaches down from the world of Mystery. He is the master of all those who have had neither a worldly master nor a worldly initiator. Such is the case of the Sufi who, before any contact with a human master, before any of the historical affiliations on this earth which are passed through successive human generations, receives his affiliation directly from the one recognized as master by all those "without a master." The personal guide is preeminently manifest in the person of Khiḍr, and it is profoundly significant that a large group of Shi'ites should have identified him with the Twelfth Imam, the Hidden Imam.

There are indeed two stories of visions which tell us successively of a meeting by Rūzbehān with Khiḍr in person, then with two sheikhs who are the very "image" of the mystic pilgrim and who reveal to him the esoteric rank he has now attained. Having reached the western region of darkness, Rūzbehān, like Khiḍr, finds there the light (the vision of the angels enfolded in the light of the setting sun) and the Source of Life in the form of a Sea of Light. The initiation received directly from Khiḍr took here the shape of eating a piece of fruit. Rūzbehān wrote: "At that time I knew nothing of the higher theosophical science, and behold I saw Khiḍr. He gave me an apple, an apple from which I took a bite. 'Eat it all,' he said, 'as I have eaten it all.' It seemed to me that there was an immense sea stretching from the Throne to the Pleiades, and I could see nothing else. It was like the irradiation of the sun. Then, without my willing it, my mouth opened and this whole sea of light entered, not a drop remained unabsorbed."

This initiation is confirmed by another dream vision whose symbolic figures indicate with all the precision of an archetype the degree of spiritual plenitude attained. All created beings are revealed to the visionary as enclosed in a house; numerous lamps provide a brilliant light, but a wall keeps him from entering. So he climbs onto the roof of *his own* lodging, where he finds two very beautiful people in whom he recognizes *his own* image. They appear to be Sufis and smile at him affectionately. He notices a hanging pot under which a delicate and pure fire is burning without smoke and fed by sweet-smelling herbs. At this moment one of the visitors unfolds a cloth, and brings forth from it a bowl of very beautiful form and several loaves of pure wheat. He breaks one of the loaves into the bowl and pours over it the contents of the pot, an oil so fine as to appear a spiritual substance. Then the three together eat a kind of communion meal. Rūzbehān continues:

> Then one of them asked me, "Do you know what was in the pot?" "No," I answered, "I know nothing about it." "It was oil of the Great Bear which we gathered for you."
>   When the vision was over, I meditated on it, but it was not until some time later that I realized that this was an allusion to the Seven Poles in the heavenly pleroma (*malakūt*) and that God had bestowed upon me the pure substance of their mystic grade, that is, the rank of the Seven who are invisibly spread over the surface of the world. I then turned my attention to the Great Bear. I noticed that it formed seven openings, through all of which God showed himself (*tajallī*) to me. "My God," I cried, "what is this?" He said to me, "These are the seven orifices of the Throne."[5]

It is impossible here to pursue and comment on the hundreds of visions related by Rūzbehān in the pages of his spiritual diary. What they reveal to us is the secret of his passionate love of beauty, his ecstatic adoration of the faces of beauty which he knows he has previously contemplated in another world. Out of this secret, there grew in him the sense of the amphibology (*iltibās*) of visible things, the multiplication of symbols which he interpreted without falling into the snare. It could be said that he lived in constant intimacy with a heavenly world of sumptuous splendor, revealing to him the magnificence of benign beings invisible to ordinary perception. His universe can only be described in the terms he uses himself: in the pages of his diary there appears an endless succession of angels whose beauty is both delicate and superhuman, of prophets, of houris, of gardens, and of celestial music. Remarkably dominant are the often repeated splendors of flaming dawns and the profusion of rose gardens, white roses and red roses, shadowed rose bowers, the divine presence shining forth in the splendor of a red rose.

Certainly we are far from the phenomenon of "unhappy consciousness." There is not even an equivalent to be found in the feeling shown by the mystic to have left behind him the *tauḥīd* professed according to the norms of common exoteric consciousness and of legalistic religion. This feeling appears in the consciousness of every Sufi, but only to turn, precisely at this point, into a feeling that all contradiction has been resolved. Here again, to bring to an end the case of Rūzbehān, is the story of a particularly eloquent visionary dream. Rūzbehān was aware that in order to remain faithful to the presence of his inner God, he might have

---

[5] Cf. Corbin "Soufisme de Ruzbehan," pp. 65–67. I hope that an edition of the diary (i.e., *Kashf al-asrār*) will follow that of the *Shaṭḥīyāt*.

to be thought a mangy sheep by the conventional Muslim. Such was the case of those called the *malāmatī*. Ḥāfiẓ of Shīrāz, the mystic poet and compatriot of Rūzbehān, was later to be one of them. Rūzbehān reveals their affinity in one of the visions in which to him the contradiction between the One and the Many is resolved, a contradiction that exoteric theology refuses to face and is, therefore, powerless to overcome. He writes:

> When I was young I had a sheikh who was a man of great mystic knowledge. He was a *malāmatī* sheikh whose true character was hidden from ordinary people. One night, I was looking upon a vast plain in the Plains of Mystery, and behold I saw God in the guise of this sheikh at the entrance to this plain. As I approached him, he made a gesture showing me another plain. I went toward this other plain and again I saw a sheikh like him, and again this sheikh was God. Once more he gestured showing me another plain; and so forth until he had shown me seventy thousand plains, and each time at the approach to each plain I saw a figure like the one I had seen at the first. I said to myself: God is nevertheless unique, one, undivided, transcending numbers, great or small, as well as sameness, contradiction, and similarity. Then I was told: "Such are the theophanies of the eternal attributes, since they are limitless." At that moment I felt the grip of the esoteric realities of the *tauḥīd* from the sea of magnificence.

3. MUḤYI 'd-DIN IBN 'ARABI (d. 638/1240)

In connection with the initiatory dreams of Rūzbehān, it is fitting to refer to evidence afforded by Ibn ʿArabī, one of the greatest theosophists and visionary mystics of all time (born at Murcia, in Andalusia, in 560/1165, died in Damascus in 638/1240). Having treated at length elsewhere the visionary experiences that marked the whole of this great sheikh's life and work,[6] I limit myself here to two references. Both disclose a life of intimacy with a mysterious heavenly beloved and would lend themselves to comparison with the narratives in Rūzbehān's diary. Ibn ʿArabī declared: "In whomsoever active imagination does not operate, never will he reach the heart of the question." Not only has he himself provided a far-reaching theory of imaginative cognition (which profoundly influenced Mollā Ṣadrā of Shīrāz in the sixteenth century), but, by his own testimony, he had received a full measure of this visualizing or visionary

---

[6] H. Corbin, *L'Imagination créatrice dans le soufisme d'Ibn ʿArabī* (Paris: Flammarion, 1958).

imagination; and he made use of it with remarkable lucidity of consciousness. He confessed:

> This power of the active imagination developed in me to the point that it presents my mystic beloved to me visually in a bodily, objective, extra-mental figure just as the Angel Gabriel appeared bodily to the eyes of the Prophet. At first, I did not feel strong enough to look at this figure. It spoke to me. I heard and understood. These apparitions left me in such a state that for many days I could not take any nourishment. Each time I went to the table, the figure was standing at the table's end, looking at me and saying in a language I could hear with my ears: "Will you eat while contemplating me?" It was impossible for me to eat, but I did not feel hunger! I was so full of my vision that I stuffed myself and became drunken in contemplating the figure to the point that this contemplation took the place of all nourishment. My good appearance astonished my friends who knew of my total abstinence. The fact is that I continued for a long time without tasting a bit of food, not experiencing either hunger or thirst. All the while this figure was never out of my sight whether I was standing or sitting, moving or resting.[7]

This visionary event forms both the prelude and the source of the colossal work *al-Fotūḥāt al-Makkīya (The Spiritual Conquests of Mekka)*. This prelude, which is actually the product of long spiritual maturation, is presented as an extraordinarily lucid dialogue, at the border of conscious and transconscious, between the human ego and his divine alter ego. Ibn ʿArabī was in the process of finishing his turns around the Kaʿba when behold, in front of the Black Stone he met the mysterious being whom he recognized and described as "the evanescent young man, the Silent-Speaker, who is neither living nor dead, the simple-complex, the embracing-embraced," all terms with alchemical overtones, amassed to symbolize the *coincidentia oppositorum*. At this moment, doubt overtakes the visionary: Perhaps this procession is nothing but a living man's ritual prayer over a corpse (the Kaʿba)? "Behold the secret of the temple," the mystic young man said to him, "lest it escape you." The visionary suddenly saw the temple of stone become a living being. He then understood the true spiritual rank of his visitor. Kissing his visitor's right hand, he asked to become his disciple, to learn from him all his secrets. He would teach nothing else. But the visitor spoke only in symbols, his eloquence but riddles. At a mystic sign of recognition, the visionary was overtaken by so powerful a love that he lost consciousness. When he was

---

[7] *Ibid.*, p. 277.

himself again, his visitor revealed to him, "I am Knowledge, I am He who knows, and I am He who is known." [8]

4. NAJMODDĪN KOBRÀ (d. 618/1221)

A converging movement of primary importance in the history of Islamic spirituality took place at the beginning of the thirteenth century. Ibn ʿArabī emigrated from Andalusia toward Syria. The disciples of Najmoddīn Kobrà from Khwarezm in central Asia fled before the oncoming Mongols toward Iran and Anatolia. Both masters have, by their influence, left a decisive imprint on the theosophy of Sufism. We spoke earlier of the expressions "invisible guide," "witness in Heaven," as characteristic of Najm Kobrà's vocabulary. What they convey is a spiritual experience of the same type we have come to know through the visionary tales of Rūzbehān and Ibn ʿArabī.

Najm Kobrà seems to have been the first of the masters of Sufism to fix his attention on the phenomena of color, the colored-light sensation the mystic may perceive in his spiritual states (sensible optical perception is not involved). He set about describing and interpreting these colored lights as indications of the mystic's state and the degree of his spiritual advancement. His influence has made itself felt in his direct and indirect disciples: Najm Dāya Rāzī, ʿAlāʾ ud-Daula Semnānī, and others. His work, known to us now in an edition by Fritz Meier, is immensely rich.[9]

In relation to the theme of this Colloquium, this is essential: what the mystic ardently seeks and experiences is not a collective relationship with a god who is the same for all, a relationship shared by all in like manner. On the contrary, it is always a matter of a unique, individual relationship of the lover and the beloved which cannot be shared; the mystic has no part in a religion of a "common father"; the relationship he experiences is not "filial" but "uxorial" * (whence the symbolism common to all types of mysticism). The individuation of an unshared relationship cannot be manifested, shaped, or expressed except by means of a figure that *bears witness* to the presence of the alone with the alone and for the alone, in the dialogue of their *unus-ambo*. The figure of the "witness in Heaven," of the "personal suprasensible guide," bears

---

[8] *Ibid.*, pp. 208, 278 ff.
[9] Fritz Meier, *Die Fawāʾiḥ al-Ǧamāl wa-fawātiḥ al-Ǧalāl des Naǧm ad-dīn al-Kubrā*, Mainzer Akademie der Wissenschaften und der Literatur, Veröffentlichungen der Orientalischen Kommission, Bd. IX (Wiesbaden: Franz Steiner, 1957); cf. H. Corbin, *Physiologie de l'homme de lumière dans le soufisme iranien*, Académie septentrionale, Ombre et Lumière, Vol. I (Paris: Desclée de Brouwer, 1961).

* In French the opposites are *filialité* and *uxorité*.

witness precisely to this relationship. It is so much the hallmark of a theophany perceived by love alone, responding to the feeling of an "uxorial" tie, that its most characteristic manifestations, the flaming-light phenomena, bearing witness to the rejoining of "like with like," appear whenever a state of love reaches paroxysm. The mystic experience described by Najm Kobrà thus rejoins the forms and experiences of celestial love characteristic of Iranian Sufism. We refer here to two texts. The sheikh wrote:

> When the circle of the face has become pure, it gives off light like a spring emptying water, so that the mystic has a feeling [by his awareness of the suprasensible] of flashing lights irradiating from his face. This flashing appears between the eyes and the eyebrows. It continues until it covers the whole face. When this happens, there appears before you, facing your face, another Face, equally of light. It also radiates light, while behind its transparent veil a sun becomes visible which appears to be animated by oscillation. Actually this Face is your own face, and the sun is the sun of the Spirit who comes and goes in your body. Later, purity submerges all your person, and behold you see before you a person of light [shakhṣ min nūr] from which lights also irradiate. The mystic notices these lights proceeding from his entire person. Often the veil falls revealing the whole reality of the person, and it is then that you perceive all with the whole of your body. The opening of interior vision [baṣīra], the vision's organ of light, begins with the eyes, continues to the face, followed by the breast, finally by the entire body. It is this person of light before you who is called the suprasensible guide [moqaddam al-ghaib] in Sufic terminology. He is also called the suprasensible "personal master" [shaikh al-ghaib]; or "spiritual balance of the suprasensible" [mīzān].[10]

Najm Kobrà lavished other names on it: "sun of the heart," "sun of certainty," "sun of faith," "sun of knowledge," "spiritual sun of the spirit." Even more explicitly, the sheikh declares: "Know that the mystic has a witness [shāhid], who is called the personal master in the suprasensible world. He raises the mystic to Heaven and it is in Heaven that he appears." [11]

It is significant that the personal guide in the suprasensible world should thus be expressly identified with the shāhid, the "witness of contemplation," the central figure in the meditations of those whom Rūzbehān describes as the "faithful of love." The idea of the shāhid

---

[10] Meier, op. cit., sec. 66, p. 31 of Arabic text.
[11] Ibid., sec. 69, p. 32 of Arabic text.

enters into a mystic doctrine of a love that binds the beloved of this world to a "witness in Heaven" in his manifestation as the "guide of light" because of an epiphanic relationship between them. We learn this from the following confession, in which, naturally, the phenomena depend on a physiology of "suprasensible perception." Najm Kobrà writes:

> Behold, while living in Egypt, in a river village on the Nile, I was taken by a passionate love for a young girl. Day-in, day-out, I hardly ate or drank, so that the fire of my love became extraordinarily intense. I breathed in flames of fire. Each time I sent forth such a flame, behold from Heaven *someone* also breathed in a flame that came to meet my own breath. The two flames came together between Heaven and me. For a long time, I did not know who was in the place where the two flames met. At last I understood that it was my *witness in Heaven*.[12]

Elsewhere, to illustrate the motif of the rejoining of "like with like" Najm Kobrà said: "Each time a flame goes up from you, behold a flame descends from Heaven toward you."[13]

5. SHAMSODDĪN LĀHĪJĪ (d. 912/1506)

In the fifteenth century, in 877/1473, Shamsoddīn Lāhījī wrote, in Persian, a summary of Shi'ite Sufism as a commentary on a long poem, also in Persian, *Golshan-e Rāz* (*The Rose Garden of Mystery*), which had been composed in the preceding century by a famous mystic from Azerbaijan, Maḥmūd Shabestarī (who died in 720/1317 at the age of thirty-three). This long poem has remained a *vade mecum* for all Iranian Sufis. Interspersed throughout Lāhījī's commentary itself are memorabilia that afford precious witness to mystic experience. We offer here three of these ecstatic confessions. The first tells of a vision during which all being is heard by the mystic in a song of ecstasy, "Ego sum Deus." One detail (the snare holding the foot) is somewhat reminiscent of the opening of Avicenna's "Tale of the Bird." The two others introduce the motif of the Black Light (*nūr-e siyāh*).

Shamsoddīn Lāhījī writes:

> One night, after prayers were finished and the liturgical recitation prescribed for the nocturnal hours, I continued to meditate. Absorbed in ecstasy, I had a vision. There was a *khānqāh* [a Sufi

---

[12] *Ibid.*, sec. 83, p. 39 of Arabic text.
[13] *Ibid.*, pp. 206–210.

> lodge], extremely lofty. It was open, and I was inside the *khānqāh*. Suddenly I saw that I was outside. I saw that the entire universe, in the structure it presents, consists of light. Everything had become one color [*yak-rang*], and all the atoms of all the beings proclaimed "Ego sum Deus" [*Anā 'l-Ḥaqq*] each in the manner proper to its being and with the force particular to each. I was unable to interpret properly what manner of being had made them proclaim this. Having seen these things in my vision, an intoxication and an exaltation, a desire and an extraordinary delectation were born within me. I wanted to fly in the air, but I saw that there was something resembling a piece of wood at my feet which prevented my taking flight. With violent emotion, I kicked the ground in every possible manner until this piece of wood let go. Like an arrow shooting forth from the bow, but a hundred times stronger, I rose and moved into the distance. When I arrived at the first Heaven, I saw that the moon had split, and I passed through the moon. Then returning from this state and absence [*ghaibat*], I found myself again present.

These last lines are an allusion to the koranic verse on the splitting of the moon. Of course, the reference is not to that heavenly body's physical mass, but to *bāṭin al-falak*, the esoteric Heaven of the Moon, the attainment of which constitutes the first step of mystic ascension.[14]

Two other memorabilia report in gripping terms two perceptions of the Black Light, which is beyond the perception of the rational intellect. We do not dwell here on this notion of the Black Light in the spiritual experience of Sufism,[15] but simply insert a translation of Lāhījī's Persian text. It involves a visionary experience in a dream, either during sleep, or in a state halfway between sleep and wakefulness. Lāhījī writes:

> I saw that the Black Light covered the entire universe, so completely that everything had the color of this light. Intoxicated and light-headed, I was submerged in this light. Rays of this light joined in me, and rapidly pulled the whole of my being upward. It is impossible for me to describe how with each pull I was raised up several millennia so that I was given access to the first Heaven and saw there many strange and wonderful things. From there, another pull, and I was lifted to the second Heaven. And so it continued, each new pull leading me from Heaven to Heaven. In each Heaven I saw an infinite number of marvels. Finally I reached the Heaven of the Throne ['*arsh*, the Sphere of Spheres]. There, without quantity, quality, or dimension, the light of the theophany [*nūr-e tajallī-ye*

---

[14] Cf. H. Corbin, *Trilogie ismaélienne*, Bibliothèque iranienne, vol. 9 (Paris: Adrien-Maisonneuve, 1961), p. 121 n. 157.
[15] On the concept of the Black Light, cf. Corbin, *Physiologie de l'homme de lumière*, pp. 219–237, and *Trilogie ismaélienne*, pp. 154 ff.

Ḥaqq] shone upon me. I saw the Divine Majesty without modality. During this theophany I was completely annihilated to myself [fānī moṭlaq] and without consciousness [bī shoʿūr]. Then I came back to myself in this world. Once again the Divine Being appeared to me. Once again I was annihilated to myself and placed outside all limitations. Everything happened as if I no longer existed, then I came back to myself in this world. Then the Divine Being reappeared, and I again ceased to exist. But once I had found my superexistence in God, I saw that this absolute light [nūr-e moṭlaq], was I [man-am]. Whatever fills the universe is I; other than myself there is nothing. The eternal being, the demiurge of the universe is I. Everything is subsistent in me. In this mystic state, strange and wonderful theosophical knowledge was imparted to me concerning the inner being of the universe; for example, the theosophic understanding of these questions: Why the Throne [ʿarsh, the Ninth Heaven] is so crystalline as to have no star in it? Why the totality of fixed stars is in the eighth Heaven? What is the reason for a different star in each of the other Heavens? Why do angelic beings not show themselves visibly in the world of the elements? and other similar questions which cannot be expressed as they ought to be, and which only the mystic who has experienced them can understand.[16]

Since it contains all the great themes of mystic experience, so complete an ecstatic confession would require a long commentary. Moreover, Shamsoddīn Lāhījī has left us still another account of the Black Light experience. This time there is a difference of tonality in the visionary dream.

Writes the sheikh: "I saw myself present in the world of light. Mountains and deserts were a rainbow of colored light, red, yellow, white, blue. I experienced an overwhelming nostalgia for them. I became as, though struck by madness and was carried outside myself by the violence of the presence and of the deep emotion I experienced. Suddenly I saw that the Black Light had enveloped the entire universe. Heaven and earth, and everything in them, had all become Black Light and now I submerged myself totally in this light, losing consciousness." [17]

Here, the Black Light reveals the very secret of being, which can only "be" as "made to be." All being has a double face, a face of light and a face that is black. The average man sees only the face of light, the face of day without understanding it—the apparent evidence of his act of existence. His black face, seen by the mystic, is his poverty. He lacks whatever it takes to be; he is incapable of providing for himself in order to be what he has to be. This is the inessence of his essence. The totality of his being is the face of day and the face of night; the face of light is the shap-

---

[16] *Ibid.*, pp. 172–173.
[17] Cf. Corbin, *Physiologie de l'homme de lumière*, p. 231.

ing of his inessence into an essence by the absolute subject. The vision of Black Light in Lāhījī has something in common with the second of the ecstatic confessions of Mīr Dāmād which we discuss next: the "great hidden outcry of the beings," the "silent outcry" of their metaphysical anguish.

6. MĪR DĀMĀD (d. 1041/1631)

Mīr Dāmād is one of the most powerful spiritual figures in the Safavid renaissance in Iran, one of the principal masters of what is called the School of Ispahan, and master of thought for several generations of Shi'ite philosophers and theosophists. Mollā Ṣadrā Shīrāzī, his most famous student, and many others with him, prove how false it would be to speak of a paralysis in Islamic thought because of rigid, exclusive Aristotelianism. There is no doubt that the phenomenon of this philosophical renaissance is peculiar to Iran, and, again no doubt, it was specifically stimulated by the problems that the Shi'ite prophetology presented. In any event, there is here neither paralysis nor exclusive Aristotelianism. A type of *ishrāqī* philosophy predominates; that is, it brought together, according to the wish of Sohrawardī, the deepened philosophical formation of a metaphysician and the spiritual experience of the mystic. Mīr Dāmād is a difficult author. He has a solid reputation as an abstruse philosopher, but he has at the same time the vibrant soul of the emotive mystic.[18]

He has left us two ecstatic confessions. The first is particularly characteristic of Shi'ite spirituality, in the sense that the motif of the personal guide, which we have met in several guises, assumes here first and foremost the form of the Imam, which literally means the "guide." We saw that in Twelver Shi'ism, one or more of the twelve Imams could be involved. In this case, it will be specifically the first Imam who teaches the visionary how mentally to surround himself with the presence of the Fourteen All-Pure: the Prophet, Fatima the Radiant (his daughter, from whom the line of Imams takes its origin), and the twelve Imams.

This confession, which illustrates so well the outlines of Shi'ite consciousness, is dated from the month of Ramadan in 1011/1602 (Mīr Dāmād must have been then a little more than thirty years old). The dream took place in the mosque of the holy city of Qomm (88 miles southwest of Tehran). After his afternoon prayer, Mīr Dāmād remained seated on his heels, facing, as always, the Qibla. Soon he was overcome by a

---

[18] Cf. H. Corbin, "Confessions extatiques de Mīr Dāmād, maître de théologie à Ispahan (d. 1041/1631)," in *Mélanges Louis Massignon* (Institut Français de Damas, 1956), I, 331-378.

certain drowsiness; he experienced a kind of rapture. He saw before him two figures of light; and he knew them to be the Prophet and the first Imam. Then the Imam taught him a "prayer of protection." It consists of these affirmations: the Prophet is before me; Fatima the Radiant is above me, guarding my head; the first Imam is at my right; the eleven other Imams are at my left; behind me are the five Companions.[19]

The mental iconography is characteristic. The four groups are placed as in a *manḍala*. (It should be noted here that the same archetypal disposition may be found in Najmoddīn Kobrà, in a Jewish prayer, and in a figure illustrating the Robert Fludd edition of the *Summum Bonum*.)[20]

The presence of Fatima is very significant: in the center and overarching the visionary's field of consciousness (she corresponds here to Sophia-Anima). The Shiʿite consciousness of this prayer is so well revealed that it came into common usage and appears in the collections of prayer (*euchologia*). All the conditions determining the "symbolism of the center" seem united to indicate to us the bearing of this ecstatic dream.

This bearing we can understand, provided we consider all the levels embraced by Shiʿite imamology. The *plērōma* of the Fourteen All-Pure (*chahārdeh maʿṣūm*) is meditated and understood not only in the ephemeral earthly apparition of the persons composing it, but rather in the reality of these persons considered as precosmic eternal entities manifesting themselves to and on all the levels of the universe. Their eternal birth takes place in the world of the *lāhūt* (Godhead) where they are, as primordial theophanies, the divine Names and Attributes. They are all that our knowledge and devotion can attain of divinity, avoiding both agnosticism (*taʿṭīl*) and anthropomorphism (*tashbīh*). They are consequently the very referents of all conceivable relationship between the hidden deity, the *absconditum,* and ourselves. They are the operant operations of the divinity, the agents of cosmogony, while in their preeternal substance they assume a mode of being analogous to the *aiōnes* of the Valentinian gnosis, with the result that this imamology assumes in Shiʿite theosophy a role homologous to that of Christology in a theology of gnostic character. Here we can understand what was indicated above in section 1. The appearance of the Imams was the source of the *walāyat;* as such, it is the principle of the continuation of an esoteric prophetology until the end of our *aiōn*. Likewise we understand why these figures dominate Shiʿite consciousness as much in its speculative life as in its visionary dreams.

[19] Cf. *ibid.,* pp. 356–358; the complete text of this prayer is the account of initiation in a dream.
[20] Cf. Corbin, *Physiologie de l'homme de lumière,* p. 202 n. 81, and "Confessions extatiques," p. 358 n. 2.

The second ecstatic confession of Mīr Dāmād relates to an event that did in fact occur some twelve years later (1023/1614). The circumstances differ. Mīr Dāmād has become a teacher, his interior experience has deepened. The vision no longer takes place in a mosque, but in a solitary place, a private retreat. Even its date affords an indication that connects it specifically to the Shiʿite mental universe, and thereby even to the first of his visionary dreams. Indeed this date is actually the 14 Shaʿbān in 1023. It is during the night of the 14 to the 15 Shaʿbān that the anniversary of the birth, in 255/869, of the Imam of our times, the Twelfth, Hidden Imam, is celebrated by special rituals and spiritual exercises. The vision was brought on for Mīr Dāmād by the recitation of a *dhikr* using the double divine name of al-Ghanī, He who suffices unto himself, al-Moghnī, He who satisfies, He who makes suffice, who gives being. Fashioned by this meditation, the vision resembles the experience of the Black Light discussed in dealing with Shamsoddīn Lāhījī. The image implied in the double divine name brings into sudden and intense dramatic vision the Avicennian theory of the world. That Iranian Avicennism should bring forth such spiritual experiences is one of the best answers for those who would deny Avicenna any mystic qualities. No doubt they have not read him in the same manner as Mīr Dāmād read his predecessors and students. As for us, we have but to retain their testimony.

The text of this ecstatic confession of Mīr Dāmād cannot be reproduced here.[21] The language is beautiful and difficult, and rigorously precise; the richness of its visual and sonorous images is particularly striking ("the great silent clamor of beings"). The text is reminiscent of Avicenna's "Tale of the Bird," and of the narrative of Plotinus' ecstasy which inspired so many *spirituales* in Islam. "Often I awoke to myself in escaping from my body a stranger to all else, seeing in the inner depths of myself a beauty as marvelous as possible" (*Enneads* IV.8, 1). The vocabulary of the Arabic version of Plotinus recurs in Mīr Dāmād, but there is this difference: The Plotinus version is an ecstasy of triumphant joy, the ecstasy of Mīr Dāmād culminates in a paroxysm of sadness, evoked by the visual and auditive experience of total anguish. Nevertheless, when he was himself again, and had awakened from his visionary dream, he retained a nostalgic desire for it because ultimately his visions strengthened one another. Together they communicate the Shiʿite ethos which could not be better characterized than by Luther's paradox, *desperatio fiducialis*.[22] This despair, which harbors an unshakable con-

---

[21] *Ibid.*, pp. 365–371, Arab text and French translation.
[22] Cf. Corbin, the studies cited in n. 1 above; "L'Imam caché et la rénovation de l'homme en théologie shīʿite," *Eranos-Jahrbuch*, XXVIII (Zurich, 1960); "Pour une morphologie de la spiritualité shīʿite," *Eranos-Jahrbuch*, XXIX (1961).

fidence toward and despite everything, is that same mood we sense in the masters of one school in modern Shiʿism, the Shaikhī.

7. SHAIKH AḤMAD AḤSĀʾĪ (d. 1241/1826) AND THE SHAIKHĪ SCHOOL

Shaikh Aḥmad Aḥsāʾī was born to a Shiʿite Arab family in 1166/ 1753 at al-Aḥsāʾ, in Bahrein, on the eastern part of the Arabian coastal peninsula in the Persian Gulf (a region famous at one time for the tiny "socialist" Qarmaṭian state established there and visited by Nāṣer-e Khosraw in the fifth/eleventh century). Shaikh Aḥmad lived in Persia for more than fifteen years. Were it not for the enthusiasm he found there, there would never have been what is now called Shaikhism (from Shaikh Aḥmad, as *shaikh par excellence*). I can find no better way to characterize this movement, which is very much alive today (with its principal center at Kerman), except to say that at that time it was a movement of "reawakening." It was not a reformation movement in the modern sense of the term, but a restoration of the entire Twelver Shiʿite theosophy in a flowering of all the teachings of the holy Imams. Nevertheless, as a classical example of the refusal to allow theology to be degraded to pure jurisprudence, the Shaikhī school was a rupture with what may be called official Shiʿism. It continues the great tradition of Shiʿite gnosis (*ʿirfān-e shīʿī*).

The work accomplished by Shaikh Aḥmad and his five successors down to our own time is considerable. It includes more than a thousand titles in Arabic and Persian.[23] It can be said of Shaikh Aḥmad that he summarizes and epitomizes in his person the fundamental *imāmī* consciousness that is the source of all doctrine. In a short autobiography intended for his son, he relates ten or twelve visionary dreams that took place during his adolescence, their appearance having been prefaced by a number of premonitory dreams.

There was first the vision of a young man, holding a book, who taught the visionary an admirable *taʾwīl* (a spiritual exegesis) of two koranic verses (87:2-3) condensing elevated philosophic teachings. After this the young Aḥmad reacts with radical distaste to taking the study of grammar and pure philosophy as an end in itself. He begins to associate with several sheikhs, but none is able to teach him anything resembling what he had learned in the dream.

At the same time "he absented himself" more and more; he was

---

[23] Cf. H. Corbin, "L'École shaykhie en théologie shīʿite," *Annuaire de l'École pratique des Hautes-Études,* Section des sciences religieuses (1960–1961), pp. 1–59.

present to his family only "physically." "I saw then so many things that it is impossible for me to relate them." Among "these things" there is a motif that returns many times: it involves climbing to the terrace of the house (as, it will be remembered, Rūzbehān did) or climbing to the summit of some high mountain. From Heaven there descended a mysterious, intangible, unreal object that he was to catch. Then one night, in a visionary state, he saw himself entering a mosque: he found himself in the presence of three people who, he was to learn, were the second Imam (Ḥasan ibn ʿAlī), the fourth Imam (ʿAlī Zain al-ʿĀbidīn), and the fifth Imam (Muḥammad Bāqir). A whole series of dreams of personal initiation began with this vision, and this first encounter calls to mind many of the features of Mīr Dāmād's vision in the mosque of Qomm (cf. sec. 6, above). Aḥmad asked the Imam to teach him a prayer or poem, the recitation of which would thereafter suffice to provoke another apparition. A text was given, which we can read since he transcribed it in full. But afterward, even though assiduously recited, the prayer produced no vision. Finally he understood that it had been the Imam's intention to lead him to shape his interior being according to the spiritual meaning hidden in the poem.

As he himself would explain later, it was this conformation of his being, this "perfect agreement," which made possible another sequence of visions. They inaugurated a lifetime of intimacy with each of the Fourteen All-Pure: the Prophet, Fatima, each of the twelve Imams, down to the Hidden Imam. "In the Heavens, in Paradise, in a suprasensible world, and in the *barzakh,* I saw strange and wonderful dreams, figures and colors which dazzle the intelligence."

These dreams can be very exactly described as "initiatory": which they are to the point that doctrines later developed in many writings are inseparable from the teachings thus received in dreams. These visionary experiences reached their high point when Shaikh Aḥmad saw the tenth Imam (ʿAlī Naqī) in a dream holding a bundle of papers. These were the *ijāzāt* (authorizations to teach) which each of the twelve Imams bestowed on him.[24] The spiritual fact can only be recorded, seeking not so much what explains it as what it implies. The experiences of a Shaikh Aḥmad, like those of all the great visionaries, have the characteristics of a basic phenomenon (*Urphänomen*) as irreducible as the perception of sound or color. The phenomenology of religious experience ought neither to deduce it from something else, nor to reduce it to something else by illusory causal explanations. It ought to discover what form of consciousness is presupposed by the perceptions of events and worlds inaccessible to the common consciousness. On their part, the ontology and

[24] *Ibid.,* pp. 12–14.

cosmology of the Shaikhīs insist on a mode of existence for an intermediate world (the *mundus imaginalis,* cf. sec. 8, below) which authenticates and guarantees validity of visionary perception.

Shaikh Aḥmad Aḥsā'ī's first successor was his most intimate disciple, Sayyed Kāẓem Reshtī (d. 1259/1843).[25] We particularly note the fact that it was Fatima, the daughter of the Prophet and the pole of Shi'ite devotion, who in a dream revealed Shaikh Aḥmad's existence to the young Kāẓem, his rank, and that he could be found in Yazd in southeast Iran. Sayyed Kāẓem was then fifteen years of age; he lived at Resht in northwest Iran. In one way or another, and against the will of his family, he succeeded in reaching Yazd and became the sheikh's inseparable companion. The body of his own work is also considerable.

The same spiritual traits appear again in another extraordinarily powerful personality, Moḥammad Kerīm Khān Kermānī (d. 1268/1870), who was the second successor of Shaikh Aḥmad Aḥsā'ī.[26] He belonged by birth to the imperial Qājār family. As early as his adolescence, he had embarked on a program of studies comparable to that of Pico della Mirandola. He left an enormous number of writings (260 volumes) encompassing the totality of knowledge, including such scientific preoccupations as the theory of color, making him something of an Iranian Goethe.

We can only touch here on certain characteristics of the visionary forms which marked the dreams of his adolescence as they had in previous cases. These we know from a very brief autobiography. His mother had had, since before his birth, symbolic and premonitory dreams, and we have the impression that the visionary perceptions of her son form a kind of sequel to them. The autobiography relates one dream in which the young man saw a strange machine rising to the highest Heavens; there were steps, but most of the people preferred to find a seat and sit down. One of his companions tried to reach the top without success. He knew by one of those intuitions that come in dreams that whoever reached the summit would make the apparatus work and would become a guide for the others. In fact he was successful and took control of the rudder.

If we look for the source of the spiritual courage disclosed by this visionary dream, it is to be found once again in a direct relationship with the suprasensible world of the holy Imams. The autobiography relates, among others, two dreams. The first was a presentation of the eighth Imam, 'Alī Reẓā, whose sanctuary at Mashhad was the center of Iranian devotion. The second was a visitation by the ninth Imam, Muḥammad Javād, which assumed the aspect of a true personal initiation after which the sheikh announced that he had made a resolution he formulated as

---

[25] *Ibid.,* pp. 25–28.
[26] *Ibid.,* pp. 28–34.

follows: "Thereafter I was careful to scrutinize hidden things; I had the mental perception, the interior vision of the holy Imams and felt myself guided by them. Thereafter I had direct recourse to them, and no one else, for knowledge. I profess nothing that is not based on them. I acquiesce [*taqlīd*] to no one else. All my understanding results from my interior vision, from the doctrine of the Imams who guide my spiritual seeking. Nothing else." [27]

So it is that the Shaikhī school fastened on to a philosophy wherein the enormous corpus of traditions (*aḥādīth* and *akhbār*) extending back to the holy Imams bore fruit and was itself extended to the whole range of knowledge. We have only started to study this unique phenomenon.

This account of the visionary dream in Islamic spirituality is incomplete because to render it complete we should have had to gather several dreams that attest to the extraordinary importance in the most intimate life of Shiʿite consciousness of the so-called Hidden or Awaited Imam. As a child five years old, he disappeared on the very day his father, the eleventh Imam, Ḥasan ʿAskarī, died (260/873). The "minor occultation" began then. In 330/941, the "major occultation" began—it still continues—when the last *nāʾib* or representative of the Imam, having received from him an order not to name a successor, died with these words: "Now the matter belongs to God alone." These words well define the Shiʿite ethos.

I cannot even outline here the hagiography of the Hidden Imam, which is practically unknown outside the Shiʿite world.[28] But I do say this: The secret history of the Twelfth Imam, which begins with the "minor occultation," is a history of *real* events, but it is not a reality open to critical history. For more than ten centuries the figure of the Hidden Imam dominates all Shiʿite religious consciousness; it *is* indeed the history of that consciousness for the more than ten centuries that Shiʿism has lived in the company of the mysterious Twelfth Imam, lived in the secret of a passionate devotion, in the secret of an eschatological expectation that has never been trapped by imposture. The Hidden Imam resides in Hūrqālyā, one of the mystic cities of the *mundus imaginalis* (ʿ*ālam al-mithāl*). He is to be seen only in visionary dreams; if he has been encountered it is realized only after the event. Stories abound, filling volumes.

Elsewhere[29] I have given a long account of a dream experienced by one of my young Iranian friends about which he very willingly told me.

[27] Cf. Corbin, "Pour une morphologie," p. 79.
[28] Cf. Corbin, "L'Imam caché."
[29] Cf. Corbin, "De la philosophie prophétique en Islam shīʿite," pp. 104–105.

The case is particularly typical, as the dreamer, a man of less than thirty, had brilliantly completed studies in Europe and so had been exposed to all the conditions of a spiritual uprooting. The dream in question bears all the characteristics of an initiation dream. After having surmounted redoubtable obstacles, the dreamer becomes aware of the *house of the Imam* and understands that the distance that separates him from it is at the same time the measure and the meaning of his life on earth. Yet this dream, along with many another, is irrefutable testimony to the ineradicable presence at the heart of Shiʿite consciousness of the "Awaited Imam." There is no better answer to give those who would ask what all our stories mean for our times than the testimony of this young "modern" Shiʿite in modern Iran.

8. *MUNDUS IMAGINALIS* (*ʿĀLAM AL-MITHĀL*)

To bring this paper to a close, I wish simply to return to the prophetic gnoseology that makes prophetology itself the basis for the categories of a superior, suprasensible knowledge, a *hierognosis*. This gnoseology provides the visionary with precise criteria for avoiding going astray. Hence the remarkable coherence of the dreams we have been reading. This aptitude for inner vision (*baṣīra*) is a charisma of Islamic spirituality which it behooves us to keep in mind.

If we wish to understand, and understand in depth, the meaning of these visions, we do not perhaps need to be visionaries ourselves, but at least we must follow the direction of this "gesture" and work toward whatever it is they are pointing to, rather than merely to concentrate on the materiality of their gesture. We must look at whatever their finger is pointing to, rather than be content with having seen the finger point.

Our *spirituales* have been remarkably conscious of this themselves. Several times, notably in speaking of the mysterious world in which the Hidden Imam resides, we have used the words *ʿālam al-mithāl*. In order to establish the meaning or the noetic value of their visionary dreams, and of their suprasensible perceptions in general, our *spirituales* have been led to develop the ontology of a *third world* halfway between the world of sensible perception and the world of intelligibility.

Our authors identify this third world as the "eighth clime" (outside and beyond the "seven climes" of classical geography), or as the *ʿālam al-mithāl,* the *mundus imaginalis,* the imaginal world. We must avoid here at all costs the word "imaginary" which to us indicates something unreal, a qualification that presupposes the total degradation of the imaginative perception.

We are not dealing here with irreality. The *mundus imaginalis* is a world of autonomous forms and images (*moʿallaqa,* "in suspense," that is, not inherent in a material substratum like the color black in a black table, but "in suspense" in the place of their appearance, in the imagination, for example, like an image "suspended" in a mirror). It is a perfectly real world preserving all the richness and diversity of the sensible world but in a spiritual state. The existence of this world presupposes that it is possible to leave the sensible state without leaving physical extension. It could be described as a *quarta dimensio* and related to the expression *spissitudo spiritualis* used by Henry Moore, the Cambridge Platonist, to describe something similar. Sohrawardī (d. 587/1191) was the first in Islam to establish organically the ontology of this *mundus imaginalis* which became very important for ʿIbn Arabī, for Mollā Ṣadrā Shīrāzī, and for all their disciples.[30]

Neither the physical senses nor the pure intellect are the organs apprehending this world; it is grasped by "suprasensible senses," essentially an *imaginative consciousness.* As we have said, we must be careful not to confuse this imaginative power with "fantasy," or imaginal reality with the imaginary. In the West, Paracelsus already remarked, the fantasy is only a mental game without basis in nature; it is "the cornerstone [*Eckstein*] of the fools." We, on the contrary, must posit that "the imagination is the incarnation of thought in image and the placing of the image *in being.*" For this reason, imaginal knowledge apprehends its proper object with as much right and validity as the senses and the intellect do theirs.

Our writers—ʿIbn Arabī, Mollā Ṣadrā Shīrāzī, in particular—have developed considerably the theory of an imagining power (*imaginatrice*), stating carefully the criteria that permit discrimination between true imagination and what we would call hallucination. Moreover, Mollā Ṣadrā returns frequently in his books to a thesis dear to him: the active imagination is like the intellect, a purely spiritual faculty whose existence is not conditioned by the physical organism.[31]

This theory of imaginative knowledge is basic. On it, in fact, rests the validity of suprasensible perceptions, visionary dreams, and therefore, of prophetic visions without which there would be no prophetic religions. Last, it is on this third world as the realm of "subtle bodies" that these writers base their philosophy or physics of resurrection.

[30] On the *ʿālam al-mithāl,* cf. H. Corbin, *Terre céleste et corps de résurrection: de l'Iran mazdéen a l'Iran shīʿite* (Paris: Buchet-Chastel, 1961), containing the translation of many texts.
[31] *Ibid.;* H. Corbin, "La place de Molla Sadra Shirazi (*ca.* 1050/1640) dans la philosophie iranienne," *Studia Islamica,* XVIII (1962), 81–113; "Mundus imaginalis' ou l'Imaginaire et l'imaginal," *Cahiers internationaux de symbolisme,* 6 (1965), 1–26.

It is clear that the analysis of visionary dreams involves a complex of themes from which they are impossible to separate. Here we have had to limit ourselves to a few indications trying to compensate for brevity by references to earlier studies.

I close with these lines of Sohrawardī: "When you learn in the treatises of the ancient sages that there exists a world with dimensions and extension other than this world of the senses and other than the pleroma of the intelligibles, a world of innumerable cities . . . do not hastily cry 'lie,' because this world the pilgrims of the spirit succeed in contemplating and they find there every object of their desire."

That this affirmation by our *spirituales* of the existence of a *mundus imaginalis* is sometimes explained as "flight" from what one has agreed to term reality, is symptomatic of the metaphysical impotence of our time. For if one takes the trouble to analyze this concept of "reality," the rejection of the *mundus imaginalis* on its part appears very much like a flight into external reality. In fact, all the rationalistic explanations by causal reduction originate in a "poor man's philosophy" on which there is no need to dwell further. The ontology of the *mundus imaginalis* and the theory of the active imagination in Mollā Ṣadrā remind us that the human being has powers that our Western civilization has perhaps paralyzed or atrophied.

We have just heard Sohrawardī denounce those who refuse all noetic and ontological value to visionary dreams. This reaction is not then simply a so-called "modern" attitude. What the coherence of the discussion does impose is, however, a recognition that this negation proceeds from certain philosophical presuppositions.

From the beginning, a frank explanation of these presuppositions is in order. Very quickly, then, it comes out that on both sides irreducible positions have been taken which precede, and therefore exceed, all rational motivations. It is best to admit this honestly. For one reason or another, the causal reduction of visionary dreams to an explanation anchored in psychology, sociology, or history proceeds from agnosticism. We have spoken here of the "Islamic gnostics." Can a gnostic be really understood by an agnostic?

AUTHOR'S NOTE: Dr. G. E. von Grunebaum has kindly called my attention to a study that appeared after my text was written, which noted that dream visions as phases and tools of spiritual progress were already recorded for the early mystic, al-Ḥakīm at-Tirmidhī (d. probably 898). An angel would appear to his wife in a dream and ask her to communicate various injunctions or certain esoteric information, for instance, regarding the meaning of the ninety-nine names of God, to her husband. A good many of these dreams, in which the language used by the angel appears to have been Persian, were preserved by at-Tirmidhī in his autobiographical statement known as *Buduww Shaʾn;* cf. M. K. Masud, "al-Ḥakīm al-Tirmidhī's *Buduww Shaʾn,*" *Islamic Studies* (Karachi), IV (1965), 315–343 (where, p. 325, some literature is listed and the full text is edited on pp. 331–343).

24

Dream, Imagination, and ʿĀlam al-mithāl

FAZLUR RAHMAN

This paper deals not with dreams in the Muslim culture but with a spiritual aspect of late medieval Islam which can only be described as a living dream. The Arabic term used to describe it is *ʿālam al-mithāl,* the "world of images." And it is the genesis and development of this doctrine of the world of images which I discuss here.

The doctrine of a "realm of images" (*ʿālam al-mithāl*) is a specific product of medieval Muslim mysticism. (Note that the word *mithāl,* pl. *muthul,* lit. "a likeness," is sometimes applied to Platonic ideas, but the two uses are quite different.) It arose partly from philosophical prophetology, that is to say, the Muslim philosophers' attempt to establish a morphological structure of the prophetic revelation, and partly from a desire to explain certain religious eschatological doctrines. Generally speaking, the former constitutes the historical antecedent while the latter supplies the basic content of this highly interesting doctrine.

The Muslim philosophers, especially Avicenna (Ibn Sīnā, d. 1037), laid great emphasis in their prophetology on the figurizing function of imagination in the prophetic revelation. The human soul, provided it is pure and strong enough, can contact the unseen in waking life as well as in dreams: all that is required is a withdrawal of the soul from the tumult of sensory life.

This is a Greek doctrine and is clearly stated by Plutarch.[1] But just as in dreams the role of the imagination is fundamental in that it transforms the purely spiritual truth into symbols by certain laws of motion governing the movement of images, so in waking life when the Prophet receives spiritual revelation, it becomes clothed in the form of images and figures. According to Ibn Sīnā, just as dreams require interpretation (*taʿbīr*, lit. "carrying across to the other side of a river"), so does revelation require, in varying degrees, a symbolic interpretation (*taʾwīl*, lit. "carrying back to the source or the initial point"). This is how al-Fārābī and Ibn Sīnā explain psychologically the positive or technical revelation such as the Bible and the Koran.[2]

Even though imagination, according to Avicenna, plays this crucial role, he never asserts that images have an ontological existence outside the experiencing subject. In addition to this psychologico-epistemological approach to the subject of imagination, however, there are traces in Avicenna's treatise *al-Risāla al-Aḍḥawīya* of an eschatological doctrine (neither affirmed nor denied by Avicenna himself), which seem to give to imagination a quasi-ontological, if certainly not a full ontological, status. He says:

> Some scholars say that when the soul leaves the body and carries the imaginative faculty along with it [i.e., in the case of the intellectually undeveloped souls] . . . it is impossible for it to be absolutely free from the body. It then imagines that it is experiencing pains by way of the usual physical chastisements, and all that it used to believe during its earthly life [i.e., about the afterlife] would happen to it after death. . . . These scholars say that it is not impossible that the soul should imagine an agreeable state of affairs and that it should experience, in afterlife, all that is mentioned in the prophets' revelations—gardens and houris. . . ."[3]

Some underdeveloped souls are also said to become good or bad demons after death, thanks to their extraordinary power of imagination.

Who are the "scholars" mentioned here by Avicenna? He is referring possibly to Muslim esotericists, but more probably to those who professed a type of Gnostic doctrine in the Middle East where a great deal of fermentation of religious ideas existed as the result of the confluence of Semitic religion and Greek philosophy. The theory, which pre-

---

[1] F. Rahman, *Prophecy in Islam* (London, 1958), p. 72 n. 27.
[2] al-Fārābī, *al-Madīna al-Fāḍila,* chap. xxv; Avicenna, *Kitāb al-Shifāʾ*, Psychology, ed. F. Rahman (London, 1959), IV. 3; cf. Rahman, *Prophecy in Islam,* chap. ii, sec. ii and notes, pp. 36 ff.
[3] Avicenna, *al-Risāla al-Aḍḥawīya,* pp. 124–125.

supposes a considerable development in the field of eschatology, apparently aims at doing justice both to Greek philosophical principles and to the doctrine of physical retribution in some modified form. It is an alternative to the theory adopted by al-Fārābī (who sought to establish it on a koranic basis), namely, that only intellectually developed souls survive and are blessed, that undeveloped souls simply perish, and that, therefore, there cannot be any talk of punishment in the Hereafter.[4]

According to Porphyry, the human soul leaves the earthly body at death in a pneumatic encasement which it slowly discards during its ascent, and, according to another view, this pneumatic body changes according to the desires and wishes of the soul.[5] This doctrine, although it does not give to the image full ontological status, has nevertheless pushed its reality to the farthest possible limit on the subjective side; indeed, it seems to obliterate the distinction between the subjective and the objective fields, which at this stage have become irrelevant to it, on the strength of certain phenomena of abnormal psychology. Yet, it is true that it does not assert the ontological reality of the image. This transition, as far as we know, was first effected only within Islamic mysticism, and represents an attempt to rationalize certain dogmatic beliefs, particularly of an eschatological nature.

While explaining a tradition about the "punishment in the grave" to the effect that a disbeliever is stung in his grave by ninety-nine serpents, each having seven heads, al-Ghazzālī (d. 1111) first states that this number refers to the chief vices and their numerous subdivisions which destroy human happiness. But then he goes on to say that the serpents mentioned in the tradition are not merely spiritual realities but also "real things." They really do exist, although they are perceived by "another sense" with which not everyone is endowed. In this connection al-Ghazzālī also points to the phenomenon of terrifying dreams wherein one endures real fright and pain, but, whereas the fright and the pain in such dreams are real only for the experient, the serpents that assail a wicked person in his grave are objectively existent though perceptible through another sense.[6]

Al-Ghazzālī's assertion about the objective existence of the physical objects of dogmatic theology is very different from the usual orthodox formula "we know they do exist but we do not know how." He gives them a clear ontological status but also affirms the possibility of perceiving them "through another sense." And although he does not say that these objects exist in a world of their own—the universe of images or symbols, perceived through a spiritual imagination—that step, in view of

---

[4] al-Fārābī, op. cit., chap. xxiii.
[5] Rahman, op. cit., p. 81.
[6] al-Ghazzālī, Iḥyāʾ ʿulūm al-dīn, book 40, chap. 7, on The Punishment in the Grave.

the philosophical development portrayed above, was a perfectly logical one for his successors to take. This step was taken actually by Shihāb ad-Dīn al-Suhrawardī (d. 1191) who, as far as we know, was the first to announce formally the existence of a new realm between the spiritual and the physical.[7]

The motivation behind al-Suhrawardī's affirmation of this realm, which he calls the realm of "suspended images" (*al-muthul al-muʿallaqa*) or of "pure figures" (*al-ashbāḥ al-mujarrada*), is undoubtedly the validation of dogmatic beliefs; he also claims esoteric experiences of this realm. The fully developed spiritual souls, according to al-Suhrawardī, will become pure "lights," that is, spirits in the Hereafter. But those pious souls who have not thus fully developed through "illumination," and who have followed faithfully the creedal and practical prescriptions of religions, shall not be able to rise to the status of pure spirits but shall ascend to the realm of suspended images wherein they shall enjoy the quasi-physical delights of Paradise of which they had cherished hopes. Similarly, the vicious damned shall be assigned to the same realm of pure figures, but the figures they shall live with are obnoxious and torturous. It is obvious that we have here the same theory of eschatology we encountered in Avicenna, the big difference being that from subjective imagination we have passed into a veritable realm of being, from psychology into ontology.

Here we are face to face with a situation, an order of being, where imagination *takes the place of* sense perception, and al-Suhrawardī expressly affirms that it is here that the resurrection of the body takes place, the divine figures (such as angels) become real, and all the prophetic eschatological statements come true. This is al-Suhrawardī's riposte to the denial by pure philosophers of the resurrection of the body. But the difficulty remains that in the instance of the fully developed "lights," the resurrection of the flesh is rather meaningless, and al-Suhrawardī states unequivocally that these souls cannot have a body but return to their primal source. In that event, then, what happens to their bodies is not at all clear.[8] The whole question of the relationship of the realm of pure figures with the spiritual world on the one hand and with the perceptual world on the other is very obscure. On the first point, al-Suhrawardī is completely silent and the implications of his statements are, as we have seen, contradictory. On the relationship of the world of figures with the physical world, al-Suhrawardī says, "Since these Suspended Figures are not in mirrors or in any such medium and have no substance wherein to subsist [*maḥall*], it is possible that there should exist in this [physical]

---

[7] Shihāb ad-Dīn al-Suhrawardī, *Ḥikmat al-Ishrāq*, Opera Mystica et Metaphysica, Vol. II (Tehran, 1952), pp. 230, 232–234.
[8] *Ibid.*, pp. 223 ff.

world that wherein they manifest themselves. [Thus], sometimes they [actually] move into these objects wherein they manifest themselves and this is whence the demons and devils appear [in the physical realm]."[9]

Thus, although the *ʿālam al-mithāl* is created for the very purpose of serving as a place where the incredible is rendered credible and where the miraculous is somehow made "normal," the physical world is still not saved from the encroachments of the realm of figures. Indeed, the intellects of the heavenly bodies also project angels from this realm into the mundane world and that is whence the angel of revelation physically manifests himself. Perhaps a better approach to understand the realm of figures is to construe it as a sort of "unconscious of the universe" where concrete symbols of love, hate, and fear are created. But then it would be the "unconscious of the world soul." This theory, with all its extravagance, would still bring the miraculous into the physical realm. Inasmuch as the "unconscious of the universal soul" would, from time to time, make inroads into the quotidian life, a systematic path will be opened for the miraculous. Further, there arise problems about the relationship between the world soul and the individual soul, between the world soul and the individual body, and between the individual soul and the world body, which must be solved if the doctrine is to be intelligible at all.

The pure individual souls can also create new furniture in the *ʿālam al-mithāl* and even project these figures into the realm of physical reality. This is supposed to guarantee the miracles worked by prophets and saints.[10] This doctrine is affirmed both by al-Suhrawardī and Ibn al-ʿArabī (1165–1240), the famous Sufi theosophist whose fecundity of imagination created an unprecedentedly rich content for the world of figures. Since imagination takes the place of and becomes sense perception in the world of figures, and since, according to the holders of this doctrine, physical resurrection is a phenomenon of that world, it follows that in the Hereafter physical or quasi-physical reality will follow the creative activity of imagination. Ibn al-ʿArabī says:

> The [contents of the] hereafter will be eternally created on the pattern of this world. For the people of Paradise shall say to the objects they desire "Be" and they shall be. Thus, they shall not imagine anything nor shall the thought of a new state of affairs occur to them but that it shall come into existence before their very eyes. Similarly, the people of Hell shall not entertain any fear of a greater torture than they are in but that it shall be realized in them or for them. This is exactly the realization of the idea. The hereafter requires the creation of a world from this world but it will be sensible [not

---

[9] *Ibid.*, p. 231.
[10] *Ibid.*, p. 242, ll. 10 ff.

merely mental]. By the mere existence of an idea, of an imaginative impulse [*hamm*], of a volition, desire or appetite, all this shall become sensible. In this world [of physical reality] this cannot be achieved by everyone." [11]

We thus see that the phenomena of the Hereafter are imaginary-real as is the nature of the ʿ*ālam al-mithāl*. A few pages later, however, Ibn al-ʿArabī draws an inconsistent distinction: "So also God shall bestow upon the people of Paradise desires and imaginary bliss over and above that wherein they already are; and by virtue of the mere act of a person's imagining or desiring [a higher blissful state], it would be realized in him according as he wished—if he wished it to be mental it would be mental, if he desired it to be sensible it would be sensible." [12] And so Ibn al-ʿArabī's conception of the relationship between the world of sense and the world of figures is not a whit clearer than that of al-Suhrawardī.

One of the prominent effects of the belief in the world of figures is the idea, reiterated by Ibn al-ʿArabī in several places and very commonly accepted by Sufis, that a person with strong spiritual imagination can be present, or at least can be seen, in different places simultaneously by projecting (consciously or unconsciously) his images. Ibn al-ʿArabī tells a story related to him personally by Auḥad ad-Dīn al-Kirmānī who said that when he was young, he served a spiritual guide who once fell ill with diarrhea while on a journey. The story continues:

> When we reached Tikrīt, I said to him, Master, let me go and find an anti-diarrhea medicine from the owner of the charity hospital, who was sitting in his tent with his men around him. We did not know one another but when he saw me among the throng, he stood up to me, took me by the hand, showed great kindness to me and asked me what I wanted. I described to him the condition of the master and he asked that the medicine be presented which he then gave to me. . . . When I returned to the master and gave him the medicine, I recounted to him the kindness of the administrator-owner of the charity hospital. The master smiled and said, "My son! I was greatly moved by your depth of feeling for my sake and therefore permitted you to go [to the doctor]. But when you went, I was afraid lest the hospital administrator should disappoint you by paying no heed to you. I, therefore, disengaged myself from my physical frame, entered into that of the hospital administrator, and sat in his place. . . . Then I returned to my own body!" [13]

---

[11] Ibn al-ʿArabī, *al-Futūḥāt al-Makkīya,* chap. 47.
[12] *Ibid.,* chap. 65.
[13] *Ibid.,* chap. 8.

Once the world of figures is affirmed as a reality, it is impossible in the nature of things to set limits to it. For this realm is no smaller or bigger than imagination itself. Obviously, concepts of physical impossibility or logical absurdity no longer apply there. Once the flood of imagination is let loose, the world of figures goes beyond the specifically religious motivation that historically brought it into existence in the first place, and develops into the poetic, the mythical, and the grotesque: it seeks to satisfy the relatively suppressed and starved artistic urge. Much of the contents of the ʿālam al-mithāl, as it develops later, has, therefore, nothing to do with religion but indirectly with the theater. At this point, the scope of the ʿālam al-mithāl becomes larger by far even than Paradise and Hell where, as Ibn al-ʿArabī says, anything will and does happen which anybody can imagine. Ibn al-ʿArabī devoted the eighth chapter of his al-Futūḥāt al-Makkīya to the description of the furniture of the Earth which God created from a grain of clay left over from the material used in creating Adam's body. This Earth is not just a place where the spiritual appears in the form of figures or where the physical phenomena exist in a "rarefied" form. This Earth is, indeed, so vast that the physical and the heavenly worlds, Paradise and Hell, indeed, even God's throne and everything contained in all of these—animals, men, angels, spirits, and so on—are mere specks in its spatial magnitude.

It is obvious that this Earth has itself been constructed on the model of the ʿālam al-mithāl and that it is only in the shadowy realm of those systematically cultivated waking dreams that this uncontrolled delirium is possible. Let us note some of the features of this Earth. The first thing we are told is that "many rational impossibilities, i.e., things which sound reason declares to be absurd, exist there." It is only the Gnostics, however, "for whose [spectator] eyes it [i.e., this Earth] constitutes a theater." The Gnostics and the Paradisians, when they wish to enter this world, must discard their bodies temporarily and leave them down here; even the angels must be led into it by gatekeepers. Everything on this Earth, including minerals and animals, is endowed with full rational life and talks and argues. Within this Earth there are other earths, each with separate characteristics. An earth that is made of gold has everything golden, minerals, fruits, "men," and so on. But the most exquisite earth is the "earth of saffron" compared to whose women the houris of Paradise fade into insignificance.

Time varies in the different earths; a moment in one may be a year in another. Mind quickens in that world and there is no resistance to thought. "People" work there—especially in the "earth of saffron"—all for the good, but not out of a sense of obligation. Since there is no inertia in that world and no physical or intellectual "resistance," this presumably must be true of the moral plane as well. Biologically, too, the atmosphere of that Earth has extraordinary resilience, for the very moment a fruit falls from a tree, another fruit grows, or rather instantaneously appears in ripe condition. Their boats make themselves: stones attract one another by a natural force until they join together forming a boat that runs, without any resistance, in whatever direction they want to go—and races on a sea of dust! They have multistory cities and towns just as we have multistory houses, except that they can build not only by tools and physical effort, but also by mere imagination and intention.[14]

I have quoted this description at length not just to portray the richness of this visionary realm but also to point out that there is nothing there which could not just as well be contained in the Paradise concept of dogmatic theology. For the possibilities of Paradise, are, *by definition*, absolutely limitless. But Ibn al-ʿArabī has expressly said that this is something over and above Paradise. It is also to be noted that, although Ibn al-ʿArabī insists that only Gnostics can have access to this realm, there is nothing spiritual or religious about it except Ibn al-ʿArabī's statement that this realm contains a Kaʿba that, like everything else, converses and argues rationally. The Paradise of dogmatic theology is undoubtedly a place of physical comfort and enjoyment, but it is also the home of spiritual bliss. I think it would be too much to say that the theosophist is indirectly caricaturing the theological concept of Paradise, which he himself not only accepts, but elaborates in great detail. The realm has little metaphysical significance, for Ibn al-ʿArabī not only does not discuss its relationship with, say, the spiritual world, but does not place it anywhere at all in his ontological scheme. It is obviously a development of the *ʿalam al-mithāl;* but it is also obvious, I think, that it represents an attempt to "secularize" the *ʿalam al-mithāl* and to use it primarily for artistic purposes of literary creation. This purely artistic use of the doctrine, if we are right in assessing its nature, does not seem to have found any significant following, except, to some extent, in Ṣadr ad-Dīn ash-Shīrāzī, the commentator of al-Suhrawardī, who puts certain mystical places mentioned by al-Suhrawardī in the *ʿalam al-mithāl*.[15]

Although Ibn al-ʿArabī asserts that since *ʿalam al-mithāl* is of the nature of imagination, it is intermediate between the spiritual and the physical world, the doctrine is fully developed only by subsequent thinkers. The ontological position of the *ʿalam al-mithāl* is really clearly defined in the works of Ṣadr ad-Dīn ash-Shīrāzī, known as Mullā Ṣadrā (d. 1640). Certainly there was a development of the doctrine before Mullā Ṣadrā, but it is he who formulated the organic relationship among the three

---

[14] The whole of this description comes from *ibid*.
[15] al-Suhrawardī, *op. cit.*, e.g., p. 234 (Commentary).

realms. He develops the "principle of higher possibility" enunciated by al-Suhrawardī and gives it a new interpretation. In al-Suhrawardī this principle means that the multiplicity that exists in the temporal realm must first exist in the higher realm of the intellect, and he accuses the philosophers of having rendered the ultimate reality devoid of content under the guise of their doctrine of the "absolute simplicity" of the "pure intellect" or, as he calls it, the "light of lights."[16] But al-Suhrawardī does not introduce, in this connection, his realm of pure figures as a grade of being. Mullā Ṣadrā takes the principle to mean that *nothing can exist at the lowest level unless it has passed through the upper grades of "existence,"* and conversely that *nothing moves to a higher grade of "existence" without having passed through the intermediary grades.*[17] This means that everything in the temporal world has a triple existence: from the realm of the pure intellect it descends into the ʿālam al-mithāl and thence to the physical realm. Similarly, in the "ascent" where things "return" to their source, the ʿālam al-mithāl is again traversed.

It may be difficult for us to understand what the "traversing" and "return" are, since things exist at all the three levels. The only way we can understand it is what we may understand by way of union at the level of experience. When an earthly being *experiences* the ʿālam al-mithāl and the spiritual realm, it is said to "return" to its primordial source. The "eschatological return" then can mean only the permanence of this experience. This is what Mullā Ṣadrā seems to teach in his treatise on the resurrection.[18]

In opposition both to orthodox Islam and to the philosophers, Mullā Ṣadrā maintains the doctrine of universal resurrection where not only humans and animals but even plants and minerals shall "return." Therefore, "there is no natural and material existent but that it has an imaginative form in another world and its imaginative form has a rational form in still another world above it. . . . Now, the reason for saying that every sensible form has an imaginative form within by which it is constituted and to which it 'returns,' and that similarly every imaginative form has a rational form within . . . is that whenever we perceive something . . . our imagination also takes on that form . . . which subsequently also moves into our intellect as a rational form." This would not have been the case if there had not existed an organic relationship between the sensible, the imaginative, and the rational. Similarly, with the movement in the opposite direction, when we conceive something rationally, a corresponding image figurizing it comes to exist in our

---

[16] *Ibid.*, pp. 154 ff.
[17] Mullā Ṣadrā, *Rasāʾil* (Tehran, A.H. 1302), p. 352.
[18] *Ibid.*, pp. 341–370.

imagination, and when the image in the imagination becomes very strong, it comes to exist externally before our sense-perception.[19]

In fact, the whole treatise does nothing but attempt to show that the orders of reality are intimately and organically linked with one another in a source-sequence form. But then what does the "return" mean? The answer must be: a permanent state of experience of the source, and removal of estrangement from it. In order to achieve this end, Mullā Ṣadrā, following the line of earlier philosophers, gives arguments for the "return" of the developed intellects to the divine intellect. Again following his predecessors, he puts the undeveloped souls in the ʿālam al-mithāl. But in order to make imaginative experience possible not only for animal souls, but also for matter—for otherwise the "universal return" cannot be maintained—he extends the ʿālam al-mithāl to all of these and contends that even material bodies have invisible life. To the question—What is, then, the difference between undeveloped humans and the lower beings?—his reply is that human souls, even if they are undeveloped, keep their individuality after death but that the lower orders of being are resurrected only as a species—they return to their image-idea.[20]

It is important to notice the difference of opinion among Mullā Ṣadrā, Quṭb al-Dīn ash-Shīrāzī (d. 1311), and Ibn al-ʿArabī with regard to the animal souls. According to Ṣadrā, these lose their individuality and survive only as species-image, but Quṭb al-Dīn ash-Shīrāzī (pupil of a pupil of Ibn al-ʿArabī) and Ibn al-ʿArabī affirm the existence of individual animals in the ʿālam al-mithāl. Contrary to Mullā Ṣadrā, both Ibn al-ʿArabī and Quṭb al-Dīn ash-Shīrāzī make the animal souls in the ʿālam al-mithāl fully endowed with reason. For Ibn al-ʿArabī everything there is rational, including plants and material objects, whereas, according to Quṭb al-Dīn ash-Shīrāzī, the material objects do not even have life. He tells us:

> As for the elements and their composite objects in the ʿālam al-mithāl, they have no souls. But the animals are endowed with rational souls just like human beings there. Most of these souls are those which have departed from the bodies of animals [on earth] if transmigration [of souls] is correct, or if transmigration is false, have departed from human bodies [on earth] and have attached themselves to the bodies of animals in that realm, if there have still remained in them some bad qualities. . . .[21]

---

[19] Ibid., p. 355, last line ff.
[20] Ibid., p. 350, ll. 16 ff.
[21] al-Suhrawardī, op. cit., p. 232 (Commentary).

The use of reason in the world of imagination is not at all easy to understand, I might add.

During the later centuries of the Muslim Middle Ages, the ʿālam al-mithāl increases in importance and forms an integral part of Sufi spiritual culture. Without formally denying the reality of the physical world, the Muslim spiritualists—in a milieu of political uncertainty, socioeconomic imbalance, and general external deterioration—sought refuge in a realm that was more satisfying and certainly more liquid and amenable to imaginative powers. Within Sufism there arose only one voice, that of Shaikh Aḥmad Sirhindī (d. 1625), which counseled caution and sobriety. Sirhindī accepted the ʿālam al-mithāl as other Sufis did, but he sought to divest it of its ontological status and declared it to be a mere experience. In a letter to a pupil, he wrote:

> They [the Sufis] have divided this contingent world into three: the world of spirits, the world of figures, and the physical world. They have assigned to the ʿālam al-mithāl [the world of figures] an intermediate position between the world of spirits and that of bodies. They have also said that the ʿālam al-mithāl is a kind of mirror for the phenomena of the other two worlds, reflecting their contents with an image appropriate for everything.
>
> That world [i.e., the ʿālam al-mithāl] in itself does not possess any forms or figures; these appear in it as mere reflections from the other two worlds—just like a mirror which in itself does not contain any form and whatever forms come to exist in it, come [as reflections] from outside.
>
> When this has been made clear, let it be understood that the spirit, before its attachment to the body, was in its own [spiritual] realm . . . and if, after its attachment to the body, it has descended, it has done so through its love for the world of bodies; it has nothing to do with the ʿālam al-mithāl either before or after this attachment. There is nothing more than the fact that, by the grace of God, it can sometimes contemplate some of its own conditions and states [i.e., whether good or bad] in the mirror of [that] world [of images]. . . . ʿālam al-mithāl is for seeing, not for being; the place of being is either the spiritual world or the physical world.[22]

---

[22] Shaikh Aḥmad Sirhindī, Maktūbāt (Lucknow [n.d.]), III, 57.

25

Some Aspects of Inspiration by Demons in Islam

FRITZ MEIER

INSPIRATION AND THE AVOIDANCE OF THE WORLD OF SENSES

According to the concepts of the medieval Orient, inspiration usually presupposes a man's keeping the exterior world at a distance. A diviner in ancient Arabia covered himself with a cloak, and the inspired founder of Islam, Muhammad, is once hailed *muddaththir* "covered with a cloak" (Koran 74:1). Islamic mystics often secluded themselves in gloomy cells to receive inspiration. Many times the inspiration comes by night, sometimes at dawn after a night spent in vigil. Avicenna thought that men had a "vacant, freer mind" at night than by day, since the body's distractions and the shackles of the sense organs disappeared; a mystic who lived around the year A.D. 1100 says expressly that auditory communications of the heart and of the suprasensible world are more easily established at night.

VISIONS AND DREAMS

Turned away from the world of the senses a man may wake. In the waking state he may be active or

421

passive. He is active when he concentrates. In doing so he may concentrate on a thought, or an image, to lay siege to the human soul's shadowed background until it opens. This can occur whenever the Islamic mystic concentrates on the formula that has come to be called the divine mention (*dhikr*) and whenever he meditates near a tomb, for example, in order to learn something about the dead (*tawajjuh*). In the latter, we are close to meditative contemplation of an external object with intent to penetrate the world the appearance hides. This mode of breaking through to knowledge seems to have been rarely used in Islam, but could hardly have been absent from its alchemy.

Very often, we learn of inspiration bestowed on man in a passive state, but not always without his being prepared for it. On the lowest level, these perceptions in the waking state, when visual, were generally called *wāqiʿa* (visions), and, when auditory or intellectual, *ilhām* (inspiration). The attitude of a sleeping man is passive. Whatever he perceives comes to him in a dream. But dreams, too, according to the Islamic ideas, can be prepared.

When, after forty years of nocturnal vigils, the mystic ash-Shāh al-Kirmānī (*ca.* 900) finally fell asleep and saw God in a dream he asked God why He appeared in a dream after he had sought him so long awake. God answered, "It is only thanks to your vigil that this fulfillment is granted you in your dream." On the degree of purity of the dreamer's soul depended, so it was thought, the very quality of the dream. For this reason there was in Muslim consciousness at first no difference between the value of the dream and that of the vision; this value depended solely on the personality of the dreamer or visionary.

Thus, according to one tradition, Muhammad received his first revelation and became conscious of his vocation in a dream. And sometimes one sees, as in Koran 28:7, evidence of a revelation announced in a dream: it is the revelation made to Moses' mother to give her son to Pharaoh's sister to nurse; in the correspondence in which the mystic Saif ad-Dīn al-Bākharzī (thirteenth century) tells his master Najm ad-Dīn al-Kubrà his visions, asking him for their explanation, dreams and visions alternate without being assigned different values. Yet a dream that brings truth to an ordinary person is considered to be, according to a word attributed to Muhammad, no more than the forty-sixth part of Prophecy, and mystics insist that the ordinary devotee receives visions of portent only in dreams, whereas the mystic receives them also in the waking state or in an intermediate state between waking and sleep. Kubrà writes, "What the vulgar owing to the vigor of their lower nature can experience only in a dream, the mystic experiences between waking and sleep owing to the weakness of his lower nature and the strength of his noble nature." Mystics possess a gradation of concepts designating the different degrees of apparitions in the waking state.

Nonreligious inspiration may also occur during the waking state or in sleep. The Arab singer and composer, Maʿbad (d. A.D. 743), is said to have learned of his vocation in his sleep. He was dozing alongside a rock in the basalt desert when he heard a beautiful voice singing songs he later remembered. In the same way, the singer al-Gharīd asserts having heard certain mysterious voices in a dream, voices also heard by people awake; later he composed his songs from what he had heard. A minister of the caliph Maʾmūn (ninth century) believed he had heard in a dream the beginning of a letter that earlier he had tried in vain to write. Similarly poets and others not normally given to poetry received poetic inspirations in dreams.

THE CONTENTS OF DREAMS: RELIGIOUS AND POETIC INSPIRATION ON THE SAME LEVEL

Dreams, poetry, and religious inspiration were already linked in the popular consciousness of ancient Arabia, and this trinity was apt to be judged rather negatively. Doubting Meccans, therefore, rejected the results of Muhammad's ecstasies as "a tangle of dreams, trickery, words of a poet" (Koran 21.5). The profession of faith, "There is no God but Allah," made no impression on them, and they asked rhetorically, "Shall we abandon our Gods on account of a crazy poet?" (Koran 37:34-35).

Muhammad rallied to these derogatory judgments and extended them to the diviners. He denied that his words could be taken for the words of a poet or a diviner (Koran 69:41-42). But by the very fact that on the strength of his first supernatural experience—after the clarity he had seen and the voice he had heard—he had, according to his own words, believed himself to be an ecstatic diviner, he brought into the open an intrinsic kinship between himself and the diviners; the same is true for his position vis-à-vis the poets. The trait these three groups have in common with regard to lore is inspiration, and, with regard to form, rhyme. As literature, Muhammad's revelations contained in the Koran belong with the ecstatic oracles of the ancient Arabian diviners and, like those, are distinguished from poetry only by the absence of meter. The Koran and the oracles of the diviners were not written in rhymed verse but in full or fragmentary rhymed phrases. Besides, Muhammad seems to have distinguished clearly between what was traceable to inspiration and what belonged to his own thought. This distinction stems from Muhammad's inner experiences, and we have neither the right to put, nor the possibility of putting, its accuracy in doubt. But, because with Muhammad only his inspired communications are rhymed, the rhyme is the point of reference that permits us to recognize what is inspired. In other words, whatever he succeeded in expressing in rhyme, Muhammad has transmitted as inspired.

Later, in another context, the epic Persian poet Niẓāmī (twelfth century) ranks the poets immediately after the prophets.

THE MUSES OF POETIC AND RELIGIOUS INSPIRATION AND OF INSPIRATION IN DREAMS

Poetic and religious inspiration share the possibility of coming from the same inspiring spirit. This spirit is often an unknown being who calls (*hātif*). In addition, Islam distinguished among spirits, souls of the departed, and angels. Angels include those beings who, according to philosophical speculations, command the heavenly spheres and the natural phenomena. The philosophy of the Ismaili makes no distinction between spirits—demons, that is—and the souls of the departed, for it sees in the spirits nothing but souls of the dead who have not reached the maturity necessary to ascend higher. It is commonly thought that the spirits (*jinn, arwāḥ*), whether benevolent spirits or wicked demons, belong to the earth, and that the angels have their homeland in Heaven. But on God's order angels may also descend into the deepest abysses or must fulfill specific missions on earth, while, for their part, the spirits often float in the air and may even ascend to the lowest borders of the celestial spheres. According to the Islamic concept, every human being is accompanied by two angels who write down his actions, and also by a *jinnī*, or by Satan himself, who tries by suggestion to lead him into temptation either in a dream or while awake.

Although a great many pre-Islamic Arab poets were Christians and must have been familiar with the idea of an angel, in no place is there an allusion in ancient times to inspiration coming from an angel. It is always a *jinnī*. One is tempted to adopt a theory like that of Ṭāhā Ḥusain and of D. S. Margoliouth who thought pre-Islamic poetry a later falsification introduced in the Islamic era; in fact, Islam was anxious to present pagan Arabia as an area of diabolical seductions, and in more ways than one tended to be hostile to poetry. Yet a *jinnī* is not necessarily an evil spirit, and even the word "devil" seems in contexts of this order to have had fairly good overtones. Guardian genies perhaps originated with these *jinn* who have in their behavior much in common with the Latin's *genii*, although the words are not related. Closely tied to all this, we find the present Arab word for "genius-ness" *abqariyya,* which is derived from *abqar,* the name of a country of genies.

The notion of demons who inspired poets was long maintained in Islam, even if it was often only a fiction or used in the attenuated sense of our notion of genius. Each poet has his own demon; often we are even given his name. The demon inspirer of A'shà was called Mishal, that of Mukhabbal was 'Amr, that of Bashshār b. Burd was Shiniqnāq. Since demons live longer than men, later stories sometimes have encounters of *jinn* with representatives of more recent generations. The Andalusian Ibn Shuhaid (*ca.* 1023; d. 1055) pretends a voyage on his own demon inspirer as Pegasus into the land of the genies to interview the inspirers of the ancient poets. The devil himself often passed as an inspirer.

For a number of poets Islam brought a conflict between religion and poetry. The poet Kumait hesitated, uncertain whether he should follow his poetic demon, or seek the Prophet's favor. 'Ubaidallāh b. Ziyād, who stopped writing, explained, "I did not want to bring together in my heart the words of God and those of Satan." The aging Ru'ba declared his refusal to continue writing poems with these words, "How many more times must I boastfully tell you the words of Satan?" On the other hand, Abū Nuwās, who knew exactly what he was doing, placed himself on the side of the devil.

It was Muhammad himself, however, who first breeched the wall of hostility set up against poets by giving his benediction to a poet, Hassān b. Thābit, who undertook the defense of his work. Hassān was initiated into poetry by a female demon whom he had met in a street of Medina; later when Muhammad had need of a satirical poet in his fight with the Quraish, Hassān placed himself at his disposal. He was assured that Gabriel, or the Holy Spirit (in Islam they coincide), would assist him as long as he defended God and his messenger. Ma'arrī (d. 1057) recognizes there is no distinction to be made here between this protection and inspiration, although he is doubtful about poetic inspiration brought by an angel.

Later on, the souls of the faithful departed often play the role of poetic inspirers. Kaulān (probably early tenth century), a Shi'ite poet who had composed forty-nine long poems in praise of the holy family, could not finish the first verse of the fiftieth poem; he told his ill luck to the Prophet in a dream he had in Mecca. The Prophet sent him to 'Alī who, in the course of the dream, added five and a half verses which he remembered on waking. Sometimes the supernatural inspirer employs ancient magic usages, such as spitting, to initiate a human being into poetry. There is a story about an ignorant poetaster who had come to see the Persian poet Jāmī (fifteenth century) and to tell him that in a dream the holy Khiḍr had spit in his mouth. Jāmī replied, "You did not see very well. Khiḍr wanted to spit into your face and beard, but your mouth was open, and so he hit your mouth."

To another chapter belong the stories of how the poet of Persia's national epic, Firdausī, was moved to give his poetic creation a decisive direction by the appearance in a dream of his unfortunate predecessor Daqīqī, and how Niẓāmī was moved to do the same thing on one occasion after the appearance of someone unknown who called him, and on another of Khiḍr himself. Sometimes God, too, appears as an inspirer of poetry. The Persian poet ʿAṭṭār (twelfth–thirteenth century) presents his didactic poem Ilāhī-Nāma as a "divine overflow" (faiḍ-i ilāhī). The enemies of the Ashʿarite notion, according to which all activity comes from God, have not been slow in drawing from this the obvious consequences, that is to say, ridiculing the idea that poetry also had to be a gift from God.

The picture is not greatly different with regard to religious inspiration. Here too we have at first the *jinn* as inspirers. The rhymed proverbs of the diviners of ancient Arabia were considered in part the result of inspiration by the *jinn*. The Koran explains the fact that the diviners mingle the true and the false by asserting that the demons who provided them with wisdom had listened secretly to the counsels of the angels and reported what they had only half understood; moreover, in doing this, they lied most of the time (Koran 26:223). The healer of ancient Arabia, Sālim, who must be considered as religiously inspired, inasmuch as he was a kind of shamanic magician in the widest sense of the word, was thought to be accompanied by a *jinnī*. Similarly in the thirteenth century there was in Transoxania a certain Tārābī, a miraculous medicine man, who organized a revolution against the Mongol government. "By hypocrisy and feigned asceticism and piety," our source informs us, he pretended to communicate with spirits (*parī-dārī*) who spoke to him and instructed him about supernatural things. Here, ordinarily, is where the numerous conjurers of demons, who even today attract crowds, come into the picture.

With Muhammad a new era begins, an era already heralded by what we had to say about poetic inspiration: along with, or rather, above the *jinn* appear the angels that offer inspiration, thereby devaluating the inspiration offered by the *jinn*. This devaluation appears in instances like this; from the legend of the demons who had for a long time been kept in error about the death of Solomon, the conclusion was drawn that the *jinn* were totally ignorant. Often we find scenes in which it is no longer the *jinn* who instruct men, but, inversely, devout scholars who instruct the *jinn*. Muhammad would have it that his inspiration came from a being he sometimes calls a "spirit," sometimes "Holy Spirit," and sometimes "Gabriel." Other Arab prophets who set themselves up against Muhammad, but did not have as much success, also claimed to be inspired by angels. The caliph ʿUmar I was considered a *muḥaddath* or *mukallam*, a man to whom the angels speak. Similarly theosophs of a later time laid claim to wisdom received from on high, from the Holy Spirit, or from God. Possibly what they mean by this is simply a consciousness of their dependence on the grace of inspiration, or, indeed, a desire to put the responsibility for their affirmations on a higher power. Sometimes, however, there are occult experiences at the base of these affirmations. Yaḥyà as-Suhrawardī (d. 1191) maintained that he had the contents of his *Ḥikmat al-ishrāq* from the "Holy Spitter" (*an-nāfith al-qudsī*), which means the holy spirit; Mullā Ṣadrā (d. 1640) considered his *Wāridāt al-qalbiyya fī maʿrifat ar-rubūbiyya* to be an "overflow" (*faiḍ*) from above; and Saʿīdā-i Qummī (d. 1692) wrote his *Nafaḥāt-i ilāhiyya* in rhymed prose as a "presence of God"; Abū Isḥāq-i Kāzarūnī (d. 1035) improvised his sermons, and in doing so considered himself to be the spokesman of God.

The men of religion, like the poets, were subject, then, to two groups of inspirers. Islam recognized the existence of *jinn* inspirers and was especially insistent on the possibility and reality of diabolical inspiration. For these men of religion, the difference was naturally extremely important. According to the Koran the prophets themselves could be the victims of Satan. According to Koran 22:51 there was no prophet of old who had not been, while prophesying, prompted by the devil to make false declarations at one time or other. Commentaries on Koran 53:19–20 would have Muhammad himself at one time induced to error in this way. Just as during what is called the night of destiny the angels visit the representatives of the just cause, so the *jinn* arrive to mislead the representatives of error. In Islam, judges often had the same dubious reputation as "publicans and sinners" in the New Testament. Thus, one judge was told this: "If you were a teller of edifying stories, you would have two angels to counsel you, but since you are a judge, two devils accompany you, lead you away from truth, and lure you into temptation." When the Shiʿite insurgent Mukhtār (seventh century), pretended to be the recipient of revelations, the devout did not contradict him but referred him to Koran 6:121 where it says that Satan too gives revelations. We possess in a story about the old religious poet Umayya b. abī 'ṣ-Ṣalt a mythological representation of the difference between demonic and angelic inspirations. The demon who inspired him always came from the left and liked Umayya to wear black robes. If he had come from the right and if he had liked white robes, Umayya would have become the prophet of the Arabs. In another mythological tradition, Gabriel could be recognized by becoming invisible to Mohammad as soon as his wife Khadīja uncovered her hair. According to Islamic concepts, the content of an inspiration generally indicates its source. If it fits in with recognized religious tradition it comes from God or the angels. But this concept was felt insufficient by the Muslim mystics, so, since the ninth century, they developed subtle theories for distinguishing between the insinuations of Satan and the inspiration of the angels.

Let me mention in passing that a later theory of dreams asserts the existence of an angel named Rūḥfāʾīl or Ṣādiqūn or Ṣiddīqūn who explains celestial writing to the dreamer in a prophetic dream.

DEMYTHOLOGIZING AND CONSERVATIVE TENDENCIES

Belief in an inspiration accorded Muhammad by an angel constitutes an unshakable pillar of Islam which it has never renounced. According to his own concept, Muhammad found himself at the end of a long line of precursors who had been inspired in the same way. They are called prophets because their inspirations were destined to be made public and had normative validity for all mankind. Islamic theology gives the name "revelations" (*waḥy*) to these prophetic inspirations. After Muhammad's death there could be no more. For this reason the inspirations of pious Muslims received the differentiating name of "inspiration" (*ilhām*), whose recognition was not included in the fundamentals of Islam. The inspiration of poets was widely discussed, particularly in regard to inspiring spirits. Not all poets were considered inspired, but only the *fuḥūl*, "the greatest." Besides, these *fuḥūl* did not rely on inspiration only, but, as did Ḥuṭaiʾa and Dhū ʾr-Rumma, often polished their poems over a long period of time. Moreover, Dhū ʾr-Rumma differentiated clearly among poems that had come to him easily, others that had cost him a great amount of work, and still others that he owed to an inspiring demon. There were others who affirmed they owed in one and the same poem some things to the *jinn* and others to themselves. Muhammad himself was warned against altering revelation according to his own ideas, and it would be entirely wrong to believe that his revelations were independent of his thought and his will. There is a tradition that recognizes that the Joseph Sura (Koran 12) would never have been revealed had it not been for the insistence of Muhammad's community. Besides, traditions of demon inspirers of the poets no longer intervene except as an expression in mythological terms which has lost its occult background. One poet, reproached for producing so little, answered, "I do not, like you, accept everything from my genie (*shaiṭān*)." Instead of calling upon the muses, the epic poets of Persia sometimes addressed themselves to some psychic urge of their own, either of the heart or of the spirit. This urge is not always easy to define. On the whole, indigenous Arabic literary criticism does not believe in the intervention by demons in poetic inspiration. The Muʿtazilite an-Naẓẓām (d. between 835 and 845) rejects it too. It goes without saying that scientific medicine in medieval Islam is far removed from demonology.

As a religion, by contrast, Islam has sustained rather than fought conservative forces. First and foremost, Islam insists on the principle of heteronomy of human conduct. Human conduct as such, at least as far as it is successful, comes from God. Every declaration of human intention ought to be followed by the restrictive formula (*istithnā*), "If God wills." Backgammon is preferable to chess because it leaves more to chance, that is to say, to the influence of God. Before undertaking anything, one prays for success, and at the end expresses gratitude.

Then, too, Islam has expressly recognized the existence and efficacy of the *jinn* and, in calling men to faith in God and the angels, it merely superimposes a new universe on theirs, devaluating the old one to a certain degree but not destroying it. None of the ancient sources of inspiration were discarded by Islam. On the contrary, others have been added—more important ones, demanding greater devotion. Rather than replacing one team with another, the field of inspiration was enlarged. This allowed Islam to perpetuate the ancient Arab ideas of inspiration by spirits. It allowed it, further, to admit new, non-Arab demonologies, perhaps most notably the rites of exorcism of the Perso-Turkish *parīkhwān* and the African *zār*.

INDEX

al-ʿAbbās, 354, 355
Abbasid: epoch, 351; society, dreams in, 352, 356
Abbasids, 352
ʿAbdalghanī an-Nābulusī, 6, 7, 9, 360
ʿAbdallāh b. al-Mubārak, 14
Abraham, 222
Abschattungen, 185, 186
Abū ʿAbdallāh az-Zanjī, 13
Abū ʿAbdallāh b. ʿUmar as-Sālimī, 362
Abū Bakr al-Warrāq, 14
Abū Dulaf, 14
Abū Isḥāq al-Kirmānī, 357
Abū Isḥāq-i Kāzarunī, 427
Abū Muḥriz, 19
Abū Mūsà, 16
Abū Muslim, 374, 375
Abū Nuwās, 425
Abū Saʿīd al-Ḥarkūshī al-Wāʿiz, 362
Abū Saʿīd Naṣr b. Yaʿqūb ad-Dīnawarī, 359, 363
Abū Shaikh al-Mufassir, 19
Abū Shāma, 11
Abū Ṭāhir Yaḥyà b. Ghannām al- Maqdisī, 362
A-causal phenomena, 172
Activated sleep, 70 (fig. 12), 71, 80; and dreams, 69
Activity; reticular, 58; tonic, 58
Adaptation: cultural, 268, 269, 270; dynamic, 328; psychocultural, 271
Adler, Alfred, 123, 129n
Adrian, E. D., 66
Aeneid, 298
Aeschylus, 304
Aesthetics, transcendental, 185
Agamemnon, 304

Index

Aḥmad Aḥsāʾī, 402–406
Aḥmad b. abī Duʾād, 15
Aḥmad b. Ḥanbal, 15
Aḥmad b. Naṣr, 17
Aḥmad b. Ṭūlūn, 18
Aḥmad Sirhindī, 419
ʿAlāʾ ud-Daula Semnānī, 387, 394
ʿĀlam al-mithāl. See Images, world of
Alekseev, Gavril, 332
Alexander, 390
ʿAlī as-Sakhāwī, 19
ʿAli ibn Abī Ṭālib, 385
ʿAli Rezā, 404
ʿAlī Zain al-ʿĀbidīn, 384, 403
Allēgorikoi, 311
ʿAlqama an-Nakhaʿī, 17
Ambivalence, 153, 324; of motives, ancient Greece, 312
American Society for Psychical Research, 167, 170
al-Amīn (caliph), 353, 354
Amīn, Aḥmad, 375, 376
Amphetamines, 60
Amphiaraus, cult of, 314
Amplification, 128, 130n, 154, 155, 157; method of, 127
Analysis, 133, 190; dream, 139, 142; function of, 141; levels of, 142; phenomenological, 179
Analyst: attitude of, 124, 140; knowledge of dreamer by, 124
Analytic psychology, 134
Anamnesis, 311, 313
Andersson, S. A., 60
Answering dream, 377
Anthropologists, 221; psychoanalytic, 216
Anthropology, 179, 184, 213, 216; and study of dreams, 182; comparative, 183, 186; psychologically oriented, 226
Anticipation of future in dreams, 49
Anticosmos, 298; temporal, 300
Antigone, 193, 195
Antike Inkubation und Moderne Psychotherapie, 155, 157
Antithesis, law of, 296, 297
Antiworld, 298
Antrobus, J., 88
Apobasis, 313
Apodosis, 343
Aporia, 189
Apparitions, 166
Apparitions and Omens, 170
Apuleius, 315

Arabian Nights, The, 39
Arabic popular culture, dream in, 365–379
"Archetypal patterns," 147
Arduini, A., 82
Arguments, dreams used in settling, 376
Aristophanes, 299
Aristotle, 12, 121, 224, 305, 306, 308, 316
Arousal, 64; association and, 60; cortical, 68 (fig. 11); effects of, 64 (fig. 8); electrocorticographic effect of, 56; electrocorticographic features of, 65; electroencephalogram, 57, 65; emotions and, 61; impulses of, 60; reticular, 63 (fig. 7); threshold, 82, 83; unitary cortical activity during, 65 (fig. 9)
Artemidorus (of Ephesus), 9n, 35, 295, 309, 310, 313, 359, 360, 361
Asad ad-Dīn Shīrkūh, 13
Aserinsky, E., 79, 86
al-Ashʿarī, 13
Asklepieion, 314, 316, 318
Asklepios, 314, 315, 316, 317; cult of, 300
Assassins, the, 47
Association, 125, 128, 130, 130n, 131n, 149, 158, 160; and arousal, 61
Associative: process, 126; significance, arousal power of stimulations having, 61
Assurbanipal, 23, 35
Assyrian court, 350
Assyrian dreambook, 311
Astrology, 6
Atharva-Veda, 23, 296
ʿAṭṭār, 426
Auguries, 314
Auḥad ad-Dīn al-Kirmānī, 414
Aurélia, 48
Aurora, 49
Austin, J. O., 49
Australian medicine men, initiation dreams of, 338, 339
Authentication, 35, 170
Author-character, 195–198
Autochthon. *See* Tonic activity
Autonomous complex, 150
Avalanche process, 66
Avicenna (Ibn Sīnā), 386, 396, 401, 409, 410, 421
Awakening, 46, 86, 192; cortical inhibition in, 66; dream of, 44
Aylward, Rev. James, 158
Aztec culture, 323

Babylonian Talmud, 35
al-Bājī, 14
Barbiturates, 60; sleep under, 54
Bartemeier, L. H., 224

Batini, C., 68 (fig. 11)
Behavior, masochistic, 183; sadistic, 183; social, 280
Behavioral: adaptation, dreaming and, 268; change, 136
Bender, M., 83 (fig. 3), 84 (fig. 4), 89 (fig. 6)
Berger, H., 66, 89
Bergson, H., 199
Bible, 25, 410
Bidney, David, 275
Birth, process of, 192
Blind subjects and REM, 93
Blondel, Dr. Charles, 199
Blood pressure and sleep, 67
Body movement during REM sleep, 93
Bonnet, V., 62
Bonvallet, M., 60, 67
Book of the Thousand Nights and a Night, 40 n. 19
Borges, Jorge Luis, 49
Brahma, 221
Breath Body, Hopi, 241, 251, 254
Bremer, F., 54, 61 (fig. 5), 63 (fig. 7), 64, 66
Broad, C. D., 166, 167
Brookhart J. M., 62
Brushwood Boy, The, 49
Büchsenschütz, B., 309
Buddhism, 46
Buhlūl b. Rāshid, 13
Burton, Richard, 40 n. 19

Caillois, Roger, 184
Calchas, cult of, 314
Calderón de la Barca, Pedro, 47
Callaway, H., 29
Candia, O., 67
Capon, A., 67
Caquot, Andre, 368
Carneades, 306
Caspers, H., 62
Catamnesis, 311
Categories, 18; of dreams, 11, 13; of dreams, Mexican, 325
Causal dream, 218
Causality, 134, 213, 344
Central nervous system activity in REM sleep, 100
Chaos, 301
Character, social, in Mexico, 321–329
Character and dreams in Ojibwa culture, 289

Charisma, 229, 235, 406; defined, 232
Charteris, Leslie, 49
Chauvin, Victor, 371
China, folklore of, 45
Chippewa, 271
Christ, 129n, 130n
Christian: asceticism, 387; dreams, 262; esoterism, 382; hierarchs, 15; sanctuaries, 378; shrines, 304; spirituality, 383
Christianity, 130n, 262, 378, 386; primitive, 129n
Christology, 400
Cicero, 46, 307
Circular Ruins, The, 49
Claes, Elsa, 55
Clairvoyance, "traveling," 111
Clan form, Mexican family, 323
Clergy, power of, Mexico, 324
Collective unconscious, 126, 127
Commentary of the Paradoxes of the Mystics, 388
Communication: between dreamer and supernatural powers, 6; linguistic, 268
Comparative: psychology, 148; religion, 4
Compensation, 132; limitation on, 133; spontaneous, 133
Complementary situations, paranormal dreams and, 116
Complex, 126, 146, 147, 149; autonomous, 150; feeling-toned, 146; recurrent, 150; unconscious, 150
Compulsive-neurotic act, 234
Concrete monad, 180, 185
Conduct: and dreaming, 289; bad, 280
Confessions, 151
Conflict, tragic, 191, 192
Conjurer, 277, 287
Conjuring, Ojibwa, 277
Conscience, 190, 191, 192, 195, 198, 281, 328, 383
Conscious: and unconscious, interactions between, 141; insight, 141; psychic activity, 143
Consciousness, 180, 183, 186, 189, 382, 383, 391; ill-socialized, 199; imaginative, 407; intentional, 182; unhealthy, 199
Cortical: arousal, 68 (fig. 10); dynamo-genesis, 60; inhibition in awakening, 66
Corticipetal: afferences, suppression of, 55; impulses, 60
Cosmos, 297, 298, 299, 300
Countertransference, 127
Creation myth, 219, 221; as "stylized" pathogenic dream, 222
Creutzfeldt, O., 64
Crisis: cult, 234; psychiatry of, 183; situation, 170
Cult, cargo, 234; crisis, 234; healing, 314

Cultural: phenomena, 4; variables, 4
Cultural sciences, development of, 3; physiological structure of, 3, 4
Culture, 185, 186, 230, 234; Aztec, 323; Greek, 300; Hopi, 237; Mexican, 321; Ojibwa, 267–291; sacred, 231, 235; secular, 230, 233; Spanish, 323; trait-item content of, 221
Culture-hero, 229, 232, 234–235; Mohave, 220
Cure, 314; religious aspect of, ancient Greece, 315; temple, ancient Greece, 303–318
Cutaneous thermolysis, 67
Cynics, 306

Dale, Laura, 170
Daniel, 349, 368
Daqīqī, 426
Darkness, 66
Daydreams, 324
Dead Leman, The, 50
Death, 14, 15; and resurrection, 336; symbolic, 311
Defense mechanisms, 232, 233, 234, 235; culture as, 229
Delatte, A., 296
Dell, P., 62, 66, 67
Delusion, 110
Dement, William, 69, 71, 80, 83 (fig. 3), 84 (fig. 4), 88, 89 (fig. 6), 91 (fig. 7), 95, 145, 229
Demeter, 317
Demetrescu, M., 64
Democritus, 307, 308, 316
Demonic origin, 306
Demonology, 428
Demons, 305; inspiration by, 421–429
Descartes, 5, 46
Descent, patrilineal, Ojibwa, 282
Devereux, George, 216, 217, 219, 221, 222, 223, 232, 233, 235, 270
Dhū 'r-Rumma, 428
Diagnosis, 305
Diffused attention, 140
Dimoki, 242, 263
Disassociation-conflict, 143 n. 18
Disease, evil dreams as, 346. *See also* Illness
Dismemberment, ecstatic experience of, 337, 340
Divination, 25, 341, 351; lore, Mesopotamian, 342, 343
Divine, the, man's relation to, 6
Divine epiphanies, 311
Diviner, 367, 370, 423
Divinity, Hopi concept of, 241
Documentation, 168, 170

Dodds, E. R., 309
Dostoyevsky, F., 194
Doutté, E., 377
Dream: action and body movement, 96; activity, objective measurement of, 98; actor in, 33; analysis, 141–142; analyst's attitude toward, 124; answering, 377; anticipation of future in, 49; aspects of, 184; associations as means of decoding, 125; authentication of, 35; authority of, 28; "bad," in Mohave culture, 222; body movement in, 98; book, 23, 24, 295, 311; categories of, 11, 13, 18, 309; categories, Mexico, 325; causal, 218; causative function of, 223; causes, 134; characteristics of, 183; charisma, and culture-hero, 229; chthonic, 305; clairvoyant, 168; classification of, 7, 8, 9, 306, 310, 359; cognitive force of, 6; compensatory function of, 153; complementary, 39, 184, 375; complexes revealed in, 146; concern for, in Muslim civilization, 4; content and eye-movement pattern, 88–89; continuous, 147; contradictory, 296; controlling by experimentation, 173; corroboration of, 34; creative, 189, 196; cultural function of, 3–21; cultural, relationship revealed in, 329; cyclical, 45; defensive attitude toward, 120; defined, 119–120, 121, 123, 145, 229; defined as "elaborate hallucinatory episode," 97; degree of reality in, 23; destiny in, 41; details of, 126; diagnostic use of, 305; diagnostic value of, 222, 223, 307; distinction between reality and, 273; divinely prophetic, 309; duration, and length of REM period, 86; ecstatic, 400; effect of fears on, 346; ego, 151–153; elements of, 9, 10, 312; epiphany, 315; episodes, number of, 99; evil, 346; experiments, 174; exploitation of, 223; false, 8; family in, 325, 326; fast, 282, 284, 285, 286, 287, 288; fate-foretelling, 226; function and significance of, 4; goals, 134; good, 8; guillotine, 87; Hopi, 237–263; image, 189; imagery, 280; incubation, 348; initiation, 331–340, 374, 392, 406; inspiration in, 424–428; instantaneous occurrence of, 87; interference, 11; internal conflicts of, 346; interpretation of, 6, 7, 9, 35, 128, 129, 186, 271, 294–295, 303, 308, 342, 358, 368, 369, 371, 410; interpreters, 349, 350; Jungian theory of, 134; logical problems of, 23–52; manifest, 8; manifest content of, 223; mantic, 341–350; meaning of, 23; memory of, 86, 182, 199; "message," 347, 348; Mohave culture and, 221; motives, 147, 312; mystery of, origin, 51; mythological, 154; obstacle, 192; omen, 218, 223, 225, 226, 345; oracular theory of, 35; origin of mystery of, 51; parallel, 38, 49, 184, 223; paranormal, 109–118, 165; parapsychology of, 163–177; passivity of, 51; pathogenic, 213–228; patterns of, Mexico, 329; phenomena inherent in, 51; phenomenological analysis of, 179–187; phenomenology of, 119; philosophical problems of, 23–52; physiological basis of, 4; place of in Greek religion, 298; political, 17, 18; portending death, 24; positive function of, 300; possessed of cognitive force, 6; powers of, 45; precognitive, 164, 165, 168, 172, 305, 307; premonitory, 402; private, 14; process of going to, 66; prognostic use of, 305, 306; prognostic value of, 222, 223; prophetic, 21, 168, 310, 428; prophetic function of, 223; prophetic significance of, 21; pseudo-, 112; psychic, 309; psychology, 136; psychology of, 119–143; psychophysiological, 189; psychophysiology of, 77–107; rationally prophetic, 309; realistic, 171; reality and indistinguishable, 50; reality

as, 46; reality of, 23, 27, 270, 375; realization of, 190, 191; recall, 86, 95–96, 98, 100, 267; recounting, 191; recurrent, 326; relationship to waking life, 32; religious, 158–161, 303; remembered, 145, 146; revelatory significance of, 21; role of, 6, 372; role of, in Ojibwa culture, 267–291; sacrificial, 197; self-diagnostic, 224; sequence of, 139; series, cohesion of, 139; "sickness," 337; significance of, 23; social and cultural range, 4; social character expressed in, 328; social context of, 342; sociology of, 199–211; "soul-wish-manifesting," 216; state and rapid eye movement (REM) sleep, 78; studies, parapsychological, 163–177; study of, 184; symbolic, 8, 171, 348, 349, 350; symbolism of, 357, 358; symptomatic, 214; symptoms, 134; systematic study of, 48; telepathic, 112, 115, 165, 168, 307; terrifying, 411; theological augmentation through, 16; theological doctrine elucidated in, 15; theory, 216, 226; therapeutic use of, 377, 378; therapeutic value of, 123; "threshold," 193, 198; tragic, 192; transformation into significant truth, 187; trustworthiness of, 29; unrealistic, 171; viridical, 305, 307; visionary, 381–406; visions and, 421; visitors, 279; within a dream, 36

Dream and: activated sleep, 69; character in Ojibwa culture, 289; continuity of egos, 186; fantasy, 49; literary creation, 189–198; non-REM sleep, 100; novel, 51; politics, 17; quest for security, 5; rapid eye movement (REM), 87, 90, 91 (fig. 7); reality, distinction between, 50, 273; revelations, 5; sex, 346; telepathic experience distinguished, 112; the novel, 51; waking state distinguished, 27; waking world, 23

Dream as: cause of rapid eye movement (REM), 87; disguised metaphysical hypothesis, 46; element of plot, 48; expressing concrete problem, 135; expression of rationality, 327; fairy tale dispelled by awakening, 46; foreshadowing reality, 30; hallucinatory episode, 97; incarnation, 135; instrument for self-cognition, 21; "lien" on reality, 29; literary device, 46; manifesting secret desires, 30; message from gods, 304; metaphysical hypothesis, 46; objective fact, 308; omen, 164; omen and destiny, 48; oracle, 314; play (drama), 131, 146; political weapon, 19; reality, 46; reconstruction of history, 182; revelation, 7; symptomatic of reality, 20; tool of political prophecy, 18; waking state, 189

Dream-censor, 229

Dreamer: as fictitious creature, 50; attitude toward irrational by, 303; biography of, 124, 128; emotional participation of, 140

Dream in: Arabic popular culture, 365–379; cross-cultural research, 21; Greek civilization, 293–319; Islamic popular culture, 365–379; literature, 48; medieval Islam, 351–363; Mexico, 321–329; Mohave culture, 219

Dreaming: and conduct, 289; and physiology of sleep, 78; defined as imagery, progression of events, and sense of reality, 98; during non-REM sleep, 95; "fraudulent," 19; function in maintaining well-being, 99; necessity of, 267; paradoxical sleep and, 85; properties of, 98; psychophysiology of, 77; REM sleep and, 85; sense of reality in, 98; significance of, 27; sleep, 78; time spent in, 98–99, 267; universality of, 267

Dream of: awakening, 44; consultation, 376; cracked granary, 26; divination, 366, 367; enemy, 224; failure, 326; ghosts, 223, 224, 225; good tidings, 8;

marriage, 358; Nebuchadnezzar, 26; opposites, 296; Pharaoh, 26; Ptolemy Soter, 36; Shah Ṭahmāsp, 45; snake, 223, 249; strife, 308; trespass, 246, 262; war, 308; warning, 8 witch, 224
Dream of Doctor Mišić, The, 49
Dreamwork, 112, 223, 229, 233, 235
Drug-induced hallucination, 46
Duke University, 168
Dumont, S., 62
Durkheim, E., 231, 232, 235
Dustūr fī 't-ta'bīr, 357
Dynamogenesis, cortical, 60
Dynamogenetic, 62; influence, 66

Ecclesiastes, 343
Ecstasy: initiatory, 336, 337; pathogenic, 332
Ecstatic experience, 331
Education, 142; Hopi, 238
EEG (electroencephalogram), 79, 173, 174; rapid eye movement and, 80 (fig. 1); sleep and, 83; sleep cycle, 79; stages, rhythmic succession of, 79
Eggan, Dorothy, 271
Ego, 126, 151, 180, 181, 183, 185; continuity of, 186; dream, 152–153; waking, 153
Ego-centered processes, 269
Ehrenwald, Jan, 115
Einfühlung, 181
Einstein, A., 213
Eisenbud, Jules, 115, 116
Ejidos, 322
Electrocorticogram, 54–55, 64 (fig. 8)
Electrocorticographic effect of arousal, 56
Electroencephalogram. *See* EEG
Electromyogram. *See* EMG
Electrooculogram. *See* EOG
Eliade, Mircea, 251
Eliezer, Rabbi, 26
Ellis, H., 87 n. 3
EMG (electromyogram), 79, 84
Emotion: and arousal, 61; and image, 27
Emotional: change, arousal power of, 61; participation of dreamer in analysis, 140; thought, Mexico, 324
Encephalitis, 69
Enigmas, 311
Enneads, 401
EOG (electrooculogram), 89; and dreams, correspondence between, 90
Epic, 372
Epicrisis, 311

Epidaurus, 314, 317, 318
Epileptic discharge in REM sleep, 99
Equalitarian values, Ojibwa, 281
Ergodic hypothesis, 219
Escape from Freedom, 328
ESP (extrasensory perception), 168
Ethos, mystic, 381
Euripides, 299, 304, 305
Evarts, E., 81
Exodus, 349
Exorcism, 191, 429
Experience, 184; ecstatic, 331
Experiments, 174
Exploitation, 223
Exterior reality, 136
Extrareticular impulses, 60
Extrasensory perception. *See* ESP
Extroversion, 136
Eye-movement: direction and temporal sequence of, 90; in sleep, 79; patterns and dream content, 88–89; potentials, 88 (fig. 5)

al-Faḍl b. ar-Rabīʿ, 352
Fahd, Toufy, 365, 366, 371, 377
Family: maternal extended, 238–239; Mexican, 323
Fantasy, 185, 310, 324, 407
al-Fārābī, 410, 411
Fate, 5
Fatigue, 66
Fatima, 399, 400, 403, 404
Faunus, cult of, 314
Fear, 261, 346
Feedback: negative, 59; positive, 59
Ferenczi, Sándor, 224
Fetish, 190
Finality, 134, 183
Fink, Eugen, 181
Finnegans Wake, 184
Firdausī, 426
Fisher, C., 88, 91 (fig. 7)
Flicker: fusion frequency, 63 (fig. 7); stimulation, subjective fusion by, 64
Flood, 262; dream of, 246, 247, 249
Folklore: Hasidic, 40; Japanese, 40; science and, 342
Freedom, 191, 193, 197
Freiburg Institute, 171, 174
Freud, S., 77, 110, 112, 114, 121, 122, 126, 128 n. 7, 133, 134, 137, 139, 140, 141, 160, 229, 232, 235, 313, 327

Freudians, difference with Jungians, 137
Frogs, The, 299
Fromm, Erich, 114, 321, 323, 324, 326, 328
Frustration, 114
Fuster, J. M., 62

Galen, 308
Gautier, Théophile, 50
Genetic phenomenology, 181
Gestalt psychology, 185
Geste de Melik Dānişmend, La, 372
al-Gharīḍ, 423
al-Ghazzālī, 16, 411
Ghosts, twins as, 217
Gifford, E. W., 216
Gillen, F. J., 338
Gjalski, Ksaver Sandor, 49
Gnostics, 383, 415, 416
God, 5, 8, 15, 16, 137, 249, 343, 428, 429; Hopi, 241
Gods, 311
Goldfrank, F., 85
Golding, Louis, 49
Good Heart, Hopi concept of, 254, 256
Good life, Ojibwa, 281
Grand Mobed, the, 367
Greece, 293-318; ancient, 303-318; pre-Homeric, 300
Greek: civilization, dreams in, 293-318; culture, 300; element in Islamic oneirocriticism, 351
Green, Celia, 171
Growing Up in New Guinea, 156
Grubb, W. B., 28
Grüsser, O. J., 64
Grunebaum, G. E. von, 11 n. 16
Guérison psychologique, La, 142 n. 16
Guilt, 197, 244, 261; complex, 383
Guilty-innocent, 197
Gurney, Edmund, 167

Ḥafiẓ of Shīrāz, 392
Halbwachs, Maurice, 199
Hallucination, 31; drug-induced, 46-47
Hanuman, 45
Hārūn-ar-Rashīd, 12, 353
Haruspicy, 314
Ḥasan ʿAskarī, 405
al-Ḥasan b. Ḥusain al-Khallāl, 359

Ḥasan ibn ʿAlī, 403
Ḥasan-i-Ṣabbāḥ, 46, 47
Ḥassān b. Thābit, 425
Ḥātim Ṭayy, 379
Hawk, 276
Hayes, Cathy, 269
Ḥayy ibn Yaqẓān, 386
Healing, 316; cults, 314; symbolism of ancient Greece, 317
Heart rate, 79
Heavenly visitors, twins as, 217
Hegel, 179, 383
Heisenberg principle, 213
Hendley, C., 93
Heraclitus, 307
Hereafter, the, 6; concern with, 20
Hermann, H., 69
Hermes, 304
Herzog, Rudolf, 315
Hesiod, 299
Hess, W. R., 54, 67
Hidden Channels of the Mind, 170
Hiebel, G., 67
Hikwsi, 241, 250, 251, 252, 262, 263. *See also* Psyche
Himu, 241
Hindu theology, 221
Hippocrates, 224, 307, 308, 316, 317
History: as psychoanalysis, 187; significance of, 186
Hobson, J., 85
Hollós, István, 115
Homer, 223, 298, 304, 309
Homeric epics, 294
Hopi: beliefs, 254–256; concept of space, 253; concept of time, 253; interdependence, 239; kinship system, 239; learning process, 239; maternal family, 238–239; matrilocal residence, 239; mythology, 238; rituals, 248–254
Hubel, D. H., 65 (fig. 9)
Hugelin, A., 60
Ḥunain b. Isḥāq, 359
Hunches, 166
al-Ḥusain b. Ḥasan b. Ibrāhīm al-Khalīlī ad-Dārī, 361
al-Ḥusain b. ʿUbaidallāh, 357
Husserl, Edmund, 179, 181, 184, 185, 186
Ḥuṭayʾa, 428
Huttenlocher, P., 82
Hygieia, 315
Hypersomnia, 54
Hypnogenetic: mechanisms, 66; stimulation, 67

Hypnoid function, 66
Hypnotic effect of stimulation, 68 (fig. 10)

Iaso, 315
Ibn al-ʿArabī, 413, 414, 415, 416, 418
Ibn al-Bannāʾ, 10, 11
Ibn Ḥazm, 12
Ibn Isḥāq, 369
Ibn al-Kalbī, 379
Ibn Khaldūn, 356
Ibn Saʿd, 357
Ibn Shuhaid, 425
Ibn Sīnā. *See* Avicenna
Ibn Sīrīn, 360, 369, 375
Ibn Zurʿa, 16
Id-wish, 229
Iliad, 294, 296, 347
Illness, 280, 288, 307, 314, 331; in Mohave culture, 219
Image, 411; and emotion, 27; of mountain, 190; psychagogic, 110
Imagery, 98, 185, 362, 363; and REM, 87, 90, 91 (fig. 7); Hopi, 240–241
Images, 186, 401, 407; cultural, 263; suspended, 412; world of, 406, 407, 409–419
Imaginal world, 406
Imagination, 409, 412, 413, 415, 417, 419
Imamology, 381
Impulses, 133; ascending, 55, 61; corticipetal, 60; direct, 60; extrareticular, 60; reticular, 62
Incubation, 31, 300, 315, 318, 377, 378, 379; ancient Greece, 303–318
Indeterminacy principle, 213
Indians: Algonquin-speaking, 271; Hopi, 237–265; Iroquois, 216, 217; Plains, 234
Individuation, 142, 148
Industrial society, influence of, Mexico, 322, 324
Inertia, 131n, 187
Inferiority complex, 138n
Infero-superiority complex, 138n
Infratemporality, 195
Inhibitory process, active intervention of, 67
Initiation, 160, 331–340, 390; rites, 148; similarities, Siberian and Australian, 340; spiritual, 381; themes, 332
Initiatory rituals, 164
Inquisition, Mexican, 124
Insecurity, 324
Insight, conscious, 141
Insomnia, amphetamines and, 60
Inspiration by demons, 421–429

Institute for Border Areas of Psychology and Mental Hygiene (Freiburg), 171
Intentionality, 182
Interaction, Ojibwa culture, 274–275
Interdisciplinary cooperation, 4
Interior reality, 136
Interpretation, 9, 25, 26, 124, 146, 147, 148–149, 153, 173, 186, 295, 303, 305, 308, 310, 311, 346, 349, 351, 358, 360, 371; amplification method, 154; ancient Greece, 312, 313, 314; by prophecy, 368; causal, 137; direct, 366; error in, 139; final, 134; incongruous, 345; levels of, 136; medieval Islamic, 363; Mesopotamia, 342; need for, 329; objective level, 150; oneirocritic, 223; parallel, 223; perspectives of, 133; phases of, 129; pre-Islamic Arabia, 369; prospective, 137; reductive, 137; subjective level, 151; symbolic, 410; synthetic, 133, 137
Interpretation of Dreams, The, 77, 160, 348
Introversion, 136
Invention, 110
Iroquois, 216, 217
Irrational, the, dreamer's attitude toward, 303
'Iṣāmī, 12
Iserine, effect of, 64 (fig. 8)
Isis, cult of, 314, 315
Islam, late medieval, 409
Islamic civilization, 183
Islam in Mittelalter, Der, 11 n. 16
Isle of Dreams, 299
Isolation, 331
Ivanov, Pjotr, 332

Jaʿfar Ṣādiq, 384
Jaffé, Mrs. Aniela, 170
Jalāl ad-Dīn as-Suyūṭī, 13
James, William, 161 n. 2, 231
Jāmī, 425
Jasmin of Love's Faithful, 387
Jasper, H. H., 60
Jeannerod, M., 92
Jewish civilization, 183
Jinn, 427, 429
Job, Book of, 343
Jones, William, 278
Joseph, 349, 368
Joseph Sura, the, 428
Jouvet, M., 69, 78, 80
Joyce, James, 184, 231
Jung, C. G., 60, 121, 122, 123, 125, 126, 127, 128 n. 7, 132, 133, 134, 137, 139,

142 n. 16, 145–161, 170, 232, 307, 309, 310; dream psychology of, 145–161
Jung and Analytical Psychology, 157
Jungians, difference with Freudians, 137

Kachina, 238, 245, 246, 251, 255, 256, 257, 259
Kanzow, E., 82
Kathāsaritsagara, 38
Kaulān, 425
Kennard, Edward A., 252, 257
Kern, 185, 186
Khalīl b. Shāhīn aẓ-Ẓāhirī, 362
Khiḍr, 390, 426
Kipling, Rudyard, 49
ash-Shāh al-Kirmānī, 422
Kisrà Anūshirwān, 367, 368
Klein, M., 69
Kleitman, Nathaniel, 54, 69, 79, 80 (fig. 1), 82, 86, 88 (fig. 5), 95, 145
Knowledge, theory of, in medieval civilizations, 5
Koch, E., 67
Kolainī, 384
Koran, 7, 11, 19, 45, 366, 397, 410, 421, 422, 423, 426, 427, 428
Krause, D., 82
Krisis, 180, 181
Kroeber, A. L., 216, 220, 222
Ksenofontov, G. W., 333, 337
Kühnel, H., 82
Kulturforscher, 4
Kumait, 425
Kuttner, Henry, 50

Lalement, Fr., 29
Lane, Edward Wm., 376, 377
Language, 185, 186; symbolic, 327
Last Visit of the Sick Cavalier, The, 50
Lebenswelt, 180, 184, 185
Legend, 370, 371
Lehtisalo, T., 333
Leriche, René, 141
Lethargic state, 57
Lévy-Bruhl, Lucien, 217, 218, 231, 235
L'homme à la découverte de son âme, 122 n. 2
Life Is a Dream, 47
"Light of lights," 417
"Light" sleep, 70 (fig. 12)
Light stimulus, 66
Lindsley, D. B., 62

Linton, Ralph, 217
Liu, 49
Logos, 221
London Society for Psychical Research, 164, 166, 167
Lord Mountdrago, 49
Love in Mexican society, 323
Lucian, 299
Luther, M., 401

Maʿarrī, 425
Maʿbad, 423
Machismo, 323
Mach's principle, 215
MacLeod, Robert B., 273
Macrobius, 309, 310
Magic, 163, 164; thought, Mexico, 324
Magician, 370
Magnes, J., 68 (fig. 10)
Magoun, H. W., 56
al-Mahdī, 17, 352, 353
Maḥmūd of Ghazna, 16
Maḥmūd Shabestarī, 396
Malayavatī, Princess, 49
al-Maʾmūn, 353, 354, 355, 423
al-Manṣūr, 18, 352, 359
Mantic belief, 307
Marco Polo, 47
Margoliouth, D. S., 424
Matthew, Gospel of, 347
Matthews, B. H. C., 66
Maturation, interior, 138n
Maugham, W. Somerset, 49
Maury, Alfred, 48, 87
Mauss, Marcel, 235
Mead, Margaret, 156
Medicine, 4
Medieval civilizations, characteristics of, 5
Meier, C. A., 145 n. 17, 155, 157
Meier, Fritz, 394
Mélikoff, Irène, 372, 374
Memory, 199; processes, recall as function of, 97
Menninger Clinic, 167
Merleau-Ponty, Maurice, 185
Mesopotamia, 341–350
Message, distorted, 348; personal, 11
Messiah, 234–235

Mestizo, 322
Metamorphosis, 142, 284; Ojibwa, 276
Mikiten, T., 93
Mīr Dāmād, 399–402
Mohammed. *See* Muhammad
Moḥammad Kerīm Khān Kermānī, 404
Mohave, 217; culture, 219; culture-hero, 220; dream and illness in, 219; god, 220
Mollā Ṣadrā of Shīrāz (Shīrāzī), 392, 399, 407, 408. *See also* Ṣadr ad-Dīn ash-Shīrāzī; Mullā Ṣadrā
Monad, 180, 185
Moore, Catherine L., 50
Moreau de Tours, Jacques-Joseph, 121
Moruzzi, G., 56, 62, 67, 68, (fig. 10)
Motivation, 4, 134n; Ojibwa, 279, 280; psychological phenomena, 4; unconscious, 329
Mouret, J., 92
Muḥaddath, 427
Muhammad, 19, 385, 422, 423, 424, 425, 426, 427, 428
Muḥammad Bāqir, 384, 403
Muḥammad Javād, 404
Muḥammad al-Mahdī, 385
Mukhtār, 427
Mukallam, 427
Muḥyī 'd-Dīn Ibn ʿArabī, 392–394, 407
al-Muʿtaḍid, 18
Mullā Ṣadrā, 427. *See also* Ṣadr ad-Dīn ash-Shīrāzī; Mollā Ṣadrā
al-Muntaṣir, 355
Murphy, Dr. Gardner, 167, 170
Mūsà, 353
al-Musayyab, 357, 358
al-Mustanjid, 356
al-Muʿtaṣim, 355
Muzaffar ad-Dīn, 19
Muzio, J., 91 (fig. 7)
Myers, F. W. H., 167
Mysticism, 383, 409
Myth, 186, 300, 314, 327, 366, 427; creation, 219, 221, 222; Greek, 298, 299, 318; interpretation of, 154; north Asian, 333; Ojibwa, 275, 278; Yakut, 332
Mythology, 311

Najm ad-Dīn al-Kubrà. *See* Najmoddīn Kobrà
Najm Dāya Rāzī, 394
Najmoddīn Kobrà, 386, 394–396, 400, 422
Narcissism, 138
Narcolepsy, REM sleep in, 99

Nāṣir-i Khusraw, 13
National Institute of Mental Health, 77 n. 1
an-Naẓẓām, the Muʿtazilite, 429
Near East, 4; ancient, 341–350
Nebuchadnezzar, 349
Necromancy, 350
Nectanabis, Pharaoh, 35
Negative feedback, 59
Nemesis, 194
Nervous: activities, suspension of, 53; control, 53; system, physiology of, 61
"Nest," Ojibwa, 283
Neurophysiology, 4; of sleep, 53–71
Neurosis: effect on consciousness, 142; obsessional, 234
New Testament, 427
Nexus, 214, 215, 216, 217, 218
Nicol, Fraser, 170
Niebyl, P., 93
Niẓāmī, 11, 424, 426
Nodier, Charles, 48
Non-REM: awakening and "thinking," 97; recall, 95; sleep, 85, 100
North Wind, 277
Nosological entities, 221
Nuʿmān, 367, 368

Object: as proof of dream's reality, 33; level, 135, 137
Objective: level of interpretation, 150; psyche, 161; reality, 10; spirit, 180
Objectivity, 273
Obsession, 51, 191
Occult phenomena, 164
Odyssey, 223, 294, 296, 298, 309 n. 24; latent content of, 223
Oedipus, 191–198; complex, 327
Oedipus Rex, 193
Ohnet, Georges, 139
Old Testament, 221, 343, 344, 349, 368
Omens, 222, 295, 312, 341, 342, 343, 345, 347, 367
Oneiric image, 190
Oneirocritica, 9n, 131, 159, 295, 310
Oneirocriticism, Arab-Muslim, 351
Oneirocritics: Arab, symbolism of, 357; Arab-Muslim, 359; medieval Islamic literature, 359–362
Oneiromancy, 35, 297, 361; in Abbasid society, 356; medical, 377, 378; scientific, 369
"On the Nature of Dreams," 145
Oppenheim, A. Leo, 23, 226
Oracles, 305
Origen, 383

Origin, aspects of, 181
"Orphée Noir," 205 n. 7
Oswald, I., 89, 92
Ovid, 298

Pale Blue Nightgown, 49
Palulukon, 237, 242, 243, 245, 246, 248, 249, 255, 258, 259, 260, 261, 262; ceremony, 257–260
Panacea, 315
Pao-yu, cyclical dream of, 45
Papini, Giovanni, 50
Paradoxical sleep, 69, 71, 78; features of, 81–85; spike discharges during, 93; triggering mechanism, 81. *See also* REM sleep
Parallelism, 340
Paranormal, the, 163
Paranormal phenomena, 172
Parapsychology, 109, 168, 215; defined, 163
Parapsychology Foundation, 167, 173
Parapsychology Laboratory, Duke University, 168
Parīkhwān, 429
Patriarchal family, 323
Patrilineal descent, Ojibwa, 282
Pentobarbital, 62
"Perils of Pauline," 139
Perceptions, 146. *See also* ESP
Personality: change, 14; integration of, 142; receptive-exploitative, 326
Personal messages, 11
Persons: other-than-human, 274, 275, 277, 278, 280, 281, 283, 284, 285, 287, 288; role of, in Ojibwa culture, 274
Phantasm, 185
Phantasms of the Living, 167
Phenomena, spontaneous, 167
Pindar, 294, 304
Plains Indians, 234
Plato, 46, 304, 305, 308, 316
Pliny the Younger, 296
Plotinus, 401
Plutarch, 410
Podmore, Frank, 167
Poet, 370; conscience of, 198
Poetry, 428
Pompeiano, O., 67, 68 (fig. 10)
Popov, A. A., 334
Posidonius, 306
Positive feedback, 59
Praxis, 183, 186, 187; *practico-inert*, 187

Precognition, 110, 164, 165, 166
Predestinarianism, 15
Prediction, 341, 342, 346
Premodern civilizations, characteristics of, 5
Premonitions, 367, 402
Principles of Psychology, 231 n. 6
Prognosis, 305, 306
Projection, 137 n. 12, 138n
Projection-perception, 138
Prometheus, 297
Prometheus Bound, 304
Prophecy, 8, 13, 219, 223; dream interpretation as, 368; political, 18
Prophet, the, 15, 372, 373, 376, 378, 381, 393, 399, 403, 404, 410, 425
Prophetic revelation, 409
Prophetology, esoteric, 400
Prophets, 25, 384, 385
Protasis, 342
Protention, 181
Protest, 126
Proust, Marcel, 182 and n. 7
Pseudomagic, 163
Psychagogic image, 110
Psyche, 250, 252, 263; cult of the, 317. See also Hikwsi
Psychiatry of crisis, 183
Psychic activity, conscious, 143
Psychical research. *See* Parapsychology
Psychoanalysis, 25, 215, 219, 222; function of, 133; history as, 187; humanist, 321, 328
Psychoanalytic theory, 224
Psychocultural adaptation, 271
Psychological: balance, 132; phenomena, 4, 5
Psychology: analytic, 134; comparative, 148; *Gestalt*, 185
Psychophysical basis for dreamer's awareness, 9
Psychotherapy, 134
Psychotic, 232, 233
Puberty, 282, 283
Pulse, 79
Punishment, 247; Ojibwa, 280

Qānṣūh al-Ghūrī, 13
Quṭb al-Dīn ash-Shīrāzī, 418

Rabīʿa b. Naṣr, 370
Rabīʿ al-Qaṭṭān, 15
Radin, Paul, 283
Ranson, S. W., 54

Rapid eye movement. *See* REM
Ratio, 309
Rationality, 143
Rationalization, 190
Realist theory of knowledge, 5
Reality, 415; exterior, 136; interior, 136; object as proof of, 33; objective, 5, 10; ultimate, 5; worldly, 5
Realization, 190, 191
Recall, 95–98; non-REM, 95; rate, REM sleep, 86
Receptive-exploitative character, 326
Rechtschaffen, A., 92
Recurrent complex, 150
Redfield, Robert, 272
Reductive-causal method, 134
Reflex responses, peripheral nerves, 79
Religion, 23, 381, 386–387; comparative, 4; Eastern, 148; Greek, 293, 297; Hopi, 237; Mexico, 323, 324; mythical content of, 190; shamanism in, 340
Religious experience, 331; varieties of, 161
REM (Rapid eye movement): awakening, 86; experiments, 174; of blind subjects, 93; period, unique behavior during, 79; period as time of dreaming, 98
REM and dream imagery, 90, 91 (fig. 7); causal relationship between, 92
REM sleep, 78 ff.; arousal threshold during, 82; body movement during, 93; cardiorespiratory variations in, 94; central nervous system activity in, 100; dream recall during, 100; epileptic discharge in, 99; function in maintaining well-being, 99; in narcolepsy, 99; memory processes in, 97; peripheral motor activity in, 100; respiratory rate in, 84 (fig. 4); temporal association with dreams, 100. *See also* Paradoxical sleep
REM sleep and: dreaming, 85; stimulation, 99
REM technique, 173
Remembrance of Things Past, 182
Republic, 305, 316
Resistance, 126, 131n, 140; emotional, 138n
Respiration in REM sleep, 84 (fig. 4)
Respiratory rate, 79
Retention, 181
Reticular: activating system and sleep, 66; activity, 58; arousal, 63 (fig. 7); formation of waking state, pharmacology of, 60; impulses, dynamogenetic action of, 62; structure, functional depression of, 67; theory, 60
Reticulocortical activation, 71
Resurrection, 417; death and, 336
Resynthesis, 133
Revelation, 5, 20, 51, 428
Rhine, Dr. J. B., 168–170
Rhine, Louisa, 170, 171
Richet, Charles, 168

Richter, Jean Paul, 46
Ritual theology, 234
River Yumans, 216
Roffwarg, H., 89, 91 (fig. 7)
Róheim, Géza, 216, 230, 235
Romanov, Timofei, 332
Romanticism, 46
Ronsard, Pierre de, 8 n. 4
Rorschach test, 165, 219
Rosenzweig test, 165
Rossi, G. F., 69, 70 (fig. 12)
Ru'ba, 425
Rūḥfā'īl, 428
Rushaid, 13
Russell, Bertrand, 214
Rūzbehān of Shīrāz, 387–392, 395, 403

Saba (Sheba), 366
Sacrifice, 197; ancient Greece, 315
Sādiqūn. See Rūḥfā'īl
Ṣadr ad-Dīn ash-Shīrāzī, 416, 417, 418. See also Mollā Ṣadrā; Mullā Ṣadrā
Saḥnūn, 15
Saʿīdā-i Qummī, 427
Saʿīd b. al-Musayyab, 18
Saif ad-Dīn al-Bākharzī, 422
Saif dhū Yazan, 371
St. Augustine, 151, 152
Saladin, 17
Sālim, 426
Samoyeds, 333, 334
Sane Society, The, 321 n. 1, 328
Sannwald, Dr. Gerhard, 171, 172, 173
Sartre, J. P., 183, 187
Satan, 428
Saṭīḥ, 368, 369, 370
Satūq Bughrā Khān, 13
Sayyed Kāẓem, 404
Scienza Nuova, 184
Scipio, 310
Security, quest for, 5
Self, nature of, 273
Semitic peoples, origin of, 366
Sense perception, 412, 413
Sensory: impulses, reduction of, 66; stimulation, lessening of, 66
Serapis, cult of, 314

Servadio, Dr. Emilio, 168–170
Sex in Mexican society, 323
Sexual symbol, 260; smoke as, 262
Shaman, 220, 221, 232, 233, 234, 235, 370, 374, 426; Siberian, 331–340
Shamanism, 164, 340
Shamsoddīn Lāhījī, 396–399, 401
ash-Shaʿrānī, 11
Sheba. *See* Saba
Shiʿism, 381, 382
Shiqq, 369, 370
Sickness, 334. *See also* Illness
Ṣiddīqūn, 8. *See also* Rūḥfāʾīl
Sidgwick, Mrs. Henry, 167
Sleep, 185, 186; activated, 69, 70 (fig. 12), 71, 78; barbiturates and, 60; blood pressure and, 67; center of, 54; cortical and reticular characteristics of waking activity, 69; darkness and, 66; electroencephalogram, 57; eye movements in, 79; fatigue and, 66; going to, 66; interruption of, and dreams, 71; light, 70 (fig. 12); light stimulus and, 66; neurophysical problem of, 53–71; non-REM, 85; onset stage, 83; "paradoxical," 69, 71, 78; "passivist" concept of, 58; passivity of, 67; phenomenological analysis of, 179–187; physiology of, 78; process, active character of, 58; recurring phases of, 69; REM, 78, 79; undisturbed, and recall, 86; unitary cortical activity during, 65 (fig. 9)
Sleep and Wakefulness, 145 n. 1
Sleep as: active processes, 58; a function, 53; functionally deficient nervous condition, 58
Smarra, 48
Snake as sexual symbol, 262
Snake Dance, Hopi, 242, 246, 255
Snake Priests, 246, 261
Snake Society, Hopi, 242
Snyder, F., 85
Social: character, 329; character, Mexican, 327; control, Ojibwa, 280, 281; interaction, Ojibwa, 277; structure, Hopi, 238; structure, Mexican, 321
Society, teleological, 184
Society for Psychic Research, 171
Sociocultural system, Ojibwa, 279, 289
Sohrawardī. *See* al-Suhrawardī, Shihāb ad-Dīn
Sommeil et les rêves, Le, 48
Somnolence, barbiturates and, 60; electroencephalogram, 57
Songs, Ojibwa, 283
Sophocles, 198, 313
Soul, rule of, 180
Space, Hopi concept of, 253
Spanish: conquest, 323; culture, 323

Spencer, B., 338
Spike discharges during paradoxical sleep, 93
Spirit; objective, 180; rule of, 180
Spirit of the Breath, 241
Spiritual Diary, 388
Spontaneous phenomena, 167, 168; documentation of, 166
Stability, quest for, 5
Steller, G. W., 30
Stepanov, Michail, 337
Steriade, M., 64
Stimulation: and REM sleep, 99; hypnotic effect of, 68 (fig. 10)
Stimulus, external, during REM period, 99
Stoicheia, 312
Stoicism, 296
Stoics, 306
Story of a Soul, The, 158, 160
Strauch, Dr. Inge, 174
Subconscious, 192; use of, 373
Subject-object relation, 161
Suetonius, 296
Sufi prophetology, 384
Sufism, 381, 383, 397, 419
al-Suhrawardī, Shīhāb ad-Dīn, 384, 386, 407, 408, 412, 413, 414, 416
as-Suhrawardī, Yaḥyà, 427
Summum Bonum, 400
Superego, 229, 281; tribal, 249
Supernatural the, 6, 163; concern with, 20; powers, communication with, by dreamer, 6
Supernormal, 164
Supero-inferiority complex, 138n
Supratemporality, 195
Suśruta Saṃhita, 24
Swann's Way, 182 n. 7
Swett, J. E., 67
Symbolic: interpretation, 410; representation, 269
Symbolism, 229, 296, 357, 362, 363
Symbols, 190, 327; sexual, 260, 262
Synesius, 309, 310

Ṭabarī, 367
Taboo, 218, 282, 346; food, 287
Ṭāhā Ḥusain, 378, 424
Ṭāhir b. al-Ḥusain, 354
"Tale of the Bird," 401
Talmud, 7 n. 2, 35, 38; Babylonian, 25

Tārābī, 426
Taʿṭīr al-ānām fī taʿbīr al-manām, 360
Teleological: future, 183; society, 184
Telepathic dream, 115, 168, 307. *See also* Dream, paranormal
Telepathy, 110, 164, 165, 166, 170
Telos, 183, 184
Temple cures, 303–318
Terzuolo, C., 61 (fig. 5)
Thematic Apperception test, 165
Theology, Hindu, 221
Theophany, 379
Theorēmatikoi, 311
Therapy, 317
Thérèse of Lisieux, 158, 160, 161
Thoumin, R., 378
Thousand and One Nights, The, 371, 372, 377. *See also Book of the Thousand Nights and a Night*
Time, 415; Hopi concept of, 243
Titiev, Mischa, 251
Tonic activity, 58, 67
Topos, 347
Tortures, initiatory, 331
Totemism, 213, 287, 311
Tragedy, 192, 193, 195; origin of, 191
Tragic knowledge, concept of, 191
Transcendental ethics, 185
Transconscious, 393
Transference, 114, 137, 142, 315
Traumarbeit. See Dreamwork
"Traum und Telepathie," 112
"Treatise of Dreams." *See Atharva-Veda*
Trophonius, cult of, 314
Truth, absolute, 5; psychological, 5; significant, 187
Tscholko, Ivan, 337
Tuareg, 377
Tulsidas, 45
Tunku Abdul Rahman, 12
Ṭuraifa, 366
Ṭūrasān, Sultan, 373
Twins, theories concerning, 217
Tylor, E. B., 272

ʿUbaidallāh b. Ziyād, 425
Ullman, Dr. Montague, 173
Ulysses, 184, 231 n. 3

'Umar b. al-Khaṭṭāb ('Umar I), 18, 427
Umayya b. abī 'ṣ-Ṣalt, 427
Unconscious, 126, 186, 325, 326; activity of, 143; autonomy of, 133
Unconscious complex, 150
"Understanding" defined, 121
Unitary cortical activity, 65 (fig. 9)
United States, influence of; in Mexico, 324
Universe, limited or closed, 5

Value-meaning-affect matrix, 221
Van Eeden, Dr. Frederik, 167
Van Reeth, Dr. P. Ch., 64 (fig. 8), 67
Vera, 49
Verification, 168, 170
Vico, Giambatista, 184
Vigil, 377
Vigilance: continuous, 69; effect of amphetamines on, 60; reticular theory of, 60
Villiers de l'Isle-Adam, P. A., 49
Vikrāmāditya, King, 49
Virgil, 298
Virginity, Ojibwa, 282
Virility, 323
Visions, 382, 422; diary of, 388; initiation, 331–340; significance of, 27
Vorgegebene Welt, 185

Wakefulness, 57, 185; behavioral, 80
Waking state, 58, 421; accentuation of, 64
Wallace, A. F. C., 216
Wallace, W. J., 216, 222
Water Serpent, 237–255, 261, 262; as giver of life, 256
Weaning, 239
Weaver, Rix, 311
Weber, Max, 230, 232, 235
Wellhausen, J., 379
White, Rhea, 170
Whorf, B. L., 252
Wild Surmise, A, 50
Winds, 286; Ojibwa culture, 276, 277
Wisdom literature, 343
Witchcraft, 220, 223
Witch of Endor, 350
Wolpert, E., 94
Wolpow, E. R., 60
Woman in Mexican society, 323

Word, the, 221
Word-association, 146–147
World, in Greek civilization, 298

Xenophon, 304, 305

Yakut myths, 332
Yaʿqūbī, 19
Yūnus b. ar-Rabīʿ, 13

Zambrano, María, 184
Zār, 429
Zateejev, Sofron, 332
Zener cards, 168
Zeus, 304, 317